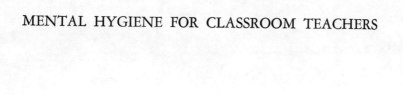

MENTAL HYGIENE FOR CLASSROOM TEACHERS

How many children will come close to a realization of their potential? Which of these will be committed to an institution for mental illness? How can teachers encourage the first outcome and deter the second?

Mental Hygiene
for Classroom Teachers

HAROLD W. BERNARD

Professor of Education
General Extension Division
and
University of Oregon
Oregon State System of Higher Education

Second Edition

McGRAW-HILL BOOK COMPANY, INC.

New York   Toronto   London

1961

MENTAL HYGIENE FOR CLASSROOM TEACHERS

TO EVELYN M. BERNARD

PREFACE

Questions asked by teachers have, as in the first edition, formed the background for the outline of this volume. Why is mental hygiene of such importance? How do I know a wise procedure for handling children who differ so widely? Why is it so difficult to reach certain children who have problems? What routine things should be done to preserve and improve mental health? What special approaches are available to classroom teachers? How can I better understand myself?

The answers to such questions are not single or simple. Each pupil is the product of his own widely different potential and experience. However, there are understandings that can be developed and approaches that are generally effective. Many teachers have expressed their appreciation of the first edition of this book, especially of its practical suggestions. This volume continues the emphasis on applicability, but new chapters have been added. One of the new chapters reflects the growing recognition of the impact of social class on the attitudes, behavior, and aspirations of pupils; it calls attention to the loss of human resources due to the difficulties experienced by lower-class pupils in staying and succeeding in school—difficulties experienced despite their intellectual potential. Another addition is a reflection of the growing interest in providing special attention for the slow learner and for those with unusually high intelligence. The increase of special services—social workers, psychologists, and psychiatrists—in the schools is recognized in another new chapter.

A few of the chapters have remained much the same—except for condensation; but new lights on the nature of adolescence, discipline, and the role of music and art in self-realization have resulted in complete rewriting of many chapters. The condensing of material has meant that despite the addition of three new chapters this volume is about the same size as the first edition.

Part 1 defines mental health and mental hygiene and indicates what can and must be done. The nature and needs of children and adolescents are described. Social class is discussed in terms of its impact on pupils and its implications for teachers.

Part 2, the major subdivision of the book, deals with approaches to mental health through ordinary classroom techniques. Discipline, teaching methods, teacher personality, and children with problems are all discussed as part of the context in which pupils must be understood and individually treated. The importance of teacher personality in salutary human relations is a focal emphasis. The part ends by raising some questions about the wisdom of certain school practices of long standing and by outlining some approaches which are generally effective.

Part 3 shows how some teachers have used art, music, writing, literature, drama, and play as means of understanding and helping children. Special services are described so that teachers may know what takes place in individual therapy and how the necessary support may be provided when the pupil is returned to the classroom. Finally, the limitations involved in rebuilding personality—when it is necessary—are discussed so that teachers may be realistic in their hopes and expectations.

Part 4 deals with the most important theme of all: the mental health of the teachers themselves. Suggestions are given which may serve to make their life and work more enjoyable.

It is hoped that many of the readers of his book will find their skepticism about the advisability or utility of the suggestions turned into a feeling of gratification. Many students who have studied these approaches have said that their study of mental hygiene has been one of their most profitable professional experiences.

It is certain that ultimate wisdom for using mental hygiene practices in the schools has not been achieved. If this presentation stimulates teachers to read further and to experiment, it will have served a worthwhile purpose. It is hoped that this book may serve in the synthesis of novel and experimental ideas with tested practices. Teachers will find that a sincere effort to bring about improvement will not only encourage and help pupils toward more complete and well-rounded development but also add much enjoyment to the life of teaching.

Harold W. Bernard

ACKNOWLEDGMENTS

Many persons have materially assisted in the preparation of this volume and my gratitude is herewith expressed. Alta Diment has continued as a typist and proofreader for this edition. The Audio-Visual Department of the Portland Public Schools, through Kingsley Trenholme, provided the photographs used in illustrations. Former students who provided ideas at certain points include Donald James, Janice Schukart, Jean Bauer, Hazel Van Cleve, Margaret Perry, Janet Smith, Eleanor Powell, and Verna Hogg. Among those who read and criticized chapters are Ruth Halvorson (art), Mary Padovan (art), Leora LaRiviere (reading), and Dr. Ralph Goldner (special services). Dr. LeRoy Pierson and Dr. John Schulz, Portland Extension Center, read various chapters and helped with the outline as well as suggested specific points of emphasis. Dr. Norman Gronlund, University of Illinois, gave concrete, specific, and helpful suggestions at numerous points throughout the entire book. Dean James W. Sherburne, General Extension Division, and Daniel W. Fullmer, Portland Extension Center, helped materially by providing teaching schedules that made pursuit of this work possible.

Thanks are also due to the many publishers who freely granted permission to quote copyrighted material. The size of this debt is reflected in the footnotes which accompany quotations.

Harold W. Bernard

CONTENTS

PART I

Basic Considerations

CHAPTER 1

MEANING AND IMPORTANCE OF MENTAL HYGIENE

Few of the many challenges faced by adults transcend that of making the most of our rich human assets—of keeping children and youth mentally, physically, emotionally, and spiritually sound. This is the challenge and the opportunity shared by teachers through adoption of the mental hygiene viewpoint. During childhood and youth the basic patterns of thought, feeling, and behavior are being established; and teachers can do much toward forming the foundations of adult happiness and effectiveness. Admittedly, parents are a major influence, but they do not typically have the same opportunity as teachers for formal study of the behavioral sciences, which might enhance their beneficent influence.

Knowledge is available today which would greatly facilitate more harmonious living. More refined and intimate scientific knowledge is continually being made explicit. The big obstacle is the task of putting proven principles into actual operation. There is no use in asking who is primarily responsible. Parents, of course, since they control children during the most impressionable years, are initially in the most strategic position. Social workers, statesmen, community leaders, church workers, and the ordinary citizen play a part, but they do not have continuous contact with children.

Teachers are a powerful group of men and women who have studied the nature of individual growth, who have become acquainted with the techniques for teaching new behaviors, and who deal with people while they are still very much in the process of "becoming." Teachers might well take the initiative in putting into active operation the way of life which can justly be called mental health. We must stop "passing the buck"—blaming parents, society, and material conditions—and act on the

3

assumption that teaching the dynamics of mental health must begin with immediately available avenues. We cannot wait for psychiatrists and psychologists to solve all the problems for us. We cannot wait for improvement of all those factors which condition mental health outside the school to be realized before taking some steps. Teachers can afford to become acquainted with fundamental principles of mental health, because to know and apply them will result in greater personal satisfaction and in greater service to a rapidly changing civilization. The question why something should be done is relatively easy to answer. The major part of this book will deal with the problem of *how* teachers can help more effectively in building mental health.

Governmental Recognition of the Problem. A significant step toward the achievement of better mental health for the nation was taken in the passage of the National Mental Health Act in July, 1946. This Act formally recognized that mental health is a problem of great consequence. The Act does three things: (1) It gives recognition to the fact that mental hygiene means more than care for those already mentally ill, (2) it implies that mental illness is preventable, and (3) it makes funds available for the study and dissemination of knowledge. The purpose of the Act is to provide

> . . . Federal support for the development of preventive mental health services in the States and communities, for research and for training of professional personnel. The goal of this program is to give every American the opportunity to achieve good mental health—to help him to live in peace with himself, his neighbors and the world.[1]

The provisions of the Act are threefold: (1) training of mental health personnel, (2) research directed toward the problems of mental illness, and (3) development by the states of preventive mental health programs in the community. The provisions are put into action by making grants to institutions for improving their facilities and for supplying training stipends to selected graduate students. There is no intent to take over the functions of states in caring for the mentally ill but to help the states by removing stigma from mental illness and to replace superstition with scientific facts about the causes and prevention of mental illness.

Teachers may find a clue to their responsibility for mental health in the concluding words of the brochure which describes the Act, "But the ultimate development of sound mental health programs depends on the local men and women who are closely in touch with the resources and needs of their community and who are deeply concerned with bringing optimum mental health to all their neighbors."[2]

[1] Federal Security Agency, Public Health Service, *The National Mental Health Program*, Mental Health Series, no. 4, June, 1948, Foreword.
[2] *Ibid.*, p. 7.

By virtue of the Act, the Federal government accepts a part of the responsibility for promoting mental health as it does for controlling cancer, tuberculosis, and venereal diseases.[3] Just as there remains much to be done about tuberculosis and venereal diseases by residents of local communities, so in the field of mental hygiene people must awake to the importance of the problem and take an active part. Just as teachers have played a dominant role in spreading knowledge about physical health and improving attitudes toward it, they must take a leading part in the attack on mental illness. In fact, the teachers' part can be even greater in mental health education than in physical health education, since some mental health problems are caused by school situations and others are aggravated by school conditions. Teachers, by direct effort, can remove some of the causes and aggravating factors of mental illness. They need not rely entirely on the effectiveness of their verbal instruction, as they had to do so largely in the successful attack on physical health problems.

That something can be done to improve conditions of mental health is indicated by data compiled during the decade after passage of the Act. In 1956, for only the second time since statistics have been available, there was a decrease in the patients resident in mental hospitals. Although more people were taken in, the rate of discharge was at an all-time high (13 per cent increase over 1955). It is felt that the decrease of 1.3 per cent of residents was due to the use of new therapies and long-range programs for improvement of care.[4]

International Recognition of the Problem of Mental Health. Six hundred persons from thirty-two countries met in Copenhagen in 1957 for the tenth annual meeting of the World Federation for Mental Health. Physicians, psychiatrists, pediatricians, psychologists, and educators discussed a variety of problems, ranging from child rearing and adoption to delinquency and insanity.[5]

The United Nations Educational, Scientific, and Cultural Organization devoted its 1952 annual meeting to the problem of mental health. The report on the meeting was published under the heading of *Education and Mental Health,*[6] and one reviewer stated, "The worlds of children and

[3] The growth of interest in mental health is shown in increased congressional appropriations for the National Institute for Mental Health, which in 1948 were $4,250,000 as compared with $52,419,000 for fiscal 1959. "No Longer Alone," *Annual Report,* New York: National Association for Mental Health, 1958, p. 6.

[4] *Facts on Mental Health and Mental Illness,* Bethesda, Md.: Public Health Service, U.S. Department of Health, Education, and Welfare, 1957, p. 5.

[5] Betty Barton, "World Federation of Mental Health," *Children,* 4:235, November–December, 1957.

[6] W. D. Wall, *Education and Mental Health,* The Hague, Holland: UNESCO, 1952. Distributed in the United States by International Documents Service, New York: Columbia University Press, 1955.

youth would be transformed in a wink were responsible educators and leaders in domestic affairs to act in terms of the scientific knowledge and interpretation it presents."[7]

Recognition of the Mental Health Problem by Educators. Individual educators have recognized the problem of mental health, and frequent references to its importance are made in books dealing with philosophy, psychology, methods of teaching, and personnel work. A number of books deal exclusively with the techniques of improving mental hygiene conditions in the classroom. It is recognized that

> Prevention depends upon diagnosis of early symptoms, in which the teacher can help. The growth of mental health as a positive, robust quality takes place in association with intellectual and emotional development, a function of the school. A third important step toward improving the welfare of all of our children is the provision of a mental health program. Mental hygiene should be introduced more generally into our school studies, and the principles of mental health should be recognized in the organization and administration of the school program, and mental health specialists should be available to those who need treatment.[8]

Recognition of the problem is an important step, but certainly not the only one. It will probably be a long time before enough specialists can be prepared to meet the insistent needs of even one out of twenty students. Some steps toward meeting these needs have been taken. The state mental health society of Michigan aided the schools in presenting an eight-week television course on mental health. Schools and colleges throughout the country are using a bibliography, prepared by the National Association for Mental Health, for students who wish to study various aspects of mental health.[9] Courses in mental hygiene will be a forward step, but the attitudes toward self, others, work, and responsibility, and the daily living habits which the teacher encourages in pupils have basic significance. There is much that can be done immediately by teachers to create a school environment conducive to mental health and to help children who have minor symptoms of maladjustment. Administrators have the responsibility of encouraging their teachers to study mental hygiene and of providing opportunities for the teachers to work with individual students and their problems of mental health.

Recognition of the problem of mental health is also reflected in the

[7] Howard Lane, "UNESCO on Mental Health," *Children,* 4:30, January–February, 1957.

[8] National Education Association of the United States, *Proceedings of the Eighty-seventh Annual Meeting,* Vol. 87, Washington, D.C.: The Association, 1949, p. 325. By permission of the National Education Association.

[9] "No Longer Alone," *Annual Report,* New York: National Association for Mental Health, 1958, p. 14.

introduction of college courses in mental hygiene. An examination of college catalogues indicates that most of the institutions for preparing teachers have courses in mental hygiene and personal adjustment. In addition, there are mental hygiene emphases in courses in educational psychology, child development, and psychology of adjustment, and in the courses dealing with teaching methods. In some states, work in the area of mental hygiene for both teachers and administrators is a requisite for certification.

Another indication of the growing awareness of the problem of mental health in the schools can be noted in the number of articles in professional magazines dealing with the subject. In 1955 the National Society for the Study of Education, which has since 1902 been publishing yearbooks on important problems in education, for the first time devoted a volume to mental hygiene in the schools.[10] In 1957 the National Association for Mental Health ceased issuing one of its publications, *Understanding the Child*, which was devoted largely to mental hygiene in schools. This action was taken because the association felt that so many teachers had become aware of the problem, and so many articles were appearing in other professional magazines, that it was no longer necessary to devote a publication exclusively to mental hygiene in school. Numerous educational conferences have sections, and sometimes continuing themes, of mental hygiene as a working basis. Many teacher in-service programs revolve around the problem of improving the mental health conditions of the school.[11]

THE EXTENT OF MENTAL ILL-HEALTH

Evidences of Mental Ill-health. Statistics on the extent of mental ill-health reveal something of the seriousness of the problem we face. It is estimated that one out of every ten babies born today will be hospitalized for mental illness at some time during his life.[12] In view of these statistics, the warning that "the schools cannot wait for some dimly seen 'ideal' time before they launch a large-scale offensive against the greatest disabler of all diseases: mental illness,"[13] is more pertinent than ever.

It is estimated that, of forty elementary pupils, two will spend some time in an institution for treatment of a psychosis, five will need psychiatric care, ten or more will have their marriages terminated by the

---

[10] National Society for the Study of Education, *Mental Health in Modern Education*, 54th Yearbook, Part II, Chicago: University of Chicago Press, 1955.

[11] Jane B. Rath, "Description of a Workshop Project in Mental Health," *Mental Hygiene*, 43:360–367, July, 1960.

[12] *Facts on Mental Health and Mental Illness*, p. 7.

[13] Robert H. Felix, "The Teacher's Role in Mental Health Defense," *School Life*, 31:3, January, 1949.

distress of divorce, and many will find it necessary to consult physicians for "functional" ailments.[14]

There are many who will fail to realize the best of their potential, who will find it impossible to be happy, who will suffer from minor mental and psychosomatic disturbances, yet will not be sufficiently maladjusted to be committed to institutions or to seek help. These, too, should be recognized as a vital part of the problem of mental health.

During World War II it was found necessary to reject for military service, because of mental and emotional instability, 38 per cent of those examined—and this, supposedly, from that group which we consider to be in the "prime of life."[15] More than one marriage out of four ends in divorce; this, too, is a symptom of inability to adjust. Increasingly the excessive use of alcohol is being recognized to be more than an unfortunate habit; it is a symptom of inadequacy in facing the exigencies of life and an attempt to escape routine pressures. In 1956 there were over five million excessive drinkers in the United States of which 1,254,000 were with complications (some diagnosable mental or physical disorder or both—formerly called "chronic alcoholics").[16] This is a rate of 4,520 per 100,000 of the adult population or roughly one out of twenty-two persons manifesting this one symptom of mental illness.

Delinquency is a symptom of mental illness, a symptom about which exact statistics are difficult to obtain because methods and viewpoints vary and because communities attempt to protect themselves from the unfavorable light of revealing facts.[17] Nevertheless, there has been an increased incidence of delinquency since World War II. There was an increase of almost two and one-half times in the number of juvenile court appearances of children 10 to 17 years old from 1949 to 1957, while this age group as a whole increased only 25 per cent. In any one year this represents only 2 to 3 per cent, but if all in the 10 to 17 age group who had ever appeared in court were included it would be about 12 per cent of the total age group.[18] Realization of the fact that the great majority of delinquents are, or were at some time, in school is a sobering thought for teachers.

The violence and shouting that have attended attempts to integrate schools are evidences of fear, suspicion, and insecurity. Racial discrimination would be bad enough if the mental hygienist had to contend only

[14] B. Y. Glassberg, "Whole Child," *Childhood Education*, 34:206–208, January, 1958.

[15] *What Are the Facts about Mental Illness in the United States?* Washington: National Mental Health Committee, 1956, p. 3.

[16] Mark Keller and Efron Vera, "The Rate of Alcoholism in the U.S.A.," *Quarterly Journal of Studies on Alcohol*, 19:316–319, 1958.

[17] William C. Kvaraceus in William F. Jenks (ed.), *Mental Health and Special Education*, Washington: The Catholic University of America Press, 1957, p. 139.

[18] Max F. Baer, "The National Juvenile Picture," *The Personnel and Guidance Journal*, 38:278–279, 1959.

with the chagrin, deprivation, and isolation suffered by the persons discriminated against. But the fact is that those doing the discriminating are indicating the symptoms of fear, selfishness, inflated egotism, and emotionally distorted thinking. Their lives are coarsened and stultified by the pain they inflict on others. Fortunately much progress has been made in recent years—for which educators can justifiably take some credit.

Mental Health as a Social and School Problem. If to the statistical indications of the need for the mental hygiene viewpoint we add the everyday symptoms of mental illness, the situation becomes even more striking. These indications cover a wide variety of phenomena. They include children at home who are excessively jealous of the status, or imagined status, of their siblings. They include parents who are working under the conviction that their children are unduly restricting their personal liberty. Pupils who hate school and are truants on every possible occasion can be added to the category of the mentally ill. Pupils who have good mental ability but who fail not only to work up to their capacity but even to achieve minimum standards are revealing symptoms of mental ill-health. Youngsters who have not learned techniques for getting along harmoniously with their peers are failing to acquire the happiness which gives evidence of sound mental health. Adults who are unhappy under the pressures of their occupational responsibilities are evidencing a lack of adjustment to the realities of life. The numerous persons who seek medical attention for ailments for which doctors can find no organic cause are, in large proportion, the victims of mental illness. The almost universal traits of jealousy, suspicion, surliness, temper displays, blaming others, moodiness, and transient unhappiness must be considered normal; but when they become chronic and excessive, they too must be added to evidences of the need for applied mental hygiene. It is with good reason and considerable insight that the designers of the Constitution of the United Nations Educational, Scientific, and Cultural Organization assert in the preamble (italics not in original):

> The Governments of the States parties to this constitution, on behalf of their peoples, declare that *since wars begin in the minds of men it is in the minds of men that the defenses of peace must be constructed;* that ignorance of each other's ways and lives has been a common cause throughout the history of mankind of that suspicion and mistrust between the peoples of the world through which their differences have all too often broken into war.

Still another picture of the seriousness of the problem of mental ill-health can be obtained by examining in detail the life situation of one individual who has properly been termed "mentally ill." This individual may be living a lonesome and fearful life in the presence of bickering parents. He learns only slowly, if at all, the basic elements of social adjustment; he is rejected by the children at school as being a crybaby or a poor sport and is jeeringly forbidden to partake in group activities. His worry over lack of acceptance causes his mind to wander in school, and the teacher reprimands him for being inattentive. A teacher conference with his parents may do nothing more than provide the parents with an opportunity to air their mutual difficulties before a third party, resulting in no advantage to the child. The child then decides to get away from school and home by truancy and running away—only to be seized by police authorities. Then because the child had "done nothing," he decides that next time they get him he will at least have had the satisfaction of having "done something." It is easy to visualize this young person in jail, planning "jobs," taking drugs, getting some cash at the end of a gun; for we know that these things do take place. Behind the newspaper headlines about crime and violence are experiences of individual sorrow, hate, frustration, and tragedy.

The Future of Mental Health. There are some who would have us believe that the incidence of mental breakdown is increasing, that the number of people in mental hospitals is growing faster than is warranted in terms of the increase in population. While the figures on commitments are not to be questioned—they do indicate an increase—there is no real reason to believe that mental illness is affecting a larger proportion of the population than it formerly did. The statistics may be deceptive unless the following notions are realized. (1) There is an increasing recognition of the symptoms that indicate mental illness, therefore more of the maladjusted are identified as so being. (2) The changing concept of mental illness has contributed to a lack of accuracy in interpreting statistics. (3) There are constantly growing facilities for taking care of the mentally ill, so that one case may become and remain a "statistic" more readily now than previously.

However, one very sound reason for considering the possibility of an increasing incidence of mental illness has to do with the fact that more people are living to advanced ages now than at the turn of the century; and longevity is continuing to increase.

Date	Per cent of total population over age 65
1900	4.1
1950	8.1
1960	8.9 est.
1975	9.4 est.

SOURCE: U.S. Bureau of the Census, *Census of Population: 1950*, vol. II, *Characteristics of the Population*, part 1, *United States Summary*, table 39; *Current Population Reports, Population Estimates*, ser. P-25, no. 39, table I, and ser. A, no. 78, Aug. 21, 1953.

The older a person becomes, the greater the probability that he will suffer from mental breakdown (Table 1-1 and Fig. 1); for example, while those between the ages of fifteen and twenty-four constitute about 12 per cent of the population, they make up about 10 per cent of first

Table 1-1
First Admissions to Mental Hospitals and Total Population by Age Groups

Age group	First admissions	Per cent of first adms.	Population in thousands	Per cent of population
Under 15	1,181	1.2	69,129	37.0
15–24	9,546	9.9	22,132	11.8
25–34	17,727	18.3	23,990	12.8
35–44	18,231	18.8	23,066	12.3
45–54	14,825	15.3	19,283	10.4
55–64	10,644	11.0	14,745	7.9
65–74	11,265	11.6	9,579	5.1
75 and over	12,645	13.1	4,847	2.6
Unknown	667	.7		
Total	96,731	99.9	186,771	99.9

SOURCE: U.S. Bureau of the Census, *Statistical Abstracts of the United States: 1957*, 78th Annual Edition: 1957, pp. 24, 83.

admissions; and while those between fifty-five and sixty-four constitute about 8 per cent of the population, they account for 11 per cent of first admissions.

Not only are older people apparently more prone to mental breakdown than are younger persons, but studies show that the rate of breakdown

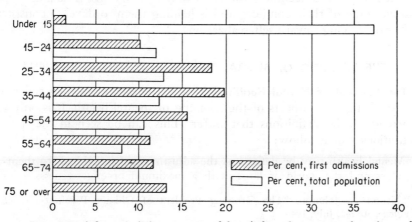

FIG. 1. Per cent of first admissions to mental hospitals and per cent of total population, by age groups.

for the older people is increasing.[19] Prolonging life may give a greater chance for incipient mental illness to become manifested. It may be that the lives of persons who were predisposed to mental disease have been saved by modern medicine only to have the weakness become apparent in later years. Science, while saving the body, has not yet taught how to cope with the problem of saving the mind. On the other hand, some of the commitments of older persons are not really the result of emotional maladjustment but the result of their having no other place to live.

No doubt organic factors have much to do with the breakdown of older people. The process of physical degeneration works toward reducing the size of organs, changing intercellular and supporting tissue, altering blood vessels and circulation. Healing after injury and disease is less rapid than in the earlier years.[20] But even if the pervasiveness of organic factors is admitted, the role of mental hygiene is significant. The way the older person thinks about his organic decline will influence his effectiveness. His willingness to accept an altered plan of life should attend changed physical status; besides, his attitude will affect the extent and speed of physical changes. Therefore, even considering organic alteration, the problem of aging is still largely a problem of mental hygiene.

There are certain questions for the classroom teacher to consider. Ideally, provision against the ills and uncertainties of old age should begin in the early years of life; that is, good habits and a healthy outlook must be established, symptoms of mental ill-health must be identified, and individuals who give evidence of such symptoms must be treated. These provisions are the best defense against maladjustment. If the classroom teacher can help his pupils establish these goals of mental hygiene, it means that he is becoming aware of minor symptoms, is helping pupils resolve some of their conflicts, and is helping them to develop consistent habits of striving toward self-realization.

THE MEANING OF MENTAL HEALTH AND MENTAL HYGIENE

The Concept of Mental Health. People are rather closely agreed upon many of the basic aspects of the meaning of mental health. It is only the wording of the definitions that differ. This can be seen in the quoted definitions which follow:

Mental health may be defined as the adjustment of individuals to themselves and the world at large with a maximum of effectiveness, satis-

[19] Nelson A. Johnson, "The Growing Problem of Old-age Psychoses," *Mental Hygiene*, 30:442, July, 1946.

[20] Clark Tibbits and Wilma Donahue, *Aging in the Modern World*, Ann Arbor: University of Michigan Press, 1957, pp. 51–62.

factions, cheerfulness, and socially considerate behavior, and the ability of facing and accepting the realities of life. The highest degree of mental health might, therefore, be described as that which permits an individual to realize the greatest success which his capabilities will permit, with a maximum of satisfaction to himself and the social order, and a minimum of friction and tension. This implies a stage of such well-being that the individual is not conscious of unsatisfied tensions; does not show socially inadequate or objectionable behavior and maintains himself intellectually and emotionally in any environment under any circumstances.[21]

A "mature, healthy person" is extremely difficult to define; indeed, a clear-cut and complete definition is impossible at this time. Suffice it to say that [he] is one who is able to live at relative peace with himself and with his neighbors; who has the capacity to raise healthy children; and who, when these basic functions are accomplished, still has energy enough left over to make some further contribution to the society in which he lives.[22]

Marie Jahoda, making a report to the Joint Commission on Mental Illness and Health, suggests six major categories for conceptualizing the often vague term *mental health:*
1. An attitude toward one's self in which self-inspection leads toward acceptance of weaknesses and pride in strengths; a clear image of what one really is and identity with it so that one is motivated toward inner stability.
2. Growth and development toward self-realization of one's potentialities; a blending of one's total personality toward achieving the best of what one might become.
3. Integration of personality involving a balance of psychic forces, a unified outlook on life, and some capacity for withstanding anxiety and stress.
4. Autonomy of action in which the individual determines behavior from within instead of drifting with the impact of present stimuli—independence in the face of difficulties.
5. A perception of reality which is relatively free from what one wishes things might be and which involves his being attentive to and concerned with the welfare of others.
6. Mastery of the environment through (*a*) the ability to love, (*b*) being adequate in love, work, and play, (*c*) competence in human relations, (*d*) capacity to adapt oneself to current circumstances, (*e*) ability

[21] White House Conference, *Preliminary Reports,* New York: Appleton-Century-Crofts, Inc., 1930, p. 465.
[22] Paul V. Lemkau, *Mental Hygiene in Public Health,* 2d ed., New York: McGraw-Hill Book Company, Inc., 1955, p. 132.

to draw satisfactions from one's environment and (f) willingness to use problem solving approaches in the life processes.[23]

The foregoing passages indicate some of the underlying concepts of mental health. Mental health involves (1) continuous adjusting rather than a static condition and is therefore a progressive goal. It is an ability to cope with the present and in all likelihood to adjust satisfactorily in the future. It involves (2) physical, mental, and emotional phases of adjustive behavior as well as habits of work and attitudes toward situations and obstacles. Hence, mental health is (3) a point of view one takes of *all* phases of living. The concept includes (4) a social phase—referred to in the definitions by such words as "socially considerate behavior," "satisfaction with the social order," and "contributions to society." Mental health is not simply the absence of disease but is (5) a process of optimum functioning and maximum self-realization. For those who are ill it is a matter of getting well, for those who are "getting along" it is a matter of improvement, and for those who are robust it is a matter of maintaining and continuing achievement.

Mental health for teachers is a state in which they are effective in their work, take satisfaction and pride in the activities they pursue, manifest cheer in the performance of their duties, and are humanely considerate of their pupils and their professional coworkers. This is a large order— perhaps too large an order—but the ongoing nature of mental health holds a saving feature. Working toward improvement and attaining some betterment are evidence of mental health in its dynamic concept.

Mental health in the classroom can be emphasized in similar terms. It involves students who are effective, or successful, in the activities of the classroom. The mentally healthy student is one who gains satisfaction from the achievements he is experiencing, and who has reason for doing so. Because he is effective and has satisfactions, he is cheerful about his work and his associations. And finally, the mentally healthy student is one who can work for and with others as well as by himself. He is not a lonesome personality; rather, he takes pride in knowing how to live happily and productively with others.[24] And by virtue of these characteristics, he is forming the habits and attitudes that create in him a confidence that problems should be and can be aggressively attacked.

The Concept of Mental Hygiene. Mental hygiene can be defined more easily than mental health, because it is simply the means by which the process of mental health is realized. Beyond this very general statement the explanation becomes more difficult, because mental hygiene is a way of life and so involves all that influences what one feels, says, and does.

[23] Marie Jahoda, *Current Concepts of Positive Mental Health,* New York: Basic Books, Inc., 1958, pp. 23–64.

[24] Reynold A. Jensen, "Guest Editorial," *Mental Hygiene,* 42:145, January, 1958.

In the classroom, it involves the plans, the objectives, the techniques, the materials, the physical conditions, and the teacher himself, as they shape the classroom atmosphere as a whole.

The inclusiveness of the meaning of mental hygiene is indicated in the following:

> Just as public hygiene is concerned with the health of people who are well as much as with the illnesses of those who are sick, so mental hygiene has implications for everyone. In its broadest sense, the aim of mental hygiene is to help all persons achieve fuller, happier, more harmonious, and more effective lives.[25]

Mental hygiene involves developing an understanding of oneself and of others. It involves capitalizing on one's intellectual potential, gaining satisfaction from positive emotions, and controlling the manifestation of negative emotions. Inasmuch as mind and body are but aspects of the total organism, mental hygiene means applying knowledge with regard to keeping in as good physical health as possible and knowing what to do in the event of illness.

Broadly speaking, the mental hygiene program in the school should do two things: (1) It should seek to remove as many as possible of the conditions which hamper the realization of mental health and should seek to diminish the impact of those hindrances which cannot be removed. (2) The mental hygiene program should seek, in terms of the maturity of the pupil, to develop attitudes that will encourage a sensible attack upon problems; and it should seek to develop tension-tolerance for the unpleasant aspects of life that, at least temporarily, cannot be changed. It should, in brief, aim at the highest degree of self-realization for each child in all areas of his school experience.

The Prospects of Mental Health. Individual school systems in which mental hygiene has been given special emphasis report gratifying results of improved school atmosphere and pupil behavior. For example, in Indianapolis, a program of mental hygiene was developed, including, among other things, the following: screening of prospective teachers in training institutions, presentation of an in-service course in mental hygiene (which in one year enrolled over 400 teachers and administrators), employment of psychological consultants, emphasis on functional citizenship in classrooms, special provisions for exceptional children, elimination of segregated schools, provisions for school-community recreation programs, establishment of a committee to study and make recommendations for teacher welfare, and continuing research on, and evaluation of, the total mental hygiene program. The results were a reduced rate of

[25] Laurance Frederic Shaffer and Edward Joseph Shoben, Jr., *The Psychology of Adjustment*, 2d ed., Boston: Houghton Mifflin Company, 1956, p. 483.

delinquency (one-fifth of the national average), reduced racial tension and acceptance of the Negro as an individual, reduced teacher turnover, better placement of pupils in appropriate curriculums, widened participation of pupils in extracurricular activities, increased community sensitivity of the role of the teacher, and heightened awareness of the need of children in both school and community.[26]

A study of Locust Point, a section of Baltimore, Maryland, indicates that even the "direst prophecies of dependability and instability may be brought to nought" by an effectively planned and executed program of mental hygiene. The data show that an educational program planned to fit the needs of people who are potentially poor, through inheritance and cultural conditions, may serve to make them dependable citizens. Dr. Ruth Fairbank, director of the follow-up study, gave teachers the major credit for turning the human liabilities of Locust Point so largely into community assets.[27]

In San Francisco, where 800 "atypical" children were treated in accordance with their needs, only four of them appeared in juvenile courts. This would be an enviable record if the 800 children had been "average" children. St. Louis experienced somewhat the same results when only 3.3 per cent of 1,969 students in special classes were committed to correctional institutions. The Los Angeles Institute of Family Relations reported that 70 per cent of 10,000 cases of potential divorce were prevented. This last study is not of direct concern to the school, but it does show that improved understanding can result in better human relationships.

For the most part, evidence of the efficacy of mental hygiene programs in the school must wait for better tools of evaluation and for long-term follow-up studies. In ten or fifteen years we may be able to make more valid comparisons, but at present we must depend greatly on impressionistic statements. There is good reason to believe that better understanding of the nature of mental hygiene programs plus more and better-trained professional workers will make significant contributions toward the development of mature, healthful members of our American society.[28]

Adequate adjustment is not innate or instinctive. Each new generation must learn anew the processes of effective living. The outstanding characteristic of human beings is the high degree of their ability to change.

[26] Herman L. Shibler, "Evaluation of a Mental Health Program" in *Mental Health in Modern Education*, 54th Yearbook, Part II, National Society for the Study of Education, Chicago: University of Chicago Press, 1955, pp. 271–304.

[27] Ruth E. Fairbank, "The Subnormal Child—Seventeen Years After," *Mental Hygiene*, 17:177–208, April, 1933.

[28] W. T. Vaughn, "Mental Health for School Children," *Children*, 2:203–207, November, 1955.

But without the direction and suggestion provided by the experience of previous generations, the actions of the present population would be faltering and groping. It can therefore be said confidently that the mental health of the future is dependent upon those who influence the lives of young people. The place of greatest influence, of course, is held by the parents, but a close second is the role occupied by teachers.

ASPECTS OF THE MENTAL HYGIENE VIEWPOINT

There are three phases of the mental hygiene viewpoint which concern the teacher in varying degrees. These phases, or aspects, are (1) the positive, (2) the preventive, and (3) the curative.

The Positive Aspect of Mental Hygiene. It is said that the great majority of babies are born perfect. Certainly, there are many children who seem to be happy, vigorous, and curious. They enter school with pleasurable anticipation. As they continue in the upper grades and high school, the majority of these pupils are in good mental health (see Fig. 1, which shows that these age groups do not contribute to mental illness statistics in proportion to their numbers in the total population). The task of the teacher is to help this majority achieve greater self-realization, to prepare them for life's exigencies through providing them balanced experiences of success and failure. Though these pupils have solved their problems up to now, they can be aided in developing better social skills and improving their understanding of and empathy with others. They can learn what for each of them are realistic goals. They can learn to appreciate and exploit their gifts and talents, to face and accept their limitations, to regard themselves as worthy and competent individuals, to apply themselves assiduously to achievable tasks, and thus to develop work habits of continuous value. The positive aspect of mental health is one of capitalizing on one's strengths and attempting to correct one's weaknesses.

The Preventive Aspect of Mental Hygiene. The second aspect of mental hygiene is concerned with individuals who are on the brink of mental ill-health. The preventive aspect of mental hygiene involves special programs for individuals after they have revealed symptoms of incipient mental and emotional disturbance. Thus, a child who is occasionally truant will be studied to see what his background difficulties are, in the hope that adjustments can be made before the truancy has become habitual or has spread into other symptoms.

In the main, it is in the preventive and preservative aspects of mental hygiene that teachers will find the opportunity for greatest service. They can set the tempo of learning situations and control the general social atmosphere of the classroom, and they can give attention to the minor deviations of individual behavior that give warning of later, more serious problems of adjustment.

The Curative Aspect of Mental Hygiene. Just as the preservative aspect of mental hygiene shades into the preventive, so does the preventive shade into the curative. When the teacher first encounters a certain pupil, he may discover that the pupil already has some marked deviation of behavior which cannot be considered to be within even the wider limits of normality. These borderline cases present a difficult problem to the teacher, since a precarious decision must be made whether to try to do something for the individual or to keep "hands off," because of the danger of doing still further damage. With this difficult situation in mind, one must look upon the curative aspect of mental hygiene as a technical problem that should be largely left to experts. When emotional illness is serious, the incipient breakdown may be hastened by the "help" of someone who is acting on good intentions alone. Recognizing this hazard, Robert H. Felix warns, "Don't stick your neck out. With the best intentions in the world, amateur psychiatrists can do lasting damage to the emotionally unstable. As a matter of blunt fact, learning to do no harm is one of the basic tenets of mental hygiene."[29]

What Teachers Can Do. But there is a great deal that the classroom teacher can do, short of posing as a psychiatrist. Teachers can recognize such dynamics of mental hygiene as (1) the futility of competition against odds compared with the gain of satisfaction from appropriate achievement and from sustained quality of human relationships, (2) the need children have for tasks which can be accepted with enthusiasm, (3) the fact that maladaptive behaviors are defenses against anxieties, (4) the building of self-esteem through recognition, acceptance by others, and personal fulfillment.[30] Dr. George Saslow describes psychotherapy as a problem of reeducation involving (1) a definition of the subject's habitual methods of response, (2) statement and realization of the principal alternative methods which would yield better results, and (3) practice of these methods, while maintaining contact with the therapist, until the response becomes habitual.[31] Teachers can participate in this reeducation (as will be shown in later chapters) by understanding the nature and origin of unsatisfactory responses, by helping pupils define alternatives, and by giving support—during both progress and regressions—to the

[29] Robert H. Felix, "The Teacher's Role in Mental Health Defense," *School Life,* 31:14, January, 1949.

[30] Lawrence Frank, "The Reorientation of Education to the Promotion of Mental Hygiene," *Mental Hygiene,* 23:529–543, 1939. (These points are expanded in subsequent chapters.)

[31] George Saslow, "Seminar in Psychiatry," Portland: University of Oregon Medical School, Sept. 8, 1959.

pupil as he strives to improve. This process requires patience, confidence, and time but frequently yields gratifying dividends in improved pupil conduct. There are many children whose symptoms are passing and minor but who might, if teachers evade the problem, develop persisting habits which would hamper future adjustment. One classroom teacher has stated the problem as follows:

> All of us will agree that we do something to all children whether or not it is intended. Therefore, it would be far better if teachers knew what to do.
>
> There is also the situation which demands prompt action by the teacher. Many deeds which sometimes turn out to be rather rash could be avoided.
>
> Think of all the thousands of boys and girls for whom there will never be any clinician. They are entitled to develop their whole personality which can best be done when the teacher understands the elements of good mental health.
>
> It is undoubtedly as true in mental health as in any other field that, even if the child can be seen by a specialist, the ultimate product depends upon the cooperation of the classroom teacher with the clinician. To fully cooperate, the classroom teacher needs a basic understanding of the problem.

We can look forward to, and work toward, the time when there will be a sufficient number of psychologists and psychiatrists to take care of the needs of all school children. At present the supply of such specialists is woefully inadequate, and often the cost of service is out of reach of the parents of many children. Most high schools in the United States enroll fewer than two hundred pupils and employ fewer than nine teachers. In such systems the adding of specialists involves expense which school patrons feel is either unbearable or unwarranted. Even in the larger systems which can and do employ psychiatrists or psychologists, the teachers will have to see to carrying out the recommendations of the expert. The basic fact and challenge is *if* teachers do not help, some unfortunate children will receive *no* help at all.

A great part of the good that teachers can do in improving the mental health of children lies not in what they can do *for* the child, but in what they do *in front of* the child, that is, the example they set and the classroom atmosphere they create. For this reason, a considerable portion of this book is devoted to a discussion of the factors that condition the mental health of teachers, with suggestions for removing some of the handicaps and for learning to live with the handicaps that cannot be readily removed.

Mental health is not a mystery. It is the result of scientific and empirical knowledge applied to the inevitable problems of daily living.

GOALS OF MENTAL HYGIENE

The goals of mental hygiene have been expressed above as "the attainment of a fuller, happier, more harmonious and more effective existence." Analysis of the concepts of these words may be advantageous.

A Full Existence. A full life is one in which, among other things, the individual comes close to realizing his potentialities. He will have grown and he keeps on growing, in a productive sense. This means, for teachers, that they seek better ways of doing their important work, they study and take joy in the social impact of teaching, they are not satisfied just to "get by" but want to do the best job possible. It means, for their pupils, that those who are capable of good scholastic work do it. The varied activities provided in the schoolroom permit every child to experience a degree of success.

A full life is one in which some exercise is given to all facets of the total personality—the physical, mental, emotional, and spiritual. Everyone has potentialities in these areas, and a goal of mental hygiene is to provide exercise and expression of them. Here is seen the necessity for variety in the school program. The mental aspects are fairly well taken care of, except, perhaps, that there is a lack of opportunity for superior accomplishment by gifted children. The realization of physical potentialities needs more carefully considered attention. Increasingly, attention is being given to emotional expression in art, music, drama, and dancing. As more teachers grasp the basic idea of full living, still more improvement will ensue. The increase in attention to socialization and world brotherhood is giving sensible emphasis to spiritual values.

Full realization of potentialities is an unachievable ideal. However, a very practical goal of mental hygiene in the classroom is that of *coming closer* to such realization for each child than would be possible if no attention were given to the goal. The greater realization of potentialities cannot be left to chance; it must be a seriously considered objective.

A Happy Existence. Philosophers have frequently said that when happiness is a direct objective it becomes increasingly elusive. In fact, it is difficult even to state what happiness is. The things that lead to happiness for one are not necessarily the things which make another happy. Perhaps the best way to express it is to say that, if a person feels he is happy, the observer must ordinarily believe that he is. Thus, happiness is a way of looking at things.

When a pupil enjoys his relations with his classmates, when he takes pride in his work, when his fears are short-lived, when he has opportunities to exercise all sides of his personality, and when he looks forward eagerly to the adventures of the coming day, then he is happy. Happiness is contagious. Happy parents tend to produce happy children, who in turn achieve happiness in their own marriages. In the same way, the cheer and confidence of teachers are quickly reflected in the enthusiasm and poise of their pupils.

Harmonious Existence. A harmonious existence depends upon success in two efforts—getting along with oneself and getting along with others. Getting along with oneself involves such matters as being able to decide between two attractions and, having decided, to feel no regret for having made the decision. Another requirement is to be able to accept one's shortcomings with grace—without bemoaning one's evil fate—and to be able to exercise one's greatest talents without boasting and arrogance. Harmony within oneself is similar to, if not identical with, what some have chosen to call a sound ego concept. The individual has the feeling that he is a worthy, able, likable, and loved person. This strong ego concept is largely a reflection of what key persons think about and show they think about the person concerned.[32] Hence, teachers who are proud of, have confidence in, and like their pupils are strengthening their egos and hence are tending to produce inner harmony. A harmonious existence calls for the attainment of such a degree of self-confidence that problems are attacked aggressively and worry is held to an absolute minimum. Living in harmony with oneself is certainly dependent upon eliminating such character traits as greed, suspicion, jealousy, and hate, to mention only a few of the more prevalent obstacles to achieving harmony with others and consequent inner harmony.

An Effective Existence. An effective existence may well be the summarizing result of self-realization, learning to be happy, and being able to get along with oneself and with others. It means getting the most done with the least expenditure of energy—that is, high productivity with the least waste. A person may get considerable work done, but if, in the process, he tires himself needlessly and cuts himself off from others, he cannot be considered efficient. To be "effective," he must come reasonably close to the realization of his capacities.

Use of the term *effectiveness* does not imply that an individual who accomplishes less than his neighbor is therefore ineffective. The mental health viewpoint would allow for the placement of the accolade "effective" on the truck driver who earns considerably less salary than the life insurance executive. In terms of the former's mental ability, opportunity for education, and social and economic background, his accomplishment may be very commendable.

Effectiveness should be thought of in terms of an individual rather than in terms of comparisons. Thus, the average student whose academic intelligence is low, who has to work outside of school hours, or who has

[32] Arthur T. Jersild, *In Search of Self*, New York: Bureau of Publications, Teachers College, Columbia University, 1952, pp. 25–40.

less than buoyant health, and who gets along with his teachers and peers may be effective; while his honor-roll classmate may be ineffective because he cultivates no interests beyond the academic and fails to associate with his peers.

Some years ago a college professor killed the president of his institution and the dean of the school in which he had been employed, and then committed suicide. Here was a man who had apparently achieved a position of eminence but who was described by his fellow staff members as being "a lonesome man—not mixing much." He had accomplished something, but his life could not be rated as effective, since effectiveness must be judged in terms of social helpfulness and of lack of waste.

THE CONCERNS OF THIS BOOK

Mental hygiene is a many-faceted phenomenon which has come to have local, national, and international importance. In citing evidence of the extent of mental illness, it has been suggested that something can be done about it. General statements have been made to the effect that, when teachers know the principles of mental hygiene and when schools are adapted to meet the needs of children and youth, improvement can be effected. In the remainder of the book attempts will be made to show how schools can be organized to challenge varied intellectual powers and potentialities. Suggestions are offered for obtaining socially oriented emotional release. Plans are described for achieving greater self-understanding and understanding of others.

Students of mental hygiene are requested not to become impatient because some all-inclusive, miraculous cure is not prescribed. Since mental health has many aspects, there must be many approaches to it. Each chapter directly suggests or implies some ways in which we can "chip away" at the problem of mental illness. Any person is the result of *all* the experiences he has had—the aim here is to shape as many as possible of the child's and youth's school experiences into the salubrious variety that will produce mental health. The book is based on the faith that a million teachers, doing the little things in mental hygiene with millions of pupils, will have a noteworthy cumulative effect.

Some readers of the first edition have expressed concern that there was no discussion of the distinctly abnormal—the psychotic, the criminally insane, the sex deviate, the children who hate—in a mental hygiene text. The reasons for the continued omission of discussion of the extreme deviate are (1) these individuals require the services of specialists—consulting psychologists, psychiatrists, and physicians; (2) the medical aspects of the problem are an out-of-school enterprise; (3) most teachers will encounter few such persons in the classroom, and if they do encounter one, will recognize that he needs special help; and (4) although study of these types may have implications for teachers, these implications can as readily be drawn from study of normal children, whose major problem is more complete self-realization and better development of their ego concepts.

Emphasis is placed on the development of mental health by the teacher himself. The teacher's personal and professional philosophy is discussed. The special concern of the book is to stimulate every teacher who studies it to find one or several mental health experiments or projects that he will initiate. This experimentation will not only be likely to help the pupils but will be a means of making teaching a creative kind of work. This in itself is a step toward optimum mental health.

SUMMARY

Contemporary man has learned much about controlling the physical world but seems untutored in ways of efficient living. His difficulties are reflected in statistics on the extent of mental illness, statistics that force us to recognize mental health as a problem of prime importance. The problem is being considered seriously by the Federal government, by international agencies, and by educators. Ultimately, it seems, much of the value of mental hygiene will depend on teachers.

It cannot be said with certainty that contemporary man is more susceptible to mental illness than were his ancestors, but it is evident that man must learn to live more fully, harmoniously, happily, and effectively. Teachers can do much to reveal the way of life that will make it possible for individuals to grow toward social, intellectual, and emotional maturity. This they can do by (1) putting a positive emphasis on the mental health that many already enjoy, (2) retarding further deterioration after the first symptoms of ill-health have been observed, and (3) helping to cure those who have minor disturbances.

The principles of mental hygiene are not a mystery. They are largely a matter of applying what we already know about effective living. New insights are, however, being achieved. Since too few parents will have the opportunity to learn these principles under formal instructions, classroom teachers are in the most advantageous position to help children and youth.

One should not take the view that the nation is rapidly becoming one of psychotics and neurotics. The fact is that there are many, many mature and healthy citizens. Most of the children in school are solving their problems satisfactorily. The proper view of the situation is that the cancerous growths on mental health can be decreased. Happier and more effective lives can be lived. The study of mental hygiene optimistically points the way to improvement.

STUDY AND DISCUSSION EXERCISES

1. Scan a daily newspaper for items which give evidence of the need for a widespread and constructive mental hygiene program.

2. Compile a list of the resources available in your state which are directly pointed toward the improvement of mental health.

3. Present data for and against the argument that mental ill-health has a greater incidence today than in former generations.

4. List a number of specific things a teacher might do to help pupils develop a healthy ego concept.

5. Which of the three aspects—positive, preventive, curative—do you consider to be of most importance for classroom teachers?

SUGGESTED ADDITIONAL READINGS

Beers, Clifford, *A Mind That Found Itself*, New York: Longmans, Green & Co., Inc., 1917. 363 pp.

The first part of the book is the biography of a man who "lost his mind" and fought a seesaw battle to regain balance. He won. The last part deals with his establishing "the modern mental hygiene movement."

Bonney, Merl E., *Mental Health in Education*, Englewood Cliffs, N.J.: Allyn and Bacon, Inc., 1960, pp. 394–423.

The effect of the teacher's personality on pupils and the factors which condition their mental health are discussed.

Jahoda, Marie, *Current Concepts of Positive Mental Health*, New York: Basic Books, Inc., 1958. 136 pp.

Mental health involves many human values including self-concept, realization of potentialities, how one works, plays, and loves, and the ability to face and accept one's ever-changing environment.

National Society for the Study of Education, *Mental Health in Modern Education*, 54th Yearbook, Part II, Chicago: University of Chicago Press, 1955.

The introduction and first two chapters describe the need for the mental hygiene emphasis, the role of teachers and schools, and the many people and agencies involved in a fruitful program of mental hygiene.

"No Longer Alone," *Annual Report*, New York: National Association for Mental Health, 1958. 33 pp.

The report describes the place of research, legislation, education, and cooperative effort in the attack on mental illness.

Remmers, H. H., and others (eds.), *Growth, Teaching, and Learning*, New York: Harper & Brothers, 1957, pp. 274–280, 418–427.

The first of these two readings deals with "Goals of Mental Health Education Selected by Experts," and the second is titled, "Mental Health as an Educational Goal."

CHAPTER 2

THE BASIC NEEDS OF CHILDREN

If there were an inclusive answer to the questions involving mental health, it might well be in terms of the satisfaction of human needs. One enjoys mental health to the extent to which his needs are gratified provided that fulfillment of a specific need does not conflict with other needs. Good heredity, compatible parents, organized communities, fine schools are all assets for children's mental health. But the ultimate basis for good mental health is the satisfaction of normal physical, social, and psychological needs. Moreover, the fundamental needs of children are nothing more than the fundamental needs of society.[1]

THE NATURE OF BASIC HUMAN NEEDS

The Meaning and Importance of Needs. Analysis of the various lists of needs by psychologists and mental hygienists shows that human needs are just what the dictionary definition implies; they are vital, indispensable, and urgently requisite. Organic needs, such as those for food, moisture, protection from extremes of temperature, if not satisfied will result in death. It may be that lack of satisfaction of personal and social needs would not cause death, but there is no certainty of this. It does appear, though, that denial of such needs brings about a lack of desire to live, which might hasten death. But aside from death, there are reasons for considering needs to be vital and requisite.

When needs are met efficiently, the result usually is a balanced and integrated personality. The individual becomes a happy, harmonious, and productive person, who is a source of gratification to society as well as to himself. Satisfaction does not necessarily imply that there is satia-

[1] Lawrence K. Frank, *The Fundamental Needs of the Child*, New York: The National Association for Mental Health, Inc., 1952, p. 28.

25

tion. Satisfaction does imply that needs are *on the way to being met* by a progressing and confident person. On the other hand, when needs are not met, or when their satisfaction is delayed too long, the person may become frustrated, inhibited, and unbalanced, developing a defeated, discouraged attitude. This, at best, produces a lack of activity and a wish to retreat from social contacts—it retards progress toward self-realization; while at worst, it turns the individual into a liability to society.

Multiplicity of Needs. No two authors seem to agree on a listing of needs. One writer lists forty basic needs, another gives a list of twenty-eight, many cite from five to eight, and a few reduce the list to two or three. In this book needs are classified into three categories—organic, personal, and social needs—with representative and illustrative, rather than inclusive, subdivisions. There is, of necessity, much overlapping, and it must be realized that the divisions are for the sake of convenience in discussion.

A great number of conditions must be satisfied, or on the way to being satisfied, if a person is to live and attain mental health. Other needs seem to vary in their intensity from individual to individual and according to the level of their maturity. That is, lack of satisfaction of a particular need for one person throws him completely off balance, while the same unmet need has little visible effect on another—he is only denied the opportunity for more complete development in the area which the need most intimately concerns. Thus, it appears that some children need more opportunity for exercise, love, independence, or companionship than do others. It is worth while to consider, however, that the differences may be more apparent than real. Perhaps the child who appears to need little exercise has merely learned to put up with the fact that it is inconvenient for his parents to give him any more play space. Another child may have been denied a healthful amount of loving care and tenderness and may have early developed compensations for that lack. The reason why a particular child appears not to need companionship may be that his early efforts at friendship were repulsed, or that aloofness is merely the result of his not having experience in making friendly contacts. The fact that there are apparent differences in the intensity of the need is no proof that denial, or partial denial, of the need has not had a limiting effect on development.

Needs Differ in Intensity at Various Ages. The multiplicity of needs is emphasized by the fact that living and growing seem to create additional requirements. Thus, the newborn infant seems to be content if his organic needs are satisfied. He can at first be left alone while awake, but soon he becomes restive if not cuddled and fondled. At this age he seems, from an adult viewpoint at least, not to need a feeling of accomplishment. He is satisfied with the opportunity merely to manipulate. But at the age of two or three years, there is definitely a need for accomplishment,[2] as can be seen in such enraged cries as "I can do it myself," and "Let me do it." Children of all ages seem to need a great deal of love; adolescents, however, from outward appearances, seem to be less inclined to seek a demonstrative manifestation of parental love. Babies often play in the same room without giving attention to other children (independent play) and sometimes play beside one another without playing together (parallel play). Adolescents are much aware of their need for peer acceptance; and their need for independence is also becoming more insistent.

When children are experiencing difficulty in adjusting to their physical and social environment, when they are causing their parents and teachers to be perplexed, they are in effect saying, "Some of my needs are not met or on the way to becoming met. I'm not just sure what is wrong, but I'm trying to satisfy my needs. What I'm doing is a series of experiments, which seem frequently to disturb adults." Of course, his analysis or statement is not so clear as that, but his actions are speaking for him. If teachers can learn to translate the actions of the child and to fill in the gaps of "lack of understanding," they will be helping the inarticulate child to better mental health.

The following statement, though written about exceptional children, can well serve to introduce the problem of meeting the needs of all children.

> Teachers, other school officials, and social workers often need to give parents of exceptional children help in understanding that *all* children have the same basic physical and psychological needs; that all children need an adequate and balanced diet, sufficient rest and sleep, a comfortable temperature, and activity when well and rested; that all need to be loved and wanted, to have a reasonable independence in running their own lives and in making their own decisions, to feel a sense of achievement that comes from making things and doing jobs, to win the approval of others for what they are and do, and to feel that they are worthwhile individuals who reasonably come up to their own inner standards. Helping children to find fulfillment for these physical and psychological needs is as much the task of the parents of normal children as it is of the parents of exceptional children.[3]

Adult needs which are dominant include the need for significance and mastery—a feeling that progress is being made. The day-to-day existence

[2] William V. Silverberg, "On the Origin of Neurosis," *Psychiatry: Journal of the Biology and Pathology of Interpersonal Relations*, 7:115, 1944.

[3] S. R. Laycock and George S. Stevenson, in 49th Yearbook, National Society for the Study of Education, Part II, *The Education of Exceptional Children*, Chicago: The University of Chicago Press, 1950, Chap. VII, pp. 122–123. Quoted by permission of the Society.

of the child and early adolescent is no longer satisfactory. Perhaps in old age needs become less imperious, except the organic ones. This may be due not so much to diminution of the needs as to having learned how to satisfy them. One need that is receiving attention in studies of the elderly is the continuing need of a purpose.[4] It is thought by many scholars that death may be hastened by retirement if attended by lack of purpose.

Examination of the differing intensities of needs at various ages shows that needs are continuous. There is neither a complete satisfaction nor an outgrowing of them. Although the degree of intensity may vary, a need is something that people of all ages must satisfy. Needs thus become one of the focal points around which the study of mental hygiene may center.

BASIC ORGANIC NEEDS

Nature of Organic Needs. If organic needs are satisfied, the human being will live; if they are not satisfied, he will die. Contemporary psychologists discount the notion that there is human instinctive equipment, or mechanism, that automatically will satisfy the need. While the need may be manifest in general activity or restlessness, the way of satisfaction must be learned. Moreover, there is a need for balance or moderation. Too much food, too much water, too much oxygen can be destructive to life and health. Mental hygienists are concerned with the balanced satisfaction of organic needs because physical health is one of the foundation stones of mental health.

Dietary Needs and the School. In many schools the inadequate diets of some children are improved by providing balanced meals in the cafeteria. Sometimes the only milk children get is with their school lunch. Teachers have found that pupils who board buses early in the morning need to have a bit to eat an hour or so after school begins. This may mean that the children have to eat their lunch before noon lest they become restless and inattentive. Since there is a relation between emotions and physical distress, it is easy to realize that some teaching problems may arise from improper or insufficient food; therefore, stress should be placed on a balanced diet. It has been found that adolescents are sometimes improperly nourished because of the popularity of hot dogs, soft drinks, and sweets. They must be reminded of what they supposedly learned in the elementary grades. Teaching should, also, call attention to the desirability of regular meals, eaten at leisure, and class schedules should allow for them.

[4] "Planning a Retirement Timetable," *Bulletin of the Institute of Gerontology,* State University of Iowa, 6:2, March, 1959.

Practice should be given in establishing a pleasant emotional tone for mealtime. In one school this practice was stimulated by an eighth-grade teacher who took her cue from discussion in social studies. Before the plan was started, the cafeteria was probably a typical one—considerable noise, hustling, and pushing in order to sit near a dear friend, hurrying to get through quickly so that a game of basketball could be started. A little food was dropped on the tables and the floor and left for someone else to clean up. The contrast with the later situation was remarkable.

An eighth-grade boy or girl was placed at the head of the table. This pupil chose a coworker from the lower grades to help conduct the meal in a pleasant manner. An effort was made to make the subject for conversation pleasant and interesting for everyone. There was no hurry, because it had been decided that each person was to wait for all to finish. There was a team which was responsible for table decorations. Cleanliness was emphasized, courtesy was practiced, and suggestions for improvements were asked for and respected. Consequently, the pupils looked forward to a pleasant meal; in addition, the results brought further satisfaction: student conversations and remarks led the teachers to realize that the practice was providing a stimulus for changing practices in the home. Some of the pupils were interested in having their families practice courtesy, give attention to making the table setting attractive, and control the conversation at mealtime. It is quite probable that many of these pupils would never have learned how to make a meal maximally pleasant unless some practice were provided in the school.

The effectiveness of the school's lessons on health and diet during the past years constitutes a hope for the proponents of mental hygiene, for the basic facts of mental hygiene are just as teachable as are the facts of physical health.

The Need for Activity and Rest and the School. Our schools have for a long time recognized that exercise in varied forms alternated with periods of rest and relaxation is a necessary element in children's growth. A major step toward improvement could be made by varying the amount and kind of exercise and by regulating the amount of rest *in accordance with individual needs.* Too many of our physical-activity programs are of the mass type.

In general, however, children need activity to express themselves, to develop skills that will aid their feelings of confidence and social competence, to practice physical skills that lay the foundation for adult activities, and to aid in the assimilation of experiences.[5] Children need, also, to rest to replenish their energies, or, rather, to avoid excessive tiredness—for tiredness may result in inattentiveness; in crossness, manifested in dealing

[5] Roma Gans, Celia B. Stendler, and Millie Almy, *Teaching Young Children,* Yonkers, N.Y.: World Book Company, 1952, pp. 314–328.

with other children; and in irritability, manifested in connection with the teacher's directions. Often these needs are inadvertently neglected in the home. Therefore, the classroom teacher has the responsibility to use his opportunity to help the children take some steps in the proper direction.

The Need for Activity and Rest and the Individual. Studies of the child may be made to find whether the school program is physically too stimulating for him as an individual, and if necessary, proper provisions for rest or restriction of activity are made. Health cards, on which information from periodic health examinations is compiled, are available to the teacher. Using these tools, the teacher can do two things to improve the quality of rest and exercise, to balance them to fit the individual.

First, he should give functional recognition to the facts recorded on the student's health card by the nurse or the doctor. A heart murmur not serious enough to warrant special attention might still predispose the child to tiring easily, and the warning taken from the card will make the teacher more alert to symptoms of tiredness. Defective vision may make it difficult and frustrating for some children to play in certain ball games. Digestive disturbances may indicate the need for somewhat more rest after meals than most children are taking. These are only illustrations, but they serve to show that the health card can have real significance, if it is used for more than filling the requirements of keeping a record.

Second, the teacher should watch for symptoms of restlessness, which indicate the need for more vigorous exercise than the average student is getting. The buoyant energy of some youngsters can be absorbed in vigorous play, which makes it possible for them to adjust themselves to the comparative inactivity of academic classroom procedures. A third-grade teacher reported that she often breaks class routine, in addition to regular recesses, by saying, "You have been working hard. Let's play a game for five minutes." The youngsters choose and play their game and are then ready to settle down to other work. For pupils who tire easily, the teacher may limit vigorous exercise by creating situations in which the child may help the teacher while other youngsters are playing their rougher games. In many grades, mats on which to lie are provided for youngsters during rest periods.

An integral part of recognizing the child's need for activity is that of providing him ample room for play and exercise. This is seen even in infants, who vociferously protest against being held tight or cry when their clothing prevents free movement. This need for space is recognized by school administrators and architects, who figure the size of the school and playground in terms of the probable enrollment of the schools. Thus, each child has his space for growing, exercising, and experiencing. When a school has outgrown the available play space, teachers and administrators make efficient use of the space available by staggering the recess periods. Frequently teachers wisely group the desks, chairs, and tables close together in one part of the room, so that the pupils may have more free floor space than would be available if the furniture were uniformly spaced.

The Many Implications of Posture. Posture may be closely related to diet or to the need for balance between rest and activity. Improper posture may inhibit optimum growth, adequate digestion, and breathing. Improper posture may be a symptom of insufficient sleep or inadequate diet. A decade or two ago formal exercises were regularly scheduled and the teacher reminded pupils to stand and sit properly. Now the emphasis is on the whole-body exercise, which is provided by encouraging pupils to engage in a wide variety of play. The teacher of today tries to see to it that each child sits in a chair and at a table which fit him. When desks are unadjustable, seats are assigned according to the size of the pupil, so that as good a fit as possible is obtained; and changes are made during the year to provide adaptation to growth changes. Attention is given to the eating and sleeping habits of the child by consulting with the parents. Of course, there are times when poor posture is merely a matter of habit. In such cases, the teacher may call the pupil's attention to the matter. If a child keeps his eyes too close to the paper while writing, the teacher may properly remind him to hold his head up. The teacher should not, however, overlook the fact that there may be glare or shadows on the paper, which may be helped by changing the position, or that the child may need to have his vision corrected with glasses.

Periodic Health Examinations. The periodic health examination, mentioned earlier, frequently becomes a formal procedure without adequate provision for followup. Teachers too frequently feel that examinations and followup are a responsibility of doctors and nurses; but even in very well-staffed schools, this is not the case. If the examination is to count as it should, teachers must know what the results are and be informed of the proper procedures for followup. A brief lecture to pupils by the medical staff will not be enough. Even if the followup is simply a matter of asking a question or giving a periodic reminder, the chances for success will be much greater. If the followup includes teacher contacts with the parents, so much the better. The old slogan "a sound mind in a sound body" contains much truth. While the "sound body" is not synonymous with the "sound mind," the possibility that inadequacy in meeting organic needs may result in the manifestation of symptoms of poor mental health should not be dismissed.

Heating and Ventilation of the Classroom. That temperature has a psychological effect on the individual is illustrated by the fact that productivity is highest among those people who live in temperate zones. Contrary to popular opinion, we do not do our best work on warm, sunny days;

actually, productivity is highest on days when temperatures vary from 60 to 70 degrees. Therefore, teachers must pay attention to heat and ventilation, so that the pupils may be psychologically predisposed to productive activity.

Several routine things can be done by the teacher and his pupils to overcome natural disadvantages in heating and ventilation. Ideally, the teacher should give the pupils a share of responsibility, first, to make the lesson of heating and ventilation more effective; and second, to create an additional pressure toward the feeling that classroom activities are co-operative endeavors. Among the points to which pupils and teacher should give attention are the following: (1) Adapting temperature to the type of activity, so that a temperature of 68 to 70 degrees prevails for the sedentary type of activity, and a temperature of around 60 degrees when activity is at a maximum in the classroom; (2) being sensitive to odors; unpleasant odors can detract from the pleasure derived from class activity; (3) making classroom monitors responsible for giving the room an airing when the recess periods take the children from the room; the cooler room on their return is an advantage, because contrasts in temperature should not be too marked; (4) seeing that air vents and exhaust ducts are kept open at all times when the room is occupied.

Temperatures should be carefully watched, because a number of persons in the same room will actually raise the temperature, even without additional furnace heat. Since the teacher has countless other activities to supervise, it will be advantageous to have some individuals in the class accept responsibility for controlling temperature. Many teachers give such responsibilities to slow-learning children, who would otherwise have less chance to feel that they are making a contribution to the class. Interest in the cooperative project of controlling the temperature will be more readily achieved if a temperature chart is kept.

Admittedly, attention to the details of heating and ventilation is a minor matter. It seems to be adding to the already multifarious duties of a classroom teacher. Here again, it should be remembered that mental health consists of numerous small details. It is comforting to know that "step by step we go a long way."

Sensory Acuity and the School Child. It is difficult to decide whether the need for sensory acuity is an organic or a psychological need; nevertheless, to the extent that a child is defective in vision or hearing, his problems of adjusting are more difficult. There is reason to doubt that defective vision of itself is a cause for misbehavior. Children who have difficulty in hearing are not necessarily problem children; in fact, many of them appear to be happy and well adjusted. But such defects are without doubt *contributing factors* to behavior anomalies. It follows that the way a child is treated with respect to his handicaps becomes a major factor in his reaction to any sensory defect. If the handicap is not recognized by parents and teachers, there is great likelihood that too much will be expected of the child and that pressures for school progress and social conformity may become too heavy for him to bear. If, on the other hand, due allowance is made for the handicap, the child will be encouraged to develop at a rate which for him is comfortably stimulating.

One child in the fourth grade who quarreled frequently with his classmates, who was inattentive during the giving of directions, and whose work did not seem to be in accord with his intelligence-test data was suspected of having poor vision. The teacher noted that he frequently squinted and twisted his head while looking at what was placed on the board. She tested the child by the Snellen chart and, on the basis of the results, referred him to his parents for further testing by their oculist. Glasses were prescribed, and, the day he reappeared in class wearing his glasses, he paused at the door and shouted to a boy across the room, "Hi, Johnny. I can see you from here." Increased interest in schoolwork was immediately apparent and the boy's social relations improved markedly.

There is, besides, the possibility that visual difficulty will result in a type of eyestrain that is physically uncomfortable. Smarting eyes, headaches, and dizziness make it difficult for a child to concentrate on what is going on in the classroom. The accompanying physical discomfort may tend to make him irritable, so that he has trouble getting along with teachers and pupils. Some aural difficulties may produce similar physical discomfort and thus stimulate an inattentive attitude, quite apart from keeping the child from hearing what is said during class activities. These generalizations have the support of facts, as it has often been noted that when a child is fitted with glasses, when he has wax removed from his ears, or when he is supplied with a hearing aid, immediate improvement of behavior results.

Regular and frequent physical examination of school children is, therefore, a step toward meeting their physical needs. This examination should have two major objectives: (1) to stimulate the necessary steps in having the defect remedied as early as possible, and (2) to encourage the teacher to make due allowance for the handicap. Ideally, these examinations will be conducted by a regular physician or at least by a nurse or a teacher who has had special instruction in making such examinations. The doctor, nurse, and teacher might have to cooperate in educating parents or in enlisting the aid of charitable institutions in order that adequate correction may be given the child after a diagnosis has been made. The teacher can help by seating the child where he can see or hear to best advantage and by being alert to deviations of behavior that may be explained by the defect. Obviously, such allowances are contingent upon the first step—becoming aware of the existence of the handicap.

In other ways, too, the teacher may come to realize that the child is handicapped by a sensory defect. Indications of difficulty in hearing may be one or several of the following:

1. Inability to locate the direction from which sound is coming
2. More than normal use of the hands in making wants known
3. Voice which lacks an intonation pattern and resonance
4. Difficulty in maintaining balance—frequent falling or stumbling
5. Faulty articulation and mispronunciation of common words
6. Inattention and frequent errors in carrying out directions
7. Turning the head to catch sound with the better ear
8. Cupping the hands to catch sound better
9. Frequently asking to have statements repeated
10. Poor spelling when dictation is used
11. Lack of interest in group activities
12. Peculiar posture—tilting the head into an unusual position

In addition, such indications as visible discharge from the ear, complaints of earaches, and the reporting of noises in the head should be followed up by the child's having a thorough hearing examination.

Certain other behavior symptoms may be a warning that the child is suffering from a visual handicap. The teacher should be so thoroughly aware of these symptoms that it would be difficult to overlook them.

1. Attempting to brush off something when reading or writing
2. Rubbing the eyes frequently
3. Watering eyes, bloodshot eyes and red eyelids, or frequent sties
4. Complaining of headaches or blurring of reading matter
5. Crying after reading or showing fits of temper
6. Screwing up the face or blinking excessively
7. Holding a book far away or too close while reading
8. Shutting or covering one eye while reading
9. Tilting the head to one side when reading or viewing the board
10. Frequent confusion of *m*'s and *n*'s or *o*'s and *e*'s
11. Tensing the body when looking at distant objects
12. Inattention during reading lessons, while something is being written on the board, or during field trips

The relation of sensory acuity to organic need might be stated as follows: The child has a need to have close and accurate contact with his physical environment. It will be seen in the following pages that sensory acuity will also condition the way in which the child's psychological and social needs will be met.

BASIC PSYCHOLOGICAL NEEDS

Just as the satisfaction of organic needs conditions the degree of physical health, so the satisfaction of psychological needs influences the degree of mental health. It would be difficult to prove that satisfaction of psychological needs is requisite to life; but certainly such satisfaction is necessary for complete living and for well-rounded personality development.

The Need to Feel Secure. It would be easy to get the impression that the need for feelings of security may be satisfied by considerate treatment from others. Frequently emphasis is laid on the belief that a child feels secure when he is loved by his parents, when he gets a great deal of time and attention, when his wishes are quickly satisfied, when he is not sternly disciplined, and when economic circumstances are such that these factors and his organic needs are readily satisfied.

> When a child is fed whenever he is hungry, he gets more than food—
> he gets a feeling of confidence that his needs are going to be met; he
> feels that he can trust his world. As all the successive difficult lessons
> of social adjustment come along, he has this basic security and con-
> fidence to build upon. If, on the other hand, he is left hungry and
> thwarted by an inflexible feeding schedule, he may begin to doubt
> and fear the world, and is likely to approach his subsequent experiences
> with doubt, fear, and insecurity.[6]

To a large extent these conclusions mean that the child needs to feel that adults have faith in him. He must know that he is accepted for what he is, because of his assets and in spite of his shortcomings. This faith must include adult belief in his good intentions, without giving undue attention to what his actions really are.

A secure person needs to have faith in his own ability to solve his problems, to overcome obstacles in the path of achievement, and to stand on his own feet "in the shifting sands of time." This second basis of security has all too often been overlooked. Genuine security is something which must be won. The love of adults and the affection of peers is a good starting point; but as the child grows older, he must surely become less dependent on others and more self-reliant. Therefore, the opportunity for a child to develop manual, mental, and social skills must not be withheld by overindulgent adults. This relates, among other things, to the fundamental need for freedom, for providing for unhampered development through a variety of play and work experiences.

When the factors that make for security are lacking, the inevitable

---

[6] Lawrence K. Frank, *Personality and Culture*, New York: Hinds, Hayden and Eldredge, Inc., 1948, p. 7. By permission of the present publishers, The Interstate Printers and Publishers, Danville, Ill.

result is the manifestation of symptoms of mental ill-health. These symptoms may take any of a variety of forms; but the most outstanding are, on the one hand, fearfulness, timidity, social reticence, lying, stealing, or retreat from competition, and on the other hand, overaggressiveness, bullying, exhibitionism, or other attempts to compensate for the felt lack.

Feelings of Security and the School. Ideas for fostering genuine feelings of security may be inferred from examination of the nature of feelings of insecurity. First, the teacher must be able and willing to show affection for the pupils. He must realize that intentions are not always synonymous with actions. There should be faith in the improvability of personality and behavior. The teacher must accept the pupil for what he is—in spite of his slowness in learning, his addiction to the use of foul language, his lack of cleanliness, or his impertinence and his disobedience. In addition, the teacher must help other children to accept their schoolmate—teaching them to aid, rather than hinder, him in the changes that will make him more acceptable. The latter has been done with striking simplicity by teachers who take their pupils into their confidence and explain to them that a certain boy or girl is in need of help, that his actions are a way of saying that he is having difficulty, and that although he may seem to resent their kindnesses at first, he will soon come to appreciate them and they in turn will appreciate him.

It often requires but a small amount of friendliness to show a child that he is accepted. A school principal, noted for his friendliness, showed this quality by giving a pat on the back to those who spoke to him; and pupils in the school would walk much out of their way for the chance to greet him with "Hello." The principal not only knew the names of more than 500 youngsters in the school but could give interesting little observations about their characteristics and difficulties. On one occasion, he noted a little boy crying on the front steps. He simply went over and sat beside the lad and said nothing for several minutes. When the crying ceased, he put his arm around the boy and began to talk to him about general topics. When, after a few minutes of impersonal conversation, the boy began to respond, the principal inquired about the trouble and commiserated with him. Finally he gave a gentle shove and said, "O.K. Better get going. Your teacher will miss you." This friendliness, though certainly not *the* solution to this boy's problem, helps him to keep trying to adjust as more exacting steps are taken by school personnel.

The child should be allowed enough freedom, so that he can learn to do things for himself. Instead of being given minute directions relative to what should be read, how a picture should be drawn, what the outline of a discussion should be, the child might well be permitted to try out some things for himself. Children need to develop independence if they are to develop feelings of security that are genuine. "This whole question of emotional training is not a matter of affection. I would say there is entirely too much affection in families! If there were a good deal more healthy indifference, we who happen to be in the field of mental health of children would perhaps have less to do."[7]

There is, however, a call for balance in the amount of help given. Teachers may properly cushion some of the difficulties which children have, but they should be careful not to make the child helpless by over-protection. The shy child should not be made a teacher's pet. The slow learner should not be assigned only the tasks which he can easily perform. Rather, continuing emphasis should be placed upon under-standing each pupil well enough so that opportunities will be provided for him to develop those particular talents which will give him a feeling of competence.

It should be emphasized that the need to *feel* secure is the point at issue—not the need to *be* secure. When a person can be made to feel secure in his ability to meet changing conditions, his attitude will be one that is helpful in facing the problem of continuous adjustment to an ever-changing world. If this point is kept in mind, there will be less danger of overemphasis on the aspect of security that is dependent upon one's relations with others.

The Need to Manipulate and Satisfy Curiosity. Among the human needs frequently listed by psychologists is "the need for new experiences." It is first noted in the very young child as an almost compulsive desire to touch and feel everything that can be reached. In preschool children it is manifest in their inability to settle into a routine; there seems to be an insistent drive for change in activity and experience. School children reveal the need in their constant desire to range widely and be on the go, in order to see new things and places. The adolescent shows his curiosity in his reluctance to take the good advice of older people; he wishes to find out for himself. Some adults reveal their curiosity in an avid desire to read, others devote their time and money to travel, some bend their energies to research. Even those adults whose curiosity does not seem to be strong show boredom and dissatisfaction with highly routine and static conditions. It seems probable that more adults would reveal greater curiosity if they were not afraid of meeting defeat were they to hazard a change of jobs or of living locale.

Curiosity is a valuable adjustive technique for meeting and adapting to new situations. One must know the how, when, and where of certain actions, must know what is expected and what is demanded if he is to be accepted and to become effective. "In a culture that values individual

---

[7] William C. Blatz, in *Modern Concepts of Child Development*, Progressive Education Booklet 6, Columbus, Ohio: American Education Press, Inc., 1938, p. 20. By permission of Charles E. Merrill Company.

initiative and resourcefulness, curiosity about matters that one has not learned about previously can strengthen considerably the individual's capability of acting on his own."[8]

Satisfying Curiosity in the School. Something negative often seems to happen to the curiosity of children as the result of their school experiences. The kindergarten and primary-school child is enthusiastic and eager; he is delighted that there are so many school days in the week. But his delight seems to wane in the middle grades; indeed, by the time he is in high school, he bemoans the fact that there are so few Saturdays and Sundays. It is hoped that a part of this is due to the psychology of suggestion, which would make one feel odd if he were to admit liking school. But much of the dislike for school can undoubtedly be accounted for by there being too little opportunity for manipulation, direct experience, and the satisfaction of personal curiosity. This is indicated in the following summary of conditions which favor effective learning:

1. The opportunity to engage in tasks that are suited to the background of the learner and are a challenge to him

2. A goal toward which the child can work and the significance of which he can feel

3. A learning task of such a character that the various motivating forces, such as the desire for security, the demands for activity, or the feelings of hunger, are satisfied either through the learning activity or through the general arrangements under which learning activity takes place

4. Provision for repetition, with intrinsic rewards if feasible, when skills or habits are involved

5. Situations involving problem-solving so designed that, when the child arrives at the solution, he feels he has accomplished something worthwhile, with a gain in security and status and without frustration of other motivating forces.[9]

The need to explore and to learn is a difficult one to satisfy in elementary-school children, because of our haste to have children grow up. There is too great a tendency among teachers to interpret behavior of children on an adult level. It is easy for us, with our wealth of background experience, to see the value of acquiring skill in computation. We perceive the importance of developing good taste and proficiency in reading and of practicing habits of courtesy and respect; but elementary pupils often seem to be unimpressed by the importance of such factors. Of course, many do develop "in a desirable manner," but perhaps

[8] Franklin J. Shaw and Robert S. Ort, *Personal Adjustment in American Culture*, New York: Harper & Brothers, 1953, p. 81.

[9] Ralph H. Ojemann, "Social Studies in Light of Knowledge about Children" in *Social Studies in the Elementary School*, 56th Yearbook, Part II, National Society for the Study of Education, Chicago: University of Chicago Press, 1957, p. 99.

they do it not because they realize the importance of these things, but because they wish to please their teachers and parents and because of commendable adult example.

On the other hand, there are those who seem to be little concerned about pleasing others. Getting them to see the value of formal schooling is somewhat difficult, and there is probably no easy solution. However, it is possible to study children, as they play, as they react in the classroom, as they converse with pupils and teachers, to find out what their motivations may be. These motivations can then be used as the point of departure in planning school activities. Studying baseball, learning home nursing incident to caring for a sick brother, running a candy shop, or discovering how the school heating plant works—any of these might well serve as the focal point for school activities that will motivate students to learn to read, figure, and get along with others. We must not assume that children are ready to satisfy curiosity because the syllabus so prescribes. Let's discover where they are, *by listening.* The discovery of present interest and the use of the present locus to provide opportunities for learning and manipulating are vital.

Teachers can, in recognition of the need to satisfy curiosity, seek to maintain balance between organized and spontaneous activity. Some routines are necessary and comforting, but operating on punch-clock regularity, slavish adherence to a syllabus or course of study, sticking to the text, and avoidance of wandering from the subject are guaranteed soporifics for curiosity. There must not only be a variety of activities for the group but also a variety of choice for individuals. At all grade levels, it is advantageous to provide opportunities to touch, feel, and manipulate the objects being studied. There is a tendency to give lectures and assignments too dogmatically, which results in diminution of curiosity. Having some cows' eyes or lungs available for dissection adds much to verbal explanations and textual materials. Curiosity about the meaning of citizenship, for another example, can be better satisfied by some direct contact with civic activities than by merely knowing the answers to questions in a civics textbook.[10]

An obstacle to the most advantageous use of curiosity is the haste with which teachers answer questions. Many of them seem to feel that it will be embarrassing not to know the answer to the question; hence, they answer vaguely or with half-truths rather than admit that they do not know. The more thoughtful teachers, however, feel that a pupil's question is a starting point for growth rather than a finish line. They spur pupils by showing enthusiasm for the question, suggesting sources of information, and calling for a follow-up report.

[10] American Association of School Administrators, *Educating for American Citizenship,* 32d Yearbook, Washington: National Education Association, 1954, pp. 97–98.

A high-school teacher, worried about the apathy of a seemingly bright sophomore, was pleased to be asked a question which could be readily answered. But the girl went back to her desk and settled down in deep repose. Days later another question was asked, but the teacher, not knowing the answer, suggested some sources. The girl studied them avidly and gave a class report on her findings. Another question was asked immediately, and though the teacher could answer it, he did not. He said, "This girl was not interested in looking for something others already knew—she wanted to find out for herself."

The rephrasing of the pupil's answer is another deleterious influence on curiosity. Many a teacher feels that, if the conclusion to a particular problem or study is not stated exactly as he had in mind, it is not adequately presented; he therefore puts it into the precise language that will drive the point home. Though this may satisfy the teacher, it does not satisfy the student. The student soon gets two erroneous notions. One is that he need not listen to student responses because the teacher can finally be depended on to state the proposition in proper form. The other is that as long as the teacher will give the answer anyway, there is little use for pupils to look for information. They can get it more effortlessly by listening to the oracle. But the outcome is verbalism, not knowledge, and genuine curiosity remains unsatisfied.

Much is being done in certain classrooms which suggests effective ways of recognizing and capitalizing on the need to satisfy curiosity. In the primary grades, teachers are making use of the experience approach, wherein pupils engage in some activity, trip, or excursion and then write their own stories. Youngsters in the middle and upper grades are learning how to organize into committees which are responsible for discovering and reporting related phases of information on some central topic being studied. Junior-high-school pupils visit factories, governmental organizations, businesses of various kinds and make these the focal points for periods of study and real learning. High-school teachers have long made sporadic use of field trips to give their study more vitality; but the work-experience type of study—in which part of the day is spent in school and the remainder on a paid job—seems to promise most in the area of manipulation and direct satisfaction of curiosity. Work experience adds reality to theoretical presentations made in textbooks. Four-H clubs have long recognized the value of this approach, but only small beginnings have been made in metropolitan areas. Moreover, these experiences —trips, committee work, work-experience programs—provide motivations for the more strictly academic subjects. We must be careful not to believe that verbalizations have the same fullness of meaning for youngsters, whose actual contact with the local world is extremely limited, as they do for adults, whose experiences are wider.

The Need for Achievement. Each person manifests the need for achievement not only so he will stand well in the eyes of others (note the relationship to the concept of security) but also for the satisfaction he gets from exercising his own capacities. A person may be able to type ninety words per minute, yet the superior accomplishment usually results in a desire to do even better. A student may be the best in the class in algebra, but this typically does not cause him to cease working. There is a personal satisfaction in achievement which goes beyond that of social needs. A young child resists being dressed if he can somehow get into his shirt by himself, however twisted the final arrangement may be. A father, noting the clumsy airplane made of two thick boards by his six-year-old, planed, measured, balanced, and glued one that would glide, but the son returned to his own crudely made toy. Some persons seek achievement in athletic activities, others in intellectual pursuits, while some seek achievement in improved moral living. The particular mode of achievement sought by a given person probably depends upon his talents and the environment in which he lives. But regardless of the form of the achievement that is pursued, the desire is not simply to "get by" but to get better.

Failure to gain a sense of achievement has a debilitative effect on personality.[11] The person who fails to accomplish a satisfactory "something" becomes a discouraged, inactive, and ineffective individual. He is a person who exists rather than lives. At best he is a burden to himself and at worst he is a mental case who is potentially or actually dangerous to society. Since the personality of an individual at the time of chronological maturity is a long time in the making, the first symptoms of inadequacy are likely to be manifest in the personalities of school children.

The School and the Need for Achievement. Fortunately, much is known about ways in which a child's need for accomplishment can be answered. The first consideration is the necessity for making provisions for individual differences. This means that the uniform routines which are largely characteristic of schools must be modified in recognition of basic differences in the ability to achieve. Accordingly, talents other than the purely academic must be taken into consideration. All too frequently, only special phases of accomplishment are singled out for admiration—athletics, for instance—while achievements in art, writing, dancing, and academic superiority are ignored. The teacher, by being cosmopolitan in his interests, can do much to offset these imbalances. Another requisite, in view of these differences, is that teachers avoid invidious comparisons—and there are no comparisons of individuals which are not invidious. Such exhortations as "See how well Mary does her arithmetic!" should

[11] Morris M. Pauleen, "A Training Experience in Interpersonal Relations for Psychiatric Technicians," *Mental Hygiene,* 42:82, January, 1958.

never be heard. A child should be evaluated in terms of how far he has traveled in a given time rather than in terms of his absolute status. Another factor is the desirability of having immediate and intermediate goals as well as long-term objectives. Even at the high-school level, and certainly in preceding grades, persistent application is helped by setting a series of immediately achievable goals rather than having to depend heavily on a hope of "passing" at the end of the year. Abstract symbols of achievement in the form of grades and marks may stimulate a few children, but many others find them meaningless. A special job well done, a personal curiosity satisfied, and a committee responsibility fulfilled might well constitute the immediate goals that would provide a more enduring kind of motivation. Experiments indicate that when children work at a task without knowing how they are getting along, their interest wanes more rapidly than if they can see or if they are told what progress they are making.[12] This imposes upon the teacher the responsibility of reporting progress in a way that will have meaning and value.

The need for achievement might also be stated as the need for success. Success may be thought of in terms of absolutes, while achievement can readily be thought of in relative, or personal, terms. That is, one may not feel that he has succeeded if he comes in last in a race; but having qualified for the race might justifiably give him a feeling of achievement. A high-school junior, being kidded for not making the basketball team, said, "Look at it this way, Dad, I'm not on the first team but I'm one out of seven hundred boys who was able to make either the junior varsity or varsity squads." This has some important implications for school practice. Because of differences in ability, it is impossible for all to achieve at the same level; hence, one child should not feel that he is a failure because his work is not on a par with others. A child who is making progress in overcoming his handicaps should be made to feel that he is achieving, because the degree to which one achieves conditions the strength of continued effort.

Achievement or failure should be measured not in terms of energy expended but in relation to one's level of aspiration. This situation imposes upon the teacher a double challenge. He must see to it, on the one hand, that goals are not too easily won and, on the other, that failure to achieve is not a consistent outcome for any one child. It has been found that after failure one's goals are lowered while after success one's goals are raised; that is, the level of aspiration tends to shift to reality. "This means that the level of aspiration operates as a mental hygiene factor of great significance. It constitutes a sort of governor; it protects

[12] Arden N. Frandsen, *How Children Learn,* New York: McGraw-Hill Book Company, Inc., 1957, p. 227.

the person against failure on the one hand, and against easy achievement which does not give the feeling of success, on the other hand."[13]

The Need to Be Independent. Dr. Alfred Adler, one of the outstanding leaders of the psychoanalytic viewpoint in psychology, places his major emphasis on the all-important driving power of need to overcome feelings of inferiority. We are born weak, helpless, and dependent; and life itself is largely a matter of compensating for this weakness and becoming an independent person. He regards the self-assertive impulse as the dominant driving force in life. It is an impulse that is subject to frustration from the environment and from the person's own feelings of insecurity. Thus, the need for independence is at once the force back of accomplishment and a cause for frustration and maladjustment. R. S. Woodworth asserts that Adler's view contains much common-sense truth that is applicable in daily life and is a valuable contribution to understanding personality and childhood education.[14]

The Need for Independence and the School. The importance of the need for independence gives psychological support to the theory of democratic practices in education and especially to the wisdom of providing freedom for personal activity and development. If teachers can rid themselves of the notion that prescribed curriculums and imposed authority are the sole sources of developmental education, a big step toward capitalizing on the need for independence will have been taken.

There seems to be no particular period in life when the need for independence is *most* crucial. Parents may have allowed the child ample opportunity for developing appropriate feelings of independence, and elementary teachers may have made similar wise provisions; but in spite of this, the need for independence becomes no less compelling during adolescence. While this does not imply that growing children do not need direction, it does indicate that dictatorial procedures hinder symmetrical personality development. Teachers at all levels must allow students to share in group decisions, to have a voice in the determination of their personal objectives, to make mistakes, and to encounter widely the variety of experiences that will make them progressively more independent.

The Federal Security Agency has published a bulletin[15] containing a check list which presents, in question form, many specific suggestions useful for implementing the need for independence. Ten questions have been selected for illustrative purposes:

[13] Roger G. Barker in Wayne Dennis (ed.), *Readings in Child Psychology*, Englewood Cliffs, N.J.: Prentice-Hall, Inc., 1951, p. 578.

[14] Robert S. Woodworth, *Contemporary Schools of Psychology*, rev. ed., New York: The Ronald Press Company, 1948, p. 197.

[15] Federal Security Agency, Office of Education, *How Democratic Is Your School?* 1949.

Do students in your classes have a voice in determining the projects or problems on which they will work?

Do students in your classes share in evaluating what they have done?

Is the slow learner in your classes given opportunities to do something important which he can do relatively well?

When your students cooperatively plan an activity, do they carry out their agreed-upon assignments and responsibilities?

Do you admit to your students that you are not an authority on all questions arising in class?

Do your students show eagerness to participate in student self-government?

Does the student editor of your school paper or magazine have the freedom of the press?

Do students have opportunities to share in group solutions of school problems?

Do students have a fair opportunity to defend themselves against a teacher's charge of misconduct?

Are opportunities provided for students to discuss student council activities?

Not only do these questions provide suggestions for giving young people practice in democratic activity, but they also point the way toward that self-directed behavior which so firmly undergirds the mature personality, which combines independence with cooperative endeavor.

BASIC SOCIAL NEEDS

The distinction between fundamental social needs and psychological needs is not sharp; each class of needs shades into the other. Although some psychological needs have social implications, the needs discussed in this section are fundamentally social in nature.

The Need to Love and Be Loved. Every individual needs to love and be loved if he is to develop into a happy and productive person. The importance of love, "tender-loving-care" (TLC), is often given special emphasis by pediatricians, practical doctors, and psychiatrists in their counsels to parents and prospective parents. Love cannot be simulated. Children know when they are genuinely loved and respond accordingly. It has been observed in controlled situations that children who had failed to make normal progress in weight and activity have, when they were cuddled, rocked, and talked to, made normal gains, have become more active, and have taken a smiling interest in things about them. Teachers frequently report that certain problem cases seem to stem from a lack of love in the home; they have also seen, in some instances, improved behavior on the part of the child after the parents were asked to relieve the pressure of crossness and abruptness and to provide more time for giving attention to the child. Occasionally, someone who has been seriously ill is known to have recovered—when there seemed to be no hope from medical therapy—simply for the reason that he was determined to live because of his importance to his loved ones.

It is difficult to assign, with accuracy, the outcomes of not being loved, since love itself is intangible. Various scholars have speculated, however, that lack of love may contribute to such conditions as drug addiction, alcoholism, prostitution, vagrancy, and lack of drive toward accomplishment. Even though experimental data are few, empirical observations of children in school warrant the belief that truancy, lack of application, lassitude, and antisocial and asocial behavior are stimulated by a feeling of not being loved. If love is not what "makes the world go round," at least it provides a lubricant to help life flow more smoothly.

The outgoing aspect of love—the need to love—is a reciprocal of the need to be loved. But, note that the higher the degree to which one is loved, the higher the capacity to love will develop. The person in whom this occurs has acquired one of the basic factors in personal mental health. It is this second aspect with which we are chiefly concerned, as practitioners of mental hygiene. The life of a person who cannot love, who is circumscribed by his own selfishness, can be likened to the confined orbit of a piece of chalk tied to a string. The spheres of activity are limited, there is little chance for personal as well as social development, there is no prospect for that person's becoming emotionally mature.

> In some respects, the most audacious of all the great insights that have come into the world was the apparently absurd conviction of Jesus of Nazareth that men must love one another. "A new commandment I give unto you, That ye love one another." We can easily imagine the bewilderment—even the ribald laughter—of his hearers. A world that was still very far from reaching the level of universal justice could scarcely rise to the level of universal love.
>
> In reality, this "new commandment" was not an absurd and arbitrary rule laid upon man from the outside. It was, rather, the most profound insight into man's nature that had yet been achieved. Today every psychiatrist would affirm its truth. Man is sound in psychological health to the degree that he relates himself affirmatively to his fellow men. To hate and to fear is to be psychologically ill.[16]

The Need to Be Loved and the School. Teachers can help in the fulfillment of this need (and work toward the fulfillment of their own need to love) by maintaining a friendly and sympathetic atmosphere in the

[16] H. A. Overstreet, *The Mature Mind*, New York: W. W. Norton & Company, Inc., 1949, pp. 102–103. By permission of the publisher.

classroom. They should realize that no one is perfect and that consequently shortcomings and deviations can normally be expected in their pupils. The understanding of pupils can be based on school records and medical reports, and on knowledge of home conditions and of personal interests, knowledge gained through an analytical view of pupil activities and conversations had with them. There is a secret "alchemy" for the development of warm human relationships and that secret is *taking time*—time to know and understand.

A difficulty is encountered in showing affection toward some children; for example, those who most need the affection are likely to create the impression that they do not want the attention of the teacher—when a child is most unlovely he is most in need of love. These individuals, in fact, because of having been deprived of love in the home, tend to be suspicious and aloof and are all the more in need of a teacher who will compensate for the lack of love by a patience and kindliness which will seep through the hardened protective shell.

The Need for Recognition. This need is somewhat akin to the need to be loved but is less intimate and personal. It has to do with group prestige, fame, reputation, and even notoriety. Adults in the community and pupils in the school want to be "somebody." Everyone has the need for being enough like the group to fit into it harmoniously and, at the same time, to be different enough to merit distinction. Each person needs to feel that he is worthwhile, that he has something of value to give to others, and that, because he is noteworthy, others will seek his advice, aid, and companionship. This does not mean that one cannot afford to have any shortcomings but that, because there is something about him that merits approval, these shortcomings may be overlooked.

The practical outcome of recognition is that it provides an important source of motivation. That behavior which begets recognition tends to be repeated. We can see this in the everyday acts of babies in the home when they try to do again the things which were praised or laughed at by other household members. Recognition tends to give the pupil a feeling of confidence in himself, thus providing an incentive for attacking new problems. Satisfaction of the need for recognition may come from socially undesirable behavior as well as from approved behavior.

The Need for Recognition and the School. Young people in school who receive recognition for laudable achievement, for group contributions, and for improved knowledge are no less motivated to continue their actions than is the lad who is recognized because he defies school regulations or because he arouses turmoil through his excessive exhibitionism. Some children who do not receive recognition for approved behaviors may, instead of "acting up," resort to excessive daydreaming or may tend to retreat from competition and from group participation where their efforts are scorned or ignored. Studies of factors contributing to delinquency reveal that lack of recognition for achievement at school or for importance in the home is a factor in deviant behavior.[17] In fact, a number of the common defense mechanisms may easily have their roots in a thwarting of the need for recognition. When considering not only this but other needs as well, remember that just as the symptoms for one kind of behavior may be multiple and varied, so too a single symptom may, in various individuals, indicate a number of unmet needs. Thus, discouragement, inactivity, shyness, and the like may be symptomatic of the unfulfilled need for love, achievement, or recognition.

Teachers can praise meritorious successes as well as honest efforts that are made to achieve; they can also encourage the group to recognize and praise the work of members of the class. It is necessary to avoid blame for failure, especially that due to a lack of ability.[18] Not only should one avoid the use of shame, sarcasm, and ridicule, but the one who tends to use them might well look to the state of his own mental health for an explanation of his behavior. Sometimes it is sufficient to comment on a person's assets, even though they may be some that are usually not rated as highly significant in the school—for example, neatness of dress, personal habits of cleanliness, considerate treatment of siblings, or regular attendance at some community function. At other times it may be necessary to encourage the young person to *develop* a specific asset, so that he will merit the admiration of the group. Another factor in teacher responsibility in this area, more vague but not less important, is the need to teach young people the meaning and importance of acceptable behavior. They must learn that healthful and desirable recognition is gained by means of socially oriented action rather than selfish and egocentric behavior. Moreover, this knowledge should come through experience of group activity. It cannot grow effectively out of the moralistic teachings of a class lecture.

Children learn at an early age that the satisfaction of their wants depends upon gaining the esteem of others. A safe and constructive assumption for a teacher to act upon is that the child is trying to please. His actions, from the adult view, may not seem pleasing, but it must be realized that the social skills are in the process of developing all through the grades and high school, developing on uneven fronts and characterized by progress and regressions. His actions, therefore, are not perfectly correlated with his intentions. Teachers can capitalize on knowl-

[17] W. C. Kvaraceus, *The Community and the Delinquent*, New York: Harcourt, Brace & World, Inc., 1954, p. 109.
[18] Fritz Redl and William W. Wattenberg, *Mental Hygiene in Teaching*, 2d ed., New York: Harcourt, Brace & World, Inc., 1959, p. 156.

edge of this growth pattern by (1) more readily showing approval for desirable behavior and (2) assisting children in developing the physical, intellectual, and social skills that merit approval.

Approval is an attitude similar to, but not identical with, acceptance. Needed at all times is acceptance of the child for what he is; this is fundamentally a matter of affection. Approval has to do with the actions of the child; and approval or disapproval of actions should be made known to the child. Studies indicate that children do not resent punishment which they understand and which does not seem to undermine their feelings of being accepted. But when punishment takes on a highly personal aspect, it is strongly resented.

The tendency to make comparisons is one of the errors which both teachers and parents make in regard to acceptance and approval. When a child is unfavorably compared with another, his personal worth is undermined. Such remarks as "Why can't you act like the little gentleman that Jimmy is?" are not likely to engender a spirit of emulation in a child who has a healthy degree of independence. A better approach would be, "You did such an excellent job yesterday, I'm sure that you can do it as well today" or "We all get to feeling a little 'out of sorts.' You're not acting like your usual self."

The Need for Companionship. Man is often referred to as a gregarious animal. His need to associate with others, to belong to the group, to share in the blessings of companionship seems to be deeply ingrained. Studies show that infants, in their first year, who are separated from their mothers manifest general depression and are retarded in growth.[19] Removal from the group is often an effective means of checking deviant behavior in school. Many youngsters who will persist when scolded or spanked are quickly restored to conformity when isolation is imposed on them.

The meaning of companionship—associating with others in a purposeful situation—is revealed in our own feelings of lonesomeness in a large city where we know no one, have not yet taken up a new job, or are waiting for travel connections. Companionship provides the opportunity for gratifying the need to love and be loved. Being a significant member of a group provides a substantial means of satisfying man's universal search for self-fulfillment, for response, and, ultimately, his quest for happiness.

The need for companionship is frequently seen as a special problem during adolescence. The adolescent, in trying to expand his social horizons beyond the immediate family group, strenuously seeks for attachment to his own generation. Understanding parents and teachers must

[19] Kurt Glaser and Leon Eisenberg, "Maternal Deprivation," *Pediatrics*, 18:626–642, 1956.

appreciate the adolescent's desire for conformity in dress, opinions, and action as a healthy indication of a growing personality.

The Need for Companionship and the School. The responsibility of the school should include some positive help in developing the techniques for getting along with one another. One of the first things that might well be emphasized is the inculcation of the techniques of courtesy. Practicing courteous behavior will set up a positive frame of reference for a favorable psychology of suggestion; that is, acting courteously will help to develop sympathy, tolerance, and respect for others. Personal guidance, in the form of commending actions and words that reveal respect for others, can do much toward developing the attributes that will make one a desirable companion.

Whatever can be done in the school to afford practice in democratic living will provide the most valuable aid to developing the kind of personality that will satisfy the need for companionship. Democracy is much more than a political technique: it has moral and personality implications; it is a procedure that makes good citizens. Sharing responsibility, pooling opinions, taking part in cooperative actions, and capitalizing on individual potentialities are ways of practicing the basic elements of companionship. One cannot work in groups without developing respect for the wisdom and talents of others, learning the true meaning of equality, and seeing the outcome of cooperative endeavor. Just as freedom, equality, and justice are basic elements in the concept of democracy, so too are these attributes basic to the satisfaction of the need for companionship.

PRECAUTIONS IN MEETING THE NEEDS OF CHILDREN

Command of the Fundamental Processes. The stress on the significance of basic human needs does *not* imply that, in our society, one can achieve maximum efficiency without acquiring basic academic skills. In fact, teaching the mastery of the essentials of reading, writing, and arithmetic is an obligation that rests upon adults for the raising of mentally healthy individuals.

No teacher should forget that "personality development" is, in effect, an approach to the effective teaching of fundamental knowledges. It is not an either-or proposition. Effective teaching demands the giving of considered attention to both personality and functional knowledge. Giving attention to the physical health needs of children is an approach to helping them learn "academic" lessons with greater facility. Giving attention to psychological needs is an approach to meaningful motivation. Giving attention to social needs is to recognize that motivation and purpose have many facets and many problems. Hysteria regarding the superiority of other nations in scientific development, armed might, or diplomatic skill should not be allowed to place such stress, in American schools, on academic prowess that education for adjustment is overlooked.

The pupil's learning to read, compute, and communicate is a responsibility of the school today just as truly as it ever has been. The mental hygiene viewpoint, however, merely emphasizes that this responsibility can best be carried out by recognition that the "whole child" goes to school —that learning is not simply a matter of mental activity. *At no point in this book is it the intention to create an impression that learning school subjects is unimportant.* The meaning intended is that, for satisfactory development, personal and social values and needs must be given an adequate place *with* the educational needs of children.

Danger of Overorganizing the Child's Life. Is it possible to go too far in solving the children's problems? Should children not have the experience of meeting conflict and frustration? Are we preparing children for psychological maturity if we protect them from "the slings and arrows of outrageous fortune"? Certainly, psychologists have warned us of the dangers of overprotection.

Without any danger of children's being raised in glass cages or being prevented from coming into contact with other children, the notion that they should be freely exposed to chickenpox, mumps, and measles has been rejected. The belief now is that, while children are better off if these diseases can be avoided, they need not be raised in a wholly aseptic environment. Similarly, we can encourage their seeking wide social and psychological experience without exposing them to inevitable frustration and defeat. Children learn by their successes as surely as by their humiliations and, at the same time, they learn confidence and friendliness rather than reticence and suspicion. *Helping* children stand on their own feet does not imply relieving them of all burdens. Guidance implies pointing out signposts, offering suggestions and precautions, preparing children for the journeys they are to make. It means taking into consideration their unique beings in terms of their abilities, backgrounds, and goals.

One indication that control and direction of children may be going too far is found in the evidence of overorganization in planning for the use of leisure time—particularly in the middle- and upper-socioeconomic strata. This is an insistent peril, for our changing culture demands that we learn how to use more freedom. The decrease in working hours per week since 1900 has been marked, and further decreases are indicated in both home and industry. The many laborsaving devices in use within the home have reduced the working hours of the housewife. Consequently, the constructive use of leisure time is a problem of increasing importance.

In trying to approach a solution, the schools, as well as the community at large, have instigated many programs for children (and sometimes for adults). The objectives of girl scouts, cubs, boy scouts, junior theaters, young people's clubs, teen-age night spots, and parent-children organizations are to be warmly commended. But some parents and other adults feel that these programs are provoking the danger of overorganizing the child's life, are leaving him too little time to develop his own resources for entertainment; moreover, if there are too many organizations, the individual may become dependent upon mass entertainment and community-sponsored programs and miss the satisfaction of thinking and planning for himself. In fact, it is entirely possible that the very lack

FIG. 2. Is a summer music camp an instance of overorganizing a child's life? What kinds of pupils should be encouraged to participate in summer schools? Are other needs besides the development of music skills being supplied here?

of organization-provided opportunities, paradoxically, serves as a stimulus to the development of independence and initiative in the use of leisure time.

The problem of overorganization of the child's life is illustrated by a letter from a teacher who wrote:

And I have a word to say about the kiddies who live in the X—— neighborhood or similar places. Mine go swimming at the "Y" Monday nights, piano lessons Tuesday, dancing lessons Wednesday, Cub Scouts Thursday, swimming again Friday, see the local movie Saturday afternoon, and go off on a fine day's trip with the family Sunday. In the summer they travel all over the United States and Canada. School becomes simply the place you have to go to before you can dash off some place to play. But is it even play? My children do not know how to play together, or even play alone. They have no "inner resources" because they have never had to "kill" a series of afternoons after school. They go some place where someone organizes the play for them. Again, they are never given a moment to sit down and relax. I have never seen such a huge congregation of overstimulated children! It appears that about sixteen out of my thirty-two are physically incapable of sitting at a desk for more than ten minutes, and I have two that cannot do it even for five minutes. And I swear that I am not exaggerating. Other teachers in the building are in hearty agreement. The classroom outcome of this business is that there are always five or six bolder ones who declare out loud that they do not want to do arithmetic, and what's more, they do not intend to do it! So there, too! And all day you spend pulling youngsters off the window sills and desks. They almost forget which is their desk because they are at them so seldom. Right in the middle of some group activity, Junior dashes out of his seat, runs over to Buster to get the football team lined up! And to make it even more interesting, you can't reason, discuss, or make a demand because Junior, overstimulated youngster that he is, cannot listen and comprehend at the same time! Group discussion? You never have a group.

Now the books say that discipline is, to a great extent, no problem as long as the schoolwork is of great interest to each child. He must be motivated. All I can say is, the school has nothing to offer these children whose parents can always top it at home, by traveling, or shipping them off every afternoon to some grand place. They simply make the best of school until 3:30, when they are off someplace where they can be entertained! And "making the best of school" is accomplished with the mass use of slingshots, gum, paper wads, paper airplanes, comic books, and fisticuffs.

To add a cheery note, every now and then comes a rewarding day. These, I find, are days jam-packed with movies, stories, and football games. But every day just simply cannot be like that. With superhuman effort I can plan one a week.

Several things can serve as an antidote to the above conditions. Teachers might well stress the idea that school is a place for work—in part by explanation but mainly by providing appropriate challenges, charting progress, commending effort, comparing past with present products, and seeing that experiences of success outnumber failures. Another way is to explain to parents through bulletins, handbooks, meetings, and parent-teacher conferences that the child needs free time which he himself is responsible for organizing. Finally, it should be made clear that interests are the result of familiarity, knowledge, success, and challenge.

Contrasting Effects of Freedom versus Organization. Claudia Lewis, in her book *Children of the Cumberland*,[20] raises somewhat the same ques-

[20] Claudia Lewis, *Children of the Cumberland*, New York: Columbia University Press, 1946.

tion when she compares the life of children reared in Greenwich Village with the life of children brought up in isolated communities. She indicates that the average intelligence quotient of children in Greenwich Village is higher, probably because of the many stimulating experiences they have—kindergartens, music lessons, dancing instruction, library clubs, and the like. Although children of the Cumberland have an intelligence quotient which is on an average lower than city children of the same age, they seem to possess an independence and inner tranquillity and poise which those in the city lack. Miss Lewis wonders whether it may be that rapid mental growth is purchased at the price of emotional instability. The question for teachers—and parents—is whether or not there may be some way of providing both the mental stimulation and the free time that will allow for some degree of independence in the use of leisure. The author suggests two answers: (1) encourage parents to provide free time for their children during which no leadership is given and no suggestions made, and (2) help children organize their group activities and then gradually reduce the degree of adult domination.

There are various theories of play which bear on the problem of leisure and organization. One is the theory of recapitulation (the child relives, through his play, the evolution of the race); another is the surplus-energy theory (energy not expended in growth is released in play). The recreation theory claims that play is a means of relief from the drudgery of work and routine; it recreates one's supply of energy and adds to the zest of living. This last theory supports the belief that too great emphasis on organization of play may make it seem like work.

The difference between work and play is difficult to establish. What is work for one person may be play for another. Baseball playing, for instance, may be work for the professional, but it is play for boys who voluntarily get teams together and do their "baseballing" whenever they can and wish. The difference lies largely in the motivations of the persons taking part in the activity.

Eric Erikson suggests that perspective is needed in evaluating a child's play. While the child should not be entirely dependent on prescribed duties, he does like to be mildly coerced into attractive ventures that he might never have thought of by himself. Erikson believes that children need not only time for solitary and independent play (including books, radio, TV) but also enough direction so that they may feel that what they are doing is important.

Good teachers, healthy teachers, relaxed teachers, teachers who feel trusted and respected by the community, understand all this and can guide it. They know how to alternate play and work, games and study. They know how to recognize special efforts, how to encourage special gifts. They also know how to give a child time, and how to handle those children to whom school, for a while, is not important and rather a matter to endure than to enjoy; or the child to whom other children are much more important than the teacher and shows it.[21]

Ideally, children should have enough free time so that they might derive some of the following advantages out of play: (1) improve hand-eye coordinations and neuromuscular skills by variety rather than by routine repetition, (2) provide an opportunity for self-expression and the exercise of ingenuity—use of imagination, (3) provide for the release of tensions through symbolic play (pretending injury or sickness to some member of the family who makes life unpleasant), (4) afford compensation for some real or imagined deficiency, (5) give exercise in learning the importance and techniques of social adjustment, and (6) select activities in which enough success can be achieved to bolster a stronger ego concept—of being a significant person. An examination of this list warrants the conclusion that overorganization may deprive the youngster of some of the mental hygiene values which a greater degree of freedom would provide. It is the overorganization, not the activity itself, which is being questioned.

Teachers can help in the solution of this problem by explaining the problem to parents, by providing leadership but not domination, and by giving their pupils encouragement and allowing them time to carry on free and independent activities.

SUMMARY

Need satisfaction is required if the individual is to approach maximum self-realization. The insistency of needs depends on age, circumstances, and balance. Fundamentally, these needs are organic, psychological, and social. Teachers will be most effective when they realize that these are interrelated and the pupil will be a better learner than he otherwise might be when need satisfaction in all categories is approached.

Organic needs may be less disconcerting when pupils are given or guided toward proper diets, when there is balance between rest and activity, when the physical conditions of light, air, and temperature of the classroom are controlled, and when sensory defect is remedied or allowance is made for it.

Teachers can contribute to the satisfaction of psychological needs by accepting pupils, encouraging skill development, allowing appropriate freedom, encouraging achievement commensurate with ability, and by relaxing the standards set by the average for those who have lesser present potential. The use of democratic methods—autonomy, shared decisions

[21] Eric Homburger Erikson, "Growth and Crises of the 'Healthy Personality,'" in Clyde Kluckhohn and Henry A. Murray (eds.), *Personality in Nature, Society, and Culture,* New York: Alfred A. Knopf, Inc., 1953, p. 214.

and work, participation in classroom routines—will do much to meet these psychological needs.

Basic social needs are very closely related to, and often overlap, psychological needs. Children, as do all persons, need to love and be loved, to be recognized as individuals, and to have companionship. Perhaps more than in other classes of needs, the fulfillment of these needs depends greatly upon the teacher's social and emotional maturity. Knowledge of pupil differences, or knowledge of their individual limitations, will help in giving pupils the feeling of being recognized. Encouraging pupils to develop social skills and understanding of others will aid them in the orientation which makes them desirable companions.

In meeting the needs of children, care must be taken that their lives are not overorganized. Children need both direction and freedom for independent exploration. Without imposing the burden of disturbing emotional conflict, ways must be found to encourage maximum mental development.

STUDY AND DISCUSSION EXERCISES

1. What are the limits of the teacher's responsibility with regard to physical health and sensory acuity of children?

2. Evaluate the concept of security which makes it important that the individual develop the ability to be independent and solve his own problems.

3. How does the need to be independent fit in with the theory of democratic practices in education?

4. Is it really possible to disapprove of the child's actions without disapproving of him? Support your answer.

5. Defend or criticize the statement that there is a tendency to overorganize the life of children.

SUGGESTED ADDITIONAL READINGS

Frandsen, Arden N., *How Children Learn,* New York: McGraw-Hill Book Company, Inc., 1957, pp. 241–285.

Brief case studies are used to show how emotional disturbances interfere with learning, and approaches are suggested for their alleviation. The role of parents, teachers, and teaching methods are discussed.

Frank, Lawrence K., *Individual Development,* New York: Doubleday & Company, Inc., 1955. 52 pp.

The author shows how one's internal environment, differential physical growth, language development, mental development, and culture work together to mold the emerging personality.

Lindgren, Henry Clay, *Psychology of Personal and Social Adjustment,* 2d ed., New York: American Book Company, 1959, pp. 27–43.

Need satisfaction is related to the development of the self-concept. Needs become altered and modified with increasing age.

Moustakas, Clark E., *The Teacher and the Child*, New York: McGraw-Hill Book Company, Inc., 1956. 265 pp.

Accounts are given of how creative teachers use attentive listening, art work, nondirective interviews, and free activity to help pupils develop healthy ego concepts.

Stewart, Robert S., and Arthur D. Workman, *Children and Other People*, New York: Holt, Rinehart and Winston, Inc., 1956. 276 pp.

Children become appropriately mature by having teachers and parents who recognize their needs and know how to approach their fulfillment.

Willey, Roy DeVerl, *Guidance in Elementary Education*, rev. ed., New York: Harper & Brothers, 1960, pp. 34–61.

Teaching and guidance are discussed as basic need satisfactions as related to home, school, and community.

CHAPTER 3

NEEDS AND TASKS OF
ADOLESCENTS

The promotion of mental health of adolescents is based not only on an appreciation of what adolescence is but also on recognizing what causes adolescence. If the older explanations of causes of adolescence are accepted—namely, rapid growth with resultant awkwardness and uncertainty and the achievement of sexual maturation—there is little that can be done beyond being tolerant and sympathetic. According to this view, the difficulties of adolescence are natural and inevitable. If, however, the contemporary view, which is coming to modify if not to replace the older view, is accepted, there is immediately more hope that the needs can be met constructively. The contemporary view is that the troubles of adolescence are caused by the pressures of modern civilization.

The adolescent is literally in a "no man's land" of society. There is little occasion (except in a time of war) when the work of the late teenager is needed or appreciated. The youth must necessarily remain dependent when he wants to do, and is capable of doing, constructive work. A few generations ago, the young person was an economic asset to the family; now he is a financial liability, even in his early twenties. Frequently his parents do not appreciate this shift in cultural and economic organization. A similar situation has come about with respect to marriage. Financial dependence and the lengthening of the common-school period have resulted in a strong sentiment against early marriage, despite the fact that sexual urges and prowess are at or near their peak. Shifting moral standards and an alteration of ideals attendant upon two world wars have left many adults without firm convictions. Consequently, the adolescent is too often at a loss in trying to find firm anchors for his convictions and ideals.

The author has no longing to see a "return to the good old days."

Actually the changes that have taken place in cultural organization can be turned to the advantage of adolescents. Certainly the prolonging of education can be a great advantage if educational opportunities and expectations are geared to natural growth processes, to the cultural conditions which exist, and to the unique needs of adolescents. The purpose of this chapter is to indicate some of the ways in which the liabilities of the cultural period can be turned into assets.

Adolescents have the same basic organic, psychological, and social needs as do persons of other ages, for example, the need for security, the need to love and be loved, the need for new experiences, the need for independence. Adolescence, however, is merely one phase of the continuous process of growth and development. The point to be appreciated is that the adolescents' needs, if not unique to the adolescent phase of development, are felt somewhat more poignantly than at other ages. The unique place (or rather displacement) of adolescents in society is what constitutes the major part of the problem.

THE MEANING OF ADOLESCENCE

Adolescence Is Cultural Phenomenon. Puberty, the maturation of the individual, particularly in the ability to reproduce the species, is a universal phenomenon. But in some societies the young person passes swiftly from childhood to adulthood. There is sometimes a ceremony, which anthropologists have called "pubertal rites," which marks the recognition of the individual as an adult. He can then marry, establish his own home, assume his adult role in work, be taken into the governing councils. The transition from childhood to adulthood is not so smooth and rapid in Western cultures. Growing up is accomplished in stages and by degrees, recognition as an adult is partial, and the end of the period is difficult to ascertain. Thus, one often may, by law, be allowed to marry at sixteen years of age, be compelled to stay in school until eighteen, and vote at twenty-one, and may continue in school until his late twenties. Many of the regulations and customs relating to the adolescent are, without doubt, for his own ultimate welfare, but they still constitute hazards to his assumption of an adult role.

Lack of Family Responsibility. The adolescent in the recent past was a financial asset to the family. A girl could help in the multitudinous duties of caring for younger children; or, even if she were the youngest, there was a larger chance than today—with greatly increased longevity—that she might take over the housewife's duties at the death of the mother. Cooking, baking, sewing, washing, canning, and routine housekeeping had to be done. A boy could help with some of these chores, but, at a time when the majority of families were rural, he was a valued farm hand—a man's work could be done. Today the majority of families are urban, and household appliances have greatly lightened the chores of women. Consumers' goods that might earlier have been built by males are now bought ready-made.

> Once upon a time woman's work was never done, but in the advertising [today] she toils not, neither does she spin. Our prepared meat loaf is easy-slicing, easy-eating. Just add milk. Here are the easiest cookies of all. It's no bother to make creamed dishes and creamed sauces. Mix your banana cake in three minutes. All you do is put in the water and coffee. Simply pour the batter into a pan and bake. New wonder method makes jams and jellies in fifteen minutes. Your baby will clean the plate and lick the spoon.[1]

While the above is hyperbole, changes have been wrought which make the adolescent, who feels that he has made no significant contribution to the family, financially dependent on parents. Girls and boys, as tall and heavy as or even taller and heavier than parents, must ask for money or be put on an allowance. When parents and teachers stop to realize that it is the culture of the times rather than some mysterious endocrinology of growth that causes feelings of adolescent futility and bewilderment, they will have taken a big step toward constructive help in the prolonged process of growing up. Though there may be no way of providing work which fills the need for recognition and feelings of significance, the attitude that the adult takes toward the adolescent's forced dependence can do much to make the role tolerable.

Delay of Work Opportunities. Labor legislation, in the form of child labor laws, and automation have greatly reduced the opportunity of the teen-ager—in a capitalistic culture—to rattle in his pocket a few coins which are his very own and which he may spend as he chooses. The laws and machines cannot be wished out of existence, nor would they be even if it were possible. But the fact remains that they are hampering influences in the thrust for independence. The desire for significance is thwarted in a society where the first words spoken to a new acquaintance are "What do you do?" rather than "Who are you?" i.e., "What is your family lineage?"

Technologically, there is good reason to delay the entrance of youth into the working world. The complexity of industrial processes, the ramifications of commercial dealings, and the scientific nature of production and distribution make a long period of preparation highly desirable. Educated workers who have insight into over-all complexities are needed.[2]

---

[1] Howard Mumford Jones, *The Pursuit of Happiness*, Cambridge, Mass.: Harvard Univerity Press, 1953, p. 133.

[2] Peter F. Drucker, "America's Next Twenty Years: The Promise of Automation, Part II," *Harper's Magazine*, 210:41–47, April, 1955.

But how to encourage young people to continue their education and remain dependent in the face of the need for emancipation is a difficult question.

One hopeful approach, but certainly not a remedy, is that of work-experience education. This plan, adopted in many localities, allows youngsters to work part time, at current wage rates, for example, in stores, factories, offices, garages, warehouses, and mills under school auspices and with school credit. Pupils earn money of their own, see a

FIG. 3. In what other ways can work experience be correlated with school activities? Does work-experience education have to be in the field of the student's occupational choice? How can work-experience education be initiated in a school system? Is it worthwhile?

relationship of work to school tasks, gain experience on which to base vocational choices, and have their feelings of worth bolstered. These plans require the understanding and cooperation of the whole community, but dividends are available in terms of better mental health for all those involved.[3]

The Uncertainty of Military Service. Youth do not generally object to a period of military service. In fact, war and preparation for war give some young people a feeling of doing something of significance. Unfortunately,

[3] Harold W. Bernard, *Adolescent Development in American Culture*, New York: Harcourt, Brace & World, Inc., 1957, pp. 522–526.

more constructive ways of being of service to one's fellows cannot be or have not been devised. But, in the present state of world affairs, our young people show a gratifying willingness to do what has to be done and have proved they can do it well. It is the uncertainty of the period of compulsory military service and the uncertainty of the long-range forecasts as to whether many or few will be needed that merit correction. At a time when many would like to plan carefully for their college work they must register for military service. At a time when some would like to marry they are uncertain as to the wisdom of doing so at once or of waiting until some vague time in the future. At a time when they would like to be launching a lifetime career they are thrust into other activities. After entering service, they do not know how long they will be in it.

One reduction in the numerous tensions which beset youth would be to place military service on a predictable basis. Possibly combining military training with features of the Civilian Conservation Corps, of the 1930s, would reduce some of the thwarting uncertainty which is now characteristic. In the meantime, adults might well discuss and interpret this uncertainty with youth and thus provide better understanding.

Adolescents Are a Minority Group. A century ago America was a nation young in population structure. About a quarter of the population was between the ages of ten and nineteen. Today only 14.7 per cent of the population is in that age group.[4] As greater numbers of people live to older ages, this percentage will slowly decrease further. When adolescents constituted a substantial part of the population, their numbers and importance made them recognized; as a result, our cultural mores of emphasis on youth were formed. Though there is still much emphasis on youth, there is also an emphasis on maturity. The adolescents, now a smaller minority group, suffer from the disadvantages of other minority groups to the extent that adolescence has often appeared to be almost synonymous with delinquency. The fact that only 5 per cent of youth are delinquent, despite the hazards they face, does not save them from misunderstandings similar to those suffered by Negroes, Jews, or trailer-house dwellers; i.e., sweeping generalizations are often erroneous.

While it must be admitted that not all adolescents grow up without trouble, the spectacular, the sensational view of adolescents must be discarded. Generalizations should be based upon the statistical studies of adolescents. Most adolescents do not commit violent crimes, bear illegitimate children, or habitually use narcotics. The view one takes of adolescents is important, because they, like other persons, tend to live up to what is expected of them. The ego concept, or concept of self, does not come just from within, but is also largely a reflection of the view which

[4] *The World Almanac*, New York: New York World-Telegram and Sun, 1958, p. 258.

others take of the individual. Teachers, as well as parents, should appreciate the position of the adolescent and try to see him as a normally growing person rather than as a member of a deliberately deviant minority.

Gap between the Generations. There has always been difficulty in achieving understanding between adults and the following generations of children and adolescents. It is too easy to forget the difficulties one experienced a decade or two ago. Today this gap is wider because of the rapid rate of change which characterizes our civilization. Some changes are cyclical; but, on the other hand, it is difficult to predict what employment opportunities will be. During World War II days, and for some years after, employment opportunities were high—quite unlike those of the depression years and different from work opportunities in 1958. Studies indicate that, in the high incidence of unemployment about 1960, those in the fourteen to twenty-four year age bracket are most frequently jobless—16 per cent against 4½ per cent of the total labor force.[5] Many technological changes have resulted in entirely new phenomena. Television, man-launched satellites, atomic power, and flight faster than sound were simply dreams when the present generation of parents were themselves adolescent. Social customs such as sexual morality, social drinking, and women's smoking have changed gradually but perceptibly. All these make communication between the generations difficult. As always, the good advice, "When I was a boy . . . ," tends to fall on somewhat inattentive ears. There is no presently available means to eliminate the gap. The problem is one of appreciating its existence and attempting to bridge it through understanding.

Prolonged Schooling. The average number of school years completed rose very slowly from 8 to 8½ years from 1880 to 1920. During the decades after 1920, the increase was rapid—an increase of three years to an average in 1960 of about twelve grades for white persons over the age of twenty.[6] Recent years have seen larger and larger portions of high-school graduates go to college. Two factors will probably further increase the extension of education: (1) the demand for educated workers created by automation and (2) changed sentiment toward education by the large numbers of GI college students who have established a new "college tradition" for many families. This prolonged schooling is for the ultimate good of adolescents and society, but its importance must be interpreted and emphasized for those young people who are also thinking of a job, marriage, and becoming self-sufficient.

[5] Max F. Baer, "Recent Labor Market Developments," *Personnel and Guidance Journal*, 39:340, 1961.

[6] "Educational Attainment in 1980," *National Education Association Research Bulletin*, 37(No. 2):45, April, 1959.

Many people have succumbed to the hysteria of competitive space flight, and thus are in favor of making school much tougher. "If pupils will not or cannot learn, get them out of school and make room for the brains. Produce scientists who can overtake the Russians," is the essence of their frightened contentions. But those interested in mental health, in complete self-realization for all, are unwilling to abandon the educational gains of recent years just because there are some acknowledged weaknesses in our system. Certainly we should make school "tougher" for those who have the capacity. We have in the past tended to neglect pupils who are comfortably above average or are superior.[7] But we still have substantial numbers of pupils who are doing as well as can be reasonably expected and who need continuing education—for themselves and for society. These pupils need encouragement through school pursuits in which they can be successful and studies which interest them. We will still need in our culture writers, musicians, artists, experts in the social sciences, homemakers, and informed citizens as well as chemists, physicists and engineers. Moreover, as we stress scholarship in all realms, it must be borne in mind that some famous men—Thomas Edison, Ulysses S. Grant, Winston Churchill, William Cullen Bryant, for example—did not distinguish themselves in academic pursuits. Our schools must continue to be flexible in meeting the unique needs of all.

The Need for Outgrowing Parental Ascendance. Much of the turmoil of adolescence is manifested in the struggle to outgrow parental domination. The struggle is intensified by the factors, cited above, which make independence hard to achieve. This struggle is probably noticed more by parents than by adolescents; only about one-fifth of the latter report conflict with parents.[8] However, some arguments, assertion of independence, defiance, and ill-feeling are quite normal; therefore, parents need not feel that unpleasant episodes are evidences of past failure. Parents who stop to think would probably not want their offspring to be so lacking in backbone as to act with docile obedience.

When understood as a manifestation of thwarted attempts at independence, adolescent rebellion is easier to tolerate. You also find it easier to sit by and see mistakes being made when you know that mistakes today mean fewer in the future. The errors in choice of friends, the poor planning, the low grade in subjects you could have helped your children with, are hard to take—much harder to take than the falls that accompanied those first halting steps. But even as they learned to

[7] Robert J. Havighurst and others, "The Importance of Education for the Gifted" in *Education for the Gifted*, 57th Yearbook, Part II, National Society for the Study of Education, Chicago: University of Chicago Press, 1958, pp. 9–14.

[8] H. H. Remmers and Benjamin Shimberg, *Examiner Manual for the SRA Youth Inventory*, Chicago: Science Research Associates, Inc., 1949, p. 3.

walk smoothly by being allowed to try, so will they become mature only if you let them do for themselves. . . .

Ironically, those adolescents who find the leaving of their parents and the acquisition of independence most difficult may treat their parents the more cruelly. The more the breaking away disturbs them, the more fierce and childish will be their outbursts.[9]

Teachers can make a signal contribution to the mental health of adolescents by recognizing the need to be treated as adults. They can understand the strivings for autonomy and the need to make decisions and mistakes. Further, if teachers understand the real causes, the cultural ones, which tend to produce turmoil, they will listen to the adolescent's opinions, discuss problems with him, admit the truth of some of his contentions, and point out inconsistencies in a kindly manner. If they respect the divergent views of adolescents as they would those of their own colleagues, they will foster growth toward maturity. Teachers who, instead of "laying down the law," have worked with adolescents on their problems have found that youth grow rapidly toward sensible decision making. Ways of providing such experiences abound in cooperative curriculum making, in disciplinary actions, and in the guidance of social contacts. When opportunities for adult behavior are denied in the home, it is all the more necessary that the lack be compensated for by classroom procedures.

SOME INSISTENT NEEDS OF ADOLESCENTS

There are many statements of the needs of adolescents. There is a recognition that their needs differ in intensity, if not in kind, during these years of "stress." In this section some of the more immediate, specific, and pressing needs of adolescents—needs that bear directly on mental health—will be discussed.

Peer Adjustments. Questionnaire studies of adolescents indicate that a sharply felt need is that of satisfactory peer adjustment. A baby or a young child does not seem to be greatly concerned about whether or not he is getting along harmoniously with others. Babies characteristically play with other babies only in later stages of development. By the time children have reached school age, they are concerned about having playmates and often attempt to buy friendship when they are unable to earn it; but, at least in the early grades, it is more important to the child to please his teacher than it is to please his peers. This is decidedly not the case when they arrive at adolescence. The desire to be accepted by his

[9] J. Roswell Gallagher, "Why They Rebel," *The Atlantic Monthly*, 191:70, June, 1953.

peer group has been called the strongest single control in the adolescent's life.[10]

Adolescents are attempting to be adults; they want to appear to be men or women. They have a deep-seated desire to grow away from what they feel to be the hampering influences of parental domination. The group most available to them outside the family circle is that of their friends and classmates. To appear to these to be right, significant, and properly conforming is highly important. Anxiety over seeming not to fit the pattern is likely to bring about symptoms of tension and frustration.

A first step in recognizing the importance of peer adjustment is to realize that the apparent repudiation of parents and teachers is a healthy indication. It shows that the adolescent is growing away from the need for adult support and is attempting to strike out for himself. Teachers should realize the importance of bizarre hairdos, the value of wearing skirts of the proper length, of using cosmetics, and of having a sufficient number of sweaters. The boy with his heavy brogues, tight dungarees, or dirty cords may repudiate the adult's ideas of what the well-dressed young man should wear, but to the boy these details help to make him an integral member of the crowd. This same phenomenon lies back of his assuming a dislike for school, wanting to stay out late, and being able to choose his own friends. Certainly the adoption of the current mode with regard to dress, speech, and manners is only a surface manifestation of peer adjustment, but the teacher must be careful not to underestimate the importance of conformity.

Another aspect of peer adjustment concerns the widespread notion among adolescents that they are "different." Thus, a mole, a wide mouth or a small one, the size of his nose, or the shape of his legs will be likely to bother an adolescent deeply. When the variances are barely noticeable, the reaction to them differs very little from what it would be if they were quite extreme. Marked deviations in height or weight are serious problems and should be regarded as such by the adolescent's counselors. That they often are not so viewed is revealed in the case of a girl who approached her counselor with the words "I'm too tall—and don't tell me that it really doesn't matter, because it does." It did matter to her but not to anyone else. She was erect and good-looking, was popular with girls, had all the dates she wanted, was active and successful in athletics, and had a good scholastic record.

Adjustment to Teachers. First in some lists and ranking high in other lists of the needs that adolescents feel is that of teacher adjustment. As

[10] Vincent Claypool, "What Practices in School Discipline Develop Better Student-Teacher Relationships in Junior and Senior High School?" *The Bulletin of the National Association of Secondary School Principals*, 42:3, April, 1958.

the adolescent tries to grow away from his parents, he reaches out to other adults for companionship and guidance. Hence, it is important to him that associations with teachers should be harmonious and mature. This imposes on the teacher the necessity of never laughing or sneering at the immaturity of the pupils; in fact, the teacher must take the view that the confidences given to him are of serious import. The nature of teacher-pupil contacts will determine to a remarkable degree the direction that growth will take through the adolescent years.

Inability to get along with teachers is a source of concern to the young person. In spite of the fact that he puts on a blasé front, he wishes to show his adulthood by being able to establish harmonious adult contacts. Teachers can aid, in and out of class, by respecting the opinions that are proffered, by listening and conversing rather than lecturing, by avoiding the temptation to say, "You'll find out the truth when you are older" or "You'll realize the truth when you have more experience."

Parent-Teacher-Pupil Adjustment. The adolescent's adjustment to the teacher is particularly important because the teacher helps provide a bridge between the child's world and the adult's world. The teacher is the best-known adult outside the family circle. It is therefore pertinent to say a few words of precaution about the function of the parent-teacher association at the secondary level.

The spirit behind the parent-teacher association at the high-school level is commendable. Certainly the advantage of having all those who are dealing with young people pool their resources of information and their viewpoints can hardly be questioned. However, there is a question as to the validity of the technique for gaining this cooperation. Without being dogmatically certain, the author hazards the view that parent-teacher associations at the high-school level should not be encouraged.

Examination of the fundamental needs of human beings shows that high on the list are the desires for personal significance and independence. The adolescent wishes to outgrow dependence on parents, to be recognized as an individual in his own right, and to be seen as one who is able to take care of his own problems. He does not realize so fully as the teacher how much he needs the help of adults—particularly his parents. The parents, in the eyes of the adolescent, are the ones who constitute the greatest obstacle to his achieving independence and significance.

High-school teachers are in a strategic position to give constructive help to the adolescent in the process of becoming an adult able to handle his own affairs. In the first place, there is great likelihood that the only adults whom the adolescent knows intimately, aside from his parents, are his teachers. In the second place, the teacher, by virtue of being a teacher, holds a place of prestige and eminence, from the standpoint of the young person. It frequently happens that a young boy or girl actually experiences ardent hero worship toward particular teachers. Young people, if they are treated as adults, will come to teachers with their problems. But in order that this strategic position may be capitalized on, a high degree of rapport between pupils and teacher must exist.

There is some danger that the PTA will interfere with the building of the rapport that is so essential. When a young person sees his parents talking with his teachers, he is likely to feel that he is the subject of conversation, although it may be that his feeling is not justified. He probably thinks that his teacher is abandoning him and siding with his parents—in league against him. If he gets this impression, he begins to look upon the teacher as another obstacle to his growing up and will resent his counsel and friendship.

Not all adolescents react in this way. Many of them are truly glad to have their parents become acquainted with their teachers. They are pleased when their parents attend school functions and visit their classes (on visiting days). Those who have this attitude, however, are the ones who are allowed the freedom of choice and action that is the privilege of adulthood. They are pupils who are experiencing no acute problems of adjustment in the school; consequently, they do not need help. However, some still say, "I'm embarrassed by my parents' coming to school. I try everything I know, short of demanding, to keep them away from my teachers."

A PTA will be of no particular value to any student who is not experiencing a problem. It is likely to prove a marked detriment to one who feels that parental fetters are too confining. It is, therefore, recommended that a formal organization for the teachers' getting together with parents be discouraged.

There are some advantages of the PTA which have only indirect bearing on pupil adjustment. These too need consideration, as is indicated in the following:

> The basic reason why I am interested in P.-T. A. work is that I have a conviction that a school or a school system cannot be much better than the public opinion on which it rests. At least that seems to me to be true in a democracy. If a school happens to have a good principal or if a school system has the leadership of a good superintendent of public instruction, then the school can go a little ahead of public opinion. This, however, has limits and the school which moves too far ahead of public opinion will soon find itself pulled up short. It seems to me that only as our parents and other citizens study the problems of developing children and youth can we, as educators, expect intelligent support from them. This is as true of the secondary school as of the elementary school. Citizens are bound to have *some* views regarding the school's purpose, curricula, methods of discipline, and equipment. I would much prefer

to have an intelligent opinion which is based on careful study than an uninformed one. My conception of the P.-T. A. has always been that it is a study-and-action group which discusses and deals with three main topics: (1) What schools are for, (2) What children and adolescents are like, and (3) How children and adolescents can best be helped to develop in home, school and community.[11]

This public relations aspect has real merit, especially when schools are under periodic attack from persons who make sweeping generalizations about the decadence of American education. Questioning the wisdom of the PTA in matters of pupil adjustment does not deny the desirability of interpreting schools to the public. The argument is that contact between adolescents and teachers may be threatened. When young people do wish to have parents and teachers meet, there is no reason why the meeting cannot be arranged to take place informally. It would be a valuable approach, particularly when the adolescent is to be discussed, to have him become a party to the discussion.

Determination of Purposes. Psychologists stress the fact that all behavior is caused. It is either purposive or purposeful—it does not just happen. An attempt is constantly being made by teachers to transform purposive behavior (manifest in vague strivings) into purposeful behavior (in which goals are more consciously determined and clearly seen). The adolescent is no different from any other person in regard to the purposiveness and purposefulness of behavior; but the adolescent who is making healthy growth becomes less and less satisfied with vague goals or those imposed by teachers or dictated by the curriculum. He wishes to know the reasons for doing what he does and to know particularly how these activities will be of personal benefit.

There are two major forms which the determination of purposes may take. One is the selection of a life occupation and the other is the formulation of a philosophy of life. Some individuals will have made considerable progress toward determination of these purposes, while others seem to be not much concerned with them. Even tentative determination of purposes will help them to marshal their efforts and to concentrate their energies in a society in which specialization is of some importance.

Studies of the objectives of adolescents show that characteristically there is a great deal of change and shifting of interests. Occupational choice is a developmental process.[12] Final choices of occupations cannot be expected to be made by all during the high-school years; nor should an unalterable philosophy of life be formed in adolescence. The tentative

[11] Personal letter from S. R. Laycock, formerly Dean of Education, University of Saskatchewan, Saskatoon, Canada, Nov. 25, 1952.

[12] E. L. Tolbert, *Introduction to Counseling,* New York: McGraw-Hill Book Company, Inc., 1959, p. 177.

selection of an occupation will result in exploration and study that will ultimately provide a sound basis for mature selection. Explanation or discovery of the personal benefits of academic pursuits will result in a more purposeful approach to school work.

One needs clear purposes if he is to possess good mental health, if he is to enjoy life, if he is to avoid becoming a drifter. Teachers can help by making the study of occupations an integral part of their courses of instruction, whether these courses be in mathematics, social studies, Eng lish, science, or such subjects as woodworking and secretarial training As the requirements of jobs, the background needed, the personal qualities which are requisite, and the opportunities available are discussed, the student will be better able to take necessary further steps toward preparation for his future. These same courses can serve as bases for discussions of the meaning of morality, citizenship, effective personality, and brotherhood, and thus will provide clues to the formulation of a tentative philosophy of life.

The teacher can be helpful if, in class discussions, counseling interviews, and informal conversations, he stresses the importance of determining purposes and emphasizes the normality of change of goals. The wavering nature of purposes during adolescence is recognized as an indication of healthy growth. This, of course, does not refer to such inclinations as wanting to be a cowboy on Monday and a doctor on Tuesday, but indicates that no one need be discouraged if objectives change during the course of a term's work. The important thing is that attention be given to the matter of purposes and that teachers aid by pointing out, in formal classwork as well as in informal contacts, the necessity of devoting conscious attention to their determination. The need for direction is acutely felt by the normal adolescent.

Establish Feelings of Worth. Children, adolescents, and adults, need to have a feeling of personal worth or significance. The problem for adolescents is made the more pressing, however, by virtue of changing social relations as they expand their experiential world to include more contacts outside the home. It is this need for a feeling of personal worth, as well as the need to be accepted by peers, that gives rise to the urgent desire for conformity to adolescent attitudes, manner of dress, and modes of conduct. The more an adolescent doubts his personal worth, the more servile his conformity becomes. The more firmly he believes in his own worth, the greater is the possibility for his achieving independence of thought and action.

One way teachers can help is to treat the adolescent with respect. Listen to his views, give courteous consideration to his opinions. Find occasion to praise the contributions which he makes to group thinking and action. Treat him, when possible, as though he were the adult he is trying to be. This does not mean that he should be flattered or praised when there is no justification for such encouragement. The author, advising his student teachers that a little praise goes a long, long way, was gratified to find, on each of his next few class visits, that the teachers were able to find justifiable reason for giving praise. An active search for things to praise had opened their eyes to items of merit.

Another way the teacher can help is to delegate responsibility both to the group and to individuals. This responsibility might include such things as the selection of topics for study, the choosing of committees for carrying out the divisions of work, giving these committees a voice in classroom control, and supervision of such things as heating, ventilation, lighting, and the manipulation of projectors, radios, maps, globes, and the like. Individuals can be given responsibility according to their recognized special talents and skills. This will help in two ways: first, appropriately used special talents enhance classroom welfare, and second, the pupil is given an opportunity to display his abilities. A boy who took little interest in literature and drama was known to be interested in electricity. He was encouraged to prepare and manipulate the lighting for a high-school play—which he did with high proficiency. A night or two before the big production the leading man became ill, but the lighting-effects boy volunteered to take the part. He played it well, because, while getting the right lighting effects, he had also learned the roles of all the cast, including emotions as well as words. To be able to sing, draw, or write well is something that builds feelings of worth. Residence in a particular neighborhood, knowledge of a given occupation through familiarity with the father's vocation, or knowledge gained through vacation travel to a particular region may provide the student with resources for assuming a degree of responsibility which is out of the ordinary.

Closely allied to, perhaps actually a part of, responsibility is the opportunity for self-direction and independence of decision. This fundamental concept of the current emphasis in guidance has been facetiously, but penetratingly, defined as "Seeing through Johnny so Johnny can see himself through"—the stress being placed on Johnny's ultimate self-determination. This can easily prove to be a sore point, because the decisions of an adolescent are often at variance with the matured view of the adult. But remember that if youths are not allowed the opportunity to make mistakes in their own decisions, they are denied, as well, the opportunity to select for themselves the avenues leading to success.

Quite probably, the most important factor in developing feelings of worth is that of developing skills. Teachers can assist by recognizing and encouraging latent talent. They can stress the necessity for work and effort if abilities are to be developed. They can point out how proficiency will operate to make the adolescent's life more effective and gratifying. Above all, they can make the classroom a laboratory for the development of intellectual, artistically creative, and social skills. Purposeful effort is economical effort, and teachers can aid by clarifying the goals which are desirable.

It has been suggested that creative opportunities should not be thought of as being limited to art, sports, and student activities but should include academic subjects as well. By encouraging choice of subjects and novel approaches to them—experiments, library research, critical reports—feelings of worth can be enhanced by individual expression. Instead of using limited reading lists, demanding conformity of opinion, and following routine approaches, teachers should take time to help adolescents (on an adult plane) to devise a program with some individuality.[13]

Being liked is another factor basic to feelings of worth. Many an adolescent believes that he is so different from others that his being liked is essential to his feeling of assurance. The key to the situation is a simple one; it is contained in the cliché "To know is to understand." Factual knowledge obtained by teachers from tests, past school marks, or case histories must be supplemented with the subjective data submitted by the student in his conversations, his free writing, and his artistic creations.

Closely akin to the need for being liked is the need to be recognized. A manifestation of this need is the exhibitionistic nature of much of the adolescent's behavior. If recognition can be earned through scholastic work and leadership ability, there will be less need for the loud talking, swaggering, and other attention-getting behavior familiar at that age. Adolescents can be helped by the teacher's offering opportunities for the young persons to assume responsibility, display their talents, and be recognized for the contributions they can make.

The teachers may protest that attention to the above suggestions will be difficult and time-consuming. But to the extent of their own success in helping their pupils to achieve satisfactory feelings of worth, they will count the time well spent and find the work gratifying. Moreover, in the course of time and with repeated practice, the effort to obtain these results will become easier, even habitual.

Understanding Oneself. Much of the pupil's self-understanding will come about as the result of experience. Further understanding will be gained through the indirect aid that teachers can give by promoting peer adjustment, by facilitating teacher-pupil adjustment, by assisting with the clarification of personal purposes, and by fostering feelings of personal worth. In addition, self-understanding is a topic that can profitably be attacked through direct study and discussion.[14]

[13] Lou LaBrant, "Mental-health Practices in the High-school Grades" in *Mental Health in Modern Education*, 54th Yearbook, Part II, National Society for the Study of Education, Chicago: University of Chicago Press, 1955, p. 232.

[14] Douglas F. Parry, "Experimental Practice in Improving the Emotional Health of Secondary School Students," *The High School Journal*, 35:80–88, 1951.

Repeatedly, teachers have reported that they have been amazed to find how penetrating the discussion of personal problems by adolescents can be. Class discussions, forums, group counseling, and debates have been successfully used to bring about better understanding. An example of the effectiveness shown by young people in solving their own problems is that provided by some contemporary teaching regarding the use of alcohol. Attempts to influence the conduct of young people through fear —alcoholism, drunken driving, and the negative physical effects—have produced little positive change. Approaching the problem through moralizing has been ineffective, as well. But discussions by adolescents about why people drink, what the psychological effects of alcohol are, and what limitations the use of alcohol places on personality development have led to the kind of understanding that provides positive motivation.

Preparation for Marriage. In view of the fact that practically all these young people will, within a very short period of time, be engaged in home and family relationships, it seems surprising that more direct attention has not been given to preparation for that experience. Many of the needs stressed in mental hygiene will find their fruition in the institution of marriage. Feelings of security, feelings of belonging, the desire and need to love and be loved, opportunities for personal accomplishment, and the organic needs related to sex may be realized through a successful marriage. Yet statistics show that about one out of four marriages fails and that the other three could yield greater satisfaction to the participants if more adequate preparation were provided.

Many of the lessons relative to a successful marriage can better be learned before the stress of falling in love with the wrong person or before the problems of marital adjustment have become a reality. Furthermore, the teacher is in a more advantageous position to deal with these problems than is the parent, because of the lack of emotional involvement. Miss Rosen, in her class in human relations for seniors, found, through journals the pupils were keeping, that two of them planned to elope. She offered no advice but listened, individually and then in joint conference, to their doubts, aspirations, and fears. They finally decided to delay their marriage and consult with their parents. After graduation they were married and received the help of both sets of parents in getting started.[15] Miss Rosen helped by being their confidante, by being patient, and by treating the young people as adults. It takes these things to build the rapport which is necessary if the adolescents are to be prevailed upon to write confidential journals. In view of the prevalence and imminence of marriage in the life of adolescents, it is advisable that all their teachers be well informed on marriage problems.

One of the important considerations is that, although sex is important,

[15] Clark E. Moustakas, *The Teacher and the Child*, New York: McGraw-Hill Book Company, Inc., 1956, pp. 203–204.

sex is one, and only one, of the factors that make for successful marriage. Literature should be made available to adolescents that frankly discusses sex problems, while placing them in proper perspective. It should be made clear that adequacy of personality, past history of social adequacy, the previous happiness of the young people concerned, and the happiness of their parents are equal to, if not greater than, sex adequacy in importance in marital adjustment. Unhealthy experimentation in premarital sex experiences might well be diminished if young people were instructed that sexual satisfaction is an achievement, a creation, rather than a discovery. Inasmuch as sex is mental and emotional in nature, as well as physical, it is impossible to discover whether one is "sexually adjusted" through experiences in the back of a car or in a cheap hotel room. The haste, fear, and apprehension which attend such ventures bear no relationship to the sex pleasures of emotionally mature married people. The importance of conducting sex experiences within the verbally accepted mores of our society cannot be overstressed.

In spite of Hollywood versions of romance, it is the exceptional instance in which love at first sight develops into satisfactory marriage. The more we can do to abolish the notion that "marriages are made in heaven"—that one should *find* the perfect mate made-to-order—the sooner we shall get young people to see that marriage, like mental health, is a matter of continuous adjustment. Instead of their searching for the chimerical perfect mate, they should realize that their own personal adequacy creates the perfect mate—that the determination of two people to make their marriage work is most important.

A study of the factors which contribute to divorce should be instructive to young people as they seek their mates. Differences in religious belief, marked differences in cultural background, and widely varying moral standards constitute hazards. On the other hand, differences in age, likeness or unlikeness in personality (as long as each is mature), and differences in interests are less hazardous than is commonly believed.[16] Young people can be taught to look for balanced personality in such things as having friends of both sexes, lack of complaints against parents and associates, interest in various activities, and concern for the interest and welfare of others. It is important to look for these qualities in persons with whom one dates—before one has "fallen in love."

Newly established marriages have a better chance for success if the parents of the newlyweds are happily married. If one's mate has come from a broken home, some difficulties may be anticipated. Extra care, therefore, should be taken to solve problems immediately and mutually. Many young people who come from broken homes are particularly determined that their married life will be different; thus, these people

* Ray E. Baber, *Marriage and the Family*, 2d ed., New York: McGraw-Hill Book Company, Inc., 1953, pp. 79–158.

have an advantage; however, the fact that the basic personality trends are established in one's early home remains as a peril.

Young people, even beyond high school, are often quite unrealistic with regard to the income they consider necessary in order to get married. In one survey, if marriage were to be delayed until income were up to what 75 to 80 per cent of the class considered desirable, it would not be consummated until about fifteen years after graduation from college. In other words, it is pure fantasy for an average young man to think he should provide for his wife "in the manner to which she has become accustomed." He should realize that it probably took her father some twenty years to establish his daughter's present economic level. Again, the lesson should be emphasized that a strong marriage is built not on economic advantages but upon adequacy of personality. Studies of divorce show that, where low income is cited as a cause for marriage breakdown, the actual cause is lack of maturity of personality on the part of one or both of the marriage mates.[17]

Another lesson that should be taught before it is too late is the fallacy of the notion that one can marry to reform another. A knowledge of the nature of personality growth shows that in very few instances can one just decide that a poor trait will be cast aside because of marriage. Heavy drinking, dishonesty, promiscuity, laziness, and incompetence are characterized by habits and attitudes that are a long time in forming and usually require the help of experts and much time for reconstruction.

These lessons and others related to marital success are sometimes attacked in high-school courses that deal with personal problems and social living. Even though there is no formal course which paves the way to the introduction of such material, there is much the teacher can do to supply the adolescents' need of knowledge of marital life, of life at home, where women will spend the majority of their time and men will spend a substantial proportion of their time. The personal attitudes of the teachers, the remarks they make, the advice they give can help young people to make marriage a deep source of personal satisfaction and mental health.

NATIONAL EDUCATION ASSOCIATION STATEMENT OF ADOLESCENT NEEDS

Needs of Adolescents. A list of adolescent needs which may justifiably be viewed with respect, because it was formulated by the processes of group thinking, is the list prepared by the Educational Policies Commission of the National Education Association[18] (see Fig. 4). The part that

[17] *Ibid.*, pp. 226–229.

[18] *Planning for American Youth*, rev. ed., Washington: National Association of Secondary-school Principals, 1951. Permission to use headings granted by the National Association of Secondary-school Principals of the National Education Association.

these needs and their satisfaction play in the pursuit of mental health for the adolescent is discussed under the following numbered paragraphs:

1. "All youth need to develop salable skills." Not all teachers have direct responsibility for helping adolescents develop specific vocational skills. All teachers do have a responsibility for teaching the lesson of the dignity of labor, for instilling an acceptance of the fact that people have to work, and for encouraging a willingness to do any work that has to

FIG. 4. The imperative needs of youth. Permission to reprint granted by the National Association of Secondary School Principals.

be done. Except for a brief time during World War II, the past fifty years have seen a steadily decreasing freedom of choice in the selection of one's work. While there is a heavy demand for some kinds of workers, there is a decreasing demand for others. The glamour of rocket engines, electronics, and synthetic chemistry must not blind young people to the great need for workers in management, distribution, and organization.[19] Unless adolescents realize that they will have to do the jobs that society wants and needs to have done, they will have a hazard to their mental health imposed upon them because they have failed to understand that there is a difference between developing skills and developing "salable" skills. This factor makes it necessary to shift the primary emphasis regarding vocational preparation from the field of individual aptitudes and interests to what jobs need to be done in terms of the nature of our national economy. The teacher's part is to foster a sense of responsibility, a willingness to do what has to be done, and a belief in the respectability of any job which is well done and which contributes to the welfare of society.

2. "All youth need to develop and maintain good health and physical fitness." The simple lesson of physiology needs to be reemphasized in the high school. Youth who are growing in power and in the range of their activities need to have it impressed upon them that their resources are not inexhaustible. They should know that they need adequate amounts of sleep, a sensible diet, and appropriate exercise.

In addition to the elementary facts of hygiene, the adolescent should have an opportunity to learn about menstruation, nocturnal emissions, experimental masturbation, acne, rapid growth of the nose, profuse sweating, and the development of secondary sex characteristics which are normal phases of development. Fortunately, there is a steadily growing number of teachers who are able and willing to bring these facts to the attention of the adolescent and are thus helping them to absorb the experiences of their growth and development.

3. "All youth need to understand the rights and duties of the citizen of a democratic society." The "duty" of citizenship becomes a "privilege" when mental hygiene is considered. "He who would find his life must first lose it" is not just an important lesson of Christianity; it is a sound principle of mental health. Psychologists and psychiatrists make frequent mention of the fact that a person must "get outside of himself," diminish preoccupation with personal problems, and give serious consideration to the welfare of others, if he would enjoy good mental health. When teachers provide opportunities for the exercise of citizenship in their classes, when they acquaint pupils with the current issues that are troubling the country, when they give them actual contact with governing

[19] Peter F. Drucker, "America's Next Twenty Years: The Coming Labor Shortage. Part I," *Harper's Magazine*, 210:27–32, March, 1955.

bodies and community political institutions, they are not only preparing wise voters but improving mental health. To the extent that ways are provided for pupils to practice citizenship, that they are given opportunities to participate in community projects and to engage in activities which redound to the benefit of their school, they are learning lessons of personal mental health.

4. "All youth need to understand the significance of the family for the individual and society." Many school pupils do not have adequate opportunities to learn effective patterns of family life. Since both boys and girls will find in their own later family life sources of either deep satisfaction or marked dissatisfaction, it is imperative that serious attention be given in the school to the subject of family life. Facts pertaining to the development of adjustive personalities, wholesome sex relations, care of children, and home financial management should be presented. There is much literature, written for adolescents, that can be used in family-life courses and in units of health and social living classes dealing with marriage.[20]

5. "All youth need to know how to purchase and use goods and services intelligently." Study of the purchase and use of goods is part of most high-school home economics courses, but large numbers of students do not take such courses. When one stops to think of the barrage of advertising in newspapers and magazines, on billboards, and on radio and television—a barrage to which we are all exposed—it seems that instruction in wise buying should be a fundamental part of preparation for effective living. Some teachers have attacked the problem through tying the lessons in with the study of mathematics, while others have approached it in their orientation and personal-problems classes. It can be studied from the vantage point of industrial arts classes, economics courses, and home-room groups.

6. "All youth need to understand the influence of science on human life." This need is, to an extent, being met by present courses in science. Too often, though, there are teachers who emphasize the "science" aspect to the exclusion of its "influence on human life." What is needed is a new emphasis, one which will direct attention to the fact that science is constantly functioning in daily life. Studies show that with the extension of education upward there is a decrease in the amount of superstition prevalent, but these same studies also show that even well-educated persons retain some ill-founded beliefs. Many teachers have lists of common superstitions, which they attack in the course of their instruction.

Without danger of an argument regarding the relative merits of science versus values, it can safely be stated that men must devote time to the study of the impact of science on human lives.

[20] See, for example, Life Adjustment Booklets published by Science Research Associates, Inc., Chicago.

These are confusing times. The daily headlines, evidence of fear and anxiety in high places, fill us with these same feelings of fear and anxiety. Their large black banners of war, famine, strikes, loyalty oaths, traitors, mobilization, civilian defense, A-bomb experiments, debates on aid to Europe, price controls and taxes multiply this confusion. Surrounded by radio programs and television shows on which these problems are continuously being discussed, often passionately and pessimistically, is it any wonder that children and youth, too, reflect the fears and anxieties of the adult world?[21]

Fears and anxieties are, however, subject to at least some degree of rational control. While there are many hazards, the natural and life sciences suggest ways of meeting them effectively. A recognition of and an emphasis on rational approaches can best be made when the citizens of tomorrow are learning their first facts about science. In short, the science of living harmoniously with one's fellow men should be an integral part of the science of physics, chemistry, and biology.

7. "All youth need an appreciation of literature, art, music, and nature." The theory of liberal, or general, education has emphasized this value for ages. Yet the practice has fallen short of the goal for many present-day school people. Perhaps the reason for the lack has been that the appreciation aspect has been secondary to the knowledge of the facts of literature, art, and the like. Appreciation has been achieved by those pupils who have studied under teachers who teach the lessons of shared experiences, of human insights, who enjoy these things themselves, who are sensitive to the needs and interests of their pupils. Teachers are needed who see in music and art ways of enriching personal lives, means of releasing tensions and of obtaining surcease from daily cares.

The current emphasis on producing scientists must be supplemented by recognition that, in our society, we shall also need to continue the search for values, for beauty, and for the realization of various creative potentials. We must go further than teaching preselected information; we must encourage the exercise of many forms of creativity.[22] Thus we need continued emphasis on literature, art, music, and nature. Appreciation of these areas has a dual role in mental health. In the first place, they provide an avenue for the exercise of the positive, upbuilding emotions and thus supply needs and satisfactions which help one to round out his existence. The second part of their service, not entirely separate from the first, is that they open an opportunity for the "profitable use of leisure time." Art, literature, and nature represent areas and

[21] Association for Supervision and Curriculum Developments, *Growing Up in an Anxious Age*, Washington: National Education Association, 1952, p. 4.

[22] Paul A. Schilpp, "Teaching: ' . . . The Opening of Doors,'" *The Saturday Review*, 41:16–17, Feb. 15, 1958.

activities of life which, although ordinarily given little place in the ordinary workaday experiences of the average individual, can serve to round out a wholesome way of living.

8. "All youth need to be able to use their leisure time well and to budget it wisely." This objective of education deserves more attention to-day than it did at the time it was stated as one of the "Seven Cardinal Objectives of Secondary Education." The decreasing length of the working day and the introduction of laborsaving devices in the home impose more responsibility in the exercise of freedom. The changes mean that the problem of what to do with leisure time will become more and more pressing. The second factor grows out of the first: on account of lack of education, people have turned more and more to mass entertainment. "Stupendous spectacles" and "supercolossal productions" are not necessarily detrimental, but there are few individuals who would argue that there is anything very constructive about them. As one grows to maturity and on into later maturity, this mass entertainment becomes less and less attractive, and the consequence is an impoverished oldster who is less able to handle the leisure imposed upon him. This leads to the third factor; namely, there are increasingly large numbers of people who are reaching the age of sixty-five (the traditional time for retirement)—an increase due not only to population growth but also to rapidly lengthening longevity. Utilization of leisure time is also a problem of adolescence, because the habits of youth partially determine the actions and attitudes of the same person in later life.

From the standpoint of mental health, leisure should give opportunity for expression of interests and capacities rather than merely supply entertainment or "pass-time." While some attention is given in the schools to the development of leisure-time interests which can be functional in adult life, the major emphasis is on mass entertainment. The trend seems to be toward developing championship teams which can draw huge crowds to witness the skill of a few specially endowed and specially trained performers. The fact that these few may go on to become highly paid professionals does not free the schools of the obligation to teach a more constructive use of leisure time for the school population at large.

Teachers can help, in this dilemma, by cultivating a wide variety of interests themselves, by becoming sensitive to the interests of their students, and by encouraging the development of those interests which are suited to individuals who differ in talents and background.

9. "All youth need to develop respect for other persons." This need is at the very core of mental health. Personal success in any one occupation is to a large degree determined by one's ability to get along with other persons. "Getting along" involves the establishment of respect for the rights, interests, wishes, welfare, skills, and shortcomings of others

Respect, in its turn, grows out of an intimate acquaintance with the other person and his problems. Finally, respect for others contributes to personal mental health by opening up those opportunities for "getting outside oneself" of which psychologists and psychiatrists speak so urgently. Fortunately, teachers, also, are widely aware of the existence of this need.

Two responsibilities of teachers stand out. First, the significance of respect for others should form the basis of much class discussion and illustration. Second, the organization of class activities should be so designed as to offer opportunities for exercising respect. This can be done by sharing responsibility, by calling for various skills and knowledges, and by giving recognition to the contribution of each class member.

10. "All youth need to grow in their ability to think rationally." This is another need which has long been recognized. The difficulty in getting it worked into the plan of education is that too often it has been regarded as an inseparable companion of learning. Of course, schools will never be able to anticipate in their programs of instruction *all* the problems that students will meet in the course of their lives, but some constructive approaches may be integrated into the established curriculum by changing some teaching habits.

One of the major handicaps in the development of thinking is that teachers are too eager and too ready to give answers to problems. This tends to make the student dependent upon authority for his conclusions. If the student has arrived at conclusions by himself, the experience will have helped him to develop the research techniques needed for modifying conclusions. To furnish answers is often a waste of time when the limited experience of the learner has not even prepared him to ask the questions that call for those answers. The traditional emphasis on accurate vocabulary, objective facts, and precise knowledge is still needed—asking and answering questions involves acquiring data. But teachers must, in addition, seek significant student problems which may serve as integrative threads in the use of knowledge.[23]

HOW TEACHERS CAN HELP ADOLESCENTS ACHIEVE MENTAL HEALTH

Understand the Meaning of Behavior. Much maladjustment, whether in children or in adolescents, is due to a lack of understanding on the part of parents. Further, some teachers lack adequate understanding and are unwilling to become concerned about the problems of adolescents.

[23] Benjamin S. Bloom, "Ideas, Problems, and Methods of Inquiry" in *The Integration of Educational Experiences*, 57th Yearbook, Part III, National Society for the Study of Education, Chicago: University of Chicago Press, 1958, pp. 99–101.

A first step toward remedying this handicap is for teachers to learn to interpret the behavior manifestations of individuals.

Many attempts at adulthood made by high-school students are annoying and ridiculous to adults: slang, unusual styles of clothing, fondness for old cars, imitations of adults (such as wearing club insignia, special hats or jackets, initiations, overuse of make-up, smoking), talk about night clubs, sporting events, and so forth. A school which is designed especially for adolescents cannot expect to avoid these manifestations.[24]

The parallel columns below indicate the kinds of interpretation that teachers might well attempt to make; but it is necessary to keep in mind that, because of the wide variations which exist between individuals, the suggested interpretations cannot be definitive. Moreover, the majority of adolescents will not show a marked degree of variation from what is deemed to be normal. The following material, then, suggests ways of becoming aware of those who do need special help and understanding.

Behavior	Interpretation[25]
Pretending to be ill, sudden outbursts of temper, crying, pouting, and sulking	Lack of opportunity to accept responsibility, no necessity to accept consequences for one's own acts
Engaging in fantasy, rationalizing failures, tense, and sensitive	Is faced by problems which are too difficult
Shyness, lack of initiative, complacency with present status	Has experienced repeated failure, lacks social success, has no outstanding ability
Dissatisfied and unhappy in present situation	Possesses physical defects or lacks ability to perform expected tasks
Loss of appetite, sleeplessness, tics, stuttering, excessive tiredness, or dizzy spells	Glandular imbalance, inadequate diet, excessive demands, academic and social inadequacy
Is lonely, has no corps of friends, is isolated from the group; has no confidants	Lacks opportunity for companionship, feels inadequate, may undervalue or overvalue self
Quarrels, shows no respect for rights or opinions of others, has little concern for welfare of others	Limited social experience, has been pampered at home or at school, has few responsibilities
Does not apply himself to schoolwork, has no clearly defined goals	Has not perceived the significance of schoolwork, has not earned the approval of others

[24] Lou LaBrant, "Mental-health Practices in the High-school Grades" in *Mental Health in Modern Education,* 54th Yearbook, Part II, National Society for the Study of Education, Chicago: University of Chicago Press, 1955, p. 234.

[25] These interpretations are illustrative only. For any one kind of behavior (symptom) there are many interpretations. Moreover, the causes of behavior are many rather than single. See Charlotte Buhler and others, *Childhood Problems and the Teacher,* New York: Holt, Rinehart and Winston, Inc., 1952, p. 15.

The necessity for understanding each adolescent, or knowing him intimately, can be readily seen by shifting the positions of the items in the foregoing columns. That is, another possible interpretation for "Pretending to be ill, sudden outbursts of temper, crying, pouting and sulking" might very well be "Is faced by problems which are too difficult" or "Has experienced repeated failure, lacks social success, has no outstanding ability." The intention here is merely to indicate the need for interpreting behavior as a first step in understanding the adolescent. Behavior is the individual's way of showing that his needs have or have not been met.

The column headed "Interpretation" requires but little reflection before it will reveal ways of getting at the causes of behavior. Gradually, but nonetheless surely, responsibility must be put upon the individual. His duties and obligations must be scaled to the individual's present level of development. Opportunity must be given to develop skills which contribute to the welfare of the group, and opportunity for social intercourse must be provided. Physical defects must be treated or the person must be helped to realize the actual way in which others regard such defects.

Adolescents generally are mature enough so that they too can learn to interpret their own behavior and that of others through discussion, explanation, and illustration. Such insight represents significant progress toward behavior improvement.

The School Can Provide Some Practice in Social Relations.

The adolescent years are, preeminently, a period of social development and adjustment. . . . With the oncoming of adolescence, the boy or girl becomes acutely aware of social pressures and relationships. It is this sensitivity that leads the adolescent into the conformity characteristic of the period. . . . As the adolescent grows older, he learns to react to some situations but not to others, and he develops greater self-confidence, so that he does not feel the need for dependence upon his friends. He tends, however, to remain very sensitive to the reaction of his group to his behavior. It is therefore essential that the teacher should realize the strength of these social drives and should always try to work with rather than against them.[26]

Teachers can help make transition to more mature social relationships a smooth one by giving the adolescent a chance to act on an adult level. He can be given an opportunity to recount his experiences, to exercise initiative in the formulation of plans for the class, to be responsible for finding information. Committees, panel discussions, group projects, and

[26] Luella Cole, *Psychology of Adolescence*, 4th ed., New York: Holt, Rinehart and Winston, Inc., 1954, p. 261.

class experimentation and visitation will afford many opportunities for social contacts in the form of delegating responsibility, discussing procedures, presenting and criticizing data, and evaluating what has been done.

Wider social contacts can be made possible through the encouragement of various activities. Clubs, dancing hours, hobby groups, athletic contests, and student government have all been utilized as means for social experience. These, of course, make demands on the time and energy of the teacher, since he must provide the necessary supervision and guidance. It is just such supervision, however, that the adolescent wishes to outgrow; therefore, care must be exercised to let the supervision partake of the nature of guidance rather than that of domination and direction.

Teachers can provide *maximum* practice in social relations if they establish a high degree of teacher-pupil rapport. This is so fundamental an aspect that it is a concern of this entire book. Suffice it to say here that if the teacher has a genuine interest in young people and will seek to understand them, he will be offering the most salutary help available for establishing harmonious social relationships.

Help Them Establish Goals—Formulate a Philosophy. It is not necessary or even desirable for adolescents to have a fixed and final philosophy. They should, however, be thinking about some tentative goals and be molding a tentative framework for their personal philosophy. They will have goals, whether or not teachers give them any help. They need help, however, in choosing goals which are appropriate and they need help in thinking through their goals, to see that conflicting objectives are reduced in number. Everyone has goals, but not all people have thought through them in order to give them the consistency that may justify the use of the word *philosophy* in reference to them.

A starting point, but only a starting point, around which the formulation of a philosophy could revolve might well be the following three points:

1. *Attitudes and habits to avoid.* Discouragement, excuse making, suspicion, selfishness, self-pity, and laziness are factors which make adjustment more difficult than it need be. The pupils should be led, in group discussion, to name others. They can be led to think these things through by attempting to list them in the order of seriousness.

2. *Attitudes and habits to cultivate.* Optimism, perspective, humor, responsibility, willingness to work, and friendliness are factors which tend to facilitate adjustment. What is the source of such attitudes? How can individuals develop these qualities in themselves? What is their relative merit? Questions such as these are stimulating to the critical think ing that leads to a genuine and productive philosophy.

3. *Problems that should be considered.* Questionnaire analysis of problems about which adolescents are rightfully concerned include the following: scholastic work, vocational selection and preparation, marriage, the place of religion in full living, living with one's family, privileges and responsibilities of citizenship, desirable personal habits, the relative value of temporary goals, and the major purposes of life. Do not expect that all will come to the same conclusions, but discussing the problems will help revise and systematize the thinking of each individual.[27]

The School and Better Personal Adjustment. Childhood and adolescence are crucial years in establishing acceptable and gratifying behavior patterns. Teachers must realize their responsibility for getting at the causes of misbehavior and maladjustment. They must continue to participate in the search for curricular additions and modifications that will provide varied opportunities to suit individual aptitudes of young people. The place of the teacher in helping adolescents achieve better mental health is indicated in the following:

> Everyone on the school staff makes a contribution in meeting the needs of youth. The classroom teacher is most important because he is most directly in touch with the individual pupil. He makes his contribution by setting an example of personality and personal relations, maintaining a sensitivity to the needs of individuals in the class, conducting group discussions of common personal problems, realizing the special guidance values of his subject, developing out-of-class contacts, referring students to other sources of help, and exerting a wholesome influence on the school and community environment.[28]

Meeting the mental health needs of adolescents is part and parcel of effective educational procedures.

SUMMARY

The needs of adolescents are basically the same as those of children and adults. Some of the basic needs, however, are felt more acutely during the adolescent years as the individual comes closer to the independence of genuine adulthood.

If maximum help is to be afforded to adolescents in their drive for more complete self-fulfillment, one must consider some of the problems they face in American culture. These will do more to explain their behavior than thinking that there is something in developmental processes which makes maladjustment practically inevitable. Some of these prob-

[27] Adolescents may be helped by the booklet by T. V. Smith, *Building Your Philosophy of Life,* Chicago: Science Research Associates, Inc., 1953, 48 pp.

[28] Ruth Strang, "Guidance to Meet the Needs of Youth" in *Adapting the Secondary-school Program to the Needs of Youth,* 52d Yearbook, Part I, National Society for the Study of Education, Chicago: University of Chicago Press, 1953, p. 202.

lems are (1) adolescence (but not puberty) is a cultural phenomenon, (2) today many adolescents lack responsibilities which might contribute to feelings of worth or significance, (3) the opportunity to work and be financially independent is delayed by law and by the need for education, (4) many are faced by the uncertainty of military service, (5) adolescents are a minority group subject to misunderstandings similar to those experienced by other minority groups, (6) the rapid rate of technological and cultural change widens the gap between generations, (7) prolonged schooling renders them dependent at an age when independence is vigorously sought, and (8) despite biological maturity there is a strong sentiment against their early marriage. When it is understood that these are things that perplex adolescents, we shall be in a more advantageous position to render them constructive help and guidance.

Some of the insistent needs of adolescents, which grow partially from the foregoing conditions, are the achievement of peer adjustments, adjustment to teachers, student-teacher-parent rapport and understanding, determination of purposes (at least tentatively), to establish feelings of worth, to understand oneself, and to prepare for marriage.

Teachers can aid in the satisfaction of such needs as formulated by The National Education Association by studying the nature and meaning of the behavior of adolescents. They can help provide the social contacts that are so important in all areas of adjustment—personal as well as vocational. They can help by encouraging adolescents to think through their objectives so that a foundation for an evolving philosophy of life is achieved.

STUDY AND DISCUSSION EXERCISES

1. Write a several-page account of some difficulty you experienced as an adolescent. What help did you receive? How might you have been more effectively helped? What understandings would have been beneficial?

2. Engage in serious conversation with some adolescent whom you know and get his views on marriage, military service, and occupation. Are his views sound? What are your reactions to his perspective?

3. How far can a teacher go in treating adolescents as adults? What limitations must be observed?

4. What organizations are there in your school and community which are designed to facilitate healthy contacts for youth?

5. Defend or criticize the statement that teachers are in a more advantageous position to influence youth than are their parents.

SUGGESTED ADDITIONAL READINGS

Angelino, Henry R. (Chrm.), "The Educational Program: Adolescence," *Review of Educational Research*, 30:1–92, February, 1960.

Summaries of research on the society, characteristics, development, and education of adolescents are presented.

Bernard, Harold W., *Adolescent Development in American Culture*, New York: Harcourt, Brace & World, Inc., 1957, pp. 399–432.

This chapter deals with such topics as motor vehicle accidents, accident proneness, diseases, neurosis, factors in mental illness, crime, drug addiction, and the use of alcoholic beverages.

Goodenough, Florence L., and Leona E. Tyler, *Developmental Psychology*, New York: Appleton-Century-Crofts, Inc., 1959, pp. 385–405.

Emphasis is on growth as an explanation for the behavior of adolescents, but attention is given to the adolescent's "search for personal identity."

Kettelkamp, Gilbert C., *Teaching Adolescents*, Boston: D. C. Heath and Company, 1954, pp. 320–366.

Representative problems of adolescents, attitudes and understandings needed by teachers, and techniques for gathering needed information are dealt with in this chapter.

National Society for the Study of Education, *Adapting the Secondary-school Program to the Needs of Youth*, 52d Yearbook, Part I, Chicago: University of Chicago Press, 1953. 316 pp.

This yearbook deals with the concept of needs, how they may be better met, and the relation of the needs to the academic and personal guidance, extraclass, and "work-experience" phases of school work.

United Nations Educational, Scientific, and Cultural Organization, *Education and Mental Health*, The Hague, Holland: UNESCO, 1955, pp. 154–178.

Those concerned about the unfavorable comparisons of education in the United States with European countries may profit from this chapter.

CHAPTER 4

SOCIAL CLASS AND
DEVELOPMENTAL TASKS

Teachers will be able better to appreciate the mental health needs of children and adolescents if they are better acquainted with the developmental backgrounds of their pupils. They are well aware of the tremendous impact of home influences on child and adolescent development. Sometimes, however, they do not seem to recognize that homes are as they are because they typify given socioeconomic strata of our population. Rather than simply being a good or bad home, a home is often reflecting the values which have been acquired from the immediate social and economic milieu. Rather than being a good or bad pupil, that pupil is often reflecting the ideals and aspirations that prevail in the social class in which he is being raised.

Social class structure in the United States is not a new phenomenon, but only in recent years has it seemed greatly to concern the educator. It seems to have been assumed that all pupils have very much the same background and opportunity. So pervasive are the influences of social class that it is essential that teachers expand their knowledge of social class structure.

Along with the recognition of social class, a new concept has been developing in educational circles called "developmental tasks." These tasks vary somewhat according to socioeconomic status. Understanding them will improve the teacher's appreciation of class structure and yield better understanding of the mental health needs of pupils.

THE NATURE OF SOCIAL CLASS

The idea that social classes exist in the United States is not a particularly welcome one. With justice and equality taught as dominant American ideals, the notion that opportunity is limited for some tends to be repudiated. It is true that, in the United States, class lines are not so rigid and impassable as they are in some other countries; nevertheless the fact that there are classes cannot be doubted.

Mobility. One of the reasons why social classes often go unnoticed is that the differences between them are continuous rather than discrete; that is, a given person or family may have some middle- and some lower-class characteristics. One person may, for instance, have a job that is deemed lower class but have a middle-class home. Another may have a middle-class education but a lower-class income. In short, it is difficult to distinguish between a family on the lower edge of the middle class from one on the upper edge of the lower class. Boundaries are dim and indistinct.[1]

Another reason why social class is not so apparent is the phenomenon of mobility, that is, the movement upward from a lower social class to a higher one through education, professional success, marriage, or conscious modification of behavior. Thus, the son of an itinerant worker (usually lower class) may succeed in school, become a clerk, apply himself assiduously, win promotion and higher salary, marry an upper-middle-class girl, buy an appropriate home, and raise his children in acceptable upper-middle-class tradition. Downward mobility is also a possibility. This happens when one does not strive to keep up with the rising standards of living in our dynamic culture. Inability to earn sufficient money to maintain a suitable residence, to sustain social contacts, or lack of a desire to emulate "proper" behaviors may cause one to lose status.

It takes effort to maintain or improve one's position in the social status hierarchy, for living standards for the nation as a whole are improving. Thus, the income of a laborer today will buy for him and his family all that a professional man may have had thirty years ago. The college education which is characteristic of the middle-class person today may be contrasted to the high-school education which was typical in 1920.[2]

Factors Determining Social Class Status. Money is often thought to be the major criterion of social class. It is a factor but not necessarily the most important one. Probably the prime factor is behavior. A lower-class person may make as much money as someone in a higher strata, but if he does not modify his actions to accord with those in the higher category his status remains unchanged. Education is important because through it he can learn the necessary behaviors and ideals. His chances of making the money necessary for maintaining a higher status are im-

[1] Blaine E. Mercer, "Some Notes on Education in the 'Open' Society," *Social Studies*, 45:256–258, November, 1954.
[2] Robert J. Havighurst and Bernice L. Neugarten, *Society and Education*, Englewood Cliffs, N.J.: Allyn and Bacon, Inc., 1957, p. 51.

proved. Occupation is also a factor; though one may achieve success in a high-salaried position or acquire his own business without the typical education, his chances of so doing are improved with education. Place of residence is also a factor in determining one's position in the social class structure. All of these are reflected in the following passage:

> Some of the symbols necessary include the acquisition of outward personal behaviors including manners, etiquette, and speech habits which are enforced by inward attitudes and values which have become habitual to the individual. Other necessary symbols are a personal and a family environment which symbolize higher position. These include houses, furniture, and similar symbols of status to increase the strength of his claims to higher position.
>
> All this means that a mobile person's money must be translated into a way of life which expresses high status. Such behavior is not sufficient, since, to be rated at the top, it is necessary for him to participate in clique, associational, and often family relations before he is securely placed. . . . Talents of all kinds which are highly prized raise their possessor's position and make it possible for him to acquire the other necessary symbols and to establish the relations essential to participation in the higher social ranks.[3]

CHARACTERISTICS OF SOCIAL CLASSES

Bearing in mind that a given person might have some characteristics of one social status and some of another, the following will give the teacher an idea of how intimately child behavior might be influenced. It should also be remembered that the figures given below are approximations, since communities vary in the exact proportions of each class which they might contain.

Upper Class. This small group, containing from 1 to 3 per cent of the population, possesses family wealth, belongs to exclusive clubs, is often the power behind the throne in politics, and is highly motivated to exhibit proper behavior. There is no problem of "keeping up with the Joneses," since they are the Joneses. Ostentation and publicity are not sought as they are by the class next below. Education is important but is only one aspect of proper behavior. Professional training is not important, but some sons may go into the professions of medicine, law, or architecture. They rarely enter the ministry, and teaching is virtually never selected.

Public-school teachers will rarely encounter the pupils of this group for three reasons. The group is small, even in communities where it is represented; there may be none from this class in some areas (especially

[3] W. Lloyd Warner, Robert J. Havighurst, and Martin B. Loeb, *Who Shall Be Educated?*, New York: Harper & Brothers, 1944, pp. 33–34.

in a rural region); and, finally, the children are typically sent to private schools.

Upper-middle Class. This group consists of the 7 to 12 per cent of the population which is engaged in administering business and in professional work. They are largely persons who have risen to moderate wealth through education and effective work, who are active in community and political affairs, and who live in the best residential areas of cities, in homes which are sufficiently large to accommodate comfortably the parents and the children—two or three is the typical number. The marriages are stable; both mother and father have an education which tends to be somewhat better than that gained by upper-class persons.[4]

Teachers will typically be delighted to have children of this class under their tutelage. While their intelligence may average only slightly higher than the average of other classes, they come from homes where they have been provided with good books, travel experiences, and the opportunity to read the best magazines. Most of them will have had special opportunities to develop skill in dancing, swimming, games, and musical activities which tends to give them feelings of self-confidence. They are strongly motivated to succeed in their school tasks, for they and their parents are said to have an "education compulsion." They dress well, are kept in good health, are confident and optimistic, and in general manifest the behaviors which teachers, with their own middle-class orientation, approve.

Lower-middle Class. This group consists of the 20 to 35 per cent of the population which best fits in the stereotype of the typical American family as represented in popular magazines.[5] About two-thirds of them own their own homes which border, or may even be in, the best residential districts. Marriages are stable, and the families are slightly larger than in the upper-middle class. Some of the mothers work as teachers, secretaries, and bookkeepers to supplement the incomes of the fathers who are white-collar workers, foremen in industries, building contractors, and small-business owners. They travel much by automobile, but rarely go abroad. Many have a college education, but the proportion is much less than in the two classes above (see Table 4-1). They are active in lodges and fraternal clubs and are the most consistent churchgoers of any class.

The children of this class, like those of the upper-middle class, are imbued with the importance of education, and a third of them go on to college. They are seldom discipline problems, for their parents expect them to be obedient and hard-working pupils. The average level of their

[4] A. B. Hollingshead, *Elmtown's Youth,* New York: John Wiley & Sons, Inc., 1949, pp. 89–97.
[5] *Ibid.*, p. 97.

IQs will parallel that of the groups above, but their background is not quite so rich. They dress and act in manners which are quite acceptable to teachers.

Upper-lower Class. This group, constituting the largest social class, contains from 25 to 40 per cent of the population. They are the poor but industrious blue-collar workers. They live in small but well-kept houses "on the wrong side of the tracks." The women, when not confined to the home by children, may work in factories, restaurants, or retail stores. A large fraction of them have parents who were immigrants. A third of the families are broken by divorce, separation, or death; nevertheless, they average over four children. They are consciously or unconsciously engaged in the struggle for upward mobility. Leisure-time activities con-

Table 4-1
Quota Fulfillment Indices*

Class	Non-attendant	Trade school	High school	Private school	Liberal arts college	Higher vocational school
I	6	70	79	348	494	155
II	39	24	110	168	303	132
III	60	79	106	162	164	119
IV	92	76	110	96	61	90
V	105	100	106	66	55	100
VI	151	159	82	62	18	77

* The index number of 100 indicates that one finds the same proportion of children on a social level in a given educational category that one finds in the total population.

source: James S. Davie, "Social Class Factors and School Attendance," *Harvard Educational Review*, 23:178, Summer, 1953.

sist of gathering in pool halls for the men and radio listening and television watching for all. There is little reading of books, magazines, or newspapers other than the local publications.

The pupils from this class are not quite so acceptable to teachers, because education is not especially important or meaningful to the students from this background. If the teacher were to threaten failure to a pupil in the upper grades or high school, the teacher, with his middle-class orientation, would be shocked and tend to disbelieve the answer, "I don't give a ————." Yet the pupil would probably mean it. His parents will typically not have gone much beyond the eighth grade (one-third of the fathers have less than eight years of schooling); and although parents profess a belief in education, their children tend to exceed but little the educational status of their parents.[6] With their unstable home back-

[6] Harry P. Smith, *Syracuse Youth Who Did Not Graduate*, Syracuse: Board of Education, 1950, p. 22.

grounds, these pupils tend to be behavior problems; in addition, their ideals and attitudes differ at many points from middle-class orientation. They often experiment at early ages in sex, drinking, truancy, and thievery. (Let it be noted that there are many exceptions to these generalizations.) Altogether, teachers tend to find it somewhat unrewarding to work with these pupils.

Lower-lower Class. All the rest of society looks down on the 15 to 25 per cent of the population which is lower-lower class. They are regarded as trash and do contribute disproportionately to delinquency, crime, and sexual promiscuity. However, it must be remembered that though this generalization is accurate, each individual must be judged separately, since there are a considerable number of respectable persons who are classed as lower-lower because of their poverty.[7] Parents in this group are often fatalistically discouraged, work sporadically, move frequently, and live in the poorest of dwellings. Mothers often supplement the meager income by working as waitresses, dishwashers, or domestic help. Although there is an average of 5.6 children per mother, over half the homes are broken by separation, desertion, or death. The instability of marriages leads to the terminology *tandem marriage* or *serial monogamy*. A secretary in a school in a lower-lower-class district learned, after contacting three brothers in the school, each with a different last name, always to inquire, when attempting to contact their mother, what her last name was. One mother in the course of two years had two husbands and at the time of contact was living with and contemplating marriage to still another. In Elmtown, from 20 to 25 per cent of births in this class are illegitimate.[8]

Obviously, these children are not a cheering influence on teachers. The language of the pupils is rough. Often an upper-grade girl will be reported as having sex relations with a grown man. Their dress is shabby; and on occasion it has been necessary to bathe a child, because strong odors made him offensive to others. They are often slow learners who are truant, aggressive, and destructive. They are discouraged and often feel that those higher than they "are against them." They are weakly motivated to perform school tasks and, besides, are often disturbed by the instability of parental personality and relationships. Occasionally, there is an unusually able and interested child, and, also occasionally, there is a teacher who appreciates the difficulties of these children and who works patiently with them.[9]

[7] Havighurst and Neugarten, *op. cit.*, pp. 23–24.
[8] Hollingshead, *op. cit.*, p. 116.
[9] Jessie Bennett Sams's *White Mother*, published by McGraw-Hill Book Company, Inc., New York, 1957, is a true story of such an occurrence. It has been called one of the most incisive sociological studies of our time.

THE SOCIAL CLASS STATUS OF TEACHERS

Social Origins of Teachers. Teachers come from no one type of background, but all, or almost all, are from parental occupational categories which indicate middle-class origins: farmers, 32 per cent; skilled or semiskilled, 22 per cent; managerial or self-employed, 21 per cent; clerical or sales, 7 per cent; and unskilled, 6 per cent.[10] A study of school personnel in Texas reveals that, out of 150 teachers, 3 were upper class, 112 were upper-middle class, and 35 were lower-middle class. There were none from the upper-lower class, and approximately half of the 150 were upwardly mobile from the social class status of their parents.[11]

The above shows that teachers, like others in American society, are engaged in the struggle to maintain or improve their status. Their origins, present status, and the education they must have to qualify them as teachers all combine to instill in them middle-class ideals regarding education, application to work, marriage, morality, and correct social behavior. Thus, it is through no conscious perverseness on their part that they find it difficult to identify with the great majority of pupils who come from the two lower classes. These children are, in a large degree, simply different from what the teachers were as children or from what the teachers' own children are. In many classes the author has asked the students if their mothers ever told them that they were not to play or associate with certain of their schoolmates. Those who had lived in rather uniform neighborhoods may not have been so advised, but those who lived in mixed communities had almost always been so counseled. While their parents did not use the term *social class,* they nevertheless showed an awareness of it.

Teachers, Pupils, and Social Class. This middle-class orientation explains in part, but only in part, some of the things that happen in school. One cause for concern regarding the outlook and role of teachers is that in Elmtown although class I and class II pupils received the majority of higher school marks, most of the conferences with parents were about scholastic matters; on the other hand, while most of the low marks were received by lower-class pupils, conferences with parents dealt with matters of conduct. Hollingshead also reports that although intelligence is correlated with social status, the degree of correlation is not sufficient to account for the concentration of failures in the lower social classes.[12] It would be well for teachers to examine their own procedures to see if

[10] "The Status of the American Public-school Teacher," *National Education Association Research Bulletin,* 35:10, February, 1957.

[11] Carson McGuire and George D. White, "Social Origin of Teachers—Some Facts from the Southwest," *The Teacher's Role in American Society,* Sixteenth Yearbook, John Dewey Society, New York: Harper & Brothers, 1957, pp. 362ff.

[12] Hollingshead, *op. cit.,* pp. 175ff.

there is any intentional, or unintentional, tendency for them to grade on behavior and social-class status rather than on actual academic performance. There are several reasons why teachers might regard lower-class pupils as being below their actual status or potentiality. (1) Some pupils bring a low regard for school from home and are not highly motivated. Some teachers may regard this low motivation as a rather personal affront. (2) Rather than being "naturally" mean or aggressive, lower-class pupils may bring to school worries, strain, and feelings of futility that need to be countered by acceptance, encouragement, and feelings of success. (3) Lower-class pupils have different standards of values and morality from those which the teacher has. It will take time, patience, and confidence on the part of many teachers to offset the negative influences that have surrounded these pupils from infancy. (4) Finally, there is the possibility that teachers may tend to avoid giving low grades to pupils whose parents are obviously interested in their children's success and whose parents may even create unpleasant situations for the teacher if such grades were given.

Certainly, it would be unjust to place the blame on teachers for the high rate of school dropouts of lower-class children. But teachers are in the best position to do something about it. In so doing, they will inevitably be making a contribution to the mental health of individuals and to the nation in terms of conserving the great natural resource— children. At present, the great majority of high-ability students from the lower classes are being lost as a national asset because their potentialities are undeveloped. In a study of 3,348 cases in Boston it was found that, of all boys of high-school age in the highest fifth of intelligence ratings, three times as many in the upper class as in the lower-socioeconomic classes expected to go to college. The college expectations by father's occupational category were as follows: White-collar workers, 89 per cent expected to attend college; middle white-collar (office manager, teacher), 76 per cent; minor white-collar (bookkeeper, clerk), 55 per cent; skilled labor and service, 40 per cent; other labor and service, 29 per cent.[13]

Much potential ability is lost even before the time when college attendance might seriously be considered. Of 178 Prairie City youths with IQs above 115, none from the upper and upper-middle classes has failed to finish high school, but 9 from the upper-lower and lower-lower classes had dropped out. In the IQ group of 100 to 114, none from the upper and upper-middle classes had dropped out, but 33 from the upper-lower and lower-lower classes did not finish high school.[14] Thus, it appears that

[13] Joseph A. Kahl, "Educational and Occupational Aspirations of 'Common Man' Boys," *Harvard Educational Review*, 23:188, Summer, 1953.

[14] Robert J. Havighurst and Robert R. Rodgers in Byron S. Hollingshead, *Who Should Go to College?* New York: Columbia University Press, 1952, p. 226.

social status rather than intellectual ability is the major determining factor in school attendance. It has been observed that the waste of talent in America is acute—fewer than half of the top 25 per cent of high-school graduates now are graduated from college.[15] Reference to Table 4-1 shows that this waste is largely a function of social class factors.

Several factors combine to determine how long a pupil will pursue his schooling. Parental wishes, the individual's own motivation, intellectual ability, and financial resources to support prolonged education must all be taken into account. But it is also clear that the "school's system of encouraging some students and discouraging others" also plays a part.[16]

Specifically, the teacher's natural response to the learned behaviors of the lower-class students, behaviors which are yet not sanctioned by the middle class, will make these students feel unwanted. Pupils from the upper and middle classes also tend to make lower-class pupils feel out of place—Hollingshead's study shows that friendships and dating follow class lines. The cost of participation in school activities, particularly at the high-school level, is often such that pupils from the lower classes are excluded. Inability to buy sufficient clothes to keep in style is a factor which weighs heavily on the mind of the adolescent who is so concerned with success in peer relationships. Uniformly prescribed homework may cause even the able pupil from the lower classes to fall behind in his work. Whereas the middle-class student will probably have a room of his own and books, references, and school supplies readily available, the lower-class teen-ager will tend to live in a crowded home where study facilities are lacking. Often the lower-class teen-ager will have a part-time job, necessitated by the inadequacy of family income, which keeps him from having time for, or interest in, schoolwork. The facts that his father's job does not call for much education and both parents will probably have less than average education mean that he has no model for high educational aspiration. His peers, similarly lacking in motivation, do not provide a contagious atmosphere for prolonged schooling. These factors combined with the necessity of adapting to middle-class behaviors discourage assiduous and prolonged application to school tasks. The middle-class parents, on the other hand, feel the importance of education and place it first in significance.

Hence, the teacher who would ease the problem of keeping all able pupils in school must guard against the tendency to avoid or unjustly criticize the lower-class pupils. He must seek ways to keep these pupils active and interested in student activities. He must teach pupils to regard others in terms of what they are instead of in terms of social class origins. He must be careful to avoid assignments which will discriminate

---

[15] "A Background for Public Debate," *National Education Association Research Bulletin*, 37 (1):27, February, 1959.

[16] Havighurst and Neugarten, *op. cit.*, p. 224.

against the pupil with limited study opportunities and facilities. He can do much by direct counseling—praising successes, encouraging ambitions, pointing out the necessity for education in a nation which is achieving continuously higher average educational levels.

EDUCATIONAL IMPLICATIONS OF SOCIAL CLASS

Teachers Must Recognize Social Class Differences. Each individual views the world, and himself, differently in terms of his own family background, which, in turn, is structured by the socioeconomic status of the family. The teacher must, if he is to manifest the acceptance which is an element in the mental health of pupils, avoid showing shock, surprise, or disappointment at the ideals, mores, language, thoughts, and behaviors of pupils who have an orientation at variance with his. To develop the knowledge that leads to respectful understanding, teachers can study the phenomenon of social class, using the books mentioned in the footnotes or the recommended readings for this chapter. The reading of at least one such book would seem to be an essential of sound teacher preparation. Membership on, or even a visit to, a local welfare committee would help the teacher know better the kinds of people and homes that are often the concern of aid to dependent children or welfare assistance. A walk through that portion of the community "on the wrong side of the tracks" would do much to awaken the teacher to the kind of circumstances which some children have outside of school hours. If a visit to a representative home in these areas could be arranged on a friendly basis, it would provide additional insight. Actual contact of this kind would do much to lend credibility to the notion that it can and does "happen here."

Recognize Different Kinds of Motivation and Intelligence. Not all pupils are motivated to do well on traditional kinds of academic tasks. Pupils from the lower classes, especially those in the upper grades and high school, want something directly related to the tasks they see being performed by the adults who surround them. There is an insistent imminence to the problem of making a living for those who marry and enter the working world at an early age. The ability to see long-term values is one of the marked differences between middle- and lower-class persons. Patient explanations, expressions of approval, and the continued search for subjects and approaches related to lower-class culture may help the teacher strengthen the kind of motivation which will aid these pupils in upward mobility.

It is felt by some that the intelligence tests commonly administered in schools do not give all children a chance to reveal their true potentiality. Specifically, many of the items are so phrased that they tend to discriminate against pupils who are from the lower classes, even if the item itself is essentially no more difficult than a similar item from lower-class experiences and culture.[17] Tests have been designed to impose less of a handicap on children from the lower-socioeconomic levels; these tests are purported to be somewhat more accurate in assessing intellectual potential.[18] Whether such tests do or do not result in less discrimination against some social classes, the teacher should be aware that intelligence tests are only indications, or approximations, of intelligence and not final and accurate measures.[19] Moreover, remember that certain aspects of intelligence, such as musical capacity, social adaptability, motor functioning, or esthetic or mechanical aptitude are sometimes only slightly correlated with general IQ scores. Capitalizing on such qualities, as these, may help to provide the motivation for better use of general intelligence.

Intelligence-test scores are valuable indicators and predictors of academic success, but they must be supplemented with tests of special aptitudes and discerning observation if we are to avoid discrimination. If this is not done some of the potential of many lower-class pupils will continue to be lost.

Broad Educational Goals Must Be Implemented. Studies of dropouts from school indicate that sometimes so much attention is given to the strictly academic that some pupils become discouraged. One study cites "dissatisfied with courses" as being second only to "failing grades" —the latter is probably closely related to the dissatisfaction—as the principal or contributing reason for leaving school.[20] Not that educators and school patrons have not thought about these matters—on the contrary, broad educational goals have been formulated and are practiced in some schools but a more complete implementation of them is needed. Such studies as that on the imperative needs of youth (see Fig. 4, Chapter 3), provide ample clues to how educational programs might be broadened. Since it is known that much latent talent resides in lower-class pupils, it is essential that discouragement in the form of low grades or being left out of student activities be replaced by encouragement. Differentiated curriculums—shop and commercial courses, for example—will broaden the goals but must not be thought of as alternatives for the comparative present lack of achievement for *all* lower-class pupils. Continuing em-

[17] Allison Davis, "Poor People Have Brains, Too," *Phi Delta Kappan*, 30:294–295, 1949.

[18] Allison Davis and Kenneth Eells, *Davis-Eells Test of General Intelligence or Problem Solving Ability*, New York: Harcourt, Brace & World, Inc., 1953.

[19] Denis Baron and Harold W. Bernard, *Evaluation Techniques for Classroom Teachers*, New York: McGraw-Hill Book Company, Inc., 1957, pp. 68–84.

[20] Elizabeth S. Johnson and Caroline E. Legg, *Why Young People Leave School*, Washington: U.S. Department of Labor, 1948, p. 18.

phasis on varied objectives is especially needed today, when there is the almost hysterical emphasis on college-preparatory courses and scientific education and the repudiation of "life-adjustment" emphases.

The Hidden Costs of Education Must Be Lowered. It is unfortunate that the cost of "proper" clothes should be such that some pupils feel out of place in school. In addition, other costs, in the form of club and class dues, "pep" uniforms, play costumes, class rings, yearbooks, and insignia, tend to keep lower-class students from being "in the swing" of things. A survey of 134 high schools in 29 states revealed that average costs per pupil ranged from $58.50 in small communities to $103.50 in cities over 100,000.[21] These figures do not include clothing. These costs, even several years after the survey when per capita income ranges from $964 in Mississippi to $2,858 in Delaware,[22] could well constitute an insupportable burden for a family with two or three children in school. It is small wonder that one girl in Elmtown stated that there was nothing for them in school except going to classes, studying, reciting, and going home again—they were "pushed out of things."[23]

Several things might be considered, and the school class as a whole might do the considering. Find out if the costs are essential or might be raised in some other manner than direct assessment; see if part-time jobs might be found for the needy; enlist the aid of local civic organizations in supplying scholarships, medical care, clothes, and even school lunches. These approaches could contribute valuable learning experience in addition to easing the financial struggle involved in "belonging."

Pupils Should Study Social Class Structure. Pupils probably make no effort to be snobbish and if made aware of their acquired attitudes might wish to modify them. Hence, study of the social class hierarchy could be made a part of social studies courses and could open avenues to an understanding of certain phenomena that operate in their daily lives. Celia B. Stendler has suggested a high-school course using such materials as have been referred to in this chapter.[24] W. Lloyd Warner has written a pamphlet for adolescents dealing with such topics as "You and Social Class," "How Can You Determine Your Social Class," and "Social Class and the Future."[25] Students in a high school are probably no more desirous of wasting athletic, literary, forensic, or dramatic ability which will redound to the reputation of their school than the nation as a whole is desirous of losing scientific ability and potential leadership.

[21] Paul B. Jacobson, *The American Secondary School*, Englewood Cliffs, N.J.: Prentice-Hall, Inc., 1952, p. 101.

[22] Department of Commerce, Office of Business Economics, 1958.

[23] Hollingshead, *op. cit.*, p. 202.

[24] Celia B. Stendler, "Social Class and the Curriculum," *Educational Leadership*, 7:371–375, 1950.

[25] W. Lloyd Warner and Mildred Warner, *What You Should Know about Social Class*, Chicago: Science Research Associates, Inc., 1953.

DEVELOPMENTAL TASKS, NEEDS, AND SOCIAL CLASS

The Nature of Developmental Tasks. Human needs are universal—they characterize members of society in every race and land. Similarly, developmental tasks, which are specific statements of certain needs at various ages, face everyone regardless of socioeconomic status—though the task may vary somewhat with status. These tasks are rooted in biological nature and growth, in the degree of psychological development, and in the values and aspirations of the individual as they are acquired from his larger society and specific subcultural status. The behavior which indicates success in developmental tasks differs among social classes. To the extent to which one fails to achieve his developmental tasks, he fails to have his basic needs satisfied. Hence, a developmental task is a growth and adjustment problem, stemming from biological and psychological growth and societal demands, which arises at or about a certain age in a given society. Failure to achieve the task results in unhappiness for the individual, alienation from society, and leaves him relatively unprepared to conquer his next developmental tasks. Success leads to happiness, social approval, and readiness to achieve successive tasks.[26]

In whatever way social class status influences developmental tasks, the tasks remain fundamentally the same for all socioeconomic strata. Note, however, that a specific task may have varying degrees of difficulty—that for children of one class a given task may be comparatively difficult, but another task relatively easy.

Developmental Tasks of Children. Developmental tasks of preschool children in American culture include such things as developing motor control, learning to eat and dress, learning to be a family member, achieving emotional control, acquiring language, and learning about the physical world and the rules of society.

Children of school age have such developmental tasks as the following:[27]

1. *Broadening the concept of self to include functioning in groups other than the family and neighborhood playmates.* Prior to school age social contacts have been largely with one's family and neighborhood, both of which represent a certain social class. On entering school, a child has for the first time, regular contacts with members of other social classes. The teacher, therefore, must provide guidance and counsel toward regarding all persons with respect. Typically, more freedom is afforded

[26] Robert J. Havighurst, *Human Development and Education,* New York: Longmans, Green & Co., Inc., 1953, p. 2.

[27] Headings from Stephen M. Corey and Virgil E. Herrick in Jerome M. Seidman (ed.), *Readings in Educational Psychology,* Boston: Houghton Mifflin Company, 1955, p. 40. See also Havighurst, *Human Development and Education,* pp. 25–41.

the lower-class child in achieving this task, while the middle- and upper-class child experiences more adult supervision and direct control.

2. *Learning one's role in peer groups.* The often-unwritten rules and regulations which govern the world directed by his peers, rather than by teachers and parents, must be learned and internalized. Since the culture of the school is so largely middle class, the lower-class children will find the task more difficult. These children are, also, typically less ready to accept adult dictates. Hence, they will need the sympathy, understanding, and patience of teachers as conflicts are brought to them for adjudication.

3. *Becoming weaned from total dependence on adults.* Middle-class children have an advantage here, because their parents encourage personal independence in performing household tasks and in getting around to libraries, dentists' offices, museums, and the like. On the other hand, lower-class children have an advantage, too, because they are simply let go—but less parental direction is provided in their becoming independent.

4. *Developing sexual modesty and establishing one's sex role.* The lower-class boy is taught the necessity for fighting and becoming a "man," while the middle-class boy is taught not to be openly aggressive. Lower-class girls may with impunity become tomboys, but middle-class girls are taught to be little ladies. These variant attitudes lead to conflict and, hence, lay some of the firm basis for early class discrimination.

5. *Developing the physical skills necessary in ordinary games and sports.* This task concerns boys more urgently than girls, since a boy's status so largely depends upon skill and prowess. Boys of all classes are expected to learn these skills, but while the middle-class boy may have had special training at the YMCA or country club in certain sports, the stronger aggressiveness of the lower-class boy tends to make him a vigorous participant in competitive sports.

6. *Learning the concepts necessary for daily living—time, distance, quantity, and social and personal values.* Many of these concepts (time, space, speed, temperature) are common to all American culture and are understood equally well by children from any social class. Other concepts (maid, manners, cooperation, duty, work, travel) are less well understood or are understood in a different manner by children from the lower social classes. If the teacher takes it for granted that all concepts are common, some children will misunderstand what is being attempted to be communicated.

7. *Gaining skills in communication.* Middle-class children come to school with somewhat superior skills in communication because of their experience in groups controlled or directed by adults, better literary backgrounds, and wider travel experiences. These superior skills often make it appear that they are basically superior mentally and may cause

them to be favored pupils. However, the school is the place where lower-class pupils may correct their deficiencies if the teacher is sympathetic and considerate.

Developmental Tasks of Adolescents. As individuals achieve such tasks as the foregoing they begin, with increasing age, to encounter new ones which are appropriate to their physical and intellectual development and which are thrust upon them by the society in which they live. Thus, the adolescent in our culture faces the following tasks.[28]

1. *Achieving more mature relationships with one's peers of both sexes.* Social class structure sets the pattern for enormously varied social relationships. The middle class expects its children to be successful and co-operative; adolescents are carefully led through graduated experiences in clubs, church, and community activities. Premature attachments to the other sex are frowned upon. Lower-class adolescents are frequently involved in early sexual experimentation; they tend to marry earlier and often seek adult status through activities (smoking and drinking) which are regarded as delinquent. While middle- and upper-class youngsters have opportunities for learning social skills in out-of-school activities, lower-class youth are dependent on the school for learning these social skills.

2. *Learning to accept one's role as male or female.* No particular problem is generated by this task except that in our society as a whole girls are under less pressure to adopt the traditional role of dependence and submission than formerly. They may choose a business or professional career to marriage without criticism. Boys seem to have no special difficulty with this task.

3. *Using one's physique appropriately and facing up to one's physical liabilities and assets.* In all social strata, a person's appearance and rate of growth influence acceptance and feelings of security. Schools can help by devising physical activities appropriate to various developmental levels, by teaching hygiene and the physical changes of adolescence, by using art, physical education, and biology to increase understanding of the body, and by making answers to adolescents' questions readily available.

4. *Gaining autonomy by decreasing dependence on adults.* This task is more readily achieved by those of the lower class, for they are expected to work and contribute to family living expenses. The early achievement of freedom from parental dominance, however, makes these youth less ready to accept the dictates of teachers and may cause some unexpected friction. The task is also relatively easy for upper-class youth, for parents do not need to be highly protective since economic pressures are slight. The task is most difficult for middle-class youth who must, in order to protect and improve their status, prolong their schooling and delay mar-

[28] Havighurst, *op. cit.*, pp. 111–158.

riage and work. While conflict with parents is common, they do yield to the pressures of school and teachers and make admirable students. Such factors as these make it all the more difficult for teachers to understand the lower-class students who, by comparison, are less pliable and sub-servient.

5. *Developing confidence in one's ability to become financially inde-pendent.* During prosperous times the availability of part-time jobs makes this task relatively simple for the middle and upper classes. Youth can prove to themselves that they *can be* financially independent even as they are encouraged to continue in school. Lower-class youth still feel the pressure of finances and will quit school to earn wages at a full-time job as soon as they may legally do so. The social pressures to earn a living plus the many other factors of low grades, peer discrimination, and the conflict between their values and those of teachers contribute to our failure to develop the potentialities of a substantial portion of our population.

6. *Planning and preparing for one's future occupation.* Upper-class students feel no great pressure in this task, since they so frequently follow their parents' occupation. Middle-class students choose and pre-pare for managerial, professional, business, and teaching careers; however, business and teaching are the predominant aims of their school and college pursuits. Lifework for the lower class is simply making a living; their jobs are characterized by lateral, rather than vertical, mobility. With the coming of automation, it becomes more and more necessary for the school to provide these pupils with help that goes beyond merely making them literate.[29]

7. *Establishing the attitudes and gaining the experience which pre-pares one for marriage and family life.* In the upper classes marriages are of two types, (1) stable, yet contracted early, even before economic independence is achieved and (2) unstable and lacking in intimacy. Middle-class marriages are contracted at relatively older ages and are stable. Much concern is manifested that children be supplied with salutary growth needs and prolonged education. Lower-class marriages are contracted early and are unstable. Kinsey has indicated that adoles-cents from the lower classes have a comparatively high incidence of premarital sex experience[30]—an observation supported by Hollingshead.[31] It is with this class that schools should be especially concerned with

[29] Peter F. Drucker, "America's Next Twenty Years: The Promise of Automation, Part II," *Harper's Magazine*, 210:45, April, 1955.

[30] Alfred C. Kinsey, Wardell B. Pomeroy, and Clyde E. Martin, *Sexual Behavior in the Human Male*, Philadelphia: W. B. Saunders Company, 1948, pp. 347–351.

[31] A. B. Hollingshead, *Elmtown's Youth*, New York: John Wiley & Sons, Inc., 1949, p. 239.

teaching, counseling, and peer experiences that will contribute to more stable and satisfactory marriages.

8. *Developing skills and concepts which prepare for civic participation.* Both the upper and middle class are concerned with the privileges and obligations of intelligent citizenship. Lower-class parents do not participate regularly and vigorously in civic affairs. The schools can foster improved citizenship by providing practice in school government. It must be remembered that those most in need of training will often manifest the least aptitude for it. Patience and confidence must replace the practice of withholding citizenship privileges when the necessary skills are not immediately apparent. Experiences in the form of field trips, local projects, and community surveys can provide background. Most schools provide for study of contemporary social problems, but these must be seen from the viewpoints of all social classes.

9. *Building the basis for socially responsible behavior.* Experiences away from home, especially those in school and college, broaden the understandings and loyalties of upper- and middle-class youth. Lower class students feel that they are "being kept down"; thus, their loyalties are largely to family, relatives, and the lower-class social unit. By making the latter young people an integral part of the school community, by giving them a chance to develop a feeling of belonging, by providing prolonged education, they too can develop a basis for socially responsible behavior.

10. *Gaining values and attitudes that provide a guide to acceptable and productive behavior.* Upper- and middle-class students readily accept scientific views of the material world but may have trouble with a scientific view of man. The latter sometimes constitutes a problem for alert youth. Lower-class youth are not stirred by these problems, since they either largely ignore them, or readily accept an authoritative or fundamentalist religion. The approach to sounder values for all may be through (1) stressing the importance of people and of identifying with them, (2) providing experiences for youth with peers of all social classes, (3) direct study and analysis of values, and (4) studying science under the leadership of democratic rather then dictatorial teachers.[32]

IMPLICATIONS OF CLASS AND TASKS FOR SCHOOL WORKERS

Teachers Must Understand Varied Social Values. Teachers should develop a concept of the nature and imperiousness of developmental tasks because they can then appreciate more fully the problems faced by pupils. It is too easy to conceive of school as a place where one acquires intellectual skills and where all else is secondary. Intellectual skills are

[32] Havighurst, *op. cit.,* pp. 155–156.

important, but so too are the other areas of development, namely, ethical values, attitudes toward self, social competence, and productive home, occupational, and civic life. Intellectual skills are more easily achieved when tension and unhappiness in other spheres of activity are reduced.

One inherits not only his physical and intellectual potentialities but also his social class status. Adjustment must be made to self and to society. As teachers realize that these tasks are as inescapable as are basic human needs they will give attention to them, despite their not being written into the curriculum. Just as needs must, at least partially, be met, some degree of success in achieving developmental tasks is vital in order to keep individuals working at their successive tasks not only in the class-room but after school.

> On one hand, then, education is an integrating process designed by society to help the individual understand, fit into, and contribute to or change that society. On the other hand, it is a process which requires integration both within itself and with other social institutions and processes. Finally, by this process we try to produce individuals who continue to organize their own experiences and, thereby, derive more meaning from them.[33]

One of the advantages of the developmental-tasks concept is that cultural differences are noted. Unless and until teachers understand these differing backgrounds, children will be misunderstood and be treated as though they were "just plain ornery," unintelligent, and recalcitrant. Actually, they are simply differently oriented toward school, occupations, sex morality, civic participation, and social adaptation. The need to be loved and the need for recognition and companionship, and the like, are the same for children of all social classes. Again, note, differences are continuous, and sharp differentiation between class orientation is fallacious. Generalizations—what often and typically occurs—will, however, help the teacher avoid interpreting differences in behavior as being malicious deviation from middle-class mores.

Children typically learn to place different values on competition; they express their affection in contrasting ways; they have divergent views of the property rights of others; they display varied reactions toward discipline; and they value membership in different kinds of groups. It is small wonder that teachers, with their middle-class orientations, regard so many pupils from the lower classes as problem cases. "Many teachers simply cannot communicate with lower-class children and have no idea of the beliefs and motives of these children. The children in turn trying to communicate are abashed at criticism of their language and behavior

[33] Paul L. Dressel, "The Meaning and Significance of Integration" in *The Integration of Educational Experiences,* 57th Yearbook, Part III, National Society for the Study of Education, Chicago: University of Chicago Press, 1958, p. 6.

which are quite acceptable within their own social groups.[34] Examination of the high attrition rate of lower-class students (see page 94) will emphasize the need for improved communication and understanding if schools are to take a vital role in helping *all* pupils achieve their developmental tasks. The idea that failure in school is solely the result of inadequate intelligence must be repudiated, and more attention must be given to motivation and ways of improving teacher effectiveness.[35]

The study of social class by teachers is urgent, because of the tendency to generalize from their own experiences. They must remember, too, that a substantial portion of their pupils come from lower classes and are facing, in addition to academic problems, the necessity of adapting to a school culture which has a middle-class orientation. With an appreciation of this extra task for some, the teacher might be inclined to make allowances for slower learning, inadequate motivation, and unattractive personal grooming and habits.

The Need for Expanding Cultural Contacts. Children are faced with the necessity of bridging the gap between the limited (not in the sense of being lower) culture of the home and the broader culture of life in the school and community. This is true not only in the sense of socio-economic differences but in variations in homes at any level. Many of the answers to children's questions that are given in the schools are different from those given by parents. That children are confused by this contrast is indicated by the high incidence of delinquency among children of foreign-born parents—in cases where the home culture varies most markedly from the local culture. Examples of this kind of contrast are seen in such matters as autocratic discipline when compared with the discipline of purposeful activity—"Don't take nuthin' off nobody" versus cooperation, and "You can do better than your cousin" against the notion that real accomplishment is commendable in accordance with one's ability. Contrasts exist in attitudes and actions relative to sex activities, language usage (including swearing), and views of drinking, religion, honesty, manner of dress, and personal cleanliness—to mention only a few.

Lower-class and middle-class persons feel anxious about different social as well as physical dangers. Whereas the middle-class child learns not to receive poor grades in school; not to show aggression to teachers; not to fight, curse, or have sex relations, the slum child dreads quite

[34] W. H. Burton, "Education and Social Class in the United States," *The Harvard Educational Review*, 23:248, Fall, 1953.

[35] George Williams in *Some of My Best Friends Are Professors*, New York: Abelard-Schuman, Inc., Publishers, 1958, pp. 21–34, contends that schools and colleges are failing to educate adequately the great majority of even those pupils who are quite capable of accomplishing the academic tasks set for them.

different situations. His gang teaches him to fear being taken in by the teacher, of being a softie with her. To pursue homework seriously brings disgrace in the eyes of lower-class peers. Instead of boasting about good marks lower-class children conceal high grades if they ever receive them. The slum child also fears *not* acquiring a reputation as a street fighter. He cannot afford *not* to curse. "If he cannot claim early sexual relations his virility is seriously questioned."[36]

The elementary teacher can help children bridge these cultural differences in several ways. First, he can understand that, just as there is a readiness for reading, there is a readiness for accepting cultural changes. Anger, temper tantrums, and rage are evidences of too much pushing—perhaps pushing too forcefully to adapt to a wider culture. The transition should therefore be slowed down. Smaller lessons (in cooperation, in discipline, etc.) should be given. If the child is allowed a chance to mature before he is subjected to sharp contrasts, he can accept the contrasts of our culture more readily.

Second, the teacher can study life in the different subdivisions of the community. He can have interesting and instructive experiences by visiting some of the minority groups—the Negro, the Mexican, the Puerto Rican, the Japanese section of the community. He can visit the homes of the farmers who work on shares, the homes of the day laborers, and the camps of the itinerant crop followers—people who live in trailers and one-room cabins provided by the farm owner. Some appreciation of the varying cultures can be achieved by talking with teachers from different communities and sections of the city. Teachers in "downtown" schools have a different class of pupils from those in the restricted residential areas or those in the suburban areas.

Third, the child will be helped in making the transition to a wider culture if he feels that he is recognized and accepted in that larger social group. Therefore, the teacher will help by doing anything he can to show the pupils that they are liked. The simple evidences of friendship—a smile, a few words of commendation, serenity and consistency of manner, expressions of appreciation—give the children an assurance that will be of value in promoting cultural transition.

SUMMARY

The idea of social class structure is unpalatable, but such things, as income, education, parental occupation, place and kind of residence, *and* behavior do influence one's position on the social scale. These factors condition stability of marriage, occupational choice of young people,

[36] John J. Honigmann, *Culture and Personality*, New York: Harper & Brothers, 1954, p. 323.

length and seriousness of schooling, morality, and conduct. Mobility is possible; those in the middle class aspire to higher status, while those in the upper class feel secure and those in the lower class are often discouraged and uninterested in upward mobility.

Teachers are practically all from the middle class and often have difficulty understanding and communicating with pupils from the lower class, who have different aspirations and behavior patterns. Pupils, too, unconsciously choose companions like themselves, and thus the lower-class pupil may find himself an outsider in school activities and academic work.

Social class and its concomitants result in the loss of many able pupils; therefore, it seems advisable for teachers to recognize its existence and nature, to respect different kinds of intelligence and motivation, to broaden educational goals to include the needs of lower-class pupils, to reduce the hidden costs of education, and to encourage the study of social class by all pupils.

The concept of developmental tasks is one which will help teachers implement a recognition of social class. Each of the tasks, for children and adolescents, contains implications for reducing the limiting factors of social class and should be studied seriously. Teachers can, for instance, seek to understand varied social values, help pupils expand their cultural contacts, and devise ways to help children from all classes become accepted, confident, and desirous of realizing their potentialities.

STUDY AND DISCUSSION EXERCISES

1. What might be some special hazards to mental health encountered by middle-class persons?

2. Name several specific implications for teachers which stem from the low educational aspirations of lower-class pupils.

3. Do you think it is dangerous to raise the social aspirations of children as long as society as a whole remains relatively unchanged?

4. How do you account for the low grades of children from the lower class when achievement tests do not reveal correspondingly low accomplishment?

5. What activities might the teacher conduct to improve pupils' understanding of social class?

SUGGESTED ADDITIONAL READINGS

Anastasi, Anne, *Differential Psychology*, 3d ed., New York: The Macmillan Company, 1958, pp. 505–541.

Social class differences in psychological development, education, intelligence, motivation, and behavior are described and documented.

Bernard, Harold W., *Adolescent Development in American Culture*, New York: Harcourt, Brace & World, Inc., 1957, pp. 243–273.

Attention is devoted to what can be done in the school to correct certain injustices which stem from socioeconomic status.

Havighurst, Robert J., *Human Development and Education*, New York: Longmans, Green & Co., Inc., 1953, pp. 25–158.

The nature and implications of developmental tasks of childhood and adolescence are treated in terms of social class status.

Havighurst, Robert J., and Bernice L. Neugarten, *Society and Education*, Englewood Cliffs, N.J.: Allyn and Bacon, Inc., 1957, pp. 221–241.

Comparative intelligence, achievement, and length of schooling for various social classes are among the topics of this chapter.

Hollingshead, August B., and Frederick C. Redlich, *Social Class and Mental Illness: A Community Study*, New York: John Wiley & Sons, Inc., 1958.

Mental illness and the amount and adequacy of treatment are related to social class. Teachers, like psychiatrists and psychologists, experience difficulties in communicating with the lower-class person.

Warner, W. Lloyd, Robert J. Havighurst, and Martin B. Loeb, *Who Shall Be Educated?* New York: Harper & Brothers, 1951.

This book, through case studies, shows the impact of social class on the lives of school children. The inequality of opportunity and what it means to all of society is considered.

PART II

Mental Hygiene in Teaching

CHAPTER 5

TEACHER PERSONALITY AND PUPIL BEHAVIOR

Despite beautiful school buildings, up-to-date textbooks, liberal laboratory facilities, abundant instructional aids, and huge libraries, Mark Hopkins's definition of a school is still noteworthy: that is, a school is a log with a teacher on one end and a pupil on the other. The best of facilities count for little if the teachers are inadequate in personality or preparation. Yet there have been times when teaching positions were granted to people to keep them from being charity cases, when unemployable ministers were permitted to teach, and when anyone with more than ordinary education was thought capable of being a teacher. Even today the cliché "Those who can, do; those who can't, teach" is not forgotten.

Discussions of mental health in the schools invariably stress teacher personality as the most significant factor in the mental health of children. This volume is no exception. Sometimes it deals with teacher personality directly, and when not directly, it is at least strongly implied. Certainly the suggestions made in the book are without meaning until they are translated into action and behavior by the teacher and thus become an expression of his personality. Whether we wish it or not, the most vital aspect of mental hygiene in the schools revolves about the personality of the teacher. The essential prerequisite for the maintenance of our nation's emotional and mental maturity is a body of properly trained and personally adequate teachers.

STATUS AND IMPORTANCE OF TEACHER PERSONALITY

The Mental Health of Teachers. Impressionistic accounts of the mental health of teachers have sometimes been given which lead to the belief that teachers are, in large numbers, neurotic or psychotic and quite unfit for their jobs. It must be assumed that these pessimistic reports come from those who have, unfortunately, suffered at the hands of teachers or, just as probably, are projecting their own difficulties. These spectacular reports must be examined critically.

Actually, the few studies we do have indicate that teachers are no better and no worse than the adult population at large. Unless teaching attracts either only stable or only unstable persons as recruits, there is no reason to expect that we would find any deviation from the expectation that one out of twenty persons (or teachers) would be a candidate for a mental institution. This is, in fact, what studies indicate—that teachers are committed to mental institutions about as frequently as the rest of the total population. In one study it was found that 4 per cent of the teachers sampled in one system were definite mental cases. It can normally be expected that any child will in the course of twelve elementary and high-school years, encounter two badly maladjusted teachers.[1]

These data are not surprising in view of the fact that there are virtually no, or at best only sporadic, attempts to select teacher candidates in terms of their mental health. But the data are disappointing. *One* maladjusted teacher out of a hundred is too many. Considering that in a year this teacher will have intimate contact with twenty or thirty impressionable youngsters, all of whom are developing their attitudes toward education and continued learning, are evolving habits of work and standards of value, and some of whom are not too robust, then one such teacher anywhere is too many. Perhaps the teacher education institutions, boards of education, and administrators would be more concerned if they thought their own sons or daughters might be exposed to this threat.

Without laboring the point, it can be recommended that certain things be done: (1) In selecting teacher candidates, use mental health as one influencing factor. (2) Remove some of the hazards to teacher mental health, for example, low pay, overloading, authoritarian administration.[2] (3) Arrange for group therapeutic sessions where teachers can learn to view their normal conflicts more objectively. (4) Encourage those who are identified (by themselves, their peers, or administrators) as problems to seek psychological counseling or psychiatric help.

Meaning of Personality. Personality is such a complicated and intricate thing that exact definition would require pages, but there are aspects of

[1] W. U. Snyder, "Do Teachers Cause Maladjustment?" *Journal of Exceptional Children*, 14:40–46, 73–78, 1947.

[2] Cyril C. O'Brien, "Mental Health of the Teacher," *Journal of School Health*, 25:22–24, 1955.

the concept which seem rather generally to be accepted. These would include physique, appearance, potential capacities, developed abilities, interests, ambitions, habits, and temperament. The combinations of these factors which condition one's social effectiveness and inner harmony are no less varied or important. Personality thus includes one's hates, loves, fears, likes, and dislikes.

> *Personality is defined by the particular empirical concepts which are a part of the theory of personality employed by the observer.* Personality consists concretely of a set of values or descriptive terms which are used to describe the individual being studied according to the variables or dimensions which occupy a central position within the particular theory utilized.[3]

Obviously, there are many facets of personality with which teachers must be concerned. Why is teacher personality so pervasive? How does teacher personality affect pupil growth? What are some of the personality traits of teachers which have greatest significance? How can these traits be developed? Answers to these questions will clarify the importance of a teacher's personality and serve to illustrate his influence.

School Contacts Are Continuous and Intimate. The prerequisite for optimum mental health is a nation of healthy-minded parents; but the school is a more logical place for improving mental health than is the home. Teachers have better opportunities, and are often required, to study mental hygiene. The significance of teacher personality is enhanced by the fact that the child, coming to school to learn, is typically receptive and eager. Because of the amount of time in school, the intimacy of school contacts, and the nature of school activities, it is inevitable that the teacher's personality and behavior will have a profound effect upon pupil behavior. For example, in a study of one hundred teachers and their pupils there was a statistically significant positive correlation in every one of the twenty-two personality characteristics which were measured. The investigation indicates that "it is of vital importance to the development of wholesome personality in the children, that they have teachers who possess well adjusted personalities."[4]

Teacher Personality Is Contagious. *One teaches what he is* perhaps even more than he teaches what he says. A boy will walk with the same shuffling, swinging, or strutting gait as his father. It takes a long time to eradicate "He don't," "That there thing," and "That guy, he . . ." if the child repeatedly hears such expressions in his home. On the other

[3] Calvin S. Hall and Gardner Lindzey, *Theories of Personality*, New York: John Wiley & Sons, Inc., 1957, p. 9.

[4] Sister Mary Amatora, "Similarity in Teacher and Pupil Personality," *Journal of Psychology*, 37:45–50, 1954.

hand, formal instruction is largely superfluous if the child's intimates speak correctly. Visits to two classrooms will give evidence of this kind of response. The same pupils under two different instructors act differently. If the teacher is tense, irritable, dominating, or careless, the pupils will show evidence of tensions, crossness, and lack of social grace and will produce slovenly work. If we first look at pupils and see them to be industrious, cheerful, energetic, confident, and cooperative, we can then turn to the teacher and see a poised, happy individual who knows where he is going and how he intends to get there.

Vigorous learning situations are a matter of contagion as well as of premeditated desire to learn. The teacher, for this reason, should be a learner with the pupil. He can be a competent authority without being dogmatically authoritative. Some teachers stimulate pupil responsibility in learning by saying frankly, "I'm not sure about that. Will you look it up and let me know," "I thought . . . ; but you see what you can find," or "I remember only vaguely that [the author] mentioned it in the book, [title]." Teachers who welcome a viewpoint forwarded by a pupil, show appreciation for supplementary materials that the pupil furnishes, and *are themselves gathering new data* are providing a setting for enthusiastic learning.

A child learns from his teacher unintentionally such reactions as quarrelsomeness, careless work habits, and discourteous treatment of others. The pupil will as quickly learn to be cooperative, systematic, polite, and purposeful.

> This is no process of imitation whereby the child imitates specific and discrete behaviors in order to achieve an immediate goal. As far as we can tell, it is largely an unconscious process of coming to "feel like" the "model" person with whom he identifies and to perceive situations in the same way the "model" perceives them.[5]

Teacher Behavior Is Consciously Imitated. Many things are learned as the result of conscious imitation. Kindergarten children reveal this imitative learning when they return home and "play school." The child who is the make-believe teacher of the moment imitates the voice, action, and statements of the real teacher. Imitation at this age level and much of that in the elementary grades may have little effect on enduring behavior patterns, but that little is worth considering when it relates to the child's attitude toward continuous learning. Imitation at the secondary level is a still more serious matter. Adolescents consciously seek a pattern for their conduct in some more mature person. Since they are

[5] *Fostering Mental Health in Our Schools,* 1950 Yearbook of National Education Association, Association for Supervision and Curriculum Development, Washington, D.C., 1950, p. 147. By permission of the Association for Supervision and Curriculum Development.

attempting to outgrow their dependence on parents, the model is likely to be the other adult whom they know most intimately—their teacher. This is usually a fortunate situation, because the imitated teacher will be one who is well liked, one who creates a wholesome classroom atmosphere through the influence of his personality attributes. It sometimes happens, however, that less desirable personality traits are imitated, because the youngster sees in some teacher a roughness, toughness, or sophistication that he is inclined to admire.

Many pupils at all levels, and particularly at the high-school age, make better growth if their teacher provides a model that is worthy of emulation. Basically, all children want to grow, to be independent, to develop competencies, and to achieve status. Such a declaration of independence can be heard in the two-year-old's cry, "Do it ownself"; in the six-year-old's protest, "You don't have to show me"; and in the adolescent's argument, "Frank's mother lets him. . . . " But they can't always do it themselves and they do need to be shown. Unwittingly they identify themselves with their parents, with older brothers and sisters and other more mature relatives, with movie heroes, and with their teachers.

The important thing is that the model be worthy of emulation. This does not imply that the child will be, or should be, a carbon copy of the teacher. Nor is it a matter of the teacher's choice. Whether or not he wishes to be one, he is a model, at least in part. Therefore, he should manifest such desirable characteristics as an open-minded attitude toward people and situations, a healthy regard for others—accepting them for what they are in terms of the influences which have shaped them—and a calm approach to disturbing problems. This involves acting in a mature manner with regard to the exercise of authority, the raising of important issues and the ignoring of insignificant ones, and the development of a plan to promote the growth of the mind.[6]

Improving the Personality of Teachers. It is assumed that the effectiveness of teachers is improved by their taking courses in mental hygiene, methods of teaching, and educational psychology and philosophy. Certainly, it is clear that teachers have, in large numbers, come to view pupil problems in a more enlightened manner than was the case some thirty years ago.[7] What one knows and what he does *are* aspects of his personality and are the results of his experience. However, it has been found that courses in mental hygiene do not necessarily help. Teachers who had such courses made higher scores on the Minnesota Teachers Attitude

[6] H. A. Overstreet, "The Mature Mind," *National Education Association Journal,* 39:48, 1950.

[7] E. C. Hunter, "Changes in Teachers' Attitudes toward Children's Behavior Over the Last Thirty Years," *Mental Hygiene,* 41:3–11, January, 1957.

Inventory, but they were not superior in comparison to the upper extremes of teacher-pupil relationships. The investigators felt that attitudes, good and poor, were deeply rooted in the lives of teachers and were not easily changed.[8] This we can readily accept, but it should have the effect of challenging instructors in mental hygiene, and the teachers who take the courses, to strive more vigorously to make the changes which are recommended.

Another study indicates more encouraging outcomes. Over a period of years, 40,000 teachers have participated in the work of the Institute for Child Study at the University of Maryland. There each teacher studied and built records for one child who was then studied and evaluated in a group. As a result of this participation, teachers became objective and factual in describing children. They learned principles which assist them in explaining behavior. They developed positive behavior in the classroom, for instance, increased the use of praise and encouragement while diminishing the use of isolation and reprimand. Other outcomes included the development of warm and accepting attitudes toward children. Judgments of behavior accorded more closely with that of mental hygienists. Teachers became sensitive to individual differences and to the multiple causation of behavior and were more democratic. Human relations with children and colleagues improved as teachers became more accepting of themselves. However, it is to be noted that their pupils neither increased nor decreased in their reading and arithmetic achievement.[9]

FACTORS IN TEACHER EFFECTIVENESS

There are hundreds of characteristics of teachers. Sometimes these are stated in terms of character traits, sometimes in terms of behaviors, and sometimes in terms of knowledges.[10] Even if we could "pin down" the meaning of abstract terms now in use, it would still have to be admitted that there are many variations of successful teachers. This section, presented with due regard for limitations, deals with factors over which teachers have *some* immediate control.

Personal Grooming. What one wears is a reflection of the personality and a partial revelation of the individual. Clothing, if not an aspect of personality, is nevertheless a factor which influences the behavior of

[8] P. D. Rocchio and N. C. Kearney, "Does a Course in Mental Hygiene Help Teachers?" *Understanding the Child*, 25:91–94, 1956.

[9] Richard M. Brandt and Hugh V. Perkins, "Teachers Change as They Study Children," *Childhood Education*, 34:218–220, 1958.

[10] A. S. Barr, "Characteristics of Successful Teachers," *Phi Delta Kappan*, 39:282–284, 1958.

youngsters. Children in the kindergarten and primary grades often openly comment on the teacher's dress, the costume jewelry she wears, or her shoes. Pupils in the intermediate grades may speak less frankly, but their interpersonal remarks reveal that clothes are noticed. High-school students are similarly observant.

The teacher's clothing is a factor in pupil behavior, not only from the standpoint of possible imitation and emulation—particularly, for high-school pupils—but more significantly as an element of classroom atmosphere. Cleanliness and color help generate a feeling of cheer. Comfort is desirable, because it helps condition the teacher's feeling about his work. The comment "My shoes are killing me" is often superfluous, except as it indicates the specific cause of ill humor. Moreover, practical psychologists often explain that appropriateness in the style and quality of the clothing worn immediately affects a person's confidence in himself.

Voice. The infant, in crib or arms, responds to its mother's voice before he comprehends words. When we reflect that children judge friendliness more from tone than words, we can appreciate the teacher who wisely says, "Statements of children's needs should include that of a friendly voice."

A high-pitched, strident voice expressing curt commands is indicative of a tense, uncertain teacher. A low-pitched, well-modulated voice reveals poise and confidence in self and in pupils. In mental hygiene terms, poor voice is a symptom of some difficulty. Hence, improvement of voice becomes a matter of analysis and remediation of underlying causes. These causes may be found among the gamut of mental hygiene difficulties—home conditions, marital situation, uncertainty of position, poor physical health, dislike for one's work, and the like. Hasty preparation, friction with other staff members, and lack of faith in the worthwhileness of teaching might also be factors worth attention.

Sometimes the symptom (poor voice) itself may be successfully attacked. It would be advantageous to have the aid of a competent instructor; the speech and dramatics instructor will usually be willing to help. A tape recorder can serve by giving the speaker a chance to hear himself as others hear him. If these aids are lacking, it is still possible to bring about improvement by examining habits of speaking. Is pitch too high? It may be if there is a tendency to outshout the pupils. Is the voice harsh? Straining to be heard may be the cause.

A Smile. Infants, as well as children and adults, respond to a smile with a smile. Youngsters whose teachers give this manifestation of a radiant personality find their schoolwork more interesting (perhaps because they feel recognition) and more pleasant. Furthermore, a smile has the effect of autosuggestion; for example, wearing a smile as a pretense will tend to produce a more pleasant feeling—but, of course, the inner feeling also must be cultivated.

A smile is regarded by child psychologists as one of the first evidences of the development of social behavior. It is a universally understood evidence of friendliness. A smile can do much to establish the kind of classroom rapport that makes work and learning pleasant and effective. Admittedly, this matter of smiling is a minute detail, but it is the multiplicity of minute details that produces the over-all condition known as a healthy classroom atmosphere.

Accent on the Positive. Different teachers take different views of individual children. John, a normal eighth-grader was a slow starter. One teacher saw him as lazy and dumb, another thought he would outgrow his weakness, and a third deemed him to be disrespectful, disobedient, and "playing it smart" to get his way.[11] Those with the mental hygiene orientation would view him as a child who was in need of help and understanding.

If the teacher's personality is to produce a wholesomely stimulating effect on pupil growth, it is necessary that emphasis be placed on the positive. Many teachers can find in the most troublesome pupils some virtue, point of superiority, or valuable trait. When a youngster complains, "The other kids don't like me," and the teacher answers, "But I like you. You are always polite and kind to me," the teacher is accenting the positive. He may be fully aware that this pupil picks fights and teases smaller children. The positive can be accented by reminding the boy who is slow in arithmetic that he is one of the best basketball players in the class, by indicating that a poor reader is capable of drawing beautifully, and by finding some reason for a compliment, even if it be partially fictional.

It is necessary to have confidence *in the intentions* of students, as well as confidence in their ability. The teacher may say, "I know this is a difficult assignment, but I also know that this class is perfectly able to do the work." When an unpleasant incident arises, such as the breaking of a globe, it is necessary to believe that this may quite as likely be an accident as an act of maliciousness.

Faith in the ability of students to conduct their affairs with prudence and aplomb accents the positive; whereas, the conviction that adult leadership and dominance is requisite to the conduct of student affairs would stress the negative. An example of stressing the negative is found in the case of a high-school principal who was convinced that students were unable to handle finances accurately and honestly. Monies collected at ball games, dances, and for the school annual were handled entirely by

[11] Arthur Lerner, "Teacher Problems and Problem Teachers," *Phi Delta Kappan*, 39:391, 1954.

teachers. Treasurers of clubs and classes merely reported the sums that were cited to them from the principal's office. Student resentment was strong and was manifested by destruction of school property, by frequent "sneak days," on which the entire student body would be absent. While student funds should be subject to close supervision by the school staff, student-participating experiences are a vital part of learning from cocurricular activities.

Typically, it seems that individuals do as much, and only as much, as is expected of them. Perhaps this is because our own egos force us to confirm the faith that others have in us. At any rate, accent on the positive tends to bring out the best that is in a person—the school child included. Praise instead of criticism, stimulating suggestions in place of sarcasm, a smile substituted for a scowl, and hope instead of discouragement—these are means of accenting the positive. Looking for causes instead of correcting behaviors is one of the more significant means of accenting the positive.

Competence without Dogmatism. An important factor in creating a desirable classroom atmosphere is to avoid dogmatism. A teacher can be well informed, thoroughly versed, and competent in his field without trying to show that he "knows it all." In fact, feeling sure of oneself instills a confidence that makes it possible to respect difficult views and challenging counterstatements. Thus, competence and tolerance go hand in hand; and lack of assurance breeds dogmatism.

Many teachers have reported that they had, before studying mental hygiene, tried to cover their ignorance by assuming an authoritative air. Many of us may have had the experience of taking a class from someone who was not thoroughly acquainted with the literature in his field and of finding that the teacher, nevertheless, was overpositive in his statements. This situation had the effect of creating a tension which made an unpleasant atmosphere in the class and of throwing doubt on the truth of those statements of the instructor which were sound.

Competence in one's field, or lack of it, produces an effect on oneself as well as on others. Teachers have indicated that they have had the feeling that on some days the students seemed particularly inert, that they came to class ill-prepared, were uninterested in the lesson, and were particularly attentive to distracting influences. Reflection and analysis revealed that the fault was often with the teachers. On days when they went to class unprepared, did not know just what direction the lesson would take and did not have alternative activities in mind, the students seemed unprepared and uninterested. On the other hand, when teachers were well prepared and had much to give, students seemed so eager that there was hardly enough time.

Another argument against dogmatism is that schools in a democracy can be justified only when they help students to learn to think. This requires the development of powers of criticism, of independence, and of the ability to evaluate. These in turn demand open questions, freedom from dictation, and the opportunity to make choices. Obviously, these conditions cannot exist where a key figure, the teacher, is dogmatic and authoritarian. The highest form of education can be implemented only by teachers who are competent without being dogmatic.

Respect for Pupil Differences. Some lists of teacher qualifications mention tolerance, but there seems to be a certain degree of intolerance in the word *tolerance,* the latter being defined as the quality of endurance, ability to put up with. What teachers need is to have admiration and respect for pupils. More is needed than putting up with Johnny's dirty hands and nails and with Alice's slowness in learning. The mitigating circumstances which accompany such characteristics need to be understood.

It takes a genuinely mature person to understand a child's assertions, "You're not fair," "I hate reading," and "I see no earthly reason why I should study ancient history." A teacher of literature responded to a boy's protest, "I hate poetry," with just such maturity. She said with surprise, "Why, that's just because you don't understand it." She proceeded to explain the meaning of the words and sentences and then read several passages aloud. Tears came to the adolescent's eyes and the teacher said, "Why, you appreciate this much more sincerely than the average student does." His original remark was more than tolerated, it was respected. He in turn respected the teacher and was put on the road to respecting poetry.

When a teacher is well adjusted himself, he is more likely to accept and try to understand, rather than to resent, the negative emotional outbursts of pupils. The Massachusetts Association for Mental Hygiene proved this when in working with groups of ten to fifteen teachers in psychotherapeutic sessions it was found that teachers frequently complain about traits in pupils which others saw in the complainant. Things teachers had vowed they never would do were the very things they practiced.[12]

Respect for others, like mental health itself, is not something to be achieved as the result of taking certain specified steps. It is an organismic response, involving intellectual processes, emotional behavior, and physical well-being. It is the result of conscious striving and the outcome of personal experience. Those who attempt to improve their respect will find that other elements of good mental health are being strengthened. For instance, when improvement in mental processes is sought through studying child development, psychology of adolescence, and educational psy-

[12] Leo Berman, "The Mental Health of the Educator," *Mental Hygiene,* 38:422–429, July, 1954.

chology, one will, at the same time, be taking steps toward achieving better classroom procedures.

EXAMPLES OF THE EFFECT OF TEACHERS ON PUPILS

A few studies are available which show that the personalities of teachers (including what they do as well as what they are) have pronounced effects upon pupil behavior. The following examples are designed to help prove the generalizations made in this chapter and to suggest improvements.

Two Teachers and Delinquency. A juvenile officer in a West Coast city, speaking of his work to a local service club, asserted that their city had not experienced the characteristic rise in delinquency reported in other cities of like size. He indicated that there were several possible explanatory factors. Among them he mentioned "teen-age night spots" under the supervision, but not the domination, of trained adults. The significance of organized athletic opportunities was stressed—it was indicated that no boy who participated in an organized athletic program had been in trouble during the past three years. The importance of working with parents was strongly emphasized, as was the role of teachers. Said the speaker, "I give most of the credit for our enviable position to two of the teachers in ——— High School. These teachers take time to work with individuals. They see problem behavior as an indication that pupils need help in adjustment. They investigate the pupil's problems and try to alter negative situations; when they are unable to do this, they prepare the pupil, through counseling, to meet and endure the situation. They have not only the time and faculty for helping students, but they have a keen insight into what we call predelinquent behavior. They are sensitive to behavior which presages difficulty."

This is quite different from the situation that evidently prevailed in a neighboring city. Two boys escaped from a state school for boys and in a forty-eight-hour period stole two cars, held up a store, broke into another one, fatally wounded a state patrolman, and wounded a man who finally took them into custody. A newspaper gave the following account of one of the boys:

> The youth said, "I just don't know what gets into me."
> His home was happy, he said. He didn't steal for money. He said he wasn't that poor.
> "I ran away from home three years ago and held up a place in ———
> and then went to ———. I did it because I didn't like school."

There is, of course, the possibility that the boy was what is known as a psychopathic individual—nothing could have been done for him. There is the possibility that his remark about the school was merely a way of making an excuse—a face-saving device. But there is also the distinct possibility that he could have been helped by teachers, or a teacher, who recognized "predelinquent" behavior as an indication of his needing help.

The Case of Locust Point. Dr. Ruth E. Fairbank has reported the results of a functional program of mental hygiene which worked wonders in the lives of individual children.[13] Locust Point, a section of Baltimore, Maryland, conducted a school survey which revealed that, out of a school population of 1,281, there were 166 children for whom predictions for the future were very black. Predictions were based on intelligence-test results and thorough investigation of community and home backgrounds. The group of 166 subnormal children was subdivided into groups. Twenty-two of the children had such pronounced disabilities that there was little likelihood they would be anything but charges to the community; for seventy-eight children it was predicted that they would drift through life at the lowest social level; and the remaining sixty-six, because of slightly higher intelligence, "offered only greater possibilities of their being detrimental to society."

A follow-up study, seventeen years later, revealed that three-fourths of the 122 (out of the original 166) who were restudied were self-supporting, in spite of the prevailing financial depression (1930–1931). Even the twenty-two with the darkest prognosis had made fair adjustment; prostitution, illegitimacy, and dependency were much lower than had been anticipated.

Among the stabilizing and explanatory factors in this favorable environment were school personnel who worked with parents, an organized athletic program, getting married, and finding a job appropriate to one's abilities. But, it is to the school (" . . . a modern building was eventually erected which not only serves as a schoolhouse, but acts as the social, recreational, and educational center for the entire community") and to the teachers that major credit is given for turning these inherent liabilities of Locust Point so startlingly into assets for the community. The teachers were carefully selected for their sympathetic and understanding attitude toward individual pupils. They worked with pupils not only in academic pursuits but also in matters of personal, social, and economic adjustment.

The importance of the personality of the teacher in opportunity class is well illustrated by this teacher, in whose classroom a large percentage of the very retarded children spent their school lives. She was unusually socially minded, knew the home conditions of all her pupils,

[13] Ruth E. Fairbank, "The Subnormal Child—Seventeen Years After," *Mental Hygiene,* 17:177–208, April, 1933.

was very sympathetic, and somehow or other impressed them with clear and practical ideals of decency combined with a wholesome fear of the Lord. As one girl puts it, "Miss Hannah always told me never to swear or drink or let a boy touch me, and I never did." . . .

Here, again, we find the effect of contacts in those early years with teachers who were not convictionless, but aggressively determined not to lose an opportunity to inculcate good old-fashioned morality, embodying principles of decency and respect for individual personality and cleanmindedness. The most striking result of this survey is to be found in the lasting impression made on these people in childhood by one of the teachers who came in closest contact with them. Science has no tests to evaluate the influence of personality, but the tests of life on growth and development tell the story.[14]

Teachers May Cause the Symptoms. An interesting problem for speculation is postulated by Clara Bassett as she outlines the analysis of problems in three classrooms. The following data are presented:

Behavior problem	Teacher A	Teacher B	Teacher C
Number of pupils	45	47	47
Dishonesty	3	12	43
Cheating	18	34	40
Disorderliness	18	1	47
Carelessness in work	17	9	45
Failure to study	26	5	44
Shyness	5	2	37
Tattling	4	22	37
Daydreaming	0	2	26
Unhappiness	0	0	17

Does teacher C cause the symptoms? Does the teacher's anticipation of the children's being problems prompt them to confirm the suspicion? Is teacher C merely more alert than the other two? Were the pupils under teacher C worse to begin with? Regardless of the answers which we give to these questions, there would still be doubt in the minds of most of us that we would willingly send a son or a daughter of our own to teacher C. Bassett gives the following interpretation:

Such wide variations in the number of problem children detected in classes of similar size and make-up must mean that either the three teachers stimulated their children to behave differently or they varied decidedly in their sensitiveness to the behavior problems of their children. A comparison of the above columns with each other indicates that one of the teachers consistently found a high percentage of problems in contrast with the other two.[15]

[14] *Ibid.*, pp. 186, 207. By permission of the publisher.
[15] Clara Bassett, *The School and Mental Health*, New York: Commonwealth Fund, Division of Publication, 1931, p. 50.

Statistical Evidence on Teacher-Pupil Influences. There are so many factors which condition social intercourse, so many things which cause a given behavior, that it is hazardous to say *A* causes *B*. Nevertheless, it is the consensus of school workers that the personality of a teacher is one of the more important factors that shape the responses of pupils. One of the few studies which have made this belief definitive is that of Paul L. Boynton and associates,[16] who gathered sufficient data to permit a noteworthy generalization: mentally healthy teachers have a perceptible effect on the mental health of their pupils. Seventy-three fifth- and sixth-grade teachers were studied with respect to the quality of their mental health. A similar study was made of their 1,095 pupils. Pupils who had emotionally stable and mentally healthy teachers revealed markedly better mental health and stability than did the pupils of teachers who were in poor mental health. On all measures of instability, the children who had unstable teachers made higher scores than did those who were under the tutelage of well-balanced teachers. Moreover, these differences began to be revealed in as short a period as two to two and one-half months.

The Teacher and Classroom Climate. Daniel A. Prescott has given an extraordinarily succinct statement of the relationship of teacher personality to pupil behavior. His statement and its implications should be carefully considered by every classroom teacher.

> Different people tend to create different climates of feeling among their associates; and different groupings of people show prevailing moods as different as the weather of the arctic and the torrid zones. Some groups swelter at their tasks in the heavy, humid oppressiveness of obligatory functioning, like a sea-level metropolis in midsummer. Others buoyantly undertake common responsibilities with the light, stimulating freshness of the autumn in high altitude dryness. The whole odor of life is sweet or sour, fragrant or foul, tangy or stifling, according to the moods we inhale from those around us.
>
> It is no accident that problem children so frequently come from homes broken by divorce. Their lives have been profoundly influenced by the tensions and conflicts going on about them. It is no accident that delinquents appear so frequently in certain sections of great cities. There poverty and misery are so close to riches and ostentation that inferiority is emphasized and the prevailing mood becomes bitterness. Children are extremely sensitive to the emotional climate enveloping them. Their attitudes, their ideas about what is valuable in life, and their personal goals, as well as their moments of gaiety or depression are influenced profoundly by the moods of the people with whom they come in contact. . . . These constitute learnings more important even than skills in reading or figuring.

[16] P. L. Boynton, H. Dugger, and M. Turner, "The Emotional Stability of Teachers and Pupils," *Journal of Juvenile Research*, 18:223–232, 1934.

The question must be raised, then, whether the emotional climate common in the school classrooms of the country is a wholesome climate or not. Is this climate a joyous, buoyant one appropriate to our usual picture of childhood as "happy?" Or is it dull, uninteresting, monotonous, and heavy? Or is it full of tensions, bickerings, repressions, and feelings of failure? Does the child unconsciously absorb the feeling of certainty that he has a significant role in the world and is a valuable person? Or does he get the sense that life is a jungle battle with no holds barred and his own lot a sorry one? Does the child feel that people are "with him" and that as part of a larger whole he and mankind are moving toward brighter days? Or is he led to feel that other persons are essentially his antagonists, or at least the setters of unimportant and distasteful tasks?[17]

THE TEACHER'S RESPONSIBILITY FOR PUPIL BEHAVIOR

The foregoing discussion makes it evident that the classroom teacher has a serious responsibility for the shaping of the pupil's present behavior, as well as for setting the course of future development. The kind of person a teacher is depends upon his *total* regime of living. This section summarizes *some* of the items involved in full and complete living.

Teachers Must Be Mentally Healthy. Attention should be given to physical health factors. An adequate amount of sleep, properly balanced diet, appropriate physical exercise, and allowance of time for rest and relaxation are problems which the mentally healthy teacher must solve. A task, a plan, and freedom to carry out the plan are as necessary for the teacher as for the pupil. The teacher must define as clearly as possible his philosophy of life and education. Today's philosophy will not be the same as that of next month or next year, but it should be definite so that directions for growth are clearly pointed. Teachers, perhaps more than other people because of their leadership responsibilities, need to cultivate adaptable and resilient minds. A step in this direction might be an in-service class, an experiment in school, or a planned reading project. An effort should be made to improve social relationships by actively engaging in clubs, church activities, bridge clubs, picnics, and the company of friends at dinner. The constant contact with immature students should be balanced by planned contact with adults. Emotional satisfactions must be sought. One should take time to do those extra things which are especially enjoyable. Art, drama, motion pictures, athletic contests, creative hobbies, and music are common mediums for achieving emotional satisfactions.

Perhaps, in the future, teachers will be more carefully selected with

[17] Daniel A. Prescott, "Emotional Weather," *The Educational Record*, 20:96–97, 1939.

regard to their mental health status, and perhaps they will have more readily available psychological and psychiatric help for personal problems. In the meantime, there is much that can be done by the individual teacher to preserve and improve his own mental health. A starting point is to live a satisfying life—one in which a wide variety of interests serve to keep one's mind off the petty, personal irritations of everyday living.

Teachers Need to Outgrow Their Earlier Years. The fact must be faced that each of us is the product of his previous experiences. The statement is frequently made—and there is much truth in it—that we teach as we were taught. Yet it is also true that everyone is growing. Sometimes the growth is slow, sometimes it is taking an undesirable direction. We are convinced that education is improving, but sometimes too slowly to keep pace with the changing times. Both personality growth and improvement in educational procedures will take place more rapidly *when planning charts the course of change.*

In Rochester, Michigan, a four-year in-service teacher education program was carried on in connection with some pupils (from a nearby mental institution) who were on the road to recovery and who were being returned to school. It was found that three major problems were involved. (1) Psychological education should be in the direction of giving teachers continuous support. (2) Teacher anxieties were created when educational measures touched upon previously acquired anxieties or dealt with areas where their defenses were weak. (3) The success of the program was dependent upon the "supporting" role of teachers and helping them to become more mature rather than on marking them part-time therapists.[18]

The outgrowing of one's childhood years can be attained by learning to accept oneself with both one's limitations and one's assets. We can learn to understand ourselves and others. We should stop feeling guilty about our shortcomings and create a design for living that will help us to overcome them. The first step is to recognize the problem. The next is to formulate a plan, a plan for improvement of personality and more effective teaching methods, and after that comes a need for the exercise of patience as the slow process of growth takes place.

It must be accepted as fact that everyone is influenced by his own childhood experiences. Negative experiences have created tensions and weakened defenses. Teachers are likely to punish the trivial actions which tend to arouse memories of their own childhood. Principals, it has been found, who were poor in scholarship, seem to prefer teachers who had

[18] M. L. Falick, Mildred Peters, Morton Levitt, and Ben O. Rubenstein, "Observations on the Psychological Education of Teachers in a School-based Mental Hygiene Program," *Mental Hygiene*, 38:374–386, 1954.

poor scholarship records.[19] Similarly, there are teachers who belittle the bright child, apparently because he poses a threat to their own prestige or security.

Teachers Must Consider Individuals. Teachers have for so long and have so often heard of the necessity for giving attention to individuals that it is likely to be viewed as more of the "verbiage of pedagese." But recognizing individuals and giving attention to their differences will continue to be a focal point in effective education. This is not only a matter of intellectual differences but also of socioeconomic differences, differences in motivation, and variations in personality orientation.

The touches of humor that can be used to stimulate one child are found to be completely ineffective with another. In some cases it is possible to motivate a child with mild sarcasm, while another child may be completely devastated by its use. Praise may generate further effort on the part of one child; but when it is used on another, it makes him feel so superior that he no longer sees any room for improvement in himself. Thus, it is evident that any generalized description of elements which make up a favorable classroom atmosphere is subject to error in the case of particular individuals. Teachers need to interpret these generalizations in terms of the things they know about particular pupils. Thus, while it is necessary to know the general characteristics of children of a certain age, it is also necessary to improve our knowledge about John, Mary, Alice, and Peter.

Derogatory Remarks Must Be Avoided. It is shocking to hear some teachers make spiteful, insulting, and pain-producing remarks to children. Among the vicious words which some teachers use in reference to pupils are dumb, stupid, lazy, awkward, mean, stubborn, dirty, filthy, ignorant, rude, and devilish. Such categorical evaluations are, of course, not getting at the causes of behavior; instead they are leaving lasting impressions on the youngster, who is so eager to receive the approbation of his teacher. To the experienced observer, these words reveal a teacher who does not understand the concept of causative factors in pupil personality. Hence the teacher who uses such terms is, in fact, disclosing more about himself than about his pupils. The real impact of remarks like these, however, is that they tend to give the child the feeling of being rejected and out of place.

SUMMARY

There are many factors—curriculums, methods, buildings, teaching materials, community, pupils—that influence the kind of classroom at-

[19] Paul Woodring, *A Fourth of a Nation*, New York: McGraw-Hill Book Company, Inc., 1957, p. 235.

mosphere which prevails in a given situation. The most important of these is the teacher himself. It is his personality, more than what he knows or what methods he uses, which will determine the rate and direction of the growth of his pupils. This is true because (1) school contacts are continuous and intimate, (2) personal contacts influence learning on the part of pupils, and (3) the teacher becomes a goal (both consciously and unconsciously) of growth for children and adolescents.

Some of the facets of personality that will bear particular attention on the part of the teacher are manner of dress, voice, the ability to smile, emphasis on the positive, competence without dogmatism, respect for all humans, and a confidence in the worth of each individual.

Much empirical evidence and some experimental evidence points to the immediate and pronounced effect of teacher personality on pupil behavior. The influence of teachers is known to reduce delinquency and raise the level of functioning of handicapped children. It has been experimentally verified that maladjusted teachers quickly stimulate an exhibition of misbehavior on the part of pupils.

If responsibility for influencing the behavior of school children for the better is to be properly assumed, numerous things must be done. For the present, attention will be confined to the following considerations: (1) The teacher himself must be in good mental health; (2) teachers must study means of outgrowing the negative influences of their own childhood; (3) individuals must be treated as unique persons; and (4) the handicapping effect of ill-conceived remarks and categorical evaluations must be avoided. Again let us remind ourselves that, whether we wish it or not, what the teacher is influences pupil behavior at least as surely as what he says.

STUDY AND DISCUSSION EXERCISES

1. Have you encountered, in your past school experience, a badly maladjusted teacher? What actions made maladjustment evident?

2. Visit some classroom and note any particular teacher strengths or weaknesses in terms of the data of this chapter.

3. Prepare a statement of your personal philosophy of life.

4. Describe a number of specific things which a teacher might do to manifest a consideration of individuals.

5. To what extent should paper grading, lesson planning, committee work, and so on, be allowed to interfere with a teacher's regular use of leisure?

SUGGESTED ADDITIONAL READINGS

Baxter, Bernice, *Teacher-Pupil Relationships*, New York: The Macmillan Company, 1941. 166 pp.

Personality characteristics of teachers are described in terms of their effect on the personalities and behavior of pupils.

Olson, Willard C., "Implications of the Dynamics of Instructional Groups," in *The Dynamics of Instructional Groups*, 59th Yearbook, Part II, National Society for the Study of Education, Chicago: University of Chicago Press, 1960, pp. 268–280.

The teacher as the central figure in children's group learning must know the implications of his role and be aware of the impact on pupils of grouping, school marks, and curriculum modifications.

Rasey, Marie I., and J. W. Menge, *What We Learn from Children*, New York: Harper & Brothers, 1958. 164 pp.

The authors describe what they have learned, in over two decades of work in a residential home, about children and youth with special problems.

Remmers, H. H., and others (eds.), *Growth, Teaching, and Learning*, New York: Harper & Brothers, 1957, pp. 246–273.

The readings deal with the changing attitudes of teachers, comparison of views taken by teachers and mental hygienists of behavior problems, and the elementary teacher's understanding of child behavior.

Witty, Paul A., "The Mental Health of the Teacher" in *Mental Health in Modern Education*, 54th Yearbook, Part II, National Society for the Study of Education, Chicago: University of Chicago Press, 1955, pp. 307–333.

Characteristics of good teachers, evaluation of teachers by pupils, and approaches to better understanding are considered in this chapter.

CHAPTER 6

UNDERSTANDING AND HELPING PUPILS WITH PROBLEMS

As we attempt to understand pupils, two broad categories describing the origins of problem behavior should be considered. In the first category are the antecedent, or contributing, factors to behavior, which build up over a period of time as aggravating conditions because they are neither immediately apparent nor readily resolved. Reaching out in time and space, they may go back to very early phases of the individual's life and permeate his whole existence. The second category consists of the immediate, or precipitating, factors, the sparks which set off the kegs of dynamite. While the observer may view these as inconsequential incidents, they are, in fact, the overbalancing tensions which create a leak in the dike of inhibited impulses and cause a flood of asocial and antisocial conduct.

A distinction must be made between causes and symptoms. The causes are all important. The symptoms are only indications that something is wrong. Too many teachers, as a matter of expediency, deal only with the symptoms and totally neglect to reach understanding by getting at their origin. Until symptoms are regarded as misguided attempts to adjust, an understanding of children cannot be achieved.

NOT ALL PUPILS ARE PROBLEM CASES

Difficulty in Adjustment Is Normal. As many children as adults have problems, but not all children (not all adults) are problem cases. A certain amount of indecision, some tension, temporary disturbances, and even some objectionable behavior are normal. It is prolonged tension, continuing unsolved conflicts, and habitual misbehavior that characterize problem cases. A girl who pouts because she did not get the part in a school play she sincerely wanted may be showing evidence of immaturity but should not be regarded as a problem case unless that attitude is characteristic. A boy who has a fist-fight with a classmate may be manifesting quite normal reactions to a dispute about keeping in line or custody of some article. We may regard occasional disobedience, tussling in class, or lack of application to schoolwork as an objectionable but normal pattern of behavior—but such was not the case with fourteen-year-old Stuart. Only four or five days would pass without his lashing out against his peers, several teachers reported his talking back, and his schoolwork was only very rarely acceptable. He was referred to a counselor who came to suspect an unusual father-son tension. The counselor talked to the mother, who reported continual loud arguments at home. The father had recently been discharged from a public mental hospital and demanded immediate and exacting obedience. He frequently shouted, "If you don't like it here, get out." (Stuart did once run away from home.) The mother, realizing the condition of the father and the inability of the boy to make unreasonable concessions, consented to foster-home placement. After a period of six months, with only occasional relapses, the boy's attitude toward peers, teachers, and school tasks was markedly improved. Any one of Stuart's behaviors could be considered normal, but as a total pattern, they indicated the need for help.

Diagnosis Is Based on Multiple Symptoms. If the girl who showed disappointment at not getting a given part in a play (above) becomes sullen when she is not made discussion-group chairman, refuses to play unless she can be "it," declines to talk at all unless she is recognized every time she raises her hand, then the multiple manifestations of undesirable behavior can be regarded as symptoms of continued difficulty.

The study of mental hygiene in the classroom would indeed be abortive if all pupils were seen as cases of maladjustment. Lessons in mental hygiene would be misleading if teachers were led to interpret isolated symptoms as having significance that would rightly be inferred only if there were a whole set of symptoms. Objectivity in viewing pupils calls for a recognition of the commendable aspects of behavior as well as recognition of negative symptoms.

Understanding Is Based on a Working Concept of Normality. The difficult problem of working for mental health in the classroom is made all the harder by a failure to understand typical behavior. The following facts are emphasized in order to foster that better understanding: Growth is slow, it progresses on uneven fronts, the child carries on experiments in adjustment, errors are caused by lack of experience, and the correct terminology is a *child with problems* rather than a *problem child*.

There seems to be a tendency to confuse what is normal and what is desirable. For instance, it is normal for children to encounter some learning difficulties in all the grades. Obviously, not all children can be so good as the leaders in the class in reading, writing, and arithmetic. It is normal for children to quit school as soon as they are allowed by law to do so. Even today, about 50 per cent of our population over twenty-five years of age has an eighth-grade education or one lower still.[1] The average high-school pupil will fail from one to four subjects during his secondary-school career. The average boy or girl will not be a doctor, a lawyer, or a teacher. Average individuals will, however, be parents, will cast their votes at elections, and will determine the rate of progress of civilization. Unless we remember that it is the superior individual who becomes the professional worker, clarifies the issues at elections, and formulates the policies of a nation, we are likely to expect too much of the normal (average) pupil and thereby place him under strain.

If the reader is inclined to discredit this statement of the case, let him take stock of his average pupils' learning problems, of the difficulty of putting across straight subject matter, of the average accomplishment of pupils in any grade, and of the average educational attainment of citizens in general. The teacher should stop to realize that in any grade, in any one item being measured, half the children are below average; for example, in the fourth grade at mid-term half the pupils will fall below the median score. Norms are established in just this way. Hence, typical children should not be regarded as retarded learners—or problem children.

Furthermore, our concept of normality should include the knowledge that there is no one child who will exactly fit the "hypothetical average." Each child is unique, and knowledge gathered from a textbook must be buttressed by information which leads to an appreciation of the individual. Such an understanding not only is basic to fostering mental health in school but is a fundamental of effective education. In fact, democratic philosophy includes the conviction that there are unique possibilities in both extraordinary and ordinary people. We need to encourage all boys and girls, especially in those areas where they show strengths, to reach for higher levels of achievement. Remembering that a child may be normal in one characteristic and not in another, normal in some situations and not in others, we should know each child in terms of many traits and situations rather than judge him in terms of wide generality. Teachers must have not only a statistical view but also an analytic view (which stresses differences) of normality.[2]

[1] *Education—an Investment in People,* Washington: U.S. Chamber of Commerce, Education Department, 1955, p. 21.
[2] H. H. Remmers, Einar R. Ryden, and Clellen L. Morgan, *Introduction to Educational Psychology*, New York: Harper & Brothers, 1954, pp. 5–6.

HELP CHILDREN BY LISTENING

To the extent that one feels he is an important, well-liked, worthy, admirable individual, he is free to "become," to develop, to gain stature, to relate himself positively to others. To the extent that he is insecure, that he feels he is unworthy or disliked, he must resort to various escapes and mechanisms in order to protect himself from further injury. Recently psychologists have returned again to ego concepts to account for the phenomenon of personality integration.

> They [psychologists] have reintroduced self and ego unashamedly and, as if to make up for lost time, have employed ancillary concepts such as *self-image, self-actualization, self-affirmation, phenomenal ego, ego-involvement, ego-striving,* and many other hyphenated elaborations which to experimental positivism still have a slight flavor of scientific obscenity.[3]

There are, of course, many ways of strengthening ego, some of which are suggested throughout this book; but one of these ways is through attentive, interested listening.

Listening Provides Catharsis. An attentive listener gives the confider an opportunity to make use of the principle of catharsis and to feel that he is important enough to be listened to. Freud has made it clear that getting a thing off one's chest is a potent method of dealing with frustration. People who are deeply disturbed emotionally may need the help of drugs or hypnosis to get the full benefit of catharsis; but for ordinary tensions, talking to someone in whom the confider has confidence may afford a healthy catharsis for pent-up emotions. Thus, even without giving any wise advice, the teacher may help pupils by giving them an opportunity to release their feelings.

The experience of a high-school teacher illustrates the effect that listening to a student can have upon the student. A senior dropped into the teacher's room after school hours and said that she was experiencing some difficulties for which she hoped the teacher could suggest help. The teacher immediately became serious and said, "I hope I can. What is the difficulty?" The girl then proceeded to tell her about all the troubles she was having. The English teacher seemed to have little patience with her inability to use grammar and punctuation marks correctly. Her boy friend was paying more attention to another girl than he was giving to her. She had hoped to get a certain part in a forthcoming dramatic production, but the role had gone to another.

[3] Gordon W. Allport, *Becoming*, New Haven, Conn.: Yale University Press, 1955, p. 37.

As the details were poured out, the teacher began to formulate some words of advice, but every time she was ready to say something, the girl burst forth with more of her sad story. Her parents were not so lenient about letting her go out on dates as were the parents of the other high-school girls. The teacher had in mind to say that perhaps this was because they wanted to be sure that their daughter would not encounter any unwholesome influences and that, therefore, it was an indication of the parents' love. She did not have a chance. Still more woes were bared by the suffering student. Other girls had more attractive sweaters than she had—in fact, they had two or three while she had only one. She was not sure that she had decided on the right course of study.

Suddenly the girl arose and said, "Well, thank you, Miss ———, you have helped me a great deal," and she went out of the room, leaving the teacher ready to give good advice but with no opportunity to do so. The teacher later admitted that she was not only surprised but disappointed at not being able to help. However, a day or two later, the girl stopped her in the hall and said, "Miss ———, I want to thank you again for helping me so much." There was no time to analyze the situation because the teacher was due in her classroom. But still later the girl stopped by and reiterated her thanks and said, "You have no idea how much you have helped me. Many of my problems seem much less serious now." "Then," concluded the teacher, "I realized what had happened. I had heard of the principle of catharsis but had not remembered it at the time. Inadvertently, I had simply listened, not because I had nothing to say, but because I had no chance to speak. She had gotten rid of some of her tension through talking with me. Without giving any advice, I had helped her accidentally by lending an attentive ear."

The girl had been helped in two ways. She had released tensions by talking about her problems. And, it seems probable, that she had straightened out some of her thinking by putting her problems into words rather than permitting them to remain vague worries.

Listening Builds Rapport. Listening builds rapport because it gives the individual a sense of significance, or even of importance, to have another listen to him. Most of us have at times felt almost insulted upon realizing that someone with whom (or rather, to whom) we were talking was not paying the slightest attention. Many a young woman is aware that one way to make an impression on a young man is to give undivided attention to him; instead of letting her eyes wander to other people, she keeps her gaze on him and seems to "hang on his every word." Teachers can, and effective teachers do, pay attention to what their pupils are saying and thus encourage them to express their problems completely and clearly.

Listening Provides Insight. Another advantage of listening is that teachers are enabled to find out how the pupil *feels* about his situation. It may be that the pupil has what seems to the visiting teacher to be a very good, well-ordered home. Yet the pupil may feel that he is being treated unfairly, he may suffer from unfounded jealousies toward a sibling, he may think that the home is characterized by a domineering atmosphere. What the pupil's feelings are, from the standpoint of helping him with his problem, is as important—perhaps more so—as the actual, objective situation. What these feelings are can be discovered in different ways, but one of them is by listening. It is truly said that "To know is to understand" and one way to learn is to listen.

The description of these feelings will not always come out so easily as in the case of the girl cited above. Many are loath to bare their feelings; many young children lack the facility with language to do so easily. It is therefore important that the act of listening be cultivated to the extent of its becoming a habit. When the young person can depend upon the teacher to listen to his faltering explanation, and when he knows that he will not be deluged with adult advice, he will be encouraged to recite the facts that will make possible a better understanding of his problems.

> Listening to children as they express themselves, without trying to press our thinking and feelings upon them, is perhaps one of the most fundamental ways of promoting mental health in the classroom. . . . Effective listening does not come automatically and easily. It comes only through continued practice and the desire really to understand the perceptual expressions of the other person.
>
> Children want to feel they are talking with, not to, someone. They want to know they are understood and accepted.[4]

The Role of the Listener. In order to make the most of listening as a diagnostic and therapeutic approach, it is necessary to observe certain precautions. One of these is to avoid showing shock or disappointment at what is said and how it is said. If the teacher interrupts by observing that the language is too vile, the pupil will be unable to release his true feelings. If one comments on the venom with which the pupil refers to parents, peers, or teachers the cathartic process will cease. If one is judgmental of the behaviors described, a barrier is placed in the way of further confession or revelation. Allow the pupil time to formulate his thoughts. If one feels he must keep the conversation "going" by making comments at every pause, two things may happen. One, the pupil's thoughts might get off the area which is really significant to the pupil. The other is that the time for phrasing one's thoughts is limited.

It is necessary for the listener to appreciate that self-disclosure is sometimes a difficult process. S. M. Jourard has suggested that perhaps *the* skill involved in counseling is the art of coping with the terrors that

[4] Clark E. Moustakas, *The Teacher and the Child,* New York: McGraw-Hill Book Company, Inc., 1956, pp. 42–43.

attend self-disclosure. Interest, empathy, patience, a nonjudgmental atti-tude, and avoidance of punitive words are aspects of the art of listening. Teachers cannot be of maximum help until they permit pupils to disclose how uninformed or misinformed they, the pupils, are. Teachers cannot provide the most helpful stimulation to pupils until the pupils are able to disclose the things in which they are really interested.[5]

WORKING WITH PARENTS

Most of the problems of disturbed children, we have seen, originate in their early years. Hence, it is not surprising that in order to help these children it is necessary to know something about their home conditions. Remember, parents, as well as children, are products of their back-grounds. Often the teacher can do nothing to change parents. Parents know they are inadequate and would like to change, but they cannot change their feelings and habits merely because a teacher is frank enough to tell them that they expect too much, that they are unreasonably harsh, or that they do not really accept their children. Nevertheless, knowledge of the home can help by making the teacher appreciate the heavy emo-tional burdens carried by bewildered children.

Factors in Effective Work with Parents. Teachers can safely assume that parents, by and large, have good intentions in dealing with their offspring. Most of them are seriously trying to do the best they can for and with their youngsters. However, teachers are frequently not sufficiently aware of these good intentions. Perhaps this is because teachers, having a back-ground in the psychology of childhood or adolescence, having studied mental hygiene and being able to look at children more objectively, can more readily see the mistakes that are being made by parents but neglect to give them credit for their constructive intentions. Another advantage the teacher has is that he is not so deep in emotional involvement. Point-ing out obvious errors of treatment by a parent will be easier if the teacher assumes that the parent is concerned about his child.

A second consideration is that frank honesty can be used with parents. Tact, of course, is desirable; however, when tact fails with parents, brutal honesty and the statement "You are wrong" does not always arouse resentment. Teachers who have tried the technique of forthright com-ment report that it is, more frequently than not, effective even though they dislike having to use it. Obviously, the frankness should be bolstered with as much factual information and sound theory as is possible. Where there is a question as to how far one can go in advising parents, the final criterion should be the welfare of the child concerned.

[5] Sidney M. Jourard, "Healthy Personality and Self-disclosure," *Mental Hygiene,* 43:506, 1959.

The third consideration is that when parents err, it is probable that they are either rebelling against or imitating some influence that operated in their own childhood. Many of the techniques they use on their children have been directly copied from those of their parents, whom they probably *now* believe to have done a good job. Teachers who recognize the pervasiveness of this phenomenon have not only a clue to the better understanding of themselves, but also a clue to understanding parents. If they are able to make clear to parents this general tendency, they will aid them to exert a more salutary influence on their children.

There is not necessarily a close correlation between effective parenthood and educational or economic status. Homes which operate at a subsistence level frequently provide as wholesome an emotional atmosphere as do middle-class and well-to-do homes. Genuine affection counterbalances material lacks. Consistency, with even questionable methods, may be better than sporadic use of superior methods. Acceptance of children for what they are, rather than what parents might wish them to be, is just as likely to occur in a home of poor economic circumstances as in the home where there is ample means for comfortable living. It is possible to have had formal education through the college and university level without getting any specific instruction in the nature and needs of children or without taking courses dealing with family relations.[6] Even when such specific study has been made, the application of the knowledge may fall short because of the limitations placed on the individual through childhood conditioning. On the other hand, someone who has had no extensive formal education may be fortunate enough to have enjoyed wholesome mental hygiene influences, because of the stability of his own parents, and may unconsciously apply those influences in carrying out his own parental responsibilities.

Counteracting Adverse Home Influences. There are some points at which the philosophy of the school is in direct opposition to the philosophy of the home. A teacher made a study of some of these points of conflict by having fellow teachers indicate the one or two pupils in their respective classes who were judged to be having the greatest difficulty in adjustment. She then visited the home of each of these children and found, through questioning, the following points of conflict: (1) The school taught a cooperative and intellectual approach to the solution of difficulties, while the home preached the doctrine of "Don't take anything off anybody." (2) The school attempted to get each child to compete with himself, but parents were more interested in the child's being at the head of the

[6] Eleanor E. Maccoby and Patricia K. Gibbs, "Methods of Child-rearing in Two Social Classes," in William E. Martin and Celia B. Stendler (eds.), *Readings in Child Development*, New York: Harcourt, Brace & World, Inc., 1954, pp. 380–396.

class—or at least standing well in comparison to the neighbor's child. (3) The school attempted to teach good health habits and the ideal of truthfulness, whereas the parents, perhaps unwittingly, preached to the child that other people's concern about his diet or tooth-brushing habits was none of their business, or that the child was six years old for purposes of going to school but only five when he rode on the bus. (4) The school tried to diminish the prestige of fighting, but the father was likely to say, "If you get licked at school, I'll lick you again when you come home." In addition, the investigator found that, in several of the homes from which children with adjustment problems came, the parents originally had a rather antagonistic attitude toward the school. Nevertheless, the teacher was able to make clear to the families the differences in viewpoints and to stimulate acceptance of the educational viewpoint.[7] It required both honesty and tact to accomplish this result.

Some parents attempt to compensate through their children. Pushing them toward superior academic status, urging them to hold several class offices, or to be prominent in athletics generates in the children tensions that prevent their accomplishing what they might if they were left alone. One girl in the fifth grade who had superior intellectual equipment was below grade in her reading. Diagnostic tests revealed no specific difficulty. A conference with her parents revealed that they were concerned about the girl's lack of superior attainment in reading and were coaching her at home. It was admitted that not all the reading sessions were conducted calmly and happily, but that, in fact, they frequently ended with the girl in tears and the parents in an angry mood. The teacher encouraged the parents to give up tutoring the girl and let her drift for a while. As often happens in such cases, it was only a matter of months before the girl was slightly above grade in her reading accomplishment. The most interesting phenomenon in this instance was, however, that the mother admitted she had never been a good reader and that she did not want her daughter to suffer from the same handicap. A father sometimes will push his sons into athletic competition and encourage them to aim at stardom, because in school he himself had failed to gain the glamour of being foremost in athletics.

Paul's father was a successful drugstore owner who had worked his way to achievement without much formal education. His lifelong desire had been to become a physician, but he had been unable to realize that aim. From early childhood it had been decreed that Paul should enter the medical profession. After completing his college courses without distinction, Paul gained admission to a medical school, but in the first semester failed in anatomy and chemistry. Investigation showed that his

[7] Margaret E. Onion, unpublished master's thesis, Eugene, Ore.: University of Oregon, 1946.

ability was in the lowest 5 per cent of his class and that his interests, measured by a relatively objective technique, were not at all those of physicians. Both tests and interviews showed that the young man's interests and abilities were in the business field. His failure released him from medical school, which probably was best for his ultimate welfare. The readjustment had been achieved, however, at the cost of years of lost effort and, more significantly, of creating in Paul a sense of personal inadequacy that will be difficult to overcome in any field of endeavor.[8]

Sometimes quite conscientious parents are unable to let their children grow up. Some mothers daily bring their youngsters to school or meet them after school in order to see to their safety. Many children who enter the first grade are not able to tie their shoes or put on their rubbers, because these things have always been done for them by their loving mothers. This phenomenon is not limited to the primary school. The same factor is perceived when the teen-age girl is not allowed to have dates and when the high-school boy is not allowed to go on an overnight hike with his classmates. Inability to release children may be seen even in college.

A college freshman, possessing the ability to do acceptable college work, had a mediocre high-school record, plus a hovering mother—who seemed to prevent his doing passing work. His former high-school principal reported that the mother had often consulted him about ways and means of the boy's getting better results. She was always initiating new plans to help her son. When he entered college, the mother had flown several hundred miles on three different occasions during one semester to see if she could not do something for him. In spite of all assistance, he failed in most of his courses. He was transferred to another college and, as on previous occasions, the mother made the original contact. After talking to the boy and gathering the data cited above, the college advisor suggested that the mother withdraw and let the boy take the initiative and the responsibility, himself. Her answer was disheartening, "I'll talk to him and see if he'll do it." The boy decided that he would like to try to enter a college in a remote corner of the state, but the mother was afraid that she would not be able to oversee his schedule and to attend to his studying when he should. It may not have been too late for the youth, but it was too late for the mother. No satisfactory solution of the problem was found.

Other errors made by parents that show direct results in school behavior are overacceptance, rejection, excessive dominance or submission, lack of consistency in discipline, and lack of objectivity in viewing the gifts and liabilities of their own children. There is, however, no one-to-

[8] Laurance Frederic Shaffer and Edward Joseph Shoben, Jr., *The Psychology of Adjustment,* 2d ed., Boston: Houghton Mifflin Company, 1956, pp. 173–174.

one relationship between such influences and the resultant behavior. For instance, an aggressive, bullying, dogmatically self-assertive child may have developed these characteristics from being overaccepted, cuddled, coddled, and pampered at home. Another child having the same behavior trends may be compensating for being rejected, ignored, and being made to toe the mark rigidly at home.

There are three ways in which information about negative home influences may be used by teachers. First, they can better understand the child if they have knowledge concerning the factors operative in the shaping of his personality. Second, they may occasionally be called upon by parents for counsel and assistance in dealing with child-raising problems that are tragically real, even though vaguely formulated. Information will provide the objectivity needed. Third, the information may afford clues to the pupil's more appropriate treatment in the school.

Favorable Home Influences Provide Clues for Treatment. Knowledge of negative home influences provides warnings as to procedures to be avoided. Knowledge of salutary home influences provides data to help in formulating objectives more clearly. One of the greatest assets of the home is the affection which many children experience. When a child is loved for what he is, he is developing a confidence that he is significant and worthy and that he can trust a friendly world. If, on the other hand, he is without this affection, he is likely to develop hostile and pessimistic views of the world and even toward himself.[9] Child development literature stresses affection as of prime importance. The role of affection is illustrated in a study in which doctors found that children raised in institutions had better appetites, slept more soundly, played better with their housemates, gained in weight more rapidly, and seemed to be more alert to things about them after the doctors ordered the nurses to spend an hour a day cuddling, fondling, and talking to each child. If the teacher will use a smile of greeting, a word of praise, an attentive ear, a pat on the back these minor items will add up to a child's feeling that he is significant and worthy in the classroom—ready to do his best.

Stability of environment is another asset to development that can only be weakly compensated for in the school. There is a planned and progressive change in the experiences which the child has in the school. Both subjects for study and teachers who lead him are typically changed at least once a year and sometimes more often. The home, on the other hand, remains much the same year after year. Even though the place of residence is changed—and this sometimes constitutes a hazard in the development of a stable personality—the parents remain much the same, year after year, as does the type of home in which the child lives. It has

[9] Lawrence K. Frank, *Personality and Culture,* Danville, Ill.: The Interstate Printers and Publishers, 1948, p. 7.

long been thought that frequent changes of residence are a hazard to children's mental health. But recently it has been suggested that perhaps maladjustment is not the result of change of residence so much as it is a function of the type of parents who move and the reason for the move. When stable parents move to follow their careers or to improve their positions, their children are well adjusted in school, make friends easily, and are not contributors to delinquency.[10] This suggests that pupils who move into a new school need not be quite so disturbed if they find there a welcoming class group and teacher.

The home contributes to wholesome development by providing him with possessions—things which are undeniably his own. The books, toys, clothes, tools, and furniture which are his, and his alone, give the child and adolescent a feeling of importance and significance that is fundamental to the building of confidence. A room of his own helps to provide a sense of privacy and personal security. It is a mistaken notion that youngsters should be taught to share everything they have. A cooperative attitude is more likely to be engendered if there are some things which are used in common by all members of the family and other things which belong definitely to the individuals in the family. Respect for the property of others is stimulated by a person's having things which are unquestionably his own. Much of the disrepect for the property rights of others that is manifest in children's stealing has been traced to the circumstance that these children do not have things which others may use only upon permission.

Not All Parents Will Cooperate. Some of the above information is of limited usefulness to the teacher. He may be able to use some of the ideas in talking and counseling with parents. Even the courageous teacher who is willing to attempt a reconstruction of the mistaken ideas of parents finds that sometimes the advice is ignored or even resented. These experiences lead to the often heard question "What can you do about it when your efforts to change parental attitudes fail?" The answer may seem like an evasion of the question: Try to provide, in your contacts with the pupil in the school, some of the lacks from which he suffers in the home. According to the teacher's code of ethics, teachers must avoid undermining the child's respect for the authority and prestige of his parents; so, without criticizing the methods or philosophy of the home, a teacher must try to convince the pupil, through verbal instruction and example, of the relative superiority of the philosophy of the school. Thus, for example, there might be some study of the merits of individual initiative versus competition, of cooperation versus fighting, and of cooperation versus the "chip-on-the-shoulder" attitude. Duties and responsibilities

[10] Alvin L. Schorr, "Families on Wheels," *Harper's Magazine*, 216:71–78, January, 1958.

can be assigned in the classroom which would tend to offset the barriers to growing up that overanxious parents impose. If a child seeks much attention, perhaps because of indulgence or rejection in the home, it would be good clinical practice to give that attention. But in the classroom there are other pupils who need attention; hence, the teacher might well explain that the pupils need to share it, so that others may also be recognized. When shyness indicates, and investigation of home factors confirm, that the child is rejected at home, the obvious role of teachers is to supply *some* of the affection and acceptance that has been denied.

School Can Compensate for Home Deficiencies. Often children can be helped in solving home difficulties, even when no actual contact with the home is made. The teacher and the school activities can afford compensations which make it easier for the child to absorb his difficulties. This does not imply that opportunities for parent-teacher contacts should be ignored; but it suggests that constructive steps can be taken when such contacts are difficult or impossible to establish.

> While the parent or parent-substitute often is an aggravating factor in the case of a maladjusted child, and while therapy might move ahead faster if the adults were also receiving therapy or counseling, *it is not necessary for the adults to be helped in order to insure successful play-therapy results.*
>
> The reader will notice that many of the reports in this book are of children who were in situations where there was little insight on the part of the adults toward a better way of helping these problem children. In very few of the cases did the adults receive treatment of any kind, and yet the children were able to become strong enough within themselves to withstand very trying conditions. It seems as though the insight and self-understanding gained by these children brought about more adequate ways of coping with their situations, and, since the tensions eased, this in turn brought about a certain change in adults.[11]

The above is pertinent even though it refers to play therapy. There are many ways of supplying the child with compensating satisfactions, giving him freedom, showing him how to make class contributions, and encouraging his unique creativity. There are many contributing factors in the establishment of a problem; so too there are many avenues which may be taken as a solution to a problem.

Classroom teachers can provide affection. A little third-grade girl who was making no contribution to class discussion was observed one day. She did not talk with her neighbors. Even during recess she remained quietly in her chair. There was some written work to be handed in; a few

---

[11] Virginia Mae Axline, *Play Therapy,* Boston: Houghton Mifflin Company, 1947, p. 68.

students submitted it early, and then, in a surge, the remaining pupils brought their work to the desk. The girl joined the throng and reached out to put her paper on the desk; the teacher also reached out and put her arm about the girl's waist, and at the same time she continued her conversation with another pupil. When she finished, she turned to the little girl and pulled her closer, remarking, "That's a very neat bit of work you have done." At first the girl pulled away, but in a moment she bent her head to one side and laid it against the teacher's shoulder. Without knowing anything about home conditions, one was aware that the girl needed just such spontaneous expression of affection. It need not be assumed that affection must be shown in a physical caress. Merely paying a child individual attention will make him aware of an attitude of affection.

Teachers can help make up the deficit of not having property. Materials can be assigned to individuals; it can be understood that books are temporarily the property of a particular individual; a child's assigned place at a table or a desk can be understood to be his own. Group pride in the classroom can be fostered by encouraging pupils to attend to its decoration and neatness.

Stability of environment, in the sense of meeting few strange people, cannot be arranged for in ordinary class routines; but there can be a sensitiveness to the child's problems. A word of comment from a teacher who knows a pupil to the new teacher to whom the child is going and a comment to already oriented students as to the desirability of meeting the new student with a warm friendliness will contribute to the feeling of being accepted.

By way of summary, the teacher can help students who suffer emotional deprivation or frustration in the home by providing an antidote. Knowing the conditions that tend to stimulate evidences of maladjustment will help to disclose what contrasting stimulation should be provided. It is possible so to treat the child that the school environment in some way compensates for the deficiencies of the home. Admittedly, this is only a palliative, but palliatives can help one endure pain while he is making the growth which will enable him to live with his handicaps.

USING PUPILS AS RESOURCES

Peer Culture and Adjustment. One of the more pervasive problems of mental hygiene, and an outstanding objective of education, is that of social adjustment. The National Association of Secondary-school Principals has asserted that one of the imperative needs of youth is that "All youth need to develop respect for other persons, to grow in their insight into ethical values and principles, and to be able to live and work cooperatively with others."[12] If this be true, and few would have the temerity to question it, then a knowledge of what one's peers think of him is basic to the understanding of a given pupil. Peer relationships are of importance not only in terms of immediate adjustment but also in terms of the practice they afford for later mature and productive citizenship. The teacher cannot be satisfied with his own evaluation of peer adjust-

FIG. 5. What needs of adolescents are being met by peer-group activities? Are mental and physical health needs being approached? What are some other appropriate developmental activities that might be pursued? What should be the role of adults?

ments, simply because adult values and adult views of behavior differ from those of younger people.

Apparently, one of the deepest of adolescent needs is the need to be supported and approved by his peers. The actual values of the peer group change and mature as the boys and girls grow older, and gradually they lose some of their power, partly because the youngsters have learned more about thinking for themselves, partly because they have already achieved a secure place in their own group, and partly because peer values are becoming merged with adult values instead of being in opposition to them.[13]

[12] *Planning for American Youth*, Washington: National Association of Secondary-school Principals, 1944, p. 43.

[13] Luella Cole, *Psychology of Adolescence*, 4th ed., New York: Holt, Rinehart and Winston, Inc., 1954, p. 263.

In view of this evolving set of relationships it is advisable for the teacher to supplement his observations with those of the youngster's peers.

Obtaining Peer Evaluations. A view of the evaluations placed on classmates can be achieved by the technique of directed, purposeful listening —so highly recommended earlier in the chapter. The remarks which are made in the presence of the individual, as well as those which are made "behind his back," are informative. The tone of voice in which others address the person being studied, the nicknames which are applied to him, and the nature of the questions which are directed his way are all clues to the evaluations others place on him. What is heard must be interpreted. It cannot be accepted solely in terms of what is said. Questions such as the following will help orient directed listening: What are the motivations of the individual who made the remark? Under what circumstances was the remark made? Is there a repetitive nature, or constant theme, revealed? Do the comments seem to represent a consensus of many students? Do the observations, in the teacher's opinion, seem to be justified?

Estimates of evaluation by one's peers may also be acquired from directed observation. The frequency with which a student is elected to office, the number of times he is appointed chairman of a group, the role of leadership (or the kind of follower he is) apart from formal elections, and the kind of response typically made to his suggestions all provide clues to an understanding of pupil evaluation of others. Observations may also be made of the person-to-person relationships which exist. Which individuals "pair off"? What kinds of persons spontaneously seek the company of the individual being observed? Is he on the fringe of the spontaneous groups or is he an integral part of them? What kinds of information do others seek when they question him? These questions and others of a similar nature will provide further insights into peer evaluations.

Adjustment inventories, used with due caution and as suggestive of clues—taking individual items on the questionnaire as the starting point for interviews—can assist teachers in evaluating peer adjustment.[14] It is important to go back of single items, such as the pupil's never seeking the advice of classmates or his preference for working alone, and to analyze the reasons why the response is given. Inventories may be used, before there is an opportunity to listen and observe, for obtaining an early clue to the matter of peer adjustment, and thus difficulties may be anticipated. Sociometry, which is the plotting of interpersonal attractiveness (to be discussed in Chapter 10), is an easily applied and highly informative technique for assessing peer evaluations.

---

[14] Adjustment inventories are misused if too much is expected of them (see Denis Baron and Harold W. Bernard, *Evaluation Techniques for Classroom Teachers*, New York: McGraw-Hill Book Company, Inc., 1958, pp. 127–133).

BETTER UNDERSTANDING THROUGH PROFESSIONAL EDUCATION

College Courses. Many professional courses are offered, in typical teacher education institutions, which pave the way to a better understanding of children. Representative courses conducive to such understanding may include Educational Psychology, Mental Hygiene, Psychology of Childhood, Psychology of Adolescence, The Education of Exceptional Children, Pupil Guidance, Student Counseling, Measurement in Education, and Curriculum Development. Each course of this kind carries a particular emphasis which broadens the teacher's view of the many-faceted problem of personality development.

There are two shortcomings in college courses as an avenue for understanding children. One is that too often the verbal descriptions fall short of giving a clear conception of the unique, living individual. The generalizations and stress on typical situations fail to answer the difficult question "What shall be done for individuals?" This shortcoming is intensified by the fact that the courses are often taken when the student has had only limited experience in working with children. It sometimes happens that an experienced teacher repeats a course he has had as an undergraduate. He may then exclaim, "My, there are so many helpful suggestions in this course. I cannot see how I previously overlooked such items."

The extreme youth of the science of psychology constitutes a second shortcoming. Whereas medicine, physics, chemistry, and mathematics have histories which stretch back through centuries, psychology, as a science, is slightly more than half a century old. One is amazed to find the startling contrasts which exist between a book on child psychology written in 1915 and one published today. The change and, we hope, progress are remarkable, but it must be admitted that there are still many unanswered questions.[15] This situation makes it imperative that teachers devote at least part of their time to studying contemporary developments.

Two things can be done to offset the handicap of lack of experience. One is to supplement academic study with contact with children—talk with them, play with them, watch them. The other is to keep one's basic texts so that they can be reviewed with specific problems in mind after accepting a teaching position.

In-service Education. In-service education is even more pertinent to gaining understanding of pupils than are college courses, because those who participate are currently having direct and individual experience with youngsters. What is being learned from leaders and the discus-

[15] M. F. Ashley Montagu, *The Direction of Human Development*, New York: Harper & Brothers, 1955, pp. 5–8.

sion which takes place in the study group can be weighed against immediate personal experience. There are several forms which in-service training may take. Where highly trained specialists are available in metropolitan centers, these specialists organize study groups and give teachers information relative to their particular aims and techniques for accomplishing their purposes. This would appear to be almost an obligation, since in many instances teachers have to help execute these same techniques.[16] Even where the specialists work directly with pupils (for instance, in a reading clinic), the teacher must still work with the pupil in other phases of schoolwork; therefore the teacher should know what is going on, so that he and the specialists will not be working at cross purposes.

Many universities make off-campus classes available to groups of teachers, either within a town or in adjacent towns. An expert from the university outlines the work, lectures, suggests pertinent readings, and sometimes makes a professional library available. Evening classes on the campus are widely offered to teachers within commuting distance. Such in-service training is additionally attractive, for credit is often given, counting toward degrees or special certificates. In many such classes it has been found that there is a marked contrast in the understanding and interest of teachers-on-the-job and teachers-in-preparation. The former see the wisdom of theory, generalizations, the statement of tendencies, and the existence of probabilities, whereas the latter seek specific answers to specific problems—an impossibility in view of the wide variation of details in apparently similar cases.

Teachers in small school systems may not have opportunities for group in-service education. A substitute is available in the form of correspondence courses. Here, again, owing to the fact that the teacher is daily working with pupils, the courses come alive, because they can more readily be related to current experiences. Correspondence courses possess the double advantage of (1) being financially economical and (2) requiring that the teacher do the work and hence the learning.

Another form of in-service training is that of workshops. These are often held just prior to the official opening of school (or on occasion school may be suspended for a few days in order to devote the time to the workshop). Teachers and specialists engage in study groups, the teachers being expected to give as well as to receive. Often an experimental, or demonstration, situation is provided that adds meaning to the

[16] Daniel A. Prescott, *The Child in the Educative Process*, New York: McGraw-Hill Book Company, Inc., 1957, describes how one in-service-education program works. The teacher who is interested in the improvement of mental health will find many helpful suggestions in the descriptions of other teachers' experiences as they improved their understanding of children through in-service education.

project. A sample program of a workshop in which all the teachers in a county participated for several days and which centered around the general topic, Improving the Mental Hygiene Values of a School, included the following subtopics:

> Reciprocal Relations between Reading and Mental Health
> The Teacher's Influence on Classroom Atmosphere
> Mental Ill-health Symptoms in the Classroom
> Improvement of Social (Peer) Adjustment
> The Teacher's Personal Mental Health
> Working with the Home for Better Mental Health
> Physical Health and Mental Health
> Using Sociograms and Adjustment Inventories
> Play Therapy, Art Therapy, and Creative Writing
> How Emotions Affect the Learning Process
> How Teachers Can Aid Each Other in Solving Problems
> The Unit Approach and Child Development
> Discipline and Mental Health
> Community Resources for Mental Health

The teachers chose topics that were of interest to them and worked out answers to questions which were appropriate to the topic, under the guidance of clinical psychologists, college professors, and psychiatrists— each of whom directed one of the groups.

Professional Experimentation. One source of information which leads to better understanding of children and which is available to every teacher is personal experiment. The teacher can, for instance, experiment with free play, art work, creative writing, and the use of personality inventories in an attempt to achieve more complete understanding of his pupils. He can experiment with the making of a case study, with a view to diagnosis and remediation as the outcome. A teacher will find it stimulating to take such books as Virginia Mae Axline's *Play Therapy*, Daniel A. Prescott's *The Child in the Educative Process*, Clark E. Moustakas's *The Teacher and the Child*, Edmund Bullis's *Human Relations in the Classroom*, and Julia Weber's *My Country School Diary* and to apply some of the techniques described to the study of his own pupils.

Experimentation will be additionally informative and stimulating if it is a group project. Two or more teachers can, without expert aid, apply some analytic and therapeutic approach, discuss the results each obtains and thereby achieve many constructive viewpoints. One experiment so fruitful to the group is to gather the information which goes into a typical case study of a child with problems and, then, to discuss a program for remediation.

Understanding children through personal and group experimentation and study should, of course, be supplemented with the reading of professional literature. Maximum results will be obtained from such reading if it is planned and organized. Attention should be concentrated on a particular problem or subject, so that various views will be gained.

SUMMARY

A school program designed for promoting mental health is based on certain fundamental ideas: (1) behavior is caused, (2) misbehavior is a symptom of conflict or tension, and (3) we must get at the causes and deal with them.

All children encounter some difficulty. Imperfect adjustment is normal, and teachers must be fully aware of the fact that not all children are problems—they all need help and understanding, but they should not be regarded as cases. The repeated manifestation of difficulties and the multiplication of symptoms are what indicate abnormality.

Studying the home may reveal the causes of many disturbing symptoms. Even when it is impractical to work directly with the home, the child can be given emotional release through engaging in interesting activities, he can be led into activities from which he can gain a sense of accomplishment, and he can be accepted by the teacher so that his sense of social security will be at least partially improved.

Many data helpful for understanding children can be taken from school records. Such information would include standardized test data, record of past scholastic experience, anecdotal reports of typical phases of behavior, and the evaluations formulated by previous teachers.

The teacher's understanding cannot be complete without including a view of the child as he appears in the eyes of his peers. Techniques for gaining this insight are listening to the interpersonal remarks of pupils in the class, observation specifically directed to the matter of social adaptation, the construction of sociograms, and the interpretation of the questions on some kind of adjustment inventory.

Many avenues toward the understanding of children are opened through professional education. Chief among these avenues are courses taken while one is preparing to be a teacher, in-service-training courses, participation in workshops, and correspondence courses. If these formal agencies are not available, there still remains the possibility of engaging in individual and group study and experimentation.

STUDY AND DISCUSSION EXERCISES

1. Why is there such a great temptation to be concerned with symptoms? Why is it so necessary to understand the causes of the symptoms?

2. Since conflict is normal, should an attempt be made to remove obstacles from the child's course of growth?

3. If negative home influences cannot be eliminated, what is there left for the teacher to do?

4. What steps do you advise for making professional study more functional?

5. What are some precautions which must be observed if the teacher is going to engage in personal experimentation?

SUGGESTED ADDITIONAL READINGS

Buhler, Charlotte, and others, *Childhood Problems and the Teacher*, New York: Holt, Rinehart and Winston, Inc., 1952. 372 pp.

Theoretical considerations provide the basis for helpful approaches to children with problems. Numerous case studies are used to illustrate fundamental principles.

Cutts, Norma E., and Nicholas Moseley, *Teaching the Disorderly Pupil in Elementary and Secondary School*, New York: Longmans, Green & Co., Inc., 1957. 170 pp.

General suggestions for improving class discipline are followed by discussion of specific problems, such as those presented by the physically handicapped child, the scholastic misfit, and children from broken homes.

Gorlow, Leon, and Walter Katkovsky, *Readings in the Psychology of Adjustment*, New York: McGraw-Hill Book Company, Inc., 1959, pp. 237–283.

This group of four readings deals with experiences in infancy, cultural factors, social class status, and family life as determinants of behavior.

Hymes, James L., Jr., *Behavior and Misbehavior*, Englewood Cliffs, N.J.: Prentice-Hall, Inc., 1955. 140 pp.

The author stresses the fact that bad behavior is the attempt of the individual to adjust—to relieve tensions. The emphasis is strongly upon the necessity for the teacher's getting at causes.

Olson, Willard C., and William W. Wattenberg, "The Role of the School in Mental Health" in *Mental Health in Modern Education*, 54th Yearbook, Part II, National Society for the Study of Education, Chicago: University of Chicago Press, 1955, pp. 99–124.

The authors describe basic mental hygiene factors as background for the wise use of sociometry, anecdotal records, observations, and projective technique.

CHAPTER 7

PERSONALITY PROBLEMS IN THE CLASSROOM

Adjustment or maladjustment is dependent upon the extent to which fundamental needs of human beings are met or on the way to being met. Hence, a summary of the basic causes of maladjustment is felt to be advisable, in order that teachers may realize more fully the sequential development of problem behavior. It is not enough to suggest ready-made approaches to specific problems. Each case has its unique nuances. The teacher who wishes to be a beneficent influence for mental health should know that all deviant behavior stems from a *variety of causes*. How better understanding of pupils with personality problems may be achieved and suggestions for helping them are considered in this chapter.

TYPICAL PERSONALITY PROBLEMS

The Teacher Learns about Tom. The following description, largely in the words of the classroom teacher who studied the case, illustrates many of the basic causes of maladjustment. The child concerned, as is true in a typical situation, manifested many symptoms of stress instead of resorting to but one disturbing behavior.

The first child whose name I learned this year was Tom. His behavior was different from that of others in the group. When we toured the school that first morning I explained the purpose and mechanism of the fire alarm. When the alarm was set off as an illustration, Tom rushed to me, threw his arms around my waist and hid his face in terror. It took some time to reassure him. The next day I showed a film. After the picture Tom told me he was going to be sick. I rushed him to the toilet and stood by while he tried without avail to vomit. When we talked of it afterward he told me that he was always sick when taken to a show. His medical certificate showed that he had a sinus allergy. . . .

He snorted almost continuously, despite my appeals for consideration of others. His mother informed me later that she had told him he would drive the teacher mad if he made a noise with his nose in school; and it seemed that he was having a good try at it. Children asked to have their seats removed from beside him and I did not blame them. Finally, I decided to ignore the habit but this required a great deal of fortitude.

His behavior was most immature. He was unable to concentrate on any subject for even a short time. Even for stories he had no interest, and his writing and drawing papers were always a mass of scribbles. He was solitary in his play habits out of doors. He would spend his time racing up and down the playground, often asking the teacher on duty to see him run. In group play in the classroom the children complained constantly that he knocked over whatever they were building. He talked out uncontrolledly at all times and his speech was very difficult to understand. He did take one interest and that was when we talked of nature. He would bring to school grasshoppers, caterpillars, and other specimens and for these he showed understanding and great care in handling. He would not allow any of his classmates to approach his treasures too closely. When they did so a fight would result.

When I gave the group an intelligence test I found that Tom was unable to concentrate on it and despite my encouragement he thumbed through the pages putting marks on them wherever his fancy indicated. One exception was recognition of lefts and rights. This page he did complete with a high score. I gave the test over, with him alone, a few days later. I found that under constant encouragement he finished it but the effort seemed to make him very tired. His indicated I.Q. was 92 and, as before, his score on the recognition of lefts and rights was high. I tested this capacity and he could tell me without difficulty which was his left and his right hand and on which side of a car the steering wheel was located.

After about six weeks of school we interviewed all the parents of our first-graders. When Tom's mother came she revealed her anxiety about his adjustment. She was very apologetic and was very sensitive because her neighbors sought to compare Tom's progress with that of their own children. She told me that she had had two children who had died in infancy or early childhood and that she had then adopted Tom—against the advice of her friends. About a year later she had had another baby who died in its first year. The following year she had a daughter, who is still alive and is two years younger than Tom.

Tom did not talk until the age of three. At four and a half years his speech was still largely unintelligible to a stranger. As he grew older Tom became very impertinent to his mother. He treated his sister very badly, playing all manner of tricks on her—nipping, biting, and scratching her until she would be quite overcome. Tom's mother would take as much of this behavior as she could stand and then would chastise him soundly. For a few days it would appear as if he could not do enough to make amends.

His mother had tried to understand the situation. She had read books on how to bring up children correctly but had always found herself up against his cruelty toward his sister. She felt that she could not stand by and watch . . . so she had usually resorted to chastisement. She had considered consulting a psychologist but had been discouraged by her husband, who preferred to shut his eyes . . . in the hope that Tom would grow out of it.

We carried on until November and by that time I realized that his I.Q. was higher than that indicated by the group test. He revealed this fact in many ways but he still refused to cooperate in our class lessons in any way. I decided to interview his mother again. I suggested to her that a psychologist could really help us to understand Tom's difficulties. She said she had been thinking of the matter herself and decided that she would make an early appointment. She came to school after her consultation to tell me of the result.

Tom's I.Q. was revealed by the Stanford-Binet test to be 115 but he was suffering from a feeling of rejection, which had begun at a very early age. He had tried by various means to claim the attention of his mother, developing habits such as bed-wetting and refusal to eat the food served to him. The psychologist considered the allergy to be another bid for attention and certainly the worst of his snorting has since ceased.[1]

The treatment was to be a complete change in the attitude of the mother and she has worked hard to achieve this end. All punishment was to be done by the father. The sister was sent to a nursery school while Tom stayed at home in the mornings for some time and received his mother's undivided attention. In the afternoons he came to school. The situation improved almost from the very beginning. The habit of bed-wetting was discontinued almost at once. I felt encouraged to apply a little pressure in the field of learning. I began to insist that he remain in his seat and attempt to do a small part of what the others were doing. I found that he came to resent this treatment on my part and he began to show it in various ways. Twice he wet the floor when asked to copy a bit of writing. At other times he would rise from his seat while I was working with another group, sharpen his pencil and poke the other children in the neck with it. . . . He would resort to biting and scratching until I felt that I had to spend the better part of the day keeping him out of trouble. In addition he began to steal little articles from my desk and the desks of the children. I realized that Tom was not yet ready to be asked to concentrate in any way.

Matters at home, however, had continued to show slow improvement. I informed his mother of the latest development and told her that I thought it best to give Tom every freedom in class that did not inter-

---

[1] Some students may be interested in reading Hyman Miller and Dorothy W. Baruch, *The Practice of Psychosomatic Medicine*, New York: McGraw-Hill Book Company, Inc., 1956, 196 pp. Psychosomatic conditions are illustrated in the occurrence of allergy.

fere with the other children and that I would not expect any scholastic achievement from him until he seemed ready to work at his own desire. I let him spend most of his time for the next two months in our play corner. During this time he had the company of a new child who . . . was also slow to mature socially. It was most disturbing to the lessons of others but the day came when the two of them tired of almost constant play and were glad to have a reading lesson. Tom's interest in reading has grown remarkably in the last two months. Last week in his achievement test he scored a 1.9 grade placement. He can count fairly well but still refuses to concentrate for long on anything that requires writing. I know he is capable of writing fairly well as I have seen when he wanted to please me specially; but for the most part he gives up after the first few words. Although I encourage him I do not make a point of his completing any given amount. . . . He can take part in an organized game reasonably well and he will remain seated during class lessons. His mother has helped to increase his prestige with the other children by supplying little treats for the class in Tom's name.

I have been considering the matter of his promotion to the second grade. Although he still has not developed good working habits the progress which he has made in reading leads me to believe that they may develop shortly. I also know that he is eager to go on to the second grade and I feel that he should be allowed to continue at his own rate without any repetition of what he has already learned.

This account of Tom shows many of the basic causes of maladjustment and also indicates the variety of behaviors that may result from disturbing influences. His feeling of insecurity was revealed in his conduct in novel situations. He ran to the teacher for physical protection and revealed his anxiety by becoming ill at the showing of a film. According to the psychologist's report, his allergy represented an attempt to run away from what, to him, was an unpleasant situation. His inability to concentrate reflected in his aggressiveness toward his sister and toward his classmates. A conflict in motives is revealed in the teacher's account of the mother's discipline, "Then it would appear as if he could not do enough to make amends." Conflict is further indicated in his sporadic attempts to please the teacher by doing his work.

The teacher's role in helping Tom embraces the following: (1) looking beyond the symptoms for an understanding of causes, (2) acceptance of Tom for what he is now, (3) exercising patience with the slow processes of growth—avoiding prodding which to Tom indicates nonacceptance, (4) helping Tom develop skills which will gradually generate self-confidence, (5) praising Tom for any help and consideration he can be led to give to others, (6) capitalizing on his interests by providing appropriate materials and encouraging him to share his knowledge with classmates, (7) attempting to find peers with whom he can work in small subgroups, and (8) working with parents to develop mutual understanding.

Uniform Success Is Unlikely. Teachers have often asked how it is that the cases they read about turn out so beautifully, such as the apparent improvement in Tom's conduct. Their own experiences do not allow them to report such complete and uniform success. Actually, even in clinics and in classrooms where teachers are well trained and have the help of specialists, there is frequent failure. It is probable that the cases one reads are reported *because* they were accompanied by success. Teachers may be comforted to know that others do fail, that failure to cure does not mean that the situation has not been improved, and, furthermore, that optimistic faith in the possibility of future healthy growth for children is quite as realistic as recognizing that obstacles are often difficult to surmount.

Physical Bases of Misbehavior Limit Classroom Success. Sometimes there is little or nothing that can be done for a disturbed child except to endure him. There are sometimes physical causes of aberrant behavior that will only have a psychological burden added if teachers become desperately demanding.

> *The aftereffects* of some illnesses may include quite specific kinds of behavior. Particularly disruptive is the overactive, aggressive behavior that sometimes, though far from always, follows scarlet fever, measles, diphtheria, sleeping sickness, and some other diseases. The individual is actually unable to keep quiet. He runs, charges violently into others, throws himself about, and attacks other people and their belongings. This behavior is *compulsive*, that is, entirely beyond voluntary control. . . . We've known cases that disrupted a succession of public and private schools for four or five years before the cause was discovered. *Brain injuries,* especially those received at birth, may also cause compulsive overactivity. *Deficient development of some part of the nervous system* may make a child aggressive and overactive. It may also result in mental deficiency. Some authorities now believe a defective central nervous system is associated with *schizophrenia* in children.[2]

Many times a physical disability is so apparent that we almost automatically make allowances for the child. Examples might include the crippled child, the pupil with cleft palate, the youngster with heavy thick glasses or glasses with one opaque lens. In other instances teachers may have been warned that the pupil is subject to epileptic seizures, that allowance must be made for some cardiac condition, or that malnutrition renders the child susceptible to irritability, restlessness, or fatigue.

[2] Norma E. Cutts and Nicholas Moseley, *Teaching the Disorderly Pupil in Elementary and Secondary School,* New York: Longmans, Green & Co., Inc., 1957, p. 51.

Chronic Psychological Conditions. The improvement of school situations which might aggravate misbehavior does not necessarily mean that some basic frustrations the pupil has experienced have been removed. It might be that teachers have attempted to bolster a pupil's feeling of security by praise and seeing that tasks are designed so that accomplishment results, but this may simply be a palliative for pain which persists at home. The absence or imminent absence of a father (or mother) who declares that he wants a divorce or threatens to leave home produces enough pain and confusion that nothing can be done in the school to remove the basic causes of aggression (or seclusiveness). About all that can be done is to relieve the pain temporarily in the school by acceptance, compassion, and directing the pupil into productive pursuits that lead to some self-gratification.

At times there is no present aggravating circumstance but the pupil is still fighting against the insecurity felt at some earlier time. Hank B. is an example. He had been shifted from home to home several times by the time he was in the fifth grade. But in the fourth he was finally back with his father who was fundamentally a stable and devoted father and husband. His new mother understood the difficulties Hank had met and was admirably tolerant of his odd and at times violent behavior. His fourth grade teacher had understood the source of Hank's difficulty . . . but his wild use of paints, aggressive behavior (pushing, tripping, pinching) and grimacing were nevertheless disturbing. Hank could barely sit still while the teacher kept her hand on his shoulder. While others were listening to a story Hank kept poking at the children who sat close to him. Some of these tried to ignore him but one boy struck back and the teacher had to seat them apart. It seemed that Hank, knowing the teacher was trying to be patient, kept testing the limits of her permissiveness. No perceptible improvement was noted in the fourth grade. The next year, in the fifth grade, Hank's aggressiveness had decreased but he still was unable to concentrate effectively. In one forty minute period he worked only for three or four minutes; he gazed off into space, he went for a drink twice, sharpened his pencil twice (going to the sharpener by the longest route possible). He chewed his pencil, twisted a lock of his hair. He examined a cap gun which he took from his pocket. When the teacher saw this (possession of play guns was prohibited) she took it from him and it accidently went off. The teacher was startled but noting the alarm on the boy's face she said nothing. She later reported that she felt his fright should not be compounded by a lecture or punishment. During this period Hank was supposed to be working with a group but was so isolated from them and so inattentive that he did not even miss them when they went into the hall for a conference. Thus, in the fifth grade, he was no longer distractingly aggressive, he did not seem to be deliberately testing the teacher's patience, he did not remain entirely aloof, his aimless movement about the room had decreased but he was still unable to do concerted work. Perhaps if the salutary home and school influences can continue, Hank will make further improvement but the past is too recent to expect that a few months of excellent treatment will have resulted in complete metamorphosis.

SOME CAUSES OF MALADJUSTMENT

There are always reasons for the individual's behaving as he does. Sometimes causes are obvious, sometimes they can be located through analytic study, and sometimes they are so obscure that it is difficult, if not impossible, to determine the source. In this section, some of the more common causes of maladjustment will be examined, with a view to their understanding and more successful treatment.

Causes Manifest in Feelings of Insecurity. A feeling of insecurity may be described as an attitude or conviction on the part of the individual that he is unwanted, that he is rejected by those with whom he comes in contact, that he is incompetent, and that there are factors in his environment that threaten his safety and well-being. High-school pupils who hesitate to state their own opinions on matters for fear of condemnation or ridicule, children who reveal a dread of launching some new project, and adults who are tense when meeting people are giving evidence of feelings of insecurity. Such individuals do not "feel at home" in any situation. They wait for others to chart the way and, even then, may hesitate to follow for fear of being criticized. Many of the pupils who refuse or hesitate to recite, even though their information may be adequate, present a common manifestation of feelings of insecurity as well as of feelings of inferiority. The above-cited case of Tom indicates such feelings at many points, but his case adds to the foregoing list the loss of appetite and restlessness (his inability to concentrate). Enuresis and poor sleep habits may accompany feelings of insecurity, but it must be remembered that the symptoms described may also be indicative of other deprivations of basic needs.

It must be realized that feelings of insecurity are *not causes;* they are, in fact, indications of factors that cause the feelings. Many causes of insecurity are to be found in the child's early years. There are even some who believe that children may be born neurotic, because of the child's sharing a "common endocrine pool" with his mother during pregnancy. Her tension produces secretions which in turn stimulate endocrine changes in the fetus.[3] After birth, one's parents normally are glad to supply both the child's organic and psychological needs. They feed him,

[3] M. F. Ashley Montagu, "Constitutional and Prenatal Factors in Infant and Child Health," in William E. Martin and Celia B. Stendler (eds.), *Readings in Child Development*, New York: Harcourt, Brace & World, Inc., 1954, pp. 18–19.

keep him warm and dry, and comfort him in times of stress. They rejoice in his successes and sympathize with him in his failures. They show their approval by praising his activities. They find in many instances evidences of his vast superiority to other children. The consequence is that he knows he is loved, wanted, and accepted, and he grows up feeling secure.

On the other hand, parents sometimes feel that he was born at an inopportune time, they may feel that caring for a child interferes with their own enjoyment of life, or they may feel that he is unworthy of them as their child when they compare him with the beauty, intelligence, and vigor of other babies. Often the parents recognize these feelings and their basic feeling of rejection for the child is overcompensated. They overaccept the child, they force themselves to fondle and praise him, but the child is not fooled and he still senses the rejection.

Such factors in the etiology of feelings of insecurity may persist as active influences in the grade- and high-school years. These might include harsh demands and remarks; severe and sometimes cruel punishment; demands which are inappropriate with the child's developmental level; lack of sympathy in times of illness, pain, or stress; and even direct statements that the child is a hampering influence. Other continuing influences are the bickering and quarreling of the parents, a desire on the part of insecure parents to compensate through the child, or rejection by the larger community because of race, religion, or mode of dress.

Obviously the removal of feelings of insecurity is a long-time process, starting with an understanding of the basic causes. Therapy should, of course, begin in the home, but when this is not possible the case should still not be deemed impossible of improvement. Teachers may take an interest in the child, an interest that will give him the assurance that there is *someone* who is interested in him and on whom he can depend. Opportunities for giving deserved praise should be actively sought. The reprehensible practices of shaming, ridiculing, and personal criticism should be carefully avoided. Opportunities for the release of pent-up feelings should be provided. These might well include drawing, writing, working with tools, untrammeled play, and personal interviews. There should be an encouragement for the child to develop personal skills that will replace his feelings of insecurity with a well-founded feeling of competence. It makes little difference what these skills are, whether they be academic, artistic, athletic, social, or concerned with the maintenance of personal appearance. Just as the basic causes of insecurity tend to spread into many areas of behavior, so do the feelings of confidence generated in a specific area tend to spread to other fields of activity.

Causes Manifest in Feelings of Inferiority. Alfred Adler originally formulated a concept that is at present widely used in an attempt to understand deviating behavior.[4] Briefly, his idea was that a powerful motivational force in the life of an individual was to compensate for real or imagined deficiencies or defects. Beginning early in life when the individual is entirely dependent on others for all his satisfactions, there is a struggle for power, independence, and superiority. Inability to satisfy this desire for power and independence over a period of time results in what is popularly known as the *inferiority complex.* Whether or not we subscribe to the belief that this drive to power is a natural part of the motivation of every individual, it is evident that there are many who suffer to a hampering degree from a lack of confidence, marked self-consciousness, and feelings of incompetence. A well-adjusted person, no doubt, lacks confidence and is self-conscious *in some situations;* but in a maladjusted person evidences of feelings of inferiority are shown in a major portion of his behavior. In the extreme case, symptoms of the feeling of inferiority are many; they include the conviction that others are criticizing him, the tendency to avoid meeting or being with others, the handicap of easily becoming embarrassed, projection on others of his own deficiencies or errors, and an inclination to avoid novel situations. In many cases inferiority may be indicated by compensating behavior in the form of exhibitionism or of sporadic attempts to dominate some of the situations in which the subject finds himself. Attention-getting behavior on the part of school children—making noises with the mouth, feet, or fingers; making faces or grimacing; coughing; pestering others; or being disobedient—may in many instances give evidence of this hampering feeling.

Feelings of inferiority are often vague and general. However, specific handicaps or real defects may, in some cases, be the origin of a feeling that diffuses into all areas of life. Many children, nevertheless, who do have handicaps do not suffer these feelings. It is safe to say that it is not the liability but rather the view that is taken of it that is the significant contributing factor.[5] Even the crippled child must be given the impression that he is wanted and accepted. Whether or not the child has some handicap, it is necessary for him to be accepted. *It is imperative that unfavorable comparisons between him and his peers and siblings should be avoided.* Disapproval of the child expressed in crossness, nagging, shaming, or scolding gives impetus to the development of feelings of inferiority. Remarks such as "You dummy" or "You ornery brat" can lead a child to feel *and act* that way.

Secondary-school teachers should realize that adolescence is a critical

[4] Alfred Adler, *The Practice and Theory of Individual Psychology,* New York: Harcourt, Brace & World, Inc., 1924.

[5] William M. Cruickshank (ed.), *Psychology of Exceptional Children and Youth,* Englewood Cliffs, N.J.: Prentice-Hall, Inc., 1955, pp. 22–26.

time in the development of feelings of inferiority. Unless the growing person has been intellectually and emotionally prepared for the onset of puberty (with information included as to the wide differences in age when the physical changes take place), he or she may be confused and disturbed by changes in contour, voice, the development of breasts and genitals, and the growth of hair in the pubic areas. To these physical changes must be added the problems of enlarging his world of acquaintances, the world of expanding activities, and the world of economic responsibility. Although his body is of mature size, or nearing it, laws and mores prevent his entering the working world, they delay his marriage, and they prevent his taking part in pursuits in which he sees adults engaged. Adults can see that all these restrictions are working out to his ultimate advantage, but to the adolescent himself they often seem to be an indication of personal inferiority. He is likely to point out disturbing comparisons. He tells his parents about *some* of his peers who have greater freedom. He points out instances of *some* of his pals who have quit school. He describes the jobs that *some* of his friends have been privileged to take. The situation of parents and teachers is made more difficult by the fact that to an extent he is justified in his arguments. Yet unless the problem is objectively and intelligently handled, the outcome may be an intensification of the adolescent's feelings of inferiority.

Removing or modifying the causes of inferiority feelings might include acceptance of the individual as he now is, avoidance of comparisons, praise and reward for accomplishment. Special attention should be devoted to finding some excuse for expressing appreciation and approbation. This would include scaling schoolwork to the abilities and background of the individual student, seeing to it that there is a more equitable distribution of the experiences of success and failure, seeking the development of skills which contribute to ego strength, and giving the developing pupil opportunities for self-determination that are in accord with his capacity.

Group discussion among adolescents will help them to understand their common problems much more clearly than will an "inspiring" lecture by an adult. Such group discussions can lead them to see that their problems, which they felt were so individual and personal, are shared in some manner by their peers. Learning that others of their age are having similar difficulties will help them to avoid a feeling of personal inferiority. As a matter of fact, adolescents—if they are but given a chance to exercise their ability—should and frequently do have the ability to perceive problems in a much more mature light than was formerly thought possible.

Causes Manifest in Feelings of Hostility. Feelings of hostility are a major factor in some types of maladjustment. Neurotic anxiety springs in large measure from hostile impulses of various kinds.[6] The individual senses the injustice of his own feelings of hostility and is concerned lest his impulses be revealed in action. In young children hostility is directly expressed in behaviors that are irritating to parents and teachers. Though it is probable that, in some instances, a child's striking or pinching a younger sibling is merely a matter of experimentation or curiosity, it is also possible that these actions may be an expression of hostility. Children who are excessively aggressive on the playground, resorting to name calling and fighting, may be giving evidence of the existence of such feelings. Cruelty to animals, which in some cases is due to inexperience, may at times represent a somewhat disguised manifestation of hostility—the perpetrator knowing that the animal is helpless to resist. Hostility may be further disguised by attacks on inanimate objects. Thus, the destruction of school property (writing on desks, carving initials, breaking windows) is often an indication of hostility which the individual himself does not recognize.

The causes of feelings of hostility are similar to those back of other feelings which hamper facile adjustment. Remember, a similar situation for three different children may result in three different responses—apparent inferiority, hostility, or insecurity. The treatment the child receives at the hands of adults is a prime factor in the explanation of these feelings. Parents whose own insecurity and selfishness make it difficult for them to accept the responsibility of parenthood cannot show the warm affection that might serve as an antidote for such maldevelopment. Preference for another child and comparisons that belittle the perplexed child are problems known to generate feelings of hostility. Lack of consistency in the treatment of a child is considered by some psychiatrists to be more harmful than treatment that is consistently harsh or unjust. Parents who resist the child's natural and admirable desire to grow up may arouse hostility, even though the resistance is well-intentioned as a protective measure. Interference with the choice of companions, laughing at immature choices of activities or possessions, and criticism of athletic, social, or academic interests are ways of generating hostile feelings.

All too often our futile approach to hostility is to reflect it in kind. There seems to be a conviction on the part of both parents and teachers that treatment should consist of making the hostility so unpleasant that it will no longer be expressed. While they may be successful in inhibiting the expression—often it may merely be a matter of delaying the expression until it breaks forth in some criminal behavior—the underlying feeling remains, even in exaggerated form, as a continuing source of tension.

[6] Karen Horney, *The Neurotic Personality of Our Time*, New York: W. W. Norton & Company, Inc., 1937, p. 63.

The positive approach is suggested by the underlying etiological factors. Opportunities for the indirect expression of the feelings through athletics, art activities, and personal interviews can be recommended. Appreciation of the individual's acceptable actions, expressed through praise and encouragement, a chance to choose his companions, activities, and interests will provide the needed psychological reinforcement. Perhaps, above all, there should be the opportunity for the child to associate with parents and teachers who do not look upon his behavior as an attack upon their own integrity.

Causes Manifest in Feelings of Guilt. Closely allied to feelings of insecurity and feelings of inferiority is the feeling of guilt. These are all indicative of the individual's dim self-evaluation. Experienced teachers know these persons as those who appear to be "conscience stricken" in regard to ordinary behaviors. The feeling is expressive of a marked fear of displeasing or offending others.

Evidences of feelings of guilt are seen in such behaviors as self-condemnation—in which the individual believes, and sometimes expresses the conviction, that he has done something shameful, sinful, or disgusting. Sometimes the subject, by denying himself simple pleasures, will punish himself for the wrongdoings that he attributes to himself. Evidences of guilt feelings may also be seen in the anticipation of condemnation by his peers or by adults. While not all instances of projection (blaming others for one's own errors or shortcomings) may be attributed to guilt feelings, there are instances in which guilt is the motivating factor.

The causes of feelings of guilt are similar to the causes of other feelings which lead to maladjustment. Sharp criticism, repeated condemnation, belittling comparisons, unrealistically high parental expectations, accidents for which one receives continuing blame are factors which nourish feelings of guilt. To these must be added the attitude on the part of parents that sex and genital exploration are shameful. If the child is shamed, slapped, and scolded for simple sex explorations, there is likely to develop an abnormal curiosity which, because of its mystery, becomes the more compelling. Despite the fact that he shares the feeling that it is sinful or shameful to handle the genitals, he continues the practice—only to suffer guilt feelings because of his "weakness."

> The child's physical function—first those of defecation, then his sexual desires and activities—are weighed down by moral considerations. The child is made to feel guilty with regard to these functions, and since the sexual urge is present in every person from childhood on, it becomes a constant source of the feeling of guilt. What is the function of this feeling of guilt? It serves to break the child's will and to drive it into submission. . . . There is nothing more effective in breaking any per-

son than to give him the conviction of wickedness. The more guilty one feels, the more easily one submits because the authority has proven its own power by its right to accuse.[7]

The problem is intensified at the adolescent level if ill-founded stories about feeble-mindedness and insanity caused by genital manipulation are heard. The other factor is an exposure to religious teaching which emphasizes fear, sin, and retribution. Though these beliefs seem to have diminished in popularity in recent years, there is evidence that they are not entirely extinct.

Remediation of guilt feelings may be so difficult a problem as to require the aid of a psychiatrist. However, certain preventive and prophylactic measures can be recommended. There should be an attempt through kindly interview to get one to understand his own motives, assets, and admirable qualities. Discussion with understanding adults can help the child to see that he is not unlike others. It is obvious that a more objective teaching in regard to sex is necessary. Genital exploration is a normal, *and passing*, phase of development. If the child's growth is not arrested by ill-advised teachings, the exploration will cease. (It is encouraging to note that many adolescents are being taught that sex development is an indication of approaching adulthood.) Religious teachings that emphasize love, service to others, and more complete self-realization will serve to concentrate attention on strength rather than weakness. Feelings of guilt are the result of constant and repeated pressures. Consequently, remediation must involve the slow process of growth which demands patience on the part of the adult and the avoidance of continuing error.

Conflict. Everyone, in a culture where individual freedom of choice is both an ideal and a characteristic, will experience some degree of conflict as he makes choices. When indecision is temporary and when the choice is relatively unimportant to the individual, the conflict is not frustratingly serious and it does not lead to maladjustment. But the continuance of a problem situation, with no release of the emotions involved, causes an accumulation of tensions that become increasingly provoking and maladjustive. It is this *continued state* of conflict—the unresolved problem, the accumulation of tensions—to which the psychologist refers when he speaks of conflict.

Seeds for the propagation of conflict are sown when children are asked to make decisions that are too difficult for them in terms of their maturity. For instance, a father who rewards his son for a report of good behavior at the end of the day by romping, telling a story, or by giving

[7] Erich Fromm, "Individual and Social Origins of Neurosis," *American Sociological Review*, 9:382, 1944.

a candy bar may ask, "Have you been a good boy today?" The child remembers that he had broken a glass when he tried to help his mother wipe the dishes and that she had called him a bad boy. The decision to tell the truth or to be deprived of the reward arouses conflict. Of course, one such occasion is of little consequence, but the situation repeated day after day may, and has often, become the source of conflict. School children are faced with a similar problem when the teacher asks for information the giving of which the individual feels would be a betrayal of confidence in his peers. The more highly developed the pupil's social responsibility, the greater the conflict he will suffer. Adults, too, face conflict; for example, the desire to be a companion to his children may oppose a father's conviction that devotion to his work will win them security. In all these examples, the particular problem is of less significance than its chronic occurrence.

The conflicts thus far described are conscious and recognized. Most of the conflicts, however, which lead to personality disturbance are those which are beyond the field of awareness—they are unconscious.[8] In these, the individual does not recognize the nature of his dilemma. A common example is the phenomenon of ambivalence—the existence of opposed feelings for the same person. Thus, a child may both love and hate his parents. The attempt to act as he pleases results in punishment and retaliation, which provokes suppressed hate and hostility. This may be combined with a vague fear that he will be deserted by the parents. Yet there remains the belief that they do care for him and his needs.

Unconscious conflict may arise also as the outcome of some remote experience. An unpleasant experience involving pain or fright may have occurred so long ago that there is no distinct memory of it, yet the residue remains in the form of some persistent fear or dread. Fear of closed places, fear of animals or of insects may have been generated by specific events now forgotten. The fear of insects may make the study of biology a conflict situation—the tendency to avoid them versus the desire to study a needed subject.

Feelings of guilt generated by failure to satisfy too high parental expectations may lead to conflict. Religions which stress man's sinfulness and worthlessness are often at the root of persistent personality conflicts.[9]

The resolution of deep-seated conflict may be a problem for psychological consultants or psychiatrists. It is, nevertheless, justifiable to hope that some conflicts may be avoided, some may be mitigated, and some may become bearable if positive mental hygiene principles are applied.

[8] Louis P. Thorpe, *The Psychology of Mental Health,* New York: The Ronald Press Company, 1950, p. 112.

[9] John Dollard and Neal E. Miller, *Personality and Psychotherapy,* New York: McGraw-Hill Book Company, Inc., 1950, pp. 240–241.

Acceptance of the child, forgiveness for errors, frank and objective discussion, and an attempt to understand the uniqueness of each individual will help.

THE TEACHER'S ROLE IN DEALING WITH PROBLEMS

We now turn to an examination of some evidences of difficulties in the classroom, with the aim of giving teachers further insight into treatment.

The Danger of Labels. Some adults, unfortunately, seem to feel that if the behavior of a child can be named, the struggle for improvement is virtually won. However, we still have the problem of discovering the cause and of removing it *or* of teaching the pupil to live with the persisting causative condition. In a way, medical practice is much easier. If a child's illness is diagnosed as being mumps or measles, the doctor knows what caused the difficulty. He knows, too, the precise treatment that should be administered. But a symptom of maladjustment in the psychological realm is not so revealing. It may be perfectly clear that a child is projecting his difficulties on others; but the reason why he hit upon projection, rather than upon shyness, as an escape or relief from his problem is not clear; nor is it evident what "germ of discontent" has invaded his private world. The label is only the beginning. The next steps involve the investigation of possible sources of difficulty. Furthermore, since individuals differ in their reaction to specific stimuli, it is necessary to know how the individual *feels* about his problem. Ability to name the symptoms and to evaluate their seriousness must be combined with a curiosity about what they may represent to the individual.

Seclusiveness. A number of years ago, teachers were likely to view seclusiveness or timidity with favor (because it did not interfere with smooth classroom functioning), but today they are coming to share the belief of psychiatrists that it is a rather serious indication of maladjustment.[10] Seclusiveness is a withdrawing from the world (especially the social milieu) to avoid defeat and disappointment. The seclusive individual has accepted defeat and resigned himself to his fate. It should be remembered, however, that this symptom is, in itself, an attempt at adjustment (albeit an unsuccessful one in terms of long-time adjustment). It is serious, too, because the underlying tensions are unresolved and unexpressed and hence likely to lead to later still more serious deviations.

Another significant consideration in viewing and dealing with the phenomenon of seclusiveness has to do with individual differences. Some pupils may be perfectly well adjusted yet give the appearance of shyness and timidity. It could be that in a particular situation they just feel that

[10] E. C. Hunter, "Changes in Teachers' Attitudes toward Children's Behavior over the Last Thirty Years," *Mental Hygiene*, 41:3–11, 1957.

they have no special contribution to make and do not see any necessity for pushing themselves forward.

How, then, do we judge the seriousness of seclusive behavior? Two answers are pertinent. One is that the pervasiveness of timidity should be studied. If the child is timid in all situations, if he cannot contribute even though he has something to give, and if he resists all advances, these are indications that the symptom is serious. The second factor has to do with the coexistence with other symptoms. If the only indication of possible difficulty is shyness, there is reason to regard it as being of minor importance. If, on the other hand, shyness is combined with nail biting, stuttering, inattentiveness, or sullenness, it may be regarded as needing investigation. This is the attitude taken by psychologists when they refuse to interpret specific behaviors without first knowing the individual and his accompanying actions.

When the degree and the nature of seclusiveness are judged to be abnormal, remedial steps are in order. First, there must be a search for specific causes which will in themselves suggest corrective measures. Second, the general prophylactic and therapeutic measures—accepting the child, helping him to build skills and knowledges, seeing to it that he enjoys some measure of success, and avoiding force—may well be applied.

Aggressiveness. This symptom, like any others discussed, is more or less serious according to the degree of its development. It is much more likely than the others to catch the attention of the teacher, because of its disturbing nature; however, it is probably less serious than seclusiveness, because it represents an active attempt on the part of the individual to compensate for his frustrations. In others words, to overcome seclusiveness, behavior must be both started *and* directed, whereas, in the remediation of aggressiveness, all that is necessary is to direct behavior into more constructive channels.

The fundamental cause of aggression lies in persistent frustrations, and specialists agree that redirection of the behavior is much better than to attempt to repress it.[11] Yet the latter course—by punishing or shaming the "offender"—is the one all too frequently pursued by teachers. In redirecting aggressive behavior, one teacher may use group discussion, another sociodrama, and still another give leadership responsibilities. One teacher made an aggressor the custodian of play equipment and the steward of the class. She indicated that it would be better if he secured cooperation instead of trying to control by force, and she praised him when his conduct merited approval.

Aggression may actually be stimulated by repressive discipline. The

[11] Norma E. Cutts and Nicholas Moseley, *Teaching the Disorderly Pupil in Elementary and Secondary School*, New York: Longmans, Green & Co., Inc., 1957, p. 65.

frustration generated by threats and fear of consequences manifests itself in fighting, quarrelsomeness, and destruction when the individual is not under the immediate supervision of the feared person. Since such outbursts seem to challenge the authority and prestige of the teacher, the natural response on the teacher's part is one of hostility. This, however, merely aggravates the situation.

The constructive approach to aggressiveness and its related symptoms of cruelty and destructiveness is, of course, that of determining causes and attempting to help the individual meet fundamental needs which he currently lacks. Until the specific needs are identified the generally successful approach will be to help the child adjust socially, try to make him feel worthwhile, build his confidence through facilitating achievement, and give him an opportunity to contribute.[12]

Truancy. Studies of the relationship of truancy to delinquency lead to the belief that truancy is a cause of delinquency. Actually, of course, truancy is an indication of maladjustment that may become progressively worse until it reaches the stage of delinquency. It is now generally recognized that truancy is one kind of predelinquent behavior, a precursor or warning that more serious maladjustment will ensue unless the disturbing situations in the child's life can be lessened.[13]

Two cases in the primary grades illustrate the variety of causes which might be involved. One lad skipped school because, in his words, "They just go over the same old stuff." He hid under the porch at home and read and played by himself. His father consulted a psychologist who administered the Stanford-Binet test and reported an IQ of over 135. The teacher was asked to provide the boy with more stimulating work. She was helpful and saw to it that the boy was given work to do that would more nearly challenge his abilities. This was an easy solution, for the boy was capable of working by himself and needed only to have appropriate materials provided. The other case involved a boy who was slow in his academic work but who happened to have manipulative ability. His teacher had deprived him of play materials in the hope of stimulating him to give more attention to reading. This boy was more active in seeking entertainment than was the one described above. He traveled about various parts of the city. Help, in his case, consisted of the teacher's removing some of the pressure to do academic work and permitting him more opportunity to construct. When class projects permitted, she let him help build benches, stools, light stands, and the like while the other youngsters were given the roles of actors, ushers, and musical entertainers.

[12] Katherine D'Evelyn, *Meeting Children's Emotional Needs,* Englewood Cliffs, N.J.: Prentice-Hall, Inc., 1957, pp. 70–71.

[13] Sheldon Glueck and Eleanor Glueck, *Delinquents in the Making: Paths to Prevention,* New York: Harper & Brothers, 1952, pp. 69–80.

Other factors contributing to truancy may include repressive disciplinary procedures which the child seeks to avoid. Schoolwork which is meaningless in the student's eyes is known to be the explanation in many cases. Fear of failure will keep some children from school, for they do not seem to realize that absence will only increase the certainty of failure.[14] Grading systems which are so rigid that some pupils never have a chance to distinguish themselves contribute to deliquency. In Denver, Colorado, it was reported at a conference on grading that at each report card period there was a marked increase in truancy and running away from home—a time at which local police were alert to pick up stragglers.

Youngsters in the upper grades and in high school may avoid school because they feel that their clothes are laughed at by their peers. The emotional pain caused by having ill-fitting or unpopularly designed clothing is sometimes quite acute. Closely allied to this feeling is that occasioned by being a member of some minority religious or racial group.

The cases cited may seem to indicate that the solution of the maladjustment manifested in truancy is relatively simple. Actually, numerous contributing factors are involved; therefore, it is mandatory for the teacher to learn as much as possible about the truant. Efforts should be made to cultivate friendship, not only to make the school atmosphere more inviting but also to get at the feelings of the individual child. Obviously, an effort should be made to make use of any of the particular interests the pupil has in the ongoing work of the class. Since some of the factors contributing to truancy are found in home conditions, a visit to the home is usually necessary. These visits should emphasize the worth of the child, because the tendency of parents is to rationalize their own position and to condemn the child. The need for kindly treatment and complete understanding is reflected in the lessening tendency to have "truant officers" and the increasing use of personnel counselors, among whose duties is that of dealing with truancy.

Tattling. Tattling is one of the irksome and baffling problems with which a teacher has to deal. In the first place, it is difficult to define. Jennie's report that "Frankie pushed me" or that "Sue took my pencil" certainly seems to be tattling and should probably be temporarily ignored; but ignoring is less workable when there are recurring reports of stealing or of the destruction of school property.

When tattling is chronic and characteristically involves inconsequential matters, remedial measures are in order. If tattling is obnoxious, it certainly should not be rewarded by being given recognition, but an attempt to supply the indicated need should be made. Tattling is a bid for attention; so, efforts should be directed toward finding some legitimate reason

[14] William C. Kvaraceus, *The Community and the Delinquent*, New York: Harcourt, Brace & World, Inc., 1954, p. 109.

for giving the needed consideration. It has been shown that the child seeks and should find the teacher's favor, but the esteem of the teacher should be warranted if it is to build good habits in the child. Punishment and shaming are obviously ill-advised methods of treatment, for they involve a further destruction of the pupil's security.

Other Evidences of Maladjustment. There are other evidences of maladjustment, such as selfishness, tantrums, and the chronic breaking of regulations; but they are symptoms, and the consideration and treatment of them are very like those indicated for various symptoms in the foregoing discussion.

SCHOOL-HOME-COMMUNITY TEAMWORK

A review of the symptoms of mental ill-health and the ways in which disturbed individuals act (truancy, withdrawal) should make it quite clear that school personnel cannot do the whole job of guidance or rehabilitation. The home is frequently at fault in serious disturbances, but the home itself is often upset by community factors or cultural influences. Hence, the inclusive approach to mental health is one of teamwork involving home, school, and community.

The Role of School Personnel. Too often one hears teachers say, "But, what can one do? The troubles stem from the home and we can't be expected to change that." The response to this is not a comforting one to teachers. "You can't be expected to change the home. Perhaps you can't do much to alleviate, even temporarily, the pain the pupil feels. But you are in the most advantageous position to do *something* if you will stop 'passing the buck'." Teachers, through perusal of professional literature, teachers' meetings, and formal courses—summer-school-extension, and in-service-training—have the best opportunity to become aware of the needs, the problems, and the effective approaches that will lead toward (not to) the solution of personality problems in the classroom. They can disseminate this information; they can identify the problem; they can suggest remedial measures.

This is more than a matter of going half way. It may mean going three-quarters, or more, of the way and not being very welcome then. But the job of helping parents needs to be done, and the occasional word of appreciation plus the knowledge that the job is worthwhile should compensate for the disappointing aspects which will inevitably occur.

The Resistance of Parents. Parents, by and large, want to do better. But there are obstacles to their acting as if this were true. While they want to do better, under stress when their son or daughter is in trouble, they, like all human beings, feel the need to protect their egos through the defense of excuse making and shifting the blame. Though they want the best for their children, they do not always see eye-to-eye with teachers as to what is "best." Families too are victims of circumstances and must be positively helped rather than negatively criticized.[15]

Introducing family members to mental health concepts through counseling, community meetings, and the distribution of literature can make an impression on the parent generation. But teachers have a greater hope, i.e., that of "chipping away" at the prejudices and ignorance of the generation now in school, so that in another decade or two a better generation of parents will exist, a generation that will be less resistant to change—for it is realized that personal deficiencies are often due to cultural factors rather than individual perversity.

Enlisting the Aid of Community Agencies. There are many community agencies that can help school personnel in dealing with personality problems. But in order for them to help, it is necessary that they know what the problem is and what steps they might take. This calls for communication—discussion, cooperative consultations, friendly criticism, and clearer explanations of the other's function. A typical, but certainly not inclusive, list of community agencies will suggest how teamwork can help to reduce the tension of some maladjusted children:

Agency	*Possible Function*
Family Case-work Agency	Reduction of family friction
Child-guidance Clinic	Specific suggestions for guiding children
Boy and Girl Scouts	Development of constructive interests
Church Schools	Moral training and social experience
Mental Health Associations	Provision of literature and lecturers
Library Association	Guidance of the curious and gifted
Art Museum	Development of special talents
Dramatic Clubs	Ego enhancement and social contact
Good-will Industries	Easing of financial pressure on family
Recreation Center	Development of skills; building of health
Junior Baseball	Promotion of health and leisure-time interests

The problem is more often one of capitalizing upon existing facilities rather than creating them. Since it is everyone's business to cooperate, it is no one's responsibility to see that there is cooperation. This might well be the function of the teacher, who sees the great need for cooperation in view of the limitations of his own specifically defined sphere. There may be accusations of "officiousness," "personal aggrandizement," or "megalomania," but the need for leadership is great and someone must put the welfare of the bewildered youngster above the peace of his own security. There are rewards for activity in the community. Not only does one give help to the youngster, but it has been found that teachers

[15] George S. Stevenson, *Mental Health Planning for Social Action*, New York: McGraw-Hill Book Company, Inc., 1956, p. 218.

who participate in community activities tend to be happier than those not so involved.[16]

Claude M. Fuess, commenting on the need for strengthening our educational philosophy and system indicates that, while we need buildings and equipment, we also need dedicated teachers *and* a change of national attitude. Education is a problem which must be faced by all persons, and leadership, which will involve all possible agencies, is required. Only in this way can decadence, which has undermined previous empires that have experienced too easy living, be prevented.[17]

SUMMARY

When fundamental needs are not met to the satisfaction of the individual, the condition is reflected in many different kinds of objectionable behavior. Sometimes these evidences are temporary and occur in a general context of good behavior. Sometimes the evidences are chronic and several indications of maladjustment are noted. The solution of the problem involves, in general, a better understanding of the individual and a concerted effort to bring about over-all improvement in his environment.

Basic causes of maladjustment are revealed in feelings of insecurity, feelings of inferiority, feelings of hostility, feelings of guilt, and conflicts of ideals and actions. These evidences of maladjustment are themselves, in turn, caused by lack of fulfillment of the need to be accepted or to be recognized as an individual of worth, by repressive discipline in the home and school, and by a thwarting of the need to accomplish and to be independent. Moral standards which are too difficult for the individual to comply with in terms of his maturation, as well as invidious comparisons with siblings and other children, are known to be powerful factors in the production of maladjustment.

Specific evidences of maladjustment are numerous. Representative examples include such manifestations as seclusiveness, extreme aggressiveness, truancy, and tattling. The fallacy of labeling *conduct* with a technical name is indicated by the fact that treatment for each kind of behavior is strikingly like that for other kinds. Each child must be understood in terms of his particular background, abilities, and interests, and in terms of his own view of the situation in which he functions.

It should not be expected that all cases of maladjustment will be successfully treated. Some physical factors are beyond the teacher's control.

[16] J. Murray Lee and Dorris M. Lee, *The Child and His Development,* New York: Appleton-Century-Crofts, Inc., 1958, p. 590.

[17] Claude M. Fuess, "Money Is Not Enough," *The Saturday Review,* 41:10–12, Feb. 1, 1958.

Many psychological disturbances are of such long standing that the measures taken in school will give the child only slight help. Frequently much can be done in classrooms and more will be done for mental health when parents, school personnel, and those in community agencies work cooperatively in the solution of problems which affect them all.

STUDY AND DISCUSSION EXERCISES

1. What would you consider to be the basic factors underlying the maladjusted behavior portrayed in Tom's behavior?
2. What are some reasons why we cannot expect to be uniformly successful with all the personality problems encountered in the classroom?
3. Would you agree with the teacher who says that she tries as much as possible to ignore fighting among her boys because she feels that it is a good way for them to get rid of their hostile feelings?
4. Have you known any cases of truancy which do not seem to stem from any basic maladjustment? How would the treatment of such a case differ from that suggested in the chapter?
5. What suggestions can you make for improving, or instituting, school, home, and community teamwork?

SUGGESTED ADDITIONAL READINGS

D'Evelyn, Katherine E., *Meeting Children's Emotional Needs*, Englewood Cliffs, N.J.: Prentice-Hall, Inc., 1957. 176 pp.

The author deals (in case studies) with a number of symptoms—stealing, aggression, withdrawal, truancy—and shows how they might arise.

Klein, D. B., *Mental Hygiene*, rev. ed., New York: Holt, Rinehart and Winston, Inc. 1956, pp. 474–507.

This discussion of ways in which people seek to evade reality will provide teachers with an improved understanding of defense mechanisms.

Miller, Daniel R., and Guy E. Swanson (in collaboration with others), *Inner Conflict and Defense*, New York: Holt, Rinehart and Winston, Inc., 1960, pp. 43–96.

This selection takes a close look at some of the origins of problems and conflicts and suggests how approaches to their resolution must be appropriately modified.

Rogers, Dorothy, *Mental Hygiene in Elementary Education*, Boston: Houghton Mifflin Company, 1957, pp. 350–377.

Common mistakes and helpful procedures in dealing with youngsters handicapped in speech, hearing, vision, or vitality are discussed.

Shaffer, Laurance F., and Edward J. Shoben, Jr., *The Psychology of Adjustment*, 2d ed., Boston: Houghton Mifflin Company, 1956, pp. 157–213.

The pages indicated deal with various defense mechanisms which might be met in the school but which are not confined to it.

CHAPTER 8

DEFENSE MECHANISMS IN THE CLASSROOM

Defense mechanisms are the habits which are developed to help one satisfy his motives, reduce his tensions, and resolve his conflicts.[1] They are the means by which one protects himself from failure, disappointment, or rejection. However, in the psychology of adjustment, defense mechanisms typically refer to maladjustive behaviors, which do not adequately serve to meet one's needs; that is, the mechanism may reduce tension momentarily in one area only to intensify his adjustment problems in another.

The teacher's wise treatment of defense mechanisms calls for him, first, to recognize that there is a reason for both desirable and undesirable behavior. Undesirable behavior may stem from a glandular, neurological, or other physiological defect or imbalance. Frequently the trouble is caused by continuing tension, conflict, or deprivation.

Second, objectionable behaviors must be judged in terms of possible desirable features as well as their frequency and setting. Aggressiveness, for instance, may have the positive aspect of generating initiative. Contemporary psychologists investigate causal circumstances as well as frequency and concomitants of the problem behavior. For example, a child who has been referred for study because of lying is not condemned for his behavior. We must know the nature of his lie. Is there a pattern to his lies? Is a particular category of behavior (social contacts) concerned? Is fear, desire for prestige, or longing for personal possessions a motivating factor? Are there other evidences besides lying? In short, the lying is viewed only as an aspect of behavior—not as the totality.

Third, defensive behaviors should be regarded as symptoms of difficulty. Consequently, to change the behavior, it is necessary to get rid

[1] Laurance F. Shaffer and Edward J. Shoben, Jr., *The Psychology of Adjustment*, 2d ed., Boston: Houghton Mifflin Company, 1956.

of the cause. This is a pressing problem for teachers, because it is the immediate behavior that is so bothersome; hence, there is a tendency to correct the mechanism rather than to seek the cause.

REPRESENTATIVE PERSONALITY PROBLEMS

Negativism. The habit of, or tendency toward, resisting direction, ignoring requests, or doing as one pleases in spite of rules to the contrary is called negativism. It becomes a source of irritation to the teacher, since it upsets the smooth class procedures; therefore the teacher has a tendency to curb the symptom immediately and abruptly. This tendency is aggravated when disrespect for teacher authority is read into the behavior.

Negativism is a normal phase of the process of maturing. It is an indication that the pupil is attempting to develop the healthy independence in which educators profess to believe. It may be an attempt to show that he, the negative person, is exercising the originality that makes it difficult for him to adhere to routines. Further, negativism will be outgrown when the individual sees advantage in conformity. It can, of course, grow into an extreme difficulty, and undesirable habits of negativistic conduct sometimes develop.

The cause of negativism may be demands that are, from the pupil's viewpoint, unreasonable—excessive adherence to routines, a hampering check by harsh discipline in the home, inability to perform requested tasks, or interference with activities which are in process at the time. Moreover, a contributing factor in negativism may be in the attitude of the person viewing it.

> If parents or teachers are themselves able to accept both middle age and the resulting new relationship with the younger generation, they handle with more equanimity and more stability the minor manifestations of negativism and rebellion which seem to characterize adolescence. They make fewer scenes over temporary and ephemeral "ill-chosen friendships," food preferences (dill pickles preferred to carrots), speech mannerisms, and adoration of other adults. They accept without distress their children's experimentations in literature, politics, religion, and entertainment and are able to recollect their own teen-age years of experimentation. This is not to say that the negativism of adolescence is absorbed docilely by the parents or teacher. Few people like "freshness," rudeness, or disregard of their own feelings. However, under the psychological conditions we have described, we feel the parent or teacher is able to deal, both more effectively and with less stress, with the negativism of adolescence.[2]

[2] Robert S. Stewart and Arthur D. Workman, *Children and Other People*, New York: Holt, Rinehart and Winston, Inc., 1956, pp. 126–127.

There are times when dealing with the symptom is entirely justifiable. In the interest of the mental health of the class as a whole, it may be necessary to take a decisive attitude toward a particular pupil. Thus, a student who refuses to draw a particular map in World History because, he suggests, there are better maps in books, may set a poor precedent for other pupils and for other situations, or his action may interfere with the culmination of some larger and more essential phases of the work as a whole. The need for conformity may be taught both by pleasurable experiences and by the deprivation of privilege because of nonconformity; but understanding is still important. Perhaps the pupil does not realize that drawing the map himself will help him to a better knowledge of geography.

Lying. It is difficult to formulate a precise and widely acceptable definition of lying. Some define any untruth as lying; others will not admit to lying when the truth is really none of the other's business or when the truth might do more harm than good. In fact, teaching children not to lie is a complicated problem because of the widespread acceptance of the social lie. If asked how he likes another's hat, a person of breeding may think it necessary to deviate from the truth rather than to say, "It's a nice hat for a twelve-year-old," or something else more pertinent than polite.

Respect for truthfulness may best be taught by helping the young person develop pride in his own reliability and honesty. Too often, among teachers and parents, a child is quickly censured for what he has said, because of a belief that he is lying. Perhaps his "lie" is less a matter of deliberateness than a lack of maturity sufficient to discern and comprehend what is objectively seen. Again, it may be a matter of fancy or imagination, since young children often cannot distinguish their imagination from reality. In fact, some adults have difficulty remembering the difference between what actually happened, what they wanted to have happen, and what they read that paralleled some experience they had had; or they even may not be sure whether something actually happened or whether they dreamed it. This is particularly true after some time has passed. Rather than to condemn, it would be well to help the child analyze his experience so that he can perceive it more accurately.

Children distort the truth or deliberately lie for a number of reasons. In the pre-kindergarten years children mix truth and fiction. At this stage, which in reality is only the beginning point in moral and ethical development, he has difficulty in determining the difference between what occurred and what he believes has occurred. Other children lie to see what will happen. They detect lies on the part of other children and not infrequently by their parents. When parents are obviously insincere in respect to the truth in relations with others, children follow this pattern. A child may lie to escape punishment for stealing and to satisfy the need for security. . . . When a child lies to avoid punishment, the punishment should be evaluated in terms of the event. In the case of insecurity the child should be pitied rather than punished. Lying for such a reason demands an appraisal of the forces preventing him from achieving status.[3]

The wise teacher's actions will go further than disapproval. There should also be a search for the basic causes which underlie inability to assume responsibility. There should be an attempt to distinguish between immaturity as a cause and some frustrating situation as the precipitating factor. Removal of the background factor will obviate the necessity for lying; but there will sometimes be occasion for explaining the workings of defense mechanisms to children—and to adults.

The foregoing shows the futility of treating symptoms and the value of searching for causes, of which there can be such variety. A blanket remedy for lying, or for any defense mechanism, cannot be cited because of variation in causes and in basic differences of personality.

Daydreaming or Reverie. Daydreaming may suggest that the individual is encountering such a number of frustrations in his everyday life that escape into a world of fantasy affords a welcome relief. If the reveries provide enough satisfaction, they may be indulged in to the extent that the individual will lose contact with reality and become a psychotic. This extreme is what the classroom teacher must look for in his evaluation of a particular case. Excessive daydreaming deserves attention less for what it is at the moment than for what it may become.

Demanding more strict attention from the pupil, being sarcastic or derogatory about his mental "absences," or penalizing him for missing some of the conclusions presented in the class will not accomplish anything except a change in the type of escape, if it does that much. Excessive daydreaming results from such experiences as being socially unacceptable (or imagining that this is so), taking an apologetic attitude on account of one's background (or parents), being unable to deal with the school tasks which are assigned, meeting competition which leads to frequent defeat, or fearing defeat in unpleasant or novel situations.

There are some distinct advantages in daydreaming. Few individuals would accomplish anything noteworthy if they did not daydream about it beforehand. Reverie should be encouraged to the extent that it helps determine and define goals. The teacher's task is to determine the extent to which these dreams result in action and the extent to which they become ends in themselves. A high-school boy was noted by a teacher to be somewhat lonely, sometimes engaging in reverie, and participating in work sporadically. His teacher became interested in the subject of his

[3] Cecil V. Millard, *Child Growth and Development*, rev. ed., Boston: D. C. Heath and Company, 1958, p. 359.

activity and discovered that there was a pattern to his interest, namely, forestry. Whenever a report, subject, or problem could be related to forestry or conservation, the boy was active. His dreams of becoming a forester motivated his schoolwork. But the teacher also discovered a note of unreality in the daydreams. The boy dreamed, besides, of becoming a big-league baseball player. The fact that he did not turn out for high-school athletics (his vision was corrected by heavy lenses) and had no time to play baseball on account of his paper route indicated that this second daydream was absurd. Oddly enough, he had never played in an organized game of baseball. The teacher, through questioning, got him to see how unrealistic were his baseball dreams and, at the same time, emphasized the validity of his interest and ability in forestry.

As with other defense mechanisms, daydreaming must be assessed in terms of its extent and results. When it is merely a temporary release from pressing events and when it is intermittent and transitory, it can be regarded as acceptable. If it leads to action, it can be encouraged. The excessive daydreaming that moves on to loss of contact with reality is the kind that must become the concern of the teacher.

Rationalization. Rationalizing is the assigning of false or distorted reasons to some act, completed or contemplated, about which the individual feels apologetic and which therefore needs justification. Different names have been given to this escape mechanism: (1) The *Pollyanna type* involves the saintly acceptance of unpleasant things. "My principal is very gruff and insulting; but it is just the thing I have needed all these years to jar me out of my complacency." (2) The *sour-grapes mechanism* involves telling oneself and others that the things that had been so mightily striven for were not really desired after all (in view of not having earned them). "I really did not want the part in the play because it would have made me neglect my studies." (3) *Projection* is the attempt to save face by blaming others for one's own errors, shortcomings, or failures. "I got a lot out of the course, particularly from my readings, but no one could possibly expect to make a good score on the kind of examination he gives. Why, some of the questions concerned points we never discussed in class!"

The danger of rationalizations lies in their very plausibility. In fact, the mental processes "sound" so logical that they soon begin to fool not only the listener but the relator. It is at this point that rationalization becomes a threat to mental health. The false reasons excuse the individual from an aggressive attack upon the problems of reality.

One antidote is to avoid placing the child in situations where he will need to excuse his actions. Asking for reasons why he was late, why an assignment was not completed, why he got into an argument, or why he took Mary's pencil will often force him into giving an explanation for a situation when he honestly does not understand the reasons himself. When a child says "I do not know why I did it," he is often telling the entire truth—he does not understand his own motivations.

High-school pupils can be helped to avoid rationalization by having the workings of the process explained to them—by learning that it is an evasion of personal responsibility, a distortion of fact, and an indication of the need for developing more adequate personal resources.[4] They should, at the same time, learn that the device is commonly used and that they need not consider themselves to be in poor mental health because they have adopted it. It will help the teacher to evaluate rationalization if it is remembered that this defense mechanism has both advantages and disadvantages.

> These rationalizations make thwarting more bearable. In fact, they assist in normal lowering of aspirations after thwarting. . . . The difficulty with the rationalization is that the person may distort some facts in making up a tale that is pleasing. And when one disregards facts, he runs the risk of aggravating his problems. So the person who fails to locate the causes of his difficulties in schoolwork, and hides behind rationalizations, will not learn to do better.[5]

Identification. The tendency to put oneself in another's shoes, sharing his victories and personally mourning his defeats is called identification. It is a device seldom noticed in the lower grades but quite evident in the secondary school. The desire for membership in exclusive groups is frequently a manifestation of this mechanism, and it goes a long way in explaining the intense loyalties which are characteristic of adolescents. No doubt there is some justifiable satisfaction to be achieved from such identification. Sharing the gratifications and disappointments of other people is a commendable aspect of social development.

The danger in identification lies in excessive use. For example, a girl may proudly proclaim that she is a member of a certain home room that has earned and retained scholastic honors for the school; yet her lack of responsibility for carrying out assignments and undertakings is so marked that others have to work the harder to compensate for her poor record. A boy may identify with some movie hero and advertise the superiority of the male of the species yet, may take no responsible part in personal grooming or in learning the social graces.

Treating the obvious symptom is not enough. The teacher, in order to be genuinely helpful, must know the basic causes of the feelings of infe-

[4] Jack Kough and Robert F. DeHaan, *Helping Students with Special Needs,* secondary school ed., Chicago: Science Research Associates, Inc., 1957, pp. 103–104.

[5] Lee J. Cronbach, *Educational Psychology,* New York: Harcourt, Brace & World, Inc., 1954, pp. 552–553.

riority and help the student to overcome them. In the case of the girl cited in the previous paragraph, her inability to accept responsibility may arise from her having been unfavorably compared with a sister who is superior in academic pursuits. She feels that it is useless to attempt to beat or even equal her records; so she does not place herself in the position of possible defeat by actively competing. Perhaps the boy is apologetic about what he feels to be an inferior social background and needs personal help in achieving the conviction that what he himself *does* is more important than where he comes from. A sound general approach would be to ask, "How can I help this person build a stronger ego concept?"

Compensation. As the name implies, compensation is the seeking of satisfaction or the attempt to avoid tension by increase *or* transfer of activity. The first is called *direct compensation,* in which the individual seeks satisfaction in an area of disappointment or weakness by exerting greater effort to the accomplishment of the goal; the other is *indirect compensation,* in which one leaves the disappointing field and seeks gratification in substitute activities. An example of direct compensation is seen in the pupil of average mental endowment who studies longer and more conscientiously (perhaps compulsively) than the typical student, in order to receive good grades.

A fourth-grade boy who had been retained in the third grade so obviously gave evidence of discouragement and bewilderment that he was provisionally passed on to the fourth. There he worked so diligently that he did not go out at recess and had to be told to go home after school; but he was still not doing fourth-grade work. The extra effort would be laudable if it produced results. In this case, it is regrettable that such pressures were exerted on the boy as to result in his neglecting normal, boyish activities. The mediocre student employs indirect compensation when he gives up academic achievement as a goal and devotes his energies to athletic prowess or leadership in social activities.

Compensation, as seen from the examples cited, certainly possesses some distinct advantages. The hazard lies in overemphasis. It may be, as is too often the case, that the additional effort made to become an outstanding scholar interferes with the well-rounded development of the pupil. Thus, more mental health problems are added to the burdens of the pupil. However, if the aim can be attained without the cramping of other desirable developments, then the compensation may be quite worthwhile.

Indirect compensation may have the advantage of opening additional spheres of exploration, or it may lead to distinctive achievement because of intensified drive. Its great danger is that the individual may not derive genuine satisfaction from the compensating activity. Thus, if the student continues to worry about his inability to gain distinction in academic fields, it is doubtful, from the mental hygiene point of view, whether his compensation will be satisfying. If, as the result of indirect compensation, he is able honestly to say "Academic accomplishment is not everything in the world," the compensation is more likely to be acceptable. On the other hand, if his statement is "Now, I could be satisfied if I could just get on the honor roll," the adjustive value of the behavior is more questionable.

Compensation is often not so obvious as the examples cited. Bullying may be the expression of an effort to compensate for inability to gain the wished-for degree of social acceptance. Stealing may be a compensation for being deprived of clothes or spending money such as are possessed by one's peers. Lack of courtesy often is more than a habit; it may be an attempt to cover up an inability to understand what is going on in class. Sarcastic remarks may stem from either well-founded or ill-founded feelings that other children are receiving favors. These forms of compensation are, of course, undesirable. On the other hand, such behaviors as staying after school to help the teacher, marked courtesy in dealing with fellow students, or even devoted attention to the task at hand may be indicative of efforts to compensate for various tensions. Odd as it may seem, an overly "good" child may actually be motivated by deep-seated tensions. However, the symptom would not be regarded as serious unless it were coupled with other symptoms.

The teacher may aid the pupil in three ways: (1) He may assist by trying to find areas of activity that are likely to yield compensating gratifications. This entails gathering some knowledge about the student's interests and abilities. (2) He may help by giving the pupil a more objective view of the situation, trying to show him that individuals vary in their ability to accomplish in various areas and that the very effectiveness of our society depends upon just such differences. (3) He may explain the workings of the mechanism, thus attempting to help the pupil gain an insight into his own conduct so that he may arrive at a more hearty acceptance of himself and his limitations.

Displacement. Displacement is somewhat like compensation, except that it is more temporary. It is an effort on the part of the individual to release the pent-up emotions generated by some frustrating situation.

There is a close analogy between the operation of steam in a boiler and emotion in the human organism. In both instances, safety or escape valves must be provided. If the pressure of steam, or of emotion, is increased or if the valves are blocked, the outlets of emotion repressed, and other vents not provided, an explosion is bound to occur. Sometimes there will be an accidental opening which will temporarily serve as escape valve. You have seen steam escaping through a seam or a small rust hole in a boiler; in the same way, wives, husbands, children, and other domesticated animals often serve as escape valve for "displaced" emotion.[6]

Displacement is being used by the child who twists the arm of a smaller classmate as a means of relief for having been reprimanded by the teacher or having been given a low grade. He is afraid to attack the teacher, but he can release his emotion by taking it out on another person. It is likely that a good many desks in high school are maliciously carved in an effort to release resentment aroused by autocratic discipline. Some of the derogatory remarks about teachers penciled on walls and in books are attempts to displace the emotions generated by failure or restriction.

The usual treatment of such symptoms is further discipline, deprivation of privilege, or a lowering of marks, but this only serves to intensify the situation. Although outward conformity may be secured, such conformity is likely to be temporary and, in the end, to bring on a more marked attempt at destruction or defamation. Because of this probable result, some psychiatrists ask parents and teachers to overlook "displacement" and seek the causes of the behavior. Thus, when the small child kicks his mother, the parents, instead of "tanning his hide" until he learns never to do it again, should ignore the child or quietly remove him until his "steam" has been dissipated, in the meantime seeking the basic cause of his resentment. A high-school student spoke sharply and impudently to his teacher when she returned a paper with the remark that it was not up to his usual performance. Instead of "jumping down his throat," she looked sadly at him and said, "Why, John, you're too much of a gentleman to say that." It was true, he was a gentleman; although no apology was demanded, he voluntarily said he was sorry and assured her that it would not happen again.

Displacement can be engineered to serve a constructive purpose. Play and art therapy (Chapters 14 and 16) are examples of the purposeful use of displacement. That is to say, a child's drawing of a child kicking an adult serves, to a degree, the same release function as an actual kicking would serve. Yet the uninitiated adult might be inclined to moralize about the drawing and spoil the therapeutic value. In the same way, children may displace their emotions by having, in their play, a temporarily hated adult become sick and die or be subjected to serious injury.

No specific remedy for displacement can be recommended. It is something to which even those who are considered well-adjusted might temporarily resort. Two generalizations can be made: (1) The teachers should recognize the nature of the mechanism, so that they will be able to react to it for what it is. (2) The frustrating and irritating situations which might lead to its use should be guarded against. This, of course,

[6] S. H. Kraines and E. S. Thetford, *Managing Your Mind*, New York: The Macmillan Company, 1947, p. 142.

is a very large order, since it entails such matters as a curriculum in which adjustments to individual differences are possible, a cooperative and understanding atmosphere pervading the whole school, teachers who understand and like children, and provisions for activities which will provide for the release of negative emotions.

Irradiation. Irradiation refers to the release of tensions through a number of situations, rather than through just one object or circumstance. It is revealed in the conduct of both children and adults. The individual who strikes out at everyone and everything because of some frustration is resorting to irradiation. The child who disobeys the teacher, trips another child, quarrels with his playmates, shoves his neighbors in the cafeteria line, and in general creates a disturbance wherever he goes provides an example. Much of what is generally termed irascibility is probably irradiation.

The inability to recover from tensions that result in irradiation can be partially blamed on the physical condition of the individual. Therefore, an explanation for the conduct might well include an investigation of such factors as diet, sleep, temporary infections (colds, infected eyes, boils, and the like), and excess activity that produces fatigue. Frustrations due to failure, unpopularity, autocratic classroom regimes, and being forced into unduly strenuous activities also may serve as precipitating factors. Hence, the classroom atmosphere as a whole calls for investigation if the mechanism is noticed in several children.

Withdrawal. Seclusive behavior, or withdrawal, refers to the tendency of an individual to avoid contacts with other people. It is manifest in bashfulness, reluctance to recite, playing or studying by oneself, and, in general, the "lone-wolf" type of behavior. This symptom of inability to adjust is regarded as a serious manifestation by psychologists and psychiatrists. An increasing number of teachers are becoming aware of the gravity of the symptoms; but recent studies show that, although teachers agree much more closely with clinicians than they did twenty-five years ago, they are typically less concerned about withdrawal than they are with transgressions against authority and morality.[7] Almost automatically, teachers will give more attention to such behavior as whispering, inattention, disobedience, carelessness, and lying, because these manifestations interfere with their plans and, consequently, their personal integrity appears to be challenged. Furthermore, their stand can be explained by the fact that they have to think of the welfare of the class as a whole. However, if the mental hygiene viewpoint is adopted, these disturbing overt behaviors may be less serious than seclusive and with-

[7] Manfred H. Schrupp and Clayton M. Gjerde, "Teacher Growth in Attitudes toward Behavior Problems in Children," *The Journal of Educational Psychology,* 44:204–214, 1953.

drawing behavior for two reasons: (1) Overt behavior, even though it is disturbing, serves to let off tensions, whereas the seclusive behavior permits the basic tensions to remain as "bottled up" sources of irritation. This may result in a rather complete warping of the personality, so that later adjustment becomes increasingly improbable. (2) The overt behavior, in spite of its disturbing effect on the teacher, is an attempt at adjustment. The individual is putting up *some* kind of battle against frustrations. As long as he is fighting, there is a chance that he will find a solution for his difficulties, especially if he is given some understanding guidance by his parents and teachers. Withdrawal, on the other hand, indicates a feeling of defeat—there is no overt attempt at adjustment. The teacher who would help in such a situation has the double job of overcoming inertia and guiding effort after it has been aroused.

Just as we should not regard all lying, stealing, anger, or rationalization as symptomatic of some deep-seated maladjustment, neither should we regard every quiet individual as a clinical case. There are probably inherently different strengths in the drive toward socialization; but, even accepting the idea that socialization is learned, it must be admitted that the various experiences of several individuals would amount to a considerable difference by the time the children had reached school age. E. Kretschmer claimed that certain personality types were dependent upon bodily build. Carl Jung classified personalities into the extrovertive and introvertive types. W. H. Sheldon has pointed out that certain social characteristics (as well as other personality traits) are correlated with morphological types; that is, lean people are less inclined to be highly social than those who are heavy or stout.[8] Roger J. Williams has suggested that man's organs—sinuses, heart, lungs, stomach—provide the basis for differences in personality, drive, and interests, and that if this fact were understood, it would go a long way in helping to achieve better adjustment.[9] Even though the theories of these men have not been universally accepted, the belief that there are differences in basic personality orientation, including drives toward socialization, should be given careful consideration.

If the process of socialization is interpreted to mean that all children should be friendly and outgoing, it is possible to do some of them much injustice. Forcing children into positions of leadership, companionship, recitations, and the like may actually serve to generate, instead of diminish, tensions. Shy or lone (not lonely) children, however, can be just as happy as those who are highly extrovertive.

[8] W. H. Sheldon and S. S. Stevens, *The Varieties of Temperament*, New York: Harper & Brothers, 1942.

[9] Roger J. Williams, "Chemistry Makes the Man," *The Saturday Review*, 40 (14):42–46, Apr. 6, 1957.

R. D. is a case in point. As a child, he did outstanding work in grade and high school; moreover, he spent a great deal of time reading and experimenting with his chemistry set and other projects which were started from time to time. He played baseball occasionally and well, but not with the enthusiasm of the average youth. In college he had a few friends and went out with them at intervals but seldom joined the gang. In the army he was not inclined to join in the bull sessions but liked to read and engage in serious conversations with an older person. After discharge from the army he was married, took a position as a teacher, and is apparently living a well-adjusted and happy life. It would have been possible to identify him as a seclusive individual at any time during his school life. The significant thing is that there were no other manifestations of adjustment difficulties. Thus, care must be taken to view the individual in his total behavioral situation and avoid diagnosis in terms of isolated symptoms.

Projection. A common method for saving face when a person fails, makes an error, or performs inadequately is for him to blame another person or some object for his own shortcomings. Rather than shoulder the responsibility himself, he projects the inadequacy on some person or situation. "A clumsy carpenter blames his tools" is a cliché which pertains to projection. The mechanism is used by persons of all ages; even the very young person is sometimes taught to slap the "nasty" table which bumped him on the head. Aside from the release of anger or disappointment, this serves no constructive purpose. It would be better to control one's feelings and direct energy toward overcoming the obstacle and forming the habit of facing the reality of one's deficiencies.

The James-Lange theory of emotion states that emotion results from bodily activity stimulated by the situation. The theory is commonly contrasted with the common-sense theory, which postulates that emotion is produced by the situation. William James, however, believed that emotions were *the outcome of the response* to the situation. That is, common sense would say that you see a bear, you are afraid, and you run; but the James-Lange theory says that the order of events is to see a bear, to run, and to be afraid. While the theory certainly does not explain all there is to emotion, there does seem to be this element of truth in it: giving vent to one's feelings often does tend to build up the emotion. If a person is insulted and immediately retorts with some vehement answer, he becomes more angry, whereas if he smiles and says "You misunderstand me," the feelings do not mount so high.

The James-Lange theory throws light on the evaluation of projection as an adjustive mechanism. Projection, by providing physical or verbal expression, builds the emotion to a higher pitch—even if we do not believe that the expression produces the emotion. On the other hand, if the emotion is not allowed to mount, there is a better chance that some constructive measures will be taken. Thus, the student who fails to get a desired role in a play can, instead of blaming the teacher, reflect on his past negligence about assuming responsibility, see that it has been blameworthy, and begin to plan for the improvement of his conduct. If, instead of blaming his pen for a messy paper, he can be taught to see that his own dilatory actions made it necessary for him to hurry when the work was due, he has a better chance to improve his behavior.

Efforts to help children avoid the use of projection will include various measures like the following: setting a good adult example, especially avoiding such responses as blaming inanimate objects for personal ineptness; refusing to accept projections as valid excuses for not performing satisfactorily; explaining to upper-grade and high-school students the natural workings of the mechanism; demonstrating and illustrating the need for personal responsibility in shaping the course of actions; helping pupils develop the skills which will obviate the need for projection.

It should be realized that projection is essentially an indication of emotional immaturity; hence it is perfectly normal for children of school age. However, since the habits one forms in childhood are only with difficulty overcome at a later age, projection should not too readily be disregarded as a passing phase of conduct. Many adults have not outgrown its use. An early realization of the futility and hazards of projections would help.

Malingering. The habit of feigning illness, or malingering, to avoid some unpleasant situation, has little, if any, positive advantage. It lacks the aggressive nature of attack that characterizes such behaviors as lying, negativism, compensation, or even displacement or irradiation. Furthermore, by its very nature, it encourages the development of psychosomatic disorders. An individual who feigns illness is acting under the negative suggestion of illness; the idea of illness is actively, if not dominantly, present in his mental set. As a result, he is inclined to exaggerate and call attention to any mild aches or twinges which he does feel.

Parents can stimulate the tendency of a child to malinger by being oversolicitous about his health. It is entirely reasonable that they should protect the child's health by seeing to it that he is in bed, even with minor illnesses, and they must make sure that the child's return to normal activity is gradual. But, at the same time, they must take care that the ill child does not receive an undue amount of attention that will turn illness into something pleasant for him. If he is read to more than ordinarily, if others of the family have to entertain him, if his whims in eating must be indulged, and if he is waited on a great deal, he may easily come to think that illness is an advantageous situation. He soon learns that he can be the center of attention and get his way easily by being ill and may feign illness in order to continue being solicitously treated.

Teachers must not press the child into activity when he is not up to par physically; yet they must not make him feel out of place by putting him aside when there is good reason for his not taking part. On the other hand, it is necessary to be careful not to indulge pretended illness. In order to avoid either extreme, it is important to observe rather closely the child who holds back from participation or who complains of illness. If he is active and happy when he is not being supervised and if he acts ill only when teachers are watching, he may be viewed with suspicion. A school doctor or nurse can be of assistance in such a case; but where such help is not available the teachers' judgments must suffice. If they suspect malingering, the remedy might very well be rather abrupt treatment, leaving the "ailing" one out of games and going on without him. Of course, if malingering is only one of several types of escape that the child is experimenting with, the cause must be sought in terms of wider adjustment problems.

Hypochondria. This defense mechanism is rather well defined by humor: A hypochrondiac is a person who, when you ask, "How are you?" tells you. Whereas malingering is feigning illness, hypochondria is the tendency to make the most of illnesses which are really experienced. A headache, a sprain, or an upset stomach becomes a major disability for the hypochondriac.

Hypochondria is encouraged by the outdated notion that girls who are menstruating should be very careful not to engage in physical exercise, should avoid taking baths, and should get more rest than usual until the end, or near the end, of their period. The tendency to exaggerate the discomfort of the menstrual period has been encouraged by adults who use such terms as *the sick time* or *the curse* in referring to the phenomenon. It is the consensus of medical authorities that most menstrual difficulties can be blamed upon worry, misapprehension, and misunderstanding, that only in very few cases is there any physical ground for the existing widespread impression of disability and danger from exertion.[10]

Youngsters should have pointed out to them what fun they are missing. An oversolicitous attitude should be avoided. The element of fear should be explained, and the encouraging thought should be added that many of the things which people fear never take place. Besides giving his explanation of this defense mechanism, the teacher can be helpful to its victims by his treatment of them. He can listen politely, but not with too great interest, to their complaints; and he can discourage indulgence

[10] Harold W. Bernard, *Adolescent Development in American Culture,* New York: Harcourt, Brace & World, Inc., 1957, p. 152.

toward minor ailments by refusing to accept excuses for belated work. In addition to refusing to indulge illnesses that are unimportant, the teacher might do well to search for such causes of frustration as meaningless schoolwork, unsatisfactory social relationships, the threat of academic failure, or an attempt to justify failure in attaining some office or honor.

Conversion Reactions. Closely related to hypochondria and malingering are those responses which are known as *conversion reactions*. These consist of psychological or emotional conflicts which are converted into physical symptoms. Whereas hypochondria is exaggeration of ills and malingering is feigning illness, the subject is actually sick in conversion reactions—though the ailment is psychic rather than physical. The first two must be regarded seriously because of the unconscious motivation which may lead to conversion reactions.

> Conversion reactions can run the continuum of severity from the mild headache resulting from anxiety and tension to the development of functional blindness, paralysis, and other incapacitating illnesses. Conversion reactions are symptomatic of emotional disturbances that may be rather severe. The treatment of these obvious symptoms is not of particular benefit to the adjustment of the individual; he may simply develop different symptoms. Psychotherapy is indicated. Psychotherapy for conversion patients may require considerable social learning that they failed to acquire in childhood. This takes time and effort. Because these reactions are typically acquired in childhood, the prevention of conversion reactions in children through adequate social learning experiences is important.[11]

Fighting and Quarreling. While teachers will at some time encounter the defense mechanisms described above, perhaps the most common and most immediately disturbing reactions are fighting and quarreling. As in other defense mechanisms the causes will be manifold and the approaches must be varied. The following analysis of possible causes of chronic fighting, summarizing many research studies, will help the teacher understand better all the defense mechanisms.

1. Many children in our American culture have too much done for them. Because of domination at home the individual child may become aggressive in his play group or at school.

2. Fighting often results when a child is hungry, tired, or is exposed to other physical stress. His hostility may be directed toward the person or persons he believes are responsible for his difficulties, or he may go after someone actually remote from the situation.

3. Aggressive and hostile behavior may arise when a child has met re-

[11] James M. Sawrey and Charles W. Telford, *Educational Psychology*, Englewood Cliffs, N.J.: Allyn and Bacon, Inc., 1958, p. 452.

peated failure in a situation in which he had reasonable hope of succeeding.

4. Hostility tends to develop when a child is forced to live in a home in which he is not wanted.

5. Hostility can be reduced by helping a person to gain some insight into the situation and into the behavior both of himself and of others.

6. Some children are growing up in homes and neighborhoods where aggressive behavior is considered the approved way of solving a difficulty. A child may have had countless demonstrations of this method by the adults about him. Perhaps he has shifted for himself so much that he had to use fighting in self-protection or to satisfy his need for solving difficulties.[12]

GENERAL CONSIDERATIONS

The Teacher's View of Defense Mechanisms. The general nature of non-adjustive behaviors is that they are misdirected attempts on the part of the individual to get rid of some tension or to avoid situations that he dislikes. It is important for the teacher to keep in mind that these behavior manifestations are sometimes passive (daydreaming, shyness) and sometimes active (lying, rationalization) attempts at adjustment. Some are easy to overlook and others are forced upon our attention. Acceptance of this view will lead one to investigate the causes of behavior, instead of trying to get rid of the difficulty by making demands or by shaming.

Many defense mechanisms are not to be considered serious unless they are employed to an excessive degree; for example, daydreaming indulged in to the extent of losing contact with reality, or lying practiced so frequently that it becomes difficult for the liar to tell the truth at all. But even minor use of the defensive behaviors may be serious if several of them are used by the same individual in a number of different situations. That is, a person who rationalizes some of his actions can hardly be considered a mental health case, whereas another person who does no more rationalizing but who also daydreams tends to manifest hypochondria, and characteristically remains aloof from others may warrant further study. The point may be illustrated by the experience of the writer in screening naval recruits for adaptability for service. It was found that almost all recruits answered *some* of the items on a fifty-five-item adjustment questionnaire in an atypical manner. If, however, any recruit answered any eleven or more items negatively, regardless of the seriousness of single items, he was suspected of being unfit for military service and further investigation was indicated. (As a precaution in using test data,

[12] Ralph H. Ojemann, *Personality Adjustment of Individual Children*, What Research Says to the Teacher, no. 5, Washington: National Education Association, 1954, p. 23.

it should be mentioned that the questionnaire was not the final test. Each recruit who was thus screened through eleven atypical items was interviewed to determine the validity of his responses and was then referred to the psychiatric board for further study.)

Attention to individual differences is at the core of intelligent application of mental hygiene principles. Certainly, in dealing with defense mechanisms, it is necessary to know the person who is using any of the techniques before wise action can be taken. Mental health in the classroom is dependent upon a knowledge of the individual—his past experiences, his motivations, his interests, his capacities, his limitations, his home life, his sibling relationships, and his problems of the moment. This is not an impossible order. Many teachers have stored up a great amount of such information because they are careful observers and attentive listeners. Pertinent information may be obtained from looking over the child's cumulative record. The papers a pupil writes, the pictures he draws, the way he plays may be used for gaining insight into individual behavior, as is explained elsewhere in this book. Sociograms give evidence of the child's ability to make friends and indicate the degree of acceptance he has with the group. Questionnaires, if they are used as points of departure for questioning, are of considerable value. But, let it be repeated, probably the most significant asset of all is the ability to see and hear what is daily taking place.

It is well known that children are likely to learn more about conduct from example than they will by precept; in fact, many authorities in the fields of childhood and adolescence declare that adult example is *the* factor in the development of behavior patterns. "As the teacher, so is the school" is a pertinent indication of the pupils' reactions to example. If the teacher exercises projection, displacement, rationalization, or hypochondria, he is sure to be setting the stage for the appearance of such mechanisms in the behavior of some pupils. That pupils take on the behavior characteristics of their teachers very promptly is a recognized fact. This does not imply that a teacher alone is responsible for each pupil's actions; but there is no doubt that upon the class as a whole—as far as the children's behavior in the classroom is concerned—he has a strong influence.

The Classroom Atmosphere. The treatment and avoidance of defense mechanisms are governed by many specific elements, but the classroom atmosphere as a whole also needs to be considered. This factor has to do, first of all (and again), with the behavior of the teacher, who is primarily responsible for the classroom atmosphere. It has been found, for example, that teachers who indicate that they themselves enjoy good health classify fewer of their pupils as troublemakers. Teachers who have the maturity which comes with age and experience tend also to reduce the number of problems with which they must contend.[13] The manifestation of friend-liness is a potent factor in classroom atmosphere, but it is largely absent in many schools. When there is free interchange of ideas, cooperative endeavor, the sharing of responsibility, and a feeling of personal worth, there is a better chance for the spirit of friendliness to be generated.

> Every youngster needs a friend. You as a teacher can do much to encourage friendships within your class. By stressing the positive values of each individual, by wise placement of students in work groups or committees, and by chats with students, you can do much to foster friendships in your class. The resulting good feelings may be a new experience in "good living" for some of your students. Your students will see you as a warm, understanding person who really likes them and wants to help them. If they feel that way about you, you will know you are doing a good job of making your classroom an experience in "good living."[14]

The classroom atmosphere will also be influenced by such things as clarity and personal meaning of the activities of the school. If the pupils, at any level, understand and accept as their own the purposes of instruction, the atmosphere will be more conducive to mental health. On the other hand, if schoolwork takes on the aspect of imposed tasks, the pupils and the teachers will then swelter in the oppressive weather which is generated. "Meaningful" work must necessarily be in terms of individual differences. Grades, passing, pleasing the teacher, all have different meanings for various pupils. The effect of competition must be evaluated. If all pupils are made to strive for the same goals, some will inevitably be discouraged by their lack of success, while others will gain inflated ideas of their own importance and ability.

The physical aspects of the room also must be taken into account. There are many classrooms which were designed before the significance of physical surroundings was widely recognized; but even these can be brightened with pictures (which should be changed periodically), by shelves of books and magazines, by an aquarium, by orderliness of the teacher's desk, and by an attractive vase of flowers. If pupils are allowed to participate in the decoration of the classroom, the physical aspects are reinforced in value by the children's feeling that they are personally involved.

Unfortunately, it is still true that in many schools the principal purposes are to pass examinations and to get satisfactory grades. As long as this situation remains, school will continue to be a chore. When these aims are made incidental, when they are used to secure information

[13] "Teacher Opinion on Pupil Behavior, 1955–56," *National Education Association Research Bulletin*, 34:72–74, April, 1956.

[14] Jack Kough and Robert F. DeHaan, *Helping Students with Special Needs*, secondary school ed., Chicago: Science Research Associates, Inc., 1957, p. 103.

about growth and areas which need additional attention, then they can contribute to the feeling of the pupils that they are engaged in productive and creative work.

In the final analysis, all this adds up to the inescapable, the sometimes discouraging, and always challenging fact that it is dependent upon the teacher to create a salutary classroom atmosphere.

> The teacher who is a wholesome, well-adjusted human being seems to have tremendous influence in producing the kind of atmosphere in which other human beings thrive. Friendliness, understanding, adaptability— these apparently simple elements of everyday living include some of the major factors in mental hygiene, and they are, in part at least, within the control of teachers in their own classrooms and with their own groups of children.[15]

It can readily be seen that thoughtful attention to the classroom atmosphere can go far toward avoiding the situations which will lead children to use defense mechanisms in the classroom. A wholesome atmosphere will provide a set of environmental stimuli which will ameliorate the tensions generated by out-of-school situations. The defense mechanisms already in operation will not thrive in a wholesome classroom atmosphere.

SUMMARY

Dealing with defense mechanisms in the ordinary classroom involves the following considerations: (1) Mechanisms are attempts on the part of the individual to adjust. (2) A person using one or two mechanisms should not be considered an abnormal individual or be treated as such. (3) The development of skills will decrease the necessity for using the mechanisms. (4) There should be a continuing effort to develop objectivity on the part of all pupils. (5) Keeping in good physical health will diminish the need for resorting to the use of defense mechanisms. (6) Wholesome participation in social activities is the antidote for the tensions which lead to escape mechanisms. (7) It is basic that treating the symptom should be replaced by a search for and removal of the cause. (8) Provision of a good adult example will diminish the tendency to resort to nonadjustive techniques. (9) Causes of emotional disturbances are multiple, so that the classroom atmosphere as a whole should receive the cooperative attention of teachers and pupils. (10) Participation in meaningful work will allow little time for the brooding which stimulates the development of emotional tensions. (11) There are no panaceas for the treatment of defense mechanisms, because each individual will differ from others in his reason for using them.

[15] W. Carson Ryan, *Mental Health through Education,* New York: The Commonwealth Fund, Division of Publication, 1938, p. 289.

STUDY AND DISCUSSION EXERCISES

1. Reflect on your own behavior for the past three days. Have you engaged in any form of rationalization? Was the process of any value?

2. Explain in detail why one's physical status might contribute to the manifestation of irradiation.

3. How would the treatment of a chronic fighter who is such because it is a part of his neighborhood culture differ from the treatment of one who fights because of feelings of inferiority?

4. What are some of the major considerations which teachers should observe when evaluating the seriousness of problem behavior?

5. Suggest a number of specific steps for improving the general atmosphere in any classroom.

SUGGESTED ADDITIONAL READINGS

Bonney, Merl E., *Mental Health in Education,* Englewood Cliffs, N.J.: Allyn and Bacon, Inc., 1960, pp. 70–91.

Some of the causes of aggressive behavior are described and a variety of constructive approaches for dealing with aggression are suggested.

DeHaan, Robert F., and Jack Kough, *Helping Children with Special Needs,* elementary school ed., Chicago: Science Research Associates, Inc., 1956, pp. 117–163.

The authors present suggestions to elementary teachers for giving to maladjusted children the help which they need so much.

Kough, Jack, and Robert F. DeHaan, *Helping Students with Special Needs,* secondary school ed., Chicago: Science Research Associates, Inc., 1957, pp. 96–167.

The pages indicated deal with general maladjustment, aggressive maladjustment, withdrawn maladjustment, and educational maladjustment of pupils in the secondary school.

Ojemann, Ralph H., *Personality Adjustment of Individual Children,* What Research Says to the Teacher, no. 5, Washington: National Education Association, 1954.

This series is designed to (1) help teachers become alert and sensitive to advancing human knowledge, (2) help them improve their work by supplying facts, and (3) stimulate further research. This booklet presents research implications for teachers in the area of personality adjustment.

Sawry, James M., and Charles W. Telford, *Educational Psychology,* Englewood Cliffs, N.J.: Allyn and Bacon, Inc., 1958, pp. 432–456.

Beginning with the hereditary basis of personality, the authors describe the development of interests, socialization, and maladjustment.

CHAPTER 9

MENTAL HYGIENE FOR SLOW LEARNERS AND THE GIFTED

There are three phases of the mental hygiene program: curative, preventive, and positive.[1] The curative has to do with correcting factors that produce symptoms of maladjustment and includes helping troubled individuals to take a more optimistic and realistic view of their problems. Preventive relates to avoiding the hazards which tend to produce turmoil and includes preparing persons to meet and satisfy the exigencies of life. Positive refers to efforts directed toward cultivating unrealized potential of the well.

The concern in this chapter is with all these phases as they relate to problems faced by slow-learning pupils and by those who are distinctly above average. If, from the beginning of the child's school experiences, learning challenges were appropriately scaled to his intellectual status, we could be concerned mainly with the positive and preventive aspects of mental hygiene. Unfortunately, there are various kinds of pressures (grades, passing, grade norms, unrealistic expectations) which tempt teachers to overlook individual differences and to impose, on the other hand, the tyranny of the average. Though teachers, particularly those in the upper grades and high school, are faced with all three phases, a major problem with the slow learner is getting him to utilize fully the limited resources which he does have. With the gifted child, we must be concerned with challenging him to make better use of his high potential.

SLOW-LEARNING CHILDREN

Two Kinds of Slow Learners. It is important that teachers realize that there are two kinds of slow learners. One is the pupil who, for various

[1] These are called restoration, protection, and elevation by George S. Stevenson, "Search for Mental Health," *Children*, 3:177–180, 1956.

reasons, functions as though his mental capacity were unusually low but who, in fact, has considerable unused ability. For instance, a pupil may perform poorly simply because he has a visual or auditory malfunction which keeps him from sharp contact with his environment and, in turn, from developing his intellectual potential. In school he misses part of what is said in class or fails to profit from what is on the chalkboard. He lags behind in class work, becomes bored or discouraged, and adds to the lack of sharp sensory contact with class activity the additional handicap of being inattentive. In such instances the teacher's job is to identify the nature of the handicap, then, to encourage the pupil to get glasses or a hearing aid, or to seat him where he can watch others as they talk or nearer to the chalkboard. Teachers have reported that quite marvelous transformations of personality, greatly improved motivation, and reorientation toward school tasks have resulted from the use of glasses or hearing aids. With such a pupil the teacher's job is one of restoring his confidence, convincing him that he can greatly improve his work, helping him to capitalize more fully on previously neglected potential.

Various kinds of speech defects may similarly cause a pupil to appear to be a slow learner. His hesitancy in response, his difficulty in expression, may give the impression of slow mental response. If impatience, scorn, or derision is added to the communication barrier, the individual may withdraw and compound the impression of retarded mental development.

Much the same sort of apathetic response may be engendered by emotional deprivation. Home or school conditions that inhibit communication, contribute to inability to concentrate, or result in low levels of aspiration may give rise to what appears to be true mental retardation. This phenomenon has been strikingly shown in studies which indicate that during a certain period of development a child may markedly regress in intellectual status due to being deprived of mother love.[2] Many pupils who have been thought to be mentally retarded have, after a marked change in home conditions, begun gradually to show learning ability which was previously unsuspected. The curative phase of mental hygiene can be implemented by teachers who will show the affection, the acceptance, the interest which should be characteristic of all classrooms.

The three possibilities—defective sensory acuity, speech defect, and chronic emotional turmoil—of pseudo retardation suggest a pointed implication for teachers. Since these conditions can be identified only by well-qualified diagnosticians, it might be well for the teacher to assume that the slow learners in his class have, as yet, undiscovered latent potenti-

[2] René A. Spitz, "Personal-emotional Maladjustment during Infancy," in Raymond G. Kuhlen and George G. Thompson (eds.), *Psychological Studies of Human Development*, New York: Appleton-Century-Crofts, Inc., 1952, pp. 490–496.

alities. He can seek to relieve emotional turmoil by attempting to approach satisfaction of basic needs.

The other kind of slow learner is the one who just does not have the mental ability, even under the most favorable conditions, to develop mentally at a more rapid pace. The futility of pressure, coaching, and longer work periods is indicated by the teacher who, having heard that Bill just could not be taught reading in the first grade, vowed that she would teach him in the second. She said she worked and pleaded and praised and at the end of the year, "Sure enough, he could read a little. But he had forgotten how to write his name!" For such pupils cure is not the major concern. It is a matter of protecting their ego concepts, their enthusiasm, their sociability by making them feel that differences in intelligence are no more important than differences in color of hair, height, or facial appearance.

Identification and Characteristics of Slow Learners. Mental tests are an aid to the identification of slow learners, but it is, emphatically, the consensus of teachers and psychologists that such tests are nothing more than aids. It can be said, with this reservation, that slow learners are *roughly* those with IQs somewhere between 70 and 90. However, experienced teachers know that there are some pupils with an IQ of 85 who perform as well on academic tasks as others with IQs from fifteen to twenty or more points higher. Sometimes a pupil who has been getting average or higher grades, confirmed by standardized achievement tests, will cause a teacher to say of his 85 IQ, "I don't believe it." However, when tested by the psychometrist on an individual test, the status is confirmed. Greater accuracy in the identification of slow learners is obtained by combining other measures and estimates with intelligence test scores.

Thus, of the three features of definition: intelligence quotient, educability, and social development and adjustment, the latter is now receiving its rightful place in a description of mental deficiency. This is especially true in the child under six since the former two features are often most difficult to validly determine at these ages. Thus the emotional and social maturation of the child and the manner in which he develops as part of a family group or neighborhood environment becomes a valuable and practical means of measuring retardation. It is not intended to depreciate the value of intelligence tests but to emphasize them in perspective with the rest of the picture.[3]

Estimates vary as to the number of unselected school children who will have IQs below 90. Percentages range from 12 to 22 per cent who are in

[3] Richard M. Auld, "Recent Advances in Mental Retardation in Children," in William F. Jenks (ed.), *Mental Health and Special Education,* Washington: The Catholic University of America Press, 1957, p. 79.

this category.[4] Percentages as a guide to identification are further complicated by variations in the population from which a particular school draws its pupils. For example, in one school in a large city and said to be located on "Pill Hill," since the pupils come largely from the homes of physicians and other professional workers, the average IQ of pupils in a given year may be as high as 125. A few blocks away, near a river and industrial area, the situation is quite different. There with over half the homes broken, in the typical fashion of the lower-socioeconomic strata, the average IQ may be close to that representing the upper border of the slow-learning category.

For practical purposes then, a slow learner may be identified through a combination of low intelligence-test scores, inadequate school achievement, inability to adjust socially to his peers, and lack of any compensating special abilities. When so identified, some sort of special provision must be made for these children if they are to learn techniques of adjustment to their situation and to their own limited potentialities.

Just as it is difficult to establish a sharp line of demarcation between the intelligence of slow learners and other pupils, it is similarly difficult to generalize on the characteristics of slow learners. Generally speaking, it is unwise to base identification on facial appearance, gait, or physical coordination. Nevertheless, slow learners are likely to be slow in physical and emotional maturation; moreover, sensory defects will be more prevalent among them than among the other students. They are generally not so well physically coordinated as their age mates. Their emotional expression is less well controlled. Their social adaptations tend to be awkward and immature. Development in speech is characteristically slow. However, this is not a safe prognostic factor, since we know that, although early acquisition of speech is an indication of high intelligence, delayed speech is not necessarily an indicator of low intelligence. It is worth mentioning, since there is much popular impression to the contrary, that these pupils *do not* typically have compensating abilities in manual skills or shop work.

The mental health implications involved in the characteristics of slow learners and in the processes of identifying them may be epitomized as follows: (1) Consider the possibility that the problem might be curative when withdrawal from vigorous pursuit of learning is the result of sensory defect. (2) When there is actual mental defect, scale your expectations to his indicated ability—preserving the individual's self-respect by showing that, in terms of his differences, he is doing entirely acceptable work. (3) Avoid discouragement based on intelligence tests alone, since motivation can and does cause varying degrees of utilization of what is

[4] Cecil V. Millard, *Child Growth and Development*, rev. ed., Boston: D. C. Heath and Company, 1958, p. 128.

possessed. (4) Curb the practice of shunting the pupil out of academic pursuits—he can learn many of the basic skills and concepts when they are presented appropriately—for there is likely to be *no* compensating talent in manual dexterity. (5) Most important, it is advisable to proceed slowly. Give more illustrations and demonstrations, and use concrete, tangible teaching aids, even though it does take time.

General Considerations in Teaching Slow Learners. There is no sharp line of demarcation between average, low-average, and slow learners. The crux of the situation has been well indicated by the observation that there has been too much emphasis on the *slow* and not enough on the *learning* in the phrase *slow learning*. These pupils *can* learn; however, in order to do so, the pace must be slower, the aims modified, and the content of subject matter altered. Their learning is better in the area of the concrete and the specific than in the area of concepts and abstractions. Probably one of the outstanding contributions of recent studies on slow learners is that these pupils can, in significant numbers, be made into self-supporting and contributing citizens. It is an anachronistic practice that those most in need of help are condemned to the shortest periods of education. It is well to remember that slow-learning pupils have the same needs as do human beings in general.

Retarded Children in the Regular Classroom. There has been a great surge of interest in making special educational provisions for retarded children, for experience has proven that they can in six out of seven cases be taught successfully. Even so, only about 15 per cent of these educable slow learners are able to attend special classes in public schools.[5] This means that, if anything is to be done with the majority of these pupils, it will, at present, have to be done by classroom teachers.

Education for retarded children should begin in the nursery-kindergarten years—rather than holding them out of school until they are "ready." They need, as do other children, to have social experiences, to get away from maternal overprotection, and to build slowly the background that will give them comprehension of the concepts necessary for daily living (see Developmental Tasks in Chapter 3). They should be given educational toys that will develop physical coordination. They should play with other children. They should be encouraged to do routine chores and run errands—this will probably be their lot in life at best. Academic activities must be scaled to the child's level of ability. The error expressed by one teacher, "He is now in the third grade. He just must learn to read," must be avoided. This youngster was still shy by a few months of having reached the mental age of 6.5 years, which among other things is considered essential for successful initiation of reading.

[5] Cornell Capa and Maya Pines, *Retarded Children Can Be Helped,* Great Neck, N.Y.: Channel Press, Inc., 1957, p. 51.

Application to arithmetic will come even later. It will be futile to hold them back "until they meet age-grade standards," because they will be slow at all grade levels and many routine explanations given at typical speeds will be frustrating.

Although it is not being done now, these children should be kept in school until they are eighteen, since they will, by and large, be unable to secure employment prior to that time. In high schools the combination

FIG. 6. Do service activities give the slow learner a feeling of significance? Is it right to let such experience displace some academic pursuits for the slow learner? What skills and appreciations can be developed by such activities as these boys are engaged in?

of some low-level schoolwork and part-time employment outside the school has worked successfully. The emphasis in such school programs is not vocational training but vocational education. Specific vocational skills need not be taught in school, since the jobs they take will be largely unskilled jobs requiring little academic or vocational training.[6] There should be an emphasis on the development of all those qualities which will enable them to take a self-sufficient role in community living. These valued qualities include keeping clean, paying attention to appropriate

[6] Samuel A. Kirk and G. Orville Johnson, *Educating the Retarded Child*, Boston: Houghton Mifflin Company, 1951, p. 101.

dress, getting along cheerfully with others, learning to take and follow directions, acquiring habits of promptness, dependability. Simple skills like telling time, keeping track of money, counting change, and learning safety rules are some of the things at which the classroom teacher might realistically aim. By giving them enjoyable experiences in the classroom, that is, simple tasks they can achieve, it may be possible to diminish the high drop-out rates which are now typical for slow-learning grade- and high-school youngsters.

Special Classes. Doing a high-quality job with slow learners takes more than patience, sympathy, and acceptance on the part of teachers. The teachers should have special training so that maximum effectiveness can be achieved. Moreover, children can function more freely and spontaneously when they are placed with their intellectual peers. This then comes down to a matter of establishing special classes. Here they are less likely to be embarrassed by invidious interpersonal comparisons. There is less likelihood that they will be exposed to the tyranny of the average. The teacher is much more likely to give functional recognition to individual differences. One teacher of such a class reported that pupils at 3:30 P.M. said, "Do we have to go home now?" On Friday these pupils, ranging in age-grade status from three to ten, ask, "Can't we come back tomorrow?" These questions suggest two things: one, school can be made interesting, and two, life outside of school must be rather rough for these youngsters. The questions are not surprising when we stop to think that, in these special classes, expectations and requirements are scaled to abilities.

It sometimes takes much effort toward education of parents before they will give assent to having their child placed in a group of slow learners. In one instance, the parents decided they would permit their daughter to enter on a trial basis. When they visited the class and saw that she had become eager to learn and appeared to be happy and particularly when they saw that, under appropriate circumstances, their daughter revealed more ability than they themselves had suspected, they were willing to make the transfer permanent.[7] Here all three phases of mental hygiene are illustrated—curative, preventive, and positive.

Teaching slow-learning children is not rewarding in the sense of scholastic achievement, to which teachers have become accustomed. But it is rewarding to those who have the social sensitivity to respond to the sometimes mute gratitude of the slow learner and his parents. In Oregon, when a pilot program was instituted for the mentally retarded and the gifted, the former director said, "We hesitated to go into communities with our plan for slow learners. But the fact is we found we were

[7] Pauline Kammet, "Parents' Attitudes toward Special Classes for Mentally Retarded Children," *Understanding the Child*, 20:110–115, 1951.

welcomed with open arms by parents so much in need of help. On the other hand, we found, much to our surprise, that we met resistance when certain children were not identified as being gifted."[8]

> Teaching the mentally retarded is probably the most demanding of all branches of education. It takes a truly dedicated, outstanding person to work successfully with these children: someone with a great love of people, a sense of humor, unswerving personal stability and a real understanding of child development. It is tough work, and generally offers no extra pay. But teachers who have tried it . . . will understand the former high-school teacher who said, "I never want to go back to ordinary teaching—this is far, far more rewarding."[9]

Slow-learning pupils have the same rights as others—the right to enjoy living, the right to self-realization, the right to become contributing citizens. These rights may be implemented if the three aspects of mental hygiene are made a part of their school program. The curative phase is involved when sensory, physical, and emotional handicaps are removed or modified so that pupils can come closer to achievement of their potential. The preventive is involved when the evidence is clear that average expectations are for them unrealistic. But their feelings of being appreciated, their wish to be recognized can be implemented by slowing the speed and changing the content of schoolwork. The positive phase is involved when it is recognized that slow learners are educable and can become contributors to, rather than burdens on, society.

GIFTED CHILDREN

The positive aspect of mental hygiene derives importance not only in terms of greater utilization of the potentialities of unusually bright individuals but also in terms of the improvement of society. It is a temptation to assert that this waste of human resources is one of the greatest indications of the need for a thoroughgoing mental hygiene program.

The Need for Better Education of the Gifted. The sudden realization of the fact that we do not, in the United States, necessarily have the best scientists has done much to make the present an excellent time to do a better job of educating our best pupils more thoroughly and intensively.

> The United States, with its Western tradition of human diversity and freedom, will find that it faces problems of infinitely greater complexity than does the Soviet Union. Given a smaller population with an incomparably larger array of needs and ambitions, this country will find it increasingly difficult to keep pace with Russia in every field. For the

[8] Mason McQuiston, personal interview, Portland, Ore., April, 1958.
[9] Capa and Pines, *op. cit.*, p. 65.

moment we can cope with the emergency in a piecemeal fashion; soon it will demand a radical new approach.

But wherever we look we will always face the same problem of how to train and then use effectively the most precious resource which the nation possesses: The brains of its citizens.[10]

Indications that we are not using this "precious resource" effectively are easy to find in current literature, of which a report in *Look* is representative. In more than 90 per cent of America's schools no provisions whatsoever are made for exceptionally bright children; though there is much talk, *Look's* forty-eight-state survey found only token experiments in individual schools in large-city systems. There is the suspicion, shared even by some gifted children, that it is not quite respectable to reveal "brains."[11]

The belief that brains are being wasted is more than a matter of sentimentality directed to a few students who show they are bored by the snail's pace they must maintain or to those who resentfully cover up their disdain for a teacher who dogmatically asserts he is right when a pupil can cite author, book, and page to prove otherwise. James S. Davie, studying the relationship of social class status to school attendance, found that pupils from the lower class were much underrepresented and those from the upper social class much overrepresented in college attendance. Specifically, where 100 is considered the quota-fulfillment index, when one finds the same proportion of pupils going to college as there are persons belonging to that class in the total population, the index for class I is 494 and the index for class VI is 18.[12] Thus, class I is overrepresented almost five times and class VI sends less than one-fifth of what would be proportional representation. To make the evidence of waste more striking, let it be noted that class VI contains much the larger portion of the total population. The argument that class I students have the intelligence to do college work and class VI students do not have may be in part true—but only in part. Studies of high-school dropouts show that many lower-class students who drop out have IQs higher than those of many upper-class students who stay in school. John B. Miner believes that intelligence may in part be a function of education and that the somewhat higher intelligence in upper classes is a function of their more extensive education.[13] The relationship of intelligence to length of schooling works

[10] Kermit Lansner, *Second-rate Brains*, New York: Doubleday & Company, Inc., 1958, p. 5.

[11] George B. Leonard, Jr., "The Plight of the Gifted Child," *Look*, 21:40–47, Nov. 26, 1957.

[12] James S. Davie, "Social Class Factors and School Attendance," *Harvard Educational Review*, 23:175–185, Summer, 1953.

[13] John B. Miner, *Intelligence in the United States*, New York: Springer Publishing Company, Inc., 1957, p. 83.

in both directions: low intelligence promotes a high drop-out rate and a high drop-out rate is a factor in low intelligence.

Further evidence of intellectual waste is given by a 1957 survey of the Educational Testing Service, when it was found that one-half of the top 30 per cent of all high-school students never get to college. This means that over a period of four years about a million able students fail to go to college, where they could cultivate, to their own and the nation's advantage, their intellectual resources.[14]

The need for better education of the gifted is thus seen to be an economic and a social class problem as well as a challenge to educators. This, however, should not deter teachers from attacking the educational aspect. If they can make school more challenging, help create an admiration for superior intelligence, diminish the socially discriminatory practices which now discourage some pupils, and develop enthusiasm for self-realization, they will be taking steps toward the solution of our present dilemma.

Identification of the Gifted. Identification of the gifted is even more confusing than is identification of the slow learner—because of the different methods of determining giftedness. It is estimated that slow learners make up from 10 to 20 per cent of the total pupil population and that, on the other hand, as much as 25 per cent is gifted. When leadership, artistic creativity, specialized interests, musical talent, or high motivation that is accompanied by ordinary intelligence are added to the more common measure of IQ, the number of pupils who merit special consideration runs high.

The late Lewis S. Terman set IQ 135 as the lower limit in selecting pupils to be studied for use in his four-volume series on *Genetic Studies of Genius;* he made exceptions, however, when a lower-scoring student was reported by teachers to have made a noteworthy achievement. Any child testing over 125 IQ on a Binet test is eligible for Major Work Classes in Cleveland, Ohio, if his maturity, health, and social adaptability are satisfactory. University City, Missouri, has an enrichment program for gifted students, but because of space limitations, the minimum IQ score may vary; 140 may be the low score in some years. A Portland, Oregon, child may get into special classes on the basis of exceptional talent in art or leadership and have only slightly above average test scores. More effective and realistic screening is deemed possible when, in addition to intelligence-test scores, data are obtained on interest and skill in the fine arts, musical aptitude, creative writing, dramatic talent, social leadership, teachers' observations, and parental reports.[15]

---

[14] Lansner, *op. cit.*, p. 70.

[15] Robert F. DeHaan and Robert C. Wilson, "Identification of the Gifted" in *Education for the Gifted,* 57th Yearbook, Part II, National Society for the Study of Education, Chicago: University of Chicago Press, 1958, pp. 155–192.

Actually, exact definition of the gifted is less important than making *some* provision for those who are most outstanding. As facilities expand and attitudes improve, it will be time to give more careful consideration to precise identification. In the meantime, teachers should know the factors that might be considered, because there are cases of pseudo mediocrity, as well as pseudo retardation. Pupils have been known to be so apprehensive about receiving high grades and being identified as "eggheads," "bookworms," or "brains" that they deliberately concealed their superiority. It takes potential, motivation, and exposure to develop high functional intelligence.[16] For such pupils the curative aspect of mental hygiene merits consideration. It is erroneous to state that "Genius will out." Perhaps the poet emphasizes this more effectively than does the psychologist.

> Full many a gem of purest ray serene
> The dark unfathomed caves of ocean bear.
> Full many a flower is born to blush unseen
> And waste its sweetness on the desert air.
> *Gray*, "Elegy in a Country Churchyard"

Characteristics of the Gifted. The conventional picture of the gifted child has been a slight, stoop-shouldered, myopic individual with his nose in a book. Terman's studies have done much to erase this misconception, for he found that high intelligence is more likely to be associated with health, robust physique, lack of sensory defect, and being both taller and heavier than age mates. Nevertheless, the stereotype has not vanished. These characteristics of the gifted are, of course, not enough for identification, inasmuch as correlation coefficients between physical and mental traits are low.

Perhaps the outstanding characteristic of the gifted child is that among his peers in grade status he will be the youngest. In fact, it has been said that a rough way to identify giftedness is to look up the birth dates. Another characteristic is the size of the gifted child's vocabulary and his accurate use and choice of words. His language development is so far ahead of that of his peers that people are likely to remark that he talks like a "little professor." Gifted children's perception of relationships is such that they make generalizations in a superior fashion. These things add up to an ability to do abstract or conceptual thinking at earlier ages than other youngsters and to do it in a superior fashion in the later years. This thinking will take place in all areas which interest them—scientific, historical, mathematical, or social. Teachers will note the characteristic speedy rate of learning. Herein lies the futility of attempting to "enrich" the curriculum by giving more problems. The gifted child will, as a mat-

---

[16] Miner, *op. cit.*, pp. 4–10.

ter of fact, master the fundamentals and principles involved so quickly that he actually needs fewer problems. We see here the danger of boredom and the need for recognition of the preventive aspect of mental hygiene. The gifted children keep at their projects, both self-initiated and those suggested by others, for long periods of time. Memory is, of course, notably long and accurate. Past experiences are recalled readily and they can memorize poetry or roles in plays with astonishing ease. They are characterized by a wide range of interests and have avid curiosity. Their questions are not ones designed simply to involve parents and teachers in conversation but represent an active search for answers to problems that intrigue them.[17]

Note that the characteristics are relative. Pupils of average intelligence will also possess some of these traits, though not so abundantly or with such high frequency. Moreover, note that these characteristics have some very direct implications for teaching.

Providing for the Gifted by Enrichment. Fundamentally, enrichment consists of curricular selection and the organization of learning experiences which are appropriate to the youngster's accelerated mental development. There are many ways to do this, but it emphatically is not a matter of having them do more work at the same level as that planned for the average pupil. The basic objectives of education for the gifted are the same as those for all children—to live competently with their fellows, to develop special competencies, to foster self-direction, to develop a love for learning, to stimulate critical thinking, to appreciate the cultural heritage, and to contribute to society in terms of unique abilities.[18]

Enrichment may refer to depth, breadth, or kind of educational experience. Emphasis on depth may be illustrated by the study of words. Instead of stopping after finding a definition in the dictionary, the roots of the words, its similarity to other words, its synonyms and antonyms are also sought. And there are those who enjoy this activity. One lad who when a high-school senior scored as high as the norm for college professors on a vocabulary test was in the habit of spending much of his leisure in *reading* the dictionary. The study of mathematics might be deepened by searching for algebraic solutions for the problems which could be solved by arithmetic, by encouraging study of the theory of numbers, or by studying the history of mathematics. Broadening of educational experiences will consist of supplementing the study of literature with the reading of biographies of authors or of relating the story, essay,

---

[17] Norma E. Cutts and Nicholas Moseley, *Teaching the Bright and the Gifted,* Englewood Cliffs, N.J.: Prentice-Hall, Inc., 1957, pp. 18–26.

[18] A. Harry Passow, "Enrichment of Education for the Gifted" in *Education for the Gifted,* 57th Yearbook, Part II, National Society for the Study of Education, Chicago: University of Chicago Press, 1958, p. 194.

or poem being studied to the historical period during which it was written. Broadening experiences in science might consist of reading about the lives of scientists, relating theoretical science to everyday living, or conducting individual experiments or investigations into insect, bird, fish, or mammalian life. All of these could constitute the basis for a special report in class to assure the student that the extra study is something more than just busy work.

A third-grader asked after the author had been introduced, "What kind of doctor are you? An M.D., a D.D., or a Ph.D.?" This was followed by questions about dinosaurs and space—though it turned out he planned to be a physician. His questions revealed the result of enrichment from experiences—further evidenced by books, on the table and shelves, about dinosaurs and space, at several different levels of reading difficulty. His interests had aroused those of his peers. Enrichment through varied experiences is illustrated in cases where the pupil is encouraged to carry on independent study in foreign language, mathematics, or science. The pursuit of some hobby during school-time can be encouraged as long as the pupil understands that competent mastery of subject matter is a preliminary to such activity.

Some of the foregoing suggestions may strain the teacher's imagination and creativity. Hence, it is important to enlist the aid of the pupils concerned in planning a developmental sequence of experiences. Suggestions from other teachers as to what they have done will be helpful in getting *something* started. After a year or two of experience, plans for enrichment will be more readily devised. Teachers who do *something* one term or year are observed to have many more things moving in their "three-ring circus" the following year. Not only does their experience provide data on what may or may not be effective, it seems that some experimentation makes them more alert to the suggestions in professional literature.

Planning, counseling, and checking on progress, all are time-consuming. But even a selfish view, as contrasted to an altruistic one, might still justify the expenditure. If one is worried about the "class average," one might consider that work with the gifted will do more to raise the average than will a comparable amount of energy devoted to slow learners. Moreover, pressure on the latter to achieve may result in emotional disturbance and maladjustment, whereas pressure on the gifted is likely to remove the symptoms of boredom, resentment, withdrawal, "laziness," and the like. Finally, it has been noted that whenever special attention has been given to the gifted a concomitant result is that education for the generality has been improved.[19]

The need for attention to the gifted has been recognized. The cost of

[19] Leonard, *op. cit.*, p. 46.

implementing programs is not prohibitive. Enrichment materials for gifted children in the lower grades can be effectively used in routine teaching at the higher levels. The real problems are "plain laziness" and fear of change.[20] Another consideration is the obstacle imposed by the teacher's own lack of a feeling of security. When the knowledge and beliefs of a teacher are challenged by a young pupil, there is a threat to the authoritative role of the teacher. One need not feel that he is abnormal or inadequate when these feelings arise. Let the feelings be recognized,

FIG. 7. Have substantial gains been made recently in meeting the needs of gifted pupils? How can equipment for special projects be secured? What is the comparative importance of laboratory and reading experiences in the education of the gifted?

but take steps to modify them. In the final analysis, there will be no better proof of the teacher's excellence than to have taken part in the development of a pupil who later makes a name for himself, his school, and his teacher when he emerges into the adult world. The leaders, artists, scientists, teachers of tomorrow must attribute a part of their success to the stimulating experiences that have been arranged for them.

Special Classes for the Gifted. Fundamentally, the provision of special classes for the gifted is a means of enriching their school life. But usually we mean by enrichment that which takes place in the regular classroom, while special classes take the pupil outside the classroom where he is

[20] *Ibid.,* p. 47.

placed with others who are similar to him in intellectual status and interest. Special classes are those in which pupils in a given school are grouped according to their indicated ability. The objective is to ease the burden on the teacher by reducing the range of differences which must be given attention if all pupils are to make optimum progress. Special classes may also include the provision for study of a specific subject which is not typically included in the curriculum—for instance, a class in French or German offered to able students from the first to the eighth grades inclusive. There might be a similar arrangement for those interested in art, but, typically, the students will come for special classes from one or at most three grades—it depends on the nature of the subject.

In elementary schools in various communities, special classes have been established in foreign language, art, mathematics, science, social studies, music, reading clubs, and toastmasters' clubs. In the secondary school there may be classes, such as Accelerated Geometry, Accelerated Chemistry, Advanced Writing, which are often similar in content and method to courses taught at the college level.

There are many arguments (most of which have mental hygiene implications) concerning the provision of special classes for the gifted students. The following columns illustrate some of the arguments for and against providing for the grouping that is basic in such arrangements:

1. It is undemocratic to give some opportunities which are not shared by others.

2. Leadership experiences are available for bright students when grouped with their age peers.

3. Bright and average pupils both profit from being in the same class. Leadership is exercised and inspiration is provided.

4. Bright pupils become egotistical, conceited, and haughty when grouped in terms of their ability.

5. Average pupils are stimulated to exert more effort when they perceive what others can do.

6. Pupils need to work together in school so that they may as adults be able to work together.

7. Grouping pupils may put a pupil with his peers in one class, while in another he is out of his element.

1. Democratic theory emphasizes the need for varying instruction to challenge each to do his best.

2. Leadership opportunities are distributed to pupils who are overshadowed when grouped with brighter age mates.

3. Grouping makes the teacher's task of meeting differences easier, because the range of variance is reduced.

4. Research provides ample evidence that grouping incites the bright to greater effort and accomplishment.

5. Average pupils are discouraged when their best efforts yield low results in comparison to the achievements of the bright.

6. By virtue of the things one does in life, his competitors are persons of similar status.

7. Grouping can be arranged by subjects and interests so that the range of ability in any one class is relatively small.

8. Any gifted child gains more from a given experience than an average child—his program is enriched automatically.

8. Mastering daily lessons easily, the gifted child becomes lazy and satisfied with mediocre achievement.

9. It is unfair to teachers to take the bright pupils from them, thereby lessening the gains in total class achievement.

9. Teachers are often apprehensive of the bright pupil and thus cause him to slacken effort. There is a temptation for teachers to neglect those who can work independently.

10. Grouping cannot be done precisely; therefore, some borderline pupils may be unjustly put in or kept from the bright group.

10. *Any* plan for grades, promotion, grouping, college selection, or job appointment suffers from this borderline inaccuracy.

Some of the foregoing arguments are simply personal opinion—biased, as are most opinions—while others can be supported with research data. The point of listing them is not so much to settle arguments as to indicate that, where grouping is used, there are dangers that should be anticipated and antidotes provided. Even though there may be dangers accompanying special classes and ability grouping, we cannot afford to view with complacency the data provided by Terman some years ago, i.e., while the average progress quotient of his gifted subjects was 114 (meaning that they were accelerated by 14 per cent in grade placement), their average achievement quotient was 144. This means that the typical gifted child was *retarded in grade placement* by 30 per cent.

Although children can and often do achieve remarkably in spite of being denied the special promotions they have earned, a considerable proportion of those in our gifted group languished in idleness throughout grade and high school and failed to develop the ambition or habits of work necessary to make them successful in college. The question is how much risk of social adjustment can one afford to take to keep the gifted child at school tasks difficult enough to command his attention and respect. The data here reviewed indicate that the risk of maladjustment is less than is commonly believed.[21]

Acceleration for the Gifted. Perhaps the most common technique for providing for the gifted is acceleration, that is, skipping a grade or taking two grades in one year, so that the pupil is in a higher grade than his age mates. Even this practice has diminished in recent years, because of the fear that accelerated pupils will be misplaced socially, physically, and emotionally. Acceleration is feared particularly in the primary grades when individual growth in these various characteristics is rapid and differences are wide. It is less feared in the intermediate grades when differ-

[21] Lewis M. Terman and Melita H. Oden, *The Gifted Child Grows Up*, Stanford, Calif.: Stanford University Press, 1947, p. 280.

ences are smaller, due to slower rates of growth. It is again feared at the high-school level when one might be graduated so early that he is out of place when he enters college.

The wisdom of acceleration has been investigated by Dan C. Shannon who summarized the results of studies which have spanned a period of thirty-four years. He concludes that research seems to say things to which educators prefer not to listen. It was found, for instance, that bright pupils who entered college two or three years younger than the average took more scholarship honors, took part in more student activities—including football—and were elected to more offices than their older classmates. Shyness and timidity were more frequently found in the control group than in the accelerated group. Another study concluded that, when junior high school was completed in two instead of three years, the accelerated group was slightly better in social and personal adjustment than was the three-year group—when careful counseling based on mental and physical status was part of the plan. Other studies support the view that acceleration cannot be condemned on the basis of threat to mental health. The case is similar with respect to academic achievement; for example, younger pupils do better scholastically than do students who are two or three years older (the students were matched on the basis of IQ, sex, and father's occupation). In college the same trend continues: the young entrant keeps abreast scholastically, participates in student activities, and likes the experience of acceleration. An amusing study resulted from professors' complaints about the bright but immature versus the bright but mature students in their classes. A questionnaire showed that in many cases the same student was deemed by some to be mature and by other professors to be immature. In final summary it was found that the average age of the mature group was 17.3 years while the average for immature was 17.4 years. The difference is not statistically reliable, but it appears that age is not equivalent to maturity. Of those who became nationally famous after graduation from college, the greatest percentage (29 per cent), were graduated at nineteen years of age, 22 per cent were graduated at twenty years, and the percentages diminished until only 3 per cent of the nationally known group were graduated at twenty-six years.[22]

A further argument for acceleration, even if research did not prove the case, would be that, if schools all over the country were to practice acceleration, the chances of the student's being "out of his element" in college would not be great because many of his intellectual and age peers would be there.

From the standpoint of society as a whole, one of the more cogent

[22] Dan C. Shannon, "What Research Says about Acceleration," *Phi Delta Kappan*, 39:70–72, 1957.

factors supporting acceleration is the early age at which creativity reaches its peak. In science and literature this peak tends to be reached in the late twenties and early thirties. Thomas Edison, for example, though he invented during his entire lifetime, took out the greatest number of patents per year between the ages of thirty-two and thirty-six.[23] Acceleration, resulting in early graduation from high school and college, would leave more years open for creative production prior to reaching the years of highest creativity.

As the world of automation becomes a more prominent feature of our way of life, the demand for prolonged education becomes more insistent.[24] Prolonged education may in some ways be a hazard in adolescent and early adult development (see Chapter 3). If more students were to be graduated from schools and colleges at younger ages, it seems probable that they would in greater numbers be likely to seek the higher degrees (before marriage and entering the occupational world) which are so urgently needed in a technological society. This particular problem is intensified by the fact that young men have to perform a period of obligated military service. Being accelerated in school has the double advantage of increasing the probability of (1) performing more technical services in the armed forces and (2) encouraging one to continue schooling after service.

> If we conceive of democratic education as that which attempts to serve each child according to his needs and his talents, some type of selection is needed, particularly in the secondary schools. In most of the elementary classrooms of America, youngsters are already grouped so that the gifted, the average, and the slow may each work at his own level of development. Our secondary schools need to provide more programs that give individual ability the incentive to progress as rapidly as possible.[25]

Numerous plans have been devised for providing "the incentive to progress as rapidly as possible." Some of them require that adjustments be made only within the school. Examples would be where the elementary pupil is simply promoted from the fourth to the sixth grade, or from fifth to seventh. Another is to permit a high-school student to take courses selected from those usually offered in the year above which he ranks in school. Early graduation may be effected by taking proficiency

[23] Harvey C. Lehman, "The Creative Years in Science and Literature," in Raymond G. Kuhlen and George G. Thompson (eds.), *Psychological Studies of Human Development*, New York: Appleton-Century-Crofts, Inc., 1952, pp. 464–468.

[24] Peter F. Drucker, "America's Next Twenty Years: The Promise of Automation," *Harper's Magazine*, 210:41–47, April, 1955.

[25] Waurine Walker, "An Educated People Moves Freedom Forward," *National Education Association, Addresses and Proceedings*, 95:101, 1957.

examinations in subjects which a student has not taken formally or by carrying an extra subject each year, so that he accumulates the required units for graduation in three instead of four years. Sometimes the extra courses taken are specially designed so that acceleration will leave fewer gaps in required basic knowledge.

At times acceleration may require cooperation of schools and colleges. Thus, in the Program for Early Admission to College, tenth- and eleventh-grade students may be admitted to regular standing in college if they reveal high academic ability and appropriate personal maturity. The Advanced Placement Program, sponsored by the College Entrance Examination Board, permits able high-school seniors to take college courses in high school and be admitted to sophomore standing on entrance to college if they prove their competence on placement examinations.[26] The merit of these plans has been clearly demonstrated. Most of the students who take part in them do admirable work and they avoid developing habits of indolence.

The Teacher's Role in Education of the Gifted. Teachers can study the progress of plans now in operation and become the instigators of similar plans in their own schools. They can impress upon the gifted student the value of "making time" instead of "marking time" and encourage him to add his influence to the progress of plans. They can study the typically cited objections to acceleration and ability grouping and offer appropriate counter-arguments. They can examine themselves for evidence of resentment to or jealousy for the gifted child. Their support can be given to those who, at PTA meetings or staff meetings, express an interest in capitalizing upon the talents of the gifted—our greatest national resource.

Within his own classroom the teacher can carry on a stimulating twofold program. One is to enrich the regular classroom work by encouraging extensive and intensive readings, assigning individual reports that require research, encouraging independent experimentation, providing time for special work of either an academic or avocational nature. The other is to search for evidences that some pupils, who might already have learned to conceal their giftedness, have unusual talents of various kinds.

SUMMARY

The curative, preventive, and positive aspects of mental hygiene have especially noteworthy importance when applied to slow learners and gifted children. Recent years have shown that retarded children are edu-

[26] Lloyd S. Michael, "Secondary-school Programs" in *Education for the Gifted*, 57th Yearbook, Part II, National Society for the Study of Education, Chicago: University of Chicago Press, 1958, pp. 265–266.

cable when school tasks are geared to their level and speed. It has long been known that much of the potential talents of the gifted remain uncultivated.

Slow learners are different from average children in degree, hence a sharp dividing line in terms of IQ is not sufficient—though mental tests provide clues. Care must be taken not to mistake emotional blocks to learning for slow mental development. Sensory defects must also be looked for and corrected when possible. Retarded children in the classroom need to be accepted socially, to take part in activities, to have responsibilities and to be considered as individuals. Special classes are particularly advantageous, because the teachers typically involved have special skills and because the pupil has the opportunity to function with his intellectual peers.

Much of the inadequate treatment of the gifted may be attributed to misinformation about the characteristics of the gifted. Suffice it to say that mental superiority is typically accompanied by good health, superior physique, comparatively superior sensory equipment, ambition, curiosity, and good social and personal adjustment.

One way of helping the gifted come closer to a realization of potential is enrichment. This places a burden on the teacher to plan, guide, and evaluate individual and small-group learning activities. But it pays high dividends to teachers in terms of average group achievement, to pupils in terms of self-realization, and to society in terms of cultivating human resources.

Special classes for the gifted have been objected to, because of the false belief that it is undemocratic. However, if democracy means emphasis on individual uniqueness and contributions, the objection is weakened if not nullified. Not only do gifted children not develop undesirable traits but education for all is improved when special classes are operated.

Acceleration seems to possess many advantages: greater challenge to individuals, encouragement to prolong education, and completion of formal education prior to the peak years of creativity. Research shows that acceleration does not typically create problems of social misplacement.

STUDY AND DISCUSSION EXERCISES

1. Summarize in ten or twelve statements some of the general considerations that must characterize the teaching of slow learners. (Go beyond the text for answers.)

2. What are some of the major factors (social, educational, and administrative) which condition the formation of special classes?

3. Assuming it is impractical to give special attention to more than half of those who might be considered gifted, would it be acceptable to use just the criterion of IQ as the basis for selection?

4. Do you consider that enrichment could, under favorable circumstances, be adequate for education of the gifted?

5. Under what circumstances do you think it would be undesirable to enter gifted students into college two or three years early?

SUGGESTED ADDITIONAL READINGS

An Introduction to the Education of the Able Student in Wilmington Public Schools, Part I, Wilmington, Del.: Wilmington Public Schools, 1958. 27 pp.

This pamphlet describes specific steps for planning better education of the gifted. Copies may be obtained from the Curriculum Service Center, Wilmington, Del.

Conant, James B., *The American High School Today,* New York: McGraw-Hill Book Company, Inc., 1959. 140 pp.

Several of Dr. Conant's twenty-two recommendations for improving the American high school are designed to provide more realistic opportunities and futures for able pupils.

Cutts, Norma E., and Nicholas Moseley, *Teaching the Bright and the Gifted,* Englewood Cliffs, N.J.: Prentice-Hall, Inc., 1957. 268 pp.

The role of the classroom teacher in identifying, challenging, and leading gifted students is the central theme of this book. Enrichment, special classes, and acceleration are discussed.

Kirk, Samuel A., and G. Orville Johnson, *Educating the Retarded Child,* Boston: Houghton Mifflin Company, 1951, pp. 123–250

The pages indicated deal with specific problems of educating retarded children in preschool, elementary, and secondary grades.

Kough, Jack, *Practical Programs for the Gifted,* Chicago: Science Research Associates, Inc., 1960. 192 pp.

Discussion of identification, enrichment, and acceleration of gifted students is supplemented by descriptions of existing programs.

National Society for the Study of Education, *Education for the Gifted,* 57th Yearbook, Part II, Chicago: University of Chicago Press, 1958.

If the student cannot read the entire volume on the importance of education for the gifted, their identification, and description of various plans, it is suggested that he select chapters of particular interest.

CHAPTER 10

THE MENTAL HYGIENE OF DISCIPLINE

The ability to enforce discipline was once the *sine qua non* of successful and admired teachers. Either through fear or strength the teacher had to keep pupils in submission. The birch rod and willow switch were as necessary as were slates and crayons. The motto "Learn or get out" was prominently displayed in some classrooms. The first question asked of a prospective teacher was "Can you maintain discipline?" This discipline was definitely of the authoritarian type.

The repressive concept of discipline is definitely unpopular today, if it has not been completely repudiated. But there is a possibility that, in the course of getting away from the concept, the pendulum has swung too far. There are at least a few teachers who seem to believe that there is no place for imposed discipline in a modern, successful school. Actually the idea that there should be no authoritarian discipline is as deleterious to the growth of the pupil as was the old martinet viewpoint.

THE MEANING OF DISCIPLINE

Earlier Concepts of Discipline. Although American schools were intended to prepare pupils for effective citizenship in a democratic society, the emphasis was on conformity and obedience. A pupil who questioned the word of a teacher was regarded as an upstart who deserved immediate and harsh condemnation; failure to conform was punished by the use of the hickory stick. Even inability to learn the tasks required was thought to be evidence of innate stubbornness and was punishable by a caning. E. K. Wickman,[1] in 1928, found that many teachers considered such

---

[1] E. K. Wickman, *Children's Behavior and Teachers' Attitudes*, New York: The Commonwealth Fund, Division of Publications, 1928.

irregularities as standing on the wrong side of the desk to recite, making too much noise with pens and pencils, failure to put down a pencil immediately, and not keeping straight lines in passing to be serious manifestations of behavior. Whispering, talking out of turn, leaving one's seat or the room without permission also were acts of insubordination. Looking at school regimes of the past we marvel at the toughness of spirit that made it possible for any pupils to reach a sane, hearty, and sometimes happy adulthood.[2] We may even be inclined to infer that imposed discipline is not entirely wrong. However, we are sure that such methods did inhibit the learning of some and prevent school attendance by others.

Contemporary View of Discipline. Today the aim of discipline is to secure good order and socially oriented self-direction, and the method is different. Order which stems from compulsion is not necessarily good discipline—in fact, when the external controls are relaxed, there is often a marked disruption of the "good order" which is so highly prized. Order which stems from attention to purposeful activity will usually be less than the "pin-drop-silence" type, but it will persist even without adult control. Observance of group welfare, conformity to legal requirements, respect for authority and learning, and temporarily putting aside one's own immediate wishes are lessons that must be learned.[3] Then, the hearty performance of duties and of freely chosen activities in an orderly manner with due regard given to the rights and privileges of others may be considered the goals of constructive self-discipline.

Constructive discipline may be defined as training or instruction that molds, improves, strengthens, corrects, or improves behavior. The aim is to encourage the development of each individual's unique personality, so that he can make a contribution to society that is not made by anyone else and so that he will gain the satisfaction of realizing the more complete fruition of his own strong points.

Obviously, this kind of emphasis indicates that there must be no confusion between the meaning of liberty and of license. License, which in this connection means assuming the right to do what one wishes without regard to the desires of others, must be contrasted with liberty, which means freedom to do what one wishes as long as it does not interfere with a like amount of liberty for one's associates. To have independence means that one may, without external compulsion, choose his own socially oriented actions. In a way, this concept is now at work in our schools. In the elementary school there is usually a large amount of

[2] Aldous Huxley, "Can We Be Well Educated?" *Esquire*, 47:112ff., December, 1956.

[3] George D. Stephens, "Needed: A Declaration of Dependence," *The Educational Forum*, 23:61–68, November, 1958.

teacher direction. In the secondary school direction becomes somewhat less evident—students are free to study what they wish during their study periods. In college there is practically no supervision of study—completion of assignments is the students' responsibility. Fortunately, there are numerous indications that independence can be achieved much earlier than the college level. When given an opportunity, children continually surprise adults with their ability to be intelligently self-directive.

Another important aspect of the present view of discipline is the directing of attention to causes rather than to symptoms. Imposed discipline has a tendency to follow misbehavior, whereas current discipline seeks to avoid misbehavior through expert teaching and appropriate curriculums.[4] Authoritarian discipline often gets the immediately desired result of conformity, but in far too many cases the tensions are vented maliciously. For instance, in a school where autocratic discipline prevailed and where there was good order in the classroom, pupils did not talk back to the teachers, lessons were done on time, and no one thought of running in the hallway, there was still evidence of a lack of discipline. The school building was broken into on several occasions, supplies were strewn about, books were thrown from the shelves, and there was considerable breakage in out-of-the-way places.

What methods, then, should be used in the process of disciplining? Ideally, the classroom teacher should discover that the necessity for arbitrary control should be secondary to the discipline achieved by purposeful activity.

1. We want discipline which recognizes the *inherent dignity and rights* of every human being, rather than discipline attained through humiliation of the undisciplined.

2. We want discipline based on *devotion to humanitarian principles and ideals*. In a democratic society, loyalty to the principles of freedom, justice and equality for all rather than discipline based on a narrower, more egotistic affiliation of "*my* group" is essential.

3. We want *self-direction, self-discipline*, rather than discipline based upon unquestioning obedience to a leader.

4. We want discipline based on *understanding of the goal in view* rather than discipline based on taking someone else's word for specific appropriate behaviors.[5]

Values and Outcomes of Effective Discipline. Discipline is an essential factor both in securing the optimum development of individual poten-

[4] Norma E. Cutts and Nicholas Moseley, "Four Schools of Discipline: A Synthesis," *School and Society*, 87:87, Feb. 28, 1959.
[5] George V. Sheviakov and Fritz Redl, *Discipline for Today's Children and Youth*, new revision by Sybil K. Richardson, Washington: National Education Association, Association for Supervision and Curriculum Development, 1956, pp. 7–8.

tialities and in living harmoniously and productively in social groups. Since in our society it is unlikely and undesirable that a person be supervised at all times by another who holds a place of authority, it is essential that discipline shall ultimately come from within. Although it may not be safe to call autocratic discipline a cause of maladjustment, it may safely be claimed as a contributing factor. When disciplinary measures serve to stir up and aggravate tensions, and at the same time, prohibit the release of feelings aroused, a growing, festering emotion is created. It is considered important to get the bad feelings out, in order to make room for good feelings.[6] Many children are fortunate enough to find ways to express their emotions both in and out of school; others have enough tension-tolerance to stand up under the onslaught of tension. Some, however, break down while attending school, and others carry their tensions into adulthood as weaknesses in their emotional stability.

Effective discipline will teach reasonable conformity, respect for law and for people—respect that arises from understanding and appreciation, rather than a simulated respect that arises because it is demanded. School authorities recognize that, while you can demand conformity, you must earn respect. The former respect is an outgrowth of the opportunity to participate in common problems. This difference can easily be recognized when a contrast is made between an autocratic classroom, where there are opposing camps of teacher and students, and one in which the feeling has developed that all are embarked on a common enterprise. To place much responsibility on young children with their limited maturity and experience for decision making and self-direction is expecting too much. Children can be comfortable in the presence of firm and kindly authority. Often young children are con-fused by the lack of positive direction.[7]

Another value of self-discipline is that it develops social awareness and practice in group participation. The individual, by participating in the planning and execution of policy, is brought to a realization that others have wishes and privileges that sometimes conflict with his own. He can, without making himself a nonentity, more readily accept the fact that it is occasionally necessary to consider others.

Effective discipline prepares one for significant participation in democratic processes. Conformity is required, but stereotyped activity is a restrictive influence on a functioning democracy. Democracy recognizes the worth of the individual and prizes the fact that different persons will make different contributions to group welfare. Cooperative projects,

[6] Dorothy W. Baruch, *How to Discipline Your Children*, New York: Public Affairs Pamphlets, 1953, pp. 7–22.

[7] "Ten Criticisms of Public Education," *National Education Association Research Bulletin*, 35 (4):137, December, 1957.

group activity in discipline, and other school enterprises are learning experiences; moreover, they must be a means to self-fulfillment, and not expressions of conforming for the sake of conformity.[8]

The discipline of purposeful activity tends to fulfill the basic need for satisfying curiosity. We need only look back upon our own educational experiences to know that many of the tasks which we performed in school dulled curiosity by prescribing the sources of information and the methods by which the results of study were to be reported. The avoidance of failure, staying after school, or the loss of privileges was the goal of study, rather than the satisfaction of curiosity. Many people have not had enough tension-tolerance to withstand these pressures and, even as adults, continue to avoid formal learning pursuits. It is difficult for one to be ready to take up adult responsibilities if he has become accustomed to having his plans and methods laid down for him.

Discipline in the classroom has a threefold purpose. (1) It should remove distracting factors from the teaching-learning situation and so direct activity that learning will take place in an economical fashion. (2) The mental health and physical safety and well-being of all pupils must be safeguarded while they are under school auspices. (3) Practice in conformity, cooperation, leadership-followership, and personal accountability that will prepare students for all that responsible citizenship implies should be provided.

Lack of discipline in the school and the home tends to produce unhappy children, because they do not learn the important lesson that bending to the will of others is a necessity if they are to get along in social groups. There are many adults who manifest symptoms of mental illness, which is at least partially due to their never having learned either internal discipline or the necessity for conforming to external controls. These symptoms take such forms as crime, excessive use of alcohol, cheating for selfish purposes, inability to hold a job, dissatisfaction in marriage relations, and lack of determination in pursuing an objective. There are some who feel that improper discipline in the schools is a contributing factor to increased juvenile delinquency.[9]

FACTORS IN WHOLESOME DISCIPLINE

In the following discussion the viewpoint is taken that coercion may compel conformity and lead to the performance of disagreeable tasks, but that it does not lead to genuine discipline. In addition, it is assumed that attention and effort flow from interest, that love for literature,

[8] John Martin Rich, "The Problem of Freedom in the Classroom," *Social Studies,* 50:22–23, January, 1959.

[9] "Ten Criticisms of Public Education," *op. cit.,* p. 152.

mathematics, or for social responsibilities is an outcome of effective motivational techniques.[10]

Teacher Direction Has Its Place in Effective Discipline. Do not expect that pupils will automatically be ready to assume responsibilities for self-direction. It may be necessary, initially, to call some pupils to order. No harm will be done to a "delicate personality" if the pupils understand that ultimately the teacher is responsible for acceptable classroom conduct. Governmental, business, and educational organizations all make use of specialists and experts. Children should learn that properly constituted authority is not an infringement on personal liberty.

A Prime Requisite Is to Understand the Nature of Children. This will include, among other things, the understanding that children's actions are frequently not in agreement with their intentions. Many times their conduct is the result of ill-conceived experimentation rather than malicious intent. The degree of pupil control should vary with the situation. It is natural for students to desire freedom of movement. To restrict this freedom unnecessarily is to ignore one of their innate drives. Likewise, it may be necessary to provide for rest from both physical and mental activities, inasmuch as they have a short attention span, limited physical vitality, and a lack of strength.

Understanding the interests and abilities of individuals in the class is just as necessary in constructive discipline as in effective academic instruction. Spontaneity in voice and action may be difficult for one child to avoid and for another to accomplish. *Respect for children as persons* should imply that the teacher knows enough about the background of each to be able to judge when a bit of behavior is really out of line with his nature, his background tensions, and his disappointments.

Wholesome Discipline Avoids Shaming, Sarcasm, and Ridicule. Any words or actions which belittle another person tend to undermine his sense of worth or serve to stimulate resentments that are destructive to a cheerful classroom atmosphere; therefore these measures must be heartily condemned. Sarcasm and ridicule reduce the likelihood that the school will meet the need the pupil has for security, for recognition, and, to an extent, for a feeling of companionship with the teacher—if not with fellow students. Any personal comparisons are likely to give offense. Each of us knows from personal experience alone that expressions and statements which humiliate tend to break down the group cohesiveness. Corporal punishment administered in public is one way of violating this principle.

Discipline should be based upon the concepts of courtesy and kindness rather than upon servile conformity to laws, rules, and regulations. This

[10] Nathaniel Cantor, *The Teaching-Learning Process,* New York: Holt, Rinehart and Winston, Inc., 1953, pp. 68–70.

approach, too, should be the outgrowth of pupil experiences and group discussion instead of being adopted because of a teacher's precept or prompting. The significance of the adult's example is illustrated in an anecdote about a mother who took her young son to a psychologist. When she said, "I just don't know how I can teach Tommy to be courteous," the psychologist asked her, "Do you say 'Please' and 'Thank you'?"

Keep Pupils Busy with Interesting Tasks. Interest is the identification of the individual with some object, goal, or person. Identification in this sense is not unlike the defense mechanism, since it implies a feeling of oneness with—a community of feeling. Interesting tasks are those which the pupil feels are significant to his own being and aims; he sees their relationship to his needs and wants. Busy and interested pupils have no time for acts that would keep them from their accepted goals; and activities that interfere with accepted objectives are the ones which are objectionable and annoying to the classroom teacher. This means that teachers have the responsibility for clarifying the goals and reminding students of them.

Emphasize the Rewards Which Are Inherent in the Work at Hand. While this does not necessarily imply that rewards and prizes have no place in motivation, it does imply that prizes should lead to intrinsic motivation. The more quickly the shift to intrinsic motivation—the will to carry on pursuits for the satisfaction to be found in the tasks themselves—can be made, the greater will be the assurance that continuous learning will become an experience personally desirable to the learner. Praise for work done, acknowledgment of individual contributions, and the display of results are means by which the rewards that exist in the task itself can be kept in the minds of pupils. All teachers should be prepared to answer the question "So what?" regarding subject matter, whether or not it is actually asked. The teacher who cannot figure out the best reason in the world for teaching the worst subject is likely to be ineffective.

Strict Domination Should Be Avoided. The uniformity of conduct stressed in strict domination is contradictory to the innate and acquired differences which exist between pupils. While there must be order underlying productive work, the lock-step procedures all too often used in classrooms do not bring about continuously productive activity. It has been shown above that classroom docility lasts only as long as the dominating authority is present. Work is done under compulsion rather than with spontaneity, with the result that, as an inevitable accompaniment, a distaste for work is acquired.

Recognize the Mores Existing in the Group. This factor is related to understanding the nature of children; but it takes cognizance of the fact that mores differ between one community and another. Local variations in style of dress, hairdos (including boys' styles), colloquialisms, and political and social attitudes should not be brusquely attacked by the teacher. One violation of group mores too common among teachers is demanding that pupils report the misconduct of other pupils. This encouragement of "tattling" puts the student in an equivocal position: if he reports, he is condemned by his group, and if he remains silent, he feels the disapproval of his teacher. In either case, he will suffer from indecision and doubt that will threaten his feelings of security.

Seek the Causes of Misbehavior. At times students do something just because they can get away with it; but usually misbehavior is generated by some tension or deprivation which the child feels. Even though it may sometimes be necessary to correct a pupil's actions immediately, the teacher has a responsibility to search for and, if possible, eliminate the causal factors of misbehavior. To demand conformity and obedience is in exactly the same category as commanding a pupil to give up day-dreaming, to stop projecting his difficulties, or to stop biting his nails. While a teacher may point proudly to the fact that he shamed Mary into keeping her thumb out of her mouth, he may not have noticed that Mary's insecurity now shows itself in recessive behaviors.

The point may be illustrated by the case of a boy in a geometry class who said that when he told the instructor he did not understand the explanation that had just been given by the instructor, the instructor roared, "Wipe that grin off your face, you big, milk-fed lout, or I'll toss you out the window." In another class, the lad said, near the close of the period, "It seems to me that this poem is so obscure that reading it is a waste of time." The instructor did not consider it a violation of his personality that such a statement should be made. Instead, he answered, "Well, the time's about up now, but if you'll stay a few minutes, we'll go over it together and see if we can't get meaning out of it."

Teachers Need to Have Confidence in Themselves and in Their Pupils. Autocratic procedures on the part of the teacher are likely to grow out of his feelings of insecurity. He demands strict conformity and attendance to business, because he fears that things will get out of hand. Two steps may be taken to establish the feelings of confidence that would make repressive discipline unnecessary. One is for the teacher to spend adequate time in planning and studying both subject matter and teaching procedures. The second step is to cultivate a classroom atmosphere conducive to good teacher-pupil rapport—one that will actually make it difficult for pupils to upset orderly procedures.

The teacher must also be confident that pupils are capable of assuming responsibility. Just as teachers sense and appreciate the confidence placed in them by administrators, so pupils can sense and act upon the confidence teachers have in them. They enjoy living up to expectations. If they know mature conduct is expected, they will strive for it. On occasion, a student may not be able to live up to the high level of expectation, but that situation will provide an opportunity to stimulate growth by saying "Well, this was a pretty difficult program for you, but I'm sure that next time you'll come even closer to perfect achievement."

IMPROVING MENTAL HEALTH THROUGH DISCIPLINE

The following suggestions for improving mental health through good discipline are in accord with the democratic values cherished in American culture.

Firmness Is Necessary. One of the frequently mentioned criteria of maturity is ability to consider the wishes and welfare of others. The egocentric behavior that is characteristic of childhood must yield to the more altruistic behavior that marks the true adult. Regardless of how vehemently we may declare that "They are children only once," the fact remains that there are "musts" in society. If teachers and parents do not teach the lesson, peer groups will teach it with less kindness and with less regard for consequences to the personality. A middle course must be sought between the lack of firmness exhibited in pampering the child and the repressiveness of autocratic demand. While children should not be permitted to "rule the roost," neither should good order be based on the whim of the teacher. The criterion for firmness, therefore, should be "What action, rules, and mores are in the best interest of the group?" Particularly in the beginning, teachers may even go so far as to look for opportunities to exercise their authority, so that the pupils will know that firmness will always be used. This is particularly important when the students are testing the new teacher—and this testing will take place until his reputation is well established.

Discipline Should Be Appropriate and Consistent. This is an admonition difficult to clarify, because, in order to be appropriate, measures for checking disapproved conduct must be varied. One lad had an unexcused absence, because he wanted to go swimming with some of last year's graduates. Another lad cut because he had a chance to work in someone's garden and earn money with which he could buy a cherished biology book. Appropriate discipline takes into account the individual, the time, the total situation, and the degree to which the behavior differs from the individual's typical responses.[11]

Consistency is paying uniform attention to a given kind of response

[11] Lawrence E. Vredevoe, "Practices in School Discipline," *American School Board Journal*, 139:19–21, July, 1959.

and accordingly adjusting corrective procedures to the individual. One must be sure not to overlook a given response at one time and deal with it decisively and abruptly at another time. If the teacher and the class disapprove of whispering during the time others are presenting materials to the class, the interruption should not be frowned upon at one time and ignored at another.

A Good Adult Example Should Be Set. Much behavior is learned by direct imitation and much by means of unconscious imitation or suggestion. Pupils try to imitate their admired teachers. Especially in high school, boys and girls consciously aim to pattern their behavior after teachers whom they have selected as "heroes." For this reason, the teacher's attitude toward aspects of discipline (lying, cheating, work habits, use of criticism) has direct influence on the conduct of the young people. If they hear the teacher making excuses which they know are not genuine, if they hear him laughing about having been given too much change, if they are present when he criticizes his fellow teachers and administrators, they may think of these behaviors as appropriate.

Teachers sometimes object to being considered models, because they feel that it is unreasonable to expect them to be paragons of virtue. Fortunately, they do not have to be perfect. Recently, a few practical psychologists have let parents know that occasional lapses from consistent serenity will not irrevocably spoil the growth trends of their offspring.[12] A parent may lose control of his temper once in a while without feeling that he has committed an error that cannot be corrected. Similarly, teachers need not feel that they are lost souls if they become irritated now and then. It is the teacher's characteristic, or typical behavior— most often seen by the student—that is absorbed into his own reaction patterns. If the teacher cannot always be a perfect example of self-discipline—a few do seem to approach this ideal—he can at least make a consistent effort to grow toward better self-control. It is not going too far to say that the most fortunate pupils are those who can watch their own teacher growing and learning with them. They have a dynamic, a changing, a developing model before them.

Use the Processes of Reasoning. Teachers should explain to erring students the reasons for rules and regulations in general and the reason for specific requirements in given cases. If reasoning is attempted in a moment of emotional stress, there is too great a likelihood that what is said will degenerate into wrangling and nagging. Teachers should not expect youngsters, even of high-school age, to understand their own motivation; it is, therefore, not very practical to try to reason with them by asking "What makes you do this?" or "Why do you act in this

---

[12] Ilse Forest, *Child Development,* New York: McGraw-Hill Book Company, Inc., 1954, p. 245.

way?" Too often, the child honestly does not know the answers to such questions. It would be better to try to get him to see how he would feel on the receiving end of the very behavior he manifests.

It is apparent that reasoning used for disciplinary purposes will be most effective when the conversational approach, rather than the cross-examination method, is used. The talks should take place during a period of emotional calm or neutrality; and the discussion might well begin by analyzing the problems of someone else.

Provide for Substitute Behaviors. It is wise to suggest substitute behaviors instead of simply prohibiting a specific act. Instead of the parent's slapping the child's hand, for getting into the drawer of knives, and saying "No, no" or "Stop that," it is recommended that the child be allowed to become aware of the forbidden area, but that, as a part of the total procedure, he be given something with which he may play safely. Similarly, teachers, instead of forbidding interruptions, may ask the pupil to wait his own turn and then make some thought-out contribution. Instead of the pupil's being told that he must study, an attempt should be made to discover why he is not interested in the project at hand and to help him find something that will challenge him. An effort might be made to show him why the particular project has reference to his own growth and development. If boys on a basketball trip are acting in a rowdy manner in restaurants, perhaps they need to know just how their behavior can be improved so that they will get attention for behaving as gentlemen.

Providing substitute activities indicates a recognition of these truths: that behavior is caused, that the ultimate aim of discipline is self-direction, that growth is an individual process, and that a mature individual must get along without constant supervision. Substitution is a means of recognizing that repression, at best, has only a temporary value. Repression may lead to the individual's harboring resentments and frustrations to the point of his becoming an unbalanced personality; or it may cause the pent-up feelings to be released later in antisocial ways.

Discipline Should Be Democratic. Democratic discipline has a triple advantage. (1) It is in accord with the objectives and principles of our society, (2) it tends to capitalize on individual assets and thus provides a means of stimulating growth toward adult independence and self-direction, and (3) it lessens the chances of generating habits and tensions that are harmful to mental health. These advantages can be noted in classrooms where democratic discipline has been tried; and they are given pointed illustration in experimental situations.

Kurt Lewin and associates[13] carried on a series of experiments in

[13] Kurt Lewin, Ronald Lippitt, and Ralph K. White, "Patterns of Aggressive Behavior in Experimentally Created Social Climates," *The Journal of Social Psychology*, 10:271–299, 1939.

which artificially created social climates (involving club activities) were compared with regard to their effect on the behavior of ten-year-old boys. One climate was democratic; i.e., policies were matters of group decision, goals were discussed and the leader suggested alternatives, members were free to work with whom they wished, division of tasks was left to the group, and the leader praised or criticized work impersonally. Another climate was authoritarian; i.e., policy was determined by the leader, steps were dictated one at a time, the leader designated working groups and tasks, and praise and criticism were personal in nature. The third was a laissez-faire group; i.e., there was complete freedom for group or personal decision without leader participation, the leader said he would help if asked but took no other part, groupings were determined without the leader, comments on work were infrequent, and no attempt was made to interfere.

The groups were equated as far as possible, and after six weeks the following results were noted. Aggressive actions per meeting were, for the laissez-faire group, thirty-eight; for the autocratic group, thirty; and for the democratic group, twenty. It is to be noted that in the autocratic group some of the boys showed apathetic reactions. Observers judged that the boys in the autocratic group were apathetic to actions that were not of the aggressive type; whereas, actions were spontaneous, fact-minded, and friendly in the democratic group. The boys themselves evaluated their activities. The consensus was that they disliked the leader in the autocratic group but directed their hostility toward club members; they appreciated and liked the democratic leader but felt that they needed more direction and help than they had in the laissez-faire group. If the leaders left the room, there was a sharp rise in aggression in the autocratic group; whereas, the work continued almost normally in the democratic group. Scapegoats, boys who were picked on by others, had life made miserable for them in the autocratic group—two such boys dropped out. No such instances were noted in the democratic group. Their pride in work is reflected in the statement "Rather clearly the work products of this authoritarian atmosphere seemed to be the objects of aggressive attack rather than prideful ownership."[14] There were disturbances in the democratic group, but the results as a whole seem to indicate that discipline was of the constructive type. In the autocratic group, undesirable behavior developed promptly. Results similar to those reported have been informally observed in the school classroom.

Implementing the Principles of Constructive Discipline. The underlying principles of discipline which tend to promote good mental health suggest some practices to which teachers may profitably give attention.

1. The original contact with students should be systematically business-

[14] *Ibid.,* p. 289.

like, giving the impression of purposeful activity. In order that the first day may give the impression that there is work to be done, business to be conducted, the first meeting should be of full length. The short periods which so frequently characterize the opening of school tend to detract from the serious atmosphere desired.

2. Seek to establish congeniality and friendliness by learning the names of the students as quickly as possible. Learn at once, through records or conversation, something about each student—where he lives, what his interests are, what special abilities he has, or what he does in his spare time.

3. Explain to the pupils specifically what is to be accomplished. Youngsters in the primary and the elementary school will need to have this explanation in terms of immediate goals, whereas pupils in high school may tend to be satisfied with the outlining of more remote goals. Frequent restatement of the goals and discussion of the degree to which they have been and are being accomplished will incite the students to purposeful efforts.

4. Students can be encouraged to take part in making disciplinary policy; they should also be given a part in establishing and maintaining classroom routines. Many teachers, at both the elementary and the secondary level, have discovered that giving pupils special duties to perform reduces the need for imposed controls. Recognizing and praising the pupils' contribution will reinforce their willingness to help.

5. Courtesy is a matter of spirit as well as of form; thus, a teacher should not only habitually say "Please" and "Thank you," but he should have the tone of courtesy in his voice. A visitor in almost any school can find in some classroom a teacher who is attempting to overcome the hum of activity by raising the pitch and increasing the volume of his voice. The inner poise that comes through having good mental and physical health and the confidence that comes through having work carefully planned will help to control the tensions that show themselves in a strained speaking voice.

6. Try to strengthen the pupil's feelings of personal worth. This can be done by scaling tasks to his ability. Thus, the experiences of success and failure will be more equitably distributed and ego feelings will be enhanced. A spirit of genuine friendliness is another stimulant to feelings of worth.

GROUP DYNAMICS AS AN APPROACH TO DISCIPLINE

Group Dynamics and the Teacher. Group behavior, being a factor in the need for acceptance and recognition, has considerable influence on school morale. It also significantly affects academic achievement, inasmuch as group acceptance is reflected in the ego concepts of individuals and, thereby, conditions their feelings of security and levels of aspiration. The group climate is a major determinant of the prevailing mental hygiene in the classroom. A group functions best when its parts synchronize, when there is agreement on common goals, and when cooperation can be sustained. These characteristics can best be achieved when individuals within the group are understood and encouraged to contribute to group well-being.[15]

Classroom groups are composed of a variety of individuals, with varying origins and objectives and, as such, contains cliques and subgroups. To achieve optimum growth for individuals—the socialized, the isolate, and the deviate—all must be made to feel comfortable. The socialized will present only minor problems that can be met by agreeing on common goals, by giving each a chance to contribute, and by respecting the viewpoint of each. The isolate needs to be provided with a friend, introduced to small working groups where he can feel personal support, and only gradually be made a part of the larger total group. He should be paired with those who show positive response to him (sociometry can provide clues). The friendliness of a teacher is paramount. The deviate should receive encouragement for any positive contribution he makes or abilities which he shows. The teacher can, through explanation of the reasons for deviant behavior, help even very young pupils understand the misbehaving pupil.

As the teacher shows and explains the nature of cooperative endeavor—by accepting pupils, discussing goals, and providing a positive emotional tone—there develops a *we*-feeling, which enhances the stability of the group. A division of responsibilities and roles occurs. Leaders, idea "men," powers behind the scenes, favorites, buffoons, critics, executors, and peacemakers emerge. The teachers must learn to identify and capitalize on these roles, since they provide the means for various individuals to be accepted for the contributions they make.[16]

Group Dynamics as a Disciplinary Project. Group guidance has been used as an approach to rehabilitation, and not as a punitive disciplinary measure, in the junior high schools of Santa Barbara, California. Conventional detention periods had failed to reform a number of incorrigibles who collected many demerits. Therefore, weekly meetings, during assembly periods, for eight to twelve pupils were arranged in order to discuss their problems. The counselor explained that the aim of the

---

[15] Murray M. Horowitz, "The Teacher Utilizes Group Forces" in *Learning and the Teacher*, 1959 Yearbook, Association for Supervision and Curriculum Development, Washington: National Education Association, 1959, pp. 117–118.

[16] Paul Scheidlinger, *Psychoanalysis and Group Behavior*, New York: W. W. Norton & Company, Inc., 1952, pp. 184–186.

meetings was to change attitudes so that their actions would show they could live and work with others. The group members decided on a minimum length of time after which one could then go to the counselor and ask for release. This provided an opportunity for counseling and further airing of feelings. The counselor acted as a friend and, while the necessity for observing rules was stressed, the feelings of the pupil were accepted even when the conduct was not. The counselor let it be known that pupils could be "made" to behave but that it was desirable for the pupil to accept responsibility for changing himself. In the counseling groups the pupils discussed their merit reports, reasons for being referred to the group, and ways of improving behavior. They discussed human needs and feelings. Time was taken from the group meetings for the writing of periodic reports on progress. Topics for discussion and writing included such things as grades, teachers, attendance, promotions, dates, parents, graduation, citizenship, and report cards. It was felt that the results of this group guidance were good—judging by changes in expressed attitudes and overt behaviors. The sessions indicated that pupils need the support of a counselor, the cooperation and understanding of other school staff members, and teamwork with and of their peers.[17]

Group dynamics was used with eighth-grade girls who were involved in running away from home, truancy, drinking, and sexual promiscuity. Individual counseling had proven inadequate, partially because of time limitations. Six girls met with a psychologist and their teacher, held informal group sessions, and talked freely in a permissive atmosphere about their problems. The aim of becoming self-directive and of understanding themselves and others seemed to have been achieved after eleven weekly meetings; a follow-up study made six months later showed that the girls had maintained the growth which had developed by the end of the project. There was no evidence of regressive behavior; the girls could cope with their problems and tolerate frustrations, they realized that others had problems, and they reduced their tensions by airing their feelings.[18]

Group Counseling and Pupil Achievement. The importance of group identification and support is demonstrated in several projects involving underachieving pupils in various grades. One such study involved ten underachieving second, third, and fourth-graders. These children met for two hours a day, four days a week, for a total of sixty to eighty periods. Remedial instruction and group counseling received about equal attention in each period. Some pupils were withdrawn, while others were

[17] Paul Crawford, "A Disciplinary Group Guidance Project," in Helen I. Driver (ed.), *Counseling and Learning through Small-group Discussion*, Madison, Wis.: Monona Publications, 1958, pp. 312–316.

[18] Quentin R. Bryan and Edna M. Younker, "A Multiple Counseling Project for Pre-delinquent Eighth-grade Girls," in Driver, *ibid.*, pp. 293–297.

hyperactive and disruptive in their regular classes. Music, art, drama, and dancing were sometimes included in the counseling sessions. The first sessions were used to identify problems. Later ones were designed to give insight into the nature of their problems through free discussion of wishes, outcomes of action, and attitudes. Tasks were designed which required pupils to work together in groups. Eight of ten pupils benefited from the group sessions. Gains in achievement, as indicated on standardized tests, ranged from one to three grade levels, and ability to work independently was demonstrated. It was found that ability to work in groups was correlated with success in academic pursuits. Success in working with the small group carried over into work in the regular classroom.[19]

Any class has its leaders, its show-offs, its idea men, its excutives and its peacemakers, and troublemakers. When the teacher recognizes the individuals who play these various roles, it will be easier to accomplish the major goals of education. It is true that pupils have learned and progress has been made through competition, reward, and independent application, but it is likely that even better progress can be made when we realize the motivation which is inherent in group processes. Furthermore, as group dynamics are utilized the pupil will get, in addition to his academic growth, practice in performing in groups—which in some form or another will be an inescapable part of his life. "Finally, teachers can no longer take for granted the traditional classroom organization. They must learn to deal with the classroom consciously and deliberately as a group that may thwart as well as support and stimulate the learnings for which schools assume responsibility."[20]

HANDICAPS TO IMPROVED DISCIPLINE

The improvement of disciplinary procedures will be the outcome not only of an understanding of the factors which make for good discipline but also of a realization of the outstanding obstacles with which one must deal.

Teacher Insecurity Is a Deterrent to Effective Discipline. While teacher personality is only one of many elements in good discipline, it is considered to be the most essential factor.[21] When such things as having been reared by autocratic parents, worry over financial affairs, concern over

[19] Gale E. Jensen, "Small-group Counseling for Under-achieving Primary School Children," in Driver, *op. cit.*, pp. 286–291.

[20] William C. Stanley, B. Othanel Smith, Kenneth D. Benne, and Archibald W. Anderson, *Social Foundations of Education*, New York: Holt, Rinehart and Winston, Inc., 1956, p. 127.

[21] George V. Sheviakov and Fritz Redl, *Discipline for Today's Children and Youth*, new revision by Sybil K. Richardson, Washington: National Education Association, Association for Supervision and Curriculum Development, 1956, p. 60.

job tenure, lack of harmonious relations with fellow workers and administrators, and pressing family responsibilities cause the teacher to feel insecure, he is likely to create a tense classroom atmosphere. This, in turn, reacts on the pupils, who may be stimulated to acts of misconduct or, at the very least, be disposed to emotional outbreaks. The teacher then becomes more irritated and the tension is heightened. The teacher's insecurity also may make the normal behavior of youngsters appear to him as symptoms of disobedience and rebellion. Thus, both the view and the situation are altered by the teacher's emotional state.

Inadequacy of the teacher has the same effect. If his lesson plans are superficially prepared, or if his knowledge of the subject matter is inadequate, he dreads having the students ask questions that will reveal his lack of knowledge. A teacher's inadequacy may also spring from a lack of knowledge of the general principles of child growth and the psychology of childhood and adolescence. This leads to a misinterpretation of behavior and motives.

While other factors—administration, home background, physical plant, the temper of the times—must be recognized, it will pay the teacher to look within himself when seeking to achieve a free and relaxed atmosphere in which work progresses with a spirit of enjoyment and energy.

An Outmoded Philosophy of Education Handicaps Discipline. Many books, in their entirety, have been devoted to the philosophies of education; and, still, there is by no means universal agreement on what the tenets of a sound philosophy should be. However, on a few points which relate directly to the matter of discipline there is widespread, if not universal, agreement.

One aspect of philosophy which bears directly on discipline has to do with the emphasis placed on the mastery of subject matter, as contrasted with that on pupil growth and the development of independent thought processes.[22] The two are not necessarily in opposition to each other; in fact, most desirably, they should be emphasized side by side. Many of the difficulties in discipline in the school arise because so much emphasis is placed on subject-matter mastery that individual differences in ability and interest are completely ignored. When teachers accept the view that subject matter is only a means of fostering pupil growth and not an end in itself, a long step toward more effective discipline will have been taken.

An encouraging degree of growth has taken place in recent years in the direction of evaluating what constitutes pupil misbehavior. Few teachers would agree with the attitudes and concepts which prevailed in some oldtime schools. Slowness in learning is not today considered misbehavior or innate perverseness; it is, instead, considered a symptom that

[22] Frederick Mayer, *Philosophy of Education for Our Time*, New York: The Odyssey Press, Inc., 1958, p. 156.

something is wrong—with the child, the curriculum, the method, or the teacher. Teachers today, for the most part, think that the irregularities found in E. K. Wickman's study (see the section on Earlier Concepts of Discipline in this chapter) are ludicrous. Whispering, failure to listen, and neglect of homework are still frowned upon, but they are seldom treated as serious. More recent studies[23] show that teachers' views on behavior problems are coming closer to that of mental hygienists.

Another factor relating to discipline and educational philosophy has to do with responsibility for conduct. In the past, this was thought to rest solely upon the teacher. Any attempt on the part of some adventurous pupil to suggest that pupils participate in rule making was looked upon as evidence of subversion or a rebellious attitude. Today discipline is a group concern; students have a voice in the making of regulations, they have their committees to make suggestions to the group, and they delegate responsibility to members of the group to see that the decisions are executed.

Belief That Punishment Improves Behavior Is an Obstacle to Good Discipline. A study of the history of penal methods indicates that punishment has uniformly been a failure as far as improved behavior control is concerned. The largeness of the number of persons who have relapsed into crime and who had been in institutions which use repressive methods of punishment had for a long time been attributed to the deep-seated criminality of the convict. Today, there is an increased emphasis upon the search for background causes of criminality, upon devising methods for removing or ameliorating these causes, and upon attempts to substitute better responses. This is accomplished by trying to create individual feelings of worth, by teaching productive skills, and by giving the criminal relative freedom and more responsibility. Although the press of numbers in prisons is so great that serious obstacles stand in the way of putting such methods to the test, there is widespread agreement that the rehabilitation of inmates is more likely than when the emphasis is on retribution and punishment.

Punishment imposed on pupils in the school has a still less secure basis than punishment used in dealing with criminals. The control is external and does nothing to secure the internal direction that is desirable in our society. Although punishment may produce immediate conformity, there is too much danger of later serious disorder—when the pupil is removed from the reigning authority—involved in justifying its use in school.

[23] D. B. Ellis and I. W. Miller, "Teachers' Attitudes and Child Behavior Problems," *Journal of Educational Psychology*, 27:501–511, 1936; Donald James, *An Investigation of Teachers' Attitudes concerning Children's Behavior*, Portland, Ore.: Reed College, 1950; E. C. Hunter, "Changes in Teachers' Attitudes toward Children's Behavior in the Last Thirty Years," *Mental Hygiene*, 41:3–11, January, 1957.

Punishment does something to children. Reliance on punishment does something to you, too. This is a hazard. Choose punishment over the slow, steady talking way and you will come to build a point of view about people. Increasingly you will find yourself thinking that young-sters are basically evil . . . basically uncooperative . . . out to get your scalp.

Punishment lures you into this attitude. It is so available. Turn to it and, the next time there is law-breaking, it is there again. Soon you be-come a super-censor. You stop evil from showing. . . .

There is no surge of *anti-life* inside of children. Children are humans like yourself. Life is more pleasant all around when you talk with them, explain, discuss, and interpret.[24]

Some of the possible pernicious results of arbitrary punishment include trickery or lying to outwit adults, hatred of adults, the development of attitudes of fear, manifestations of cruelty and intolerance, making the recipient feel unworthy, and creating a desire to "even the score."

Failure to Recognize Individual Worth and Differences Inhibits Discipline. Failure to recognize differences interferes with wholesome discipline in several obvious ways. (1) Attention is turned only upon the symptom. (2) Teachers tend to adopt regulations that have to do only with the act. (3) The fact that procedures of discipline have various effects on different persons is ignored. (4) External control carries with it the implication that a pupil is incapable of making wise decisions for himself. Obviously, these techniques of which the shameful consequences have been already appraised above, have no place in educational procedures which profess to be aiming at developing better-adjusted members of society, who will regard learning as a continuing and enjoyable adventure.

Expecting Control to Be Achieved Suddenly Is an Obstacle to Discipline. Since growth requires practice, there is little hope that the demand for unquestioning compliance throughout the years in school will result in self-direction as an adult. Neither at the first-grade level nor during the senior year in high school would a teacher's lecturing on the advantages of personal control result in a sudden change in the pupils' viewpoints. Small beginnings that are followed by extended opportunities for pupil self-direction provide the chances for development of the mental hygiene viewpoint of discipline.

Some teachers, particularly at the secondary level, who know that previous practice in self-direction is lacking might give up hope of affect-ing the continuity of development. Such a view is needlessly pessimistic. Learning and the development of skills are dependent upon the level of maturation of the individual. Secondary-school pupils are more mature

[24] James L. Hymes, Jr., *Behavior and Misbehavior*, Englewood Cliffs, N.J.: Pren-tice-Hall, Inc.. 1955, pp. 65-66

in physique and intelligence, and in the matter of experience, than are pupils in the elementary school. Therefore, their progress in learning self-direction will be more rapid than that of their younger schoolmates when the proper situations are provided, because they can better understand what is implied. This does not mean that the elementary teacher need have no concern about the matter because it will be taken care of later. In the first place, not all pupils go on to the secondary school. In the second place, overlearning is an economic principle of learning. The secondary pupil who has had prior practice will learn this important lesson more thoroughly. Furthermore, there is a danger that some poor past habits and conditioning of the pupils may counterbalance the favorable present environment. Teachers must begin with confidence in their ability to capitalize on the capacity youth has for growth.

SUMMARY

Contemporary educational theory emphasizes the idea that wholesome pupil control is self-directed, socially oriented behavior that stems from purposeful activity. Happy and productive citizens must learn that the welfare of others is a means of securing their own personal enjoyment of living. This is most easily accomplished when each person can perceive his own identity with the group.

Wholesome discipline can be developed when teacher direction is positive but also cooperative, fair, consistent, and attentive to individual differences. Such discipline depends on teachers who have a thorough knowledge of growth principles in general and an appreciation of the specific causes of behavior in terms of the school and out-of-school backgrounds of individuals.

The newer concept of pupil control requires that remedial measures be consistent and appropriate, that a good example of self-control be set by the teacher, and that, to as great an extent as possible, substitute activities be provided to release undesirable tendencies. Group control, based on the process of reasoning, is the major objective of discipline, because, when achieved, it is a means of developing well-adjusted individuals who will have had the advantage of practice in democratic methods.

Among the handicaps to the achievement of improved procedures of discipline in the classroom, one of the most important is the lack of fundamental security and confidence that characterizes the teacher himself. Another handicap, still centering about the teacher, has to do with accepting contemporary educational philosophy and shaking off the belief that harsh punishment has a helpful influence on the one who is punished. Other obstacles to improved discipline arise from a failure to recognize individual worth and individual differences or from a lack of appreciation of what is implied in the belief that growth takes place continuously and gradually.

It is now realized that group dynamics is a powerful means of constructive pupil control. The motivation, the sharing of problems, the release of tensions, the realization of shared difficulties, all combine to teach better conduct and to enable pupils to marshal their resources for effective academic achievement. Group-therapy sessions for improved behavior and remedial schoolwork have been found to be means of capitalizing on group dynamics.

STUDY AND DISCUSSION EXERCISES

1. Summarize what ten experienced teachers regard as being the fundamentals of good classroom discipline. Does their consensus agree with the view presented in this chapter?

2. In what way is consistency in discipline related to understanding individuals? Interpret "What's fair for one is fair for all" in terms of this relationship.

3. Can you recall, from your own experience, an example of a teacher's behavior being reflected in his pupils' behavior?

4. Cite some examples, from your own experience, of how the behavior of individuals is conditioned by the group in which they function.

5. Why do you think there has been such success in academic work and in improving behavior when group counseling has been the focal emphasis?

SUGGESTED ADDITIONAL READINGS

Baruch, Dorothy Walter, *New Ways in Discipline,* New York: McGraw-Hill Book Company, Inc., 1949. 268 pp.

The author points the way to a better understanding of the child and his emotions. Her approach is essentially constructive—not repressive.

Bernard, Harold W., *Adolescent Development in American Culture,* New York: Harcourt, Brace & World, Inc., 1957, pp. 533–566.

This chapter stresses the positive approach of providing constructive activities for youth in place of the punitive measures which follow the occurrence of negative actions.

Driver, Helen I. (ed.), *Counseling and Learning through Small-group Discussion,* Madison, Wis.: Monona Publications, 1958, pp. 281–316.

These pages contain articles examining the use of small-group discussion and counseling in elementary and secondary schools. The items briefed in the text are discussed at greater length.

Hymes, James L., Jr., *Behavior and Misbehavior,* Englewood Cliffs, N.J.: Prentice-Hall, Inc., 1955. 140 pp.

This book contains suggestions for steering the narrow course between authority, direction, and firmness and then contrasts them to the need to be gentle, permissive, and understanding.

Sheviakov, George V., and Fritz Redl, *Discipline for Today's Children and Youth*, new revision by Sybil K. Richardson, Washington: National Education Association, Association for Supervision and Curriculum Development, 1956. 65 pp.

Popularity attests to the booklet's useful implications for the classroom teacher, implications deriving from a sound basis in psychological and psychoanalytic theory.

CHAPTER 11

TEACHING METHODS AND MENTAL HEALTH PRACTICES

Children not only learn reading, writing, arithmetic, geometry, chemistry, and history; but they are, at the same time, learning certain attitudes, interests, habits, ideals, and ambitions. While he is imparting the mechanical skills of reading, the teacher of reading inevitably implants a like or dislike for reading, an interest in or a distaste for books, as well as a sense of adventure or of boredom in connection with books. The science teacher is, whether he wishes to or not, helping to develop an attitude toward experimentation and research and either a respect for accuracy or a disdain for detail. Moreover, these side learnings are often much more important than the isolated facts the pupil may be able to turn back to the teacher at the time of the final examination. Thus, the acquiring of information is inevitably accompanied by the formulation of ideals, attitudes, and goals—which become part of the teacher's responsibility.

Since learnings are complex, varied, and multiple, there is no teaching method that will inevitably lead to success. Certain emphases based on sound knowledge of the characteristics and needs of children will tend, however, to make successful whatever techniques a given teacher may use. Among these emphases might be listed the following:

1. The necessity for treating different children differently

2. The importance of gaining knowledge—as a source of personal satisfaction and as the basis for problem solving and continuing learning

3. The role of pupil activity (both physical and mental) in efficient learning

4. The greater vitality of learning activities which have meaning and purpose for the learner

5. Joyful living today as preparation for abundant living tomorrow

6. The value of cooperative learning activities as preparation for effective citizenship in a democracy

7. The necessity for clear communication between individuals in a society and between societies

These emphases are stressed in the various sections of this chapter.

GIVING ANSWERS VERSUS SEEKING ANSWERS

The Teacher's "Complex." Some teaching methods have so intimate a bearing on the mental health of school children that attention to them is warranted. One of these is the "complex" which many teachers seem to have, that is, that every question raised in class must be answered. To make it even more difficult, a teacher often feels that the answers must be phrased in the exact words that he had in mind when the question was asked. The hazards to the child are twofold: first, he is discouraged from seeking answers on his own initiative because he knows that the answer, in the end, will be given by the teacher and in the teacher's own words; and, second, the pupil acquires the erroneous notion that there is an answer to every problem. Wendell Johnson states the difficulty as follows:

> Human energy is never more extravagantly wasted than in the persistent effort to answer conclusively questions that are vague and meaningless. Probably the most impressive indictment that can be made of our educational system is that it provides the student with answers, but it is poorly designed to provide him with skill in the asking of questions that are effectively directive of inquiry and evaluation. . . . Any attempt to improve our educational system that does not involve a clear recognition of this defect of it can hardly be expected to lead to substantial reform. In fact, any attempt to reeducate a maladjusted individual that does not leave him with effective techniques of inquiry cannot be trusted to result in substantial and lasting benefits.[1]

It is basic in problem solving that a pupil should learn either that answers are not known in full or that, if known in part, they are tentative. In no other way can he expect to meet the many complex and changing problems that he must face in a fast-moving world. Raising questions which do not get answered will help prepare the child to acquire the ability to adjust to the many problems he does not meet in school. He will have a better chance to acquire the ability to do research and be prepared for the inevitable time when he will discover that there are conflicting answers to the same problem. A teacher, by not allowing a

[1] Wendell Johnson, *People in Quandaries,* New York: Harper & Brothers, 1946, p. 55. By permission of the publisher.

person the privilege of challenging the teacher's view, can do much that may destroy an individual's ability to change his own mind.

Miss M., a teacher of high-school social studies, serves as an example. She has definite ideas about the undesirability of what is currently being called the "welfare state." Students know that if they argue against her views they will be given low marks. Her reputation is so well established that some of the more adventurous students deliberately set out to bait her. They look up arguments, just for the fun of presenting them. But they know what the result will be; so, after the first six weeks or the middle of the semester, they pretend to be converted and meekly nod their heads when she presents her views.

A high-school boy related that he found it advantageous not to speak up at all in class. He wanted to present the views he heard at home (the father and mother were both in the profession of teaching and were highly respected), but because the views differed from those of his teacher, he kept quiet. On the first attempts at the presentation of conflicting views, the instructor became so angry that his face reddened and he shouted angrily at the lad. Not only is such dogmatism discouraging to the inquiring mind of the child, but it is indicative of a closed mind on the part of the teacher. Knowing all the answers and refusing the right to question is not in accord with our ideals of democracy. It would be desirable from the standpoint of mental health, as well as of effective teaching techniques, if the teacher were to be a learner with the students. It would serve to launch them upon a cooperative search for information which could result in the thrill of discovery and provide a basis for their continued growth and adaptability.

An eighth-grade teacher utilized this active searching for answers by getting the pupils to seek formulas for area and volume. Placed on a table were various objects—cylinders, prisms, cardboard rectangles, squares, and triangles. A pupil suggested that the appropriate formula be written on small cards and placed before each object. Some knew the formula for a figure or two, others thought they did, and others had an idea certain suggestions were wrong. They decided to check their books and then figure out why the formula worked. Throughout, there was genuine interest and activity. Whether rapport was the cause or outcome of this procedure, interest was apparent to the observer, who stated, "Another teacher would probably not miss the opportunity to lecture on proper and improper answers. Not Mr. J.—he was intent on getting pupils to search for answers."

> In teaching, we are interested not only in *what* is learned; we are equally interested in *how* it is learned. For example, throughout life, people face problems on which they need to gather pertinent informa-

tion, consider alternatives, make choices and test them, evaluate the consequences, and draw conclusions. Some methods of teaching help children build skills in this kind of problem-solving. Other methods actually deter children's development of such skills.[2]

THE ROLE OF INTEREST

Interest is intimately related to the concept of purposefulness. In general, whatever is done to stimulate pupil interest will also add to the pupil's comprehension of purpose.

Meaning and Importance of Interest. Interest may be defined as the spirit which exists between the individual and some object, situation, person, or activity. The "spirit" is a feeling of oneness with, or a matter of identification. It should be noted that interest is not a discovery but, rather, something that is created. Pupils are naturally interested in very few things; they create their interests by growth, maturation, and experience or contact. Interest is an active feeling on the part of the pupil. Teachers cannot *make* things interesting. They can only set up the conditions whereby the pupil is encouraged or enabled to *take* an interest.

Interest is another of those key matters which we may guardedly refer to as being most important. Many of the problems of teachers would be diminished (discipline, haphazard learning, lack of self-realization, overdependence, stereotyped responses) if they were to know and utilize the conditions which lead to the creation of interest. But perhaps the strongest justification for stimulating and capitalizing on interest resides in the fact that if we, as teachers, can help pupils develop genuine interests, we shall have accomplished that all-important goal of getting pupils to regard learning and education as a lifelong process.

On graduation from high school, what a boy loves is vastly more important than what he knows. What companions does he choose? What books does he voluntarily read? What ideals does he harbor? These are the really significant characteristics which determine his life's career. Does he chum with wholesome pals, does he read choice literature, does he enjoy good lectures, does he participate in harmless recreation, does he take an interest in civic welfare? Or, does he seek vile companions who tell smutty stories and enter into questionable escapades, does he read trashy and indecent magazines and books, does he sneer at the church, the school, good books and all serious activities?

His attitude toward society and its problems, his attitude toward religion and morals, his attitude toward duties and obligations, are vastly more important than the few items of intellectual knowledge he has gained. His spontaneous likes and dislikes, his loves and his hates, his

[2] Margaret Lindsey and William T. Gruhn, *Student Teaching in the Elementary School,* New York: The Ronald Press Company, 1957, p. 90.

longings and aversions, will really determine what manner of man he shall be.[3]

The fact that these words were written about thirty years ago does not detract from their importance. Rather, our slowness in accepting them would seem to indicate a need for more careful study of the doctrine which is proposed in them.

Techniques for Stimulating the Growth of Interest. The following proposals for stimulating interest are neither conclusive nor inclusive and it is hoped that the reader will expand each concept to fit the particular situation at hand.

1. *Provide a worthy example.* Interest is contagious and the teacher should provide an enthusiastic and confident exemplification of the love for learning. The enthusiasms of the teacher are generally quickly accepted by pupils of all ages. The bored and weary teacher tends to create apathetic pupils.

2. *Make sure the pupil understands what is expected of him.* Young children playing with complicated mechanical toys which they are unable to operate quickly become bored. Simple blocks and balls which they can manipulate will engage them for longer periods. Adults may be interested in lectures they understand but would be restless if made to sit through a presentation in a foreign language. Certainly one of the major advances in educational practice is the increasing realization of what things do, and do not, have meaning for pupils and the use of curriculums which are governed accordingly.

3. *Provide an immediate and clear goal.* Only the psychologically mature person can sustain prolonged effort directed toward remote goals. The younger the pupil, the more necessary it is to have immediate objectives. To have something to work toward and to know the possibility of attaining it in a short time are essential for creating and maintaining interest.

4. *Relate the new to what is already known.* Interests do not come out of the blue. It is natural for us to be more concerned about the welfare of our children and our next-door neighbor than about some unknown person in Tibet. We cannot expect children to be interested in abstractions when there is so much that can be done to expand their knowledge of things about which they are already partially informed.

5. *See that information is acquired.* One who cannot read is not interested in reading. One who knows no history is not interested in our national beginnings. It follows that interest is contingent upon the acquisition of information. Sometimes this acquisition involves drill and some forcing. But if drill is used with variation and if compulsion is used with

[3] F. E. Bolton, *Adolescent Education,* New York: The Macmillan Company, 1931, p. 175. By permission of the author.

discretion, the result is likely to be favorable to success. New knowledges serve as a basis for expansion of interests.

6. *Arrange for success.* There is truth in the cliché "Nothing succeeds like success." Arranging for success involves a knowledge of the capacities of individual pupils. It involves a comprehension of the difficulty of the task. It involves the provision of varied activities.

7. *Scale activities to capacities.* Success cannot be achieved in activities that are not scaled to the capacity of the individual. Two examples may

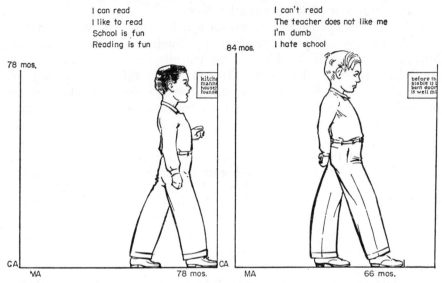

FIG. 8. The child at the left is ready for reading at the chronological age of 6.6 years (78 months). He not only learns to read but develops a favorable attitude toward learning. The child at the right, although chronologically older, is not ready for reading and develops unfavorable attitudes toward learning, toward himself, and toward the school. These attitudes may still block his reading efforts when, at the approximate chronological age of 8.3 years (99 months), he develops the mental age for reading readiness. (It should be noted that MA is only one factor in reading readiness.)

serve to illustrate the point. Among the factors involved in reading readiness is a mental age of approximately 6.5 years. If we try to force reading before this minimum age, the result is embarrassment, humiliation, boredom, and the creation of feelings of inferiority. It has been noted that a greater proportion of high-school pupils are successful in the study of algebra when algebra is studied in the junior or senior year rather than the freshman year (IQs being the same). Mental capacity is greater with the additional years, even though IQ remains the same. Unfortunately, we do not have precise and definite statements as to the optimum time for beginning most of the other school subjects. It is, therefore, the responsibility of the teacher to look for symptoms indicating that the teaching is approaching too near the frustration level of the student.[4]

8. *Encourage pupils to keep up with daily assignments.* It is discouraging to get behind. The teacher would do well to help and encourage able students who have dropped behind because of illness or interfering activities, so that they may keep up with their peers or with the course outline. Any students who are unable to progress at the normal rate should have their assignments varied, so that they may consider their progress satisfactory in terms of what is expected of them.

9. *Provide an opportunity to use what is learned.* One value of recitations is that they give the pupil an opportunity to use what has been learned. A more functional use of learned material would be to have it applied to the solution of a felt problem. Thus, utilizing knowledge of civics in launching plans for a youth recreation center would be more meaningful than putting that knowledge to use in passing a test. Nevertheless, tests have their place in arousing interest. Most of us enjoy taking the tests we see in various magazines. The difference lies in the use that is made of the results. If the test in school is the sole basis for the assigning of grades, it is likely to destroy rather than foster interest. If the test is to show present status and give clues to next steps in development, it will probably be viewed quite differently.[5] More pertinent uses of knowledge might be found in making a mural, presenting a report, preparing and evaluating a field trip, working out the solution of some school problem that involves the welfare of pupils, or participating in some group project.

10. *Help the students know what is being accomplished.* A knowledge of results is a motivating factor. Show children specifically how their reading is progressing, how their written compositions are improving, how their comprehension of the multiplication tables is growing, and how their knowledge of history is expanding. If this undertaking seems difficult, the teacher might well appreciate the difficulty pupils have in evaluating growth. Knowing what progress is being made is a positive motivating factor.[6] Examinations can be used for drawing individual graphs or charts of the results. Saving samples of work and comparing them periodically provides the pupil with a chance to assess his progress.

11. *Utilize concrete sensory material.* Verbal descriptions are difficult

---

[4] Howard F. Fehr, *Teaching High-school Mathematics,* What Research Says to the Teacher, no. 9, Washington: National Education Association, 1955, pp. 13–16.

[5] Harold W. Bernard, *Psychology of Learning and Teaching,* New York: McGraw-Hill Book Company, Inc., 1954, pp. 387–390.

[6] Pauline S. Sears, "Levels of Aspiration in Academically Successful and Unsuccessful Children," *Journal of Abnormal and Social Psychology,* 35:498–536, 1940.

for children to understand and perhaps have much less meaning for high-school pupils than is commonly thought. The vitality of learning can be increased by the use of materials that can be handled, felt, seen, even tasted. Teachers are taking advantage of concrete sensory materials when they make excursions or engage in projects, when they utilize films, phonograph records, models, stuffed animals and birds, and when they conduct experiments.

12. *See that action is full and vigorous.* Children like to be physically active; they enjoy being participants. In fact, it is difficult for them to remain passive and they will frequently find something to do if they are not led to constructive activity. The activity planned for them may include recitations, oral reading, spelling drills, the giving of reports, and encouragement of their asking questions; but it should also take such forms as making displays, going on trips, producing a play, painting, drawing, working with scissors and paste. Activity can be arranged for in the high school in much the same way—performing experiments, engaging in projects, making clothes and preparing foods, utilizing student activities (the extracurricular program) more fully, and engaging in field trips.

13. *Capitalize on feelings of belongingness.* Each pupil should be made to feel that he is a significant part of the group. This means that there must be great enough variety of occupation in the classroom so there will be something significant which each child can do. One fourth-grade teacher accomplished this by seeing that each child had some duty to perform. There was a president, a secretary, a monitor, an official guest greeter, a person to head the fire line, one to bring up the rear of the fire line, a flower arranger, a material distributor, a play-equipment custodian, an errand boy, a student-council member, and the like. It might be well to mention that requiring all pupils to do the same thing at the same time works toward destroying a feeling of belongingness, because of the great differences there are in the ability of different ones to do any given task. Belongingness is a feeling that cannot be ignored if we hope to have all pupils develop an interest in classroom functions.[7]

14. *Be alert for strong emotions that interfere with desired motivation.* No pupil, in elementary or high school, can efficiently concentrate on school activities if he is worried about the way his parents are getting along, about whether or not his father will have a job, about whether or not his sister will recover from her illness. While the teacher can do nothing about the worrisome situation, he can make due allowance for the situation by relaxing his demands, by being tolerant of inattention,

[7] Ralph H. Ojemann, *Personality Adjustment of Individual Children,* What Research Says to the Teacher, no. 5, Washington: National Education Association, 1954, pp. 14–16.

and by giving additional encouragement. Some of the interfering strong emotions are aroused by school situations which the teacher can help to solve. These disturbing conditions may be lack of acceptance by peers, difficulty in learning certain phases of the current assignment, fear of the teacher, disappointment over not having achieved some position or honor that had been sought. Certainly, the teacher can control such expression of his own strong emotions as would have a disconcerting effect on the pupil.

15. *Utilize appropriate punishment and reward.* Studies of the use of punishment show that children do not resent—in fact, they appreciate in retrospect—consistent, appropriate, and deserved punishment. However, certain cautions must be observed. Care must be exercised that punishment takes the form of correction of the deed rather than expression of the teacher's own emotion. The punishment must fit the deed and the doer. Deprivation of privilege will usually be sufficient.

Rewards are, in general, more effective than punishment as a means of motivation. Superior work, in terms of the pupil's ability, may be rewarded by the granting of some desired privilege. Commendation for progress is a reward for which all may aspire. Honor rolls, when there are other rewards for different pupils, have value. Rewards which are tied to social approval and personal status become the source of powerful motives for young people.

16. *Make use of praise.* Some would say "Make use of deserved praise," but sometimes it is difficult to find something deserving of commendation. Nevertheless, it is gratifying to the individual. "That's a beautiful hat." You secretly believe it is atrocious, but you do not want people saying so. Tell the fifth-grader, "You're a little gentleman," and he will try harder to be just that. A high-school teacher said, "You are too intelligent to be satisfied with this work," and the boy was. He did it over to live up to the praise regarding his intelligence. Being able to praise is largely a matter of discerning *something* which might be praised (not necesarily deserving praise).

Research shows that praise is, in general, more likely to be effective with introverted pupils and, conversely, that blame or censure is more likely to stimulate extroverted children. Its use is dependent on individuals.[8] This generalization does not, however, alter the conclusion that blame and censure must be utilized sparingly.

The importance of the foregoing recommendations may be brought into bolder relief if we remember the words of the unknown psychologist who said, "The intellect is a mere speck afloat upon a sea of feeling."

[8] George G. Thompson and Clarence W. Hunnicutt, "The Effect of Repeated Praise or Blame on the Work Achievement of 'Introverts' and 'Extroverts'," *The Journal of Educational Psychology*, 35:257–266, May, 1944.

Paying attention to the factors that lead to interest is one way of capitalizing on emotional factors in learning.

MENTAL DISCIPLINE AND EDUCATIONAL PRACTICE

The Theory of Mental Discipline. There was a time in educational practice when emphasis was laid on the study of the practical arts that would help pupils adjust to the needs of the time. School curriculums were built on the basis of contemporary needs. But as times changed schoolmen, pressed to justify certain subjects, found justification in the theory of mental discipline. Briefly, this theory emphasized that the faculties of the mind were sharpened or disciplined by the effort put forth in the learning of difficult school subjects. Distasteful subjects were especially valuable, from this viewpoint, because they called forth more application than subjects in which the student was interested. This theory has now been largely discarded by educational psychologists. Difficult subjects still have their place in the curriculum, because they serve a real purpose, not merely because they are difficult. Educators now seek to have schoolwork based on the needs which students feel or, at the very worst, based on needs which they are quite certain to feel at some later time.

It must be admitted, however, that vestiges of the theory of mental discipline still linger. Latin, for instance, was taught at one time because it was valuable for those large numbers of students who were preparing for the ministry. Today some teachers may feel that Latin is good for the student because it makes him buckle down to some good, hard work. When Latin is taught so as to show the derivation of English words, when it is taught in ways which facilitate the study of modern languages, or when it is taught to students who intend to study medicine, it is serving a contemporary purpose. Many teachers do accomplish this.

Many students have been exposed to fruitless courses in mathematics because of the mental-discipline orientation. When they asked why they should study algebra, they were given some such answer as "Because it is good for you," "Because you will need it to enter college," or "Because you will find it valuable in later life." Literature, history, economics, and the sciences have been justified in a similar tenuous fashion. Such vague justifications do bear fruit, but the product is not the kind desired. All too often the reaction has been a deep dislike for these subjects, a dislike that leads the student to reject them, at least insofar as he has any power of choice.

Fortunately, there are teachers who are acquainted with the fallacy of mental discipline and who justify the teaching of all subjects, whatever they might be, in terms of the needs and purposes of their pupils. The same courses may be used as the vehicle of learning, but the methods of teaching differ, inasmuch as the teachers are stressing the *transfer* values.

The Transfer of Learning. By *the transfer of learning* it is meant that learning one thing will make it easier to learn another thing; for example, the learning of Latin may facilitate the learning of English. However, transfer does not necessarily take place automatically. Even if some transfer does take place without conscious attention, there will be more transfer when certain conditions are observed in instruction. These conditions can be better understood when the conditions under which maximum transfer takes place are known, namely, (1) when there are common elements in the two learning situations, (2) when generalizations are derived, (3) when the learning is raised to the level of ideas, and (4) when the level of intelligence is high.

If teachers use these conditions wisely, they can add vitality to the pupil's learning activities and make them function better.

1. Common elements in various learning situations should be pointed out to the student. It will pay to start with having students indicate what they perceive to be the similarities and duplications among different subjects and situations. Examples which show the common factors can be cited. Explanations of pervasive elements should be given.

2. There must be specific emphasis on principles and generalizations. These should not be left to chance or depend upon the pupil's own insight for perceiving them. The general principles should be shown in many different situations, so that the student may learn them thoroughly. Let the student know that you consider the generalization to be important and stress it in reviews, drills, and examinations.

3. Whenever possible, indicate the presence of an ideal (actually, a form of generalization) which is common to various learning situations. Thus, while you are stressing neatness on a spelling or an arithmetic paper, indicate that it is desirable to apply this same ideal to care of the school grounds and the classroom floor. Just as it is desirable to be prompt with the handing in of assignments, it is important to arrive at school on time; and promptness is a quality which employers prize in employees who wish to advance. Diligent application to the task at hand is as important in committee work, the school play, the daily assignment, chores at home, as it is in playing a good game of baseball.

4. Do not be afraid to abandon a course of study or a project if it appears to be beyond the level of the students' abilities to grasp. It may not be possible to increase the intellectual level of pupils, but it is possible to recognize the differences which exist and to expect a great deal of some and comparatively little of others. The task itself may not prove too difficult if the pace is slackened.

Mental Discipline, Transfer, and Mental Health. The theory of mental discipline works against mental health for several reasons. For many students the futile and difficult subjects produce a distaste for schooling which persists beyond the rigors of the present situation. Any experienced teacher can point out examples of pupils whose interest in school activity has been thoroughly dulled by their lack of ability in dealing with numbers, with algebra, with Latin, or even with literature. The value of the mental-discipline theory may be questioned even for those who have done the work well and have received an A grade. They have studied the subject as an end in itself, rather than as a means to acquiring skills and attitudes which will bring about later productive experiences.

Dependence on the theory of the transfer of learning, on the other hand, gives education an ongoing purposefulness. The student learns the functional value of the activity in which he is engaging. He has an opportunity to see how his learning fits into the pattern of his daily living. Since the teacher is not stressing the disciplinary value of the subject, he will seek to create conditions which will awaken a lively and continued interest in the work at hand. The teacher will be interested in both the direct and the indirect values of the subject he is teaching and the student will be better able to see both kinds of values—in short, the work will touch a larger part of his entire life. All these advantages will combine to make learning more facile and to make the present an opportunity for the operation of the "law of effect." If all teachers were to accept the transfer viewpoint, it should be possible to produce a generation of children who would learn *and live* the idea that education is not a product but a process—a way of living.

Emphasis on the theory of transfer of learning is not a single or an isolated method of teaching. This emphasis implies that an effort will be made on the part of the teacher to show the elements that are common to various subjects, to school subjects and daily living, and to the activities which go on in the school and those which are taking place in world affairs. There must be an attempt to formulate from the activities at hand generalizations that will include situations likely to be met in the future. The emphasis implies, further, that the attitudes governing the conduct of school activities will be expanded to include more pervasive ideals. Finally, it implies that schoolwork at all levels will be appropriate to the maturation level of the students in any particular class.

TEACHING METHODS AND PURPOSEFUL BEHAVIOR

Behavior is either purposive or purposeful; i.e., activity has a goal-seeking nature. Teaching methods which recognize this principle will generally be superior to those which fail to recognize the factor of purpose.

The Meaning of Purpose. At one level behaviors are *purposive:* they are actions designed to maintain the equilibrium of the organism and are largely unconscious. The attempt to understand children in terms of their biological and physiological functioning is also an attempt to understand their purposive strivings. *Purposeful* behavior, on the other hand, is concerned with activities which are directed toward consciously formulated goals; it is a matter of conscious concern and effort. Both kinds of behavior are goal seeking, but purposeful behavior is controlled by a relatively clearer perception of the goal.

Teachers capitalize on the purposive strivings of the pupil when they recognize basic organic and social needs. They capitalize on purposeful strivings when they clarify goals and help pupils perceive the significance of their school activities.

> A good learning environment provides opportunity for children to examine what is important to them and to plan ways of working toward these goals. For example, a teacher, together with the class, may decide that each person should work on something he has never tried before or something which he has tried but does inadequately. Another group may be guided to undertake certain activities which lead it into the community or which require careful reading and note-taking. Cooperatively thinking through the objectives and reasons for study is certain to improve the quality of learning. Often the purposes for an activity, which originally may have been only those of the teacher, may really become those of the students.[9]

Making school activities increasingly purposeful is seen in those methods which emphasize such things as the following: school projects growing out of incidents in the pupils' lives; explanations in terms the pupils understand; activities carried on by youngsters because the activity itself is enjoyed—not because a grade will be earned; relating schoolwork to the adolescent's vocational ambitions; connecting schoolwork to topics which are being discussed by students in their free time; and applying schoolwork to the solving of some problem which the group has accepted as its own. It should be clear that purpose is not inherent in the task or subject at hand; it is rather, a part of the pupil's way of looking at the activity.

Purpose and the Elementary-school Child. The elementary-school child characteristically has a shorter span of attention than that of the adolescent or adult. This makes it necessary for goals to be more immediate in the grades than will typically be the case in high school. The production of a play after the effort of sustained practice, the meaning of a six-week grading period, passing, or graduation—these are less likely to spur

[9] *Creating a Good Environment for Learning*, 1954 Yearbook, Association for Supervision and Curriculum Development, Washington: National Education Association, 1954, pp. 238–239.

the elementary student to effort than they would the typical high-school pupil.

The immediate goal holds a lure that appeals to all of us, but it is particularly important to the younger child. Goals should represent something beyond one's present status or accomplishment, but they should not be so far beyond that their attractiveness is diminished by distance. It is futile to attempt to motivate young children to learn multiplication by citing their need for it as bank tellers or bank presidents. Learning to spell so one can be a stenographer in fifteen or twenty years will not provide much stimulation for girls in the intermediate grades. But as the pupil grows older he learns to wait for gratifications and a balance between the immediate and deferred goal is feasible. Thus, preparation for a visit to the dairy tomorrow, arranging a display for PTA next Friday, planning an informal drama for this afternoon, or making something to take to mother after school are ways of paying attention to the immediacy of children's goals. Longer-term projects may be used successfully if intermediate steps are clearly perceptible to the child. A mural begun in early October in anticipation of Halloween could be a long-term goal, because the intermediate phases of its making are concrete and visible. On the other hand, repetitious practice in a dramatic production might prove boring, because progress is less tangible.

Some authorities inveigh against the use of grades, marks, and stars because they are artificial and tend to cause pupils to lose sight of the real goals of learning. It is true that one must guard against the making of grades and the earning of rewards becoming the end purpose of learning, but these devices do possess the advantage of being immediate goals. "School marks may direct the attention of pupils, parents, and classroom teachers away from the *real* purposes of education toward symbols that represent success but do not emphasize its elements or meaning. They frequently permit and encourage the calculation of a meaningless rank in class or a composite score."[10] Thus, instead of grades which are vague and too inclusive, the immediate goal could be better citizenship, improved neatness, more effective playground organization, greater accuracy in spelling, higher speed in correct computation. These can be defined in specifics which will allow even the primary pupil to plan and chart his own growth.

Recognition of the limitations of marks may suggest some of the things that classroom teachers can do even when required to prepare school marks for the office file. First, define very clearly what each mark means in terms of pupil *development* using descriptions of activi-

[10] John W. M. Rothney, *Evaluating and Reporting Pupil Progress*, What Research Says to the Teacher, no. 7, Washington: National Education Association, 1955, p. 9.

ties other than, or at least in addition to, mere repetition of memorized material. Classroom teachers may enlist the aid of pupils and parents in defining the kind of development that is expected. Then pupil growth in those activities can be observed from landmarks estimated at the beginning of the period of instruction.[11]

The natural and serious play of children is purposive, but under guidance, it can become highly purposeful. It is an activity containing potentialities which the effective teacher cannot afford to overlook. If we wish to capitalize upon the natural growth tendencies of children, we shall have to recognize play as being an important, rather than a superfluous, activity for them. If we wish to clarify purposes for children, we shall have to take steps that will capitalize on the educational values of play.

A first step toward utilizing the child's natural interest in play will be for teachers to appreciate some of its positive contributions. Among these may be listed the following: (1) Play exercises the emotions of joy and excitement—it adds zest to living. (2) It is associated with abundance of energy and its healthful release—it is recreative. (3) It provides an avenue of preparation for adult living through the exercise of physical, emotional, and mental capacities. (4) It provides an escape from unpleasant and uninteresting situations, thus providing the child with inner resources to withstand situations that cannot be avoided. (5) It provides a means of compensatory activities; that is, the child is given an opportunity to develop skills that would otherwise remain unexercised. (6) It gives an opportunity for the child to exercise his powers of imagination, thus adding to his potential faculty for indulging in creative activity,

The elementary teacher would do well to incorporate such elements of play as physical activity, competition and cooperation, use of the imagination, and the manipulation of materials into school routines. This would involve the use of games and contests. It would involve a greater permissiveness in the school atmosphere and a more active role for the pupil in the determination of activities. Playing in sand can stimulate the search for printed materials. Production of dramas can consolidate the learning of historical facts. Managing a play store can demand the use of functional arithmetic and the study of what, at a higher level, would be called economics. Rhythm work and the use of dramatizations and impersonations can be of assistance to the speech-handicapped child, besides furnishing practice in verbal expression for typical pupils. Guessing games can serve a similar function in the development of language skills.

Purpose and the Secondary-school Pupil. The greater maturity of the high-school pupil does not make the role of purpose any less vital, though

[11] *Ibid.,* p. 9.

the need for immediate goals may be somewhat less urgent. Certainly there can be no objection to making the schoolwork varied, pleasurable, and tangible. Precise information on personal and academic growth provides both motivation and direction and *is* perhaps more important to the high-school student, because of the proximity of adulthood.

Successful teaching methods in the high school will, among other things, stress the role of schoolwork in vocational selection and preparation. Bashfulness may prevent adolescents from admitting that they are concerned about marriage and family living, but, as a matter of fact, many of them will be married in from three to five years and they are concerned about it while in school.[12] Teaching which recognizes this interest will find a receptive audience. High-school pupils are becoming more cognizant of themselves as purchasers and consumers of goods. This area of functioning, when brought into the curriculum, will serve to enliven classes in mathematics, sociology, economics, and homemaking. These young people are functionally concerned with the problem of what to do with their leisure time. This too can provide an emphasis for such courses as literature, history, language study, music, and art. They are much concerned about their relations with others—both with their peers and with adults. As they are given opportunities to study and practice social skills, they are engaged in activities which to them are purposive as well as markedly purposeful. Adolescents have considerable concern about their personal appearance. These natural interests offer clues for making the study of physiology, biology, and health education vigorous and purposeful.

Such areas of concern as the foregoing can still further cultivate effective teaching methods and capitalize on purposeful activity if the youths are made planners and doers in the classroom. If the pupils are called in on the "purposing" process by means of planning committees, they will tend to arrange for activities which are in accord with objectives that are already operative. Pupil planning is recognized as being one of the ways in which contemporary education can implement our growing knowledge about the importance of purpose in human development.

Some school systems have a student's advisory committee. This committee, usually composed of students representing the high schools in the system but sometimes including the elementary pupils also, is selected by the students and meets regularly with the superintendent. Such a group can help to inaugurate certain aspects of a citizenship program, for

[12] The "peak age" for marriage of women in the United States is eighteen years—33 per cent of eighteen- and nineteen-year-old girls are married; 48.1 per cent of all brides are under twenty years of age. Source: Bureau of the Census and U.S. Department of Health, Education, and Welfare, 1958.

example, the prevention of vandalism in school buildings, a system-wide sportsmanship program, general standards of behavior, an after-school recreation program, or the care of public property.[13]

Not only are the learnings of pupils made more vital when the pupils themselves become active doers and planners, but the technique adds to the possibility of their education's being truly functional through the practice they get in the democratic processes.

Work-Study Programs and the High-school Pupil. A movement which is apparently gaining momentum and one which adds greatly to the purposefulness of secondary education is that called work-study programs. The motive back of such programs is that education will be more vital when it is related to and correlated with the vocational objectives of youth who will soon be taking their place in the business and industrial world. There are many variations of the plan, but the central idea is that students work for part of the day and go to school the rest of the time. The work phase is supervised jointly by an industrial or a business representative and by a teacher (work-study coordinator) from the school. Not only are courses set up in the school which point toward the kind of work that the student is doing, but the coordinating teacher attempts to aid other teachers of the academic and traditional high-school courses to relate their subject matter to the work the student is doing. The work-experience type of program can do and, under proper supervision, does the following:

1. Gives students new status as individuals by teaching responsibility, developing initiative, and instilling confidence
2. Helps generate healthy attitudes toward work, provides opportunity to earn and handle money, and to understand the social-industrial world
3. Provides opportunities for vocational exploration, the evaluation of plans, and the fixing of occupational goals
4. Engenders a strong desire to learn and to remain in school, improves job opportunities after school, and develops abilities which enable them to continue their education
5. Makes schoolwork more meaningful by relating school and work and by bridging the gap between the school and the work world.[14]

[13] *Educating for American Citizenship*, 32d Yearbook, American Association of School Administrators, Washington: National Education Association, 1954, pp. 74–75.
[14] Adapted from Clifford E. Erickson (ed.), *A Basic Text for Guidance Workers*, Englewood Cliffs, N.J.; Prentice-Hall, Inc., 1947, pp. 260–361; and Bernard A. Jordon and Harry B. Spencer, "Supervised Work Experience Programs in Life Adjustment Education," in Franklin R. Zeran (ed.), *Life Adjustment Education in Action*, New York: Chartwell House, Inc., 1953, pp. 416–417.

An examination of this list will reveal that the objectives are in close accord with the specific needs of adolescents (Chapter 3) and also are in harmony with many of the principles of mental hygiene.

CAPITALIZING ON THE RESOURCES OF THE SCHOOL

Teachers as Resources. The lack of a psychologist or psychiatrist in the school does not mean that there is necessarily a lack of wisdom in dealing with children, including those who differ from their peers. While it is likely to be difficult for one teacher, who may not be prepared in clinical psychology, to deal effectively with all cases, the counsel and aid of other teachers in the school can be used to plan a constructive program. When teachers get together on a particular case and pool their wisdom and points of view, the recommendations frequently resemble the advice of experts to a remarkable degree. On several occasions, when the author has described the symptoms of a case for a group of teachers, the resulting recommendations have been commendable. If one teacher makes a proposal that is of questionable value, others are able to check the view and point out the fallacies. When a pertinent suggestion is given, it is followed by approval, or germane modifications are recommended. The pooled wisdom of the group is often accurate and complete. This is probably a result of group participation which gives practice in distinguishing fact from opinion, tends to encourage a study of pertinent literature, and provides experience in seeing differing significances in the same fact.[15]

It is likely that there are in every school individual teachers who are unusually able in dealing with particular kinds of problems. In one school, for example, the art teacher helped a number of teachers who referred children who had various kinds of problems to her. She had a mental hygiene point of view and could, through her art work, get the students to express more clearly the difficulties they were experiencing. Without pressing them, she got them interested in painting and drawing and from their work was able to understand some of their tensions. After rapport was established, the youngsters would tell her more directly what was bothering them. A city truant officer said that he was sure the work of two particular teachers who took a genuine interest in pupils was responsible for the fact that very few court repeaters came from the school in which those teachers worked, while other schools in the city had a noticeably high percentage of repeaters in the juvenile courts.

Group discussions of children's problems will uncover the ability of such resource persons as have been cited above. Further, these meetings

[15] Daniel A. Prescott, *The Child in the Educative Process*, New York: McGraw-Hill Book Company, Inc., 1957, p. 461.

will enable teachers to know better the teachers who have such gifts and interests. Even if these meetings were to result in no constructive recommendations for the pupil (and that is unlikely), there would still be great value in the preparatory study and research which accompany these meetings.

In addition to the human resources, there are material resources which sometimes go unrecognized. Books which deal with the various kinds of interests that children might have are helpful. The musical equipment of a school can be regarded as a means of tension release for some students, quite as much as it is an avenue for putting on school entertainment or as a preparation for the child's future constructive employment of leisure time. An example is an eighth-grade boy who, because he was doing less than his test scores indicated he should do academically, was encouraged to practice the clarinet, instead of plodding through routine assignments. He had enough talent to take a place in the school band and thus win some recognition. His success led him to use his class time more diligently in order that he could be sure of getting time to practice. Many communities are recognizing the wisdom of making a wider use of the material equipment by scheduling after-school activities and keeping some of the facilities in service during the summertime.

It seems appropriate to mention the use of monetary resources in providing extra individual attention and an extended school program. To expect teachers to add to their present work load the activities which are implied by the above suggestions seems unfair. More teachers and more money will be required. The value of these contributions from the standpoint of improved mental health must be sold to the administrator and the school's patrons. In the meantime, teachers will have to ask themselves who will do the job if they do not.

Pupils Are Resources. Another of the resources of the school for improving mental health is that which is inherent in the uniqueness of personality in individual pupils. Teachers are taking advantage of this resource when they call on pupils to dance, sing, recite, or perform their tricks of magic. But it can go further than this. Pupils have repeatedly proved that they can intelligently solve many problems of institutional policy, as well as the personal problems they themselves are encountering. They need only to be given a chance for discussion and evaluation.

H. E. Bullis in the book *Human Relations in the Classroom*[15a] cites numerous examples of the way youngsters in the upper grades have worked out their own problems. The technique involved was for the teacher to read to the group a hypothetical case study, which was then discussed. As the discussion progressed, the pupils shifted from the textbook case

[15a] H. Edmund Bullis and Emily E. O'Malley, *Human Relations in the Classroom,* Course I, Wilmington, Del.: The Delaware State Society for Mental Hygiene, 1947.

to their own problems. As one pupil revealed his difficulties, others in the class made suggestions as to what he might have done or should do in the future. This approach has the double advantage of helping students realize that others have problems and of their getting the suggestions from their peers rather than from adults. Group discussions engaging six to ten students, together with teachers or counselors, have been effective in reducing problem behavior, stimulating underachievers, and counteracting delinquent and predelinquent actions. Self-understanding is improved by discussing motivations, by learning that others have problems, and by reconsidering the effects of one's previous behaviors.[16] Evelyn Millis Duvall recommends that adolescents approach their problems of social and sexual adjustments through group discussions, forums, panels, and group counseling. She feels that it is up to youth as well as leaders of them to "tap the resources at hand."[17]

> Where seating arrangements and discussion techniques encourage free expression of ideas and sharing of the leadership function, children can do much to foster wholesome growth on the part of each other. A teacher as a member of the circle can help boys and girls discover how best to tap all of the various ideas and resources available within the group, and how to help each child assist the group to move along with reasonable efficiency toward its goal. Even relatively young children can be guided to see what is happening within a group—what, perhaps, seems to be holding up progress. The teacher can both demonstrate and talk about the importance of being a courteous listener and of being appreciative of each child's contribution. He can show the advantage of discussion which is "circular" rather than always directed toward the teacher.[18]

It is apparent that pupils can be used as school resources. Bringing them in on planning, encouraging them to seek materials, and opening opportunities to them for the exchange of ideas are ways of utilizing this resource. The unique talents, interests, and experiences of pupils can also be used as resources to supplement ordinary classroom recitations and projects. It is frequently reiterated that, although the United States is richly endowed with mineral, agricultural, and forest products and has a sound economy and efficient business and industrial organization, our greatest resource consists of the youth of our land. Pliable, eager, talented young men and women are the real keys to our national success.

[16] Helen I. Driver, *Counseling and Learning in Small-group Discussion*, Madison, Wis.: Monona Publications, 1958, pp. 286–303.

[17] Evelyn Millis Duvall, *Keeping Up with Teen-agers*, Public Affairs Pamphlet 127, New York: Public Affairs Committee, Inc., 1947, pp. 27–29.

[18] Camilla M. Low in *Guidance in the Curriculum*, 1955 Yearbook, Association for Supervision and Curriculum Development, Washington: National Education Association, 1955, pp. 74–75.

SUMMARY

Many influences, such as family background, preschool experiences, hereditary potential, and social and civic factors shape the mental health of pupils. When they enter school, other influences come to be felt. The teacher's personality is of great import, but so too are the kinds of methods he uses. Various methods in diverse situations and in the hands of different teachers can be commended from the mental health point of view. There are, however, certain emphases which can be endorsed and which are applicable in many circumstances.

Teachers need to guard against a tendency to answer all questions. There are several justifications for this recommendation. (1) Learning is doing, and the active seeking of answers will be more profitable to the pupil than a verbalized answer that *seems* to satisfy. (2) Answers are not likely to hold in all situations and at all times. The habit of independence should, therefore, be encouraged. (3) There is a joy in personal discovery, of which the pupil should not be denied. (4) Continuous seeking of information should be an objective of education for democratic living.

Interest can be stimulated by the teacher's enthusiasm, better pupil understanding, clarity of goals, increased knowledge, experiencing success, keeping up with what is expected, and using information that has been acquired. Personal motives, such as feelings of belongingness, guarding against strong interfering emotions, feelings of accomplishment, and satisfaction from praise and reward, tend to create and expand interests.

Teaching methods may be strengthened by teaching for transfer—pointing out common elements, formulating generalizations, stressing ideals, and presenting materials at a level appropriate to mental development. Methods are improved by stressing purposefulness—clarifying aims, setting attainable goals, and relating schoolwork to the experiences and needs of pupils.

A method that can well supplement other educational approaches is that of utilizing the existing resources of the school. These resources include the varied interests and abilities of teachers, the different divisions of the school (shop, music room, library, art room, home economics laboratory, etc.), and, above all, the resources which inhere in the uniqueness of individual pupils.

STUDY AND DISCUSSION EXERCISES

1. Can the matter of teaching method be distinguished from the personality of the teacher?

2. Should the teacher let the students know that he has convictions about certain problems? Should he try to get students to accept his views?

3. How do the purposes of elementary pupils differ from the typical purposes of high-school pupils?

4. Make a list of the resources in your school for improving teaching methods. Compare your list with that of other class members and see if your list should be extended.

5. Which of the pupils, in a particular grade or high-school class you have seen, could be used as human resources in some teaching-learning situations?

SUGGESTED ADDITIONAL READINGS

Guidance in the Curriculum, 1955 Yearbook, Association for Supervision and Curriculum Development, Washington: National Education Association, 1955. 231 pp.

Resources available to teachers in effective work with children include specialists, administrators, fellow teachers, and parents.

Kettelkamp, Gilbert C., *Teaching Adolescents,* Boston: D. C. Heath and Company, 1954, pp. 367–411.

Pupils and their experiences, films, slides, charts, tape recorders, and radio are discussed as resources in teaching.

Morse, Arthur D., *Schools of Tomorrow—Today,* New York: Doubleday & Company, Inc., 1960. 191 pp.

This book describes a number of exerimental school programs currently being conducted. Team teaching, schools without grades, television, and programs for the gifted are among the topics.

Weber, Julia, *My Country School Diary,* New York: Harper & Brothers, 1946. 270 pp.

"Purpose is at the heart of a wholesome learning experience," states the author on page 162; but she does not wait until reaching that page to show how purpose can work to make education effective.

Wingo, G. Max, and Raleigh Schorling, *Elementary School Student Teaching,* 2d ed., New York: McGraw-Hill Book Company, Inc., 1955, pp. 176–200, 328–350.

The chapters indicated deal with capitalizing on pupil resources and pupil participation in planning.

CHAPTER 12

SCHOOL HAZARDS TO MENTAL HEALTH

The urgency of the study of mental hygiene is increased by virtue of certain educational practices which are inimical to the mental health of pupils. These practices, in spite of their being well intentioned, have been mildly criticized by some mental hygienists and vehemently condemned by others, but they continue to exist because teachers have been subjected to the practices in their own schooling. Though their professional study may have cast doubt on the wisdom of these practices, the inertia of past routines retards the application of improved knowledge. Certain of these questionable practices will be examined in this chapter, in order that teachers may add their weight to a critical examination of them and then, if it seems warranted, make some effort to eliminate or modify the procedures.

SUBJECT MATTER SET OUT TO BE LEARNED

The Compartmentalization of Learning. There is no doubt that there are areas of common knowledge which every educated individual should possess; however, the plan of gaining these out of a set curriculum or prescribed text or course of study is questionable. It has the tendency to make these learnings isolated and remote from the life situations in which the knowledges could be meaningfully used. The subject matter takes on an element of artificiality, because it is not related to the out-of-school experiences of the students. Learning subject matter from this detached point of view yields a collection of mere verbalisms, rather than changed, functional behavior. For example, some pupils can correct a poorly written sentence in a workbook but continue in their personal letters and conversations to make errors similar to the ones corrected.

Historians indicate that this approach, in its day, was successful in furnishing the background required for scholarly pursuits in religion, law, medicine, and, to an extent, in teaching. To a degree, it was successful. But if we stop to consider that possibly there were large numbers who were shut out from the pursuit of formal education by the selective process that was continually going on, we may begin to doubt that it was ever very highly successful. Students with talents that were equally high but that differed from the academic were given no opportunity to develop their potentialities. Today, when children up to fourteen, sixteen, and eighteen years of age in various states are compelled to go to school, the uniform curriculum must be given studied consideration. With children of many levels of mental ability, with vastly differing strength of motivation, with diverse objectives to be achieved, the compartmentalization and fragmentation of learning is of dubious value. Many youngsters do not have sufficient insight to bridge the gap between school exercises and life applications. Many do not have the desire to apply themselves for the sake of academic recognition.

Fallacious Justification of the Subject-matter Approach. Unfortunately, some who are in a position to do effective work in bringing about changes in practice can look back on this kind of education and say, "Well, I went to that kind of school, and look at me." Such critics fail utterly to understand that they were fortunate enough to have had the abilities and experiences which made it possible for them to overcome the handicaps imposed.

On the other hand, many students rationalize their absence by saying they lack money, are needed at home, or live too far from school, when the real reason is that they see no meaningful objective for their continuing.[1] Others, without citing reasons, become habitual truants. Many stay in school but close their eyes, ears, and minds to any stimulation and sit dumbly waiting for the bell to ring and for the calendar to show them that vacation has finally arrived. Some, it is true, have the academic intelligence which makes it possible for them to do the schoolwork in a meaningful way and the general intelligence which will enable them to transfer their academic verbalizations into a relationship that will function in their lifework. However, this transfer is, to a large extent, made in spite of what is done in school, rather than because if it.

The solutions of such dilemmas are not single, simple, or static, but evidence continues to accumulate to indicate that changes should be made in what is taught and the manner in which it is taught.[2] Bright children

[1] Charles M. Allen, *Combatting the Drop Out Problem* (booklet), Chicago: Science Research Associates, Inc., 1956, p. 17.

[2] A. Harry Passow, Jane E. Beasley, and Deton J. Brooks, Jr., "Adapting the Curriculum to the Needs, Capabilities, and Talents of Individual Students," *Review of Educational Research*, 27:277–286, 1957.

need more challenge, slow learners need more time, concreteness, and specificity. Pupils of all kinds profit from ability grouping where subject matter is adapted to present and probable needs.

An Illustrative Case Study. The seriousness of the error of failing to recognize the special capacities and interests of the child has been well illustrated by a case which the author has been able to follow for a number of years. A fourth-grade boy, G., seemed to be interested only in the clay-modeling activities of the school. All the other schoolwork was apparently unattractive by comparison. He played vigorously with other youngsters for short periods but soon returned to his clay. The objects he modeled were far superior to those produced by other children. His desk was always cluttered with models of horses, houses, men, deer, chickens, windmills, and the like. He once made a complete model of a farm, including house, barn, silo, livestock, fowls, wagons, haystack, and other items, which he modeled after various pictures that he studied. But the teacher was mainly concerned with his lack of application to numbers and his inability to read well—pursuits in which this young fellow's efforts were very haphazard. Finally, the teacher decided that she would deprive him of the privilege of working with clay until he succeeded in his other lessons. But the motivation for these other things was weak and G. would idle away his time in fruitless dreaming. Soon G. hit upon the idea of staying away from school, and some time passed before it was discovered that there was no legitimate excuse for his absences.

His parents were deeply concerned about his truancy and threatened severe punishment if the absences were repeated. Apparently G. was more willing to submit to the penalties inflicted by his parents than he was to attend school regularly, and his truancy went unchecked. He lagged further behind in his subjects. He began to avoid the uncomfortable situation at home by staying away nights, sleeping in boxcars or packing crates. He got food by bumming and pilfering. As the local merchants were warned against giving him food or the opportunity to steal, his wanderings became wider. By the time he was twelve, he had traveled several hundred miles to a West Coast city and stayed away from home for a month at a time. A year later, he had signed as a cabin boy on a freighter and had been to the Orient. All this time, his interest in modeling persisted and he usually carried about with him a piece of clay, which he would press into an amazing likeness of a pig or an elk, or into a recognizable likeness of a man's or woman's head and face.

By the time he was twenty, no one expected him to be anything but a tramp. One day, a newspaper reporter found him sitting in a Los Angeles park working with a piece of clay. The reporter was struck by the skill shown in his reproduction in clay and, in talking with him, heard an interesting story of travel and adventure, which he wrote up for a Sunday-supplement story, published together with pictures of some of the things G. had modeled just to show what he could do. Two years later, another Sunday-supplement story appeared in an Eastern newspaper, describing a showcase full of models of parts of the human organism which were being displayed in a large metropolitan technical museum. It would be gratifying to report that G.'s great talent had been discovered, but unfortunately the pattern of his life seemed to have crystallized. G. was still at heart a wanderer, an undisciplined ne'er-do-well.

Some time later a personal visit with G. confirmed the stories that had been carried in the newspapers. But he was temporarily engaged as a mess steward on a freighter. His clothes were shabby, his speech was awkward, and his ability to write was slight. He had difficulty in writing some addresses and spelling even the names of his brothers and sisters. But his skill in modeling was still apparent. He pulled a piece of clay out of his pocket and made several interesting animals for the author's small sons.

One cannot help wondering what might have been the outcome if a teacher with the mental hygiene viewpoint had used this lad's talent as an approach to other learnings—if she had tied his interest in clay to a functional ability for using numbers and words. We might assume that school would have been valuable to him even if he had not learned to read or compute. His talent for modeling might have been expanded to creativeness in drawing, painting, and sculpturing at no great loss to the school. In fact, since creativity is sometimes defined as the ability of a person to assimilate the accumulated data from his experiences into varieties of thought patterns,[3] emphasis on these relationships might have been the means of making G. truly creative. Certainly, he could have had the advantage of remaining in contact with his peers instead of being forced into an adult world during his childhood. We might assume, too, that the case might have turned out worse than it did. G. might have been a delinquent and an adult criminal—a liability to society—instead of becoming merely a nonentity. Certainly a tenable supposition is that the boy could have been led by an adroit teacher to acquire the fundamentals of learning that would have contributed to the making of an artist of some importance.

Changing Emphases. In many elementary classrooms children are engaged in varied activities which have more meaning to them than an ordinary lesson in a reading or an arithmetic textbook. Their schoolwork is oriented to some experience which they have had—a trip, a visit to a museum, an excursion in the country, or the visit of someone who is recognized as having some special knowledge of interest to the group. Practical lessons in arithmetic, reading, and language are stressed through

[3] D. F. Johnson, "Creativity a New Challenge," *School Arts*, 58 (2):23–25, October, 1958.

their use in carrying out the project. Arithmetic is involved in computing transportation costs and estimating the time needed for the trip. Reading is used to give the proposed project its proper setting and to furnish fuller information on questions that are raised by the activity. A study of language is introduced in the writing of letters asking permission to make a visit or expressing gratitude for a courtesy or for supplementary information. Such work has a place in the first grade, where pupils dictate their own reading materials, put together out of some experience the children have had—a visit to a local rose garden, for instance. In the upper grades, the work of the class centers around a long-term project, such as an investigation of local forms of government or a study of local industrial activities. Practice in the fundamental processes is not incidental, nor is it neglected; it is introduced in connection with concrete situations which have an orientation in the real experiences of the pupils themselves. Drill, practice, skill contests are used—but as supplements and aids rather than the major techniques of instruction.

A thirty-school experiment has indicated that such meaningful experience as this can serve as the foundation for acquiring knowledge in the traditional high-school subjects. Even the students who went to college after studying in "progressive" high schools did not suffer any marked handicap on account of their having turned aside from a subject-matter-set-out-to-be-learned type of curriculum. Specifically, the following items are worthy of note: There were 24.7 per cent dropouts from college among the progressives, as compared with 28.2 per cent among pupils who had gone to traditional schools. The grade-point average of progressive students was 0.04 higher—of no significance, of course, except as indicating that they suffered no great handicap. Progressives lagged by 0.02 of a grade point in foreign language study. The lack of traditional prerequisites seemed to present no real disadvantage. Seventy-five per cent of the progressives were judged by their teachers to be more competent in carrying on independent work. It is in terms of the education of the "whole child" that progressive methods showed superiority; i.e., these students, when in college, listened to more speeches and music on the radio, they attended more lectures and concerts, they read more books other than textbooks, and they enjoyed more cultural pursuits. Besides, they took a more active part in campus activities, except in athletics.[4]

In spite of the fact that there are no marked immediate disadvantages that can be attributed to departure from a set curriculum and that there are some ultimate advantages in the long run—advantages which are both academic and cultural—the prescribed curriculum remains in force. It takes courage on the part of teachers and administrators to deviate from

[4] Dorothy Bromley, "Education for College or for Life?" *Harper's Magazine*, 182:407–416, March, 1941.

time-honored practices. But when the non-college pupil can be kept in school longer and when the college-bound pupil can be better prepared by means of differentiated curriculums, the uniform curriculum lauded by the survivors of yesteryear loses its tenuous justification. The differentiated curriculum, which recognizes abilities in addition to the academic and caters without discrimination to all social classes, not only promotes individual mental health but helps the nation as a whole by better use of its human resources.[5]

There are some hopeful indications. A few schools are experimenting with larger units of curricular organization than the hour-of-math, hour-of-English, stop-with-the-bell approach. English and social studies are a frequently used combination; mathematics and science are often combined.[5a] Many teachers are willing to deviate from the locally and state-prescribed curriculums; they select the topics of study from an analysis of the interests, abilities, and background of their students. Some teachers start with the prescribed text, but then at times they may go more slowly than the regulation rate and at times advance beyond the prescribed course.

This point of view does not require a repudiation of the value of knowledge and information. The value of facts and of accuracy in computation is more pertinent when the information and the practice are attached to problems that the typical school student realizes are intimately related to himself. Furthermore, it is felt that strict stressing of the subject-matter-set-out-to-be-learned may leave out some of the desirable concomitants of effective education. These include a testing of values, the development of attitudes toward work, an interest in continuing education, and practice in democratic activities.

> Education must meet the needs of the individual and must be adapted to his interests; for if he is not interested, he will not respond, and if he does not respond, he will not learn. The curriculum must be based upon these interests and these needs. In deciding whether algebra should be studied by a high school freshman, those who hold to the antithesis do not ask whether algebra is a necessary preparation for trigonometry or calculus, instead they ask whether the fourteen-year-old can grasp the principles of algebra, whether he can use it in his daily life, and whether he is interested in it.[6]

[5] For further discussion of these issues, see William H. Burton, "Education and Social Class in the United States," *Harvard Educational Review*, 23:243–256, 1953.

[5a] Ralph W. Tyler, "Curriculum Organization," in *The Integration of Educational Experiences*, 57th Yearbook, Part III, National Society for the Study of Education, Chicago: University of Chicago Press, 1958, pp. 105–125.

[6] Paul Woodring, *A Fourth of a Nation*, New York: McGraw-Hill Book Company, Inc., 1957, p. 72.

This orientation, while acceptable to many teachers and typical pupils, is not inclusive enough for all pupils and educators; for example,

> But this commitment [high school education for all] does not mean that we must set out standards at the level of the slow learner or that we must ignore standards altogether, as some educators have urged us to do. For those who can achieve them, standards are highly motivating; their effectiveness can be observed in any good graduate school or school of medicine or engineering. Obviously such high standards, if set for *all* high school students, would only frustrate the less able, yet they are necessary for those who are to be our leaders.[7]

Needs differ, mental abilities are varied, and motivations vary in strength and direction. The concept of subject-matter-set-out-to-be-learned must be examined in terms of these differences. Pupils profit from an opportunity to exercise the need for independence and, at the same time, to satisfy the need for companionship through cooperative endeavor. On account of the varied activities which are involved in new approaches, there is an opportunity to gain recognition in ways other than by ranking first on a pencil-and-paper test. Tension-tolerance is heightened through practice in solving meaningful problems. Certainly, there is a more realistic environment in which one may fill the need for manipulation and for satisfying curiosity. The experience approach tends to foster genuine psychological security, by teaching a pupil to stand on his own feet through full and balanced living today.

UNIFORM GRADING, EXAMINATIONS, AND MARKS

Grades Are/Are Not Involved in Life Situations. The Procrustean-bed analogy,[8] so often referred to in education, is most pertinent when applied to the system of grading that is so extensively used in present-day schools. The grading system would be more lifelike if every citizen were employed to do the same task at the same salary, if everyone were expected to produce the same results from his efforts. But this is not what happens in life. Employees are selected to do different jobs at different rates of pay. The day laborer is considered a success when he works regularly and efficiently, even though his salary may be only half that of a successful lawyer, professor, or doctor. Actually, all workers do not do the same thing. They tend to do the things for which they have the interest, talent, and background. They might do them even better and work more cheerfully if they did not have school backgrounds which had

[7] *Ibid.*, p. 129.

[8] Procrustes welcomed all travelers, but he forced all guests to sleep on one bed. If guests were too tall, he chopped off their limbs to fit, and if too short, they were stretched on a rack until they were the proper length.

implanted feelings of inferiority and the anticipation of failure. It is easy to imagine the frustration, resentment, and disappointment that are built up by such a situation. Like the Procrustean bed of old, the present grading system does not fit all individuals, but they must be made to fit it.

> In antediluvian times, while the animal kingdom was being differentiated into swimmers, climbers, runners, and fliers, there was a school started for their development. Its theory was that the best animals should be able to do one thing as well as another. If an animal had short legs and good wings, attention should be devoted to running, so as to even up the qualities as far as possible. So the duck was kept waddling instead of swimming, and the pelican was kept wagging his short wings in the attempt to fly. The eagle was made to run and allowed to fly only for recreation, while maturing tadpoles were unmercifully guyed for being neither one thing nor another.
>
> The animals that would not submit to such training, but persisted in developing the best gifts they had, were dishonored and humiliated in many ways. They were stigmatized as being narrow-minded specialists. No one was allowed to graduate from the school unless he could climb, swim, run, and fly at certain prescribed rates; so it happened that the time wasted by the duck in the attempt to run had so hindered him from swimming, that his swimming muscles atrophied and he was hardly able to swim at all, and in addition, he had been scolded, punished, and ill-treated in many ways so as to make his life a burden. In fact, he left school humiliated. The eagle could make no headway in climbing to the top of a tree, and although he showed he could get there just the same, the performance was counted a demerit since it had not been done according to the prescribed course of study.
>
> An abnormal eel with large pectoral fins proved that he could run, swim, climb trees, and fly a little. He attained an average of sixty per cent in all his studies. He was made valedictorian of the class.[9]

When schools abandon uniform grading we see pupils who gain appreciation for schooling, improve feelings of self-confidence and worth, and bolster their personal security.[10]

Unreliability of Grades. One of the more serious criticisms of the grading system, in view of the regard for grades by pupils and public, is their unreliability. Study after study has shown that two different teachers do not give the same grade for objectively determined equivalence of achievement in academic accomplishment. There is considerable difference between the grading standards of various schools. The same paper graded by different teachers may, and has, received scores running

[9] J. Adams Puffer, *Vocational Guidance*, Chicago: Rand McNally & Company, 1913, pp. 22–23. By permission of the author.
[10] Raymond H. Rignall, "Are Report Cards Necessary?" *Family Circle*, 41:104–111, September, 1952.

the full gamut of the grading scale. Even the same paper graded by the same teacher at different times does not always receive the same score.[11] But the most ludicrous of these situations was that in which, during a study of grading, the teacher's paper—a key to the scoring—was accidentally mixed in with the students' papers and was marked as a failure by some of the scorers.

> All parties involved—teachers, pupils, and parents—are thus placing too much emphasis on the significance of academic grades. Both the elation produced by high grades as well as the humiliation precipitated by low ones may be too extreme in view of the unreliability of the marks themselves as well as the uncertainty as to their precise implications. . . .
> One can all too readily mislead students into regarding grades and degrees as the chief goal of formal education. The symbols become more important than that which they are supposed to symbolize. . . . When marks and degrees come to mean more than does the love of learning or the joy of intellectual discovery then the purpose of awarding such academic symbols has also been defeated.[12]

Attempts to revise the grading system have been largely confined to improving the system itself and making it more objective. Thus, objective tests of the true-false, multiple-choice, and matching type have been the subject of extensive study and experimentation. The aim has been to remove, as far as possible, the personal element from scoring. Resort to the use of standardized tests is more of the same thing, but based on large-scale operations. This work is commendable, but whether it will really get to the roots of the problem is doubtful. For one thing, it does not remove the criticism that all students are still measured on the same scale. It does not allow for the cultural differences which exist within the different localities of the same city.

The Subjective Element in Grading. One of the criticisms of grading is that it is subjective, but there is some doubt that the subjective element should be eliminated in pupil evaluation. The fact is that success, in any line of activity, depends, to a degree, upon the ability to get along with others and to make good impressions. It is worth considering that the impression a pupil makes on his teacher is a worthy concern of education. The ability to express his ideas so that others will understand and consider them deserves some attention. What is needed is not a repudiation of the subjective element in grading but a recognition of it that will allow the

[11] Georgia Sachs Adams and Theodore L. Torgerson, *Measurement and Evaluation for the Secondary-school Teacher*, New York: Holt, Rinehart and Winston, Inc., 1956, pp. 25–26.

[12] D. B. Klein, *Mental Hygiene*, rev. ed., New York: Holt, Rinehart and Winston, Inc., 1956, pp. 615–617.

teacher to use it constructively. Prejudice certainly should be eliminated; but there may be advantages in considering the *total personality* of the child, rather than depending solely on his percentile status on a standardized achievement test.

The teacher's viewpoint of the marking system is intimately related to his philosophy of education. If he regards education as the mastery of subject matter, if he believes the function of the school can be stated as acquisition of facts and improvement of the mind, then grades, marks, and examinations are acceptable to him. If, on the other hand, he conceives of education as the drawing out of the individual, as a means of developing the total personality of the pupil, then he will question comparative marks and standardized grading.

The foregoing implies that examinations and tests are only a part, not an entire medium or the end, of education procedures. Tests and examinations have a constructive role to play in functional education, but their use—or rather, their misuse—leads to the logical question, What is that use?

The concept which promises some relief from the limitations of marks and grading is called *evaluation*. Evaluation is an attempt to broaden the basis for estimating the progress of a student in school. While acquisition of information is one of the elements considered, there are items combined with the evaluation which include a consideration of the pupil's background, his status at the beginning and at the end of a unit or term of work, his work habits, his attitudes, his ability to get along with others and work with them, his actual potentialities in contrast with his grade placement alone, the state of his physical health and any physical or emotional handicaps, and the like. Evaluation is, in short, a *total* view of the child, not a reliance upon the end result of mastering subject matter.

Steps toward Improvement. When the report cards of our parents or grandparents are examined with their scores of 76¼ or 92½ per cent, there is likely to be a derisive smile because of the absurdity of such grading. Over the years an improvement was devised in the form of A, B, C, D, and so on, but this made comparisons between individuals difficult; therefore, numerical values were assigned to each letter. In order to designate some honor like valedictorian or admission to a certain club, the average of letter grades is computed to three decimal places, e.g., 2.421—no less absurd than the 92½ per cent of past years. Since there is variation in pupil ability, even the letter grades are thought to have defects; so new letters have been used: N, S, and C or some similar group. In one system these mean "not satisfactory in terms of indicated ability," "satisfactory in terms of ability," and "commendable in terms of ability." But some pupils and parents (and some teachers) lament this because the same C might be awarded not only to a low-ability student for comparatively poor work but also to a high-ability pupil who with no greater expenditure of effort did much more or much better work. Others object that employers and college officials must know the grades of a student. The mental hygiene viewpoint demands that we ask the question: Does the employer's or college official's preference trans-

FIG. 9. "I don't say I *deserve* better grades, but my point is that my sense of security is being threatened during my formative years." (Charles Dennis, in *The Christian Science Monitor.*)

cend the need of pupils to be evaluated in terms of their status, progress, and specifically stated goals?

The main purpose of testing is not to grade or rank pupils but to assist classroom teachers in getting evidence of achievement of growth. Specialists in measurement have largely failed in constructing standardized tests to measure the totality of behavior. . . . They have not yet produced total understanding of the human personality which the classroom teacher must have.

The period when such procedures were uppermost and in which quotients of intelligence and achievement were computed for most children seems now to be drawing to a close. It has served its purpose in making classroom teachers more aware than previously of individual differences among pupils. It has also made them aware of the limitations of the evaluative devices that have been used. We are now ready to pass from "the quotient stage" to one in which standardized tests will provide a small tho still important place in evaluation programs.[13]

Fortunately, for those school systems which have the temerity to abolish grades and comparative report cards there is already available a tested, meaningful, and satisfactory means of evaluation, namely, the conference method—of which there are several kinds. One of these is for the teacher to go to the home of the pupil (with the parents' consent) and talk about the pupil's progress and problems, his limitations, areas of development needing attention, behaviors that are commendable or that need improvement, ways in which the parents might help the school in its program, and factors in behavior that have received commendable notice. The visit to the home has the advantage of giving the teacher a direct view of what the home situation is, thus enabling him to understand better and to make allowance for some of the actions in school that otherwise might be severely condemned. Some parents seem to be somewhat embarrassed by the prospect of a visit from the teacher. This is avoided by the teacher's suggesting a conference either at home or at school, according to the parents' preference. A school visit has the advantage of giving parents firsthand information about the school.

The teacher-parent conference is particularly valuable in the primary grades. In the upper grades and the high school, the teacher-pupil conference has been given favorable comment from those who have tried it. In this, teacher and pupil talk "man-to-man" about the progress being made, habits that should be formed or broken, and areas of knowledge and behavior that need additional attention. This method has the advantage of making the student a more active participant in the evaluation than he ordinarily is when the letter or numerical grading system is used. The conference has the advantage of letting a student know not only why (on what basis) he was evaluated as he was but also exactly how (the meaning of scores) he was evaluated. The opportunity it offers for better understanding between the teacher and the pupil would make further experimenting with this plan worthwhile.

The objective of all grading systems should desirably be to promote growth and to chart next steps. This objective is perhaps nowhere better

[13] John W. M. Rothney, *Evaluating and Reporting Pupil Progress*, What Research Says to the Teacher, no. 7, Washington: National Education Association, 1955, p. 7

served than in the use of pupil self-appraisal. This plan calls for a detailed statement of the various aims, objectives, and desired outcomes of the learning situation. The aims are made clear to the students at the beginning of the term—in many places the students have participated in the formulation of the objectives—and then each student is given the chance, periodically, to evaluate his own progress toward the attainment of the goals. In the meantime, the teacher will have evaluated the student in terms of

FIG. 10. Are teacher-parent conferences superior to report cards as a means of evaluating pupil progress? Can individual differences be better provided for when conferences are used as evaluations? What are the major objections to teacher-parent conferences?

the same objectives. If there is any discrepancy between the two evaluations, teacher and pupil get together to discover the reasons for the differences.

Analysis of current educational literature clearly indicates a trend away from grades and marks to the viewpoint of evaluation. Educational texts a decade ago, in dealing with the subject, discussed means of making grades and marks more objective and precise. Now the tendency is to broaden the base and make use of the mediums inherent in the concept of evaluation. Anecdotal records; representative bits of work; health histories; the results of periodic intelligence tests and achievement tests;

reactions to the responses made on personality inventories; teacher-teacher, teacher-pupil, and teacher-parent conferences—all these become a part of the broadened concept.

THE DILEMMA OF NONPROMOTION

Threat of Failure Is a Negative Incentive. There are some administrators and some teachers who believe that, in order to maintain standards, a certain percentage of the pupils in a class must be failed. They argue that, if the threat of failure is removed, the pupil will have no incentive for working—the result will be to foster dilatory work habits.[14] Many teachers feel that threat of failure is a questionable practice. When they hear that two students were failed, they ask "Why did they fail? What was done that should not have been done? What was left undone that should have been done?" This viewpoint clearly puts the blame where it ought to be placed. A failing student is an indication that the teacher is failing to adjust goals and content to individuals or that inflexibility in the curriculum demands that the child fit the school rather than the school fit the child's needs and development.

There are many arguments for and against the practice of automatic promotion; some of them are epitomized in the following parallel lists:

Against Social Promotion	*For Social Promotion*
Annual promotion eliminates the incentive of competition.	Causes of failure are manifold; retaining pupils does not remove all causes.
The threat of failure will cause pupils to apply themselves.	Repeaters do not learn more in two years than the nonrepeater of the same mental age learns in one.
Elementary repeaters do better work the second time.	Over half the repeaters do not improve, and one-eighth do poorer work when repeating.
Nonpromotion tends to keep pupils with their academic and social peers.	The range of abilities continues to be wide, and the frank facing of differences leads to adjustments in teaching.
Nonpromotion upholds academic standards.	The curriculum should be adjusted to children, not to mythical standards.
Nonpromotion tends to avert unjustified feelings of competence and worth.	Nonpromotion typically intensifies children's emotional instability.

Although some studies are not favorable to the policy of 100 per cent promotion, research does deal the nonpromotion adherents a heavy blow. Achievement tests administered to pupils of equal ability show that those promoted on trial make greater gains than do those who are required to

[14] Robert J. G. Barlow, "Social Promotion—Asset or Liability?" *School and Society*, 87:88, Feb. 28, 1959.

repeat the grade.[15] Moreover, the study of pupils and the use of guidance *leads* to the enrichment of the curriculum which, in turn, seems to have the best effect on the personality structure of pupils. Providing lifelike school situations, allowing for variety, and emphasizing the strengths and interests of pupils provide for positive motivation.[16]

Newer Practices in Promotion. Experienced teachers often question the practice of passing the student when he has not "come up to standard," inasmuch as they feel that it is kinder to fail the student immediately than to postpone the imminent failure. They assert that the student who is socially promoted will get inflated ideas about his abilities. It is probably true that some will get such ideas, but a far greater number of them will know, without grades, marks, and failure, that their work in academic lines does not measure up to that of their peers. Students from the first grade on have a rather clear conception of their comparative ability. Rather than to shame and humiliate large numbers of students by not promoting them, it would seem to be a simple thing to be quite frank in a personal interview with the unseeing one or two students, who are apt to get inflated ideas about their academic prowess.

> Worst of all, failure results in the pupil being branded as a failure by his schoolmates, his relatives, and his friends. Failure incurs the risk that the pupil will develop an inferiority complex and acquire a grudge against the school and society. When a pupil fails school, there is danger that he is being prepared for failure in life.[17]

Fortunately, the resolution of the promotion dilemma can be side-stepped by using the ungraded school organization. Since various practices of promotion or nonpromotion do not seem to produce the desired results, the classification of subject matter and materials on the basis of the psychological characteristics of learners, instead of by grade level, seems advisable. This was done in Appleton, Wisconsin, by reorganizing the eight elementary-school years into three blocks—kindergarten, two years; primary, three years; and intermediate, three years. Pupils progressed steadily under provisions for slow, average, and bright pupils. It is felt that the following advantages accrue from this plan: (1) Each child progresses according to his own idiosyncratic growth rate, (2) no child repeats a grade; instead, he is allowed to progress more slowly than do others, (3) no child is a "failure," inasmuch as his program is adjusted to fit him, (4) placement can be readjusted at any time during the three-

[15] "Ten Criticisms of Public Education," *National Education Association Research Bulletin*, 35 (4):149, December, 1957.

[16] David Segel, *Intellectual Abilities in the Adolescent Period*, Bulletin 6, Federal Security Agency, Office of Education, 1948, pp. 22–24.

[17] Ward G. Reeder, *A First Course in Education*, 3d ed., New York: The Macmillan Company, 1950, pp. 300–301.

year period, (5) placement is based on physical, mental, emotional, and social growth, and (6) the elimination of unrealistic pressures is conducive to good mental health.[18]

If teachers are restricted by state or local curriculums and feel that these represent a minimum of accomplishment, instead of serving as guides to teaching, then the idea of failure is hard to remove. However, some teachers have the courage to hold out for the belief that the student's going to another grade or class will be more educative than his being again subjected to the frustration of remaining in a failure situation for another semester or year. Effective pupil guidance will avert much of the prevailing practice of failing. If conditions conducive to mental health are to prevail in our schools, the negative threat of failure must be replaced by more positive lures to educational achievement.

HOMEWORK

The Dubious Values of Homework. Closely allied to the threat of failure is the necessity for the student's doing homework in order to complete the work of his grade, class, textbook, or syllabus. Requiring a prescribed amount of work from all pupils seems not unlike requiring all to weigh a certain number of pounds or to run a hundred yards in a certain number of seconds before he can be passed. Recent criticisms of education, stating that schools are "soft," are intensified by comparing American education with the ostensibly greater success of certain European systems and provide arguments for the homework adherents. The fact that pupils in America have widely varying abilities, that they come from varied socioeconomic backgrounds, and the universality of education, as contrasted to the competitive and selective nature of the European systems, is ignored in these criticisms.[18a]

In the first place, homework assignments are likely to magnify rather than to reduce the range of individual differences in academic achievement. The youngster who is having difficulty in keeping up with his peers is also likely to be the one whose home influences are distracting. He may have other work to do—a paper route, caring for babies, or extensive home duties. The home conditions may be crowded, so as to prevent privacy for study or even a place for spreading out books and papers. On the other hand, the able student probably has a room or a

---

[18] John I. Goodlad, "Illustrative Programs and Procedures in Elementary Schools" in *The Integration of Educational Experiences*, 57th Yearbook, Part III, National Society for the Study of Education, Chicago: University of Chicago Press, 1958, p. 191.

[18a] See, for example, C. Winfield Scott and others (eds.), *The Great Debate: Our Schools in Crisis*, Englewood Cliffs, N.J.: Prentice-Hall, Inc., 1959, pp. 7–43.

table for a study place, while others in the family are willing to tune down the radio out of consideration for him, and able assistance may be available. These conditions may tend to give him a feeling of superiority over his less fortunate but equally intelligent classmate.

In the second place, young people, including those of high-school age, need to have time for play and social development. School attendance should not demand of the student a monastic devotion to academic pursuits. He should be encouraged, especially during the winter months, to play and exercise in the open air. A foreign-born mother of two girls, both of whom had been graduated from college, stated in broken English, "We hear so much about how advanced European students are. True, some can stand the pace, but no note is taken of those who contract tuberculosis and have mental breakdowns because they must study all the time."

> Excessive tension and a sense of pressure are often associated with homework. If a pupil is not able to resist the appeal of television or student activities, he may begin to think of himself as lacking in purpose and will power. Late hours spent in study and failure to complete assignments may make a conscientious pupil depressed and anxious.
>
> For mental health, children and young people need to engage in worthwhile out-of-school tasks suited to their individual capacities. Homework should supply such tasks and reasonable freedom in carrying them out. Whenever homework crowds out social experiences, outdoor recreation, and creative activities, and whenever it usurps time that should be devoted to sleep, it is not meeting the basic needs of children and adolescents.[19]

In the third place, homework is likely to create a poor learning situation, both in school and at home. Those who know they can do their work easily at home are likely to make little use of their study time in school, thus forming poor work habits when work should be given first place and tending, besides, to prevent those who cannot work profitably at home from finishing their work at school. At home, proper guidance is likely to be lacking. When the parent is not able to give competent instruction, the student is likely to become confused; and even parents who are academically capable are likely to be emotionally so involved with their children that they make tense taskmasters.

Meaningful Homework. Now that some of the heat of the argument has been dissipated, it may be admitted that there is a place for some kinds of homework. If a class—in social studies, for example—wishes to find out about adult reactions to some situation (radical attitudes, perhaps),

[19] Ruth Strang, *Guided Study and Homework*, What Research Says to the Teacher, no. 8, Washington: National Education Association, 1955, p. 18.

then a discussion with the parents would serve the double purpose of gathering information and including the parents among the resources of the school. It would also offer a basis for mature conversation on an intellectual level and thus tend to promote social maturity. Some of the work involved in the solution of a problem might include activities which cannot be carried on in school—a visit to a museum to gather information for a report, a trip to the local library to get materials not available in the school library, or another trip to obtain pamphlets from the chamber of commerce. Such undertakings should not be assigned to all pupils, but those who have the time—without infringing on their home duties—should be asked to make the visits. Finally, homework done on a volunteer basis should be permissible if the teacher knows that it will not interfere with the well-rounded program of activity that a mentally healthy child should have. For example, a pupil who is known to be spending time on homework when it can be adequately done during school hours might be discouraged, but one who normally has social and recreational interests might be given encouragement to make a special report on a supplementary book or to dig up some information from encyclopedias or other reference volumes, which would go beyond the scope of time available during school hours.

Homework and Preparation for College. There are some teachers who believe that unless the student has been disciplined through homework, he will be inadequately prepared for college. This may be of importance to some prospective college students, but the risk of impairing eyesight because of inadequate lighting and of harming physical health because of furniture ill-fitted for study, and the restriction of exercise and the possibility of inadequate sleep for students not going to college will still place homework in the questionable-practices category. Moreover, proper work habits can be instilled in short working periods as well as in longer ones. The student who has learned to make good use of his time will not, as a rule, have difficulty in adding more hours of work in college, for he will have the advantage of additional maturity and an atmosphere where study has traditionally occupied some of the evening hours. As a matter of fact, the maintenance of a balanced schedule of exercise, recreation, and work is as important in college as it is in high school. Children and young people do not learn to work well by being forced. They learn, instead, to dislike work and they repudiate it when the compulsion is gone. They do learn to work properly when the tasks are meaningful and when rapport with the supervising adults is high.

The evaluation of homework depends in part on the grade placement of students, in part upon the out-of-school conditions of pupils, in part on their intellectual status, and in part upon the adjustment of assignments to these factors. In summary then, let it be understood that no unequivocal support or repudiation can be given to homework. The same routine lessons and tasks for all pupils (uniform homework) receives no support from research. Individualized homework—that which considers interests, abilities, and home conditions—may be recommended in limited amounts in the upper grades. It seems likely that the enjoyment of meaningful and appropriate assignments will be as sound a preparation for college as will the forced fulfillment of uniformly prescribed homework. "Flexibility in the kind of assignment must replace uniformity, with the objective of developing voluntary effort, initiative, responsibility, and self-direction in the student."[20]

AUTHORITARIANISM

The Unhygienic Nature of Authoritarianism. Authoritarianism refers to the practice and philosophy of depending on absolute, inflexible standards as goals for thinking and behavior. Creeds, customs, pronouncements of experts, official dictums are the source of authority for making decisions and directing action. Conformity is expected and deviation from it is culpable in such orientation. While it is recognized that there is a place for competence and leadership in pupil control and individual development, authoritarianism must be listed as one of the school hazards to mental health.

Besides traditionalism, authoritarianism is a constant danger in education. The autocratic spirit prevails too often among some administrators who regard the teaching staff as being part of the hired help. A hierarchial spirit in education is contrary to the ideals of democracy, and it creates frozen individuals on the top and fearful persons on the bottom of the scale. The democratic spirit ought to develop more patterns of genuine cooperation between administrators, teachers and the community. . . .

The authoritarian teacher demands conformity on the part of his students. They thus are not required to think for themselves, but to accept the word of the teacher as absolute truth. Undoubtedly, the authoritarian spirit of German learning contributed to the rise of National Socialism. In German schools the teacher was often regarded as an idol; to contradict him was a form of heresy. . . .

If we stress in education preconceived truths, absolute standards, memorization and drill, if we discourage independent decisions, we create students who lack initiative and self-reliance, and who are always potential tools for dictatorships.[21]

[20] "Improving Homework—Suggestions for Teachers and Parents," *National Education Association Research Bulletin*, 35:30, February, 1958.

[21] Frederick Mayer, *Philosophy of Education for Our Time*, New York: The Odyssey Press, Inc., 1958, pp. 156–157.

There are several reasons why authoritarianism is harmful to mental health. One is that it limits the opportunity to practice the habit of independent thought. Another is that it obviously restricts the opportunity for independent action, which we have seen is a fundamental human need. Freedom to grow, practice in standing on one's own feet is a prime requisite to the development of healthy feelings of psychological security. Empirical and experimental data indicate that dictatorial procedures tend to stir up an attitude of resentment, thus inhibiting the development of harmonious relationships.[22] The incentive of cooperative endeavor should replace the negative stimulation of domination. Finally, authoritarianism conflicts with the ideals, if not the practices, of the adult society for which we purport to be preparing school pupils.

Contrasts to the Pattern of Authority. There are some encouraging deviations from the pattern of authority which so largely characterizes our society. Numerous teachers are experimenting with plans for giving students a voice in their own classroom control and government through committees, councils, and group legislation. Often this does not take the form of student government but allows the students a chance to discuss various problems of control that are related to learning situations. Student discussion of educational objectives, selection of areas to be studied, and the self-determination of learning responsibilities are plans that tend to diminish external adult control and increase student self-direction.

Reduction of authoritarianism does not mean the removal of direction and control. It is a matter of deciding what conditions are most likely to foster the development of effective social and personal behavior. It is a question of whether docile conformity is as good for the individual and for society as the development of feelings of identification and the fostering of habits of making contributions to the functioning of one's social group.

The mental hygiene implications of authoritarianism are clear. On the one hand, the child subjected to dominating authority may learn to conform blindly, becoming a submissive individual incapable of doing things on his own initiative. He waits for direction, permission, and approval. He may develop lasting fears of provoking the displeasure of those in authority. On the other hand, a child may fight so hard against adult authority, coercion, emotional deprivation, and being forced into some preconceived mold that he is unable to live with himself or others. He may store up his feelings of resentment against authority, while conforming to the desires of those in power; but when he is released from the area of authority to which he has become accustomed, he repudiates all authority. This sometimes happens when young people who have been models of behavior in the home go away to college, where their

[22] See Kurt Lewin studies cited in Chap. 10.

social and moral behavior deviates sharply from its older pattern. Instances occur within the teaching profession itself. Teachers who in earlier life have conformed to a domineering father may live in fear of displeasing their supervisors; or they may react to the earlier influence by deliberately flouting the administrative regime. One teacher who was exceedingly dictatorial in her teaching methods, demanded pin-drop silence, and was subject to fits of temper in the classroom is known to have been brought up strictly in an authoritarian home.

Authoritarianism is related to oppressive discipline. The person who believes in absolute adult authority is likely to be the one who feels justified in enforcing rules and regulations by means of corporal punishment, the uniform application of penalty without regard to individuals or situations, and by the use of fear as a deterrent. Even a cursory examination of the literature of mental hygiene will show that these attitudes and practices are in direct contradiction to the teachings of mental hygienists.

Restriction of Freedom. There are many ways in which the restriction of freedom is manifest in the typical school. Among these may be listed (1) a concept of class routine in which sitting in chairs or at desks for the whole period is expected and sometimes enforced; (2) a set curriculum, which restricts the freedom of the pupils to exercise self-direction; (3) school rules and regulations which students have had no part in formulating; (4) the teacher's fear that, if he allows spontaneous activity, the class will get out of hand; (5) the relative lack of opportunity to choose and pursue activities which are outside the realm of traditionally conceived educational subjects; and (6) lack of freedom to pursue knowledge beyond the bounds of texts and references.

The approach to the extension of freedom in the classroom might well begin with the teacher's seeking greater freedom for himself. This should mean that the teacher is willing to devote time and intelligence to the cooperative solution of administrative problems. Those teachers who are quick to resent direction from above are often the ones who are first to complain about the time required for the discussion of administrative problems. Although teachers should be on guard against encroachments on their right to freedom of speech, they must not mistake freedom for license. The right to teach what and as they like should be limited by the teacher's code of ethics and the framework of democratic philosophy.

The teacher, to a large extent, has within his power the privilege of extending the freedom of his pupils, even in the typical school situation. He can, for instance, allow them to move around to get materials and supplementary references, he can encourage trips to the school library, and he can encourage students to plan and execute field trips and excursions. He can provide opportunities for the students to select the topic of study and the approaches that are to be used in the study. He can help students organize their own plans of classroom government and encourage them to select competent executive officers. Teachers have found that the pupils are capable of admirable self-direction and that many classroom tensions tend to disappear when freedom is extended.

> By way of summary, it is the conviction of those who choose to regulate their affairs in the light of the democratic principle that individual freedom or opportunity for self-realization are increased as people learn to fashion their actions, institutions, and arrangements along lines suggested by their own reason rather than by accepting the reasoning of others. The process of intelligence, however, must be guided by consideration for the rights and potentialities of each individual; as well as by the possibility of securing increased individual benefits through cooperative action. This faith in the superiority of the democratic ideal over any other known social principle as a guide to the good life suggests that it is the most valuable cultural possession of democratic groups. As such, the ideal must become a part of the thought and practice of the young. Schools are needed to teach the democratic ideal, and the American secondary schools have a special responsibility for fulfilling that function.[23]

SUMMARY

A few prevalent school practices are harmful to mental health. A set curriculum interferes with the need to be independent and to develop one's own purposes. The set curriculum interferes with his fulfilling the need to manipulate and to satisfy his curiosity. It attempts to force children into the same mold, regardless of their unique backgrounds, proclivities, and experiences.

Uniform grading interferes with the need to be recognized for what one is rather than for what others think one should be. It tends to destroy feelings of personal worth among those who cannot fill the academic requirements for passing and graduation, or among those who might require a slower pace.

The practice of failing students tends to bring forth feelings of shame, inferiority, and insecurity. It tends to prevent the child from engaging in social intercourse with his physical peers. Failures frequently result in behavior manifestations of truancy, destruction, seclusiveness, bullying, and shiftlessness.

Homework, instead of bringing a child up to standard, tends to widen individual differences. It places undue emphasis upon the virtue of aca-

[23] I. N. Thut and J. Raymond Gerberich, *Foundations of Method for Secondary Schools,* New York: McGraw-Hill Book Company, Inc., 1949, pp. 17–18.

demic superiority. But probably the strongest condemnation of homework is directed at the child's being deprived of opportunities for health-giving, developmental, free play. Physical exercise is as essential to good mental health as mastery of the fundamentals. Neither should be allowed to assume undue proportions in the child's life.

Perhaps one of the most condemnable practices in school is that of authoritarianism. Certainly, viewing the school as preparation for democratic living, we cannot allow dogmatic authoritarianism to interfere with the need for freedom or with the need for developing unique potentiality and creativity, as has been the experience of some other nations of the world.

Fortunately, there are hopeful indications that many of these questionable practices are now being challenged in some of our schools. Teachers can implement and hasten the better practices by study and experimentation.

STUDY AND DISCUSSION EXERCISES

1. Can you cite, from your own experience, some instance of a child's being thwarted by the inflexibility of school requirements?

2. Could "progressive" practices be justified if there were no superiority in academic tests on the part of "progressive" students?

3. Evaluate some newer practices in grading and marking that you have seen employed.

4. Under what conditions would you deem nonpromotion to be advisable? Do your professional colleagues agree with you?

5. Under what conditions would you judge homework to be of value to elementary pupils? When would it be advisable for high-school students?

SUGGESTED ADDITIONAL READINGS

Conant, James B., *The American High School Today*, New York: McGraw-Hill Book Company, Inc., 1959. 140 pp.

One of America's foremost educators analyzes some of the weaknesses of secondary education and proposes precise steps for improvement.

DeHaan, Robert F., and Jack Kough, *Identifying Students with Special Needs*, secondary-school ed., Chicago: Science Research Associates, Inc., 1956. 94 pp.

Kough, Jack, and Robert F. DeHaan, *Identifying Children with Special Needs*, secondary-school ed., Chicago: Science Research Associates, Inc., 1955. 91 pp.

These two books, one for elementary and one for secondary teachers, tell what to look for in discovering pupils with special talents, developmental handicaps, and physical and sensory defects.

Rothney, John W. M., *Evaluating and Reporting Pupil Progress*, What Research Says to the Teacher, no. 7, Washington: National Education Association, 1955. 33 pp.

Limitations of conventional marking practices and ways to improvement are examined in the light of research findings.

Strang, Ruth, *Guided Study and Homework*, What Research Says to the Teacher, no. 8, Washington: National Education Association, 1955. 33 pp.

This book presents, on the basis of selected research, the pros and cons of homework and suggests methods of improving pupil work habits.

Woodring, Paul, *A Fourth of a Nation*, New York: McGraw-Hill Book Company, Inc., 1957. 288 pp.

Progressive and traditional education, provisions for bright and slow-learning children, the integration of learning experiences, and the training of teachers are discussed pro and con.

CHAPTER 13

CONSTRUCTIVE CLASSROOM APPROACHES TO MENTAL HEALTH

One of the major reasons why the concept of mental health must be a classroom emphasis is that, typically, too few specialists are available. Moreover, many children who need help are not in such dire difficulty as to warrant the aid of specialists; they merely need to be more adequately understood, so that optimum opportunities for development will be open. For these reasons, constructive approaches to mental health that are now being used—and can be more widely used—should be emphasized and clarified. Here, as elsewhere in this book, the focus is on meeting the needs of pupils—which itself depends on better understanding of individuals.

SCHOOL RECORDS

School Marks. Repeated studies of traditional marking systems (using letters or numbers) indicate that there is great variation of the meaning attached to each grade.[1] An A or a B assigned by two different teachers may indicate quite different levels of accomplishment. One teacher may mean by an A that the pupil is doing a high quality of work—in the upper 5 or 10 per cent of the class—while another teacher's A may mean that the pupil is serious, industrious, conscientious, and socially considerate and that, in spite of his doing only average quality of work, he is doing his best. Administrative policies also may differ. Some principals may require that all pupils receive passing marks, while others may recommend that a given proportion of the class should fail. Herein lie

[1] Theodore L. Torgerson and Georgia Sachs Adams, *Measurement and Evaluation for the Elementary School Teacher*, New York: Holt, Rinehart and Winston, Inc., 1954, pp. 29–30.

the defects of the letter or numerical grades so widely used in the United States.

Enough is known of these defects that teachers in a given school would find it advantageous to hold a series of staff meetings to discuss the meaning and implications of the marks given to pupils. Even if the system were to remain unchanged, out of the discussions might grow a better understanding of the meanings, as well as the limitations, of the grades on the pupils' record cards. An understanding of what teachers of preceding classes meant by the grades they assigned would make it easier for the present teacher to know whether a given pupil would be likely to need help in becoming better adapted socially or whether he should put initial emphasis on finding additional stimulating work for him of an academic nature.

While a teacher should be on guard against being influenced by the grade previously assigned, he can be helped to avoid biases in his own grading by making comparisons with previous marks. A teacher who had rated the work of John as outstanding was surprised to see that John's previous grades were substantially lower than those being given him at present. This made her pause to examine her own evaluation, and she discovered that John's work—as well as his attitude toward his peers— was distinctly mediocre. Upon reflection, she felt that she was "over-grading" John because she enjoyed his cheerful smile and the profuse courtesy and consideration he always extended her. This resulted in her giving more attention to both his social adjustment and his specific academic difficulties.

The teacher should bear in mind some of the major functions of grading: (1) The pupils should know exactly what the marks are for and how they might be improved. (2) Some marks should be for seriousness of endeavor rather than for comparative accomplishment. (3) Marks should in some way show the student what his next educational steps should be. (4) Marks should be mutually understood by administrators, teachers, pupils, and parents. (5) Marks should be clear enough to provide the next teacher some practical clues for the next steps of development to be pursued. (6) Consistently poor marks of a pupil should challenge the teacher to a closer examination, or reexamination, of his teaching methods and educational philosophy.[2]

Anecdotal Records. An anecdotal record is a verbal description of some typical aspect or incident of the pupil's behavior. Unfortunately, the anecdotal record has been misused by some teachers who record bizarre or unusual events. This breaks down the purpose of the device, which is

[2] It is the author's conviction that these functions can best be served through evaluation conferences between pupil and teacher at the secondary level and between teachers, pupils, and parents at the elementary level (see also pp. 66 and 269).

to give a representative view of the child so that objectives and evaluations of growth can be established. Anecdotal records should be made periodically throughout the term in order to formulate a basis for improved procedures. This kind of record is designed to improve professional insight, to present means for a better understanding of the child. It should be specific and should include a variety of incidents. Dates, persons, and actions should be objectively recorded. The following are illustrative examples of the descriptive nature and variety of good anecdotal records.

Oct. 10. While I was working with a group in reading, Chester's group was working at their tables. The work was a check-up on a story that the group had finished with me. [This is the setting or situation.] It was not long before I saw Chester with a game in a corner of the room. I went to him and asked him, "Chester, have you finished your work so soon?" He answered, "No ma'am, I was just playing this game awhile." I said, "Go to your seat and finish your work." He looked at me with an expression that seemed to say either, "I don't know what you mean" or "I don't want to." By this time my patience was a little ragged, so I said, "Chester, go to your seat immediately and finish your work." He went to his seat slowly, looking back a time or two at the game corner and stopping a time or two. [Note that the description includes the action by Chester, the reaction of the teacher, direct quotation of what each said, the teacher's description of her own mood, Chester's reaction to her directions, and the mood in which he responded.]

When the period was up, of course, he had not finished his work; so when playtime came I said, "You have had part of your playtime. Now you can finish your work." He mumbled and whined, "What for?" I answered, "I believe you know why."

When the others started out the door to the playground, Chester started too. I said, "You may not go." He turned red and stuck out his lips in a pout. Then he started to cry. "Chester, if you will stop pouting and get down to work you will be finished in time to have some play." A few children who had overheard the conversation said, "Miss C, that is the way he did all last year." [Note the new setting, the actions, reactions, direct quotes, and mood cues.]

After all the children had left the room I stayed to see that Chester settled to his work. After I was sure that he didn't need any help I went to the playground. In about ten minutes he was there with his paper all finished. I commended him on his work. He smiled, thanked me and went to play. [Note that the episode is completed to reveal the outcome.][3]

The *series* of anecdotes as a whole gives a clearer picture of the pupil's patterns, problems, and motivations. His view of companions, attitude

[3] Daniel A. Prescott, *The Child in the Educative Process,* New York: McGraw-Hill Book Company, Inc., 1957, pp. 155–156.

toward school and home, major interests, strengths and weaknesses will become more apparent and give clues for a better understanding of him. It is not implied that this technique is a panacea, but it is a readily available, easily manipulated device, which any teacher can use. As he works with the technique and sees the pertinence or the uselessness of certain entries, it will increase in value.[4]

Cumulative Records. The cumulative record is a card or folder for recording or filing information which can be valuable in terms of achieving a better understanding of the development of individuals. Typically, this record will contain such items as the name, birth date, birthplace, and sex of the child; parents' names and ages; number, age, and sex of siblings; socioeconomic status of family in terms of languages spoken, occupation, and place of residence; the pupil's health history—illnesses, operations, and physical handicaps; school history—attendance, scholarship, samples of work (dated), conduct reports, student activities; scores *and dates* of standardized tests; ratings of personality characteristics including anecdotal records and sociometric data; outside activities including jobs or home responsibilities; records of observations made in school, on the playground, or of work or social activities; interviews with the pupil or his parents; and records of former attempts to solve particular problems.

It may appear that a great deal of work is involved in keeping such a record, but it should be remembered that, as in the case of all problems, it is out of the data accumulated that a solution will appear. While some of the data are of a confidential nature and probably should not be shown to the pupil, there are some things that can be recorded by the pupil himself in the middle grades and on through high school. It is desirable to keep the data recorded to a minimum because considerable time must be spent on keeping the record up to date and because a mass of carelessly chosen and hastily recorded material is so overwhelming to the teacher that all of it is ignored. On the other hand, the cumulative record provides such an excellent developmental record of the pupil that its potentialities should not be overlooked.[5] While the time devoted to recording information may seem to be futile when pupils encounter no difficult problems of adjustment, there is a great saving of time when there is an immediate situation that requires study and attention. Moreover, since the record is cumulative, it must not all be done at one time or by one person. In some school districts cumulative-record forms have

---

[4] Suggestions for the use of anecdotal records is given in Willard C. Olson, *Child Development*, 2d ed., Boston: D. C. Heath and Company, 1959, Appendix D, pp. 467–473.

[5] J. Murray Lee and Dorris May Lee, *The Child and His Development*, New York: Appleton-Century-Crofts, Inc., 1958, p. 294.

been constructed by committees in which consideration has been given to conciseness, ease of recording, and pertinency of data.[6]

STANDARDIZED TESTS

Standardized-test data are a part of the cumulative record, but since testing takes place even where there is no plan for cumulative records, it is being treated separately. Moreover, the widespread misuse and misinterpretation of test data demand special attention.

Using Standardized-test Data. Many valuable insights into pupil behavior and growth are afforded the classroom teacher in the form of standardized tests if the results are wisely viewed. But, if tests are to serve their maximum usefulness, there must be due regard for their limitations and a knowledge of what they do and do not do. We might well begin our understanding of tests by appreciating what they are. Any test is only a sample. A psychological test is a sample of behavior. An intelligence test is a sample of intellectual behavior. An achievement test is a sample of academic knowledge. We must carefully avoid thinking that a test is a *measure* of anything. The sample is a valuable indication of the whole thing (personality, knowledge, intelligence), but it is not *the thing*.

If we accept the thesis that an intelligence test is an indication of ability to adjust, we can immediately see that there are various kinds and phases of intelligence. The typical intelligence test indicates to a marked degree the kind of intelligence that is required for academic work. It does not indicate with a dependable degree of accuracy what we might call social intelligence. It does not indicate the energy, motivation, and habits that condition the effectiveness of intelligence on wider realms of adjustment. Achievement tests are subject to similar limitations.

Tests are approximations. That the implications of this statement are not appreciated is revealed in teacher-made remarks, such as "I have an IQ of 118." "He's hopeless. His IQ is only 88." When did the teacher get a score of 118? It was in his junior year of high school. What was the test? He could not remember. Was another test given to the youngster who had scored 88? No, he had been assured that the validity and reliability of the test were high. An experienced user of tests knows that on equivalent forms[7] of a test an individual might as easily make a lower

[6] An illustrative cumulative-record form is shown in Harold W. Bernard, C. Evan James, and Franklin R. Zeran, *Guidance Services in Elementary Schools*, New York: Chartwell House, Inc., 1954, pp. 188–193.

[7] Equivalent forms of a test are two or more tests covering the same material. The questions differ but are of the same degree of difficulty. *Theoretically*, if both tests were administered to one individual in successive hours, the scores would be identical.

score on the second test as he would a higher one. A lower score on an equivalent test given at the end of the term does not necessarily indicate a regression of intelligence. The significant point to be considered is the trend of scores that can be perceived as the result of a periodic program of testing. We can now modify our statement of the meaning of a test by saying: *A test is an indication of the individual's present status in whatever is being tested.* In reporting test results we should say, "Frank indicated an IQ of approximately 118, in January, on Form B of the Otis Self-Administering Test of Mental Ability, Intermediate Examination." With such orientation, one would not be surprised to find the score achieved on the California Test of Mental Maturity, Intermediate Form, somewhat at variance with the Otis results.

The need for precaution in evaluating test results is well illustrated by the remarks of a superintendent of a home for the feeble-minded. He said,

> I have often been asked what the critical score for commitment should be. I must say that I cannot answer the question. It all depends. Some children with an I. Q. of 70 are socially inept and incapable of any degree of self-dependence. Some children with an I. Q. of 50 are quite capable of doing work on a farm or in the home. Often we find that individuals with an I. Q. as low as 50 are socially adequate and have special capacities that would make it unwise to place them in an institution.

The fact that the tests to which he referred were administered by competent psychometrists on an individual basis might well lead teachers to view quite critically the test results obtained from group tests.

Intelligence tests are valuable indicators of the mental growth of individuals. While an IQ gives some idea of the pupil's potential, it is more pertinent for the teacher to know his mental age. Two children in the second (or the eighth) grade may have different IQs but be of the same mental age. It is the mental age that gives the quickest clue to the pupil's present learning ability. For example, assuming that a mental age of 6.5 years is required for the successful beginning of reading, a child with an IQ of 80 will be ready by the time he is about eight years old, when, at his rate of development, he will reach the requisite mental age.

Achievement tests, if they are intelligently interpreted, can be of service in offering motivation. A visitor to a seventh-grade class noted with some concern that the results of an achievement test had been posted on the board in histogram form. When there was an opportunity to question a child as to how he felt about having the results posted, the visitor was surprised to find that the pupil, although not ranking high, was well satisfied. He said, "Well, it's true that I am not the highest in the class, but look at the progress I have made. Frank is still ahead of me, but look how far I have come since the first of the year" (see Figure 11). "Here I was at the beginning of the year," indicating A, "and here I am now," indicating A'. "Frank was here," indicating B, "but he progressed fewer points than I did," indicating B'. Both pupils should feel proud—Frank

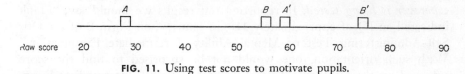

FIG. 11. Using test scores to motivate pupils.

of his rank and the other child of his growth. Achievement tests should be used to provide an idea of the pupil's relative strengths and weaknesses, to evaluate his rate of growth, and to make rough interschool comparisons. Certainly it is a misuse of achievement tests to base grades upon them, to coach students to come up to prescribed norms, or to fail to take into consideration socioeconomic factors and curricular approaches when rough comparisons of schools are being made.

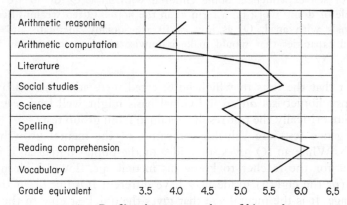

FIG. 12. Profile of test scores for a fifth-grader.

A questionable use of achievement tests is for the teacher to view the results for a particular pupil and then become concerned about his relative weaknesses to the extent of ignoring his strengths. Moreover, a given child might on an achievement battery make scores that vary as much as three or more grades from his low to his high score (see Figure 12). This typically causes the teacher to be alarmed about the comparative weakness and to begin a remedial or coaching program. So much attention is devoted to remedial speech, reading, and arithmetic in teacher education institutions that the typical teacher has become remedial-minded; much less emphasis is given to the development of strengths, especially the talents of the gifted pupils.[8] Yet, from the standpoint of mental health, since people are happiest when they use their talents in ways which they enjoy and which society deems valuable,[9] it would seem wise to encourage the development of strengths, instead of emphasizing heavily, through hastily agreed-upon remedial programs, his lack of competence. Moreover, there is the possibility that the self-assurance and level of aspiration generated will cause the pupil to apply himself assiduously to learning in the area of weakness.

Uses and Limitations of Standardized Tests. The wise use of tests, including achievement batteries, should entail knowledge of what standards or grade and age norms mean. The norm is the average score made by hundreds of pupils who, at a given age or in a given grade, took the test during the process of standardization. These norms should not necessarily constitute goals for individuals.

Arthur E. Traxler asserts that tests may be of value by

1. Giving a general picture of the mental ability of pupils in a given grade,

2. Being used as an aid in developing curriculum and teaching methods,

3. Helping teachers assess ability and achievement of class groups,

4. Aiding the study of individual pupils,

5. Indicating pupils' ability level in command of tools of knowledge,

6. Providing clues for the diagnosis of strengths and weaknesses,

7. Helping teachers and counselors understand pupil interests,

8. Providing clues to the assessment of personality (though tests in this area are less dependable than tests in other areas),

9. Providing part of the information on which to base guidance toward educational and vocational goals, and

10. Helping to study and assess changes in pupils over a period of years.[10]

Misuses of standardized tests would include the following: (1) basing grades or marks on the results, (2) categorizing pupils on the basis of their scores, (3) believing that test scores are infallible, and (4) refusing to use them at all, because they have limitations.

Standardized tests need not be rejected entirely because of their inherent limitations, but it is necessary to exercise skill in interpreting the results. "In other words, he [the practical person] takes the very com-

[8] Clifford W. Williams, "Characteristics and Objectives of a Program for the Gifted" in *Education for the Gifted*, 57th Yearbook, Part II, National Society for the Study of Education, Chicago: University of Chicago Press, 1958, p. 148.

[9] Robert J. Havighurst and others, "The Importance of Education for the Gifted" in *ibid.*, p. 9.

[10] Arthur E. Traxler, "Using Tests in Schools," *The American School Board Journal*, 139:11–13, July, 1959.

monsense point of view that the proper thing to be done under the circumstances is to make the best possible use of such tools as exist, while waiting for better ones to be developed."[11]

Personality Inventories. Personality inventories make an appeal to teachers in view of their need to understand individuals. But it appears that, at present, these instruments must be viewed with skepticism. One reviewer asserts that such questionnaires seek the pot of gold at the foot of the rainbow—that our need to aid in personality adjustment leads us to accept "instruments of very low objective value."[12] Another says that when the results are not clearly dangerous, they are "superficial and lacking in clinical sense."[13] George G. Thompson finds it surprising that personality inventories continue to be used despite the preponderance of negative research findings regarding their value.[14] Actually, it is of much greater value to know *why* a child acts in a particular manner (an item which inventories do not reveal) than to know just where he ranks comparatively. For example, there is a high-school youth who answered "Do you have headaches?" with a "Yes." (When he was in the first grade he had had a headache after a smallpox vaccination.) "Yes," he had walked in his sleep. (His mother said that when he was three he walked in his sleep while they were visiting his grandparents.) "Yes," he had dizzy spells. (When he stooped to a lower shelf in a library for a time, he was dizzy after he straightened up.) "Yes," he had some unusual fears. (Two years ago he was afraid when some boys dared him to wade across a swollen, icy stream during the spring floods.) If his score had been taken at face value, he could have been rated a neurotic. When the reasons for his answers were considered, there was no cause for concern.

Questionnaires may be of some value if the atypical answers are used to narrow the range of possible difficulties that should be explored. It is easy to discover if the atypical answers center about some particular area, e.g., home, school, health, social adjustment, or emotional control and emotional manifestations. But again, the important thing is not that the questions are answered atypically, but that they lead to the discovery of *why* they were answered as they were. It is not too much to say that *the raw, or interpolated, score on an adjustment inventory should not be recorded in a permanent record*, where others might misunderstand its import. Results should be used by the present teacher for discovering those who need help and who might otherwise escape detection and for narrowing the range of areas that warrant further investigation.

[11] C. C. Ross and Julian C. Stanley, *Measurement in Today's Schools*, 3d ed., Englewood Cliffs, N.J.: Prentice-Hall, Inc., 1954, p. 134.

[12] L. F. Shaffer in Oscar K. Buros (ed.), *The Third Mental Measurements Yearbook*, New Brunswick, N.J.: Rutgers University Press, 1949, p. 56.

[13] Douglas Spencer in Buros, *ibid.*, p. 58.

[14] George G. Thompson, *Child Psychology*, Boston: Houghton Mifflin Company, 1952, p. 614.

PERIODIC REVIEW OF EDUCATIONAL OBJECTIVES

On-the-job details may keep the teacher from recalling the many-faceted goals of education. At the cost of reiteration, some of the goals will be repeated here with the plea that teachers stop to think what the personal and professional implications of the objectives are.

The Seven Cardinal Principles of Secondary Education. The most widely known statement of educational aims is probably that issued by the 1918 Commission on the Reorganization of Secondary Education. The items included are (1) good health, (2) command of the fundamental processes, (3) worthy home membership, (4) vocational efficiency, (5) civic efficiency, (6) worthy use of leisure time, (7) ethical character. Even a little reflection will help a teacher realize that a constructive approach to classroom problems and improved mental health would result from a serious attempt to put these objectives to work in the classroom.

Mid-century Committee on Outcomes in Elementary Education. A committee composed of representatives of the Russell Sage Foundation, Educational Testing Services, United States Office of Education, and the Department of Elementary School Principals of the National Education Association formulated the following goals for elementary education: (1) physical development, health, and body care, (2) individual social and emotional development, (3) ethical behavior, standards, and values, (4) social relations, (5) understanding the social world, (6) developing concepts of the physical world, (7) esthetic development, (8) skill in communication, and (9) understanding quantitative relationships.[15]

A critical examination of these objectives is quite likely to lead to the conclusion that some objectives are neglected as the price of achieving others. In the above list it is not indicated that ethical behavior is more or less important than understanding the social world or promoting physical health. The periodic review of such statements is helpful in maintaining a *balanced* emphasis when pursuing the well-rounded development of pupils.

Purposes of Kindergarten Education. Educational leaders at all levels, whether preschool, elementary, or secondary, seem to grant similar items a place of importance in terms of objectives. This can be seen in part by noting the aims of kindergarten education.

1. To train the child more readily to adapt himself to his environment.

2. To teach the child to realize that the privileges and rights he formerly had as an individual cease to be his alone, when he becomes a member of a group.

3. To teach the child to associate with those outside his family group.

[15] Nolan C. Kearney, *Elementary School Objectives,* A Report for the Mid-century Committee on Outcomes in Elementary Education, New York: Russell Sage Foundation, 1953, pp. 52–120.

4. To develop the power of self-control.
5. To provide for many children an enriched environment.[16]

Educational Policies Commission's Statement of Objectives. In 1937 the Educational Policies Commission of the National Education Association formulated the following categories in terms of living in American democracy:

The Objectives of Self-realization
The Objectives of Human Relationships
The Objectives of Economic Efficiency
The Objectives of Civic Responsibility

These objectives have been further studied and presented in terms of detailed descriptions of behavioral characteristics by a committee working for the Educational Testing Service, the Russell Sage Foundation, and the National Association of Secondary-school Principals.[17]

Using Educational Objectives. It is not enough to read or memorize such lists as the foregoing. Each teacher should periodically review, and use as a check list, the various sets of objectives to see what can be done to make any particular item functional. No marked or sudden improvement in teaching can normally be expected, but gradual improvement is made more probable.

Detailed study of educational objectives can serve as a center of profitable professional meetings. An attempt should be made to interpret these in ever more specific terms. As each teacher tells what he thinks can be done to implement the objectives, others will see additional avenues for making the objectives functional.

Teachers at Newberg, Oregon, took part in a five-day workshop in which both elementary- and high-school teachers studied the objectives stated by the Educational Policies Commission. Committees were organized to deal with a limited number of items under each of the four heads. Reports were made to the entire group. At the end of the workshop, such remarks as the following were made: "I've gained many ideas that I will begin using immediately." "These objectives are really challenging." "I have a better appreciation of the work of high-school teachers." "I've overlooked a bet—my colleagues have a lot of valuable ideas." A beginning teacher said, "I just finished studying these objectives at college. Now I see them in an entirely different light." The author was especially gratified about this one: "Mental hygiene has long been

[16] *The Articulation of the Units of American Education,* Seventh Yearbook of National Education Association, American Association of School Administrators, Washington, D.C., 1929, p. 69. By permission of the American Association of School Administrators.

[17] Will French and Associates, *Behavioral Goals of General Education in High School,* New York: Russell Sage Foundation, 1957, pp. 58–65.

a major interest. It is helpful to see how it can operate in daily class activities."

CONSTRUCTIVE USE OF EXISTING ASS_ 5

It would be desirable to have in each school a guidance clinic staffed by trained specialists whose function is to help teachers in the solution of their problems. The number of such clinics is increasing, but the vast majority of schools do not have such services. Many resources for helping children, such as a manual arts shop, an art room, athletics, homemaking facilities, which are mentioned in this section, are readily available in many schools which do not have clinics. Even where the clinics *are* available, it is necessary for the teacher to appreciate these resources to be used for helping children, since he will, in the final analysis, be called on to carry out the recommendations of the specialists.

Teachers. Teachers differ in their interests and talents and each seems to establish interpersonal bonds with some kinds of persons better than with others. Here, for instance, is a high-school English teacher who is also interested in the subject of biology and has an affinity for shy individuals. She did exceptional individual work with an average, but serious, high-school pupil, who was interested in becoming an engineer. This same boy did not appeal to the coach, because the boy was neither interested in the school teams nor eligible for them. Here is a mature sixth-grade teacher who is warmhearted and good-natured toward aggressive, loudmouthed preadolescents. She is fully aware of what acceptable behavior is, and these rough, tough boys come to her for private talks in which she asks them questions and laughs with them in order that they may arrive at a better understanding of how they look to their classmates. She realizes that their aggressive behavior is often a cover for tensions they can hardly recognize.

Here is another teacher who was, herself, a product of a broken home. She is not a maudlin sympathy giver, but she is exceedingly well qualified to deal intelligently with those pupils at all grade levels whose difficulties seem to grow out of a feeling of insecurity generated by their broken homes. Here is a male teacher who is deeply interested in both boys and science. He helps many pupils come closer to full realization of their capacities by recognizing and broadening their interest in natural phenomena. After school and on holidays, he and some boys can frequently be found in the science laboratory, making their own investigations and preparing demonstrations and displays to be used for later classes.

Such teachers, through their unique interests and personality appeals, can often help other teachers reach particular boys and girls. You may have difficulty in reaching one of your pupils, but if you will call upon such teachers for assistance, they can help to solve your difficulty. An interest on the part of some pupil can be expanded in much the same way that a tension generated in a specific class will irradiate into other phases of the pupil's work. The English teacher mentioned above influenced two shy pupils (in one school year) to take a more active and aggressive part in other classes than her own. The sixth-grade teacher was able to influence the conduct of "toughies" to such an extent that other teachers found them less obnoxious in situations not involving her guidance. The teacher who was interested in boys and science is given credit, by the local juvenile officer, for averting many cases of delinquent behavior in the community.

The handicap to using teachers as resources for mental health rests largely within ourselves. Instead of trying to conceal our own inability to cope with a given situation by criticizing the teacher whose approach is different, we need to develop the magnanimous attitude of acknowledging that each teacher in his particular way can make a special contribution to pupil growth. This advantageous use of teacher resources also involves knowing fellow staff members. As we listen to their accounts of the day's work, we can get some idea regarding their orientation toward pupils and their problems and find out how their views can be used to the greater advantage. Our social contacts with colleagues will help us to develop a knowledge of their interests and hobbies, which they are often most willing to turn to the advantage of pupil growth.

The teacher must feel free to ask for help. No single individual can do all that is necessary to know the child, the parents, the community, as well as the content he is teaching. He must do what he can by himself, but he must use whatever assistance is available. Special teachers in music, art or physical education are helpful. The teacher needs to use them to help evaluate proposed activities and to help in establishing class plans. If he waits until the project is planned and seeks help only when something goes wrong or uses the special teacher apart from other activities in the classroom, he is missing opportunities to grow through the use of these specialists. Similarly in the secondary school, where communication among departments is difficult, grade level meetings which bring teachers together to learn from each other are essential. Secondary teachers may not know even the serious physical defects of the students unless central planning provides for the sharing of information.[18]

Pupils. Pupils are a resource for the better adjustment of others which is all too frequently overlooked. It is necessary to dispel the notion that children are naturally crude and cruel. Certainly, instances of teasing

[18] *Creating a Good Environment for Learning,* 1954 Yearbook, Association for Supervision and Curriculum Development, Washington: National Education Association, 1954, pp. 187–188.

seem to indicate that children enjoy the suffering of others. But instead of being the outcome of some innate depravity, this conduct is more likely to be due to the lack of experience, to the lack of thoughtfulness, or to the leadership of some particular youngster who is in need of help and understanding. A little guidance by the teacher will do much toward changing the orientation of thoughtless pupils and converting their actions into constructive help.

A teacher who anticipated some difficulty for a dark-skinned Mexican child in a school where all the other youngsters were white devised a unit on Mexico, its culture, and its role in world economy. But she went further; when the Mexican boy was out of the room she led a discussion on how her pupils might absorb him into their group. The answers came largely from the class members and the actions which followed were highly gratifying. The youngsters "fell all over themselves" to be friendly. There seemed to be, for a time, a danger that they would spoil the newcomer. But he was soon an integral part of the group in an atmosphere of normal friendliness. There might not have been any difficulty, but because a deviant is so often distrusted, the concern of the teacher seems to have been justified.

Youngsters can be useful in bringing supplementary materials to school which will serve to make formal learnings more concrete and personal. A unit on Japan was enlivened by the pupils' bringing in trinkets, war souvenirs, and *National Geographic* magazines. Often the pupils' own experiences can be advantageously turned to account—their travels, the stories an uncle has told about his adventures, films that they have seen, and stories that they have read.

Pupils can be potent factors in creating a congenial atmosphere in the school as a whole. One list of the ways by which pupils may become resources indicates the following areas of activity: (1) the creation of a "check-up" committee to see that the library is kept neat and free of litter; (2) the establishment of a "luncheon club," whose function is to make lunches pleasant and congenial; (3) making students responsible for helping those who have been absent to catch up with their work—thus warding off the discouragement that is a forerunner of uninspired work; (4) pupil participation in the planning and conducting of field trips; (5) formation of a courtesy committee, whose duty it is to help visitors find what they want and be made to feel welcome; (6) discussion of the substitute-teacher problem and the formation of a committee to plan a procedure whereby the substitute's dilemma would be mitigated; (7) control and responsibility for safety in the classroom, corridors, playground, and adjacent streets.[19]

[19] Paul R. Mort and William S. Vincent, *Modern Educational Practice,* New York: McGraw-Hill Book Company, Inc., 1950, pp. 149–153.

Teachers are daily discovering that youth hold tremendous resources for the solution of all kinds of problems. When given a chance, they assume responsibilities that surprise even the most experienced. Education periodicals contain many short accounts of such activities. The book, *Educating for American Citizenship*,[20] describes numerous instances in which youth accomplished much in realizing their own potentialities as well as improving their communities. Teachers who would give young people purposes which will serve to direct their energies into constructive channels must first develop a trust in their sincerity, energy, and intelligence. Wise use of the resource will develop it more fully.

The Manual Arts Laboratory. Even in small schools there are specialists who can do much to promote wholesome pupil growth—the athletic coach, the home economics teacher, the librarian, and the music teacher. An instance of what these specialists can accomplish is found in an account of a manual-arts teacher's work toward the achievement of better mental health for his pupils.

This teacher had, through the years, become increasingly sensitive about other teachers' sending him slow-learning boys who could not make the grade in academic work. Some bright lads were taking a good deal of work in manual arts, but they were ones who had caused trouble of various kinds and were sent to him as a means of getting rid of them. When he was taking a graduate course in education, it was pointed out to him by the instructor and by fellow class members that he might well accept the situation as a challenge to do something really constructive for the boys who were sent to him. This he readily decided to do, because, he recalled on reflection, he *had* materially helped a few of the boys who had been working with him.

He stopped trying to produce works of art in the shop. He gave up trying to maintain rigid classroom discipline. Instead, he treated his shop as a place where boys could work off their tensions. He gave direction in the development of manual skills as boys indicated their interest. He talked with the boys informally whenever they were willing. At all times he was friendly. In an atmosphere of freedom and fellowship, the lads felt that they could confide in their instructor, because their tales went no further. The instructor did not refer problem cases to higher authority.

Under these conditions, the boys began to have a pride in what they could produce. They took good care of that part of the school which they liked; so the shop was kept neat in appearance and was systematically run by the boys themselves. But this was not the total result. As the instructor became familiar with the stories of the boys, he helped them to develop more constructive attitudes. He showed them that their

[20] *Education for American Citizenship*, 32d Yearbook, American Association of School Administrators, Washington: National Education Association, 1954.

accomplishment could be duplicated in other areas of activity. He further helped by conferring with other teachers about particular pupils— dropping hints as to how they could be helped: Johnny needs lots of praise. Frank needs to receive stern challenges. Bill enjoys having a position of leadership and will carry his responsibilities well. Jimmy will take orders if they are firmly given. He had attained the understanding on which these hints were based, through the individual study of each boy. He talked with them a great deal and did even more listening. Teachers continued to send troublemakers to shop classes, but their attitude was different. Instead of trying to get rid of the disturbing individuals, they now had the feeling that something could be done for these boys.

The concreteness of the end products of the manual arts shop and *the opportunity for physical movement* probably contributed to the effectiveness of the situation in the foregoing report. Most of all, it depended on the *teacher's orientation.* Much the same thing has been done by others in connection with music, home economics, and athletics.

Home Economics. Homemaking activities in the school deserve consideration from the mental hygiene, as well as from a practical, viewpoint. It was a home economics teacher, for instance, who solved the problem of an overlarge girl, who was not even in this teacher's classes. Shortly after entering the ninth grade, this girl became known to teachers and pupils as a rough talker and a fighter. Her violence toward boys actually frightened some teachers. Many of the others wanted to help, but it was the home economics teacher who, by speaking to her casually in the halls, finally got her to talk. It developed that she felt ashamed of her clothes and her appearance and took it out on pupils who dared to tease her. Used clothes donated through the PTA were made over in the home economics classes. The girl was fitted out with garments that were suitable for her age, size, and coloring. She was given some specific information about skin care and hair dressing. The outcome might seem magical to those who are unaware of the importance of physical appearance to the adolescent. The girl's conduct became friendly and ladylike. Her mental superiority showed itself in her marked leadership in academic studies. It was the consensus of teachers that they had a new girl in their classes.

EXPERIMENTAL APPROACHES

Reading for Mental Health. Teachers have long felt that the emphasis on the mechanical skill of reading should be accompanied by an emphasis on the development of good taste in selection. All too often the matter of taste is left to the individual judgment of the teacher, who is likely to feel that his coverage of appropriate books for all age levels is too limited.

Concrete, specific, and detailed help in the matter of selection has come from the American Council on Education. "Biography, fiction, and drama offer readers an opportunity to identify emotionally with human beings who are in interaction with their fellows. They provide access to the feelings of other people in a way otherwise offered only by face-to-face contacts."[21]

Sociometry and Pupil Adjustment. An experimental approach which is frequently used by teachers to improve understanding of pupil relations, that is, to provide clues for better adjustment, is that known as sociometry. This is the study of the likes and dislikes, the lines of communication, existing between individuals within a group. The graphical plotting, called a *sociogram*, reveals at a glance the mutual attractions and rejections within a class (Figure 13). The study is based on a questionnaire that consists of items designed by teachers for the specific purpose which each teacher has in mind; typical questions are similar to the following: Whom do you consider to be your best friend? Which of the students in the room would you like to have as your best friend? If all the pupils were to work in pairs on a mural, whom would you select? Who would be the best chairman of a panel discussion in social studies? For whom would you vote as class president? Who would be the best substitute in the absence of the teacher for a short period of time? Frequently, students are asked to give both a first and second choice. In a typical situation one student will be chosen by a number of his classmates, while one will not be chosen by anyone in response to a given question—and still another will, sometimes, *never* be chosen. Results are then tabulated for each question. A solid line may indicate a first choice and a broken line, a second choice. Girls are represented by circles and boys by squares in the illustrative sociogram (Figure 13). Individuals are identified by initials within the box or square. The relative isolation or popularity of individuals is indicated by the cluster of directional lines.[22]

Examination of the sociogram quickly and realistically shows how well a pupil is absorbed within the group. The objective of the sociogram is to group, or regroup, pupils so that the expressed choices of pupils are put into effect, so that each will be relatively at ease as he works with others with whom he feels most comfortable. An underchosen child should be placed with his own first choice, if possible, and mutual choices should be respected. "Among the many teachers who have used sociometric choices

---

[21] American Council on Education, *Reading Ladders for Human Relations*, revised and enlarged edition, Washington, D.C.: American Council on Education, 1949, p. 1. By permission of the publisher.

[22] Various approaches to sociometric study, including the sociogram, are described in Denis Baron and Harold W. Bernard, *Evaluation Techniques for Classroom Teachers*, New York: McGraw-Hill Book Company, Inc., 1958, pp. 145–161.

and continued their arrangements over a period of time, none have reported more than temporary disturbances, and all have found their classroom atmosphere and working morale have increased markedly."[23] This reshaping of groups according to pupils' choices helps them to find security in the roles which others recognize as their areas of competence. The

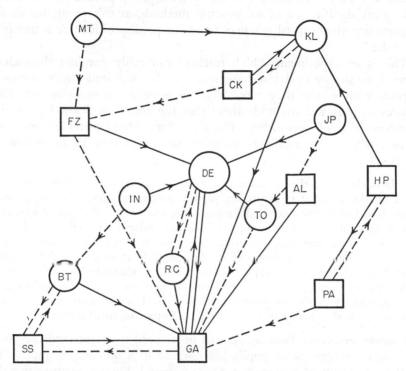

FIG. 13. Sociogram based on responses to "Who would be the best substitute in the absence of the teacher?" DE (girl) and GA (boy) are mutual first choices; DE and RC are mutual second choices. GA was a first choice of two boys and four girls; DE was a first choice of two boys and three girls; KL was a first choice of two boys and one girl, etc. In the matter of second choice, there is more variation but clustering (known as *stars*) is still evident. MT and JP are neither first nor second choices of any individual and consequently on this question are known as *isolates*.

sociogram is of value in that it reflects the values of pupils, which may at times differ from those of the teacher. Teachers are sometimes surprised when the sociogram shows a particular individual to be relatively isolated, in spite of his recognized abilities. Sociometric study has shown the need for regrouping pupils in such situations as playground activities,

[23] American Council on Education, *Sociometry in Group Relations*, Washington, D.C.: American Council on Education, 1948, p. 47.

seating in the cafeteria, control of traffic, classroom organization, or membership in clubs. Several schools have discovered, for instance, that there is not enough opportunity for boys and girls to know one another. The value of such a study of grouping, *and regrouping as conditions change,* is reflected in the following words: "Only as children participate as active agents will they ever become aware of what group procedures can mean. The great significance of sociometric methods, at this point, lies in the opportunity they afford teachers to create predisposition for active give and take."[24]

This is an experiment which teachers can easily conduct themselves. They have simply to devise some question that will lead pupils to choose persons with whom they would like to associate in specified activities. However, it is well to understand that the results will not be a major transformation of personality. The sociogram should provide some clues as to small, but cumulatively effective, steps that may be taken toward improvement of social ease.

> It is clear that the remedial aspects of the sociometric process cannot be taught as easily as the technique for procuring data. Effective plans are based upon the entire educational preparation and the special education in guidance and counseling of the particular individual. . . . Many teachers have been surprised that steps that were taken to improve the social structure of a group showed such little change in a follow-up evaluation after a period of months. This is characteristic of all attempts at change where life histories of persons as well as the social structures of particular groups are involved. There is some encouragement from the theory of the cumulative impact of small differences.[25]

Informal Projective Techniques. The great need to understand the problems and motivations of pupils has resulted in a number of approaches to the assessment of personality. One of these is known as projective devices (see Chapter 14), a means by which the individual "projects" himself into a neutral situation and gives it a meaning or interpretation according to his own orientation. Since formal techniques require special training for use and interpretation, teachers have used informal devices which, although results are approximate and indicative, do provide some tentative clues to personality adjustment.

One informal device is to use pictures as a point of departure for getting the pupil to tell a story. Older pupils may be encouraged to write the stories which the picture prompts them to construct. The story will often

---

[24] *Ibid.,* p. 82. By permission of the publisher.
[25] Willard C. Olson and William W. Wattenberg, "The Role of the School in Mental Health" in *Mental Health in Modern Education,* 54th Yearbook, Part II, National Society for the Study of Education, Chicago: University of Chicago Press, 1955, p. 111.

contain elements of a problem which the pupil is facing—at home, in school, or in peer adjustments. Fears and anxieties, hopes and aspirations may be revealed to teachers who are attentive and understanding readers and listeners. Of course, answers to problems cannot be uniformly expected, though there may be indications, and the clues provided may well suggest next steps.

Another and somewhat similar approach is the unfinished story. The teacher simply relates the first few lines of a story and then asks the pupils to complete it. For example, one might begin, "Johnny was a twelve-year-old boy. One day he started to school a little late and as he was hurrying along the street he heard a strange sound coming from between two closely set buildings. He hesitated, then stopped, and peering into the gloom he saw a wet, cold little puppy huddled in a little hollow. Now you finish the story." Many times the pupil's story will be imagination rather than a projection of feelings and problems, but occasionally some valuable clues as to interests, empathy, responsibility, ethical standards, or hopes will be revealed. Three things are necessary in introducing the story: (1) It should concern a character with whom the pupils can identify; (2) it should be in an area pupils wish to explore; and (3) it should be flexible enough to allow for the expression of personal feelings.

Movies and Filmstrips. Motion pictures provide perhaps the easiest means for permitting pupils to identify with the characters involved. Typically, films are used to teach something, but they can also be used as avenues for understanding individuals. If the teacher will watch the reactions and facial expressions of pupils, he may get some ideas regarding sensitive areas or attitudes toward situations. Discussion will often reveal the feelings of pupils toward the right and wrong behavior or of how they feel they would respond to the situation depicted. Again let it be stressed that the use of films or filmstrips in this context is to understand rather than to teach.

SUMMARY

Clinical assistance and trained personnel for aiding pupils to make better adjustments to school and life situations are desirable. But existing conditions are short of the ideal. It remains for teachers to make the best use of available facilities and assets if the many pupils who need help are to get any assistance whatever.

School marks can be used more constructively if they (1) are clear to the pupil, (2) recognize both effort and accomplishment, (3) indicate next steps, (4) are helpful to parents, next teachers, and administrators, and (5) lead to teacher self-appraisal. Anecdotal records, case studies, and standardized-test data are clues to improved understanding. Periodic reviews of educational objectives will help both the tyro and the experienced teacher to check the value of various activities carried on in the classroom.

Existing assets for mental health in the school include fellow teachers with their various experiences, unique interests, and differing educational backgrounds. The manual-arts shop, the art room, athletic activities, homemaking activities, and the like have proved to be constructive approaches to the solution of the problems of particular pupils. The pupils themselves can give mutual aid if they are given the opportunity. We need only to put into practice the democratic ideals which we profess.

Experimental approaches, readily available to ordinary classroom teachers, have proved to be effective in improving mental health. One of these is the selection of books which are appropriate to specified age levels and types of problems. The adjustment of pupils is improved through their seeing their own problems from a more impersonal point of view, i.e., in the experiences of others. Their adjustment is also made easier by their realizing that others have experienced the same kinds of feelings that are bothering them. Having pupils tell a story about a picture, finish an incomplete story, or react to movies can serve to provide clues for teachers' improved understanding.

STUDY AND DISCUSSION EXERCISES

1. List as many arguments for conventional marking practices as you can, then ask others to criticize their validity.

2. Observe some class member, in and out of class, and make two or three anecdotal observations which convey a representative view of him.

3. What kinds of test data do you think would constitute a minimum for primary pupils? For elementary pupils? For high-school pupils?

4. Have some experienced teacher tell how he has used pupils as a resource for more effective learning experiences.

5. Have some class member who has read a book listed in *Reading Ladders for Human Relations* tell how it might be used to improve personal adjustment.

SUGGESTED ADDITIONAL READINGS

Baron, Denis, and Harold W. Bernard, *Evaluation Techniques for Classroom Teachers*, New York: McGraw-Hill Book Company, Inc., 1958, pp. 223–241, 243–260.

The selections deal with the shortcomings and alternatives of current grading practices, and the use of tests as supplementary data.

Bullis, H. Edmund, and Emily E. O'Malley, *Human Relations in the Classroom*, Course I, Wilmington, Del.: The Delaware State Society for Mental Hygiene, 1947. 222 pp.

This volume contains specific suggestions for helping junior-high-school pupils to see their personal problems in perspective.

Lee, J. Murray, and Dorris May Lee, *The Child and His Development,* New York: Appleton-Century-Crofts, Inc., 1958, pp. 257–297.

A number of ways of learning more about peer-group relations are described and careful explanations of sociometry are included.

Morse, Arthur D., *Schools of Tomorrow—Today,* New York: Doubleday & Company, Inc., 1960, pp. 27–40.

The chapter indicated describes the elementary schools in Appleton Wis. which have no grades, no report cards, and in which pupils are neither promoted nor failed.

Staff of Intergroup Education in Cooperating Schools, *Reading Ladders for Human Relations,* rev. and enl. ed., Washington: American Council on Education, 1949. 115 pp.

Background suggestions are followed by chapters which deal with eight areas of human relations. Books on each area are suggested according to their appropriateness for pupils of various ages.

PART III

Special Classroom Approaches to Mental Health

CHAPTER 14

ART AND MUSIC AS MENTAL HEALTH APPROACHES

Because of the intricate make-up of human personality, it is improbable that any simple answers will be found for developing effectively adjustive individuals. The multiplicity of human needs and their varying strengths in different persons make it clear that the use of a given technique must be adapted to the person, time, and circumstance.

Several of these needs can be satisfied, at least partially, through various art and music mediums. For example, the fulfillment of the need for activity, to satisfy curiosity, to achieve, to be independent, and the need for release of tension can be facilitated through art mediums. Study of the use of art in effective education thus assumes an important place in the program which the teacher devises for better mental health. Fortunately, the techniques are simple enough to make it possible for every teacher, including those with limited art education, to use them effectively. It is a matter of understanding and applying basic principles such as those briefly indicated in this chapter.[1]

ART AND PUPIL DEVELOPMENT

The Meaning of Art. There is much variety in the definition of art. Thomas Munro states that art is a name given to many different kinds of human products and activities, and he then proceeds to distinguish among twenty-two different meanings.[2] From the standpoint of mental hygiene, we can say that art refers to a kind of behavior in which creative imagina-

[1] Further study, using such references as appear in the footnotes and in the list of recommended readings, is strongly encouraged.
[2] Thomas Munro, *The Arts and Their Interrelations*, New York: The Liberal Arts Press, 1949, pp. 49–107.

tion is channeled into constructive areas. The traditional concept of art is that it "is a significant expression giving form and order to a human being's reaction to his environment."[3] It is a means of meeting human needs, involving both activity and feelings, through the use of materials.

The Greeks were careful to distinguish fine arts from the practical, or industrial, arts. Today we are not so sure that a sharp distinction should be made between the "practical" and the esthetic. Full and efficient func-

FIG. 14. How should the worth of art activities be evaluated? What are some of the mental health values of art work? How can art work be correlated with academic pursuits?

tioning in the practicalities of life demands that humanistic and spiritual studies be recognized in man's striving for freedom and individuality.[4] Although art, through the centuries, has been thought by many to be "art for art's sake," today there is more emphasis on art for complete living.

The forerunners of the contemporary concept of *art in education*, Rousseau, Pestolazzi, and Froebel, believed that it was a factor in stimulating harmonious child development. However, some took the view that art in our earlier schools was too formalized, too strictly related to geom-

[3] Charles D. Gaitskell, *Children and Their Art*, New York: Harcourt, Brace & World, Inc., 1958, p. 12.

[4] Peter Viereck, "The Unadjusted Man," *The Saturday Review*, 41 (44):13–15, Nov. 1, 1958.

etry. The newer concept, as it has been developed up to now, emphasizes capitalizing on *every* individual's capacity for creativeness, however limited the capacity. It holds firmly to the principle that art demands freedom, whether the medium be dancing, painting, modeling, music, drama, or creative writing. The primary objective of art in education is personal self-expression which will satisfy the needs for accomplishment, freedom, exploration, and individual worth, and is not the superiority of achievement that calls forth appreciation by others, which will be known as *art*. Unless these facets of individual creativeness at all levels are kept in mind at all times by the teacher, art as a means of creative mental growth for all cannot be effective.[5]

Art in Contemporary Education. Today, instead of producing pictures with proper balance of shape, location, and color, by using prescribed strokes and standard instruments, *each* child's creation is appreciated in terms of what it reveals about his motivations and stage of development. Instead of emphasis on proficiency in painting, modeling, and dancing, stress is placed on the release of tensions and the expression of unique interests. Skills are not repudiated, but they are of secondary significance and, instead of being taught first, are taught when needed.

Learning can be more concrete when pupils have a chance to handle materials and make pictures and models of some of the objects and situations which they are studying in their academic classes. Thus, in place of the highly verbalized readings and discussions which are too characteristic of the ordinary classroom, art opens an avenue to concrete, individual learnings in the form of seeing, feeling, and, above all, doing.

There is also the opportunity to develop constructive hobbies for many pupils, not only for the few who happened to have outstanding talents for drawing, painting, dancing, and acting. Since superior creativity is not an outstanding criterion, more pupils are encouraged to exercise their freedom in creating things that are satisfactory to them. Any experienced teacher, or parent, will have noticed how enthusiastic children are over their crude drawings, the makeshift playthings they create, and even the shuffling dances they spontaneously perform. The adults will note also how easily discouraged the children become over suggestions for improvement and the offers of assistance that seem to have a critical tone.

The contemporary concept of art presents a challenge to personal growth on the part of the teacher himself. First, there is the opportunity to read about art and education, art therapy, and child study through art activities. One teacher, uninitiated in the field of art, after expressing doubt as to the worthwhileness of art, decided to look into the technique and concluded,

[5] Viktor Lowenfeld, *Creative and Mental Growth*, 3d ed., New York: The Macmillan Company, 1957, p. vi.

I felt some doubt of its suitability since art has seemed to be so much less important than the so-called tool subjects. However, even a little research soon developed a healthy enthusiasm in the subject and the conviction that worthwhile art experiences in the school are a necessary part of the child's school life in helping him develop a wholesome personality; and important for the teacher in helping her to understand the abilities, the thinking, the personalities and the problems of her pupils.[6]

Second, there is an interesting field for personal and professional experimentation. All teachers can give their pupils freedom to draw, paint, and model what and how they choose. It is a matter of placing materials before pupils, showing an interest, and giving encouragement. The teacher can then take note of peaceful or violent scenes which are depicted, the cautious or abandoned use of materials, the care with which the finished product is treated. What is seen can then be correlated with what he knows about the child from school records, relationships with classmates, conversations with the parents, information gathered from other teachers, and his previous observations of the child in other activities. If then he is not too anxious to draw conclusive viewpoints from the art activities alone, he will have gained a better understanding of the child. He may, in certain instances, already have helped the child by allowing freedom of expression. One teacher summarized her attempt at better understanding through art, as follows:

> Ruby, a heavy-set girl, unattractive and untidy in appearance, has had difficulty "fitting in" with her group. Both girls and boys take pleasure in making fun of her. She is not accepted. She has a low I. Q. and cannot do much of the academic work. She has always had a great interest in art. Her ability in craft work has been greater than that in painting, although her habits of work were very careless. Last year she spent considerable time in art and craft work, and found some satisfaction in successfully completing some good projects. Her ego was further helped when much of her work was put on display, and a doll that she made was one of a group that was sent on tour to California and all through Oregon.[7]

Fuller appreciation of the potentialities inherent in art activities in the classroom will be obtained when the teacher has himself worked in the mediums of paint, clay, color, carving, and the like. He can aid his pupils

[6] Elsa H. Gillison, *The Use of the Projective Technique in Art for Primary Pupils*, unpublished master's thesis, Portland, Ore.: Oregan State System of Higher Education, 1949, p. 6.

[7] Janet C. Smith, *Art and Therapy*, unpublished master's thesis, Portland, Ore.: Oregon State System of Higher Education, 1950, p. 27.

in drawing a line, using a brush, pulling the clay, if he has had practice with these things himself. Such practice is widely available today in the form of evening classes, in-service–training groups, and summer study. One teacher said upon entering an art class that she hated art and her only reason for being there was that she was required to earn two hours' credit in the field; at the end of the term, however, she thanked the art teacher for the most enjoyable experience she had had for some time.

THEORETICAL CONSIDERATIONS

Art as a Supplementary Activity. One of the basic principles of mental health is that a full, happy, and harmonious life demands the exercise of one's *various capacities*. Since individuals differ in both the kind and the amount of talents and propensities they possess, it is obvious that a uniform curriculum for all children is not going to afford youngsters equal chances to exercise their capacities. It is precisely at this point that art can be highly valuable; that is, it offers such variety of activities—using carpenter's tools, sewing equipment, a paintbrush, and the like—there is a likelihood that more children will find something to do that is interesting and meaningful.

There is no inherent difference between fullness of activity and artistic activity; the latter is one with being fully alive. Hence, it is not something possessed by a few persons and setting them apart from the rest of mankind, but is the normal or natural human heritage. Its spontaneity is not a gush, but is the naturalness proper to all organized energies of the live creature. Persons differ greatly in their respective measures. But there is something the matter, something abnormal, when a human being is forbidden by external conditions from engaging in that fullness according to his own measure, and when he finds it diverted by these conditions into unhealthy physical excitement and appetitive indulgence.[8]

Art can also be supplementary to the usual school program by way of illustrating and making definite the program devoted to the tool subjects.[9] Thus, in one classroom, arithmetic was carried beyond the realm of abstract numbers by a teacher who encouraged her pupils to build models of hour glasses, construct (and use) an abacus, build a sundial, and make various three-dimensional shapes out of cardboard. The pupils, in addition

[8] John Dewey, "Foreword" in Henry Schaeffer-Simmern, *The Unfolding of Artistic Activity*, Berkeley, Calif.: University of California Press, 1948, p. x. By permission of the publisher.

[9] Jack Kough and Robert F. DeHaan, *Helping Students with Special Needs*, Chicago: Science Research Associates, Inc., 1957, pp. 67–68.

to the fun of creating, had the advantage of seeing and feeling, rather than just hearing and reading. They did the latter, too, for the teacher encouraged their making reports, based on research, which were illustrated with the objects constructed.

As the teacher uses art to vivify his academic program, he is also opening a way for those who are slow in other phases of classwork to gain satisfactions. Thus, a sixth-grade teacher utilized a mural to clarify the pupils' study of geography. The project was carefully planned beforehand by the group as a whole and then by the smaller groups. The chalkboard was roughly divided off into small sections and two or three youngsters were made responsible for filling each separate section of the mural. There was overlapping between the sections, as sky met water and field met hilly country. Pictures of mountains, villages, streams, farms, roads, ships, and airplanes were drawn on the mural. It was interesting to see how the pictures changed and developed as the youngsters talked and read more on the phases of the program for which they were responsible. Most notable was the behavior of an undersized, overaged boy who previously had been creating a disturbance in the class by smart talk and unnecessary noises. But the teacher reported that, after the mural was made a part of the classwork, he asserted himself firmly on the side of maintaining such a state of order that both his own work on the mural and that of all others in the class would progress steadily. And, according to the teacher's further report, although he was still not a leader in academic work, he was demonstrating that his retardation was not entirely due to lack of ability. Upon encountering problems dealing with his section of the mural, he was reading and computing as he never had before.

Art as a Projective Technique. In general, the term *projective techniques* refers to a means whereby a more or less neutral situation is given meaning by the individual responding to it. Thus, the Rorschach blots, the pioneer projective method, are merely symmetrical but unstructured blobs of ink—such as anyone could make by placing a large drop of ink on a piece of paper and then folding the paper—which are meaningless. The subject responding to the blots tells what he sees in them, thus placing himself dominantly within the situation. Evaluation of what the subject puts into the blots is made on the basis of speed of response, movement or action, the parts to which he responds, and the effect of color on the subject's response and behavior. The subject *projects* himself into an unstructured situation and gives it the meaning which is representative of his innner self. Other projective techniques, H. A. Murray's thematic apperception test (TAT), word-association tests, play techniques, finishing a story that the tester tells only in part, as well as finger painting and other forms of art work, operate in basically the same way; i.e., the subject gives meaning to the situation and thus reveals what he himself is.

L. K. Frank defines a projective technique as "a method of studying the personality by confronting the subject with a situation to which he will respond according to what that situation means to him, and how he feels when so responding."[10] However, the projective technique may also be a means of therapy. As the individual projects himself into stories, dramas, and his own models and pictures, he may get rid of some of his tensions. Through stories and pictures the child can make some of the things happen that he would like to have happen. He can be a hero and satisfy some of his basic needs; he can make people suffer who are causing him pain, but he can do it in a way that will actually not hurt others.

Often it is not by choice that an individual (particularly a child) keeps his troubles to himself; it is a matter of his not being able to put into words his feelings, thoughts, and felt, but vague, difficulties. Knowing that something is bothering the child, we may ask, "What is the matter?" The answer "I don't know," or perhaps "Nothing," is not an indication of stubbornness or lack of confidence in the questioner but a revelation of an inability to verbalize (see Figure 15). This condition is well illustrated in the case of a nine-year-old who was not doing well in his schoolwork and who had other reactions indicative of some trouble. His teacher gave him colors and paper for finger painting and let him go to work. He filled the paper symmetrically with colors and designs, starting at the upper-left-hand corner, working in panels across the paper. After he had finished, the teacher praised the color and the order and then asked him what story he was telling. With the aid of the designs and colors he was able to let out his difficulties. A certain black shape was a piano on which he was required to practice; a red, dagger-shaped object above represented a clock that slowly ticked off the required practice time. Another slender and vertical dark slash was his father telling him he was a sissy since he could not play ball as well as he should. A big, yellow circle told about the day his father took him to a Coast League baseball game. The boy's frustrations and desires had become clearer to him as he worked with the troubles, and although he had formerly found that he could not describe his problems, he was able, with the aid of what to an uninformed observer would be meaningless blotches, to express his difficulties in words quite clearly. With her new understanding of the boy's behavior, the teacher was able to go to the parents and work out with them a plan of treatment that promised good results and hope for better adjustment of the boy.

The Teacher and Mental Hygiene through Art. The teacher does not have to be a skilled artist in order to get some values from art. It is necessary not to overgeneralize on the basis of insufficient data, but this does not

[10] Lawrence K. Frank, *Projective Methods*, Springfield, Ill.: Charles C Thomas, Publisher, 1948, p. 46.

FIG. 15. Scissors and paste picture: The picture was made by cutting shapes from colored paper and pasting them on a gray sheet. The heavy water line is dark blue, the boat and bird are green, the fish are yellow.

Freddy's description of the picture: This is a picture of a man fishing. You can't see the man because he is lying in the bottom of the boat asleep. See all the fish around there to be caught if he was awake. He could have a lot of fish to eat. (Teacher's question: Why was he asleep?) He was too tired to work that day and went fishing. He was too tired to fish, so he slept.

This is what the teacher found by investigating Freddy's story a little further: Freddy's father is shiftless, dishonest, and a heavy drinker. He gets in trouble and is in jail occasionally. He takes days off from work to fish once in a while. Last summer Freddy (a fifth-grader) picked berries to make enough money to feed the family (mother and two sisters) while the father was in jail (serving a six-months term for robbery).

preclude the possibility of experimenting and drawing tentative conclusions. Listening to what is said about one's art work or supplementary interrogation may lead to insights.[11] It may be that further study will result in sharpened insight that will lead to uniform interpretations; but at present there seems to be no danger in the teacher's using art for what it is worth in providing for individual differences, in encouraging varying degrees of creativeness, in allowing more pupil freedom, in vitalizing other phases of the school program, and in gathering tentative, supplementary data about the motivations of particular children.

The ease with which art can be used in the classroom is illustrated by a student teacher. She ordered the materials she thought she would need—glue, paper, paints, colored chalk, cotton—and encouraged her pupils to illustrate what they were studying about in geography. Each morning, the youngsters were so anxious to get at their mural and their display table that they prepared their lesson thoroughly, in an attempt to understand better what they were depicting. Two children who had worried the student teacher by their restlessness during previous recitations were as anxious to get into the swing of things as were the others.

ART MEDIUMS IN THE CLASSROOM

It has already been indicated that literature, dance, drama, and personal adornment are included in the broad concept of art. However, for convenience in discussion, this section will be limited to a treatment of the graphic and plastic arts. Remember that these mediums are not sharply differentiated in their value and use. What is said about one may also logically be said about another.

Brush Painting. Brush painting gives pupils a chance to utilize colors in projecting their thoughts. The brush may be regarded as another tool for expressing the mind and the heart. Pictures have been described as thoughts projected upon a surface in an organized manner and, as such, the teacher gains a view of the hidden inner self of the child. The picture will indicate the child's motivations, the colors may be used as clues to the predominating emotional pattern, and the detail will give indications of comparative maturity.[12] Children indicate their notion of the relative significance of objects and situations in their environment, thus

[11] Willard C. Olson and William W. Wattenberg, "The Role of the School in Mental Health" in *Mental Health in Modern Education*, 54th Yearbook, Part II, National Society for the Study of Education, Chicago: University of Chicago Press, 1955, pp. 111–113.

[12] Florence Goodenough has devised an intelligence test, the "Goodenough Drawing Test," for young children. It consists of drawing a man and is graded according to a standard scale, one point being awarded for each of fifty-one details enumerated.

allowing the teacher to get a view of each child's conception of his world. (Although another medium is used, Figure 16 shows such a conception.)

Finger Painting. The direct use of hands in paint is somewhat messier than brush painting, but it has the particular advantage of letting the user feel, as well as see, what he is producing. It seems, too, that children get a certain satisfaction from the slick and sticky feeling of the paint, quite apart from any creative satisfaction. Studies indicate that the way one works with the paint, both as to bodily posture and the use of the finger-tips, palms, or even the forearm, is an indication of certain personality trends. For example, the child who delicately pushes the paint about with one finger may have been taught to be fussily clean. He fears adults might object to his making a mess. One who plunges in with both hands feels free to explore and experiment. Clearly these illustrate the fact that a child's actions are his language of behavior. Likewise, the kinds of colors selected and the amount of paper that is used provide clues to personality. At present, there is not sufficient agreement upon just what these things mean to make direct diagnosis advisable, but when the trends are added to other observations, clues to understanding may be uncovered. However, there is no need to shy away from the technique as a means of creative activity and as a means of getting the child to objectify his feelings to the extent that he can tell others what he is painting.

Clay Modeling. When working with clay, fingers get soiled and desks, doors, and drawers will have smudges on them; nevertheless, children get pleasure from the work. Perhaps they find in the attendant dirtiness a release from the home and school requirements to keep clean and orderly. Clay gives a chance to correct errors; one may try and try again without wasting material. The physical strength required to press and pound the clay into shape affords release of emotions, as can be seen in youngsters who smack the desk loudly with a chunk of the material and strike it with their fists and elbows. Some find satisfaction in making a man (perhaps daddy or the principal) and then pounding it into a shapeless mass. Child therapists feel that such actions are better than damming up feelings of hostility or direct attack—if one dared. Details often concern the youngsters. Some third-graders have been observed to use toothpicks to scratch eyebrows and nostrils on the animals and faces they were making.

Carving and Woodworking. Working with tools will require some instruction regarding safe use and proper care of them, since defective tools are dangerous; but beyond that, the same freedom can be given children in this as in the other arts. Woodworking calls for use of the larger muscles, which are more developed than is the coordination involved in painting, and is therefore likely to give satisfactions to more pupils. If teachers can be satisfied with the slow process of growth, practice in

FIG. 16. A drawing used for pupil understanding. This picture was drawn at the request of a remedial reading teacher who asked, "Draw me a picture of your home, will you?" Noting the prominence of the hands in the upper figures she asked, "Where are your hands?" The answer was, "I can't, [show them] I have my coat on." The lad had a chronic case of eczema which caused feelings of inferiority and shame. The teacher worked on these feelings rather than the mechanics of reading and soon had him achieving at his expected level. One might also wonder about his feelings of acceptance in the home. His brother (Sammy) was in junior high school and was on a par with his dad (Did). His mother and his infant brother form another focal part of the family scene. Unimportant little Freddie (eight years old, in the third grade and unable to read) was by himself with an enveloping coat to hide eczema.

woodworking can pave the way for a gratifying and useful hobby. As in working with clay, the muscular exercise will be a relief for rapidly growing children who resist the relative physical inactivity of the classroom. An additional avenue for creativity is provided by making work in the shop available. Although it must be realized that those with limited mental ability do not compensate by having skill in manual activity, it can safely be said that woodworking, calling for a different kind of ability, is another means of providing for individual differences. Gary, for instance, by constructing with wood, obtained release from out-of-school tensions involving rejection. He had talent for this activity, was interested in accomplishment, and found emotional release in hammering and sawing. His aggressiveness waned as his success helped him to establish a place for himself in his group.

Ruth Halvorsen, art supervisor in the Portland, Oregon, public schools, recommends the art of carving and whittling as worthy of more attention. It is an undeveloped art which youngsters engage in with eagerness. She recommends the use of balsa wood for those who have a tendency to pick at their faces and bite their nails. It gives them something soft to tear at and shape. Pine is recommended for those who like to overcome pressures and who wish to construct. Hardwood can be used for those who have lots of physical strength and like to feel the pull of their muscles as they create.

Other Mediums. The foregoing do not exhaust the possible avenues of artistic creation and exercise. Other mediums which might be used, depending upon circumstances of appropriateness and availability of material, include the following:

> Pencil, charcoal, crayon, and chalk drawings
> Poster drawings and paintings
> Metalwork—tin, copper, and sheet aluminum
> Leatherworking—tooling
> Making Christmas decorations of colored paper, tin cans,
>   and papier-mâché
> Making dolls and costumes for them
> Wall murals and stage scenery
> Making puppets and putting on plays with them
> Making stencils and working with them
> Weaving with paper and string

Advantages similar to those discussed in the earlier part of this section are inherent in the above-listed mediums: freedom of activity, opportunity for varied accomplishment, physical activity providing for emotional catharsis, initiation of constructive leisure-time activities, carrying learnings beyond the strictly verbal stage, and opportunity for the teacher to obtain an additional viewpoint of the child.

If the use of these various mediums is to achieve the results indicated, the point made so frequently by the experts must be kept in mind: Free the child—do not impose adult standards.

ART AS A TECHNIQUE FOR PERSONALITY ANALYSIS

Limitations of the Technique. As yet, not all the data on art as a means of personality analysis have been gathered. Authorities differ in their interpretation of what certain colors, themes, size, and location mean in terms of revealing personality trends. Interpretation is all the more difficult inasmuch as it is known that children may draw, construct, and paint and choose colors as a matter of imitation or of convention and not of self-expression. Further, an art production may be a spontaneous creation, an interest of the moment, with no significance as to persistent personality traits. Without regarding the child as an artist, we can infer the need for caution from the following quotation:

> A picture may contain profound suggestions of sublime tragedy or poignant sentiment, even though the artist himself did not feel them very keenly. . . . A playwright can express in words the emotional attitudes of hatred and jealousy and an actor can portray them without either of them feeling there attitudes strongly himself. Similarly, a painter can represent the facial expressions and gestures that tend to stimulate an emotion in others, without feeling it himself. He can express and represent madness, and yet be quite sane. . . . It is hard to infer from the finished product just what steps were involved in its conception and execution.[13]

Many personality problems do not have their origin in one specific bit of difficulty. Instead, the causes of a problem may be, and most often are, multiple. Hence, the art product that represents only one phase of difficulty does not give an indication of the entire situation. Just as children use similar defense mechanisms in response to different situations, so too will they use similar art products in response to varied stimulations. We may be equally sure that one child who draws minute pictures in one corner of the paper does not do it for the same reason that another does. Two children may show black predominantly for quite different purposes. Considerations such as these lead to the conclusion that analysis through art must be approached with a good deal of caution. The tech-

[13] Thomas Munro, "Creative Ability in Art, and Its Educational Fostering" in *Art in American Life and Education,* 40th Yearbook, National Society for the Study of Education, Bloomington, Ill.: Public School Publishing Company, 1941, pp. 311–312.

nique can be used by the classroom teacher as a supplementary source of data; but for the present, detailed analysis through art should be left in the hands of the expert.

The Classroom Teacher as Analyst. There is no reason why the teacher cannot experiment freely with the use of art as an approach to understanding, provided he recognizes that results are questionable. It is interesting and always informative (even though results are negative) to try a new technique. Experimentation in analysis through art can serve to add variety to a job that at times becomes routinized. The art productions of a child can be understood better and the child can be better understood through them when the teacher has other information about him (see Chapter 13). The very least contribution that art can make is that it will raise some questions: Is this child inhibited? Could this represent some sex conflict? Is this youngster hiding some strongly aggressive or destructive desire? Art mediums will be more helpful and communicative if the precaution is heeded that single productions are less valuable in analysis than are several by the same child. When several are studied, trends can be noted (dominant themes, favorite colors, persistent kinds of action) and changes will begin to take on significance.

One teacher has used her own drawings to assist pupils in verbalizing their feelings (Figure 17). Before presenting the stick figure to a pupil she studied his cumulative record and all test results. Sociograms were used as supplementary information. A preliminary hypothesis of possible causes of behavior and scholastic problems was formulated. The interpretation of stories and involvement in class discussions of personal problems were used to test certain of these hypotheses. Then, through the figures, she attempted to discover (1) basic needs not being met at home, (2) areas of frustration, (3) areas of social inadequacy, (4) fears or apprehensions, and (5) directions of feelings of love or hate. These procedures eventually resulted in a girl's mother seeking the aid of a psychiatric social worker, a father's reducing pressure on a son to compensate for his own felt shortcomings, and a mother's giving more time and attention (including new and pretty clothes) to a daughter who had previously been neglected.

Sample responses to the stick figures in Fig. 17 include the following: Picture 1: Pupil C, "Not anybody plays with her." Pupil B, "She don't want to show her report card." Pupil A, "She's bawling her out 'cause she didn't come home." Other pupils said: "She's scared to go in 'cause she was bad in school." "She don't like to hear her talk so much." "She's talking to the principal." Picture 2 elicited the following: Pupil B, "He didn't like that boy." "The dad is mad at the report card and said the boy is lazy." "The dad is holding something away from the boy 'cause the kid did something he didn't like." Other pupils said: "The

FIG. 17. Stick figures used to encourage the verbalization of feelings.

boy should leave." "He's swearing 'cause the boy did something bad."
"He's not going to give him any money." Responses to Picture 3 included
from pupil C, "He's going to say, 'Leave me alone'," and "She wants to
hug her daddy"; and from others: "She's going to put spiders down his
neck." "She wants to tell him something and he's always too busy."
Pupil B responded to picture 4 with "He don't understand the lesson, it's
no use." " . . . or he might be hungry, he'll feel better after lunch." "He

tried to work the arithmetic too fast and he missed a lot." Other pupils said: "Her voice hurt his ears." "He has a headache."[14]

Personality analysis through art will be on safe ground if the conclusions drawn are tentative only, waiting for the support of corroborative evidence. Tentative conclusions can lead to remedial hypotheses. As an hypothesis, put into action, yields success or failure, it will be modified and the tentative conclusions will be revised.

Even when we conclude that art in the hands of the classroom teacher is not a highly accurate analytic technique—and ignoring the therapeutic value of freedom in art activities—there still remains the best reason for the teacher's use of the technique; i.e., children may find it easier to describe the meaning of their art than to answer direct questions about their difficulties. Children who resist any direct show of sympathy are likely to find it easier to respond to interest taken in their work and can be led on to a confidential relationship, which will help the teacher in analyzing their behavior. Art can help in getting at a child's story.

MUSIC AS AN APPROACH TO MENTAL HEALTH

Music has been called the universal language and, as such, appeals to persons of all ages. Yet, its use in schools has been limited, because of the emphasis on superiority of performance and the lack of teachers who can themselves perform competently. Fortunately, the newer emphasis is upon participation rather than perfection, and the use of records, tape recorders, and radio has made some of the advantages of music available to all teachers. Emphasis is on reducing the gap between music entertainment and satisfaction and that of the concert and opera variety so that the rank and file can share the joys of music.[15] Because the advantages of using music in education and suggestions on how to use it are similar to those pertaining to art in general, the material here is merely epitomized.

Advantages of Music Activities in the Grades and High School. *Music provides one more medium for expressing interests and creativity*. Thus, may a student not particularly active in government, art, athletics, or debating find a means of participation in activity leading to accomplishment and recognition.

Music serves to broaden the curriculum. It may be used as a subject of study—appreciation classes, chorus, band, or orchestra—or it may serve to supplement other subjects—records of folk or patriotic songs in the social studies or music from foreign lands in the study of language.

[14] Eleanor A. Powell, "Improving Classroom Atmosphere through the Use of Projective Techniques," unpublished manuscript, Portland, Ore., Spring, 1958.

[15] Russell V. C. Morgan and Hazel N. Morgan, *Music Education in Action*, Chicago: Neil A. Kjos Music Company, 1954, pp. 2–3.

Music provides for physical release of tensions, not only when performing in groups but also when alone. The piano, drums, cymbals, tuba, trombone, trumpet are all especially demanding in terms of physical energy. The energy released has been found to be helpful to the mediocre as well as the skilled performer.

Music provides for emotional catharsis. Music when properly organized and appreciated has a definite and specific emotional impact.[16] Though this may differ in various individuals, there is elation, sympathy, strength, and fortitude to be felt in given persons on hearing or performing given selections. This may explain why music has not been highly successful as therapy for mental patients—its effects are variable.

Music provides invigorating motivation and is also an inducement to relaxation. As is clearly indicated by its use in church, sound movies, and television, music is an important device in establishing a mood.

Music is a special capacity in some persons. For the musically gifted person, competence will provide an opportunity for leadership and prestige. Hence, for some, it provides a compensatory activity for failure, or felt failure, in other areas.

Music provides an avenue for group participation. Although athletics receives more enthusiastic group approval, because of our social mores, music is an approach to the same group approval and hence will elicit a degree of participation that for some would otherwise be lacking. Pride in what the band, chorus, or orchestra does is a real incentive to social identification.

Music is a means of broadening and enriching life. A great and rather "hard-boiled" scientist, Charles Darwin, is given credit for the following statement:

> If I had my life to live over again, I would have made a rule to read some poetry and listen to some music at least once a week; for perhaps the parts of my brain now atrophied would thus have kept active through use. The loss of these tastes is a loss of happiness and may possibly be injurious to the intellect, and more probably the moral character, by enfeebling the emotional part of our nature.[17]

Music can provide experiences in the constructive use of leisure time. Not only do some adults find their participation in school music has led to an individual hobby of value to them for expression and release of tension but some have found themselves continuing their interests in glee clubs, choirs, bands, and orchestras.

[16] James L. Mursell, "Growth Processes in Music Education" in *Basic Concepts in Music Education*, 57th Yearbook, Part I, National Society for the Study of Education, Chicago: University of Chicago Press, 1958, p. 152.

[17] Quoted by Peter Viereck, "The Unadjusted Man," *The Saturday Review*, 41 (44):14, Nov. 1, 1958.

Music is a means of fostering international understandings. Folk songs and foreign music have served in many schools to hasten the assimilation of pupils of minority groups and children of recent immigrants. In this process the majority group has perceived that national variations are often superficial and temporary and not fundamental differences in personality structure.

Suggestions for the Advantageous Use of Music. Making use of the advantages of music requires a teacher who is himself sincere and appreciative of music. It is the teacher's job to make the work enjoyable rather than to let it become an academic task. The emphasis must be on producing a consumer who enjoys the musical art.[18]

The music activities must be within the capacity of the pupil. Thus, blocks of wood, sand blocks, tom-toms, maracas, triangles, cymbals, castanets, jingle sticks, tambourines, and bells are used in rhythm bands in primary grades. Choral groups and orchestra may begin in the middle grades. Part singing, bands, and orchestra have long been used to the special advantage of some pupils in the upper grades and high school. While there should be emphasis on wide participation in the latter activities there should be no objection to forming expert groups for the more talented pupils.

There should be an opportunity for appreciation *and* performance. Dramatizing music, identifying the instrument with the lead, raising hands when certain previously indicated passages are played, or accompanying recorded orchestral selections with a rhythm orchestra allow both for appreciation and performance.[19] Music has been used for accompaniment to other school activities—to reading, typing, painting and craftwork, and as mood music for mechanical drawing. Its value in physical education classes is recognized but sometimes neglected.

Pupils should be exposed to a variety of good music. This should include not only the classics of the great composers but also our own national folk songs, patriotic pieces, and the folk songs of other nations. Moreover, the pupils should have an opportunity to select what is to be heard and to suggest activities (listening quietly, clapping, and humming or singing along with a record) that, on occasion, might capitalize on their choice.

The creative opportunity inherent in music should not be neglected. Pupils, especially the older ones, should be encouraged to compose musical and dramatic productions. The level may not be high, but with

[18] J. F. Gould, "On Winning Enemies to Music," *Music Education Journal,* 44 (2):58, November–December, 1957.

[19] Ruth Bampton, "Music Appreciation—1958," *Music Education Journal,* 44 (4):76, February–March, 1958.

the emphasis on participation rather than perfection, the results may be generally gratifying to all and of special benefit to some.

An Illustration of Music in the Classroom. There are many ways of using music and the following account must therefore be regarded as illustrative rather than representative. The description does serve to lend specificity to some of the advantages and suggestions cited above. Mrs. Layman, a second-grade teacher, offered this account as she played records and described the children's reactions:

> I'm not talented in art and I feel that I could not give my youngsters much help in that area; but I do love music and I thought I could share my enthusiasms. I simply played records I like and asked them to respond. It was explained that a composer had a story he was telling in the language of music. Sometimes I told them what the story was about, like "The March of the Toy Soldiers." Pupils were asked to see if they could see these little soldiers get out of their boxes and march as the trumpet called them and the band played.
>
> Music can tell them to do something—we call this mood music. I asked them to tell what they felt like or felt like doing when I played another piece. I asked them to demonstrate. They were told that whatever they did was right. This gave Jerry a chance to shine. He has a brother two years older who is a complete extrovert and very competent. Jerry's attempts to imitate usually end in failure. After the piece was played Jerry said it made him feel like a rabbit hopping across the plain and stopping now and then to nibble the grass. His demonstration was applauded by all. Others soon began giving their versions. Susan said it made her feel like a butterfly. "Butterflies can go even faster than birds." Irene said that she could see two fairies who were coming to play with her. Irene is often seen on the playground apart from all the others. Her need for companionship was thus more strongly emphasized to me. Other girls said it made them feel like ballet dancers. I got the impression that some were by now simply agreeing with others so I promised some more music another day.
>
> When I played one of my most favorite pieces, I was in for a surprise. The girls all had original and interesting responses but the boys said it did not make them feel a thing. They just sat. I tried another and this time some of the boys felt like Indians on the warpath. A group of three boys got up and put on an impromptu dance. Afterward I asked them to tell what their story was. Jimmy said he was murdering a gas station (of all things), because they had a lot of money there and he wanted it. The other two fell in with the story and said they were running away. They, I'm sure, had not planned this story and they simply followed up the one started. But it is true that during the dance they did show fear and act as though they were running away.
>
> I would say that any music that appeals to you merits a trial. You

may be disappointed but you may get some surprising responses. It seems that one of the essentials is to provide them with a wide variety of selections. It is fun and I think it aids in understanding individuals.

Mrs. Layman's account shows that she is teaching pupils to be good listeners, since they are engaging both body and mind in responses involving thinking, feeling, and doing.[20] The basis is being laid for the further development of appreciation and one cannot help but wonder why convention so inhibits older persons that few can feel the responsiveness demonstrated by these second-graders. It is hoped that upper-grade teachers will experiment to find whether, through developing good rapport, the sophisticate of the preadolescent and adolescent age cannot learn to respond with a similar richness of feeling.

ART AND MUSIC IN THE TOTAL EDUCATIONAL PROGRAM

Art activities can serve to supply answers for some of the perplexing general problems of education and can implement some of the general objectives of education.

Developing Rapport through Art and Music. Rapport may be defined as a relationship characterized by a feeling of harmony, accord, and belongingness. Oneness between teacher and pupils would be shown in perseverance in work, acceptance of responsibility, a sharing of disappointments and successes, and a confidence that what is sought can be accomplished and is worthwhile. Art and music activities that are properly directed contribute to each of these characteristics of rapport.

Physical harmony may be fostered through flower arrangements, the display of paintings (both those of the masters and those of the pupils), and the color and variety inherent in models, craftwork, and the dolls and puppets that are constructed. Murals which are jointly undertaken by committees of the class give an opportunity to develop social harmony through exercise in cooperative endeavors. Mood music can be played during certain activities. The variety of activities that may be introduced to the class by various art mediums gives each child a chance to do some things in which he can be relatively successful and thus contributes to his feelings of belongingness.

A feeling of oneness between teacher and pupils is generated by the facts that (1) in art, adult standards are not imposed, and (2) it is incumbent upon the teacher to take each pupil "where he is." Since art work is viewed as expression of personality, each person's or group's work is meritorious, even though of low artistic value; thus the recognition that

[20] William C. Hartshorn, "The Role of Listening" in *Basic Concepts in Music Education*, 57th Yearbook, Part I, National Society for the Study of Education, Chicago: University of Chicago Press, 1958, p. 287.

is received fosters rapport. Responsibility is stimulated by cooperative group undertakings, by the necessity for caring for tools and materials so that others may find them ready to use, and by the fact that each person can make some contribution to the ongoing activities. When a child fails to recite in a creditable manner or when he makes an outstanding recitation, there is typically little sharing of his feelings by other class members; but when his success or failure conditions that of others, there is a point of fusion for class morale. The feeling that the activities of art and music and the study which accompanies them are worthwhile is buttressed by the fact that learnings are concrete—results can be seen, heard, and felt, as well as discussed.

Art and Music Activities Simplify Motivation. Interest, enjoyment, success, understanding, and purpose are elements in motivation. Each of these is complicated by the existence of individual differences. Art activities, by virtue of the amplitude of alternatives, offer possibilities for meeting these differences. In addition, the opportunity to feel, see, and do adds motivating force. Such motivation can, of course, be secured only if art activities are made part and parcel of the academic learnings. Art, music, and subject matter should serve to illustrate, make definite, and amplify one another. If the teacher will but suggest one or two ideas as to how the two can be correlated and then give the students freedom to explore, they will themselves take care of further working out the correlation.

The discerning teacher will secure from art activities the most advantageous dividend in terms of motivation, that is, an insight into the emotional make-up of the child. His responses will give indications of his fantasies, will help to reveal the problems he feels, will indicate his ambitions, and may help to uncover talents not called into play before. His work will, in short, tend to reveal his private inner life. The teacher must be careful not to attach too much significance to an isolated response, but continued study might well reveal persistent trends of personality development.

Art and Music Have Therapeutic Values. It should be remembered that the vast majority of pupils have no pronounced problems of adjustment. Aside from minor disturbances that are quickly settled, most children are successfully meeting the situations of their daily lives in a process of continuous adjustment. Art activities, for these youngsters, merely provide opportunities for varied self-expression. There are, however, those whose adjustment problems are not easily solved. Experimental evidence supports the statement that art mediums are a successful means of releasing emotions, including aggressive impulses, and of projecting thoughts (see Figure 18).

Art and Music Contribute to Facile Human Relationships. Many educators, philosophers, and statesmen have agreed that the foremost problem of the

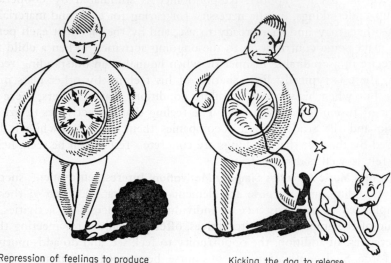

Repression of feelings to produce
shyness, timidity and general
unhappiness

Kicking the dog to release
strong emotion

Fighting, quarreling, pouting
to hide or express feelings

Expressing one's feelings through
socially approved mediums

FIG. 18. Ways of expressing or dealing with tensions.

world today is that of human relationships. Certainly, one of the leading objectives of contemporary education is that of socialization. Anything the teacher can do to foster harmonious human relationships attests to his proficiency. Art and music activities are in many ways socializing forces. Individuals may achieve the feeling that they have created something of merit for the group, that they have taken part in the joint endeavor and contributed something to it. The accomplishment of one becomes the success of all. The admiration that a pupil wins from the teacher gives him a warm feeling, which grows out of affection and attention. Children who are not adept at expressing themselves in words become more closely attached to others by being able to communicate with them through art.

Art and Music Develop the Inner Resources. Art and music, in all their manifestations, provide in many ways for the constructive use of individual resources:

They can give exercise to many facets of personality, including talents that might otherwise remain undeveloped.

Their many mediums make possible their use by great numbers of individuals who differ in capacities, talents, and interests.

They furnish release from emotional tension by satisfying fundamental human needs and by providing means of self-expression through desirable and essentially creative channels.

They aid in communication and thus make for easier and happier human relationships.

They add to the beauty and symmetry of everyday life by stimulating appreciation and skills that will be of value not only in the esthetic, but also in the utilitarian aspects of life.

They foster an awareness and appreciation of the works of masters, thus contributing to well-rounded development.

All these considerations may be summarized by saying that art helps to develop the inner resources that will help children become adults who are independent and possess initiative.

SUMMARY

Art and music activities deserve serious consideration in the mental hygiene program of the school because of the many human needs they can efficiently serve. Art, in order to serve the functions of self-expression, socialization, and release must be regarded as a supplementary and correlative area of activity and not be set apart as a distinct subject in the curriculum. Thus, art can be used (1) as a means of enriching the core curriculum, but also (2) as a means of esthetic pleasure and for expressing the personality.

Art productions and activity can serve as a projective technique for both analysis and therapy. Fortunately, the teacher can use the therapeutic aspects of art without placing too great emphasis upon art as a technique for analysis. The therapeutic values can be realized, because through the use of the many mediums available, it is possible to recognize functionally individual differences among students. They are especially valuable in aiding the child to verbalize his own thoughts and feelings.

Art and music add strength to the total educational program by aiding in the development of teacher-pupil rapport, by strengthening motivation, and by providing for emotional release. Better human relations are fostered through art and music activities, both because they offer a means of communication and because they are particularly well suited to co-operative undertakings. But the educational results are not only social. Many of the values are personal, for art can lead to the establishment of constructive habits in the use of leisure time and constructive use of the inner resources.

STUDY AND DISCUSSION EXERCISES

1. Gather some children's creative art work and attempt to interpret the product in terms of their personality characteristics. If possible, verify your views from more objective data.

2. How might art be used to supplement the teaching of arithmetic in the sixth grade? Could art be used in a chemistry class?

3. What could you personally do in the field of art to enhance your use of it with pupils?

4. Does the distinction between expert performance and appreciation and participation in regard to music seem to you to be valid?

5. What are some things the teacher who cannot sing well or play some musical instrument might do to bring music into the classroom?

SUGGESTED ADDITIONAL READINGS

D'Amico, Victor, *Creative Teaching in Art,* rev. ed., Scranton, Pa.: Inter-Textbook Company, 1953. 257 pp.

Each chapter tells what can be expected of children of different ages in terms of painting, sculpturing, pottery, and crafts.

Gaitskell, Charles D., *Children and Their Art,* New York: Harcourt, Brace & World, Inc., 1958. 446 pp.

The author suggests ways in which the teacher may develop the understanding and skill needed to guide children in many art mediums.

Gaitskell, Charles D., and Margaret R. Gaitskell, *Art Education during Adolescence,* New York: Harcourt, Brace & World, Inc., 1954. 116 pp.

The nature of adolescents and the specific ways in which art can help them meet physical, mental, emotional, and social needs are described.

Lowenfeld, Viktor, *Creative and Mental Growth*, 3d ed., New York: The Macmillan Company, 1957. 541 pp.

This is a text for elementary and secondary teachers which describes the use of art at all levels for growth in creative expression.

Mursell, James L., *Music and the Classroom Teacher*, Morristown, N.J.: Silver Burdett Company, 1951. 304 pp.

The author, well versed in the psychology of music, describes how the most can be made of music appreciation and participation in various grades, for various pupils, and for various purposes.

National Society for the Study of Education, *Basic Concepts in Music Education*, 57th Yearbook, Part I, Chicago: University of Chicago Press, 1958, pp. 215–355.

Various authors deal with the role of music in general education, the music curriculum, the art of listening, and functional music and have a message for teachers who are beginning their work in music education.

CHAPTER 15

UNDERSTANDING AND RELEASE THROUGH WRITING AND READING

This chapter deals with the release of tensions and the satisfaction of basic needs through the use of creative writing and developmental reading. Because of its simplicity, creative writing is gaining in popularity as a technique for classroom diagnosis. Too often reading is simply an exercise, but many realize that it can supply building materials for stable personality.

Creative writing may be classed with those approaches which are called *projective techniques*. It, like other projective methods, can be used as a means of getting at the "inner man" of the total personality and understanding the private world of the subject. The thoughts, problems, and conflicts of the individual that are so difficult to express orally may sometimes be written, since another person is not present. The difficulty of expressing tensions in words is a common symptom of personality maladjustment which creative writing tends to circumvent.

Creative writing is not a panacea for inarticulateness. It is, however, an approach. Neither is reading a panacea, but it is a process which, step by step, may lead to encouragement, ambition, creative ideas, and in time of trouble to consolation.

FUNDAMENTAL NEEDS AND CREATIVE WRITING

Contemporary Life and Creativity. It can be said with some truth that opportunities for creativity seem to be fewer today than in previous generations. The active satisfaction of making an outfit of clothes, a quilt, a rug, a chair, or a chest of drawers has been replaced by the relatively passive process of placing one's money on the counter and receiving a ready-made, stereotyped article. Even the earning of the money may involve a routine, monotonous activity. Along with the advantage of saving time through the purchase of ready-made products must go the disadvantage of giving up opportunities for self-expression and creativity. Even the time saved is likely to be used in passively watching mass entertainment and crowd spectacles. The high development of art on the stage or the screen indirectly robs the observer of chances for participating in an amateur production. Professionalism in sports has tended to reduce the number of local adult teams in football and baseball. Certainly it is the consensus of mental hygienists that one of the hazards to present-day mental health is the decline in the number of avenues for personal creativity.

Children too, suffer from the lack of creative opportunity. Middle- and upper-class children are generally provided with ready-made toys, though they often cast these aside to invent their own games with cans, sticks, and mud. Elaborate formal programs, devised with the best of adult intentions, push them into preconceived patterns of behavior and, consequently, leave them with little opportunity for creative independence. Early in the school years, radio occupies an abnormally large portion of their free hours. Television, even more attractive to children than is radio, offers no more stimulation to the creative impulse.

There are both scientific and empirical evidences that creative activity is significant in promoting good mental health. The first is, of course, that creativity gives one an opportunity to exercise and develop his capacities. It is thought that some misbehavior in school can be justifiably attributed to the fact that the curriculum does not present a wide enough variety of activities for fulfilling the needs of the many children who are forced to go to school. Bright children, though not characteristically trouble-makers, often get into mischief in order to satisfy an urge for activity in some other pursuit than class routines. Tensions, moreover, may have developed, not through absence of opportunity for creativity but because of parental incompatibility or lack of economic means. These tensions may be indirectly released through participation in various creative enterprises. Another reason for the significance of creative activity, not un-related to those mentioned above, is that it provides a means of therapy for those who are already mentally ill. It is a technique widely used in institutions for mentally, emotionally, and socially maladjusted persons.

Creative Writing and Mental Health. The statements made about creativity in general hold for creative writing as well. It can be an avenue for accomplishment and an approach to satisfying the need to achieve and create. It affords an opportunity for self-expression and personal growth. There can be no doubt that, given an appropriate setting, writing can provide relief from tensions and thus serve as a means of therapy. If too many rules are not imposed, it opens an opportunity for recognizing and dealing with individual differences. In addition, creative writing may serve to give the discerning teacher an insight into the motivations of individual students and thus can become a means of diagnosis or, at least, of additional understanding. This understanding may well lead to the suggestion of some means of therapy which will go beyond the writing itself. This advantage will be seen somewhat more clearly, later in the chapter, through the analysis of pupils' writing, but the point is emphasized in the following words:

> What Dr. Campbell [a practicing psychiatrist] said, in effect, was that the patients who were brought to him because they had been judged to be seriously maladjusted or even "insane," showed one chief symptom: *They were unable to tell him clearly what was the matter.* They simply could not put into words the difficulties with which they were beset. Surely no one who has made it his business to help people in trouble has failed to observe their relative inarticulateness.[1]

It is entirely possible that, if more opportunity could be provided for free and for creative writing while children are young, there might be considerably less inability to express oneself and to get rid of frustrating tensions.

Psychologists and educators have recommended creative writing as a stimulus to personality development. It is a means of making one's own problems impersonal and thus more open to solution. Writing is rich in possibilities for objectifying emotional conflicts. But perhaps the greatest advantage of being free to write and being encouraged to do so is that of "letting off steam." Teachers who have supplied the samples of writing shown below have all mentioned this factor. Though they are not just sure how it works, they report that their pupils have seemed to feel better after writing about something that surprised or bothered them. A sealed kettle over a flame may explode, but provide a vent and it sings.

RELEASE THROUGH CREATIVE COMPOSITION

Relatively few teachers have experimented with children's compositions as an approach to understanding—too often the emphasis is on spelling, organization, and neatness. If, however, the emphasis is on the message, there is not only a real incentive to improved presentation but also diagnostic and therapeutic values. Starting with an appreciation of the merits of creative writing, the teacher can develop his own technique. For example, much of the material in the subsection dealing with creative writing by secondary-school pupils was derived from the experiences of a teacher who, having read a few accounts of the possibilities, decided to experiment on her own. She reported with surprise and gratification how

[1] Wendell Johnson, *People in Quandaries*, New York: Harper & Brothers, 1946, p. 15.

much she learned about her pupils when they clearly understood that they were free to express themselves as they wished.

Preschool Children Express Themselves. Dorothy Walter Baruch, consulting psychologist, has advised creative expression for preschool youngsters. Mothers were encouraged to write down the mutterings of their disgruntled children. Instead of requiring children to obey, to conform, the mothers were asked to permit release of "bad" thoughts, to accept the children, and to let them know that their feelings were understood. A four-and-a-half-year-old girl chanted the following and her mother wrote it down:

> I don't like skin on milk,
> Or skin on custard pudding.
> I don't like skin on cocoa.
> I don't like skin.
> Except just skin on me
> Where skin ought to be.[2]

Rapport was established when the mother said, "You don't like lots of things!" "No, I don't!" the girl replied. A four-year-old boy felt better after his mother had read to him fifteen times what he had said and she had written:

> You make me do things
> I don't want to do.
> I hate to do things.
> I hate you.[3]

After the repetition of these lines, the youngster gave his mother a big hug, jumped down from her lap, and ran off chanting the lines to himself.

Creative writing can be utilized from the very beginning of school experience. If the teacher can get rid of false notions of propriety, he can encourage pupils at any age to drain off some of the venom of their feelings by having them write their thoughts. Further therapy is accomplished by having what they have composed read back to them.

Elementary Pupils Express Themselves. When youngsters have acquired the skill of writing, an atmosphere of freedom will encourage them to sublimate their feelings in creative expression. Baruch reports the case of a group of fourth-graders who sat enthralled as they listened to their teacher read aloud the things they had written.

THE WICKED MAN

Do you know who the wicked man is? I know but I won't tell. He looks like a guy named Bill. He's very wicked. He doesn't like

[2] Dorothy Walter Baruch, *New Ways in Discipline,* New York: McGraw-Hill Book Company, Inc., 1949, p. 176.
[3] *Ibid.,* p. 178.

anybody. And he can do what he wants to them because he's very big. He's a giant. He says to his father and mother, "Lie down," and they have to because he's so big, and they're scared of him. "Yes, Bill," they say. "Yes, Bill. All right, Bill. Yes, Bill. Yes."

So they lie down and he steps all over them with his big feet. He kicks them and steps on them and they cry and cry and beg for mercy. So he finely gives in in case they'll promise to be good.[4]

Mrs. Natalie Robinson Cole, a teacher of fourth- and fifth-graders, in Los Angeles, reports, "I found myself learning more about these children and their lives than I could hope to learn in years in any other way."[5] Her first step was to give up thoughts of academic approach and artistic criteria of what it means to be creative. She was simply concerned with freeing her pupils to express themselves and believed that they could lead the way. She felt that their first writing was rather poor and lifeless, but then she conceived the idea of a wall newspaper. Youngsters whose work was judged to be meritorious had their work posted on the newspaper. Gradually, materials were composed that seemed truly creative, even though none of them seemed very remarkable.

Mrs. Cole felt that, while she was gaining understanding, the pupils were gaining self-respect. When she expressed interest in what pupils said and wrote, she felt rapport and friendliness growing stronger. It was not until the end of the third term that she felt she could encourage pupils to reveal their innermost feelings. She talked with them regarding the funny ideas that adults have about some of the difficulties she had experienced in her childhood, and the pupils wrote. Some of them thought it would be all right to have their pieces read to the class, but others wrote secrets, just for their teacher: "I don't like people who is teasing me, and lot of other thing, and I don't like the bedbug and don't like to stay home and I don't like people who call me skinnybone and Uncle Sam and dirty pig and a rat, and the worst they call me is a Jap."[6] Children, too, need to get things off their chests—to profit from catharsis.

Free writing has a double-barreled impact for the child. First, it helps him to get rid of the festering tensions that might otherwise break out in trouble. Second, "They [creative activities] permit the child to explore with impunity his confused and often resentful feelings about life experiences which he does not yet understand."[7] Too often the need for a child to satisfy his curiosity is thwarted by adult conceptions of propriety.

[4] *Ibid.*, p. 185.
[5] Natalie Robinson Cole, *The Arts in the Classroom*, New York: The John Day Company, Inc., 1940, p. 105.
[6] *Ibid.*, p. 130.
[7] William E. Henry in *Fostering Mental Health in Our Schools*, 1950 Yearbook, Association for Supervision and Curriculum Development, Washington: National Education Association, 1950, p. 258.

A third concomitant of creative writing, no less valuable to the child, is that it gives adults clues to the child's private world, which is such a powerful, though unseen, factor in motivation. A remedial teacher, of the Portland (Oregon) Schools, asserts, "We as remedial teachers, working with children having emotional-social blockings, feel that the creative expression of writing, drawing, painting, and the like offer clues for us in better understanding our children." Mary Padovan, visiting teacher, also of the Portland Schools says,

> Some of the children who are referred to us find it difficult in their first interviews to express their feelings and to discuss their problems. They are helped to do this by the visiting teacher in various ways. One of them is writing. They often can write what they feel either in story form, in poetry, or in connection with pictures which they draw. I have one girl who writes poetry when she feels sad. She doesn't understand why she has written it, but her poems are a clue to us.

However much this improved understanding may help the child, there is enrichment for the teacher, quite apart from increased professional competency. Says Mrs. Cole, "Through giving children confidence, the teacher will gain confidence, through sharing their troubles, her own heart will become lighter, through enriching their experience, she also will be enriched."[8]

Mrs. Hazel Van Cleve, a third-grade teacher, took her pupils to the Union Pacific shops to gather common experiences for doing classwork. Her report of the reactions of one boy illustrates the value of emphasizing creative writing.

> My third-grade "Roundhouse" takes all engines, in any condition in which they arrive, and attempts to recondition them for roadability. It is with this "Roundhouse" and with these seven- to nine-year-old engines that the experiments and experiences are taking place for this study.
>
> Johnny Engine was towed in with a pressure-damaged boiler, no headlight, and a lost toot. His father gave up golf—with cups and trophies attached—to help live his life. His mother lives for her family but said, when she brought him to school in his sixth year, that she could do nothing with him. He and his high school sister live on a semi-bickering basis at all times. An older boy, several doors down his street, physically derailed all small engines. Johnny saved his steam and made life miserable for his sister. He has a furnished basement room for his hermit existence where he dwells with bugs, snakes, and what have you. He could imitate a cricket and one bird but stood, with longing eyes, on the sidelines of all games and activities and would not sing a note.
>
> Water pours less frequently from his boiler these days, the pressure of his engine is rising, his whistle can toot four bird calls and innumerable songs, and his headlight was beaming when he handed me this.

[8] Cole, *op. cit.*, p. 137.

The Humming Bird

One sunny day in April
I saw a humming bird.
At first I saw his color
And then his hum I heard.
Of moss and twigs he built his nest.
He likes it the very best.

Johnny has other emotions to express:

"Once upon a time there was a train. His name was Chug Chug. He was a smart train. He lived in the Union Pacific Station and was one of the best trains. But one day something bad happened. He was coming to a cross track. He turned to the left and there coming toward him was a streamliner. He thought to himself, 'I wish I had turned to the right, then this would not have happened.' The two trains met with a big loud thundering crash. Chug Chug was repaired in a month and a half and from that day on he thought."

One may not look into his mind to see the dreams he dreams but creative writing is like a mirror, it reflects the dreams he dreams. Time, kindness, and understanding will open the book of his life, page by page, so that one may read what is written therein that one may help erase ugly marks of experience and straighten pages wrinkled by unthinking hands.[9]

Secondary-school Pupils Express Themselves. It is easier for some pupils to describe specific difficulties in written form than it is to talk about them. This is because the individual writes in privacy and hence does not feel any pressure from the physical presence of another. For example, a fourteen-year-old boy who was known to be having difficulty in his home situation was asked by his teacher to write about "An Ideal Parent." Her hope was that he would write not about his difficulties but about a desired solution. The boy wrote as follows:

The ideal parent should be understanding of boys and girls and should try to help them in a way in which not to offend or hurt their feelings. The parent should be able to play with the child and make him feel as though he is safe in bringing up any questions which he feels he should know. He should take his child to a baseball game sometimes and basketball, also to ice hockey sometimes too. The parent should take the boy on camping trips and let him go camping alone with his friends.

L. lived with his mother, his father having left them when L. was very small. His mother worked to support herself and the boy and, although she took definite interest in his work and activities, apparently was often

[9] Hazel Van Cleve, *Creative Writing as an Emotional Outlet for Children*, unpublished master's thesis, Portland, Ore.: Oregon State System of Higher Education, 1951, pp. 5–6, 35–36.

too tired to give the attention L. desired. The teacher felt that he relieved his frustrations by showing an ideal state of family existence, that
his dissatisfaction was mollified by his having shown the sort of family
life he would like to have. It is entirely possible that L. would have felt
disloyal if he had directly criticized his mother and would have continued to be restive if he had contained his feelings completely; but in
his writing he could "beat around the bush" by referring to "boys and
girls" and "the child."

Another example of the release through free writing of tensions generated by a family situation is afforded by J., a girl in her senior year.
This girl had often spoken to the teacher about her parents and about
both her older and younger sisters. There was no observable tension between J. and her older sister. In her writing, however, J. showed that she
felt that her own superiority in years should give her some decided
prerogatives over her younger sister. It became obvious in her writing
that at least some degree of tension was aroused by a violation of what
she regarded as her rights.

> An ideal younger sister should realize she is younger and doesn't
> deserve the same privileges her older sister has, such as staying out late.
> The ideal sister should realize that the older sister deserves more privi-
> leges and should wait her turn. The average sister doesn't however. She
> demands the same privileges her older sister has, which, if she gets them
> aren't good for her because she grows up too fast. Sometimes this can
> work the other way and keep the older sister from receiving privileges
> due her because of the younger sister.

No doubt J. felt better for having "taken down her hair." But another
facet of free writing is suggested by the above. Might not J.'s observation about an older sister suggest that J. has been receiving the very
privileges which she would like to deny her younger sister? The attempt
to get an answer to this question will lead the teacher to a better understanding of J. Moreover, a discussion of the possible interpretations of
what was written will help J. to achieve a better understanding of herself.

The teacher of another girl who had hostile feelings toward her
younger sisters reports that K. was entirely justified in writing as she did
about the sister, who was very well known to the teacher.

> An ideal sister would do her own washing and ironing and would
> not leave it for someone else to do. She would let you study in peace,
> not blast the radio or play the piano. She would not spend all the
> morning in the bathroom so you could have a chance. She would be
> cheerful about doing things with the family even if she preferred to do
> something else, and she would not get angry when told that she couldn't
> go out on a certain night. She would not complain about not having

enough clothes when she saw some other member of the family buying something she wanted. She would not pout.

K.'s mother is a widow and K. feels that she has a definite responsibility for helping affairs along. The teacher reported that she believed K.'s writing proved to be a real catharsis for the tension generated by her conflicting feelings—loyalty and responsibility for the family, as opposed to resentment against her spoiled and sulky sister.[10]

The three foregoing illustrations dealing with family situations might better be called *free* writing than *creative* writing. The writing of C. illustrates an aspect of writing involving fantasy and might more properly be called *creative*. C. was a senior of high intelligence and extreme shyness. She was so timid that she did not volunteer to talk in class and, when called on, spoke in a whisper even though she had the correct answer and an abundance of information to impart. Her friends reported that she had no dates. She was so quiet that it was doubtful whether boys noticed her. She was not particularly attractive physically, but she had a charming manner, which, unfortunately, was hidden from those who did not take time to get acquainted with her. The following was written by C. at the time the teacher was encouraging free writing. It shows that she felt what was so obvious to others.

> Just a few minutes ago, Jane found herself in third period class. Someone hurriedly asked her for some paper, and then he almost instantly returned it. Well, why doesn't he make up his mind? she thought, with an annoyed expression on her face.
>
> A hoarse whisper broke the silence between the teacher's questions. "Read it," said the squeaky voice.
>
> Then she saw a scrawl on the other side which was almost impossible to read because the ink had faded near the end, but two words couldn't have been clearer: "dance—Saturday?" The senior with the blond crew cut grinned bashfully across the aisle.
>
> "Me?" she asked unbelievingly.
>
> "Who else?" was the reply.
>
> She automatically nodded in the affirmative, turned her head, gulped loudly, and tried to look studious. The period finally came to an end. The blond shuffled along beside her giving a few vague details and then vanished. Her eyes followed the retreating figure.

C., without doubt, received a certain vicarious satisfaction from her fantasy, but she also received a more direct and constructive satisfaction. The teacher, without being alarmed about the degree of fantasy revealed in the writing, knew that it might easily be carried too far. She de-

[10] Janice Schukart, *Achieving a Better Understanding of Adolescent Problems through Creative Writing*, unpublished master's thesis, Portland, Ore.: Reed College, 1950, p. 40.

termined, since the rapport was high, to look more closely into the situation to find why the girl was so shy that she resorted to a make-believe boy friend. A private conversation revealed that the girl felt inferior because of an older brother who had distinguished himself in academic activities. Although her brother was only two years older, he was in his junior year at Stanford and had made a brilliant record in an engineering course. C.'s parents had never criticized her for lack of diligence or scholarship; yet in the presence of friends and relatives, it was always her brother who was the focal point of conversations about the family. She had acquired the feeling that she would never be able to equal her brother's record. The teacher was able to show C. that her contributions in class were valuable, that she was at the head of her class in examinations, and that she possessed a naturally warm social personality that could easily make her popular. The teacher made free use of praise in an attempt to compensate for the feelings of inferiority that were revealed by the girl's actions, further indicated in her writing, and objectified in their conversations. Before the end of the year, C. had become more active in class activities and was seen more frequently in groups of pupils in which boys were occasionally included.

Certainly creative writing and perhaps fantasy are evident in the writing of a fourteen-year-old junior-high-school lad who has felt the pain of social discrimination. One cannot read his poem without being convinced that P. was both *objectifying* his feelings and shrugging off the hurt at the same time.

> Pretty Anna May Malone
> Had a heart as hard as stone;
> Every year since she was eight
> She has been my best playmate.
>
> I half loved that Irish kid
> 'Til she said just what she did,
> Said for me her love was through
> 'Cause she'd heard I'm half a Jew.
>
> She doesn't need to feel high-toned
> 'Cause her dad kissed the blarney stone.
> I don't think I know it all
> 'Cause my dad had a wailing wall.
>
> Time will show you Anna May
> The big mistake you made today.
> It's the truth I'm half a Jew
> But that's the half that cared for you.

It is easy to conjecture that this might be a better world, one in which there were markedly fewer interpersonal actions and remarks, if more adults of today had been led by understanding teachers to express their feelings in writing, as P. did.

Even if it were denied that writing such as the foregoing samples does much, or even anything, to release tensions, it can hardly be questioned that writing gives an opportunity for rounding out one's personality through self-expression. In the following sample no tensions are apparent. Nevertheless, the teacher was rendering the pupil a mental health service by stimulating her to express her joy of living. The poem is a source of satisfaction to both teacher and pupil.

> We praise Thee, dear Lord, for the things of earth,
> For each dainty flower,
> For all of nature's beauties.
> We praise Thee, O Lord, for things above the earth,
> For the love of our Father,
> For the beauty of the skies,
> For all the things we may touch,
> For the beauty of things we may see.
> For all that surrounds us,
> Dear Lord, we thank Thee.
> For Thy bounteous goodness,
> Thy radiant love, Thy sweet forgiveness,
> Dear Lord, we thank Thee.

SUGGESTIONS FOR USING CREATIVE WRITING

It seems somewhat paradoxical to make suggestions for directing creative writing, inasmuch as freedom is a basic aspect of the technique. The success attained by any one teacher in the use of the technique will depend more upon his adaptation of the procedures than upon his ability to follow directions. If this precaution is kept in mind, some helpful suggestions, derived from the experiences of teachers, can safely be made.

Keep Criticism at a Minimum. Perhaps the communication of ideas would be simplified if first place were given to the idea instead of to the form of presentation. Instruction in spelling, punctuation, grammatical form, and logical presentation has its place but not to the extent of excluding something to communicate. Just as a father can break down his young son's interest in a game of catch by constantly pointing out errors and remarking that the lad is throwing like a girl, so the teacher can weaken a pupil's interest in expression by constantly criticizing form and usage. Teachers might well take a hint from the technique of some athletic coaches, who first let their tyros swim or play basketball or tennis and then, *only after a beginning has been made,* start to call attention to a detail or two at a time, taking care not to spoil the fun by overcoaching.

It is not expected that grade- and high-school students will equal the form and precision of a famous novelist or poet. It is worthwhile to consider that the grammatical details can become *aids* to the clear expression of ideas—ideas that have been nourished, encouraged, and cultivated through an understanding attitude on the part of the teacher.

Rapport Is Necessary for Free Expression. Rapport, a basic element in all effective teaching, is especially necessary if students are to reveal their inner selves in what they write. In addition to "knowing" through the cumulative data about his complete background, the teacher must know enough in general about the *age group* with which he is dealing to be able to recognize the seriousness of their feelings and responses. He must certainly maintain confidences.

It would not do for a teacher to make an assignment from which he wished to get understandings about pupils on the first day with a new class. Asking them to describe their pet peeves will not be a successful project until the pupils have gained, through contact, some confidence in their new teachers. Even after a period of acquaintance, it is unlikely that materials which possess diagnostic values will be obtained from pupils on the first or the second attempt. This is true not only because the teacher is relatively strange but also because the students have probably not had sufficient experience in considering their feelings objectively.

Maintain Balance between Nondirection and Prescription. It is necessary, in working toward creative writing, to give directions without being so explicit as to inhibit free expression. Thus, students would not be *told* to release their feelings in their writings or to purge their resentments by vehement expressions. In fact, it is well to keep from them the impression that an analysis of their motivations is being sought through their writing. Aside from telling the students to be frank in the expression of their feelings and ideas, it will be enough to suggest some topics from which they may make a selection, or ask them to choose a topic of their own if they are not satisfied with the suggestions. Topics which teachers have used with success include the following:

> My Ideal Boy (Girl) Friend
> A Good Teacher
> A School I Should Like to Attend
> My Biggest Wish
> What Makes a Good Sister (Brother)
> Things That Irritate Me
> My Pet Peeve
> How to Have Fun
> What Religion Does for Me

Other topics that fit the time, tenor of the class, and age level of the students will readily occur to the teacher.

Supplement Clues from Free Writing with Other Information. Free writing is suggested as but one source of information to be used as a *partial* explanation of behavior. Whether knowledge about the child precedes understanding his compositions, stories, and poems or whether information gleaned from the writing precedes an understanding of the individual is a debatable point. Nevertheless, insight into the behavior of a pupil can be gained from his writing, and his writing becomes more comprehensible when supplemented with knowledge about his home conditions, school progress, persisting sources of frustration, social adjustment, and physical handicaps or illness. It is not enough to know that K. (pages 339–340) resents the behavior of her sister; it is also vital to know that she has some justification for her feeling.

When rapport is high, free writing is most valuable when it is to serve as the subject of discussion, or the reason, for a personal interview. Emphasis should be upon further expression from the pupil and care must be exercised that the interview does not become an occasion for offering an overwhelming amount of tutorial advice. The teacher should, instead, be intent on asking questions which will lead to an extended unfolding of the thoughts the pupil may have. As he talks beyond the point of his writing, he will often come to a better understanding of his own problems.

The Writing Should Be Observed for What It Is. Free writing is a subjective report and should be regarded as such. The purpose is to find out how the student feels, not necessarily what the facts of the situation are. If anyone *feels* handicapped, if he *feels* that he is being discriminated against, if he *feels* that he suffers deprivation, the person who wishes to help him must regard these feelings as important aspects of the problem. When an individual is disturbed his feelings are often more important than the objective facts. In cases in which the person is unjustified in his feelings, they are still factors which must be considered.

The significance of discovering the individual's personal feelings regarding a situation is well illustrated in the case of a sixteen-year-old youth who lived in a mining community. He was handsome, had an admirable physique, and possessed athletic ability. He belonged in a superior group in intelligence and had a good school record. Actively sought by both boys and girls, he was responsive to their overtures. His home was average for the community, neither pretentious nor dilapidated. He had an attractive younger sister, of whom he seemed to be proud. His mother welcomed her son's friends, gave them ice cream, cookies, pie, or cake when they came to the house and then left the room, giving the youth free run of the rooms they wished to use. She was active in community and school affairs and still had time for her children. B.'s father, who was a hard worker, held a responsible position in the mine in which he was employed. He supplemented his income by preaching in the small local Protestant church. Certainly, from an objective view, there seemed to be nothing lacking in B.'s home situation. A case worker would have given the home situation a high rating.

But B.'s conduct indicated some deep-seated conflict. His schoolwork fell markedly, he became truant, he worried his parents deeply by frequently getting drunk, and he got into sexual difficulties with some recent graduates of the local high school. He was heartily condemned by the adults of his community, and his peers began to consider it somewhat risqué to associate with him. He was finally arrested for disturbing the peace in a drunken brawl in a pool hall. It was the juvenile officer to whom he was remanded who discovered the cause of B.'s troubles—a feeling of shame and resentment toward his father. It irritated him to be called "Preach," or preacher's son; therefore he had engaged in the alcoholic and sexual episodes to convince his peers that, whatever his father might be, he was certainly not a sissy. This case was not solved through writing, but it does show that the feelings are extremely significant, often more significant than the facts of the case—thus the reason for suggesting *free* writing.

PRECAUTIONS AND LIMITATIONS

Creative Writing Does Not Always Indicate a Problem. The value from creative writing does not accrue only to those with problems. Actually, freedom to express oneself in writing is of inestimable benefit to the "normally" developing individual. He can through writing enlarge his horizons, express the various facets of his personality, develop his capacities. Without doubt many children—perhaps the majority—can endure the trifling tensions and ordinary obstacles they meet. Free writing for them is not a matter of therapy; it is a prophylactic.

All children can thrill to the joy of accomplishment that accrues from recognized creative effort. Every child, and adult too, can clarify his thoughts and feelings about his milieu by capturing them in the written words. Every child can experience the joy of giving when his composition is read. Every child may expand his appreciation for the good, the true, and the beautiful by developing the precise vocabulary that fits his feelings. Every child can profit from knowing that his surges of appreciation for the beautiful are shared, commendable, and eminently worthwhile.

The feelings that are acted out in the creative process are, however, not always the socially disapproved resentments and hostilities. They are often the more positive feelings of love and affection which the child in his naïveté may be loathe to express more directly. They are often new and only partially formed ideas which the person cannot yet verbalize, but can only feel and experience. The creative process permits him to explore these new ideas and to live them out in a world uncritical and unbiased.[11]

Writing Does Not Always Provide Release. Particularly in the upper grades and in high school, one's writing may be the mere performance of a task. The child writes what he thinks the teacher will appreciate or what will earn him a good grade. Of course, this too is an indication of personality trends, but the real person is so completely hidden that to attempt to analyze the writing is futile. It is therefore necessary to bear in mind that too much should not be read into anyone's creative products. There is too great likelihood that the work may be stereotyped in terms of what the one who is writing thinks is expected of him. But writing is an approach that, for many, will provide some release, satisfy their creative urge, and permit them to explore their social and physical milieu with impunity.

READING FOR UNDERSTANDING AND RELEASE

Mental Health Values of Reading. Literature, if read and appreciated by elementary- and high-school pupils, can make contributions to their mental health by helping to supply basic needs. Good books can give one a feeling of adventure and new experiences. Some can help pupils to understand and improve their social relationships. Books can provide spiritual adventure and guidance, can help to console one in time of trouble, and can show the power and pervasiveness of ethical and moral principles.

Some books lift one's aspirations when he is selecting goals and activities. One can face the facts—the realities—of life through books and thus be better prepared for such exigencies when they become personal. Certainly, books provide one of the ways of making life fuller, more harmonious, happier, and more effective. However, not just any books will do this and our concern here will be to try to show the teacher how he can provide guidance in book selection for and by pupils.

Choosing Books for Children and Adolescents on a Personal Basis. Interest in books would best be begun in the home by parents who themselves do wholesome reading. But parents, like teachers, need guidance in

[11] Henry, *op. cit.,* p. 259.

selecting children's books. This is a difficult task with so many well-printed, attractively illustrated ones available. A simple criterion can be helpful: Good children's books must be good adult books; that is, if the book will appeal to children, it should also appeal to adults, e.g., *Alice in Wonderland, Black Beauty, Little Women.*

An adult, who has responsibility in shaping the reading interests of children, should spend some of his own free reading periods planning and preparing for constructive reading experiences. A teacher who has taught in all the grades from fourth to seventh consistently makes reading a part of the enjoyable experiences of her pupils. She reads aloud, she asks for reports and reactions, she suggests books, and she brings children books that are of special interest to them. Each year, for instance, she watches for the Newbery Award book (see page 349) and then, after study, she reads it aloud in class. This experience is a pleasurable one for pupils, as is attested to by the rapt attention given to the reading. She provides a model for oral presentation. She raises the level of thinking through discussion. One cannot know, of course, but the idea is inevitable—these stories help children in facing their own problems.

"Of the making of books there is no end" and the task of choosing from the plethora of authors and titles may seem insurmountable. There are some guides that provide directions, however. For instance, let it be said that past publication does not necessarily outdate the book. Hence, one's own experiences may serve as an indication. *That Year at Lincoln High* by Joseph Gollomb was fascinating to this author in his youth and years later drew an enthusiastic response from his teen-age son. Although the latter noted things that are now outdated (the score in basketball games was much lower than at present), the ideals expressed, the attitudes revealed, and the excitement are current.

Professional Resources as Book Guides. A second source of guidance might be—if one lives in a university town—the instructor of Children's Literature, who will typically be delighted to render assistance. Children's librarians in local libraries give similar aid. One's fellow teachers should be able to give substantial aid. Two sources of ready help are The Children's Book Council, Inc., 50 West 53d Street, New York, and The Association for Childhood Education International, 1200 Fifteenth Street, N. W., Washington 5, D.C.

Periodically in *The Saturday Review* there is a section on children's books that discusses recent publications in terms of age levels, interest areas, fiction, science, people, places, fantasy, humor, and so on.[12] Probably the best way to keep abreast of the best in children's literature is by

---

[12] See, for example, "Books for Young People," *The Saturday Review,* 43 (42): 30–31, Oct. 15, 1960.

referring to the *Children's Catalog*.[13] Not all children's books are listed in this catalogue, since to be included, a book must receive enough votes from a board of collaborators. Hence, being listed is indicative of merit, but in addition some books are starred and some are double-starred. The esteem of a double-starred book is indicated by Louisa May Alcott, *Little Women;* and the caliber of a single star is indicated by Sir James Matthew Barrie, *Peter Pan.* A bimonthly periodical devoted to literature for children is *The Horn Book*, which contains articles about authors, outstanding books, and discussions of the place of literature in the development of young persons. This magazine also contains a section of annotations on new books. Another section deals with new books for the high-school age; these books consist mainly of adult books that would appeal to the teen-ager. Major publishers advertise their most recent lists of titles for children and young people.

A book about books for parents and kindergarten teachers is *Books before Five*, the diary of a librarian turned mother.[14] It reveals some penetrating glimpses into the lives and development of children before they enter school. The countless ways in which books that are selected in terms of interest and maturity can help in progressive development are described. Another book about books for parents is *Bequest of Wings*,[15] which is the story of a family's pleasure in growing together with the aid of books. The author takes her title from Emily Dickinson, whose words express the convictions and belief of book lovers everywhere:[15a]

> He ate and drank the precious word,
> His spirit grew robust,
> He knew no more that he was poor,
> Or that his frame was dust.
> He danced along the dingy ways,
> And this bequest of wings
> Was but a book. What liberty
> A loosened spirit brings!
> —*Emily Dickinson*

Also by Annis Duff, of interest to both parents and teachers, is *Longer Flight;* its chapters are devoted to the use of books in the search for moral

---

[13] At the time of this writing the latest edition is *Children's Catalog: A Classified Catalog of 3,204 Children's Books Recommended for Public Libraries*, with an author, title, and subject index, 9th ed., rev., New York: The H. W. Wilson Company, 1956, for which the 1957 and 1958 supplements have also been published.

[14] Dorothy White, *Books before Five*, New York: Oxford University Press, 1956. 196 pp.

[15] Annis Duff, *Bequest of Wings*, New York: The Viking Press, Inc., 1946. 204 pp.

[15a] Centenary edition of *The Poems of Emily Dickenson*, Boston: Little, Brown & Company, 1930.

and social integrity, the magic of the theater for young and old, the joy of a beginning reader as he learns of the adventure in books, and the thrill of history. As children approach their teen years they are introduced to the classics in literature and to the helpful work which librarians do.[16]

A guide which teachers will find inspirational as well as specifically helpful is *Children and Books*.[17] Part 1 deals with the needs of children, choice of books in terms of these needs, and the backgrounds of children's literature. "Sing It Again," Part 2, is a discussion of mother-goose rhymes, ballads, verse, and poetry—all with illustrative examples which serve to guide the teacher's selections. Part 3 is devoted to folk tales, fables, and myths. Part 4 deals with the imaginative world of modern and historical fiction. "Stranger than Fiction," Part 5, is a description and illustration of the use of biography in expanding one's literary horizons. Science is also a part of the world that is stranger than fiction. Part 6 throws light on frequently asked questions about comic books, television, radio, and motion pictures.

The teacher who is looking for highly selected lists of books for children will find them in the Newbery Medal Books and the Caldecott Medal Books. The first is an annual award for "the most distinguished literature for children," and has been given since 1922. The second, given since 1938, is best picture book of the year. The awards are determined by a committee of librarians from the American Library Association which receives recommendations from librarians, teachers, and children. Information about the current awards is given in *Publishers' Weekly*.

Mental Health through Literature. Probably the first step in generating the necessary interest in reading is that of aiding in the development of skills that will make reading pleasurable. One likes to do what he can do well. Occasionally a poor reader will do more than average reading, but he is definitely the exception. Hence, teachers have the simultaneous task of teaching skills and fostering interests. Word attack, stress on vocabulary growth, and emphasis on the message and its implications will stimulate both skill development and interest. The teacher's own knowledge about and enthusiasm for books is fundamental—the reading lessons must be enjoyable.

The need for variety and for reality is seen even in the primary grades. Typically, the reading books describe a boy, a girl, a baby, a pet, and a father and mother who have unlimited time for children—everyone is always in the best of temper. All are neat and clean and live in a suburban home, apparently of the upper-middle class. There are no Negroes and no Orientals in the life that is portrayed. Even children object to this "all

[16] Annis Duff, *Longer Flight*, New York: The Viking Press, Inc., 1955. 269 pp.
[17] Mary Hill Arbuthnot, *Children and Books*, rev. ed., Chicago: Scott, Foresman and Company, 1957. 684 pp.

light and sweetness" theme. A variety of books, or a supplementary library, is a requisite in the first grade. This need is even more apparent as children grow and their paths of development diverge more widely. These considerations emphasize the importance of book selection as described above.

Since books supply answers to topics of interest, the pupil's own preferences should be honored. Here is an area where adult standards should not be allowed to intrude too prominently. One teacher in the sixth

FIG. 19. What is the difference between remedial and developmental reading? Does the teaching of reading skills have a place in the high school? Should good readers use such an instrument as is pictured here?

grade told about a girl who read rapidly, comprehendingly, and extensively, but everything she read was about horses. The teacher was concerned because of the lack of variety and tried to encourage reading on other subjects, but to no avail. She later learned, when the girl was in the eighth grade, that the avid interest in horses had finally passed and the girl was reading widely and still had enthusiasm. The sixth-, seventh-, and eighth-grade teachers had no explanation, but all had learned a little lesson about patience in waiting on the slow processes of growth.

Particular and individual problems in mental health can be approached through recommending specific books to children. It would be impractical, within the scope of this book, to mention specific authors and titles, but there are three books that can supply a handy reference for locating such books. One is *The Wonderful World of Books*,[18] another is *Children and Books*,[19] and the third is *Reading Ladders for Human Relations*.[20]

Mental health is derived from many things, experiences, and thoughts. Step by step our lives are built for better or worse. Some words of Emerson suggest some of the progress which may be made with the aid of books:

> We owe to books those general benefits which come from high intellectual action. Thus, I think we often owe to them the perception of immortality. They impart sympathetic activity to the moral power. Go with mean people, and you think life is mean. Then read Plutarch and the world is a proud place, peopled with men of positive quality, with heroes and demigods standing around us who will not let us sleep.
> —*Ralph Waldo Emerson*

Teachers who have the mental hygiene point of view may encourage the taking of these small steps toward maximum self-realization by revealing the encouraging messages contained in wisely selected books.

SUMMARY

Creative writing is only one of many ways to secure improved behavior and closer identification with school tasks and to achieve a better understanding of children. Its significance is derived from the difficulty of stating one's problems orally, from the need for creative activity in a mass culture, and from the need for release from tensions.

Creative writing can be used at all school levels, even the preschool and primary levels, where, however, the teacher must do the recording for the children. High-school teachers who have gained rapport with their students feel that written work allows pupils to release tensions that they are somewhat dubious about expressing—yet which, once expressed, provide a means of gaining balanced activity and wider perspective.

Suggestions for capitalizing on the advantages of creative writing are simple but important. It is necessary to keep criticism of form, punctuation, and usage at a minimum, though pupils, nonetheless, often ask for help as they discover that they have ideas they wish to convey to others. It is vital that teachers should not show shock at the ethical values indicated in writings. It is necessary to give some direction, to suggest ideas

[18] Alfred Stefferud (ed.), *The Wonderful World of Books*, New York: The New American Library of World Literature, 1952, pp. 53–57, 123–135.

[19] Arbuthnot, *op. cit.*, pp. 404–424, 558–573.

[20] Staff of Intergroup Education in Cooperating Schools, *Reading Ladders for Human Relations*, rev. and enl. ed., Washington: American Council on Education, 1948. 86 pp.

and themes, but not to make prescriptions. Writing must be observed for what it is—a limited view of a many-faceted personality. It does not always indicate a problem. Nor does writing always serve as a release valve. Even pupils who do write freely and creatively must have other avenues of expression.

Reading, as an approach to mental health, lends perspective in evaluating one's problems, grasping new ideals, and expanding experiences. To serve these functions, materials must be selected to suit the age, maturity, interests, and background experiences of the reader. Not only must books be suitable, but the key adults must be enthusiastic about books and children. Books about books will serve to give parents and teachers the needed guidance.

STUDY AND DISCUSSION EXERCISES

1. Explain the meaning of projective techniques, using the root of the word in your explanation. In what way is writing a projective technique?
2. Describe some situation in which you have used writing (not necessarily compositions or poems) to relieve pent-up feelings.
3. Why is it so necessary to have supplementary information about a pupil when attempting to interpret his writing?
4. What are the names of some books you have enjoyed when you were a child? Do you think they would appeal to young people today?
5. Elaborate the statement "There is no expression without impression" in relation to reading and creative writing.

SUGGESTED ADDITIONAL READINGS

Applegate, Mauree, *Helping Children Write*, Scranton, Pa.: International Textbook Company, 1949. 173 pp.

Suggestions for teaching and interpreting children's writing and for encouraging their productivity are given.

Arbuthnot, Mary Hill, *Children and Books*, rev. ed., Chicago: Scott, Foresman and Company, 1957, pp. 2–36.

Children's needs which can approach fulfillment through books and the role of adults in generating literary appreciation are discussed.

Cole, Natalie Robinson, *The Arts in the Classroom*, New York: The John Day Company, Inc., 1940. 137 pp.

This book would be pertinent reading for the chapter on art, but it is included here for the very fine chapter dealing with creative writing.

Witty, Paul A., "The Improvement of Reading Abilities" in *Adult Reading*, 55th Yearbook, Part II, National Society for the Study of Education, Chicago: University of Chicago Press, 1956, pp. 251–273.

This chapter will be of interest to teachers in terms of their own development of reading skills. High-school teachers will find, in addition, some suggestions for improving their professional work.

CHAPTER 16

DRAMA, PLAY, AND DANCE AS ANALYSIS AND THERAPY

Some of the many techniques for understanding pupils and guiding them to fuller realization of their potentialities will be favored by some teachers. Other teachers, because of their unique backgrounds, will prefer different techniques. However, dramatic presentation has been used as a teaching method—particularly effective in the social studies—at all levels of education. Psychodrama and sociodrama are approaches to understanding which have been praised by many who have given them a trial. The "dramatic" approach has settled many difficult problems of interpersonal relationships.

Role playing is effective, it is easy, and it is enjoyable. Expensive equipment is not necessary; in fact, it is not advisable. No extensive preparation is needed. The ingredients are simply a teacher who is willing to try something new and a few students who would like to have some fun. *Play and psychodrama* are opportunities for the expression of difficulties which are too complex for the individual to express directly in words. *Play and drama* permit the expression of vaguely formulated feelings that in more formalized situations could not be expressed. The freedom of the situation permits the individual to reveal his feelings without fear of censure.

Play analysis and play therapy are, likewise, techniques for understanding and creative expression. Personality analysis through play is an attempt to understand pupils' motivations by observing them in the untrammeled activity of play. Play therapy is the opening of an opportunity for the child to get rid of tensions by projecting his feelings in the neutral situation of make-believe.

ROLE PLAYING IN THE CLASSROOM

Definition of Terms. *Role playing* means simply that a given person is assuming the status, actions, and feelings of another. It should be distinguished from *role taking* which is the studied and rehearsed assumption of a character in a formal play or drama where one follows dialogue and actions with little improvisation.[1] *Role playing includes both psychodrama and sociodrama.* Briefly, *the former has to do with personal, or individual, problems; the latter is concerned with social, or group, problems and processes.*

Psychodrama denotes a situation in which an individual has an opportunity to live through some problem he has encountered. It involves physical action, which goes beyond mere verbal expression or relatively passive listening. Psychodrama is concerned with the problem of a particular individual, but the activity involved must necessarily take place in a social situation. Spontaneity is an essential element of the process. The individual, to as great a degree as possible, must be freed from the inhibitions of adhering to prescribed form and content. He must be freed from feeling a need to have his actions approved, *if* he is to be spontaneous in action. Formally planned actions and precise words, though these are characteristic of drama, are not a part of the situation involved in psychodrama. However, the situation should be approximately described, but detailed prescription must be avoided. Psychodrama, then, may be defined as an unstructured but not unplanned role-playing situation in which a given individual actively and spontaneously lives through a problem he is experiencing.

Sociodrama is an extension of psychodrama. The elements involved are much the same, except that sociodrama is primarily concerned with a social dilemma or defect in social functioning. It is essentially a "living through" of experiences common to group members which have left blocked and buried emotional responses.

The distinction between psychodrama and sociodrama is tenuous since both must necessarily involve more than one person. Both are projective techniques (see Chapter 14) in that the participants express themselves freely and spontaneously. Since directions are at a minimum and the words used are expressions of the situation as viewed by participants, the dramatic production assumes the structuring given by the actors. *What one does is thus a projection of himself.*

Elements Involved in Role Playing. Freedom is an essential aspect of the psychodramatic technique. This includes space for freedom of movement, as well as psychological freedom. A cleared space on the floor will suffice, but it is advantageous to use a raised platform. The elevation adds to the impression that the situation is not a duplication of one's own status. Moreover, the teacher must explain that it is essential to act and speak spontaneously and that no censure or punishment will result from portrayals.

[1] Gertrude A. Boyd, "Role Playing," *Social Education,* 21:267–269, 1957.

The more characters can be willingly drawn from the group, the better. No pressure should be placed on the individual for whom the psychodrama is designed to get him to participate. It is to be hoped that, as he sees the other youngsters having fun, he will wish to take part too. There should be as many actors as the stage and the situation will accommodate; the remainder of the group are called upon for suggestions, for observations, and for evaluation. All the members of the group should feel that they have a part in the production. The objective for the players and for the teacher is not that of dramatic entertainment but communication.

The teacher should define the situation but should not suggest any solutions. When the general nature of the problem is understood, he should step aside and allow the actors to improvise. Words of encouragement are in order, but suggestions or questions are likely to thwart spontaneity and inhibit free activity.

The essential elements involved in psychodrama, when it is used as an approach to the resolving of social conflicts, may be summarized as follows: (1) Setting the scene by selecting for study something the youngsters have read or something to parallel or duplicate an actually experienced conflict; (2) previewing the story or verbally reconstructing the incident, preparatory to having role players volunteer; (3) the presentation of the scene by pupils; (4) analysis by the group of the situation as it was played by the actors; (5) reenactment of the conflict, with a view to improving the relationships; (6) teacher-pupil discussion and evaluation of the patterns of behavior which were witnessed.

Role playing gives the youngster a chance to practice in a neutral setting, where he can perform without danger of failure. Parents have used the technique in preparing their children for a trip to the dentist or in anticipation of a tonsillectomy. Teachers can use it to prepare for some new experience; for example, to practice desirable conduct on a long bus trip, proper behavior on a conducted tour of an industrial plant, or the like. It has been observed that there is considerable carry-over from the practice scene to the actual situation. It is this carry-over that makes role-playing techniques so significant a tool in teaching. In addition, there is the value of added variety in teaching methods. Individuals gain real insight when they deal with definite, perceivable, and concrete situations, instead of depending upon verbal abstractions. Instead of the teacher's moralizing about the distinction between right and wrong, the pupils themselves modify their behavior by participating in a situation in which approved responses may be exemplified or disapproved responses may be objectified.

Objectives of Role Playing. A major purpose of role playing is to avoid the accumulation of tensions, which are an inevitable part of vigorous living. It seeks to replace the use of defense mechanisms (fantasy, over-compensation, delinquency, excessive irritability) with more construc-tive approaches to difficulties. Thus, sociodrama is an attempt to en-courage harmless expressions of partially formed feelings of hostility or apprehensiveness.

Sociodrama, as a teaching technique, is an instrument of effective moti-vation and a means of developing truly sympathetic understanding. An-other educational objective is to encourage creative expression. In view of the prevalence of commercialized, routine, and passively receptive kinds of leisure-time pursuits, it is increasingly important that creative ac-tivities become highly specific educational objectives.

Psychodrama is another approach to the meeting of individual differ-ences. There are some who will find verbal expression an easy and natural response. Some youngsters are capable of painting or drawing situations that give the teacher a better understanding of them. Others are willing and able to respond in a counseling situation. But no one technique can satisfactorily reach all children. Even if these observations were not true, there would still be the advantage of presenting a challenging variety of meaningful situations to relieve monotony.

Psychodrama, as can thus be seen, has a threefold objective: It is a means of diagnosing the vaguely felt difficulties of some individuals; it is designed to provide therapy through the active release of tensions in a situation where freedom is encouraged; and it affords an excellent learn-ing situation because it involves personal participation.

CONDUCTING ROLE-PLAYING SESSIONS

Preparation for Role Playing. Whatever the grade level in which the psychodramatic technique is to be used, there should be a discussion of the nature of the project. It deals with problems with which all class members are in some way acquainted. It offers a chance to act in the situations as the pupils would spontaneously behave. Situations and characters are taken out of life. It is a way of learning how others feel. These factors are brought into relief through discussion and questioning rather than by telling. As the pupils get experience in role playing, the significance of what they are doing should be reiterated, so that there may be an increasing understanding of what is being sought.[2]

The theme for the psychodramatic presentation must be one that involves persons who feel somewhat as the would-be performers feel. The theme might come as the result of what the pupils are studying in school; that is, perhaps the life of an immigrant, a visit to an orphanage, the employment of a member of some minority group. It might come

[2] Jenora Boniface, "Role-playing in the Kindergarten," *Grade Teacher*, 76:31, October, 1958.

as the result of some incident that has occurred on the playground or some incident that has made the headlines in the newspapers. Such topics as Our New Baby, How the Safety Patrol Works, and What We Do on Halloween, have been used in the lower grades. Perhaps a story that is read and discussed may be used, or the theme may come as the result of the discussion of some incident a pupil has related.

The foregoing indicates that a *representative* situation must be chosen. The next requirement is that the pupils must want to take part. After the situation has been described, the teacher will call for volunteers for the various characters. If any youngster says that he does not feel like playing, that is sufficient reason for his being excused, though the teacher should look for a chance to involve him in the situation sometime later, perhaps in a different role from the one he had shunned.

The third requirement concerns the attitude of the teacher. Not only the students, but the teacher, too, must feel enthusiastic about the presentation, so that an atmosphere of freedom may be created. The results will be unsatisfactory if the pupils feel that they must participate, or that they must act in a way that will gain the approval of the teacher.

Selecting the Theme. Sociodrama involves a warming-up process. This may be done in a variety of ways, depending on the cultural situation and the maturity of the pupils. It involves an answer to the question, "What are your problems?" but these words *must* be circumvented. The following questions representative of the sociodramatic technique are suggested by Helen Hall Jennings:

1. What situations are there in which you think you don't now know how to deal with what happens and in which you wish things would happen differently? *When does this kind of situation come up and who is in it with you?*

2. In what situations do you find someone doesn't understand you as well as you would like?

3. In what situations do you find someone understands you very well, just as much as you would like?

4. In what situations do you find it hard to decide what to do or to make up your mind what to do or say—seem not able to express yourself?

5. In what situations do you go right ahead and have no difficulty making up your mind what to do or say?

6. What situations come up which make you angry or very much annoyed?

7. What situations come up in which someone gets very annoyed or angry at you?

8. What situations happen to you which make you very happy?

9. What situations happen to you which make you very sad?[3]

[3] Helen Hall Jennings, "Sociodrama as Educative Process" in *Fostering Mental Health in Our Schools*, 50th Yearbook, Association for Supervision and Curriculum Development, Washington: National Education Association, 1950, pp. 271–272.

It can be seen from the above that in sociodrama there is an attempt to make the situation quite specific. The characters—age, sex, and status—are carefully defined. The situation is clearly outlined. The exact locale of the incident is determined. But the actions to be portrayed and the words to be spoken are not discussed: these are to be an outcome of the spontaneous feelings of the participants.

Enacting the Situation. There can be no prescription at this point. The participants must be allowed and *encouraged* to portray what they feel. It is not time to stress grammatical correctness or to censure actions or feelings. In fact, it is desirable for the participants to vent their feelings, because it is through this release that they get a better understanding of themselves and others.

The Followup. After the initial presentation, the teacher encourages a discussion and criticism of what has been portrayed. Further analysis of the situation and the actions is made. Recommendations for improvement are suggested and discussed. A second presentation is then prepared and a new cast of characters is selected. The chosen ones must again be from among volunteers. Perhaps by this time some of those who were originally reticent may wish to participate; if so, then they must be put in roles somewhat removed from those they would be taking in the real situation. Repetition of the scene followed by discussion and analysis will contribute toward thorough learning of the situation, which will make for the greatest transfer into the real problems of the pupils.

An Illustrative Example of Sociodrama. A group of sixth-grade boys were playing a game of football on the school ground. A Japanese boy in tackling one of the participants tore the latter's new Roy Rogers shirt. The owner of the shirt was very much disturbed, but although he was strong, he was too cautious to engage in battle with the Japanese. It was easy for him, a recognized leader in the group, to enlist the aid of some of his mates in thoroughly roughing up the unfortunate offender. When the boys returned to the classroom, the teacher realized that something had happened, but she asked no questions. When the story leaked out in a few days, the teacher felt that an injustice had been done. She decided to use the psychodrama to see if the situation could be clarified. She asked whether the pupils would like to put on a little skit, and many thought it would be fun. Next she outlined a situation—"a little Negro boy has just entered school and has few friends. Who would like to take the part of the Negro?" One of the pals of the boy with the torn shirt volunteered. "Our scene is in the art room, where there are several groups working; some are making a cooperative mural. I'd like to have three boys work on this mural." Volunteers were obtained. "Two other boys are working on a model airplane. Who will they be?" Torn shirt and another wanted that role. "Now our Negro is by himself, working on some finger painting, and after working awhile, he spills some paint and it splashes on the new trousers that one of the mural workers is planning to wear to a scout pack meeting immediately after school. You take it from there."

The boys knew their teacher and they entered the situation heartily. There was a resentful response from the wearer of the "soiled trousers." And the finger painter responded in kind. Others got into the scene and there was some pushing. After a few minutes the rest of the class was asked to criticize and comment. Some immediately pointed out that the spilling was accidental. Arguments ensued, but they were hopeful rationalizations rather than convictions. The scene was replayed with new participants, though the teacher said that the original players had participated enthusiastically. When the scene was replayed, it was acknowledged that soiled trousers had been hurt but that he might be more gentlemanly in his behavior. The offender expressed regret over the incident and volunteered to help clean up.

The teacher was not content to let the lesson be indirect. She proceeded to discuss the situation of the torn shirt as she had heard it. There were some attempts at justifying the rough retaliation, but the consensus was that the action had been unjust. The leader of the group, finally admitting that he had been wrong, decided to apologize and shake hands. His action was acclaimed by students and teacher.

The foregoing incident is not intended to furnish a pattern but to indicate that the technique is relatively simple, as far as classroom use is concerned, though correction of a chronic situation or some deep-seated personality trait would require more extensive treatment. The teacher was willing to try, she had previously planned, but she also had to improvise. Once the scene was set, however, the pupils took over competently and with commendable results. The situation could have been occasioned by some act of discourtesy, by failure to carry out a designated and reasonable responsibility, or by an argument over who should have first choice in using a reference simultaneously sought by two pupils.

Role Playing as an Instructional Technique. Psychodrama and sociodrama can be used as supplements to other teaching mediums. Youngsters can be encouraged to show how they would like orchestra members to act when they come from another school to present a program. This will give them insight as to how to behave when they are the visitors. Understanding and feeling for others can be improved. This may involve a thoughtful attitude toward a stutterer, someone who has cerebral palsy, or a crippled child who is to become a member of their class. The class can be helped to realize how any newcomer can be made more comfortable.

Role playing can be used to promote emotional control. Youngsters will profit from seeing how their own temper tantrums, pouting, pushing, and fighting appear in the eyes of their classmates. Emotional control may also be improved through the tension release that is provided in the vicarious activity of dramatic play. Conflict situations can be resolved by seeking improved avenues of approach (though this may not be an aim of the pupils). This was seen in the torn-shirt situation. Other conflicts may involve obedience to the teachers, respecting somebody else's property rights, and priority in the use of classroom equipment.

The learning situations that have become routine may be enlivened by the acting out of some of the supplementary aspects, e.g., historical and literary incidents. This will have the added advantage of stimulating spontaneous and creative responses.

Dramatic situations are frequently used to aid in the overcoming of fears. The pupil's attitude toward academic examinations or visual, dental, and medical examinations might be depicted. The pupil's attitude toward the principal might properly become the subject of role-playing techniques.

DEVELOPMENTAL, ANALYTICAL, AND THERAPEUTIC VALUES OF PLAY

Play, during childhood, is a serious business. It takes a long time for a child to organize his experiences and to fit people, objects, and events into categories and concepts so familiar to adults. His fumbling efforts often frustrate a child who lives in a world too big and resistant. But in play he can manipulate, organize, rapidly change, and rearrange his smaller world of toys and materials; and if given the time, materials, and opportunity to experiment in his own way, he can find himself, right himself when he has gone astray, and gradually learn how to get along with himself and with others in a large and complex world.[4]

It is the purpose of this section to acquaint the reader with the results of contemporary thinking and experimentation in the area of play as a tool for better education and as an avenue toward more vigorous mental health. Suggestions are given for utilizing play as something more than physical exercise—though that, too, is of real importance.

Using Play for Understanding. Play, as a projective technique, gives the observer clues regarding the player's motivations.

You can learn from what the children play. Give them ample time for make-believe. This will tell you where they are ripe to go ahead.

[4] Lawrence K. Frank in Ruth E. Hartley, Lawrence K. Frank and Robert M. Goldenson, *Understanding Children's Play*, New York: Columbia University Press, 1952, p. ix.

It can suggest the books they will get the most out of hearing; the trips they are ready for you to take them on; the ideas they want to talk over and develop.

Children need play-time and you need it too. This is listening and seeing and observation-time for you. You pick up clues on where they are most ready to begin.[5]

As the teacher watches a baseball contest, a game of tag, or youngsters playing house, he will see that some are characteristically hostile and noncooperative while others are friendly and cooperative. The behavior in such situations is not invariably a symptom of personality orientation; however observation does create an awareness of what to look for. Hostility and obstreperousness are not native endowments but are clearly the results of experiences and reactions to experiences that are peculiar to the individual.

Knowing the child's behavior pattern, the teacher can devise play situations that will reveal more clearly the advantages or handicaps the child has encountered. For example, a group of primary youngsters can be encouraged to play house. Some who play mothers will be kind to their doll-children, will talk to them, and humor them when they "cry." Others will be cross, will spank their "babies," and threaten them with "bad men" or with promises to put them to bed. The boys who play father will help with the dishes, rock the "baby," and converse about what went on during the working day. Other "fathers" will settle down in a chair to read and will loudly demand silence of others in the household. These things the teacher already knows, having seen such play activities many times. What is not so thoroughly appreciated is that such scenes give valuable insight into behavior. Consequently, some teachers (and some parents, too) have a tendency to try to correct behavior by suggesting, "That's not the way to act toward your little girl," "It would be nicer if you spoke kindly toward your husband," or "You should try to make everybody in the home happy."

Mental health is much more likely to be improved if teachers and parents were to reflect on the significance of the statements "Child behavior reflects parental handling" and "Pupils' actions reflect teacher attitudes." The clues obtained from play situations would lead to a more thorough search for the fundamental causes of undesirable behaviors. Improved behavior could then result from the removal of aggravating situations, instead of depending on futile platitudes, such as "People will not like you unless you are nice."

[5] James L. Hymes, Jr., *A Pound of Prevention*, New York: New York Committee on Mental Hygiene of the State Charities Aid Association, 1947, p. 54.

The film *This Is Robert*[6] shows, among other things, play as a means of improved understanding. Robert, aged five or six, was given a sizable jar of cold cream, which was then placed on a large sheet of paper. Next he was covered with an apron and was told simply, "Do what you want with it." He proceeded vigorously to spread the cold cream all over the paper, then he skated in it, placed a dab or two on the wall, and then began to work on the floor beyond the confines of the paper. The interpretation of this action, coupled with similar observances in other play situations and supplemented with objective information, was that Robert felt the need to explore to the utmost the boundaries of his freedom. He wanted to see just how far he could go before being controlled. Here was only a *clue*—the cause of his need to find the limits of freedom was undetermined. Investigation indicated that he was the son of professional parents, that his care was largely turned over to a succession of nursemaids and to grandparents who were at times indulgent and at times demanding. His reaction was to find out in every situation how far he could go before being reprimanded. A step toward remedying this tendency was a talk with the parents as to the need for a healthier regime. Further, it was felt that there would be some improvement from the catharsis that was afforded in the permissiveness of his many play and school activities.

Basic Principles of Play Therapy. The teacher's responsibility for a number of pupils makes it impractical to attempt to transform the classroom into a play-therapy situation. However, it will be instructive to examine the basic principles of permissiveness and acceptance, which the successful therapist must recognize and utilize, and to seek some approximation of them. The following items tend to promote both the therapeutic and prophylactic aspects of play:

1. The therapist must develop a warm, friendly relationship with the child, in which good rapport is established as soon as possible.

2. The therapist accepts the child exactly as he is.

3. The therapist establishes a feeling of permissiveness in the relationship so that the child feels free to express his feelings completely.

4. The therapist is alert to recognize the *feelings* the child is expressing and reflects those feelings back to him in such a manner that he gains insight into his behavior.

5. The therapist maintains a deep respect for the child's ability to solve his own problems if given an opportunity to do so. The responsibility to make choices and to institute change is the child's.

6. The therapist does not attempt to direct the child's actions or conversation in any manner. The child leads the way; the therapist follows.

7. The therapist does not attempt to hurry the therapy along. It is a gradual process and is recognized as such by the therapist.

[6] New York University Film Library, New York.

8. The therapist establishes only those limitations that are necessary to anchor the therapy to the world of reality and to make the child aware of his responsibility in the relationship.[7]

A look at the above principles, sound ones for mental hygiene in general, shows that many of them have been anticipated in other parts of this book. There is a need for an atmosphere of friendliness—which is all too frequently absent. In discussing human needs the value of acceptance has been stressed. The necessity for giving the pupil an appropriate degree of freedom, permissiveness, has been mentioned as a basic ingredient of harmonious growth processes. While "reflecting back" the feelings of the child, as mentioned above, has previously not been stressed, stress has been placed instead—as was necessary—upon the worth of a sincere and continuous effort to understand the feelings of children. Respect for the child's ability to solve his own problems has been anticipated in the passages devoted to freedom and the granting of responsibility. Although the idea of not attempting to influence the child's action cannot be put to use in all phases of classroom work, the importance of free expression is strongly emphasized in the chapters dealing with art mediums and creative writing. The futility of hurrying has been specifically stressed in the incidental discussions about fundamental characteristics of the growth process. The necessity for imposing limitations—but only those which are just and proper in terms of children's needs—has been treated in the chapter on constructive discipline.

It thus becomes apparent that implementing, to some degree, these basic principles of play therapy is not impossible. Many of them have been, and are being, utilized by classroom teachers in their daily work. Virginia Mae Axline gives point to this generalization when she says, "Looking about for the prophylactic measures necessary to prevent serious maladjustment on the part of the pupils, the schools have incorporated in their programs some very admirable developments."[8] She encourages teachers to attempt to adopt, or at least to experiment with, them. "Yes, the therapeutic principles have implications for educators. They bring forth unbelievable results. Teachers are invited to try them out, if they haven't already done so many, many times."[9]

Play as Group Therapy. One of the recognized functions of education is the improvement of group relationships. Growth and development of individuals is greatly influenced by group values, feelings, and attitudes. The treatment of the mentally ill has been approached through tech-

[7] Virginia Mae Axline, *Play Therapy*, Boston: Houghton Mifflin Company, 1947, pp. 75–76. (Each of these principles, summarized in her Chap. 7, is elaborated in Chaps. 8–15, pp. 77–138.)

[8] *Ibid.*, p. 141.

[9] *Ibid.*, p. 159.

niques known as *group therapy*, and its effectiveness has been proved in many instances by marked improvement. The aim of such treatment is to bring about identification of the individual with such groups as the family, the play group, or members of the class. Fundamentally, the technique consists in giving the individual an opportunity to be himself freely, without fear of censure or disapproval.

Of course, the classroom teacher cannot be a true therapist, because his responsibility to the class precludes allowing children who are markedly maladjusted to do just as they please. "For anyone who has had much experience with normal children, especially in the atmosphere of a crowded classroom with the ever-present necessity of enforcing discipline, the assumption of these attitudes may prove particularly difficult."[10] However, devising play situations in which children are permitted to act freely, even for limited periods, may serve to give the teacher insight into the motivations of some who are not marked deviates and will allow the child the opportunity to express some of his feelings and get rid of some of his tensions. He will, as the result of seeing how his projected feelings influence others, be taking a step toward his own self-understanding.

The elements of group-play therapy are few in number. No individual need be aware that he is being studied. He is simply one of the participants. The teacher is calm, poised, and friendly with the participants but does not give praise for either words or actions. The atmosphere is one of permissiveness within limits of propriety. The teacher is alert to the expression of feelings and reflects them back to the child so that the child may understand their significance. Reflecting the child's feelings requires neither criticism or approval. It is merely a means of emphasizing the child's expressions. "You do not like your sister," "You are getting along fine," and "You want to make someone angry" are statements which do reflect his feelings to him, but the statements imply no criticism. As the child projects his feelings through play situations, he gradually gains a better understanding of the effect of his feelings on others.

Play as a Teaching Device. Play techniques have been successfully used as an approach to the improvement of learning processes. Robert E. Bills experimented with retarded readers, some of whom gave evidence of emotional maladjustment and some of whom were regarded as well adjusted. In both instances, he concluded that reading improvement could take place in a relatively short time by capitalizing on the basic principles summarized in the above section.

Taking a group of third-graders who were retarded in reading and who manifested emotional maladjustment, Bills worked with them indi-

[10] Lydia Jackson and Kathleen M. Todd, *Child Treatment and the Therapy of Play*, 2d ed., New York: The Ronald Press Company, 1950, p. 56.

vidually and in groups with the play technique. For the first three weeks, the children worked with the experimenter in forty-five-minute individual sessions once a week. During the last three weeks, he had individual sessions and group sessions; thus, during the entire six weeks' period each child had about six individual sessions and two or three group sessions (depending on regularity of attendance). Both group and individual sessions were of forty-five minutes each.

> As a result of play therapy experience it was concluded: (1) significant changes in reading ability occurred as a result of the play therapy experience, (2) personal changes may occur in as little as six individual and three group play therapy sessions, and (3) there appears to be no common personality maladjustment present in this group of retarded readers.[11]

He felt that the improvement was due to the release of emotional tensions in general, which enabled the pupil to use his natural abilities to fuller advantage.

Bills later experimented with retarded readers who gave no marked evidence of emotional maladjustment, though there were in some cases minor personality disturbances. The results were similarly encouraging.

> (1) Significant increases in reading ability resulted from a nondirective therapy treatment of the emotional maladjustments which some retarded readers exhibit. (2) The gains in subject matter ability are directly proportional to the amount of emotional maladjustment present in the child. (3) When a child gains from nondirective therapy his gain is well-rounded and not specific to any one subject matter field.[12]

The last point is of particular interest to the classroom teacher, since it indicates that the personality strength obtained from an atmosphere of permissiveness, friendliness, acceptance, and leisureliness tends to promote all-round adjustment. This adjustment makes it possible for the child to capitalize more fully on his potentialities and thus to give a good account of himself.

Equipment also has significance. It has been found that an approach to disturbed children in clinics is to provide toys, crayons, paper, and chalkboard so the child may busy himself with these until rapport has been established.[13] Since play is so important to children, it seems that

---

[11] Robert E. Bills, "Nondirective Play Therapy with Retarded Readers," *Journal of Consulting Psychology*, 14:148, April, 1950.

[12] Robert E. Bills, "Play Therapy with Well-adjusted Retarded Readers," *Journal of Consulting Psychology*, 14:249, August, 1950.

[13] Hyman S. Lippman, *Treatment of the Child in Emotional Conflict*, New York: McGraw-Hill Book Company, Inc., 1956, pp. 44–45.

similar approaches might be used in dealing with low achievers in classrooms; i.e., instead of driving straight ahead with academic work, approach it through permissiveness and play.

Many speech problems are caused—or, at least, aggravated—by emotional pressures. When children detect disapproval of their vocal expressions, they come to think of themselves as being disapproved and condemned. But in the play atmosphere they gradually realize that they need not be perfect in order to be accepted. When they are loved and respected in spite of their imperfections, they gain a feeling of security that makes them more eager to show improvement that will be commended.

Play as a Builder of Morale. There are many profitable uses of play techniques in the lower grades. The make-believe situations that are spontaneously created by children can be observed with an eye to discovering their inner feelings. If they wish to handle their blocks and dolls roughly in the kindergarten, it may be well for them to feel free to do so. Quite possibly, this will be better than storing up the negative feelings, only to have them burst forth in outright attack on playmates. In the elementary grades the children can express their feelings in the games they play. Boys should be permitted to play roughly with one another in their football games and cowboy and robber activities. Hasty interference in the name of socialized conduct can prevent girls from giving expression to their feelings in their free-play activities.

It will be necessary, in the classroom, to place restrictions on the expression of hostilities, but this should not call for complete repression. The teacher should accept the child as he is. Perhaps he is antagonistic and resentful and manifests laziness. But his behavior can be changed, and it will be most likely to change in a favorable direction if he is not rejected because of his present objectionable conduct. The teacher can be friendly. The resultant warmth will do much to provide for those individual differences about which we talk much and do little. The teacher can seek to recognize and understand the feelings of a child. Though teachers should not attempt to read too much into the behavior of free play, they can get clues to understanding that can then be corroborated by reports from other teachers, personal conversation, cumulative records, discussions with parents, and other sources of data. More permissiveness in the selection and carrying out of school tasks can be granted. This will have the double advantage of freeing the child and of stimulating his growth toward desirable educational aims.

Therapeutic Play in the School. As part of the guidance program in a public elementary school in New York City, a room was set apart for the exclusive use of therapeutic play groups. A guidance coordinator, a social worker, and a psychologist were available together with the limited services of a psychiatrist. It was recognized that children bringing to their classrooms the effects of family discord and neighborhood tensions were in need of therapy before they could adjust to the demands of the school. But since clinical services were not available, teachers, under the supervision of the specialists, volunteered to conduct the play groups.

The room was equipped with simple materials—tables, chairs, work benches, sandbox, and sink. Play equipment was that commonly used by children in the lower grades—dolls, doll furniture, paint, easels, clay, paper, and games. The sessions were neither programmed nor structured. The adult in charge was a permissive, accepting, and neutral individual. Aggression was permitted within the limits acceptable to the children and the situation. Each group met for an hour a week; some children had been in the groups for as much as four years.

While it is not suggested that this approach is a complete tool for therapy or that it is a substitute for clinical treatment when it is required, it was felt that

> . . . therapeutic effects do emerge and many of the children function better in the classroom and in the neighborhood as a result of their participation in the specialized play group.
> Children who are deprived in some measure of the emotional security which grows from the love of understanding parents or whose deprivation is acute because they are exposed to even more negative emotional experiences in their homes are in desperate need of positive surrogate identifications. Only with such support can the threatened ego receive some sustenance against the overwhelming impact of destructive forces. The play group is an attempt to meet some of the needs of such children.[14]

DRAMATIC CLASSROOM ACTIVITIES

Puppetry. Puppetry may be used to encourage creativity, to brighten school experiences, to relieve tensions, and to vent animosities—thus solving problems. In a manner similar to play therapy, the child may express his unwholesome emotions, the direct expression of which is forbidden or frowned upon (the child who crushes the clay father-figure instead of kicking his father). How this works is illustrated by Miss Temple, a fifth-grade teacher.[15] Two boys decided to play catch rather than to join the group, but all the balls were in use, so they simply

---

[14] Mortimer Schiffer, "A Therapeutic Play Group in a Public School," *Mental Hygiene*, 41:193, 1957.

[15] James A. Smith, "Teaching Creative Thinking," in Vincent J. Glennon (ed.), *Frontiers in Elementary Education, IV*, Syracuse, N.Y.: Syracuse University Press, 1957, pp. 74–82.

wandered off. They happened to find a ball in the grass and began to play. They were joined by a third boy who claimed the ball was his and showed them his initials on the ball. Disgruntled, the two retorted, "Finders keepers, losers weepers." A fight ensued. Miss Temple stopped the fight, explaining that a rule had been broken. They all talked as they returned to the classroom. After a cooling-off period, she stated to the class that there was a problem needing solution and asked the boys if they would like to show their feelings through the use of puppets. She chose puppets because guilt feelings can be more easily expressed when faces are hidden behind the small stage. The episode was repeated and again Miss Temple stopped the fight—its being against school rules. The boys were then asked to tell how they felt. Other students were drawn into the discussion and three other pupils were asked to replay the drama. Further discussion dealt with feelings, values, social approval, and sportsmanship. Not only was a situation modified but also a problem solving and creative situation had been engaged in by the pupils.

One of the major values of puppetry is that of helping individuals to understand one another.

> It is apparent that putting oneself in another's place is not an easy achievement, nor do all people find it possible to accept either themselves or other people. There is much evidence of the ease with which people blame each other for this or that difficulty or failure. There are too few incidents making the most of the assets in personal, family, and community life as against our readiness to emphasize and highlight problems.[16]

Puppetry lends itself admirably to the resolution of group problems when pupils are encouraged to make suggestions and then carry those suggestions into dramatic fruition.

Puppetry in the schools should embrace not only the construction of the puppet (Figure 20) but also the dramatic production in which the puppet performs. A hand puppet may be made by taking a nine-inch square of cloth, filling it with a wad of kapok or cotton, inserting a cylinder of cardboard to accommodate the manipulator's forefinger, and shaping the head. Tie the corners, and paint on the hair and face. Tie the dress onto the head. The puppet is ready for action.[17] Stress should be placed on the creative process rather than on the technical proficiency. It is deemed desirable to have the designer of the puppet also be its voice and manipulator. Though the voice of another pupil might be more suitable in terms of dramatic production, the puppet should not

---

[16] Jean Schick Grossman, *How to Use Hand Puppets in Group Discussions*, New York: Play Schools Association, Inc., 1952, p. 10.

[17] See *ibid.*, pp. 46ff. for more detailed instructions.

be taken from its maker—forsake achieving artistry. Puppetry can involve the group as well as an individual, if part of the plan is to permit the class to discuss characterization, revised dialogue, and new action. Group discussion can be used in improving staging and scenery. Care must be taken that creativity and individuality are the prime considerations. Moreover, hand puppets rather than the complicated strings of marionettes are generally found to be more suitable for school use.[18]

FIG. 20. Pupil-made hand puppets.

Dancing. In view of the many developmental and instructional values in dance, it seems unfortunate that more use is not made of it. Dancing involves practice in bodily control and movement. It requires individual responsibility and group cooperation. It enlists some of the advantages which are inherent in music. Once the boys in a class have overcome their misguided notions that it is a sissy activity, it serves as a form of motivation. It can provide supplementary activity for the study of history

[18] Marjorie Batchelder and Virginia Comer, *Puppets and Plays,* New York: Harper & Brothers, 1956, p. 170.

and geography. Physical education groups make *some* use of dancing; however, its value justifies *more* extensive use.

Dancing may be introduced through square and folk dancing. Records which contain stirring music and calls are available with accompanying instructions, which when studied make it possible for teachers with little experience to conduct gratifying activity. These dances are suitable for youngsters from the very beginning of their school experiences. From these dances it is a short step to improvisation. While improvisation is usually more enjoyable to the experienced dancer, it has been found to be feasible and interesting to the neophyte.[19] The teacher's encouragement to do what the music tells one to do is often enough to make primary pupils give it a try. Older pupils will need to overcome the effect of convention, but with teachers who enjoy dance and appreciate its values, this too can be accomplished. It has been suggested that, when pupils appreciate the effort, strength, and balance which is required to be a good dancer, the idea that dance is beneath one's dignity will diminish. When dance is seen as a means of improving posture, gaining strength, developing coordination, and achieving bodily control, the enjoyment of creative activity will have a chance to evolve. Using these approaches in a summer camp for boys resulted in the boys' trying, learning a few steps, teaching them to girls, and taking a lasting interest in dancing.[20]

Girls too, have the job of overcoming convention as they approach the dance. They feel that they might be embarrassed by the unusual movements and postures. One teacher found that it was much easier to overcome their reticence if the girls held something in their hands. Straight sticks, balls (about the size of a volleyball or a basketball), and hoops (somewhat smaller than the popular hula-hoops) were quite helpful. Passing the ball from hand to hand, over one's head, between one's legs, and across one's back, all in time to music, resulted in easy introductions to dance movements. The sticks and hoops accomplished the same objectives. After these preliminary sessions, modern and free dance were more freely practiced.

The possible effect of dance on personality is illustrated in the case of a shy, plain looking, and somewhat untidy eighth-grade girl. The principal was interested in square and long dances and decided to introduce them to the pupils at the noon hour during the rainy season. Boys and girls both responded enthusiastically and soon they were performing with skill and grace. The shy girl was a star performer from the be-

[19] Gertrude Lippincott, "Dance Improvisation and Technique," *Journal of Health, Physical Education and Recreation*, 29(1):32, January, 1958.

[20] Fred Berk, "Creating Interest in Dance for Boys," *Journal of Health, Physical Education and Recreation*, 29(4):58–59, April, 1958.

ginning. She seemed to blossom out and become more cheerful, more companionable, and gradually took better care of her hair and clothes (without any direct suggestions). Her schoolwork improved markedly. As a reward for the excellent performances, the principal arranged for the group to present some of their dances at PTA meetings and at assemblies in other schools. Unfortunately, the girl's mother objected on religious grounds to her dancing and forbade her continued participation. Ordinarily, the principal did not interfere with such edicts, but when the girl regressed to her previous shyness, untidiness, and mediocre schoolwork he intervened. After explaining to the parents all that had happened, they admitted that they had noticed the changes of behavior in both directions and decided to give their permission to reenter the dance group. Again change was noticed, but this time, the girl developed even further in desirable directions.

LIMITATIONS AND PRECAUTIONS

The full use of psychodrama, sociodrama, play, and dance as analytic and therapeutic measures is a job for specially trained clinicians. It is not expected, nor desired, that teachers should turn their classrooms into clinics. However, the danger is not in play and drama but in overinterpretation. Participation in a dramatic situation does not necessarily mean expression of personal feelings; much is mere imitation. The actor may sincerely be trying to do what he thinks the character would do—and his thoughts might stem from having read or heard about the situation.

These techniques should not be thought of as panaceas. In spite of the teacher's doing all he can to create a friendly and permissive atmosphere, there may still be hidden tensions within the pupil. The fact that progress has been made by some pupils does not mean that all problems have been solved. There must be a continuing search for approaches that will fit the immediate situation and the particular individual. Moreover, it is entirely possible that some children need to feel that their conduct is censured. (The fact that someone cares *enough* about them to be concerned about their conduct may give them an additional sense of security.)

The classroom cannot become a psychological laboratory. The desire to help a child who is experiencing difficulties should not obscure the ever-present responsibility for directing the growth of the happy children, who make up the bulk of the classroom population. It may be unfortunate, but permissiveness for one may have to be limited in the interest of the welfare of the entire group. Here the precaution becomes a matter of balance. Permissiveness leading to destruction and personal attack must be avoided. Restrictiveness leading to dependence and submission must likewise be avoided.

When these precautions are held in mind, the techniques become an interesting field for experimentation—one that will result in professional growth, besides providing additional opportunities for pupil growth. The fact that there are dangers and limitations should not be allowed to intimidate the teacher. There are dangers involved in the teaching of arithmetic and reading, too, if the teacher is lacking in kindliness, humility, and sincerity. The necessity for understanding children is so great that no opportunity to expand this understanding should be overlooked.

SUMMARY

Role playing is a projective technique in which an attempt is made to understand the individual or permit the release of his feelings. It involves certain basic elements, namely, actors who are willing to identify themselves with the situation, an orientation to the situation (oral description by the teacher or the reading of a story), the acting out of the situation, analysis and evaluation by the players and the audience, and reenactment and evaluation by pupils and teacher.

The objectives of free play are to stimulate personal contact, afford practice in verbal communication, give an opportunity to engage in cooperative endeavor, and to stimulate mutual respect. Free play provides an opportunity to gain insight into feelings that are too perplexing to be expressed orally. The basic elements required in its use are synonymous with good teaching methods and sound teacher personality. Friendliness and warmth characterize the teacher-pupil relationship. The child is accepted as he is. There is freedom for the child to express his inner feelings and thus grow in self-understanding. Puppetry and dancing have been used to achieve purposes similar to those accomplished by role playing.

The classroom teacher who attempts to use these techniques—and the attempt is worthwhile—must observe certain precautions: (1) Overinterpretation must be avoided. (2) Permissiveness should not be so great as to endanger other children or property; neither should restriction be so great as to inhibit healthy independence. (3) The classroom must not become a clinic. There are too many children who are normally healthy and happy to make it reasonable for one child who is encountering difficulty to monopolize the teacher's time.

STUDY AND DISCUSSION EXERCISES

1. In what ways are play and creative drama similar to creative writing, painting, and drawing?

2. Organize a committee to plan the outline for a sociodrama, and experiment with its production in class.

3. Observe a group of youngsters (any age) at play. Of the questions that arise, which do you think would merit further investigation?

4. Give your own evaluation of the proposition that free play has therapeutic value even when the child's motivations are not understood.

5. What are some specific procedures a teacher might carry out in order to make more use of dance in the classroom?

SUGGESTED ADDITIONAL READINGS

Batchelder, Marjorie, and Virginia Lee Comer, *Puppets and Plays*, New York: Harper & Brothers, 1956. 241 pp.

Suggestions for making puppets, planning the play, staging the production, developing and presenting the drama are given in sufficient detail as to allow the teacher to experiment with such projects.

Hartley, Ruth E., Lawrence K. Frank, and Robert M. Goldman, *Understanding Children's Play*, New York: Columbia University Press, 1952. 372 pp.

Blocks, water, clay, finger painting, and toys are discussed in terms of specific values for fostering healthy personality development.

Jackson, Lydia, and Kathleen M. Todd, *Child Treatment and the Therapy of Play*, 2d ed., New York: The Ronald Press Company, 1950. 159 pp.

The authors seek to provide an improved understanding of the theory basic to play therapy.

Shaftel, George, and Fannie R. Shaftel, *Role Playing the Problem Story*, New York: The National Conference of Christians and Jews, 1952. 78 pp.

This booklet describes role playing, at various grade levels, as an approach to better human relations in the classroom.

CHAPTER 17

SPECIAL SERVICES IN SCHOOL AND COMMUNITY

A common reaction of teachers, on reading about the multitudinous responsibilities involved in preserving and creating conditions of mental health, is that "The task is overwhelming," "We are only humans—we can't do it all." There are advantages in taking a humble view, but it would be unfortunate for them to be discouraged by the size of the task. In the first place, no teacher needs to feel that he is alone. In the next class, there may be another professionally minded, well-intentioned teacher to pursue the goals. In the second place, it is well to remember that there are many ways of making contributions to pupil development. One's methods may vary from those of another *good* teacher and still be effective. A teacher cannot be expected to be equally proficient with all pupils. Failure to reach some pupils is quite normal. Finally, there is an increasingly large number of specialists whose services are available in schools; they, too, may treat some children who have problems and may give sound advice to teachers in other instances.

Teachers will profit from familiarity with techniques used by specialists, for these techniques will suggest approaches which can be used directly, or with modifications, in the classroom. The knowledge of special services will encourage teachers to gather pertinent information on cases they refer, thereby facilitating the work of the specialists. Most important, teachers should be acquainted with the work of specialists, since the child will, after examination and treatment, be returned to the classroom. When teachers comprehend what has happened in these cases they can more readily establish and maintain classroom conditions that will supplement the work of specialists.

MENTAL HYGIENE IS A COOPERATIVE AFFAIR

The Need for Teamwork. It is universally agreed that the major foundation for good or poor mental health is laid in the home. However, we must hasten to say that neither the home nor the school—nor any other institution—is solely the source of mental health or illness, and it must be added that it is rarely ever "too late." Except for inherited or congenital mental disorder, the human personality is constantly in the process of becoming.

John M., a fourth grader, was truly a "trial" for his teacher. He was inattentive, "smart-alecky," aggressive, and constantly on the move. He was referred to the school psychologist who found that he was in the intellectually superior group (IQ 120 on the Stanford-Binet), hyperactive, and easily distracted. The school nurse reported no readily observable reasons for referring him for special medical examination—though she did say that to avoid all questions such an examination should be scheduled. It was agreed that repressive discipline would probably aggravate the problem since the teacher had noted that reprimands or denial of privileges was almost always followed by John's attacking smaller children after school. . . .

The teacher tried patience, threats, pleading, praise, and finally settled into a periodically hopeful, but ordinarily discouraged, policy of resignation. On one occasion she took John to the principal's office with the remark, "He's no worse than usual but I can't take it any longer. You watch him a while." John sat by the school secretary talking to himself, playing games with his hands, grimacing, and sometimes getting up to do a little jig. The secretary's attempts at conversation were ignored. The principal's counseling was greeted with a glassy-eyed stare. It appeared, for all the response given, that his IQ might be closer to sixty than to twice that.

It was finally decided—since John's conduct tended to become more violent as the day wore on—that John should be allowed to come to school only for half days. It appeared that the stimulation of school resulted in his getting "wound up" more and more tightly. The visiting teacher went to the home to explain the projected plan. She found a woman disheveled, incoherent, and apparently dejected. This was John's foster mother who regarded him as a problem that no one should be asked to bear. She had enough to do taking care of her own two children. John's true mother, remarried, would not listen to the proposal that he might be helped by spending some time with her. When the father heard of the plan to keep John in school only half days he went to see the principal and teacher. His words spoken slowly, calmly, and thoughtfully ran about like this, "I know that teachers who will put up with him at all have a terrific task. But the worst thing that could happen to him would be to keep him at home another half day. I have his mother [foster mother] under psychiatric care now but she is not ready to care for John. I've had John to the psychiatrist, too, but he says that he could not get anywhere with John until the mother has improved. Could you try just a little longer to put up with him?" The teacher said, "Sure, send him along. We have done it for five months— I guess we can take it for another four."

John's behavior did not improve. But he was passed on to the fifth grade. His new teacher had heard all the stories of the year before plus having access to all the records which had accumulated. At mid-year John was not so disconcerting. When he was not participating with the class—which was most of the time—he sat drawing circles, making spitwads and dropping them on a target on the floor. He picked up the ammunition so there was no mess. His writing was up to standard for fifth grade; his arithmetic was below, and his reading was slightly above, the third grade level. When he did participate he made acceptable, but not brilliant, contributions but was unable to assume real responsibility. He was now "controlled" but still "undirected." . . . Progress had been made but the conditions were by no means fully corrected.

It was felt that the permissive atmosphere which the fourth grade teacher had created had only led him to test the limits of freedom— frequently and vigorously. But credit was given, by the school psychologist, to the fourth grade teacher for having made much progress even though it was not highly ostensible. The fifth grade teacher, continuing the permissive regime, found John somewhat more tractable. There is hope that John will soon find that he can be acceptable and will be able to devote his intelligence to the achievement of school tasks that are commensurate with his indicated level of ability.

The foregoing case illustrates the need for teamwork. Teachers spotted and brought to the attention of school authorities a case in need of special study. The visiting teacher made an investigation of the home. The psychologists supplied data on intelligence and personality trends. The father sought the aid of specialists and enlisted the aid of school personnel. The community child-guidance clinic was consulted, but in this case the psychiatrist thought there was little that could be accomplished by direct work with the child. Each of these persons contributed something to the understanding of John and together they devised an apparently sound approach.

The Family as a Factor in Mental Health

In the nature of the case, the mental hygiene point of view cannot be limited to one or another group, or to any selected class of experts. The home, the school, the church, the community, child guidance agencies, social workers, psychiatrists, and clinical psychologists must all devote some of their efforts, and lend their support to a total program of mental hygiene. No one agency can be expected to do the job alone. Nevertheless, it is incontestable that of all these different agencies which play a part in helping to reduce the incidence of maladjustment and mental disorder in our children, the most prominent and the most important is the home.[1]

It is likely that in most cases there is little that the teacher can do to improve the home. Short of psychological counseling or psychiatric therapy, it is not likely that words of advice from the teacher can have much effect. It is not that parents repudiate the advice so much as it is a matter of being unable to act consistently on that advice. It is known, for instance, that the most dangerous home influence on children is incompatibility of parents. However, parents' incompatibility is not intentional. It is the result of their childhood experiences, the present pressures which are exerted upon them, and the fact that emotional states do not readily respond to rational processes.

There are things the teacher can do. One is to find and report to parents something that will make them proud—the child's ability to do logical thinking (even when his arithmetic score is low), his creative art products, his cooperativeness with others, his athletic ability, his laudable school citizenship. In showing parents that teachers think well of the child, the parents may in turn tend to treat the youngster more respectfully. Second, the teacher's manifested concern may result in the parent's seeing more clearly their own need for concern. Third, the teacher's discovering and understanding the nature of home conditions will result in greater tolerance of deviant behavior; as one teacher said, "When I see the unwholesome conditions of the home my thought is not 'Now I can see why he acts as he does,' but 'I marvel at how he can act as well as he does.'"

The Community as a Factor in Mental Health. The community is one of the factors that molds the pattern which the family will take. Certainly there are sufficient studies of delinquency, crime, and immorality to show that children, youth, and adults respond to the growth influences of the community. Crowded living conditions are clearly a factor in the low ego concepts which lead to promiscuous sex relations. Those people who live in run-down and marginal areas (across the tracks or by the mills and storehouses) tend to have low regard for the property rights of others. If children have little space to play, they develop defiant and defensive attitudes toward the adults whom they bother with their noise and vigor. If the recreation spots are limited to taverns and movie houses, children have little chance to participate in the activities that hold maximum developmental prospects for them. If recent immigrants are massed to-

[1] A. A. Scheiders in William F. Jenks (ed.), *Mental Health and Special Education,* Washington: The Catholic University of America Press, 1957, pp. 151–152.

gether, there is increased difficulty in becoming assimilated into the dominant culture.[2]

There are also some positive aspects of community organization; these may be measured in terms of resources of personnel. Many communities provide space for play, athletic equipment, and personnel for supervision and coaching. In some there are children's art classes, children's theaters, children's science museums. But the major resources, as far as help for teachers in the field of mental hygiene is concerned, are the boy and girl scout leaders, the social welfare workers, public health nurses, YMCA and YWCA workers who can often supply pertinent observations to teachers and specialists. Increasingly, ministers are receiving training in mental hygiene and their potential contribution should not be overlooked.

This brief mention of community factors and community workers is indicative of the fact that mental hygiene is not solely a school function. Perhaps some assurance may accrue to teachers through realizing that others are concerned with mental health problems, even though their specific work is called by another name. Too, teachers should know that, if someone will make the approach, the chances are that effectiveness for all will be improved through coordinated effort.

ROLES OF SPECIALISTS IN MENTAL HYGIENE

There are a large number of specialists whose services may supplement the work of teachers. Sometimes these specialists are school employees, sometimes they are employed by various community agencies (Child Welfare Association, Mental Hygiene Society), and sometimes they are engaged in private practice. Inasmuch as the work they perform is much the same regardless of their institutional connection, it seems appropriate to describe the services they perform rather than to emphasize their community role.

Counselors. Sometimes counselors have training as psychologists plus some teaching experience, but more frequently they are teachers who have evinced interest in this kind of work and made efforts in summer or evening classes to prepare themselves. Sometimes counselors are simply teachers who have proven they are skilled in human relations, who easily establish rapport with students, and who take on counseling duties as a part of their work load.

When a teacher finds a student whose symptoms do not respond to routine techniques or when he is too pressed for time to attempt a solu-

---

[2] August B. Hollingshead and Frederick C. Redlich, *Social Class and Mental Illness,* New York: John Wiley & Sons, Inc., 1958, p. 125.

tion, he may refer the pupil to the counselor. The typical procedure is to attempt to get the pupil to tell his side of the story regarding the reason for referral. Disturbed pupils, however, often reveal no apparent desire to talk. Without pressing, the counselor asks questions, fully expecting terse answers but hoping that his own relaxation, interest, and friendliness will "draw the student out." Sometimes a mild suggestion may be offered, but sometimes the statements "I'd like to hear more. Please come back tomorrow at ten," will end the initial conference. In the meantime, records are consulted, teachers are talked to, and points for praise are sought. Later sessions may elicit more response. Constantly the aim is to get at *how the student feels* and to obtain objective descriptions. Finally, some specific suggestion is made, but care is exercised to see that the pupil is not overwhelmed with good advice. Sometimes no suggestions are made; it seems, occasionally, that the student releases enough emotional tension during the counseling that he can face his difficulties with a little more courage. Well-trained counselors will recognize the limits of their own competence and refer the more serious cases to clinics or psychologists.

The following characteristics of a good counseling relationship provide insight into the counselor's role as well as suggesting means of improving one's work as a teacher. The counselor and client get along well—they can communicate. Emphasis is placed on the positive rather than the punitive. By sticking to the problem and avoiding shock or censure, the counselor conveys the impression that the pupil can say what he wants. There should be an atmosphere of mutual trust. The student should be active and should be free to make his own choices. The feelings and thoughts which are expressed must be viewed as being normal and understandable.[3]

The School Social Worker. The school social worker is one who has studied sociology, family living, and often welfare work. For the most part the social worker is a woman who has had experience in classroom teaching plus additional training. Her job is one of making a study of the home to see what part community, home, and parental methods and relationships might play in causing problem behavior. She collects information which will be helpful in charting a course of action for the child and then makes the necessary contacts and arrangements for referring special cases to psychologists, welfare agencies (in the case of parental neglect), or clinics. Often her work involves interpreting the work of the school to parents with the aim of altering parental attitudes and behaviors.

[3] J. Murray Lee and Dorris May Lee, *The Child and His Development*, New York: Appleton-Century-Crofts, Inc., 1958, p. 585.

The school social worker, then, is basically a troubleshooter and expediter in cases involving individual children. In practice, due to the fact that there are usually more problems than they can handle, local rules are set up limiting their activities to certain types of cases or to a quota of cases from each school. However, their help is wisely invoked wherever serious psychological difficulties are suspected.[4]

Special Teachers. Awareness of the importance of reading in our complicated culture has made the lack of appropriate progress in this skill a genuine concern of teachers who have the mental hygiene point of view. Of all the special services provided in schools, an expert in reading is most readily available. This person is one who has knowledge of the specific study of the causes of retardation and of ways of correcting the deficiency. The following observations indicate something of the general nature of the work done by remedial teachers.

Tests are given to determine whether the child is retarded in relation to his intellectual status or just in terms of average grade-norms. A child can read only up to his mental age—and to ensure the greatest accuracy in assessment of intelligence, individual tests are administered. Often tests, observations, and teachers' reports indicate that the first step is one of personal adjustment rather than direct attack on reading deficiency.

The remedial teacher must have a pupil load which enables him to do the work thoroughly; that is, it is considered better to make two years of progress with thirty pupils than to make one year of progress with fifty pupils. Moreover, since the child himself is likely to feel discouraged and inferior because of his reading deficiency, it is important that work be thorough enough to avoid further failure. Having to make still another start tends to find the pupil increasingly apprehensive and hesitant to try. Hence, students should be selected in terms of their motivation to improve and in terms of their indicated potential.

The remedial teacher often helps parents and classroom teachers to understand the nature of the difficulty. This helps the child by reducing unnecessary emotional tensions aroused by low reading achievement.[5]

Further insight into the special knowledge required of remedial teachers and the nature of their work is provided for classroom teachers in a list of things parents should know:

1. Reading retardation is not necessarily due to a low level of intelligence. Many youngsters at grade in other subjects are behind in reading. There must be concern over *causes* since neurological damage to language centers of the brain, faulty language development, or poor initial teaching may be the root of the difficulty.

[4] Fritz Redl and William W. Wattenberg, *Mental Hygiene in Teaching*, 2d ed., New York: Harcourt, Brace & World, Inc., 1959, p. 425.
[5] E. W. Dolch, "So You Are Going to Be a Remedial Teacher," *Elementary English*, 35:12–18, January, 1958

2. Reading retardation is linked to failure in growing up. Parents and teachers must learn how to encourage and praise efforts at independence without "pushing" the child so much that he feels unloved or unwanted.

3. Often reading difficulties are linked to feelings about competition in the home and school—interpersonal comparisons should be avoided.

4. Objectivity and self-respect are requisite to success in remedial reading. Here experts are needed because teachers, succeeding with most pupils, may become emotionally involved in the failure of one pupil.

5. It must be recognized that the school is only one possible factor which might cause failure. Lack of intellectual stimulation or reading material in the home or disdain for reading among one's peers must also be considered.

6. It is possible that haste and overemphasis on reading, due to emotional turmoil, may aggravate the problem.

7. For reasons not yet fully understood, boys fail in reading more often than girls. The chances that there exists a temporarily slower developmental rate for boys might be a factor in lessening pressure on boys to achieve at norms for the various grades.

8. Since children are individuals and there are many different causes for reading difficulties, retarded readers require the help of qualified diagnosticians and technicians.[6]

It can be seen that, in order to capitalize on the ramifications of the foregoing points, the remedial teacher should desirably have specialized training. It is true that some get into the work because of their interest and realization of the great need for such services. Most, however, have prepared for their work by having taken advanced work in remedial instruction, courses in child development, psychology of exceptional children, educational tests and measurement, diagnostic techniques, and laboratory work in a psychoeducational clinic.

Another rather common special teacher is the speech correctionist. For such work special training is essential, because some speech defects may become progressively worse if the teacher, even with the best of intentions, uses incorrect approaches. This however, only makes it the more necessary that classroom teachers know something about what the correctionist does.

"Well, to tell the truth, I never knew what the correctionist did with Jimmy. He went out of the room twice a week for a half-hour of speech, but I never heard about what he did during the time. Finally, at the end of the year I got a report for his cumulative record. By that time it was too late for *me* to help him."[7]

[6] Mary H. B. Wollner, "What Parents Should Know about the Retarded Reader," *Education*, 78:14–21, September, 1957.

[7] Charles Van Riper and Katharine G. Butler, *Speech in the Elementary Classroom*, New York: Harper & Brothers, 1955, p. 148.

The speech correctionist has had much work in psychology, including such courses as Motivation, Abnormal Psychology, Psychological Assessment, and, of course, has made a special study of speech itself—speech sounds, types of defects, and specific remedial procedures. Ordinarily he has done clinical work, under supervision, with children. Disability in verbal communication has such profound effects upon the personality of pupils and remedial work is such a complicated process that high standards are set for such workers. Those who achieve such standards are professionally certified by the American Speech and Hearing Association.

Speech defect is in large measure a symptom of persistent emotional turmoil. The correctionist therefore works in terms of building rapport and self-confidence. Depending on the type of difficulty, there are particular exercises and regimes which may be used. For example, articulation difficulties call for emphasis on the pupil's need to listen attentively. Phonetic sounds are emphasized, the structure of words is studied, group work is utilized, and drill is in order. In stuttering the first concern is that of achieving emotional balance. The individual must come to appreciate his own worth, pressure and embarrassment must be circumvented, and hurry must be avoided. Delayed language has many causes; therefore, first steps *must* include careful diagnostic analysis and, then, therapy will be varied according to the findings.

Psychologists. Formerly, school psychologists were largely concerned with the administration and interpretation of tests; today this work is supplemented by counseling pupils, working with parents, providing therapies, and helping teachers. The psychologist's training leads him to search for causes; the clues are drawn from tests, observations of the child, talks with the child, conversations with parents, and reports from teachers. His job is to interpret all the data he can obtain, not being content with a set of test scores.

There is considerable variation in the functions of school psychologists, depending on their training, inclinations, and what is expected of them by teachers and administrators. In general, though, their role is that of assisting school personnel to enrich the education and growth of all children. In addition, they are expected to perform the following specific functions: (1) Evaluate and interpret the intellectual, emotional, and social development of pupils, (2) identify exceptional children and help plan appropriate educational and social experiences for them, (3) develop ways to facilitate the learning and adjustment of pupils, (4) conduct research and use research findings to solve problems, and (5) diagnose educational and personal disabilities in order to collaborate in planning programs of reeducation.[8]

[8] Norma E. Cutts (ed.), *School Psychologists at Mid-century,* Washington: American Psychological Association, Inc., 1955, pp. 30-31.

The nature of help which the teacher may expect and of the services a child might receive is reflected in the training of school psychologists. While there is no nationwide requirement of these workers, many of them have a background including courses in some of the following areas: educational and psychological diagnosis, dynamics of individual development, group and interpersonal relationships, research methods, psychological statistics, experimental psychology, learning theory, and personality theory. Some have had only two years of graduate work, while others have had as much as four—including a period of internship. In the latter case the doctorate degree in education or psychology has been earned.[9]

The question is frequently asked by teachers, "How do I know when special help should be sought?" It would be highly gratifying if a definitive answer could be given, but it is not easy. Harry N. Rivlin states that as simple and defensible rule as any is that when the case really gets interesting then special help should be sought.[10] The accessibility of help will make a difference. If specialists are readily available they should be consulted when doubt begins to arise in the teacher's mind. Consultation with other teachers, with supervisors, and with the principal may also be helpful in resolving this dilemma. Certainly any time that the teacher's repertory of helpful procedures has resulted in no perceptible change in the pupil's behavior, then, he should seek help.

The teacher is the one who is most likely to see the daily behaviors that indicate the need for help and typically it is he who will initiate the steps leading to the pupil's referral to a specialist. This he does by filling out a formal referral sheet, which contains his description of the child's symptoms, recent group-test data, notes on health made by the school nurse, school-attendance data, special interests, the teacher's account of peer relationships, and the evaluation of scholastic ability and achievement. Then the psychologist supplements this initial report from talks with teachers, parents, and others who may have contact with the child. Next, he works directly with the child, giving individual tests, analyzing drawings, conducting diagnostic play sessions, and often progressing to therapeutic play or counseling sessions—including both directive and nondirective approaches. Sometimes the remedial approach involves working with parents to encourage their changing attitudes and methods. If it seems that the child needs psychiatric help, the psychologist typically acts as the liaison agent.

[9] Teachers interested in achieving the status of school psychologist may find a description of the functions, qualifications, and training of school psychologists in *ibid*.

[10] Harry N. Rivlin, "The Classroom Teacher and the Child's Learning," in H. H. Remmers and others (eds.), *Growth, Learning, and Teaching*, New York: Harper & Brothers, 1957, p. 416.

Sometimes the remedial approach suggested by the psychologist is simply one of modification of the school program—in contrast to therapy for the child or his parents. Revision of the program of studies by the classroom teacher, obtaining the services of a tutor, referral to a teacher of remedial reading or arithmetic, or capitalizing on the resources of the school (facilities such as shop, art room, or library) are all possibilities.[11]

Conducting case conferences is a significant part of the psychologist's work; he calls together all those who are involved in the case, approaches are suggested, and plans are formulated. One important aspect of the case conference is that it becomes a wide avenue of learning—especially for classroom teachers.

The importance of the teachers' knowing something of the nature and difficulty of the psychologist's work is reflected in teachers' remarks: "Nothing happened," or "He's back, but he is just the same as he always was." The psychologist's answer could be a rephrasing of the physician's remark, "We're medical men, not miracle men."

The results of therapy will often not be reflected in immediate improvement of the child's behavior. It took him a long time to develop his abnormalities and it is reasonable to expect that it will take much time to outgrow them. It is possible that the child has knowledge of appropriate behavior, but when returned to the classroom, he is unable to translate his knowledge into the behavior which he and others would approve. If the classroom has contributed to the maladjustment and if the structure of the pupil-teacher relationship remains the same, it becomes a formidable obstacle to the child's adjustment. When teachers fail to understand the purposes and processes of therapy, there is likely to be impatience with small gains in conduct. It is desirable that formal recognition on return to the class be avoided and that, at the same time, an effort be made by using praise and encouragement liberally to see that he participates.[12]

Psychiatrists. Psychiatrists are specialists in the field of medicine whose concern is diagnosing, understanding, and treating mental illnesses. They have, in addition to their basic training as physicians, an additional year or two of study in mental and nervous disorders which are complicated by psychological factors. They use data from any sciences—genetics, physiology, neurology, biochemistry, anthropology, and psychology—in diagnosing their patients' ailments. Because of the inclusive nature of their analysis and treatment, the psychiatrist frequently works as the head of a team which includes clinical psychologists, psychiatric social workers, and play and occupational therapists. Drugs, electric shock, and surgery

[11] Katherine E. D'Evelyn, *Meeting Children's Emotional Needs*, Englewood Cliffs, N.J.: Prentice-Hall, Inc., 1957, pp. 158–159.

[12] Palmer A. Graver, "Facilitating the Results of Therapy," *The Elementary School Journal*, 58:166–169, December, 1957.

may be employed when conditions warrant; the procedures used by clinical psychologists and psychoanalysts are also frequently used. Like the psychologists, the psychiatrists too may use projective techniques, play analysis and therapy, interviewing, and counseling in both analysis and treatment; mention of the variety of approaches used by a psychiatrist should help the classroom teachers appreciate the improbability of their achieving uniform success with problem pupils. Moreover, disorders such as toxic psychoses, syphilitic infection of the brain, and brain damage due to injury would not yield to the procedures used by teachers, school specialists, or psychologists. Furthermore, any mental illness primarily caused by organic factors is complicated by the patient's and society's reaction to the condition; and, conversely, disorders primarily of psychological origin may be manifested in organic (somatic) abnormality.

Thus, with the realization that psychological factors played an important role in mental illnesses formerly considered as purely organic in nature, and conversely that organic processes were of significance in many functional mental disorders formerly considered purely psychological in nature, there was a fusion of organic and psychological viewpoints into the holistic, or psychosomatic, approach to *both* mental illness and physical disease. With this newer point of view, every physical and mental illness in terms of diagnosis, understanding, and treatment, becomes both an organic, medical problem and a psychological one.[13]

Perhaps it is in the realization that it is the whole person, living in his particular community and cultural milieu, who must be understood and treated that psychiatrists make their most significant contribution to mental health.

PROCEDURES USED BY SPECIALISTS

Case Studies. When a child is referred to a psychologist or psychiatrist, it is necessary to make a detailed analysis of the background factors and present circumstances of the case. If data are complete there is a greater chance that constructive solutions will be achieved. Sometimes these data are collected on forms (or personal history blanks) and usually include information relating to the following areas:

1. *Initial data.* This item will include identifying characteristics, such as name; sex; exact age; address; grade in school; religion; father's name, occupation, and education; mother's name, occupation, and education; nationality; and the names and ages of brothers and sisters.

[13] James C. Coleman, *Abnormal Psychology and Modern Life,* Chicago: Scott, Foresman and Company, 1950, p. 55.

2. *Abilities.* Included here will be mental-test data, results of tests of special abilities (art, music, mechanics), formal observations such as the anecdotal record, and informal observations.

3. *Educational background.* It will be informative to know the age at which school was begun, schools attended, regularity of attendance, evaluations by previous teachers, former relationships with classmates, the pupil's present attitude toward school, and achievement-test data. The latter are valuable for evaluating present status.

4. *Home and neighborhood.* Pertinent data will have reference to the characteristics of the home: the physical—spaciousness, conveniences, and cultural aspects (reading material, radio, play equipment); mental and physical health of parents, siblings, and relatives; whether or not the home is stable; and what is its characteristic emotional tone. Significant neighborhood items are opportunities for play and recreation, financial and cultural aspects, and distance from and means of conveyance to school.

5. *Health.* Comparative strength and vigor, physical handicaps, frequency of physical examinations, attitudes toward health and cleanliness, disfigurements (scars, birthmarks, odd features), operations and corrective therapy, and dental record are data which may signify the sources of difficulty.

6. *Social adjustment.* Such things as friendships, loneliness, ability to cooperate, dishonesty, selfishness, sensitiveness, resentfulness, and self-control are representative of the kind of entries that may prove of value. Relationships with peers, siblings, parents, and other adults may be noted in terms of the foregoing characteristics. It is extremely important to record the individual's personal reaction to his social contacts.

7. *Interests.* Play and reading interests, vocational ambitions (or lack of them), hobbies, family and sibling interests which are enjoyed in common, and interest in school activities are likely to be profitable entries in the case history. Anecdotal records are a valuable source of information. Standardized interest blanks can serve as a *starting* point for a detailed analysis of special interests, but it must be remembered that interests change and grow—and test data should not be allowed to discourage exploration of new areas.

8. *Contacts with agencies.* If the child has been serviced by any social agency, try to obtain the information recorded and the recommendations made. If the child has been in a juvenile court, give the date, charge, findings, and disposition of the case. Unfortunately, there is no uniform dictate as to who is responsible for coordinating the use of data, but the specialist is in an advantageous position for obtaining such information.

9. *Behavior.* Much of the above does concern the behavior of the individual being studied; however, attention should be *specifically* directed to manifestations such as the following: dreaminess, nervousness, bully-

ing, dependence, tantrums, persistence, moods, initiative, truthfulness, excuse making, work habits, obedience, tact, humor, and the like.

10. *The individual's reaction.* All too often ignored in outlines for case studies is provision for getting at the individual's feelings in connection with his situation. It takes time and careful listening. Perhaps playing with a child, working with an adolescent in shop or laboratory will open the verbal gates. Getting one to discuss the story he has written, the picture he has painted, or the figure he has molded or carved may lead him to reveal his feelings. But whatever the technique, the necessity of getting at the individual's reaction is real and insistent.

11. *Steps to be taken.* On the basis of the above data, the specialist makes some tentative summary and recommendation. The recommendation may be something for the family or the school to do. If it is a recommendation to the pupil himself, it is important not to overwhelm him with good advice. Confine suggestions to one or two items. If these are heeded, it may then be appropriate to make further suggestions.

12. *Followup.* This part of the case study is, also, all too often omitted. Actually, it is just as essential a part of the entire procedure as a recommendation. There are three reasons for its being of major importance. (1) The parents, the teachers, or the child need some checking to see if progress is being made. They may need to be reminded of the importance of carrying out recommendations. Well-timed questions about progress serve to stimulate the parents, teachers, or the child to persist in efforts for improvement. (2) The followup helps the specialist evaluate the effectiveness of his study. He will be able to save time on the next study by noting shortcomings and strengths of the present one. The followup serves to refine the procedures and strengthen the recommendations. (3) The followup is likely to provide further information that can serve to modify and strengthen the effectiveness of continuing assistance.

One other observation on the case study should be noted: *Data do not supply the diagnosis.* Instruments do not make the diagnosis for a medical doctor. He must interpret the data in accordance with his training and experience and in terms of the interrelationships of the data. Similarly, the data of the case study must be interpreted by the specialist. He must weigh one factor against another. Validity of the data must be estimated. He must know how the subject feels—not just what conditions surround him. Hypothesizing is necessary. But one fellow's guess is *not* as good as another's. The specialist has laid the foundation for making diagnoses.

Case Conferences. An essential part of the work of the psychologist who serves as therapist and the psychiatrist is to conduct case conferences. Here, after studying the various facets of the case, psychiatrists, psychologists, social workers, and teachers discuss the case. Approaches are suggested and contributing factors are discussed. Theory and experience provide guides. The conferences have merits beyond individual cases, inasmuch as all those who work with the child involved see not only what others are doing and see the role of their own contributions but gain insights which place them in an advantageous position for working with other cases.

The Child Study Center of the Pennsylvania Hospital in Philadelphia has clinics for children and adolescents. Teachers who work with children in the classroom situation function side by side with specialists. It is felt that a result of this teamwork is the providing of mental health education for professional and lay persons in the community. Evaluating the results, Dr. Nixon says, "We believe that the Center's activities in mental health education, with its emphasis on reaching out to persons who work with children, has possibilities for indirect positive effects which stagger the imagination."[14]

Play Therapy. A technique much used with preschool and primary children to help them absorb and redirect their negative emotions is play therapy (see also the section on Developmental, Analytical, and Therapeutic Values of Play in Chapter 16). It is a slow process involving a half-dozen to twenty or more sessions, in which the therapist tries to reveal his faith, acceptance, and respect for the child in order to convince the subject that he is considered to be a worthy individual. The atmosphere is one of permissiveness, short of injury to other persons and wanton destruction of property. The therapist avoids both approval and disapproval of the child's action and verbalizations during therapy, since the latter would inhibit the release of feelings and the former might arrest progress, because the child might limit himself to actions and expressions which have earned him approval.

Typically the therapeutic process progresses through definite stages. At first there is hesitancy and doubt. As he gains confidence that he will not be reprimanded, his feelings of hostility, fear, and anxiety are given generalized expression. He will attack toys indiscriminately and express hostility to people in general. Then the expressions are focused more sharply and superficially—toys substituted for parents and teachers whom he dislikes are attacked and destroyed. This victory may then lead him to attack the therapist or some other person, physically or verbally; for example, one boy "accidentally" shot the therapist with a dart gun, another kept poking and striking the therapist with a slender switch. In the next stage the child is less consistently hostile and ambivalence is revealed. Attacks alternate with expressions of affection, such as spanking and then

[14] Norman Nixon, "A Child Guidance Clinic Explores Ways to Prevention," *Children*, 4:9–14, January–February, 1957.

feeding a doll baby. Finally, negative feelings begin to diminish and there is a more consistent display of positive feelings which are in accord with reality. It should be noted that "the therapeutic process does not automatically occur in a play situation. It becomes possible in a therapeutic relationship where the therapist responds in constant sensitivity to the child's feelings, accepts the child's attitudes, and conveys a consistent and sincere belief in the child and respect for him."[15]

It can be seen from the foregoing that there could scarcely be a reproduction of a typical play-therapy session. The child, the situation, and the stage of therapy would result in varied descriptions. However, the following episode may give some indication of the ways feelings are expressed and therapy is facilitated. The subject is Carol, a four-year-old who suffered stomach pains during mealtime and pulled and twisted her hair so violently that she was partially bald. Carol looked like a stepsister whom the mother hated. Carol's mother had stepparents who were alcoholics and Carol's mother, who was scrupulously clean, lived in a seven-room house with three other families. Her mother felt that Carol was selfish, inconsiderate, and unruly, while the therapist saw in Carol a frightened, confused, hostile, and love-hungry child.

FIFTH PLAY SESSION WITH CAROL

C: (*Kneels in sandbox and builds with the sand.*) Four years ago a rock—a rock felled on this house. So we call it a part of the house.

T: Four years ago a rock fell in it?

* * * *

C: (*Plays in the sandbox.*) She turns it up herself, and she plays all around and has a lot of fun. That's the way it should be. She used to laugh, but not Mama.

T: She laughed, but her mama didn't, hm?

C: Her mama used to holler all she could. She'd holler and holler and holler. All she wanted was a house. Not a big house. Just a little girl's size.

* * * *

C: (*Plays in the sandbox.*) Now she says now it looks like a house. She screams out, and ever since she's crying. It's different, this house. First the daddy left the mother, and now the mother left the daddy.

T: Mm-hm. Daddy left Mommy and Mommy left Daddy.

C: So you know what she did? She build herself a house her size. She crashed down the house to make her own house.

T: She made a house all of her own.

C: Nobody lived in it except her, and everybody's happy now. Except her. So she's cut her's off again.

[15] Clark E. Moustakas, *Children in Play Therapy*, New York: McGraw-Hill Book Company, Inc., 1953, p. 9.

T: She didn't want her house attached to theirs.

C: So she moved it down to California, and they didn't like it. But she loved it. And they didn't like it.

T: So she moved away.

C: And she brought water for her house. A little water. Water in a tub for her house. All around the house, water, water, water. And her house is bigger. And her house is bigger and bigger and bigger. Finally she wanted it hooked on again. So you know what she did? She moved again and hooked hers on. So they were glad. And their family wasn't happy. Before, they were happy and she wasn't happy. So what's the difference?

T: She's happy now, and they aren't.

C: So she crashed her house down again and made another one. If they wanted to hook on she didn't mind.

T: She would let them hook on, hm?

C: Only how could they hook on, the way they had built it?[16]

At the end of the twenty-first session Carol's mother felt that Carol was much changed. She was helpful, got along with others better, talked in a more mature manner, and prayed that there should be no more trouble between her mommy and daddy. The case and the therapeutic process demonstrates what all parents and teachers should know: When a child is most unlovely, he is most in need of love.

Projective Techniques. There are a number of approaches to both analysis and therapy which are grouped under the heading of projective techniques. In general, a projective technique involves a situation where an amorphous or neutral situation is given meaning by the subject. For example, the Rorschach blots are blobs of ink of symmetrical patterns. Since the blobs are actually without definite form, what the individual reports seeing in the blot is what his view of the blot puts there—it is a projection of himself. What he sees there is what his background, rather than the present situation, leads him to see. In the Murray Apperception Test, pictures are presented which might mean many things. What the subject describes as being seen is a projection of his own personality. In the Sentence Completion Test, the subject is given a few words and told to complete a sentence from the key words. In the Story Completion Test, he is given the first few lines of a story and then is asked to complete the story.

The projective techniques supplement the previously mentioned sources of information as aids to understanding the motivations of the subject. One of the advantages of projective techniques is, in fact, that they require the support of a many-sided study of the individual before the findings can be used with confidence. These approaches may serve as therapy— telling what one sees, how one feels, how a story ends, making dolls do

[16] *Ibid.,* pp. 89–90.

certain things, and freedom to play as one wishes provide some release from tensions and render the subject more amenable to other forms of psychological treatment.

Therapeutic Counseling. The type of counseling most familiar to teachers is vocational and academic counseling with some emphasis on personal counseling. The specialist, too, may do some of his work in all these areas, but the emphasis is upon personal adjustment. It is realized that splitting counseling into various areas is but a matter of convenience in theoretical discussion, for in living these are all functionally related. For instance, what is done to facilitate appropriate choice of vocations and school curriculums also has bearing on personal adjustment. Conversely, personal adjustment is a factor in wise choices *in* other areas.

The major purposes of counseling are (1) to assist the individual in choosing his goals—whether in the areas of vocations, school subjects, or the selection of life's values, (2) to help the individual clarify his motivations and understand their roles in choice making, and (3) to evaluate progress that is made toward these goals. Counseling is a two-person situation in which one, the counselor, helps another individual, the client, to make better adjustments to his environment. In order to do this it is necessary to know the client intimately, to offer him help, and to show him that the counselor is a steadfast friend. The counselor is trained to see beneath the surface manifestations of problems and the client's verbal description of them.

Therapeutic Counseling: Directive. During the 1930s and 1940s, counseling, particularly in schools, tended to be more directive and informational than it is today.[17] The counselor worked by questioning, listening, making suggestions, and sometimes giving pointed advice. After listening to the problem, asking questions for clarification, and having established the necessary basic friendliness, the counselor would explain the motivations, discuss the wisdom of certain past actions, and suggest means whereby improvement in adjustment could be wrought. Considerable emphasis was placed on the gathering of objective facts. This would include the attempt to get the client to assess his progress toward any particular goal in terms of his status at a previous time as compared with his status in the present, rather than in terms of the average status of others.

An important task of the counselor is to establish rapport between himself and the client. He must lead the individual to have faith in the counselor's judgments and recommendations. Some difficulties are known as *situational;* that is, they arise out of external conditions that cannot be altered by therapy. The counseling can still, however, be of value, because the supportive role in which the therapist has cast himself lends enough support to his friend, the client, to tide him over the trying cir-

[17] Jane Warters, *Techniques of Counseling*, New York: McGraw-Hill Book Company, Inc., 1954, p. 336.

cumstances.[18] These observations might be summarized by saying that the aim is to bring about enlightened self-understanding and objective appraisal of the external situation. Help must be given the client to commit himself to a set of values. Thus, counseling is basically the business of cultivating confident human beings.[19]

Therapeutic Counseling: Nondirective. There are many authorities who feel that the type of counseling described above limits the individual's chances for becoming independent and self-directing. It is believed that advice and suggestions pointing to changes in one's behavior, or life style, may threaten the individual's ego. These people feel that, instead of the counselor-centered orientation, the emphasis should be on client-centered counseling. The basic theory is that each person (particularly adolescents and adults) has within himself, given a suitable opportunity, the potentialities for resolving his own difficulties. This approach is known as *nondirective counseling*, in which the therapist is a sympathetic listener. He tries to show his concern, friendliness, and acceptance to the client. He avoids showing shock when intimacies or misdeeds are recounted. He does, however, show that some things are more important than others by saying "uhuh" in different tones, or if the response at certain points is irrelevant, by remaining silent. The therapist may repeat a statement in a questioning tone to show that it conflicts with something said earlier or to get the individual to explain it further. The thinking required in amplifying or restating the item is one factor in helping the client to straighten out his confusion.

Some people feel that nondirective counseling is too slow a process. Many clients do not have the resources, even with encouragement, to achieve the necessary insights incident to a resolution of the difficulty. They object to the passive role of the counselor who takes little part other than listening. "A counselor may take a directive role without necessarily taking on the characteristics of a mother hen. A review of case notes of certain non-directive counseling interviews gives one the helpless impression of being cast adrift in a sea of words, with no land in sight."[20]

The proponents of nondirective counseling answer such criticism by saying that any counseling, if thorough, is necessarily slow. They point out that the ultimate outcome of successful counseling is that of making the individual sufficiently understanding and resourceful that he has the strength to resolve his difficulties himself, rather than to depend on others.

---

[18] John Dollard and Neal E. Miller, *Personality and Psychotherapy*, New York: McGraw-Hill Book Company, Inc., 1950, p. 389.

[19] E. G. Williamson, "Counseling in Developing Self-confidence," *Personnel and Guidance Journal*, 34:398–404, March, 1956.

[20] H. T. Morse in Melvene D. Hardee (ed.), *Counseling and Guidance in General Education*, New York: Harcourt, Brace & World, Inc., 1955, p. 16.

Actually, as one studies the theories and methods of both kinds of counseling, it appears that the differences, in many cases are small; the desired outcome is the same in both methods. Without being nondirective, the directive counselor also aims at self-sufficiency and indicates that the problem is that of making the client see himself so clearly that he can "see himself through." This insight, they maintain, can be facilitated by advice and explanation. It seems unfair to brand one type of counselor as laissez-faire and the other as authoritarian when both emphasize the fact that a major factor is to provide companionship, sympathy, and understanding to the client who has need of them.

Group Psychotherapy. Group psychotherapy was initiated on an experimental basis, because of the time-consuming nature of individual treatment. Success was achieved, and in the process, it was discovered that part of the beneficial results were obtained *because* there was a group. The free discussion with peers, the realization that others had problems, the sympathy engendered in groups had therapeutic values quite apart from the time saved.

The essence of group therapy is that a small group of persons are brought together by a therapist, who encourages them to describe their problems and feelings. The therapist conveys his sympathy for the members' emotionalized attitudes and, with a minimum of direction, emphasizes the desirability of interaction between members.[21]

> The premise of group psychotherapy is that the human individual is a "group animal," seeking a satisfying niche in his social setting; that he is a social product, whose inhibitions and repressions are motivated by the mores of the group; that difficulties in adjustment and failure to express his emotional troubles are the result of his inability to face the group and to find his place in it. He must repress his thinking and adapt to the demands of a complex group, and his failure to achieve this adaptation produces a neurosis or a psychosis. Place this individual who has failed in the more complex setting into a small group which is friendly to him and which is composed of others suffering from allied disturbances, and he will become enabled—when he learns to understand the problems of others—to associate himself with them, to release his aggressive tendencies, his hates, his loves and his wishes, without accompanying sense of guilt. By working out his difficulties and achieving adjustment in the small group, he becomes able to face the large group (the world) and to handle his emotional problems, social or other, on a normal basis.[22]

[21] Leon Gorlow, Erasmus L. Hoch, and Earl F. Telschow, *The Nature of Nondirective Group Psychotherapy*, New York: Bureau of Publications, Teachers College, Columbia University, 1952, p. 24.

[22] L. Wender, "Group Psychotherapy: A Study of Its Applications," *Psychiatric Quarterly*, 14:708, 1940.

Group therapy is much used with young children in a recreation setting. The major requirements are space and competent direction. The free activity given to predelinquents has made possible status- and ego-developing experiences, which enable them to cast aside the status-gaining techniques, which are used in gangs. In Los Angeles where well-planned and well-staffed group activities have been provided, it has been found that vandalism and delinquency are surprisingly low for an area such as that in which the recreation center is located.[23]

Psychodrama and Sociodrama. The technique of psychodrama has been used in clinics as well as in classrooms.[24] Its essence is suggested in the word itself: *psycho,* having to do with the mind and *drama,* meaning action or play.

> It is really mind in action. In a way we can say that a psychodramatic session is like life in its highest potential. Life, as you are living it, with the one difference that all the inner forces that you have are coming out. The psychodrama is, therefore, a vehicle by means of which life is lived under the most favorable and most intensive kind of circumstances.[25]

Psychodrama is designed to help individuals get a better perspective on their problems by acting out their feelings; then, perhaps, by assuming another role, they attempt to portray the effects of these feelings on others. Acting out these feelings puts them in a different light. The client sees that other persons may be kindly, sympathetic, and understanding. Moreover, he discerns the interest and concern of others in stressful situations. The release obtained from the verbalization and activity is another factor in dealing with tensions.

The advantages of role playing are that an individual can reassess his problems by enacting them in a neutral situation; the therapy is carried out in a social setting such that communication is facilitated. The responses are such that individuals come to feel that they are not alone in their problems. Role playing has been successfully used in homes for juvenile delinquents, child-guidance clinics, and in courts of domestic relations.

Medical Therapies. Psychological approaches are not the only ones which have resulted in improved adjustment. Endocrinology has for a long time resulted in the cure of specific mental and emotional disturb-

[23] Warters, *op. cit.,* p. 369.

[24] For the use of psychodrama as a classroom technique, see "Role-playing in the Classroom," in H. H. Remmers and others (eds.), *Growth, Teaching and Learning,* New York: Harper & Brothers, 1957, pp. 236–242.

[25] J. L. Moreno, "The Psychodrama," in Johnson E. Fairchild (ed.), *Personal Problems and Psychological Frontiers,* New York: Sheridan House, 1957, p. 281.

ances. Electric shock and insulin shock therapy has been used successfully to effect cures in certain types of mental illness. Psychosurgery, in which fibre tracts of the prefrontal lobes are severed, is used as a "last resort" technique. Hesitancy in its use is due to the irreversible nature of these operations.[26] Chlorpromazine and reserpine have attracted attention in recent years due to their power to quiet, or "tranquilize," disturbed and assaultive patients. Psychiatrists are hesitant to evaluate the total therapeutic value of these drugs and the consensus is that they do not cure but do render the patient more susceptible to psychological treatment.

TEACHERS AND SPECIALISTS

Improvement of School Programs. Probably first in importance in the relationship of teachers and various specialists is that of improving competence in the classroom. It is considered to be a healthy trend when, with limited special help, most of the specialist's time is spent with teachers. Thus, instead of helping only a few pupils, the specialist is able, indirectly, to assist many; he accomplishes this by consulting with teachers regarding particular "problem children" and by letting the teacher be the one to carry out what has been mutually decided upon as a sound program. Another advantage of the relationship is preferred when teachers sit in on case conferences. This opportunity not only broadens the teachers' understanding of behavior in general but also provides clues as to how a particular child should be treated after he returns to the classroom from therapy. Too frequently, the pivotal role of the teacher is overlooked; consequently, he has little to go on when his turn comes to provide the best educational environment for a convalescent child.

Another approach to improving school programs and teachers' services is the provision of classes or seminars in which theoretical considerations are studied and, then, used to discuss specific cases the teachers have encountered. This not only gives them professional advice but also allows them to discuss, with a feeling of freedom, certain conflicts which they encounter.

Working with Children. Knowledge of the work of specialists is helpful to teachers in several ways. One is that they are better able to spot the children who are having difficulty. Not all children are so obvious about their tensions that they misbehave and draw attention to themselves with vigor. Teachers should learn to recognize also the minor, but persistent, behaviors that indicate trouble, for example, shyness, failure to achieve commensurate with indicated ability, nervous tics, excessive daydreaming.

[26] Sol L. Garfield, *Introductory Clinical Psychology*, New York: The Macmillan Company, 1957, p. 328.

They will better know, if they are dealing with specialists, when they need special help. Clues are also provided when the youngster does not respond to particular therapies. Another advantage of knowing how specialists work is that teachers will better know the kinds of information (listed above) which will be most helpful. Finally, the teacher, as was previously mentioned, can contribute to the continued development of the child on return from therapy only when he knows what the aims and methods of the therapist are.

SUMMARY

The heavy task of aiding those young people who deviate widely from the norm must be a cooperative endeavor involving the teacher, the specialist within the school, and often, the experts who work privately or in agencies outside the school. Even in simple cases, the welfare of children can best be served by teamwork between parents, teachers, and community workers. Understanding the nature of families and communities helps both teachers and specialists to play a more sympathetic and effective role in mental hygiene.

Counselors, using both directive and nondirective methods, work to understand children's problems, help them clarify goals, indicate to clients the progress being made, and, in so doing, act as understanding, respectful, and accepting friends. A psychologist has several tasks: He is a consultant for teachers, works with parents, makes analytic measurements for himself and other specialists, and conducts therapeutic processes. Visiting teachers may execute the double task of advising teachers and of helping all concerned to appreciate the part which families and community environs play in molding pupil behavior. Remedial teachers advise their professional coworkers and help pupils to overcome specific individual deficiencies.

Psychologists and psychiatrists work in a variety of ways. Typically they begin with a case study, assembling data from a variety of sources and on many items which may prove pertinent. Case conferences involving all those who have knowledge about the child concerned are common. Play therapy is a much used technique with children. Directive and nondirective counseling are used with more mature persons, who have experience enough to understand or, through self-knowledge, to come to understand their own problems. Group psychotherapy has the double advantage of saving time and capitalizing on group processes. Role playing has been found to be helpful to many persons in getting them to achieve new perspective on their problems. Add medical therapies to the list of techniques and it can be seen that the cooperative work of many specialists is needed in a comprehensive mental hygiene program.

STUDY AND DISCUSSION EXERCISES

1. Explain the importance of getting some account of how the student feels about his problem.

2. What are some of the specific data needed by a remedial-reading teacher before work with individual children should be initiated?

3. Prepare a concise summary of the characteristics and methods you believe are most vital to a superior counseling situation.

4. Can you think of any way in which group psychotherapy might be simulated in the classroom?

5. What do you consider to be the ideal relationship between teachers and specialists? Why are the relationships sometimes not ideal?

SUGGESTED ADDITIONAL READINGS

Garfield, Sol L., *Introductory Clinical Psychology*, New York: The Macmillan Company, 1957, pp. 104–172, 192–342.

Methods of appraising personality (rating scales, questionnaires, projective techniques) and therapeutic techniques (counseling and group therapy) are described.

Lemkau, Paul V., *Mental Hygiene in Public Health*, 2d ed., New York: McGraw-Hill Book Company, Inc., 1955. 450 pp.

The promotion of health is a task to be accomplished by the teamwork of psychiatrists, psychologists, social workers, law enforcement officers, ministers, teachers, and parents.

Moustakas, Clark E., *Children in Play Therapy*, New York: McGraw-Hill Book Company, Inc., 1953. 218 pp.

The psychological bases and essential conditions of play therapy are described and numerous consecutive play sessions are reproduced.

Ohlsen, Merle M., *Guidance*, New York: Harcourt, Brace & World, Inc., 1955, chaps. 12, 13.

Some of the techniques of counseling—the do's and don'ts—described herein provide valuable suggestions for improving one's work as a teacher and broadening the understanding of the counselor's role.

Rosecrance, Francis C., and Velma D. Hayden, *School Guidance and Personnel Services*, Englewood Cliffs, N.J.: Allyn and Bacon, Inc., 1960, pp. 4–23, 102–165.

The pages indicated deal with the concept and role of guidance and the work of school psychologists and school social workers.

Warters, Jane, *Group Guidance Principles and Practices*, New York: McGraw-Hill Book Company, Inc., 1960. 428 pp.

School group work can help provide students with experiences that can aid them in learning to live more effectively and creatively. Techniques used by teachers are described.

CHAPTER 18

LIMITATIONS AND PRECAUTIONS REGARDING MENTAL HYGIENE

New discoveries and insights will add to man's potentiality for development, but it is unlikely that all the secrets of successful living will ever be discovered. The key to perfect mental health is probably as elusive as the Fountain of Youth or the Pot of Gold at the foot of the rainbow. There is, however, substantial basis for hope that ways to better mental health can be attained. Now that much attention is being given to mental health, it is possible that progress, already gratifying in the past fifty years, will be more rapid. The theories and beliefs upon which we operate today will be refined—some of them will be discarded and new emphases will be added to others. In the meantime, it should be profitable to look at some of the factors which warn against going to extremes in accepting certain aspects of the mental hygiene viewpoint.

THE NEED FOR A BALANCED VIEW

Most Children Are Normal. The very definition of *normal* indicates that deviations are the exceptional thing. Teachers must then remember that many of the case studies in mental hygiene treatises deal with only a small proportion of the population. We have been concerned, for the most part, with the *one* in the statement "One out of every twenty of us is, has been, or will be in an institution for mental illness." Lest we develop an unbalanced view, it will be well, periodically, to reflect on the fact that there are nineteen out of the twenty who are in reasonably good mental health. Only by bearing in mind that there are many well-adjusted persons in both the school and the larger social environment can we maintain the perspective that is conducive to personal mental health. *Most children are normal.*

One mentally unhealthy person does not make a neurotic society. One symptom does not make a mentally sick person. Even persons who are known to be in good physical health may have an occasional headache, suffer a sprain from time to time, or now and then have trouble sleeping soundly. Anyone working in the field of human relationships, as do teachers, must realize that it takes a whole bundle of traits to make up the total personality and one error in conduct, one objectionable trait, does not make a maladjusted child. Of the forty million students enrolled in schools and colleges today many will be discourteous, will engage in disapproved sexual activities, will steal, but will grow into what we consider normal adults. Some will have been helped by teachers and others just seem to "grow out of it." Admittedly some will get worse and will ultimately meet tragedy that might have been avoidable. Teachers, it can be seen, are facing normal situations when they are perplexed or angered by pupil behavior. Too, it is normal that there should be some failures as we attempt to help pupils.[1]

Discarded Theories May Be Proved Valid. The need for a balanced view of the theories of mental hygiene is demonstrated by the fact that some of our older theories may again become popular. The belief that children should be loved, cuddled, and indulged was popular in our grandmothers' day. In the 1920s the opinion prevailed that satisfying the child's physical needs was sufficient. It was felt that spoiling the child could be avoided by failing to pick him up when he cried, by giving him no sympathy when he got bumped, and by sticking to a strict schedule when his whim varied from the clock. Today the consensus is toward showering him with love and meeting both psychological and physical needs. It has even been suggested that the stroking, fondling, patting that an infant receives in his first few hours is a factor in getting his gastrointestinal and respiratory systems to functioning properly.[2]

A firm hand which was capable of dealing out some well-deserved punishment was once considered to be requisite to intelligent parenthood. Later, the popular theory was that punishment should be strictly avoided and that substitute activities should be sought for the wayward child. Neither theory has been uniformly accepted or rejected. Many books on child development are today reservedly admitting that, quite conceivably, punishment may not do the child any harm—in fact, it may be of real benefit. Certainly, it is not easy to find unequivocal answers to the many problems that parents and teachers encounter in the complex

[1] Clark E. Moustakas, *The Teacher and the Child,* New York: McGraw-Hill Book Company, Inc., 1956, p. 224.

[2] M. F. Ashley Montagu, *The Direction of Human Development,* New York: Harper & Brothers, 1955, p. 129.

job of providing the most beneficent influences for harmonious child development.

This does not imply that no guidance is afforded by the "experts." There seems to be little doubt that we are making progress. But past experience indicates, both in child raising and in formal education, that the reaction to a particular theory (which has come to seem erroneous) is often so violent that the "swing of the pendulum" carries us into another extreme, almost as reprehensible as the original misinterpretation. It would seem reasonable to go on record for one theory, i.e., that our new programs will continue to emphasize the need for attention to individual differences. In short, together with the sound advice offered by "experts," there must be some common sense contributed by the daily practitioner.

Both Heredity and Environment Shape Personality. A balanced view of the interacting influences of both heredity and environment is fundamental. Since it is the environment which we, as teachers, can modify, we cannot afford to lose faith in its stimulating and limiting values. All that we can do for children lies in the area of shaping their surrounding circumstances. At the same time, it is vital to remember that heredity sets limits for development. If this fact is not recognized, there is the possibility and the likelihood of losing hope regarding our effectiveness. Some of the best efforts of teachers come to naught. As a matter of fact, the changes might have proved to be very wise ones, had not the scope of their effectiveness been so markedly limited by the restrictions imposed by hereditary capacity.

If an extreme view of the relative importance of either heredity or environment is accepted, there is a likelihood that the child will be harmed. On the one hand, an extreme environmentalist might tell a child the ghastly untruth, "You can do anything you want to, if you just work hard enough." Such a statement is more than a falsehood. It is an ultimately destructive belief. There are people who will *never* run 100 yards in ten seconds, who—no matter how much they practice—will never play like Artur Rubinstein or Fritz Kreisler, who could not pass the courses in a traditional college no matter how many years they might study. Heredity sets limits which may not be transcended, no matter how favorable the environment. One of the virtues of present-day schools is that there is less emphasis on making everyone do the same thing at the same time and at the same pace.

The extreme hereditarian makes just as great an error as the unyielding environmentalist. He may mouth the clichés "You can't keep a good man down" and "Genius will out." There is no way of knowing how many good men have been kept down. Certainly, there is evidence that not all those who have IQs high enough to indicate marked superiority actually achieve the competence that results in what we call genius. The teacher who looks at the test score of a youngster, finds it low, and then asserts that he will be unable to teach him anything is leaning toward an extreme hereditarian view. The practical danger of this view is that the hereditarian feels that there is no hope for the person with limited gifts and that no particular stimulation need be provided for the gifted individual, whose success is thought to be inevitable.

A balanced view of this controversy by the teacher means that he will take every child where he is, with regard to his unknown hereditary make-up, and will do as much as he can for him. For the slow learner, this would mean the exercise of patience in evaluating small amounts of progress; for the child with greater potential, it would mean the provision of as much stimulation as possible in the form of extra study, additional projects, and a great variety of activities. It would mean, for either child, watching to see that symptoms of nervousness do not appear— nail biting, restlessness—as the result of what, for him, is too much stimulation. The balanced view calls for maintaining constant hope for development, no matter how little there is with which to work.

> As in other organisms, human diversity is partly genetically and partly environmentally conditioned. However, human environments are determined chiefly by the cultural tradition transmitted by instruction and learning, not by physical and biotic factors as in other organisms. There is no sharp cleavage between human heredity and human environment: genes do not transmit any "unit characters," either physical or psychological or cultural; the genes determine, jointly with the environment, the path which the development of a person will follow.[3]

The idea that environment plays the important role in personality structuring is also supported in the following:

> Because of man's greater learning powers organic heredity as such has smaller effects upon his behavior than it does in lower animals. This is perhaps equally significantly stated the other way round: because organic heredity plays so small a role in man's social development, what he learns through the socialization process plays a vastly more important part in his development than it does in nonhuman animals.[4]

Environment does shape the personality, but it is only a contributing factor. Other factors which must be considered result from the interac-

---

[3] Theodosius Dobzhansky, "Inside Human Nature," in Lynn White, Jr. (ed.), *Frontiers of Knowledge in the Study of Man*, New York: Harper & Brothers, 1956, pp. 17–18.
[4] Montagu, *op. cit.*, pp. 86–87.

tion between the organism with its environment; among them may be listed such components as metabolism, physical health and vigor, the will to succeed, and, of course, the mental capacity of the individual.

The Influence of Early Childhood. Typical of the many statements regarding the great importance of early childhood experience is the following:

> Childhood experiences and the memory of these experiences as the years go by leave an indelible impression on the individual's personality. The child whose childhood has been happy has an entirely different outlook on life from that of the child whose early years have been marked by constant friction, sadness, and emotional tension. . . . The memories of those unhappy experiences will never be completely forgotten, nor will the effect on his personality ever be entirely eradicated.[5]

While the statement is accurate, the reader must be careful to pay attention to all parts of it, i.e., "never be *completely* forgotten" and "nor . . . *entirely* eradicated." In short, the early childhood experiences do not finally and irrevocably shape the adult personality. General trends may be established. Bases are laid for later growth. But the personality, the individual, is growing in some direction during the entire life span.

Many authorities believe that some neuroticism in our society is due to the anxiety and hurry of American mothers to toilet train their babies. The proddings, promptings, and pressures to which the baby is subjected in the attempt to train him early is thought to bring about a state of tension that persists throughout life. Under the impact of this view, contemporary approaches to toilet training are changing. Today the advice is to wait until the child can talk a little and until there is some assurance that he can understand what is wanted. Furthermore, it is felt that more important than the time and the technique of training is the over-all emotional atmosphere of love, acceptance, and admiration, which will more than compensate for errors in child-rearing tactics.

The entire hope of education and the development of better mental health rests on the assumption that growth is continuous. That teachers do not ignore early childhood influences is revealed in their efforts to get information about prior experiences. This knowledge is used, by the wise teacher, as a step in formulating plans for the future.

Teachers Need Not Succeed with All Children. There is need for a balanced view as to how much can be accomplished with each child. It is possible, and probable, that even the best of teachers will fail with some children. It may be that a child readily finds in one teacher a similarity

---

[5] Elizabeth B. Hurlock, *Child Development,* 3d ed., New York: McGraw-Hill Book Company, Inc., 1956, p. 554.

to an adored parent, while another teacher is such an antithesis to his parents that rapport is difficult or impossible. Conversely, the fault may be with the teacher. Perhaps subconsciously he sees in the child such a contrast to his ideal of what a child ought to be that it is difficult for him to give a warm acceptance.

A balanced view, therefore, will accept the idea that failure with some children is pardonable but that success with some is necessary. Of course, "the old college try" should be manifested in every case, new approaches should be devised, and new theories pondered and tested. Some other teachers, however, might succeed where you have failed. Perhaps you may have paved the way for their success without your knowing it. Outside the school there are influences which may bring about improvement, where the school as a whole has been unable to effect visible results. When teachers evaluate results, they must be objective—giving themselves credit where credit is due, blaming themselves when errors have been committed, and taking neither credit nor blame when the occasion warrants.

Contemporary Beliefs May Be Fallacious. We should like to believe that scientific knowledge has reached such a stage that we labor under no fallacious beliefs. Surely, scholars of previous generations felt that their insights were such that chances for error were few. Many people think that views of mental hygiene, the nature of the learning process, theories of education, and methods of child rearing are subject to being carried to extremes. Errors, therefore, according to this view, are due to too much stress on the replacement of that which is repudiated. The latter may be true. Contemporary theories, based on experiment and data from controlled observation rather than on intuitive and astute guesses, are, however, more than swings of the pendulum.

Evidence can be found to support the notion that tentativeness is necessary. The belief that formal discipline (improving the mind through strenuous mental exercise) should be discarded has been accepted by most psychologists. Yet there are a few stalwarts who feel that there may still be virtue in carrying on mental activity which has no immediate practical result aside from the activity involved. John B. Watson's idea that a child should be let alone—not cuddled and spoiled—and thus should learn to absorb his own difficulties was almost completely replaced by the idea that love, cuddling, and protection are vital parts of a favorable environment. Today one finds indications of reversion toward the Watsonian theory—that children should not be overprotected, that they need to encounter conflict in order to learn to meet difficulties.

It is difficult to say just what the contemporary idea of the significance of thumb sucking is. One can find firm adherents to almost any of the following beliefs:

Thumb sucking should be firmly prohibited by slapping, using bitter-tasting applications, or splinting the thumb or elbow.

The habit should be approached in a positive manner; i.e., many interesting toys or an all-round wholesome environment should be supplied.

The habit results in deformity of teeth and jaws and makes the child more liable to disease.

It will not affect the growth of teeth and jaws, since it takes tremendous and continuous pressure to alter tooth and jaw formation.

It is caused by the child's not exercising his sucking "instinct" sufficiently—his milk is obtained too easily.

It is caused by the child's having to work long at sucking and by the child's associating satisfaction and comfort with sucking—his milk should come more easily.

Steps should be taken to eliminate the habit, since the longer it continues, the harder it will be to break.

Let the child alone, for the natural growth process results in abandonment of thumb sucking.

Let him know you disapprove.

Forget about it, since calling attention to it in any way only intensifies the habit.

And with this we come to a truth in mental hygiene, "Problems are frequently not so serious as the attitude that is taken toward them." Perhaps it is parental anxiety that is the real problem. Whatever conclusion one draws, using thumb sucking as an example, it seems clear that there is a possibility that contemporary beliefs may be found to be fallacious.

Much the same dilemma exists in education. Contemporary articles debate the issues: Place more stress on the academic and forget this life adjustment education; children's interests are a poor guide to the selection of curricular content; if the pupil can't keep up with the class, find some place other than the school for him; cut out the frills—art, music, drama —and get down to the hard facts of mathematics, science, and language.[6] However, we can be sure that whatever conclusions are drawn from these issues will have undergone further refinement twenty years hence.

Much Concern about Mental Hygiene Is Dangerous. Teachers studying mental hygiene may be overimpressed and, as a result, think they find in the pupils overwhelming evidence of maladjustment. There is a danger in too much introspection; there is danger of hasty analysis which proceeds on the basis of insufficient background study. The study of mental hygiene

[6] H. G. Rickover, "The World of the Uneducated," *The Saturday Evening Post,* 232(22):19ff, Nov. 28, 1959.

must be approached with a firm intention that no one idea shall be emphasized to the exclusion of related factors and contrasting ideas.

One of the explanations for the present high incidence of mental disorder in our society is that people have too much time for introspection. This situation is reflected in the following:

> What of the American housewife? Blessed with labor-saving devices in quantities envied by her sisters abroad, she suffers least from overwork. Yet, commented the U. S. report, "neurosis is common in the housewife," though not necessarily any more so than the rest of the population. And despite all her gadgets, she often complains of fatigue.[7]

Robert Coughlan emphasizes the prevalence of too great concern when he says that, as medical science has reduced the probability of child mortality, parents have become less absorbed with keeping their children alive and have worried about mental health. "The final result might be thought of, in the language of the times, as a 'neuroses-neurosis'; that is, a neurosis brought on by excessive fear of neuroses."[8]

Should we, on the basis of such observations, stop thinking about the problem of mental health and let life and growth take its course with no attempt at guidance? A "Yes" answer to this question would seem to be undesirable. There should be an evaluation of assets, an emphasis on constructive living, as well as an attempt to eliminate negative traits and avoid harmful habits. A balanced viewpoint cannot require the suppression of thoughts about mental health.

UNPROVED BELIEFS

It would be the part of *absolute* honesty to say that *none* of our beliefs in the realm of psychology have been proven, in the sense that there are incontestable answers or that all the data are known. In this section a number of beliefs will be discussed in an attempt to show why precaution is needed. There is no intention, however, of creating the impression that the beliefs mentioned are more questionable than others that might be named.

There Is a Norm for Conduct. Actually there is no precise, or even approximate, definition of what is normal. There are "normal" height-weight tables, but careful scholars warn that there is no established norm *for individuals*. Each person must be regarded not in terms of averages but in terms of body structure and bone formation. A child deviating 10 pounds from the table may, in terms of his bodily organization, be quite normal. Normal intelligence is spoken of, but, even when it is

---

[7] "Queen with Flat Feet," *Pathfinder*, 57:30, Oct., 4, 1950.
[8] Robert Coughlan, "How to Survive Parenthood," *Life*, 28:114, June 20, 1950.

judged within limits as 85 to 115 or 90 to 110 IQ, there is realization that other factors, such as drive, sociality, and experience, condition the "normality" of the resultant behavior. The reasons for difficulty in establishing norms for conduct are easily seen. Individual differences in the possession of specific traits are extensive. The combinations of traits within an individual vary greatly. Individual, community, and cultural demands vary from place to place and from time to time.

Normality of behavior, from the mental hygiene viewpoint, is similarly perplexing. In fact, "any behavior may become a problem if it is regarded and treated as such by the adult to whose care and training the child happens to be entrusted."[9] Thus, whispering may be a symptom or a problem to some teachers, although to others it is a normal manifestation —often of interest in class activities. Thumb sucking, it has been seen, is regarded by some as a bad habit or symptom of difficulty, while others regard it as a normal phase of growing. Masturbation is a shocking behavior to some observers; to others, including some psychiatrists, a passing stage of development. Children's lying must be immediately corrected, according to some; but others regard it as a normal response to certain kinds of stress.

Normality of behavior is more an individual matter than a kind of behavior. Bed-wetting is "normal" for a four-year-old—he lacks the discrimination of maturity. Lying may be normal for an adult—the social setting must be considered. "Normality" becomes a matter of time, place, and person involved. Next comes the question of how much? Some lying, stealing, bullying, procrastination, daydreaming, rationalization, and projection may be viewed with equanimity; but too frequent a manifestation of these behaviors may be a matter of concern.

These observations should not be interpreted as indicating that there is no workable concept of the meaning of normality. They point out only that precision is lacking and tentativeness in judgment is consequently required. Practical implications of the import of these considerations should include the following: (1) One cannot generalize as to the importance of a given type of behavior without some regard for the individual concerned. (2) A given behavior has little significance in isolation. Various traits take on meaning as they are seen in relation to other traits; not one symptom but a number of them in combination is the crucial consideration. (3) The cultural milieu and developmental background of the individual must be considered when evaluating behavior.

Types of Body May Influence Personality. The notion that fat men are jolly and that lean men are treacherous has been thrust aside as an outdated superstition. Kretchmer's theory of morphological types is in dis-

---

[9] E. K. Wickman, *Children's Behavior and Teachers' Attitudes,* New York: Commonwealth Fund, Division of Publication, 1929, p. 50.

repute among contemporary psychologists. We may agree with these conclusions, since they conflict with data emphasizing the continuity of differences; that is, there is not a trimodal or bimodal distribution of body types. Rather, extreme types are merely the borders of considerable numbers of "averages" (see Figure 21). Yet the idea that body type does influence personality keeps coming into notice. W. H. Sheldon[10] holds to the theory that bodily physique is normally characterized by a certain type of personality. The error of discrete types is avoided. Three major types are listed: endomorph—abdominal predominance (fat type); mesomorph—predominance of bone and muscle (athletic type); and ectomorph —long, delicate bones with large surface in proportion to mass (lean type). Measurement of an individual is recorded on a scale having 7 for the extreme and 1 for the minimum. Thus a pronounced endomorph

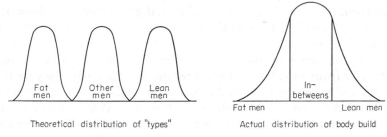

Theoretical distribution of "types"   Actual distribution of body build

FIG. 21. Distribution of types of body build.

would be a 7-1-1. A mesomorph would be a 1-7-1, and an extreme ectomorph would be recorded 1-1-7, but these extremes are rarely encountered. The sum is not always 9, and an average individual representing an extreme in no body type would be a 3-4-3, or 4-3-4. Other variations might be 2-3-5, 1-2-6, and the like. Thus continuity of description is provided for and the notion of discrete types is avoided. It is not necessary for personality organization to follow a discrete type with such a basis. One does not naturally need to be a jovial fellow, a glutton, an aggressive athlete, or a lonely scholar; he may, without deviating from his body type, have some combination of these qualities.

When two brothers are observed to have distinctly different personalities, we immediately say that of course their heredity is different. Then too, their environments, while superficially the same, are different because one of the boys is older. But according to Sheldon's theory, it is possible to suppose that their body types, being different, predispose them to divergent personality organizations. We have seen scholars who are endomorphs and scholars who are ectomorphs, salesmen who are fat and

[10] W. H. Sheldon and S. S. Stevens, *The Varieties of Temperament*, New York: Harper & Brothers, 1942.

salesmen who are thin. This would seem to indicate that interests are not greatly influenced by morphological type. But there are unanswered questions: Is it not possible that the endomorph gains his scholarly inclination at the cost of emotional stress and strain? Is it not possible that the lean salesman has to force himself to be pleasant and friendly? Does not the extremely lean man find that, in spite of ability, he does not enjoy the athletic competitions which are so highly satisfactory to the mesomorph?

Closely related to the concept of body types is the biochemical constitution of the individual—which in fact may go far toward explaining individuality. It has been proved that "normality" actually embraces a wide variation in organic make-up—as it does in psychological and social characteristics. For instance, paranasal and sinus tissues of one normal child may be twenty times larger than those of another normal child. In an ordinary breath, one healthy young man may breathe about 350 cubic centimeters, while in another the tidal air amounts to about 1,300 cubic centimeters; and the breathing-frequency rate may vary from 4 to 20 respirations per minute. Heart beats in 182 normal young men varied from 45 to 105 beats per minute. The capacity of normal hearts to pump blood varies from 3 to almost 11 liters per minute. Similarly, the very shape of hearts and stomachs vary as do the routes which digestive juices take. Because of these and other differences Roger J. Williams believes that the study of human constitution will contribute more to the understanding and solution of human problems than physical and social anthropology together have thus far been able to accomplish.[11] It seems reasonable to expect that these differences might go far toward the explanation of individual differences in motivation, energy, interests, aptitudes, and appetites.

Interesting speculations by the classroom teacher might be derived from such data. Let it be assumed that the bodily type does not predispose an individual toward a particular kind of personality development, thereby causing some interests and activities to be more natural and gratifying than others. Even without this assumption, we know that some youngsters enjoy social dancing, others are thrilled by athletic pursuits, some require no urging to produce artistic creations, and many need no prodding to devote themselves heartily to their books. Yet, in our attempt to see that each child is *adjusted*, we urge him to select a partner and get into the swing of things; we give sales talks about the development of the mind and body, to get him to join the athletic activities; we impress upon him that all children should cooperate in the making of the room mural; and we tell him "You can learn to enjoy your lessons if you work hard enough to gain a little success." It is not a question of repudiating the ideal of "well-rounded development." The argument is that

[11] Roger J. Williams, *Biochemical Individuality*, New York: John Wiley & Sons, Inc., 1957, *passim*.

too much prodding may impose greater personality stress than would come about through the child's remaining a wallflower, a side-lines observer, or a mediocre scholar. It would seem reasonable to believe tentatively that bodily organization rather than being a foolish fancy, may be one of the important factors in explaining differences in personality.

Discipline Warps the Personality. Broad aspects of discipline are dealt with elsewhere in this book. The purpose of the present discussion is merely to question the belief that discipline warps the personality. There is no quarrel with the view that discipline should be positive, that it finally should come from within the individual, and that imposed discipline should be held to a minimum. The point raised is that some discipline of the stern, imposed kind may at times be both appropriate and constructive. In fact, young children may feel a heavy burden imposed on them when they have to make choices without adequate background; thus, these children are actually relieved by imposed authority. As a matter of fact, imposed discipline that is not unduly harsh, inconsistent, and incomprehensible is often appreciated in retrospect. Most adults are products of the era of firm discipline and do not resent it. Real adjustive values accrue from adhering to social requirements.

> If, from our psychological counseling of hundreds of parents and their children, we were to pick the most common cause of mental and emotional instability, sense of failure and inferiority, it would be the practice of letting children act according to their likes and dislikes instead of according to principles. By not doing what they disliked they had failed to acquire the habits and abilities which produce competence and self-reliance.
>
> On the other hand, the secure child is the child who comes to know what his parents stand for, and that they cannot be shaken from their standards by his arguing or wheedling. This is the kind of authority that children learn to respect, because it is the authority not of force or of age but of impersonal principles. Where the parents are sure of their principles, the child will be sure of his parents.[12]

There must be both yielding to external authority and a chance to explore and discover as one exercises his capacity for independence. Just as the parent must not rob the child of opportunities to learn the invaluable lesson of conformance, so the teacher must see that, in his attempt to make school life enjoyable, he does not remove the challenges that stimulate development. Let there be concessions when the issue is minor. Let both parents and teachers stand firm when a significant principle is at stake.

[12] Henry C. Link, "How to Give Your Child Security," *The Reader's Digest,* 58: 40, March, 1951. Adapted from Henry C. Link, *The Way to Security,* New York: Doubleday & Company, Inc., 1951.

There Is a Correct Way to Rear a Child. Authorities in child psychology, advising that wise parents must do this or that, make it appear that there is a specific way to raise children. The fact is that some parents whom we would judge to be far from ideal have children who are more healthy mentally than others who have been "raised by the book." Thus, in spite of notable swings in the popularity of certain theories, healthy adults have come from homes dominated by sharply contrasting practices. This should give parents confidence to believe that the errors they have made are not necessarily irrevocable. It should give teachers a feeling of confidence that children can be helped, in spite of negative backgrounds. Dr. Benjamin Spock says:

> Don't take too seriously all that the neighbors say. Don't be overawed by what the experts say. Don't be afraid to trust your own common sense. Bringing up your child won't be a complicated job if you take it easy, trust your own instincts, and follow the directions that your doctor gives you. . . .
> It may surprise you to hear that the more people have studied different methods of bringing up children the more they have come to the conclusion that what good mothers and fathers instinctively feel like doing for their babies is usually best after all. Furthermore, all parents do their best job when they have a natural, easy confidence in themselves. Better to make a few mistakes from being natural than to do everything letter-perfect out of a feeling of worry.[13]

There are many ways of rearing healthy and happy children. Whatever techniques are accepted, applied by mature adults, and backed by good intentions, a wholesome acceptance of children, and *consistency* of application, the results are likely to be gratifying.

The element of consistency, in this triad, is no mean contender for first place. Children must know, and be able to depend on the consistency of, what is expected and what is required of them. Children taken from poor homes and placed in good ones—studies show—still long for the things to which they have been accustomed. During the bombing of London, children who were removed from their homes to the quiet of the countryside showed more personality disorders than did those who remained in the midst of the noise, excitement, and fear. Youngsters who are old enough to express their feelings in words object to moving from one community to another; and among the contributing factors to personality disorders one often cited is "frequent change of residence." Yet it has been found that "trailer-family" parents who are stable, industrious, well-educated persons who follow skilled trades in dam,

[13] Benjamin Spock, *The Pocket Book of Baby and Child Care*, New York: Pocket Books, Inc., 1946, pp. 3, 4.

bridge, and highway construction have well-adjusted children. Apparently it is the reason for change of residence—a negative one, escape from unhappiness or restlessness, or a positive one, the desire to do one's job combined with the pioneering spirit—rather than the change itself that is the crucial factor in determining the direction one grows.[14] It must be concluded, from these evidences, that the actual conditions in which a child grows are no more important than the basic psychological factors which lie back of them.

There Is a Correct Way to Teach. There is considerable controversy regarding the relative merits of progressive teaching and traditional teaching—as though there were two ways to teach, one of them better than the other. As a matter of actual analysis, there are times when it is difficult to see that so-called "traditional teaching" is any different from "progressive teaching." An eight-year study was conducted with thirty schools, to determine the effectiveness of progressive education. The interesting outcome was that superior accomplishments through progressive education were matched, in other areas, by the accomplishments of "control" students from traditional schools. But it is also worthy of note that some of the progressive schools made few significant changes in their procedures, while others made quite radical changes—both acting under the name of progressivism. As in the matter of child rearing, the conclusion seems warranted that the spirit back of the method is as significant as the method itself.

The following appeared in a set of principles governing a sound teacher education program: "In the teacher education program, the methods and techniques of the professional staff should exemplify the type of modern teaching considered most desirable for the level and purpose for which the instruction is given." Can there be such a thing as "the type"? An instructor, in order to provide such an exemplification, would have to be a veritable chameleon. Just as there are many kinds of personalities which are effective in the classroom, so too are there many types of teaching which are effective.

Results of carefully controlled experiments on teaching methods are often published in professional literature. One cannot but be impressed with the success of these experiments. It appears that our own techniques should at once be modified. But there is reason to pause—there is a factor that is exceedingly difficult to control or to measure—the enthusiasm of the teacher. The experimenter, in his enthusiasm for the new, kindles eagerness in the students. Thus, the human element must be considered in connection with all successful teaching procedures.

Teachers should know that it is unnecessary to imitate the successful

[14] Alvin L. Schorr, "Families on Wheels," *Harper's Magazine*, 216:71–78, January, 1957.

practices of another. It is always possible that, in terms of his particular personality, the methods he has developed are best for him. This assurance, however, carries with it a liability. A technique that is successful with one child may not work so well with another. It may, therefore, be necessary to deviate from customary practices, in order to be of maximum help to a child who is different from those met earlier. The teacher can profitably pay attention to practices which others find workable, so that his own ways will be modified to meet immediate circumstances. The teacher should not seek for the best method but for a continuous modification of practices that will challenge different students and serve to maintain his own enthusiasm.

THINGS WE DO NOT KNOW

How Learning Takes Place. *Learning* is defined as "the modification of behavior through experience." But no universally accepted explanation of the nature of these modifications has been made. No doubt, scientific proof of the nature of these changes would be of value to educators. In the meantime, we do not operate in a vacuum, in spite of not knowing what learning is, because *we do know a great deal about the conditions under which learning takes place.*

It is safe to say that the conditions under which the most rapid modification of behavior takes place would include, to a degree, the following: (1) Motivation on the part of the individual—action begins with the organism. Learners must give attention to *the* stimulus which must be selected from among all the stimuli that might possibly be given attention at one time. (2) A personal goal must be attached to the motivation process. The learner must (if learning is to be most economical) have a clear perception of that goal. (3) The acceptance of the goal generates tensions within the individual. Lack of knowledge prevents release of these tensions. (4) The learner casts about for a way of resolving the tension. From all possible alternatives he must select one to try; if it does not work, he attempts another alternative. (5) Successful responses are fixed through association with the familiar, through appropriate drill, and through satisfactions derived from successful attack of the problem. It is further known that speed of learning is dependent upon the intelligence of the individual, his relative maturity, his past experiences affording him an associational background, the difficulty of the problem in terms of the foregoing, and the strength of the motivation.

A Desirable Combination of Environmental Influences. It must also be admitted that we do not know just what combination of environmental influences will produce the best adjustment in individuals. When books, such as this, undertake to describe the optimum influences for pupil development, one might become dejected upon realizing that the best conditions have not been supplied. Actually, there is no sharp line between what is good and what is poor. There is, however, a distinguishable difference between what is best and what is worst. It is the former with which we are mainly concerned in trying to establish better conditions for mental health.

Life is easier for some than it is for others. Two persons (theoretically) might live in the same environment, yet grow into different personalities and enjoy different degrees of mental health. If these two started with the same inherent potentialities, we are forced to believe that it is the combination of environmental factors that produced the difference. Perhaps some kind word, an evidence of love or confidence, a helpful act, in the midst of a whole assortment of negative influences, was sufficient to pull one of the persons through to better adjustment. Thus it is that some children who seem to lack love, who have no basis for security, and who possess few material advantages nevertheless develop into healthy, confident individuals. On the other hand, a person who appears to have all the advantages manifests multiple symptoms of mental ill-health. Some seemingly isolated factor in his environment was evidently "the straw that broke the camel's back."

The Meaning of Abnormality. Teachers studying mental hygiene invariably ask, "How do I know when I have an abnormal child in my class?" The question is not easy. It varies with the individual, the situation, and the frequency of the manifested symptoms. It is possible to answer the question only for those individuals who differ widely from the "norm"; as the borderline cases are studied, the answer becomes increasingly difficult. In short, it is easier to distinguish a psychotic individual from a normal one since the psychotic has lost his hold on reality— than it is to distinguish a neurotic from the normal.

Abnormality, then, cannot be described in terms of absolutes. It is not simply a matter of *how far* one may differ from others in such characteristics as aggressiveness, sociability, and self-confidence before he is judged to be abnormal, but abnormality is also a matter of who, when, and where. An example may serve to clarify the problem. Is a child who daydreams abnormal? The answer may be "Yes" if the following conditions prevail: The child has a degree of physical health and strength that would make action easy for him; he engages in reverie when other children are finding satisfaction in vigorous action; he is "lost in his world" when stimulating circumstances surround him. Daydreaming, however, would not be considered abnormal under the following conditions: If the child were crippled and thus had inactivity forced upon him; if inactivity were imposed as punishment or by adults who did not appreciate his need for activity; and if the stimuli which surrounded him had little significance in terms of his background. Abnormality in the classroom, then, is something which is highly relative.

THE PARADOX OF OBSTACLES

Because children need to grow in their ability to absorb tensions and overcome obstacles, teachers often ask the pertinent question, "Should we attempt to remove all obstacles from the child's path?" The answer, of course, is "No," and again a word concerning caution in the approach to mental hygiene becomes relevant.

Obstacles and Conflicts Have Stimulation Value. It is entirely possible for children and adolescents to be overprotected. Psychologists, psychiatrists, and teachers have all encountered individuals who are faced with problems of present and future adjustment precisely because they have never been allowed to meet difficulties, to get into trouble, or to experience disappointment. Such persons have become so dependent that they are immediately lost when the guiding hand is not present.

> The child who has been overprotected but controlled at the same time usually does not present disturbing behavior to his environment. His binding dependency on his mother prevents his making contacts with other children and so he has not learned the art of relating himself to them. He feels different and isolated, and resents his mother whom he blames for his unhappiness.
>
> The child who has been overprotected and indulged presents a serious problem in adjustment. Accustomed to having his own way and to feeling secure in the protection of his mother, he will continue to live on the basis of the pleasure principle. He will be unable and unwilling to accept frustration and will lack the capacity to give of himself to others.[15]

Teachers can recall occasions when they have made assignments which they had thought might be too difficult, only to have the students respond by doing the work very satisfactorily. It seemed that placing additional obstacles in their way resulted in their getting down to work seriously and producing more than was expected. In our own lives, we have often been challenged to do something that was more than ordinarily difficult because we were told that it was more than we could do. Ordinarily, a game of tennis or of bridge is more highly enjoyed, even in defeat, when the competitor is a worthy one than when the opponent is an unskilled one.

Barriers to progress and obstacles in the way of satisfaction call for the growth of the individual. They demand that one gather his resources for attack. They require that one develop skills and acquire information that will facilitate achievement. Among the criteria of psychological maturity must be included the ability to endure hardships and an attitude

[15] Hyman S. Lippman, *Treatment of the Child in Emotional Conflict*, New York: McGraw-Hill Book Company, Inc., 1956, p. 145.

that looks on problems as a challenge to growth. These aspects of maturity are achieved as the result of work and struggles.

The problem for the mental hygienist becomes a matter of determining, as far as possible, which obstacles have healthy stimulation value and which are likely to cause tensions that will end in frustration. Obstacles so large as to leave little reasonable chance that the pupil will be able to attack them successfully should be removed. Obstacles appropriate to the pupil's level of maturity should be allowed to serve as sources of stimulation. Specifically, if the child has reached the mental age of six and a half years and has other indications of being able to learn to read, then, in spite of the fact that he might find it somewhat difficult, appropriate pressure might well be put on him to acquire the skill. On the other hand, if there is a pupil in high school whose intelligence is such that others like him have in large measure failed to comprehend algebra, it would seem logical to wait for further maturity or to find some other area of study for him. A parallel example might be cited in the realm of social adjustment. A new pupil in school has so many adjustments to make that it would be desirable to call on other pupils to be friendly and courteous to him, so that his adjustment would be made easier. Conversely, a pupil who has long been in the class and who has made many of his adjustments might well be left alone in a struggle to get along harmoniously in a class discussion of student government. These situations are schematically represented in Figure 22.

Some factors are beyond control. The fact that some obstacles in the way of pupils are not within the power of the teacher to remove throws further light on the question, "Should we attempt to remove all obstacles from the child's path?" Everyone must face obstacles, even some that are in the form of overprotection. Teachers should then not be too deeply concerned about removing *some* obstacles that will make growth somewhat easier. In spite of the fact that as much as possible is done to remove obstacles that have little or no stimulation value, tensions and frustrations will remain. Just as one becomes a healthy adult by avoiding illness in childhood (it is no longer recommended that children be deliberately exposed to childhood diseases) so it might be that one gains strength by victories rather than by facing unnecessary or insurmountable obstacles. The removal of the more troublesome hazards will make it possible for the individual to face the inevitabilities with greater equanimity.

Suppose that as much as seems desirable has been done to make learning pleasant—clear explanation of purposes, help when needed, encouragement, appropriate tasks—the pupil may still have to live with the fact that his parents are anticipating divorce. The help he receives in school toward accomplishment, recognition, and attainment of security will increase the probability that he will be able to absorb the conflicts

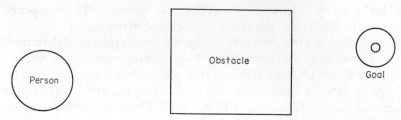

Problem: An immature individual faced by an overwhelming obstacle. Result—tensions leading to frustration and personality disintegration.

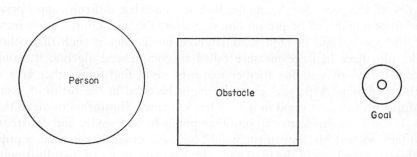

Solution 1: Help the individual to grow by providing preparatory experiences or merely by temporarily setting aside the obstacles until further maturation has taken place.

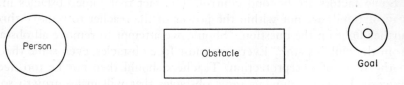

Solution 2: Reduce the size of the obstacle so that it is appropriate to the present level of maturity of the individual.

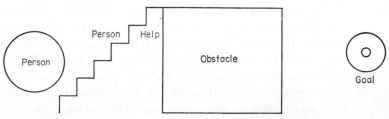

Solution 3: Give the individual help (suggestions, physical assistance, understanding) that will enable him to climb over the present barrier. Provide a progressive sequence of steps to be taken.

FIG. 22. Schematic representation of techniques for dealing with obstacles generated by the home situation. A pupil laboring under the handicap of financial poverty—poor clothes and inadequate diet—should not suffer from the additional burden of being required to master chemistry and Latin lessons which are beyond his intellectual level. Children suffering physical handicaps—heart dysfunctions, crippling, low vitality— should have their burdens lightened by being guided into activities which substitute for athletic prestige.

Of course it is necessary to guard against assuming too soon that things are beyond control. It is possible that an understanding and audacious teacher might help incompatible parents see how important it is, for the welfare of the child they love, to settle their differences. It may be that the teacher could work toward marshaling community resources that would help children overcome their poverty. Allowing time for additional mental maturity to be achieved may solve some academic questions.[16] There is hope that medical treatment may serve to reduce the liabilities imposed by physical handicaps. But the fact remains that these are likely to be insurmountable handicaps. Teachers need not be concerned about removing too many of them. In spite of the best efforts, some handicaps will remain.

> There is no way in which we can go through life without being, many times over, witness to conflict and involved in conflict. If, therefore, we have no creative wisdom regarding it—if we merely act on frightened or hostile impulse each separate time—there will be a great many occasions when we fail to do what might be done in behalf of emotional health and sound human relations.
>
> About some conflicts, of course, nothing needs to be done. They are simply an overflow of life's vitality; and the person who hurries in to stop them and smooth things over is likely to seem more like a meddler than a peacemaker in the great sense of that term.[17]

Teachers and Teaching Need Not Be Perfect. Teachers sometimes feel futile, because they realize that, with much to be done, they are so far from perfection. Others are not particularly concerned, because they feel that what they do is only "a drop in the bucket." It is important to achieve some balance between these extreme views.

Certainly there are many adults who have triumphantly survived many negative experiences in school. They have been exposed to dogmatically exacting teachers, to teachers who took no pride in their work; they have been given meaningless tasks to perform; and they have had to work with limited materials. Sometimes these negative factors stimulated growth.

---

[16] Research reveals that many failures in algebra could be avoided if it were taught in the junior instead of the freshman year of high school.

[17] Harry Overstreet and Bonaro Overstreet, *The Mind Alive*, New York: W. W. Norton & Company, Inc., 1954, p. 232.

But, there were also those who were frustrated by these experiences, and for them school became so distasteful that they stopped going at the earliest possible moment. Perhaps the reason why the average school achievement in the United States has risen about two years over the average in 1940 is that some frustrating obstacles in the schools are being removed.[18]

It is vital that there should be enough difficulty in school tasks to call for the expenditure of some energy. Fortunately, there are discernible clues to help teachers determine what is too much and what is too little in the way of requirements and motivations. When children begin to show symptoms of nervousness in the form of irritability, inattention, emotional outbursts, sullen resignation, or chronic disobedience, it may be well to become critical of existing methods and demands. When children appear bored, spend their time in annoying others, and develop dilatory work habits and excessive daydreaming, it is time to wonder whether the tasks are appropriate to the capacity of the individuals concerned. The need for balance is patent.

Child psychologists point out that the chronically happy, tolerant, and satisfied parent is a sickly sweet example for the child. A parent who becomes disgruntled and cross over a child's actions—though he does not reject the child—is establishing a more normal condition for development. He is providing the child with an experience that he is bound to meet in later life. Similarly, in the classroom there need not be a pallid tolerance for all kinds of behavior. Pupils have to learn that conformity to behavior requirements is a requisite part of effective social functioning. Normal human beings are not uniformly and incessantly cheerful and tolerant. A teacher need not be a paragon.

THE WORLD BEYOND THE CLASSROOM

Family Influences. Due credit must be given to the vast number of families that provide beneficent environments for wholesome growth—interested and proud parents who provide material comforts, medical and dental care, informative trips, and developmental pastimes. There are, however, negative situations that complicate the job of teaching and confound the practitioners of mental hygiene.

Fifteen-year-old Jane Doe came to the girls' counselor for a tardy slip—hair disheveled, clothes awry, and reeking with tobacco smoke. Because her school work was not in accord with tests indicating ability the counselor had been looking for a chance to talk with Jane—who was

[18] "Educational Attainment of Americans," *Research Bulletin of the National Education Association*, 36:82–83, October, 1958.

resentful of the question, "Why are you doing such poor school work?" After fifteen minutes in which the counselor tried to establish a friendly tone, Jane finally poured forth a long tale of woe. "It came too spontaneously to be made up," the counselor reported.

"How can I study? It's impossible to keep my mind on history or biology. First thing when I enter the door I start getting the devil. 'Why don't I get better grades? Why don't I keep myself neat? Why don't I do my home work? Why don't I help around the house?' There's never a moment of peace. I don't dare bring home friends to listen to my mother's tirade—and then the criticism of my friends which follows my going out. We never have a meal in peace. Dad eats and runs. Mom accuses him of chasing women. Sometimes there are days when I see him only a few minutes at supper. Yak, yak, yak, nag, nag, nag. I hear it all the time. It even runs through my head at school. Biology? History?"

This continued for over forty minutes and the counselor could do nothing but listen. "What advice does one give? How can you show friendliness? What will happen if the feelings are not subdued?"

There is no ready answer. But one can be friendly—which the counselor was. Jane came to the office occasionally to report afterwards. The counselor talked with the mother and tried to reveal how the girl felt. There was some change, but a human being's personality is not rebuilt with the use of a few words. Teachers can recognize the situation—if they will listen before they condemn. But the fact remains that the family sometimes constitutes an influence that places severe limitations on what the school can do.

Community Influences. Upper- and middle-class children have many advantages. They can belong to youth organizations, they have privileges in the adult golf and athletic clubs, they have dancing lessons and parties. But another, and large, portion of the population have no such opportunities.[19] The following, while perhaps not typical, may be considered representative (it concerns a gang that wanted to "go social" rather than antisocial); it indicates the problem posed by community factors in major metropolitan areas.

The music blares loud and fast, in rock 'n' roll or Latin rhythms. The meringue is a favorite. But fast music finally stops and one of the slow rock 'n' roll tunes that drags in thick, halting harmony fills the room, and the boys are standing by girls. Couples embrace, and it is then the duty of the attendant minister to see that the technique used in this dance is "fish" and not "grind." If the feet are moving, it is "fish" and legal; if the only movement is in the bodies that are, in either case,

[19] From 40 to 65 per cent, depending on community, of the population is estimated to belong to the lower-lower and upper-lower classes. Robert J. Havighurst and Bernice L. Neugarten, *Society and Education,* Englewood Cliffs, N.J.: Allyn and Bacon, Inc., 1957, p. 18.

pressed together, it is "grind" and the offenders will be tapped on the shoulder by the minister and asked to start "fishing."

At eleven o'clock it is over, and the kids return to the street. Boys without girls may go to a candy store and gather at the jukebox for still more music; some seek the shelter of tenement hallways to work out their own singing arrangements. Those who leave the dance with dates often go to the hallways too—but not to sing. There is of course no such thing as "getting the family car" for "a drive in the country." Necking has to be done in the hallways. For more serious sexual adventures, the refuge is the roof. This can be dangerous, for there are often older adventurers strolling the rooftops—but they rarely find another place to be alone.

Whatever the after-the-dance adventure, there is always, at last, the return to the street; the last place to linger before going back to an over-crowded tenement room. Tomorrow there will be the clubhouse again, and next week, again, the dance.[20]

Teachers may again ask questions about what is to be done. How do we motivate these minority groups to do schoolwork? How do we compensate for racial prejudice? How do we develop strong ego concepts in the midst of overcrowding? How is violence against teachers avoided among groups less socially motivated than the above indicated gang? There is no capsule answer, no panacea. Teachers can recognize the problem, they can respect the dilemmas, they can offer the palliative of acceptance and understanding, but these do not dissipate the tensions, the aimlessness, or the futility of immediate reconstruction of the community. The limitations of mental hygiene in the face of community influences are disheartening.

The street would be the same. The Conservatives have gone social and thereby changed their relation to society, but society is still as it was. The dope pusher is still in the doorway and the bopping gang is still in the neighborhood. The same temptations are met every day, and the million factors that made the members of the club once fight continue to be a part of their life in the city's worst slum. Norm Eddy understood, as Louie did, that in the long run the kids must find something more than a new routine and a place to meet to keep them out of the troubles of the past. The Conservatives have wrung from society a clubhouse; but not a cause.[21]

Other Factors. There are other factors beyond the classroom that impose limitations on the teachers. The mental health of school pupils is conditioned by the mental health of adults in the community at large. Education of these adults is a major problem and will not be solved in a generation. Poverty is a condition that affects the outlook of both chil-

[20] Dan Wakefield, "The Gang That Went Good," *Harper's Magazine*, 216:41–42, June, 1958.

[21] *Ibid.*, p. 43.

dren and adults. Racial discrimination limits the opportunity of those who are discriminated against and, fully as serious, limits the perspective of those who discriminate. The threat of war and atomic annihilation is a world problem of mental health—as is overpopulation, famine, filth, and ignorance. Narcotic addiction, excessive drinking, embezzlement, stealing, gangsterism, duplicity in highly placed persons not only are symptoms of mental illness but are also contributing factors to feelings of futility, anxiety, and hopelessness.

These are factors which limit the effectiveness of mental hygiene in the classroom. They are cited not with the view of discouraging the continuation of efforts but as indicative of the fact that teachers should *not* become discouraged when their efforts—though well-intentioned and intelligent—do not effect miraculous changes. While not all pupils can be salvaged, some of them, through the efforts of individual teachers, are directed to the achievement of constructive citizenship.

SUMMARY

The need for balance and for perspective has been emphasized throughout this book. Extreme beliefs and theories are as likely to occur in the field of mental hygiene as in any other area of endeavor. Some theories change because they are erroneous, others because they have been overemphasized. Heredity, for instance, must be given its due share of credit, but environment is also important. New theories can be given respectful consideration, but care should be exercised to avoid overemphasis, since some new theories may later be found defective. There should be a balance between excessive self-concern, too much introspection, and the view that one ought to "just let things happen." The middle ground lies in objective study and experimentation.

Experience and experiment may yet prove that there is a place in constructive child development for external discipline and belief in certain theories of morphology. The diverse theories of child development indicate that there is no one best way to rear children. In a similar vein, the wide variations of personalities and teaching methods among successful teachers testify that there is no one ideal "teacher personality" and no single successful method of teaching. It appears, however, that adaptability and enthusiasm in both teachers and parents are most desirable factors. Teachers should not expect to be uniformly successful with every child's problem they attack.

We do not know just how learning takes place, but we do know a great deal about the conditions under which learning takes place with relatively greater accuracy. We do not know, with precision, what constitutes an ideal environment for healthy child growth.

Sufficient barriers to development will always remain; it is wise, therefore, to remove unnecessary obstacles. Some things are beyond the control of either teacher or pupil—family influences, community factors, and certain world conditions. Teachers can help pupils prepare for these by providing a kind of immunization against difficulties, by seeing to it that difficulties are equitably distributed among all pupils. Human fallibility and precautions needed in mental hygiene are not so much reasons for discouragement as they are challenges to improvement.

STUDY AND DISCUSSION EXERCISES

1. Why do two sets of parents who use entirely different techniques in dealing with their children both seem to achieve a degree of success?

2. What precautions are necessary for applying the idea that teachers need not succeed with all children?

3. Cite some instances in which obstacles and conflicts seem to have had a beneficial effect upon a child's development.

4. What are some factors in a child's life that seem to be largely beyond control by the teacher? Can anything be done to ameliorate them?

5. What limitations imposed by the school do you think are the most serious handicaps to mental health?

SUGGESTED ADDITIONAL READINGS

Dobzhansky, Theodosius, "Genetics: Inside Human Nature," in Lynn White, Jr., (ed.), *Frontiers of Knowledge in the Study of Man*, New York: Harper & Brothers, 1956, pp. 1–18.

Human variability has its basis in biological factors, but its development is dependent on physical and psychological movements.

Garrison, Karl C., *The Psychology of Exceptional Children*, rev. ed., New York: The Ronald Press Company, 1950, pp. 468–484.

A number of situations are mentioned that must be remedied or improved before the "potential citizens of tomorrow" can realize fulfillment.

Havighurst, Robert J., and Bernice L. Neugarten, *Society and Education*, Englewood Cliffs, N.J.: Allyn and Bacon, Inc., 1957, pp. 158–178.

Using the concept of life space, the authors show how the community shapes the responses of children. It is indicated that the psychological life space may differ from physical environs.

Lippman, Hyman S., *Treatment of the Child in Emotional Conflict*, New York: McGraw-Hill Book Company, Inc., 1956, pp. 3–55.

These chapters will increase the teacher's appreciation of the limitations within the classroom when dealing with disturbed children.

Redl, Fritz, and William W. Wattenberg, *Mental Hygiene in Teaching*, 2d ed., New York: Harcourt, Brace & World, Inc., 1959, pp. 505–515.

The authors emphasize that mental hygiene represents only one of many problems faced by teachers. There are gaps in our knowledge which limit effectiveness.

The Teacher's Mental Health

CHAPTER 19

A POSITIVE VIEW OF THE
TEACHING PROFESSION

Our problems are frequently not so serious as the attitude which we take toward them. For teachers the statement is most pertinent when it is brought to bear on the evaluation of teaching as a profession. There are many who are happy, confident, creative, and satisfied (though not complacent) as they perform their educative tasks. Others, surrounded by similar demands, working conditions, challenges, and opportunities fret about restrictions, obligations, and overwork.

This chapter is written with the specific objective of attempting to influence teachers to see all the good they possibly can in their profession. Admittedly, there are drawbacks, handicaps, and justifiable criticisms, which are presented as challenges to improve the situation. There are also some unequivocal advantages. These are presented to stimulate teachers to appreciate more fully the many values which may accrue from teaching. If the reader detects an undue bias in the presentation, he should remember that there are sound mental hygiene reasons for attempting to generate a positive psychology of suggestion.

REPRESENTATIVE VIEWS OF TEACHING

Advantages Enjoyed by Teachers. If we were to concentrate on some of the positive values of the profession, instead of complaining about and magnifying the disadvantages, there would be greater probability that we could increase our corps of inspired and inspiring teachers. Admittedly, this is a slanted view. Even if it were to mean shutting our eyes to the negative factors (which is unnecessary), it is a psychological fact that growth is more frequently stimulated by optimism than by pessimism—for teachers quite as much as pupils. For the sake of their own mental health, teachers are asked to review, criticize, and evaluate some of the following advantages:

1. *Teaching offers an opportunity for professional achievement.* A fundamental human desire is to accomplish. In the toddler who insists upon feeding himself and in the person in late maturity who reacts strongly against compulsory retirement, the desire to achieve is evident. Teaching is not unique in providing opportunities and challenges to accomplish, but it is notable for the extent and variety of the avenues it opens to those who would do something that is widely recognized as significant.

There is the challenge to vitalize one's teaching by using contemporary materials, by keeping abreast of current experiments, and by capitalizing upon improved teaching aids. There are abundant stimulations contributed by both general and specialized education periodicals. Extension and correspondence courses, workshops, in-service training classes and committees, and summer schools afford both stimulation and means to professional achievement. There are some, of course, who look upon these as burdens. Others perceive and act upon the principle that an effective personal life and genuine emotional security are based upon the process of *continual* growth. The improvement of service and increase in one's sense of accomplishment and personal worth coincident with continued study will eliminate some of the cause of worry and feelings of insecurity.

2. *Teaching stimulates one to keep abreast of the times.* Effective teachers of our time must not only know what is going on in the professional field but must also be acquainted with the events of the world at large. Teachers have the responsibility of possessing information upon which to base effective handling of the many questions that pupils ask, even though these questions seem at times to be only on the periphery of the immediate lesson. This does not demand that teachers should know the answers to all questions. Nevertheless, some information about what is going on in contemporary society is part of the equipment that each of us has a right to expect to find in the teachers of our children. Keeping the interest of curious pupils alive is one way in which teaching becomes the most creative of jobs. Such information can be gained from a sensible reading of newspapers; news magazines; periodicals devoted to information, evaluation, and criticism; and serious books by informed authors. Participation in community activities is more and more coming to be considered not only an opportunity but an obligation,[1] as stress is placed on the fact that much education is gained outside the formal school. Even if we were to ignore the contribution which keeping

---

[1] "First-year Teachers," *National Education Association Research Bulletin*, 34(1):26, February, 1956.

abreast of the times makes to effective teaching, there would still remain the personal advantage accruing from the fact that one's intellect is kept high by virtue of its vigorous use.[2]

3. *Teaching contributes toward personal satisfaction.* There are few jobs which can be regarded as more important than teaching—one exception, probably, is parenthood. America has grown in size and developed in complexity largely by virtue of a firm faith in the personal and civic value of education. While it must be admitted that there are critics of education, especially when it comes to the matter of support, the consensus is much like the following:

> The school is society's formal instrument for moulding the young, for transmitting the cultural heritage, for inculcating these values, ideals and modes of behaviour on which both the continuity and the evolution of humanity depend. . . . From the choice which the teacher makes as to what to teach and what to omit, from the values implicit in the curriculum, from the pedagogical methods, from the rewards and sanctions used to evoke effort, the child, not perhaps always consciously but surely none-the-less, draws his own conclusions. He reacts to the values implicit in his school and to some extent incorporates them into his growing personality.[3]

There are few patrons and few parents who, despite apathy in financial support, do not recognize the importance of the job the teacher performs. Hence the personal satisfaction of teachers in feeling that their role is of prime importance in shaping the lives and thoughts of youth is well founded.

4. *The hours of work are reasonable.* A six-hour day and a thirty-hour week would not, of course, account for all the time involved in effectively fulfilling the responsibilities of teaching. However, the work beyond the scheduled day can be done at one's convenience, leaving time for the hobbies and personal-growth activities which are so fundamental to sound mental health. Teachers, generally speaking, are not on call as is the doctor. They are not subject to interruptions of work due to strikes ordered by some professional labor organizer. They are uniquely situated with regard to the observation of many holidays. Even when the summer is devoted to study, these months bring freedom from routine class duties and a marked change in emphasis. Moreover, this study brings personal as well as professional growth and thus promotes mental health. Julia Miller, a retired teacher being honored as Iowa's oldest coed, stated,

[2] R. L. Thorndike, "Growth of Intelligence during Adolescence," *Journal of Genetic Psychology*, 72:11–15, 1948.

[3] *Education and Mental Health*, The Hague, Holland: United Nations Educational, Scientific and Cultural Organization, 1955, p. 21.

"When my mind is busy the rest of me gets along all right."[4] There are summers, too, during which the teacher feels no obligation to attend school. Though freedom is fundamentally a state of mind, it must be admitted that the hours of work are such as to promote a feeling of freedom.

5. *The income is steady and assured.* In many localities, the teacher's pay is much too low, particularly in view of the human responsibility involved, but the income is assured. Barring gross incompetence and moral turpitude, the teacher once employed can feel confident that his employment will continue—at least, through the school year. This allows for systematic planning, which makes it somewhat easier to get along with a salary that is often close to being inadequate. Even though one is not reengaged in a particular community, the need for teachers makes it quite probable that a position can be found in another location. When a particular school board tires of a teacher, it is not necessary for him to find another type of job and thus forsake his training and experience. As a matter of fact, this assurance of employment and income is one of the reasons why many who would like to have larger incomes still continue to teach.

6. *Teaching is clean work.* There are few jobs which can equal teaching in either physical or psychological cleanliness. A little chalk dust, some scraps of paper, bits of mud, and the characteristic disarray of work in progress constitute whatever there may be of physical uncleanliness or confusion. Doctors and dentists have contact with the diseased and decayed; lawyers have to deal with the exacerbations of human emotions; and businessmen encounter much in the way of craftiness, selfishness, and greed. Teachers for the most part deal with people before they become decayed or distorted; or at the worst, these unhappy conditions are caught in the making. Psychologically pupils in both elementary and secondary schools are typically confident, cheerful, and enthusiastic as contrasted to the anxiousness, disillusionment, and pessimism of many adults. It is small wonder that the community regards teachers as a most honest, stable, and reliable group of persons when they are surrounded by these salutary physical and psychological influences.

7. *Teaching provides contact with the enthusiasms of youth.* This apparent advantage may also have its negative aspects. It is possible that the optimism, enthusiasm, and confidence of youth are not at all times sound. Perhaps through close contact with these traits, teachers may tend to overlook some of the hazards of life today. On the other hand, the dire forecasts of adults have a disheartening effect. William H. Mikesell recommends adopting an optimistic attitude in the following words: "As good suggestion, optimism (1) discovers and makes opportunity; (2)

---

[4] "Adding Life to Years," *Bulletin of the Institute of Gerontology,* 5:2, Iowa City, Iowa: Department of Publications State University of Iowa, January, 1958.

organizes the mind and raises efficiency; (3) grows by its own momentum; (4) is strengthened by its own expression; and (5) invites others to promote it."[5] The last point indicates the direct advantage teachers have through contact with the enthusiasm of youth.

8. *Teaching involves a variety of work.* If variety is "the spice of life," then teaching is well seasoned. The very definition of mental health, "the adjustment of individuals to themselves and to the world at large with a minimum of effectiveness, satisfactions, cheerfulness, and socially considerate behavior and the ability to face and accept the realities of life,"[6] implies that mental health is dependent on well-rounded development. It follows that a life occupation which automatically furnishes variety will be conducive to good adjustment.

The challenge to improve techniques and keep abreast of the time, mentioned above, infuses variety into teaching. Even though the subjects taught and the daily schedule may vary little from year to year, there can be variety in content and method. More variety is added by the so-called "extracurricular" responsibilities. The teacher may share, too, in such specialized functions as curriculum reconstruction, counseling, testing and evaluation, the nature and use of teaching aids, research, and the like, which may ward off a tendency to feel that teaching is a boring occupation. If none of the above provide variety there is still that which inheres in the differing nature of the pupil population making up the teacher's class each year. There is always the variety presented by new faces, different backgrounds, varying interests, and the inevitable differences in personality.

9. *The profession has a stimulating degree of internal criticism.* The tendency of teachers to criticize their own methods and effectiveness has some disadvantages. However, this critical attitude has an advantage, in that it prevents complacency and thus stimulates growth. It is frequently pointed out by medical authorities and mental hygienists that self-satisfaction contributes both to mental ill-health and to the phenomenon of senescence. Internal criticism should, however, be thoughtfully examined, so that the disadvantages of creating discouragement in the heart of the teacher and implanting the elements of disrespect in the minds of school patrons will be diminished.

10. *Teaching affords association with professional coworkers.* Objective studies indicate that there are persons engaged in teaching who do not have the kind and/or amount of personality traits that are desired in the teachers of our young people. On the other hand, the great

---

[5] William H. Mikesell, *Mental Hygiene*, Englewood Cliffs, N.J.: Prentice-Hall, Inc., 1939, p. 156.

[6] National Committee for Mental Hygiene, *Mental Hygiene Bulletin*, 9:1, January–February, 1931.

majority of teachers are healthy, happy, and admirable. Teaching, because of low salaries and questionable status in the eyes of the community citizens, tends to attract consecrated persons—they are typically
motivated by the ideal of service to others. Other professions, too, have
the opportunity of association with professional coworkers. Colleges in
general are becoming more selective in admission policy and those accepted for teacher education are more carefully selected and better and
more extensively trained. Teaching is attracting those seriously interested in a professional career.[7] All these factors result in one's being
associated with above average colleagues.

When called into military service, teachers effectively assume leadership in a wide variety of military activities. The ease with which they
make their adjustments is frequently commented upon by the regular
(life-career) military personnel. Dr. James F. Bender, director of the
National Institute for Human Relations, told the Connecticut Education
Association that school teachers were the top candidates for wives and
listed ten specific reasons to justify the statement.

1. They are above average in health, beauty and intelligence.
2. They have a deep affection for children.
3. They are eager to marry, wish to bear two or more children.
4. They have well-protected jobs, safe during a recession.
5. They have nice voices and don't talk too much.
6. Their regular hours and frequent vacations permit them to be good
housewives.
7. Their studious habits and common sense are invaluable to young
men starting in business or a profession.
8. Their high ideals make them lovable, tender, sympathetic and understanding beyond the average.
9. They are established in jobs and ready for marriage at the golden
age for it—22 to 25 years.
10. Divorce is rare among teachers.[8]

Studies of the mental health of teachers show varying results, and
opinions vary still more widely, but at least some studies indicate that the
mental health of teachers is slightly above that of the average run of the
population as indicated by the percentage of institutionalization. The educational requirements of the profession are for a minimum of education
beyond the average of the general population, and the actual average
is somewhat higher than the required minimum. Thus, a teacher has an
opportunity for contact with informed people.

[7] "The Postwar Struggle to Provide Competent Teachers," *National Education
Association Research Bulletin*, 35(3):119–123, October, 1957.
[8] International News Service, Hartford, Conn., Nov. 4, 1948.

Besides the objective evidences of the quality of associations available within the profession, there are some subjective estimates that point to the same factor. A continual process of "weeding-out" takes place. Teachers who are unable to conduct themselves in accordance with the mores of the community in which they work find that they are unhappy and quit, or the officials in charge do not reissue their contracts.

11. *Love of teaching.* A number of advantages accruing from teaching have been cited, but perhaps the major justification for choosing and staying in the profession is simply that teachers love to teach. For many there need be no other justification. The National Education Association conducted a survey of teachers, seeking to find the advantages and criticisms that influenced choice of work. In a section for free comments, a third of all the remarks dealt with the theme, "the love of teaching and the rewarding sense of achievement that comes from work with children and young people and contributing thru their lives to a better future."[9] The 1,100,000 teachers in this study did not regret their choice. If they had it to do over again the great majority of women (80 per cent) and a solid majority of the men (about 57 per cent) would make the same choice.

Criticisms of the Profession. There is some evidence that teachers often do not have the positive view of their profession that is most conducive to vigorous mental health. This impression may be gathered from comments made by teachers about the negative aspects of their occupation, such as complaints about low salaries, the difficulty of working with youngsters who manifest no ardent desire to learn, the unreasonable demands placed upon them by narrow-minded members of the school board, and the necessity for attending many afterhours school functions —to cite just a few. A more concrete evidence is that, at teacher workshops, institutes, and conventions, it is almost a tradition for speakers to criticize the methods, materials, and philosophy of instructions and be applauded for it. By way of contrast, the meetings of other professional people are likely to be occupied with reporting progress made, discoveries unearthed, and techniques improved. This does not imply that no examination of past deficiencies should be made; but it is probable that the mental health of teachers and improved respect from the public would be enhanced by a little less "internal" criticism and more show of professional pride. Another evidence, quite like the foregoing, is that education periodicals carry many articles criticizing teachers and teaching. There are other articles, to be sure, dealing with successful projects, improved techniques, and gratifying experiments, but these seem much less newsworthy than the negative reports. The most severe indictment, however, is that occasionally a teacher who has not the courage to get out of

[9] "The Status of the American Public School Teacher," *National Education Association Research Bulletin*, 35:41, February, 1957.

the profession will advise a younger person, "By all means, do not entertain seriously the idea of ever becoming a teacher."

The Point of View and Advantages of Teaching. Many of the above-cited "advantages" may be regarded as disadvantages. For example, having to deal with the enthusiasms of youth may test one's patience beyond endurance. Variety of work may possibly interfere with developing a high degree of competence in any one area. The hours of work may be too long, considering the amount of mental and emotional energy consumed during the time spent on the job. Internal criticism has been known to reach the point of engendering discouragement. Steady and assured income does not, in a capitalistic and competitive society, adequately offset a salary which is too low. Pressures put upon the teacher to attend evening classes and summer school are certainly a burden to many teachers. The fact remains, however, that one can take the point of view, which is conducive to mental health, of recognizing the real advantages. An individual has much choice, indeed, in regard to the kind of psychology of suggestion which shall operate.

DISADVANTAGES THAT NEED ATTENTION

It would, of course, be unwise to recommend a distorted view of any profession—a view that ignores problems needing study and action. Some of the things that need to be done to make teaching a still more salutary influence for mental health warrant the attention of even the most optimistic of teachers.

Community Demands Must Be Evaluated. One of the frequently cited disadvantages of teaching is that the community makes unreasonable demands on the teacher. It is probably true that "where there is smoke there is fire" and that some communities do make unreasonable demands. The dividing line between what is a reasonable expectation and what is an unreasonable demand is not easy to establish. For instance, many people do not regard the teacher's smoking as a matter for public concern—certainly not as an indication of immorality. In most cases, it is unreasonable to insist upon nonsmoking teachers. However, in a community composed largely of a particular religious group which views smoking as an evidence of moral turpitude and in which most adults abstain from tobacco, the demand is reasonable. It seems unreasonable that teachers should be expected to do all their buying in the particular community where they earn their salaries—especially if prices there are high and a wide selection of goods is not available. In individual cases, requiring the teacher to live in the community may be unreasonable. For instance, a teacher was given the ultimatum that she would have to live in the community or her contract would not be renewed. It made no difference that she lived six miles across the river with her mother, who owned her own home, and that in the school's community there was a marked housing shortage caused by a rapid growth in population. On the other hand, a school board required its teachers to live in the community because the teachers who were living in adjoining metropolitan areas were too frequently late to work because of heavy morning traffic.

Most teachers have not been hampered by any such stated restrictions. For the most part, the community makes only one demand, an entirely reasonable one, that teachers be gentlemen or ladies. If you were to view yourself as a parent, realizing the great influence of the teacher, you would probably be inclined to support this requirement. A child is a parent's most priceless possession. "Isn't it fair to assume that 'of them to whom much is entrusted, much will be expected'?"[10]

Most teachers do not feel that they have been unnecessarily hedged in by community demands. Much more frequently the problem is one of anticipation of restriction by beginning teachers than it is an actuality reported by those with experience. The following may be considered typical of the experienced teacher's attitude:

> As for one's personal life within teaching, I have never been able to believe the refrain that to choose to be a teacher means to renounce many of the so-called pleasures of normal human existence; that one's living will become public conversational property, subject to close scrutiny and governed by someone other than oneself. While it is true that people in a community are often very much interested in their teachers and the lives they live, I have never sensed that it is a malicious interest.[11]

It is probable that, if the teacher takes seriously the responsibility of seeing to it that children are absorbed into the constructive phases of community life, there will be less occasion for feeling that community demands are unnecessarily restrictive.

Teacher Loads Should Be Reduced. It is a fundamental postulate of psychology that learning is an individual matter. However, the results of studies of class size related to effectiveness are highly variable. Some teachers in some subjects can teach fifty or more pupils effectively. Others, and in other areas, may find a class of ten too large. Part of this is due to the teacher himself and to his concept of what constitutes good teaching and part is due to the problem presented; for instance, teaching deaf, slow-learning, or otherwise handicapped children is more effectively done in small groups. In the primary and elementary grades effectiveness

---

[10] Pauline Dudley, "I'm Glad I'm a Teacher," *National Education Association Journal*, 38:579, 1949.

[11] *Ibid.*, p. 578.

is often curtailed by inability to cope with individual differences, as well as by the emotional strain that is generated under the pressure of many different and energetic individuals. Excessively large classes are a handicap to both teacher and pupils.

Teachers' Salaries Should Be Improved. Great gains have been made in recent years in the absolute amounts paid to teachers. Unfortunately, for the sake of mental health, salaries in some states are still pitifully low. Even in states where salaries are high and recent gains have been recorded, the gain is frequently more apparent than real; that is, the purchasing power of the dollar has declined so precipitously that the higher salary of today purchases less than the lower salary of an earlier decade.[12] Consequently, financial worries are just as troublesome now as then. The most unfortunate consequence of all is that the monetary remuneration is not sufficient to attract into the profession as many fine young men and women as would like to come and as have the qualifications. It is, therefore, suggested that teachers continue to work on the problem of improved salaries, *but through organized and directed effort in their professional organizations,* rather than by means of the carping criticism and querulous discussions that have all too frequently been their futile protest.

Working Conditions Should Be Improved. Many school systems have made pioneering steps in the direction of improving working conditions for teachers. Use of the school building by teachers for purposes of recreation, when they are entirely free from supervisory responsibilities, has been granted. This includes use of the gymnasium, time for reading the new acquisitions to the library, use of the arts and crafts laboratories, designated periods to work in the woodworking and mechanical arts shops, and scheduled use of the school for parties for themselves and their friends without interruption by pupils.

Teachers' lounges are being provided in many currently constructed buildings. There must also be arrangement for planned periods when the teachers can use the rooms, free of student interference. Each teacher should have an hour a day, between 8:30 and 4:00—or whatever the school hours are—which will be his own. If it is necessary for some teacher to be on duty between 12:00 and 1:00, then he should have time to eat a leisurely and uninterrupted lunch between 11:00 and 12:00 or between 1:00 and 2:00. The "coffee break" in industry and business has

[12] Lowered purchasing power of the dollar, the fact that federal income tax was not applied to teachers' income prior to 1939, and rising state income taxes have not been offset by salary increases. Even the low economic level attained prior to World War II by teachers has not been maintained. Source: "Salaries and Salary Schedules of Urban School Employees, 1956–57," *National Education Association Research Bulletin,* 35:79, April, 1957.

been found to result in improved efficiency. It may be less easy to measure similar improved efficiency in teaching, but it is there in the form of stronger morale and more purposeful energy. It is to be hoped that administrators and the public will soon realize that these benefits are not gifts to the teachers, not a "coddling" of prima donnas, but an investment in better teaching effectiveness.

Provision should be made for medical examination *and treatment*. The annual examination to see whether the teacher is free of tuberculosis is not sufficient. Medical examinations should be frequent and thorough enough to serve as a preventive, as well as a cure. Proper planning should make it possible for teachers to avail themselves of adequate treatment. Perhaps we are still a long way from it, but the medical care provided should include psychiatric services. Availability of such psychiatric services will be a long step toward the education of teachers in their application of mental hygiene principles in the lives of young people.

Other Factors Needing Attention. Other aspects of teacher welfare which would result in a better mental hygiene setting might well include the following: (1) Provision for participation in the administration of the school; (2) improved policies relating to sick leave, so that teachers would not have financial strain added to their illnesses; (3) extension of retirement programs, so that the threat of aging would not hover so ominously; (4) salary schedules which would provide incentive for staying in the profession and motivation for the improvement of services rendered while in it (many salary schedules are attractive to young persons, but when examined by the older person or the younger one with foresight, the schedule gives too little assurance of continued improvement); (5) help for teachers through wider provision of special services for children—mental hygiene specialists, vocational guidance experts, academic counselors, reading specialists, visiting teachers, and school nurses—will reduce some frustrations.

THE TEACHER'S ROLE IN THE PROFESSION

Teaching presents opportunities and privileges in proportion to the individual's ability to profit from them. In this section, some of the characteristics of good teachers will be examined for the purpose of helping both experienced and neophyte teachers set some goals for personal development.

Personality Traits of Good Teachers. There has been a great deal of speculation and much research (for the most part inconclusive) regarding the question, What are the personality traits of a good teacher? The opinions of experts have been solicited. Professional coworkers have been queried. Children have been asked to name the qualities of personality possessed by their most liked and most effective teachers. But the answer remains elusive.

A study of twenty highly selected teachers was conducted to see what characteristics might distinguish them from other teachers. Some of the items identified were the following: they were better groomed than average, were church members, were strongly identified with their parents, had superior school records, enjoyed being and working with children, disliked clerical work, were friendly toward administrators, had wide interests, enjoyed friends, and felt that teaching was significant work.[13] Yet the author knows a teacher who apparently had all these traits (except that she also enjoyed clerical work) and who puzzled her principal and teaching colleagues by failing because of chronic disciplinary trouble. This exception is noted to convey the idea that what is significant as one teacher's assets may be relatively unimportant in another's success. What makes one teacher a liability may in another case be just the thing that presents a challenge to students of another instructor. The above list, and many others, place intelligence high on the list of teacher qualifications; and, in general, it is not to be denied that most wise principals will select those teacher candidates who have demonstrated intelligence. One principal of a large city system who had a reputation for selecting outstanding teachers told the story of making a particular effort to hire a relatively slow-learning teacher. He knew her before she entered college—in fact, had encouraged her to enter and take an education major. She had difficulty in college, and the principal, who knew some of the college officials, interceded in her behalf. "Evaluation," rather than "grading," was applied and the girl got her degree. She had been teaching a number of years when the principal told his story and he concluded with "Heaven help the administrator who tries to take her away from me without letting me know he is bidding for her services. She is one of very few who really knows what learning difficulties are, and she does an excellent job in the _____ [a minority group] section of my city."

Enthusiasm, optimism, initiative, and resourcefulness are qualities frequently mentioned in lists of teacher attributes. Again, these factors are, in general, highly desirable. But some successful teachers replace enthusiasm with a high degree of order and teach students both information and desirable personal habits. Some students are stimulated by pessimistic teachers, some are motivated more by routines than they are by a variety of approaches. An occasional student will intentionally select a teacher who has a reputation for being sarcastic—a trait that is almost universally condemned.

[13] J. C. Gowan, "Summary of the Intensive Study of Twenty Highly Selected Women Teachers," *Journal of Experimental Education,* 26:115–124, December, 1957.

Moreover, qualities which are desirable at one level of teaching may be less necessary for a teacher of another level; for example, the factor of considerateness is ranked high by supervisors of the elementary grades, while it receives a very low rank among high-school teachers.

What, Then, Are Good Teachers Like? It is difficult to define the successful teaching personality. The problem is not answered by resorting to precisely defined lists of isolated traits. A more fruitful approach to finding an answer to the question is to abandon the trait concept and to examine teachers at their work. This approach has been used by two national organizations. The results, described in the following paragraphs, provide some definite statements of skills and knowledges toward which the teacher might work.

1. *The answer given by the American Council on Education:* The book *Teachers for Our Times,* published by the Council, lists the following as qualities needed in teachers:[14]

> They should have a respect for the growth and freedom of personality.
>
> They should have a feeling of genuine community-mindedness manifested in friendly relations and a willingness to adapt themselves to local mores.
>
> They should be able to deal rationally with personal and educational problems.
>
> They should possess skill in cooperation, so that "we" feelings and "we" objectives are facilitated.
>
> They should possess knowledge and skill in professional areas.
>
> They should not only possess knowledge but see to it that their fund of information is continually growing.
>
> Teachers must be able to translate their knowledge into terms that are understandable to the particular individuals whom they are teaching.
>
> Teachers must have a friendliness with children—a genuine affection for young people.
>
> Friendliness must be reinforced with an understanding of the growth and development of children.
>
> They should possess extraordinary understanding of society and be in accord with the underlying convictions which characterize that society.
>
> The teacher should be an effective citizen not only in society in general but also within the restricted environment of the school.
>
> Teachers should possess skill in the evaluation of the activity and progress of their pupils and also the ability to evaluate themselves.
>
> Teachers should have a profound conviction of the worth of teaching.

2. *The answer given by the U.S. Office of Education:* Frances V. Rummell, after describing in detail the characteristics and activities of teachers who were deemed to be "distinguished examples of the best professional

[14] Commission on Teacher Education, *Teachers for Our Times,* Washington: American Council on Education, 1944, pp. 154–173.

talent in the Nation's classrooms today," made the following generalizations about them:

> First, professionally alert, they are not sitting out the teacher crisis on remote little islands of self-containment. Several of them have had drawn-out struggles with their souls in order to stick to teaching when better-paying jobs from outside the profession tempted them. But at least all of them see teaching as the way to make a rich life, if barely a living. Whatever they doubt, it is never the importance of their work.
>
> My second generalization—not unrelated to the first: these teachers have plenty of convictions about their profession. For example: If it is considered conventional for an elementary teacher to aspire to a high school position, and for a high school teacher to aspire to a college position, or for any classroom teacher to aspire to an administrative post, then these teachers are unconventional. Moreover, they are impatient with the mores of a profession that perpetuates, in its own ranks, the tradition, "The higher the grade the greater the professional prestige" (and consequently the salary) of the teacher.
>
> Third—and this generalization may be surprising until we think it through—these teachers had nothing whatever to say about taboos on personal liberties. I wanted to find out how good teachers manage to put up with all the little indignities that, in some communities, reduce the profession to a state of nervous dissimulation or colorless neutrality. But there simply was not any active problem of the kind. The teachers felt no cramping restrictions because there weren't any. For all the freedom of social mores they enjoy, they could be doctors, lawyers, or merchant chiefs.[15]

Specialist Rummell then goes on to remark that these qualities are not enough; they must be blended together in a workable pattern. The blending agent is artistry in human relations, a matter which is difficult to define, but which is easy to observe in democratic classrooms. She does, however, indicate what she believes to be some of the factors which constitute "artistry in human relations."

> As might be assumed, persons who are gifted in the art of human relations have a high degree of sensitivity to children's problems. These teachers may not call it mental hygiene when they understand and help to condition social behavior, but what else could this teacher have been talking about when he said to me, "No normal kid is ever deliberately bad. He's goaded by something. It's up to the teacher to find out what." . . . They talk in human terms of good will, of stumbling personalities, of creating an atmosphere of dignity for the child. They talk about un-

---

[15] Frances V. Rummell, "What Are Good Teachers Like?" *School Life*, 30:9–10, July, 1948. This is the second of two articles, both of which are highly recommended for reading and study, dealing with the question of "Good Teachers." The first is in vol. 30 (June, 1948), pp. 4–8, and the second in vol. 30 (July, 1948), pp. 7–11.

derstanding the child and about the urgency of teaching him, by example and by precept, the principles of democratic living. . . .

Above everything else, these teachers are realistic about the high calling of their profession. They are poignantly aware that under their influence this raw material may also change its very destiny.[16]

Such summaries as the foregoing may appear to be disheartening to those teachers who do not feel that they possess these qualities and attitudes. But they can and should be considered as goals toward which to

FIG. 23. Is attendance at professional meetings an opportunity or an obligation? What are some other ways to pursue personal and professional growth? What is a proper balance between the pursuit of professional and personal interests?

work. Even the outstanding teachers reported by Rummell felt that there was work to be done, "they are not sitting out the teacher crisis on remote little islands of self-containment," they are actively engaged in trying to improve their work.

Rummell did not mention it, but a fourth conclusion should be drawn from her articles, i.e., "Good teachers are growing teachers." In every one of the teachers she described, this factor is evident. Some of them were experimenting within their classes, others were applying techniques they had read about, many attended summer school regularly, others

[16] *Ibid.*, p. 11.

availed themselves of opportunities to engage in workshops and evening classes. Instead of viewing these activities as hazards or drawbacks, they regarded them as opportunities. From the standpoint of personal growth and individual mental health, active study and experimentation is helpful; from the standpoint of effective teaching, it is essential. "To think is to grow and in growing we live."[17]

Good teachers are mentally healthy individuals. Thus, in addition to professional traits and behaviors, it is vital that their personal life outside the classroom must provide satisfactions. The healthy personality will find satisfaction in contact with adults, teachers and nonteachers; provision will be made for physical exercise and repose; hobbies which give play to a variety of capacities should be followed; pleasures for the sake of pleasures must find indulgence.

THE TEACHER'S CODE OF ETHICS

Administrators sometimes say that many injustices to individual pupils would be averted if teachers were acquainted with, and would recognize, the "Teacher's Code of Ethics." Such knowledge, widely practiced, would result in further strengthening the profession. But acquaintance with the code of ethics has an intimate personal advantage for the teacher, as well. To those who are contemplating entering the teaching field it should be a kind of test for their own aptitude for teaching. If they can subscribe to the statements in the code, they are more likely to find satisfaction in their work. It should provide those who are now teaching a means of evaluating their own role in giving additional prestige to their profession. It is highly recommended that teachers become thoroughly acquainted with the following statements regarding the ethics of teaching. If the statement needs improvement, the way to accomplish it is through constructive criticism and group action—not by personal repudiation.

ETHICS FOR TEACHERS

Code of Ethics of the NEA[18]

We, the members of the National Education Association of the United States, hold these truths to be self-evident—

[17] Edward J. Stieglitz, *The Second Forty Years*, Philadelphia: J. B. Lippincott Company, 1952, p. 209.

[18] The accompanying code of ethics, adopted in 1952, on recommendation of the Standing Committee on Professional Ethics, is a revision of previous codes. Used by permission of the National Education Association of the United States, Washington, **D.C.**

—that the primary purpose of education in the United States is to develop citizens who will safeguard, strengthen, and improve the democracy obtained through a representative government;

—that the achievement of effective democracy in all aspects of American life and the maintenance of our national ideals depend upon making acceptable educational opportunities available to all;

—that the quality of education reflects the ideals, motives, preparation, and conduct of the members of the teaching profession;

—that whoever chooses teaching as a career assumes the obligation to conduct himself in accordance with the ideals of the profession.

As a guide for the teaching profession, the members of the National Education Association have adopted this code of professional ethics. Since all teachers should be members of a united profession, the basic principles herein enumerated apply to all persons engaged in the professional aspects of education—elementary, secondary, and collegiate.

FIRST PRINCIPLE: The primary obligation of the teaching profession is to guide children, youth, and adults in the pursuit of knowledge and skills, to prepare them in the ways of democracy, and to help them to become happy, useful, self-supporting citizens. The ultimate strength of the nation lies in the social responsibility, economic competence, and moral strength of the individual American.

In fulfilling the obligations of this first principle the teacher will—

1. Deal justly and impartially with students regardless of their physical, mental, emotional, political, economic, social, racial, or religious characteristics.

2. Recognize the differences among students and seek to meet their individual needs.

3. Encourage students to formulate and work for high individual goals in the development of their physical, intellectual, creative, and spiritual endowments.

4. Aid students to develop an understanding and appreciation not only of the opportunities and benefits of American democracy but also of their obligations to it.

5. Respect the right of every student to have confidential information about himself withheld except when its release is to authorized agencies or is required by law.

6. Accept no remuneration for tutoring except in accordance with approved policies of the governing board.

SECOND PRINCIPLE: The members of the teaching profession share with parents the task of shaping each student's purposes and acts toward socially acceptable ends. The effectiveness of many methods of teaching is dependent upon co-operative relationships with the home.

In fulfilling the obligations of this second principle the teacher will—

1. Respect the basic responsibility of parents for their children.

2. Seek to establish friendly and co-operative relationships with the home.

3. Help to increase the student's confidence in his own home and avoid disparaging remarks which might undermine that confidence.

4. Provide parents with information that will serve the best interests of their children, and be discreet with information received from parents.

5. Keep parents informed about the progress of their children as interpreted in terms of the purposes of the school.

THIRD PRINCIPLE: The teaching profession occupies a position of public trust involving not only the individual teacher's personal conduct, but also the interaction of the school and the community. Education is most effective when these relationships operate in a friendly, cooperative, and constructive manner.

In fulfilling the obligations of this third principle the teacher will—

1. Adhere to any reasonable pattern of behavior accepted by the community for professional persons.

2. Perform the duties of citizenship, and participate in community activities with due consideration for his obligations to his students, his family, and himself.

3. Discuss controversial issues from an objective point of view, thereby keeping his class free from partisan opinions.

4. Recognize that the public schools belong to the people of the community, encourage lay participation in shaping the purposes of the school, and strive to keep the public informed of the educational program which is being provided.

5. Respect the community in which he is employed and be loyal to the school system, community, state, and nation.

6. Work to improve education in the community and to strengthen the community's moral, spiritual, and intellectual life.

FOURTH PRINCIPLE: The members of the teaching profession have inescapable obligations with respect to employment. These obligations are nearly always shared employer-employee responsibilities based upon mutual respect and good faith.

In fulfilling the obligations of this fourth principle the teacher will—

1. Conduct professional business through the proper channels.

2. Refrain from discussing confidential and official information with unauthorized persons.

3. Apply for employment on the basis of competence only, and avoid asking for a specific position known to be filled by another teacher.

4. Seek employment in a professional manner, avoiding such practices as the indiscriminate distribution of applications.

5. Refuse to accept a position when the vacancy has been created through unprofessional activity or pending controversy over professional policy or the application of unjust personnel practices and procedures.

6. Adhere to the conditions of a contract until service thereunder has been performed, the contract has been terminated by mutual consent, or the contract has otherwise been legally terminated.

7. Give and expect due notice before a change of position is to be made.

8. Be fair in all recommendations that are given concerning the work of other teachers.

9. Accept no compensation from producers of instructional supplies when one's recommendation affects the local purchase or use of such teaching aids.

10. Engage in no gainful employment, outside of his contract, where the employment affects adversely his professional status or impairs his standing with students, associates, and the community.

11. Co-operate in the development of school policies and assume one's professional obligations thereby incurred.

12. Accept one's obligation to the employing board for maintaining a professional level of service.

FIFTH PRINCIPLE: The teaching profession is distinguished from many other occupations by the uniqueness and quality of the professional relationships among all teachers. Community support and respect are influenced by the standards of teachers and their attitudes toward teaching and other teachers.

In fulfilling the obligations of this fifth principle the teacher will—

1. Deal with other members of the profession in the same manner as he himself wishes to be treated.

2. Stand by other teachers who have acted on his behalf and at his request.

3. Speak constructively of other teachers, but report honestly to responsible persons in matters involving the welfare of students, the school system, and the profession.

4. Maintain active membership in professional organizations and, through participation, strive to attain the objectives that justify such organized groups.

5. Seek to make professional growth continuous by such procedures as study, research, travel, conferences, and attendance at professional meetings.

6. Make the teaching profession so attractive in ideals and practices that sincere and able young people will want to enter it.

SUMMARY

If an objective view is adopted we must admit that there are some negative aspects attached to teaching, e.g., low salaries, community pressures, duties beyond those regularly scheduled, and the feeling that the work of every teacher should be improved. The objective view must also admit that there are many positive advantages. Worthy of consideration among the advantages are (1) opportunity for professional advancement, (2) stimulation to keep abreast of the times, (3) personal satisfactions of achievement available, (4) reasonable hours of work, (5) an assured and steady income, (6) cleanliness of the work, (7) contact with the enthusiasms of youth, (8) variety of tasks involved, (9) a healthy degree of internal criticism, (10) opportunities for association with professional coworkers. In the final analysis, judgment is largely dependent upon the viewpoint which individual teachers develop and adopt.

Among the disadvantages that warrant attention are (1) amelioration of unreasonable community demands, (2) reduction of teacher loads so that genuine attention can be given to individual differences, (3) improvement of teachers' salaries, (4) improvement of working conditions so that better provision is made for the well-rounded life, and (5) depending on the local situation, participation in administration, sick leave, retirement provisions, salary schedules, and the provision of social services which will increase educational efficiency.

Each teacher must see to it that individual responsibility is assumed for the enhancement of the profession. Our first responsibility is to develop those personal traits that will count toward maximum effectiveness. Friendliness, enthusiasm, optimism, initiative, and resourcefulness are worthy of continuous cultivation. Joy in one's work is achieved by actively seeking personal growth. All these things add up to an artistry in human relations.

> In teaching, you have an opportunity to be a creative artist, administrator, scholar, business executive, salesperson, personal counselor. Teaching will call forth every hidden bit of talent you may have, every bit of knowledge you have somehow attained, and always leave you with a thirst for more experience, more learning.[19]

Study and application of the teacher's code of ethics may contribute to the profession of teaching in three ways: (1) presenting a test of suitability for those who are contemplating the work, (2) providing a means whereby teachers can evaluate their own roles, and (3) offering some concrete criteria of mental health.

STUDY AND DISCUSSION EXERCISES

1. Are any of the so-called "advantages" cited in the text not really advantages? State your reasons.

2. What, if anything, should the classroom teacher do about the criticisms of education and teaching that are published periodically?

[19] Pauline Dudley, "I'm Glad I'm a Teacher," *National Education Association Journal*, 38:579, November, 1949.

3. Draw up a plan for improving working conditions within some school with which you are well acquainted.

4. Suggest some plans for improving a specific desirable trait of teachers. Compare your results with a classmate who has devised a plan for improving another specific trait.

5. How can the code of ethics make a contribution to your personal mental health?

SUGGESTED ADDITIONAL READINGS

Bruce, William F., and A. John Holden, Jr., *The Teacher's Personal Development*, New York: Holt, Rinehart and Winston, Inc., 1957. 346 pp.

Personal growth is approached through emphasis on democratic orientation and application of the scientific method.

National Society for the Study of Education, *Mental Health in Modern Education*, 54th Yearbook, Part II, Chicago: University of Chicago Press, 1955, pp. 307–374.

These chapters deal with the mental health of teachers, growth through teacher education, and improved mental health through better knowledge.

Overstreet, Harry, and Bonaro Overstreet, *The Mind Alive*, New York: W. W. Norton & Company, Inc., 1954. 333 pp.

Designed to help one understand himself in terms of man's common conflicts, the book has particular force for teachers who must know themselves in order to understand others.

Perry, Bliss, *And Gladly Teach*, Boston: Houghton Mifflin Company, 1935. 315 pp.

Bliss Perry's reminiscences provide a clue to the rich advantages which are possible for a creative teacher. The book will provide inspiration for developing those traits which make for artistry in human relationships.

Stanley, William O., Othanel Smith, Kenneth D. Benne, and Archibald W. Anderson (eds.), *Social Foundations of Education*, New York: Holt, Rinehart and Winston, Inc., 1956, pp. 577–624.

Characteristics of a profession, barriers to the professionalization of teachers, academic freedom, and the teacher's code of ethics are among the topics discussed in these readings.

CHAPTER 20

THE TEACHER'S PHILOSOPHY—
IN THE SCHOOL

Mental hygiene, as a way of life for teachers, must consider many details of professional relationships. The previous chapter dealt with the pros and cons of teaching, the next one deals with the teacher's personal philosophy, and this one considers some details of professional philosophy. We shall leave the formal philosophies of education—idealism, realism, and pragmatism—to another professional course. Here the concern is with some everyday problems of functioning in the total school program. They will be discussed under the headings of various responsibilities.

RESPONSIBILITY TO PUPILS

America's Faith in Children. Americans have manifested a faith in children since the beginning of our national history. Constant emphasis has been placed on the importance of bringing about the fullest realization of the potentialities inherent in children. As each new community was established, three important steps were taken: building a home, building a church, and building a school. But this faith in children is but a reflection, or perhaps a manifestation, of other basic faiths. The ideals held by Americans are what have made the kind of people we are, the kind of government we have, and the kind of schools in which we study. These ideals—these faiths—are worth reviewing because of their importance for teachers and teaching.

1. *Americans have an abiding faith in freedom.* This faith is manifested in the establishment and maintenance of popular government. But it is recognized that freedom involves responsibility and accountability, so that one person's freedom and popular government is dependent upon abundant educational opportunity for all. Teachers are at the heart of this ideal.

2. *Americans have held consistently and persistently to certain moral values:* individual responsibility, priority of man over institutions, common consent and cooperation, devotion to truth, judgment of *all* men in terms of common moral standards, the high value of brotherhood, the right to the pursuit of happiness, and the complementing of material values with spiritual values. Teachers must make these common moral issues a part of their work.[1]

3. *Americans have a respect for personality.* Though it is recognized that there are differences in ability, this respect for personality is reflected in the words "All men are created equal." All are deserving of respect, all are entitled to freedom, all are worthy of justice. Differences in personality, in potentiality, are fundamental to our way of life. It is obligatory that teachers recognize and stimulate the development of these essential differences.

4. *Americans stress the significance of self-development.* Our schools and our national life are posited on faith in growth processes. We do not believe that we have reached perfection, but there is a conviction that (*a*) our culture is superior to others and that (*b*) we are on the way to higher realization.

5. *Americans believe in the reign of group intelligence.* We are convinced that reason, coupled with idealism, can perpetuate and improve the heritage in which we take such pride. Debate, discussion, persuasion, and the pooling of opinion are regarded as the techniques for revealing group intelligence. The habits that are involved in these techniques are not inborn; they must be developed by experience and education. Teachers are of highest importance in seeing to it that all these faiths are implemented through faith in children.

Implementing Our Faith in Children. The preservation of American democratic ideals is not possible without the enlightenment of its components. There must be an abiding loyalty to basic convictions.

> In a changing society there is always some difference between what the society is and what it wants to be, between its practices and its ideals. Thus the educational system, being part of the culture, has two supplementary functions: to be a mirror that reflects the society as it is, and at the same time, to be an agent of social change and a force directed toward implementing the ideals of society.[2]

If our democratic society is to work well, education must be universal and must be planned to produce citizens who are responsible preservers of the good and innovators for the better. Faith in freedom can be

---

[1] Educational Policies Commission, *Moral and Spiritual Values in the Public Schools,* Washington: National Education Association, 1951, pp. 18–27.

[2] Robert J. Havighurst and Bernice L. Neugarten, *Society and Education,* Englewood Cliffs, N.J.: Allyn and Bacon, Inc., 1957, p. 261.

perpetuated by allowing pupils in the school to see it in operation. They can exercise freedom by taking part in planning procedures, by being permitted freedom of movement and discussion, and by learning that what each one does has a bearing on the functioning of his peers. Moral values can be enhanced by emphasizing individual accountability, by practicing democratic processes, and by pointing out the existence and functioning of spiritual orientations.

Respect for personality can be cultivated by recognizing the contributions that are uniquely made by each pupil. This would mean, among other things, that the teacher does not establish some one, single criterion of accomplishment; for some pupils will, of course, excel in academic accomplishment, but others can make their contribution through physical skill, artistic creations, leadership qualities, or mechanical proficiency. A functional faith in self-development is dependent upon a recognition of the different potentialities residing in pupils. A teacher must understand, first, that mental, physical, emotional, and spiritual growth have significance, hence, there will be no overlooking of any of these as increased knowledge is sought in school. Second, he must realize that growth in any area will take place at different rates in different children. The lock-step tradition of education is not in harmony with our present interpretation of fundamental ideals.

It should be a simple matter to put into practice our faith in group intelligence. Many teachers are making use of discussion, debate, individual reports, and pupil participation in planning and evaluation to make their classwork more effective. They are, at the same time, giving pupils a chance to recognize the practical wisdom of the group. Each year brings an increase in the use of such procedures. Making provision for the exchange of information and opinion is not the difficult part of the procedure. What needs emphasis is the manifesting of confidence in the conclusions derived by the processes involved in the meeting of minds. Teachers who recognize the merit in group intelligence and, when possible, encourage translating the conclusions into action are doing more than teaching; they are helping to perpetuate our cultural heritage.

The Teacher and the Child. If those in the focal position for reflecting America's faith in children—teachers—are to perform their proper function, they must keep acquainted with new discoveries and the reconstruction of old theories relating to the nature and needs of children. This responsibility is partially discharged by their studying academic courses in biology, psychology, anthropology, sociology, mental hygiene, and philosophy. Some of this responsibility can be discharged through the reading of professional literature. It is necessary to go beyond the general and to know each child; this can be done by the following approaches: talking with the child, studying his play activities and interests, attempting to interpret his drawings, encouraging him to express his inner feelings in writing, using standardized tests of abilities, knowledges, and personality trends, keeping anecdotal records and cumulative folders, and making contacts with his parents and other teachers. It is worth mentioning that those teachers who have worked these approaches into an organized pattern of activity do not feel that such activities require too much time.

There is also the necessity for constantly improving one's academic specialty. In the elementary grades this might well take the form of becoming thoroughly acquainted with the constantly swelling store of materials that are designed to help meet individual differences in abilities and interests. A teacher should know what books and what materials will be most appropriate for expanding a pupil's immediate interests and knowledges. Secondary-school teachers must know their academic specialties so intimately that they can translate the materials into a functional relationship with the contemporary problems of adolescents. The continued effort of the teacher to expand his knowledge of subject matter will have the twofold effect of offering the pupils more wholesome stimulation and of satisfying his own need for growth and development.

As a factor in the teacher's philosophy in the school, responsibility to pupils has a vital significance. It means that the teacher must identify himself with the concepts and ideals that have motivated Americans from the very beginnings of our national existence. It means that these ideals will be translated into action in the techniques and materials that are used in the instructional process. Particularly, it means that the democratic ideal of respect for individuals will be practiced in everyday school life. Finally, the teacher's philosophy should embrace a desire for continuous growth of professional knowledge involving (1) the study goals or purposes of education, (2) the methods, materials, and situations that can best implement the goals defined, and (3) the study of various fields of knowledge.

RESPONSIBILITY TO ADMINISTRATORS

Little has been said in this book about the role of school administrators in an effective mental hygiene program. This neglect is not because the part played by administrators is a minor one, but because the book is directed to the classroom teacher. As a matter of fact, administrators can make a significant contribution to pupil mental health if they will apply to their own practice of administrator-teacher relationships many of the suggestions which are given in this book for teacher-pupil relationships. However, here we shall concern ourselves with the teacher's responsibility to administrators.

Loyalty. Dwight D. Eisenhower has stated:

Teachers need our active support and encouragement. They are doing one of the most necessary and exacting jobs in the land. They are developing our most precious national resource: our children, our future citizens. They can do their best only as we show them our appreciation and offer them our individual help.[3]

When a teacher accepts a contract, a formal bond between himself and the community is established. The official representative of the community is the administrator. It should reasonably be expected that teachers give to the administrator and the community the loyalty which Eisenhower asserts can reasonably be expected from citizens. Specifically this means attending meetings, carrying out instructions, keeping records, making reports, and honoring the constituted authorities of the school. This does not imply being blind to faults and overlooking shortcomings, but requires that, when criticism is pertinent, it shall be made through properly constituted channels. Two alternatives remain, both of which are professionally inadequate and both of which threaten mental health values for all concerned. One is to keep stolidy silent and let the feelings of injustice and futility fester within. The other is to let off tensions through general complaining, criticism, and faultfinding to any who will listen—fellow teachers, parents, friends, the public in general, and even to pupils. Both of these alternatives are more likely to aggravate than to solve difficulties. Teachers' meetings and conferences, on the other hand, permit the exchange of opinion that will develop a more balanced perspective and enhance the chances of a constructive solution. The teacher must give administrators credit for wishing to have the most effective educational system it is possible to achieve.

Cooperation. Cooperation is a two-way proposition and a friendly, openminded teacher will stimulate a reciprocal attitude in the administrator. Even though there are *some* autocratic and picayune supervisors, it should be admitted that most of them have arrived at their positions because of demonstrated ability. The actual fact is that where there is a lack of cooperation it *sometimes* grows out of the teacher's own insecurity. It would be well to believe in the competence of the supervisor and to be slow about taking umbrage at his suggestions. Too many teachers feel that suggestions which are actually proffered for improvement of educational practice are intended as attacks on them personally.

It will, then, be the part of practical wisdom to give supervisors credit for professional insight when it comes to evaluating the sincerity

[3] Dwight D. Eisenhower, Speech at the National Education Association Centennial Birthday Party in Washington, Apr. 4, 1957.

of their suggestions for improvement. If, as sometimes happens, super-visors are themselves insecure, they may find gratification in carping criticism. In such a case, the teacher (for his own sake) would do well to be objective about the criticism and try to see if his own response can be such as to improve professional relationships. Such a response is an indication of the teacher's own good mental health, since it represents an attempt to understand others. Moreover, only a mature personality can accept criticism graciously, especially when it is not wholly justified.

Teachers are individuals and consequently all strained relations between them and administrators are not caused by supervisory inefficiency. One tends to criticize that which he does not fully understand. One tends to resent suggestions which interfere with his customary pattern for teach-ing. One tends to question the philosophies which do not accord with his own experience. Nevertheless, it will be well to remember that the administrator is a person who himself has problems and difficulties. He is the buffer between the school and the wider community and is himself in need of help and understanding. A number of the sections of the Code of Ethics of the National Education Association have to do with coopera-tion (see Chapter 19).

Participation in Administration. A familiar attitude, up to the 1920s or 1930s, was "As the principal so is the school." With notable exceptions, the administrator was a virtual dictator—the formulator and executor of policy.

> Historically, secondary education has not generally carried all of these [democratic] responsibilities and certainly not for all youth. In the past and in other countries it admittedly has been selective, exclusive, aristo-cratic, and keyed to less democratic and even authoritarian social set-tings. . . . We can no longer afford the luxury of a program of youth education which does less than its utmost to defend and promote the goals of American democracy. The last vestiges of authoritarian edu-cational philosophy and of outmoded psychology must be routed out and their places taken by an educational philosophy born of the full applica-tion of the principles of democracy to all of life.[4]

Today administration is coming closer to the democratic ideal. A feel-ing has developed that the school will present a firmer front when teachers have participated in the making of decisions. Participation in administra-tion is just that and nothing more. The administrator must consider the views of many persons and, in the final analysis, *he* is responsible to the community for the execution of policy. Some teachers feel that time spent in administrative council is an unwarranted interruption of their

[4] Will French, J. Dan Hull, B. L. Dodds, *American High School Administration: Policy and Practice*, New York: Holt, Rinehart and Winston, Inc., 1951, p. v.

time. Many of the matters discussed are not of immediate personal concern. While this is true, there are also many matters that are of direct interest. Unless teachers willingly participate in the discussion of matters that are not of personal concern to them, there is likelihood that the machinery for their discussion of the more intimate topics will not be operative. All too frequently, the teacher who resents encroachments on his time is the one who is quite ready to criticize the policy that does not give attention to his views on matters of salary, sick leave, curriculum, and reporting.

Attitude toward Authority. An individual attitude toward authority is one criterion of psychological maturity. The opinion is justifiable that authority, and respect for it, may be required until the growing person has taken the steps preliminary to socially oriented behavior. One has not the right to flout the authority of the home, of the school, or of society. If demands are unreasonable, attempts should be made to shift to democratic determination. But until the requirements are changed, through being challenged and reconstructed, adherence to them will serve the advantage of all concerned.

Modern education is a highly specialized institution. It is not to be expected that any one individual will have all the answers to all the questions. Individuals who have specialized in particular areas of competence should have their opinions and their authority respected because of their greater knowledge and competence. As others grow in their knowledge and as better approaches are substituted, the authority of the "top man" is rightfully examined. Abuses of authority occur when the authority of one individual is not challenged by others who are competent. Thinking does not have to stop because one person has achieved a position of prestige.

Teachers who expect pupils to respect authority—and they should expect it—must themselves manifest the same attitude. A mature person is ready and willing to admit the superior wisdom of the visiting teacher, the school nurse, the custodian, the supervisor, the principal, and the superintendent in *their* spheres of authority. Conversely, it is to be hoped that these specialists will yield respect to the teacher in his realm of competence, that is, his intimate knowledge of individual pupils in the classroom. The ideas they have for improvement of methods, materials, and techniques for dealing with individual pupils should be in the form of suggestions. Authority should be questioned, it should be constantly improved, it should be cooperatively determined; but it should be respected.

When authority is accorded its proper place, when there is participation in administration, when there is cooperation, when there is loyalty, there is greater likelihood that high morale will be characteristic.

Teacher morale is composed of many things. Relations with coworkers, parents, and children, working conditions, living conditions, health, social activities, interests outside school, leisure-time activities, and continuing professional growth are among the basic elements of high morale. Each teacher has a double responsibility in this connection—contributing to the morale of others and maintaining his own morale.[5]

Morale is thus seen to consist of many things. It calls for clearly de-fined purposes which one is determined to achieve. The nature and degree of cooperation between professional staff members, school patrons, and pupils must be considered. Morale demands confidence, understanding, sympathy, and mutual consideration of group members. It demands faith in growth, optimistic hope for improvement, and respect for differences. In all of these ingredients, a respect for special knowledge and competencies is implicit.

RESPONSIBILITY TO FELLOW TEACHERS

Human Relations and the Classroom Teacher. "There is no doubt that people are most important in the learning environment. The learner is dependent upon teachers, principals, parents and friends for ideas, attitudes and opinions."[6] The generalization that success in any line of work is largely dependent upon one's ability to get along with others is certainly apropos to success in teaching. Yet a typical study indicates that, among the top mental health hazards for teachers, several might be included under "deficiencies in adult human relations." W. C. Kvaraceus, reporting a study made in a mental hygiene course at the University of Illinois, listed the hazards that were mentioned by thirty or more teachers out of a group of sixty-seven. "Conflicting personalities among teachers" and "jealousies among school personnel" ranked third and fourth on the list (heavy teacher load and overcrowded classrooms were in first and second places).[7] Besides these, the total list of twenty-seven items mentioned thirty or more times (out of sixty-seven) included the following situations that bear on adult human relations: "teachers in conflict with administrative policy," "administrator-teacher personality conflicts," "criticism by superiors," "teachers criticized in front of pupils," "teacher cliques exclude new teachers," and "lack of understanding among personnel of exact responsibilities of each staff member." Thus one-third of the

[5] John U. Michaelis and Paul R. Grim, *The Student Teacher in the Elementary School*, Englewood Cliffs, N.J.: Prentice-Hall, Inc., 1953, p. 408.

[6] *Creating a Good Environment for Learning*, 1954 Yearbook, Association for Supervision and Curriculum Development, Washington: National Education Association, 1954, p. 7.

[7] W. C. Kvaraceus, "Mental Health Hazards Facing Teachers," *Phi Delta Kappan*, 32:349, 1951.

hazards to teacher mental health are the outcome of ineptitude in getting along with others.

Your Role in Cooperation. Each teacher, in view of the two-way nature of cooperation, should do what he can to invite cooperation from others. It might be well to preface specific recommendations with a concept of cooperation—an activity in which individuals voluntarily participate, carrying it forward with consideration of the roles of others. The following suggest ways in which this concept may be made operative.

1. *Stress the "we" idea.* When seeking cooperation, try to give the impression that others have a contribution to make in a joint undertaking. If they can be made to feel that they are working *with* rather than *for*, they will participate more effectively. When you are the one who is asked to contribute, even though your role may not be effusively acknowledged, you can have the satisfaction of knowing that you have helped. When another teacher asks to use the lesson plans you have so laboriously formulated, give them gladly in the interest of better teaching, rather than in the resentful attitude that the other teacher "certainly is lazy."

2. *Seek help.* One hears that "The way to make a friend is to get him to help you." It gives almost anyone an expansive feeling to be able to help another. For example, if you have a pupil whom you do not know how to handle and you ask someone, "What would you do?" this indicates that you respect the other's judgment.

3. *Be helpful.* If we wish cooperation we should be cooperative. A request for help might be looked upon as an imposition on time and energy, but it can also be considered an evidence of the other's respect for your ability or knowledge. If you must refuse, let the reason be a truly valid one rather than an elaborate rationalization.

4. *Listen attentively.* A man who took a beautiful and famous woman to dinner, one night, was highly complimented by her gracious behavior. After briefly glancing around the dining room to see who was there, she gave her entire attention to him for the rest of the time. By looking at him and listening to him, she enhanced his feeling of worth. Many of us have been resentful toward teachers who, while ostensibly talking to us, continued to mark papers, read letters, or give directions to others. Such treatment makes us feel that the person who gives it has no real concern with our presence.

5. *Be courteous.* The habitual practice of courtesy and good manners tends to facilitate social functioning; discourteousness is a handicap. Courtesy begins with such simple matters as calling people by name, saying "Please" and "Thank you," and, in general, respecting the individuality of the other. But perhaps the strongest reason for advising courtesy is not because of the effect that it has on others but because

assuming the manners of politeness will tend to cultivate the spirit of respect for others.

6. *Share an emergency*. It seems evident that one of the ways to get bountiful aid and eager assistance is to encounter some tragedy. A flood, a fire, famine, or widespread disease brings forth a hearty response of helpfulness from the more fortunate.[8] Some of the personal tragedies of pupils awaken full and genuine expression of humane interest. Hence, when a problem is encountered by the teacher, it affords a good opportunity for establishing cooperative endeavor with other teachers. The problem need not be one involving death or serious illness. The problem might be, perhaps, not being on the ball team, failing to make the school orchestra, or heartsickness over not having clothes like the other pupils, for these are also emergencies that cannot always be met by routine procedures.

7. *Reveal purposes*. Clarity of goals is no less important when it involves the gaining of cooperation than it is in teaching. If the principal wants a special report in a hurry, he would do well to tell why it is so important. If the teacher wants help from others, he should be willing to explain in detail—and patiently—the entire setting. The value of this is illustrated by military leaders in their studied attempt to reveal to noncommissioned personnel just what the significance of their job is.

Animosities and Jealousies. Even superficial observation of the typical school staff brings to light evidence of animosities and jealousies between staff members. Little asides, direct criticisms, and innuendoes indicate a lack of harmonious adjustment. But these defects become increasingly evident during intimate personal conversations with individuals.

One reason why we cannot afford to indulge in jealousy, animosity, and suspicion is that the welfare of the school as a whole is diminished by such behaviors and attitudes. These things are not just personal, they have a direct bearing upon maintaining a healthy environment for children. The second reason for concern is that the individual cannot emotionally pay the price involved. One may be successful in hurting another's feelings through some snobbish remark or insult, but the giver of the hurt also suffers injury.

Teachers must, as should others, beware of the rationalization inherent in the statement "I'm telling you this for your own good." The words, translated into truth, would say, "I'm telling you this because of the personal satisfaction I get out of making you appear inferior to me." Two practical bits of wisdom from the Bible might serve to give a more constructive orientation to the temptation to criticize: "Let him who is

[8] Harry Estill Moore, "Some Emotional Concomitants of Disaster," *Mental Hygiene*, 42:45–50, January, 1958.

without sin be the first to cast a stone," and "A soft answer turneth away wrath." The tendency to criticize others can also be weakened by studying the implications of the mental hygiene statement: He who describes the personality of another is in reality revealing himself. Our knowledge of projective techniques should warn us that what is seen in others is conditioned by one's own personality make-up.

When New and Old Teachers Meet. A big step in the improvement of teacher-teacher relationships would be for each to make an effort to understand the problems of the other. The teacher who has previously taught in the community should try to realize that a new teacher may have some very valuable ideas. Perhaps some of the school customs—pupil discipline, classroom methods, and so on—would benefit by some overhauling. Even the teacher who has had no experience in any school system may have some ideas that are worthy of trial. Suggestions such as "This is the way we do it here" should be withheld until the new teachers have asked for help—and they will, provided that they do not feel that they *must* carry out the advice, in spite of convictions to the contrary. Similarly, the evidence of unfriendliness and indifference, though infrequently encountered, should be further reduced.[9]

Often the newcomer tends to discourage the proffering of friendship by his adherence to recent theory and by his disdain for approaches that have been formulated by experienced teachers over the years. Any reference to "old fogies" should be studiously avoided. The beginning teacher should beware of the temptation to criticize the "outmoded" methods of others, which in terms of their particular personality attributes are highly successful. Yet these same techniques may not be appropriate for the beginner.

A cordial relationship between the new teacher and the holdover will be facilitated by the same factors that are stressed in teacher-pupil relationships, namely, recognition of the uniqueness of personality, respect for varied backgrounds, a genuine friendliness based on maturity of personality, and a faith in the integrity of the purpose of the other.

Responsibility to Staff Workers. An area too frequently passed over lightly in professional relations is that concerning staff workers—the custodian, school secretary, and cafeteria workers. These are frequently persons with as much background for the performance of their jobs as many teachers have for their work. Just because the main function of the school is the teaching of children, it should not result in staff workers' being looked down upon or made to feel inferior. As a matter of fact, it is often easier to obtain a substitute teacher than it is to obtain a suitable substitute for a staff worker. Their jobs call for faithfulness and technical

[9] "First-year Teachers," *National Education Association Research Bulletin*, 34:36, February, 1956.

competence and their absence will occasion more immediate inconvenience than will that of a teacher.[10]

Unthinkingly, teachers sometimes cause the work of staff members to be unnecessarily burdensome or unpleasant. Teachers often command the custodian to cart away crates, do cleaning jobs off schedule, or make immediate repairs. Teachers will sometimes ask the secretary for hurry-up duplicating jobs, raid the supply room, or preempt the use of the telephone as though the secretary did not have to plan, organize, and schedule her activities. She has to make reports which require promptness on the part of teachers, she has to maintain stock supplies if the teacher is to have what he needs, she needs to be thought of as a person and friend if she is to act as a buffer when meeting disgruntled parents. The cafeteria worker—as well as the custodian and secretary—sometimes needs the support of teachers in protecting him from discourteous and inconsiderate pupils. The teacher, who is primarily responsible for the youngsters while in school, should not place staff workers in the position of having to assert authority which they do not possess and which they do not wish to assume.

RESPONSIBILITY TO THE COMMUNITY

Respect for the Mores of the Community. Some communities differ from the typical to a marked degree. Here, for instance, is a neighborhood, settled years ago by Quakers and today largely inhabited by Quakers. There are no beer parlors within the town limits and relatively few of the adults smoke. None of the teachers in the three-school system smokes. It seems reasonable that the adults in such a community should wish new teachers to subscribe to the predominant behavior. The feeling that sentiment against smoking is unreasonable might well be countered by a feeling on the part of those in the town that a new teacher has no right to attempt to impose his behaviors on those who think differently. For such reasons, the teacher is advised to learn about the mores of the community before accepting a position in the school. If he cannot bow to the prevailing mood, a position should be sought elsewhere.

Here is another community in which dress is conventionalized to conform to the religious orientation. While the teachers are not expected to clothe themselves in the conventional garb, they should not deliberately adopt extremes in dress just to show how narrow the inhabitants are. Such conspicuous nonconformity could be construed as an attack on the religious tenets and customs of the community, and the insecurity which might be generated in pupils would be harmful, in terms of mental

[10] Van Miller and Willard B. Spalding, *The Public Administration of Schools,* New York: Harcourt, Brace & World, Inc., 1952, p. 376.

health. This does not mean that pupils' questions should be avoided, but it cautions that our answers should be dispassionate. The slow process of continuous education should be trusted, without insistence that marked change is urgent. Practical use of these suggestions calls for the application of a quality so frequently mentioned in mental hygiene—balance.

> Friendly respect for others is, of course, basic to the establishment of sound community relations. Such relations are desirable in all citizens, but have a special importance for teachers. Because communities recognize the powerful influence of teachers on young people, they tend to be particularly concerned with the character of their views and general behavior. Strains are bound to arise when local standards differ—as they often do—from those to which a given teacher has been accustomed. Evidently, give and take is the right way to relieve these strains—but this requires mutual understanding based on genuine acquaintance.[11]

The viewpoint which is being recommended here is simply another application of the view that is recommended for dealing with pupils. Individuality must be respected. We must believe in the sincerity of motives of the other. We should realize that different interpretations of the same basic set of facts are possible.

Acquaintance with the Community. The statement, introduced earlier with respect to pupils, "To know is to understand," is pertinent to effective work in the community's schools. A thorough and growing knowledge of the community is basic to the entire viewpoint presented in this volume. Without this knowledge, one cannot work effectively with individual pupils, their unique backgrounds, and problems. Familiarity with the community conditions the teacher's effectiveness and, consequently, his own satisfaction derived from his work.

> The teacher is the *surrogate of middle class morality*. Parents expect the teacher to be a better model of behavior for their children than they are themselves. Although parents may smoke, drink, and gamble, they want the teacher to avoid any behavior that they think might be bad for children or adolescents to imitate. In this respect parents may be following a sound principle, for the teacher, especially the young teacher dealing with adolescents, is often a more effective model for youth than is the parent. As a consequence, the teacher is expected to practice the personal virtues of the middle class—correct speech, good manners, modesty, prudence, honesty, responsibility, friendliness, and so on. At the same time, certain other middle class virtues, such as competitiveness, striving for financial rewards, or independence of authority, are less likely to be valued in teacher behavior.[12]

[11] Commission on Teacher Education, *Teachers for Our Times*, Washington: American Council on Education, 1944, p. 158.

[12] Robert J. Havighurst and Bernice L. Neugarten, *Society and Education*, Boston: Allyn and Bacon, Inc., 1957, p. 387.

As we think through our objectives in education and study the implementation of the principles of democracy, the significance of the community becomes more evident. If we would understand the child's attitude toward work, toward discipline, toward cooperative endeavor, and toward morality, then we must know his cultural background. If we would understand the adolescent's attitude toward liquor, sex, and occupation, we must know his cultural background.

> As the teacher investigates the character of the community and works to improve it, she never loses sight of the young children for whom she is primarily responsible. In what kind of neighborhood does each child live? What sort of house do his parents provide? Has he brothers and sisters? Where and with whom does he play? What do his parents do? Where do they work? What do they do for recreation? Where do they shop? What language is spoken at home? Is the family new or well established in the neighborhood? Does the family take part in community activities; if so, in what are members most active? These *and many other questions* the teacher will ultimately answer if she is to plan wisely the experience for the children.[13]

There are several approaches to obtaining knowledge of a community. One is to make a personal visit. Another is to make the original study with the pupils. Still another is to undertake the study under the guise of education in-service. A group of rural teachers undertook such a study in a workshop and found that the following areas contained valuable educational material for pupils: a large nut orchard, a dairy, a turkey farm, a farmers' cooperative canning plant, a Catholic monastery, a local garage, and other enterprises. As a result of their study, they compiled a mimeographed booklet listing the names of people who could be contacted to arrange a visit, exact descriptions as to the roads to be taken, and a brief description of some of the things that could be seen. The most gratifying outcome of the workshop was, however, the assertion of the teachers that they enjoyed their teaching more because they were better acquainted with their community.

Interpreting the School. It is easy to be aware of, and assume responsibility for, the need for interpreting the school when there is some acute issue at stake. When a bond issue is to be floated which would mean an increase in salary, when the system of pupil evaluation is to be changed, or when additional pupil services are to be added, there is a sporadic effort to portray the school in its best light. But all too often, the necessity for continuous interpretation of the school is left to the administration. The sentiment "My job is to teach" also all too often prevails.

Actually, responsibility for interpreting the school cannot be avoided.

[13] Helen Heffernan (ed.), *Guiding the Young Child*, Boston: D. C. Heath and Company, 1951, p. 37.

Whether the teacher wishes to admit it or not, he is interpreting the school. Through the life he leads, the attitudes he expresses, the organizations to which he belongs, he is viewed by school patrons as a representative of the school. Pupils go home and report on the school as it is seen through their particular teachers. Thus, those things which are done to implement the objectives of mental hygiene in the classroom are avenues of interpretation. Finally, responsibility for interpreting the school cannot be avoided because of its prime necessity. School patrons have all had *some* experience with the school and they, justifiably or unjustifiably, have some very definite notions about the teachers, the methods, and the materials to which their own children should be exposed. However, this should not blind us to the fact that parents have good intentions. Informed parents will not oppose changes, costs, or reasonab'e personal assistance intended for the welfare of their children. They want and they deserve explanations. They, as has been emphasized with respect to teaching young people, deserve to have the objectives clarified.[14] This demands continuous attention and is just as deserving of studied approaches as are instructional techniques or curricular changes.

There are many ways in which the teacher can take his part in school interpretation. The friendliness he manifests in meeting patrons provides a view of "the school." Participation in civic organizations gives an indication that he is interested in the welfare of the community at large. The vast majority of teachers (80 to 90 per cent) live in the community and feel that they are accepted by it. They are active in community affairs, especially in church identification (91 per cent) and participation. But their record in voting and political activity is somewhat lower than the national average.[15] This latter is probably because of the historical transiency of the profession and partially because of laws or customs which discourage political activity. All these roles—citizen, leader, individual, scholar, patriot, friend, and brother—played by teachers are a means of school interpretation. Direct contacts with parents during back-to-school evenings, school visitation by parents, and parent-teacher evaluative conferences are highly effective. But perhaps the most continuous and inescapable public relations which teachers carry on are those resulting from the impressions made on students.[16]

No one teacher can achieve perfection in all these roles, but each is capable of attempting to come closer to the goal than he now is. This

[14] James L. Hymes, Jr., *Effective Home-School Relations*, Englewood Cliffs, N.J.: Prentice-Hall, Inc., 1953, pp. 11–34.

[15] "The Status of the American Public-school Teacher," *National Education Association Research Bulletin*, 35:31–34, February, 1957.

[16] National School Public Relations Association, *It Starts in the Classroom*, Washington: National Education Association, 1951, p. 6.

attempt will work for the benefit of both the pupil and the school patron. However, the greatest advantage will accrue to the teacher. The effort to become a teacher of "large intellectual and moral stature" will serve to get one out of the hampering confines of narrow self-concern. Above all, the unequalled opportunity to be a molder of the minds of children and youth, to share in discovery and improvement, and to have power-with rather than power-over makes the responsibility of continuous interpretation worthwhile.[17] All these challenges and opportunities offer specific and tangible goals toward which to direct one's own growth.

The behavior of pupils is another medium by which schools are interpreted. People gain impressions about the schools not only from what youngsters say about their teachers but from the way the pupils reflect in their actions the influence of the teachers. No experienced teacher who is worthy of being identified as a teacher has failed to find numerous occasions on which he was quite willing to say, "That is one of my pupils." We have seen times—at a school play production, in sportsman-like conduct at an athletic contest, upon school visiting days—when we were quite proud to say, "Those are youngsters from my school."

Finally, schools are interpreted by direct intent. Participation in parent-teacher organizations provide many opportunities for telling what the ideals and purposes of education are. Teachers are frequently invited to speak before civic and social groups on various phases of schoolwork. Visitation of the pupil's home is a means of interpretation that is highly recommended by administrators and commended by those teachers who have given it serious trial. School visiting days, or evenings, are sometimes regarded by teachers as interruptions in their work or impositions on their time. They present, however, one of the very effective means of interpreting the school. Finally, it is worth mentioning that the polite greeting of school patrons can lead to serious conversations that serve to portray the school.

SUMMARY

Concern about one's philosophy is important from professional, social, and personal viewpoints. Teachers should share America's faith in the ability of the school to bring forth maximum development of children and youth. In order to put this faith into practice, it is necessary to respect human differences, both in achievement and in capacity for achievement. Further, this faith should extend beyond the individual to a respect for group intelligence. To a very large extent, this involves no startlingly new knowledge about children, but a plan for using what we currently know (though knowledge will go on evolving).

[17] "The Rewards of Teaching," *Time*, 72(22):52, Dec. 1, 1958.

One's professional philosophy must include a consideration of responsibility and loyalty to and cooperation with administrators. For the most part, it is safe to assume that the administrators are motivated by high ideals and serious professional purposes. When the opportunity is presented, teachers may well be willing to participate in administration, though it is necessary to bear in mind that, in the final analysis, the administrator is the executor of policy.

Cooperation with one's fellow workers is a two-way concern, and the individual should be sure that his attitude is such as to invite cooperation. Too often the neglect of courtesy and of sharing inhibits cooperative endeavor. Courtesy to and cooperation with staff workers—secretary, custodian, and cafeteria workers—should be a vital part of the teacher's philosophy in the school. Both the old and the new teacher each might well give thought to ways by which the other may be made more comfortable and secure in his attempt to cooperate.

The teacher's philosophy should consider community relations. This should include a respect for the established mores of the community. If these seem to need changing, the different backgrounds of the "unenlightened" should be acknowledged and respected. One's responsibility to children involves a responsibility for knowing the community in which they live and will—many of them—continue to live. Community relations involve attention to interpreting the school and educating the community—*on a continuous basis.*

STUDY AND DISCUSSION EXERCISES

1. Using either past or present experiences, try to analyze the reasons why a particular administrator has made loyalty and cooperation difficult. What could be done by the teacher to help change the situation?

2. Explain your own attitude toward teacher participation in the development of administrative policy.

3. Make some additional suggestions, beyond those listed in the chapter, for bringing about better cooperation between teachers.

4. Cite some instances in which a school secretary, custodian, or cafeteria worker has had his work made more difficult by inconsiderate teachers.

5. Which area of school interpretation by teachers do you feel is most important? Which is of least importance?

SUGGESTED ADDITIONAL READINGS

Barzun, Jacques, *Teacher in America,* Boston: Little, Brown & Company, 1945.
This book deals with many aspects of education in a witty and thought-provoking manner. The teacher's role is emphasized throughout.

Highet, Gilbert, *The Art of Teaching,* New York: Alfred A. Knopf, Inc., 1951.

The qualities of outstanding teachers, the methods they use, and descriptions of great teachers in the past are discussed. Many practical points for consideration in the teacher's philosophy are suggested.

James, William, *Talks to Teachers on Psychology,* New York: Holt, Rinehart and Winston, Inc., 1899 (new ed., 1939). 238 pp.

It is said of William James that he wrote psychology like a novel. The result is an interesting and decidedly practical presentation of the role of teachers and the ideals they might well hold.

Lindgren, Henry C., *Mental Health in Education,* New York: Holt, Rinehart and Winston, Inc., 1954, pp. 507–535.

Lack of status, overcrowded classrooms, power over children, and threats to basic needs make it necessary for teachers to be concerned with their own mental health.

National Society for the Study of Education, *The Dynamics of Instructional Groups,* 59th Yearbook, Part II, Chicago: University of Chicago Press, 1960, pp. 30–50.

The ever-evolving roles of teachers—extraclass, administrative, instructional, and personality models—are discussed.

Zirbes, Laura, *Spurs to Creative Thinking,* New York: G. P. Putnam's Sons, 1959, pp. 36–54.

"Creative teaching" is discussed as a sensitive, insightful guidance designed to develop and fulfill the creative potentialities of individuals and groups.

CHAPTER 21

THE TEACHER'S PHILOSOPHY—
ADULT MENTAL HEALTH

There are many opposing viewpoints regarding what is good and the nature of the good life. Various major philosophical viewpoints—pragmatism, realism, idealism, Stoicism, or Platonism—are sometimes contradictory but more often complementary. What one philosophy has as a central point may be peripheral to another. Thus, it is impossible to satisfy everyone with one statement though the attempt to do so will probably continue. While we may be unable to agree on details there are some items that appear to merit consideration by anyone, including teachers, who seek to design their own well-thought-out system of values. This chapter is not intended as a prescription for an adult's—the teacher's—philosophy; rather, it is a proposal of items that seem to merit serious evaluation as the teacher attempts to bring his total functioning to a higher level.

EXERCISING THE FACETS OF PERSONALITY

A balanced philosophy should in some way recognize the need for exercising the major facets of personality. Good mental health can best be maintained when, through careful planning, some recognition is given the physical, mental, emotional, and spiritual components of personality.

Exercising the Physical Aspect of Personality. The importance of physical well-being is recognized in all statements of the objectives of education. Teachers emphasize to their pupils the significance of keeping in good health, from the first grade on through high school. But all too frequently, they seem not to recognize the importance of physical-health precautions in their own lives. For example, teachers sometimes neglect to get a sufficient amount of sleep, they hurry their meals, they often pay too little attention to having a balanced diet, and—perhaps, worst of all—they become so engrossed in the round of their daily activities that they neglect to take appropriate physical exercise. All these need to be taken into account in formulating a confident and energetic attack on the problems of teaching.

No blanket prescription can be made regarding the proper amount of sleep for a particular individual. Each person should study his own needs and see to it that his daily schedule provides for an amount of sleep that will fill his needs. A pragmatic test is to study how one feels on arising. If sleep is fitful in the early morning hours, it might be well to try allowing for fewer hours of sleep. It is more likely that the majority hate to get up and have difficulty in awakening. These people should experiment by going to bed earlier. Experiments indicate that regularity of sleep habits is important; hence, one should weigh carefully the temptations to interrupt the regular sleeping schedule.

Serious attention should be given to eating leisurely meals, in enjoyable physical surroundings and in good company. Too frequently the press of hall duty, responsibility for supervision of the school cafeteria, and the need to make a few minutes' more preparation for a "one o'clock class" may cause teachers to eat hurriedly. Sometimes this is unavoidable, but planning may help. If teachers have noon duties they might request the administration to allow for free time before or after the school lunch hour, they might work shifts with other teachers or arrange class schedules so that another teacher might double up in chorus, physical education, or shop activity—thus allowing one teacher free time for leisurely eating. Even if this cannot be controlled during the noon meal, something can be done with regard to the morning and evening meals.

Many opinions express the belief that exercise is essential to good health and mental and bodily vigor. When it comes to proving that exercise is a *sine qua non* of health, conclusive evidence is lacking. People who exercise regularly show no distinct superiority in resistance to disease, longevity, and vigor on the job over those whose only exercise is walking from the house to the garage. One thing can safely be said in favor of moderate exercise, taken with some degree of regularity: those who take such exercise report that they *feel better* when they exercise regularly. Exercise, in order to contribute to health, must be appropriate to one's age and be scaled to his daily work habits. Many exercise too energetically and too compulsively; too much is crowded into the weekend.[1] The right physical exercise can help relieve headaches, stiff neck, cramped muscles and improve appetite after a day replete with hurry and tensions.

[1] Lemuel C. McGee, "The Suicidal Cult of 'Manliness,'" *Today's Health*, 35:28–30, January, 1957.

Equally as important as exercise are regular periods for rest and relaxation. Ideally, it is to be hoped that such periods will be designated in the teacher's schedule. There is little reason to believe that while pupils need rest and recreation periods interspersed through their work, teachers are capable of carrying responsibilities continuously through the day—including what should be periods of rest and recreation. If the ideal situation does not exist, it becomes all the more important for teachers to plan a rest and recreation time for themselves outside school hours.

Plans should be made for periodic health examinations and the prompt relief of minor ailments. The excuse generally given for neglecting these is that they represent another pressure on already strained finances. It is hoped that the time will soon arrive when medical benefits will be more generally available to teachers; in the meantime it is important that prompt care of minor ailments should be considered a fundamental routine matter. One of the more important phases of the treatment of both physical and mental ailments is early identification and early treatment. The generally accepted verdict is that it is actually cheaper, in the long run, to pay for regular examinations and the treatment of minor ailments, than it is to pay the costs of later, more serious illnesses.

The following items might well serve as a check list for the observance of health habits. It is designed for older people, but teachers, too, are growing older: (1) Take care of personal appearance—one tends to feel well when he looks well; (2) pay attention to weight and diet; (3) provide for exercise and rest—including sleep; (4) take periodic physical examinations—for hearing and vision, teeth, the digestive system, the heart, and the circulatory system; (5) without becoming a hypochondriac, pay attention to psychosomatic complaints, and (6) recognize physical limitations.[2]

Recreation, in the form of hobbies, which will often also afford opportunities for the exercise of the mental and emotional aspects of personality, can be of considerable benefit to one's physical health. Recreation is more than mere rest; it stands for the re-creation of the individual through the exercise of interests and potentialities, which are given too little recognition in one's work. There need be no specific prescription as to what hobbies teachers should adopt. Whatever they might be, because they involve the mental, physical, and emotional exercise of personality, they will offer ways of enriching life.

> The busy executive and the routine clerk need hand-skill hobbies for escape from the tensions and pressures of their daily work. Learning how to make things with tools and wood, with paints and brushes, or at metalwork, bookbinding, weaving, and at other arts and crafts, will improve

[2] Jeanne G. Gilbert, *Understanding Old Age*, New York: The Ronald Press Company, 1952, pp. 312–322.

both the quality and quantity of your day's work. At the same time your hobby can be developed to become a rewarding major occupation in retirement.

In other ways, find time and opportunity to enjoy the creative use of your hands. Gardening can be creative, so can making enlargements of your favorite photographs, learning to make home repairs, making flies for next summer's fishing and developing musical skill with its coordination of hand and mind.[3]

Preferably, hobbies should be creative rather than the "pass-time" variety of the spectator type. The main requirement is that hobbies be interesting and enjoyable to the person concerned. In one group of eighteen teachers, the following hobbies were represented: making dolls, assembling scrapbooks on particular themes, fishing, gardening, stamp collecting, ornithology, numismatics, cooking, knitting, crocheting, "being a pal to my son," reading (mentioned in three or four cases), boating, skiing, and training race horses. The sad part of this particular situation is that almost half of the teachers felt they were perhaps stealing time when they were pursuing their hobbies.

Time for oneself, whether it be devoted to activity or rest, is significant in both mental and physical health. But there is a need for balance. There is little reason to doubt the validity of the following statement by William James, a philosopher of widely acknowledged wisdom, though it was originally formulated in 1899: Writing of the value of tranquillity and meditation, he said, "I beg you teachers to think a little seriously of this matter. Perhaps you can help our rising generation of Americans toward the beginning of a better set of personal ideals."[4]

Elsewhere, he said:

> Your intense, convulsive worker breaks down and has bad moods so often that you never know where he may be when you most need his help—he may be having one of his "bad days." We say that so many of our fellow-countrymen collapse, and have to be sent abroad to rest their nerves, because they work so hard. I suspect that this is an immense mistake. . . . [the] cause lies rather in those absurd feelings of hurry and having no time, in that breathlessness and tension, that anxiety of feature and that solicitude for results, that lack of inner harmony and ease, in short, by which with us the work is so apt to be accompanied, and from which a European who should do the same work would nine times out of ten be free. These perfectly wanton and unnecessary tricks of inner attitude and outer manner in us, caught from the social atmosphere, kept up by tradition, and idealized by many as the admirable way of life, are

[3] Ray Giles, *Begin Now—to Enjoy Tomorrow* . . . , new ed., Newark, N.J.: The Mutual Benefit Life Insurance Company, 1957, pp. 43–44.

[4] William James, *Talks to Teachers on Psychology*, new ed., New York: Holt, Rinehart and Winston, Inc., 1939, p. 74. By permission of the publisher.

the last straws that break the American camel's back, the final over-flowers of our measure of wear and tear and fatigue.[5]

Exercising the Mental Aspects of Personality. It has long been believed that intelligence declines slowly after reaching a peak in the early or mid-twenty years of life. Recent data offer some hope that the rate of decline can be checked by vigorous use of the mind.

> Those who write confidently about the relationship between age and intelligence may some day have a rude awakening. . . . There is experimental evidence to support the claim that those who continue to apply themselves to learning of verbal materials all through life are able to maintain their efficiency as learners better than those who do not have such a history.[6]

While teaching is a challenge to mental development, the challenge is not great enough to permit further exercising of mental capacities to become incidental. Gaining more knowledge about the subject matter being taught, keeping abreast of scientific, cultural, and political trends, and studying new viewpoints of child and adolescent development may provide some of the mental activity that is required in a healthy life. But this constant attention to school-related mental activities may not furnish the well-rounded development that is a goal of mental health. Reading and study carried on just for the sake of curiosity, quite apart from any function it might play in effective teaching, is a pursuit worth considering.

> Reading is one of the good things in life. It is good in itself and, like a good wine, needs no bush. Reading is a factor of great importance in the individual's development. Persons who read do so for many different reasons, as different as men are different one from another. We read for the rich enjoyment that comes from sharing the experiences of a penetrating mind or following the magic of a master storyteller. We read as one of the tasks of daily living. We read, particularly in these confused times, to understand the trials that beset mankind and to help keep even our sense of balance in a changing world. We read, consciously, to advance ourselves either in our social spheres or in our fields of endeavor. We read because we seek to understand many viewpoints and to evaluate many situations in order that we may bring an intelligent interest to our community life and to our daily work. We read to escape the world of reality just as we must read to live in that world. We read because we like to, and we read because we must.[7]

[5] *Ibid.*, pp. 214–215. By permission of the publisher.

[6] Oscar J. Kaplan, "Psychological Aspects of Aging," *The Annals of the American Academy of Political and Social Science*, 279:35–36, January, 1952.

[7] David H. Clift in *Adult Reading*, 55th Yearbook, Part II, National Society for the Study of Education, Chicago: University of Chicago Press, 1956, pp. 2–3.

One of the most stimulating lecturers the author has heard was the late Elwood P. Cubberley, who wrote or edited many of the early twentieth-century books in education. He once said that he never studied after nine o'clock at night. As an undergraduate student, as a graduate student, and as professor and dean, he had stuck to this rule. His reading after that hour was for enjoyment. In fact, certain evenings were designated for free reading and only for exceptionally desirable substitutions were these evenings set aside. The consequence of this reading was informative and entertaining lectures that were punctuated with pertinent side remarks relating the subject at hand to many phases of life that might easily have been overlooked. An occupational hazard sometimes mentioned by teachers is that dealing so extensively with the immature minds of students, the teachers may begin to think like children and adolescents. Collateral reading and free reading can help to supply a contrast.

The choice of companionship is an important consideration. Careful cultivation of adult friendships may offset the danger of developing arrogant and domineering habits, which seem to be encouraged by extended contact with children. The accuracy of the teacher's information needs to be challenged frequently by association with age peers in and out of school.

The challenge of improving knowledge may be met in part by active participation in school committees. Such responsibilities, far from being an imposition on the teacher's time, are opportunities for exercising and developing the intellectual aspects of personality. The same thing may be said for lively participation in community affairs. In order for one to be a contributing member, there is the need for him to keep informed about what other communities are doing with regard to the particular problem concerned, be it delinquency, improved police protection, how to deal with vice and gambling, or how to improve the volunteer social services of the community.

Exercising the Emotional Aspects of Personality. Many teachers, although they express appreciation for their profession, admit that the emotional strain is great. They feel extremely tired at the end of the day, not because they have expended a great deal of physical energy, but because of the emotional tensions that are created by having to deal with the restlessness of pupils and the numberless problems presented. For this reason, conscious attention to a living program that provides for a healthful emotional release is most important.

The intimate relationship of the various facets of personality is well illustrated in the bearing of physical exercise on the release of emotions. Numerous teachers, as well as adults in other occupations, find that walking, swimming, and participation in games and sports noticeably affects their feelings after a tense day of work. The physiological effects of strong emotion are such as to prepare one for vigorous physical activity. The supply of excess energy, caused or accompanied by certain glandular activity, demands activity which will consume that excess.

In addition to the wisely directed release of negative emotional energy, there is the need to cultivate the upbuilding emotions. Love has been proved to be an emotion so important that it is listed among the fundamental needs of humans, for adults quite as much as for children. Teachers need to love and be loved. While marriage may not be essential for every person, it does seem that for the great majority this institution is highly important in the accomplishment of well-rounded living. Undoubtedly, there are many well-adjusted persons who are not married and many poorly adjusted persons who are married. Statistics show, however, that married people have somewhat better health and longevity than do the unmarried, as a group.[8] Words are inadequate for condemning those anachronistic school systems that will not hire married women as teachers. It seems that the administrators of such schools must be forgetting the welfare of children, for economic reasons. Fortunately this absurd custom appears to be disappearing.

Some of the many ways of exercising the upbuilding emotions will appeal to one person and some to another. Many get true enjoyment and benefit from listening to music. Others are emotionally soothed by taking solitary walks. Some find in motion pictures, dramatic productions, dance recitals, or art museums, a source of exercise for the mild, positive emotions. Individual hobbies of musical production, craftsmanship, drawing, painting, and various handicrafts are means of rounding out the orbit of activities and enjoyments.

Recognizing the emotional aspect of personality is not confined to cultural "highbrows"; much can be said in favor of the excitements of amusement parks, sports spectacles, travel to the many beauty spots of our own country and of others. However, these are relatively passive, rather than creative, means of release. The main point to be considered is that each one of us has the capacity for expressing many kinds and degrees of emotion and will find that the inevitable irritations of vigorous living can often be made more bearable by our taking advantage of diversions which give exercise to our emotional capacity. What is done for developing physical vigor can also contribute to the healthy exercise of emotion. And certainly many studious activities are meaningless without their emotional concomitants of satisfaction from achievement, the stimulus of new experiences, and the feelings of security stemming from the continuing development of our own competence.

[8] "Mortality Lowest in Married Population," *Statistical Bulletin,* Metropolitan Life Insurance Company, 38:4–7, February, 1957.

Exercising the Spiritual Aspect of Personality. For many, religious devotions are the source of the benefits which have been recommended in mental hygiene programs. A religion, such as Christianity or Judaism, which emphasizes the importance of love for and devotion to fellow men is stressing a sound principle of mental health. It must be admitted that there are those who accept the form but not the essential practices of sane religion; and there are those who rely upon a deity to solve their problems, instead of taking positive action themselves. However, religion can be, and is for many people, a means of attaining the fullest meaning in life.[9]

One advantage of religion, when it stresses love for others, is that it helps a person to get outside himself. It makes more probable his being genuinely concerned with the problems of others.

> Christ says to the teacher, "Make the interests and aims of each of your scholars your own." Whether a teacher is a Christian in the profoundest sense of the term depends not in the least on whether he is a Catholic or a Protestant, a Conservative or a Liberal. It depends on whether the teacher has his own point of view, his personal interests, and then regards the scholars as alien beings to be dealt with as the rules of the school may require and as his own personal interest and reputation may suggest; or whether in sympathy and generous interest he makes the life and problems of each scholar a genuine part of the problem of his own enlarged nature and generous heart. The greatest difference between teachers, after all, is that in this deepest sense some teachers are Christians and some are not.[10]

The fact that the above statement was written in 1910 does not by any means make the thought outdated. Notable psychologists and psychiatrists place similar emphasis on the importance of religion in living a well-rounded, mature life.

> Recent decades have in fact seen a promising *rapproachement* between science and the church. As the sciences of human behavior have advanced, religious leaders have found that the discoveries and techniques of those sciences can help them to understand and deal with the aspirations and problems of people. More and more have they joined hands with psychologists, psychiatrists, sociologists, social workers, and general physicians to mutual advantage. These professions and disciplines have been brought in as consultants and as participants in the curricula of

[9] See Harold W. Bernard, *Toward Better Personal Adjustment,* 2d ed., New York: McGraw-Hill Book Company, Inc., 1957, pp. 390–414, for more extensive discussion.

[10] William DeWitt Hyde, *The Teacher's Philosophy In and Out of School,* Boston: Houghton Mifflin Company, 1910, pp. 77–78. By permission of the publisher.

seminaries, and clinics for mental disorders have been established in association with some churches.[11]

The time spent in religious devotion is, for some, a period of mental and physical relaxation. The soft, slow music of the organ and the choir helps to bring peace of mind that makes for physical and mental repose. Thoughts about the Almighty lead to a perspective of viewpoint that reveals a plan transcending our personal desires and makes it somewhat easier for us to bear our own minor burdens. This gives the mental repose that leads to more complete relaxation. Belief in a deity who cares about us personally contributes to the emotional poise which, in the long run, will help to prevent the accumulation of tensions that makes it so difficult for us to achieve relaxation.

Some may question the idea that man has a spiritual side of his nature, equal or parallel in importance to the mental, physical, and emotional aspect of personality. However, anthropologists have found that there are no men, anywhere on earth, who do not have a religion—a reaching out toward some power which is mightier than they are. Powerful and intelligent as man is, there seem to be times when the stresses of life are too much for him, so he seeks help and guidance from his particular deity— God, Jesus, Buddha, Mohammed, or Allah. Precisely at this point religion makes its great contribution to mental health. A religion that gives a person the assurance that there is help available for him, and, at the same time, leaves responsibilities for him to carry out, makes it easier for him to face his problems with fortitude.

SATISFYING HUMAN NEEDS

Other chapters have dealt with the human needs which must, at least in part, be met if children are to achieve and maintain mental health. Here the concern is with the basic needs of teachers which must be on the way to being satisfied if they are to achieve personal and professional competence.

The Need to Love and Be Loved. We hear and read frequent discussions that deal with the necessity of loving and being loved. Children have a right to be loved because of what they are—children. But teachers, as well as other adults, must earn that right by what they do. Satisfaction of this need for adults must come not so much from being loved as from loving. As teachers, we must implement the need by stressing the outgoing kind of love.

[11] George S. Stevenson, *Mental Health Planning for Social Action*, New York: McGraw-Hill Book Company, Inc., 1956, p. 225.

Emotional inclusiveness is a sign of health. It is by no means the same thing as liking everybody equally well, or in the same way. It is, rather, what we might call a *good will reflex:* a spontaneous affirmation of life; a sensitivity to other people's rights and feelings that does not have to be laboriously lumbered into service on each separate occasion; a capacity to enjoy a wide range of sharings, from those with a dearly beloved intimate to those with a passing stranger; a sense of there being in the world not just a few people who are worth while, but of there being an abundance of people worth knowing and liking.[12]

In some way our philosophy must embrace the need to contribute to the welfare of others. Clinical psychologists know that those who fail to recognize and express the need for outgoing love (emotional inclusiveness) are likely to be unpopular, abnormally introverted, and unhappy. Their lives are cripplingly circumscribed by the restrictions imposed by their selfish motivations. Of course, one's orientation in this respect is conditioned by prior experiences, but poor orientation can gradually be overcome by practice of "Do unto others . . . "

Two simple suggestions are proffered for satisfying the need to love. (1) Study the nature of people and the background of individuals, so that the understanding which is fundamental to love may be gained. (2) Act as though you loved others, so that a positive psychology of suggestion may function.

The Need to Accomplish. There are countless opportunities in the teaching profession to approach satisfaction of the need to accomplish. Every pupil who has not realized the full potential of his capacity (hence, all the pupils) affords an opportunity for something of importance to be done. Study after study of the mental health of teachers indicates that those who are happy and mentally healthy are the ones who study their responsibility and their pupils so that accomplishment of their aims counts toward their own benefit and that of their charges, as well. Accomplishment requires effort, but that effort pays rich dividends in better mental health.

The Need for Security. Except perhaps for very young children, satisfaction of the need for security cannot be bestowed upon anyone; it must be earned. This fundamental aspect of security has been well expressed by Emory Alvord, an "agricultural missionary" in the Bantu region of Southern Rhodesia.

I believe more firmly than ever in the infinite potential in people—any people, all people. But their improvement must come always from within themselves. I have no faith in handouts of any kind, economic or spiritual.

[12] Harry Overstreet and Bonaro Overstreet, *The Mind Alive*, New York: W. W. Norton & Company, Inc., 1954, pp. 138–139.

Abraham Lincoln once said, "You cannot help men permanently by doing for them what they could and should do for themselves." We need to inscribe that statement large across every plan we make these days.[13]

There are two implications for the teacher: First, his own security is dependent upon individual effort and competence. Second, the citizen of tomorrow—our pupil of today—should be taught that his security depends largely on a psychological orientation calling for personal endeavor.

The Need to Develop Tension-tolerance. Basically tension-tolerance is an outgrowth of one's fundamental physical, emotional, and intellectual equipment and of his prior experiences. But the view one takes of problems may be altered by study and reflection. It is therefore advisable to realize that problems, difficulties, and obstacles may stimulate personal growth. Unpleasant experiences, unless they are so disastrous as to result in personality disintegration, are means of inoculating one to endure further conflicts, which are an inevitable accompaniment of vigorous living. A person develops tension-tolerance not only by saying he will face adversity but also by confidently dealing with the adversity. Moreover, tension-tolerance may also be fostered by deliberately taking inventory of the good things about, when the foreboding items press so hard for recognition.

> Be still, sad heart, and cease repining;
> Behind the clouds the sun is shining;
> Thy fate is the common fate of all,
> Into each life some rain must fall,
> Some days must be dark and dreary.
> *Longfellow,* "The Rainy Day"

The Need to Be Independent. In some instances, it would be more to the point to admonish administrators to give their teachers a chance to be independent. But since this book is addressed to classroom teachers, let them understand that their independence should be earned by proving that their methods are such as will warrant approval. If attention is devoted to *earning* independence, the bellicose conception of independence, that it is part of a person's birthright and something to be maintained by personal warfare, will be avoided. A healthy independence should be thought of as a reward for consistently recognizing the rights, interests, and welfare of others. As a matter of practical fact, society will permit independence only to those who do manifest concern about the welfare of others.

[13] Liston Pope and Clarence W. Hall, "The Man Who Founded a People," *The Reader's Digest,* 58:55, March, 1951. Condensed from *Christian Herald* and used by permission of *The Reader's Digest.*

The Need for a Task, a Plan, and Freedom to Carry Out That Plan. This three-faceted human need is the very essence of personal philosophy. Teachers have their task—a task which society recognizes as of prime importance. Their experience and training should contribute to their making and remaking of plans, without which there will be much dissipated effort and many disappointing results. If their plans are democratically and humanely oriented, they will, in the majority of cases, have the freedom to execute those plans.

The problems, from the standpoint of philosophy, are patent: (1) The task of teaching needs to be repeatedly and continuously thought through, so that there is maximum adjustment to the exigencies of the time. (2) Plans need to be varied, to be reconstructed, for many reasons; not the least of these is that teachers need to avoid getting "into a rut." (3) As in the case of independence (a mere rewording), freedom must be earned in terms of its orientation to others.

Other Basic Needs. There are other basic needs which must be satisfied if optimum mental health is to be consummated. Satisfaction of social needs such as the desire to be recognized, to be considered worthy, to be admired is as essential to the adult as it is for a child. The need for companionship, in spite of its close relationship to the need to love and be loved, deserves separate consideration.

The satisfaction of needs is a continuous problem. Like other aspects of mental hygiene, a need does not remain "satisfied"; we can only work toward *being on the way* to its satisfaction. Incorporating the concept of needs into one's functional philosophy will tend to give them the continuing attention which they deserve.

POSITIVE PRINCIPLES OF MENTAL HEALTH

Another approach to the teacher's personal philosophy can be made by incorporating into that philosophy those values and action patterns which are conducive to good mental health. The following, as positive principles of mental hygiene, are means of exercising the various aspects of personality and of satisfying fundamental human needs.

Maintain Sound Physical Health. Maintaining health, we have seen, embraces several considerations, such as getting sufficient sleep, paying attention to a sensible diet, providing for rest and recreation, getting whole-body exercise appropriate to one's age level, and taking care of minor ailments before they become aggravated. The value of this item is indicated in the ancient ideal, "A sound mind in a sound body."

Seek to Understand Your Own Conduct. Because of their involvement in human development and motivation, teachers are in an advantageous position for seeing themselves more objectively. If the studies of psychology and mental hygiene are viewed as opportunities for recognizing one's own motivations, conditionings, and learnings, as well as those of pupils, they can promote self-understanding. While there is a risk that too much self-analysis may be harmful, there is also the possibility that, by studying such courses, one can, through exercising discretion, make evaluations of himself and his progress. Psychology and mental hygiene, studied primarily for the sake of understanding pupils, can also strengthen our ego concept by emphasizing the importance of our work, can teach us to use constructive self-criticism, can help us develop positive attitudes toward our own handicaps by seeing how others have faced their shortcomings.

Seek to Improve Relationships with Others. The teacher's relationships with his pupils are of prime importance in effective teaching. Attention should be given to improving adult relationships, as well. We should all selfishly profit from taking more time to be friendly, both to youngsters and to adults. It is a psychological fact, as well as a religious principle, that the giving of yourself to others builds a stronger and more harmonious personality. Seeking to improve social relationships, while primarily giving exercise to the emotional phases of personality, most frequently also provides some intellectual stimulation. It is said by the devotees of friendship that any of us can learn from the lowliest of persons.

Establish Confidential Relationships with Selected Individuals. Having a person in whom we can confide our problems and to whom we can complain about our disappointments and boast about our accomplishments provides an emotional catharsis that tends to prevent the build-up of unwholesome tensions. Psychoanalysts have significantly helped people in trouble by serving as intimate confidants. The benefit of "getting it off your chest" or "taking down your hair" has been experimentally proved to have a psychological basis.

The person who is selected as this intimate confidant must be a person who is capable of holding intact the secrets which are confided. Concern lest the information should go too far may well create tensions that are as dangerous as those that would result from the repression of the original problem. The confidant must be free of the neurotic tendency of oversuspiciousness. For example, if he were to confide in you and later were to feel that he had discovered in the conversations of others evidence that you had betrayed a confidence, even if you had in fact held it inviolate, there would be difficulties for both of you. Thus, at times it may be necessary for one to discourage a friend from telling too much about himself. However, an intimate confidential relationship of this kind will serve primarily to provide wholesome exercise of the emotional aspect of personality, but inasmuch as it also makes for better understanding of ourselves and others, it exercises the mental phase of personality.

Face Stress and Strain with Poise. This admonition may appear to be futile, in that it involves lifting oneself by his bootstraps, as it were. It is valid to ask the question, Can I stop worrying just by saying that I will not worry? It may be that it is no more possible for a person who faces strain not to be excited about it than it is for a person who is ill to get well by saying that it is foolish to be sick. But as a matter of fact, even the latter is a practical possibility. There is a psychology of suggestion that makes it possible to get rid of *some* illnesses that are *apparently* physical in nature.

There are some suggestions for achieving poise that go beyond the determination to be more poised. For one thing, it will be well to reflect on the fact that other people have troubles, too, and yet seem, in general, to go on enjoying life. Past experiences tell us "This too shall pass away." We have but to reflect on the experiences of last year to realize that many of the things that worried us somehow or other did not greatly change the major course of events, that some of the things which seemed tremendous at one time now appear to be trivial matters. We need to realize that for each of us, just as for the pupils we teach, one event does not make a lifetime.

Another fact to take into account in seeking emotional poise is that some things are beyond our power to control. It does no good to fret about anything that is personally unavoidable. Finally, it may at times pay to take the Pollyanna attitude that even evil or disliked things and events may hold advantages for us. Realizing that obstacles in our own lives can serve as a stimulant to growth is a step toward facing strain and stress with poise.

Substitute Planning for Worry. There are many people who believe that worry has a place in a mentally healthy life. Assuredly anticipation of difficulties, planning for eventualities, formulating hypotheses in advance do have advantages. In fact, it is advisable and necessary that data be gathered, that alternatives be devised, that solutions be tried; however, these constitute directed thinking—not worry. Worry may be defined as a form of circular thinking that goes over and over the same things without arriving at a workable or even a tentative conclusion; therefore, when, after a problem has been thought through, there seems to be no present solution, it is probably just as well—at least for the time being— to apply the solution suggested by the song title of the thirties, "Let's Put Out the Light and Go to Sleep."

Planning gives exercise to the intellectual phase of personality; the repudiation of worry is a recognition of the fact that the emotional phase of personality can be overtaxed. Worry, as circular thinking, means that normal conflicts develop into nerve-racking frustrations. Problems remain bottled up. They are intensified and become festering centers of diseased emotions. Dr. Peter J. Steincrohn in his book, *How to Stop Killing Your-*

self, says that worry is one of the ways to "slow suicide."[14] We worry to the extent that we are unable to make decisions. The remedy is simple. Force yourself to make a decision. All the data on any problem are never completely assembled. We must act on tentative decisions. Planning, or directed thinking, making decisions, and acting on tentative conclusions are steps toward bringing about the diffusion of the slow poison of worry.

Achieve Security through Developing Skills. Teachers who have realized the importance of developing skills in children in order to give them improved mental health will realize that their own security can be strengthened by skill development. This might take the form of developing greater competence in subject matter, of an improved understanding of the course and nature of child and adolescent development. It may take the form of becoming an authority in some phase of educational activity other than classroom teaching—such as being a curriculum specialist, becoming a guidance expert, an authority in mental hygiene, or an expert in testing, or seeking to improve the status of education as a profession.

Work therapy is effective in helping those who have broken under mental and emotional strain; it is also effective in maintaining good mental health. The skills that are developed to improve one's work thus contribute to a greater enjoyment of work and aid in hearty devotion and application to the daily tasks that are required.

Give Both Work and Play a Place in Your Life. A building contractor who was highly successful before World War II worked so hard that he had a breakdown. His family was broken and his career interrupted by military service, but he decided that success was spelled in terms of living, not the accumulation of wealth. Today he is again a successful builder, though not so compulsive about his work. He works hard but plans free time to fish, hunt, and travel. His new wife and daughter are an integral part of his daily living. He has discovered what more people should realize—mental health is a matter of balance.

The integrative person is one whose various and multiple drives are harmoniously coordinated and act together toward some inclusive purpose.

When your adjustments are integrative you satisfy all of your motives as they function in an interrelated system, without the overemphasis of one drive or the slighting of another. Furthermore, good adjustments are integrated with respect to time. Representations of the past and the future are brought into the present by appropriate symbolic processes,

[14] Peter J. Steincrohn, *How to Stop Killing Yourself,* New York: Wilfred Funk, Inc., 1950.

speech and thinking, so that behavior is determined by goals other than the most immediate ones.[15]

Many fundamental needs are most effectively approached by engaging in constructive work. Such requirements as the need for achievement, the need for recognition, the need for approval, the desire for adventure, relief from worry, the need for security are well served through devotion to one's work—in whatever socially approved line it may be. It has long been realized that a sense of dignity and craftsmanship in labor contributes much to one's ego strength and satisfaction—to one's happiness.[16] The really permanent satisfactions and significance of man reside in his work.

But work alone does not necessarily ensure balance. If more of man's capacities are to be exercised, work activities must be supplemented with recreational pursuits. Ideally, one's leisure-time activities should be in contrast with his work, so that there is a greater chance for the exercise of all capacities and for the fulfillment of all needs.

Certainly, the teacher need have no compunction about regularly scheduling a period of leisure. The release of tensions through play will make for a more enjoyable classroom atmosphere for his pupils. His exercise of different capacities will give him more common ground upon which to meet and understand pupils who have varied interests. His recreations will carry him into wider areas of the community and reveal new avenues for making the teaching of subject matter increasingly functional. His play will refresh him after the tedium of classroom problems.

Giving both work and play a place in your life is a matter of relativity. It is not an either-or proposition. Some people devote themselves so assiduously to their work that they have no time for play. But this is at the cost of a threat—frequently a realized threat—to personality integration. Others derive so much pleasure from play that they have no time for work. But pleasure is bought at the cost of that more enduring quality called "happiness."

Give Attention to the Present Situation. Giving attention to the present situation is simply a matter of applying good common sense. Certainly, nothing can be done to change behavior already enacted or events previously transpired, but—and this is highly important—past errors should be avoided in present actions. The importance of living fully and completely today was well illustrated, though it took some time for the lesson to be appreciated, for the author some years ago by an army cap-

[15] Laurance F. Shaffer and Edward J. Shoben, Jr., *The Psychology of Adjustment*, 2d ed., Boston: Houghton Mifflin Company, 1956, p. 152.

[16] Howard Mumford Jones, *The Pursuit of Happiness*, Cambridge, Mass.: Harvard University Press, 1953, pp. 116ff.

tain. At the time, the author was an educational adviser in a Civilian Conservation Corps camp, living in the temporary barracks characteristic of that organization. The room was barren, wide cracks showed in the floor and walls, and the only furniture was a bunk. An apple box was nailed to the wall to hold shaving gear and a few books. A blanket was nailed over the window to cut off the winter cold. A gunny sack on the floor served to add to morning comfort, pieces of 1- by 12-inch board were nailed together for a chair, there was a straw tick on the bunk, and some packing boxes served as a table. Simple living was the order of the day because of the temporary situation. We anticipated being ordered to another location with the melting of the snows. The captain lived on an entirely different scale. His room had attractive draperies, there was a hooked rug on the floor, he had a box-spring and inner-spring mattress, there were some pictures on the wall. An overstuffed chair, a bedspread, a bookcase with several books, and a radio contributed to comfortable living. One evening the question was asked, "Captain S., why do you have all these comforts when you know that we'll be ordered out of here in the near future?" (We were moved within four weeks.) The answer was immediate and clear-cut, "Well, I'll tell you, Bernard—something you may take a long time to realize—this temporary living turns out to be a very permanent thing."

It seems certain that many of us need to absorb this lesson. We live and work for better things tomorrow, next week, or next year. In the meantime, our lives are running their course. We are forming habits that make it increasingly improbable that we shall retain the capacity for full and complete living. The soundest, perhaps the only, approach to facing the uncertainties of the future with equanimity is to attack with vigor the problems of today.

Appreciate the Humor in Daily Situations. One way to make living enjoyable today is to attune ourselves to the humorous events that are continually happening. There are many things that may serve to "brighten the day with a smile" if we but look for the amusing elements. Perhaps the first step to be taken is to realize that the world might possibly get along without us, we shall be able to appreciate some of the ridiculous aspects of our own behavior. Most of us, at some time, have stood off and gleefully evaluated the creations women wear on their heads. Many opportunities have been afforded us to grin knowingly at men's conceit. Most men (judging from their own reports) seem to think that they are personally and individually "God's gift to women." With due consciousness of our own facial limitations, we might possibly find reason to smile at the odd appearance of eyes, ears, nose, or mouth of even some national figure.

In the classroom both the behavior and the remarks of students give plenty of opportunities for amusement (though we must be careful never to offend a sensitive pupil). Young children make many ridiculous errors when they attempt to introduce new words into their conversations. Hilarious answers to questions are given in oral and written quizzes. These latter may well make us pause to examine the meaningfulness of our teaching, but they can, nevertheless, serve to entertain and amuse us. On one occasion the author noticed suppressed humor in a class of teachers when they heard one of their members, complaining about the spelling of his eighth-graders, say, "They can't hardly spell nothing."

A sense of humor and a capacity to avoid taking oneself too seriously will be helpful for anyone—particularly, for a teacher. Yet this point of view may be easily lost unless it is consciously cultivated. William C. Morse and G. Max Wingo regard a sense of humor as one of the most essential qualities of a teacher. Many minor upsets can be handled smoothly if one looks at the lighter side and avoids viewing them as major catastrophies. A false sense of dignity makes it difficult for teachers to admit mistakes and tends to make them fearful of deviations from conventional procedures. Humor reduces tension and encourages better pupil control.[17] While one's fundamental personality trends are much the same in and out of the classroom, a sense of humor can be strengthened by deliberate exercise in any place.

Just Do the Best You Can. The idea of just doing one's best is not a philosophy of mediocrity. It is not a laissez-faire or opportunistic doctrine. Rather, it is an attitude of common sense, an aspect of facing reality, and a means of obtaining balanced activities and sensible perspective.

An incident which took place on a firing range well illustrates the practicability of just doing one's best:

> A candidate for a marksman's medal was making excellent progress and one day the range supervisor said, "I think you should shoot for record now." The rounds for rapid and slow fire at 25 and 50 yards were shot and the targets were examined. The requisite score had not been achieved.
>
> The supervisor said, "I'm not surprised. You were trying to do better than you can do. Listen, you *can't* do any better than you *can* do, can you?"
>
> The answer obviously was "No."
>
> "Certainly not. No one hits the bull's-eye every time. The best marksmen miss now and then. In fact, they don't try to hit the center with every shot. They just do the best they can. You'll do much better if you just do the best you can. Here's what happens. If you try for perfection,

[17] William C. Morse and G. Max Wingo, *Psychology and Teaching*, Chicago: Scott, Foresman and Company, 1954, pp. 302–306.

you jerk the trigger when you have the sights lined up with the target. Jerking throws the gun out of line and, by the time the gun fires, you are way off center. Just do the best you can, keep squeezing, keep squeezing, *squeezing* and come as close as you can. Often you will feel that you are off target, but keep squeezing and, by the time the gun fires, you will be back on your target—or nearly so. You can't be perfect. *Just keep squeezing and come as close as you can.*"

There are many suggestions for improved living and improved teaching in this book. None of us can achieve perfection on any point, much less on all points (25 and 50 yards at rapid and slow fire). But each of us can do better. We can keep steadily trying (squeezing) and doing the best we can. If one were to try to be perfect in understanding all children, in encouraging creativity, in teaching all the lessons children should learn, he would not have time to achieve balance in cultivating friendships, in pursuing his own creative hobbies, in giving attention to the preservation of physical health.

Just doing the best you can will prevent the development of a distinct hazard to mental health—that of perfectionism. Frustration is to a marked extent caused by failing to do what one sets out to do. The housewife who wants her home kept immaculately clean will become frustrated. The businessman who will brook no errors or shortcomings from his employees is headed for difficulty. The teacher who expects all her pupils to surpass the national average on an achievement test is going to be dissatisfied. The truly healthy person is not going to be satisfied with just anything, but he will see the wisdom of being content with doing the best he can.

Capitalize on the Mental Health Values of Religion. It has been previously noted that the human personality has four major facets, though they may not be sharply differentiated in the living person. These facets are the mental, physical, emotional, and spiritual. A number of mental hygienists and psychiatrists give religion an important place in the development of the well-rounded individual—the mentally healthy person.[18] The late Joshua Liebman has made a noteworthy contribution by showing how closely the aims of mental hygiene parallel the lessons and aims of religion.[19]

No individual is ever sufficient unto himself alone. Human nature is such that every person desires to be at least somewhat dependent upon another who is stronger than himself. A belief in God satisfies his desire. The individual feels secure because of the faith he has in a Supreme Being. His need is especially great if he has no fellow humans to whom he can turn. Moreover, worship, including prayer, is a form of catharsis,

[18] Harold W. Bernard, *Toward Better Personal Adjustment*, 2d ed., New York: McGraw-Hill Book Company, Inc., 1957, pp. 411–413, for representative views.
[19] Joshua Loth Liebman, *Peace of Mind*, New York: Simon and Schuster, Inc., 1946.

and catharsis is always good for one who is in trouble. Mental hygienists, far from being opposed to religion, welcome the positive contributions that religion can make.[20]

Religion has, through many centuries, proved its value as an avenue for such achievement. We can no more expect to receive the benefits of spiritual values by mere waiting than we can expect to achieve efficiency in our profession without working. Attending the services of a chosen church is a first and fundamental step. We need to be periodically reminded of our spiritual obligations. We need some concrete suggestions as to how our religion can be implemented. The hymns and music encourage at least a momentary slowing down of the tempo of life. Prayer provides a kind of emotional catharsis from the press of irksome problems. The very architecture of the church stimulates a feeling of firmness and permanence in a rapidly changing world. Active participation in church provides contact with others who—though they may be presently far from ideal persons—are seeking improvement in their way of life. The minister, priest, or rabbi (by whatever title he may be known) will not limit his help to only those active in the church; it is reassuring to know that in time of need he is known and is available to all. The teacher, for his own mental health as well as for the welfare of his pupils, might well reexamine the contributions that a balanced religion can make to joyful and harmonious living.

> Lord, who am I to teach the way
> To eager children day by day?
> So prone myself to go astray.
> I teach them knowledge, but I know
> How faint the flicker and how low
> The candles of my power do glow.
> I teach them power to will and do,
> But only now to learn anew
> My own great weakness through and through.
> I teach them love for all mankind
> And all God's creatures, but I find
> My love comes lagging still behind.
> Lord, if their guide I still must be,
> Oh, let the eager children see
> Their teacher leaning hard on Thee.[21]

Learn to Enjoy Living. Perhaps this suggestion is not so much an additional point as it is a summary of the foregoing. Perhaps, too, it is some-

[20] Herbert A. Carroll, *Mental Hygiene: The Dynamics of Adjustment*, 3d ed., Englewood Cliffs, N.J.: Prentice-Hall, Inc., 1956, p. 273.

[21] Used by permission of the author, Leslie Pinckney Hill, State College, Eau Claire, Wis.

thing like advising a person to lift himself by his bootstraps. Nevertheless, the fact remains that happiness, the enjoyment of living, is an outstanding characteristic of mental health. Chronic unhappiness is a symptom of the existence of problems that have not been solved and are not on the way to being solved.

> Happiness is the glow that attends the integration of the person while pursuing or contemplating the attainment of goals. The state of happiness is not itself a motivating force but a by-product of otherwise motivated activity. Happiness is far too incidental and contingent a thing to be considered a goal in itself.[22]

The enjoyment of living will normally result from the maintenance of good physical health, from understanding one's motives and capacities, from sound human relationships, from balance between work and play, from arriving at and acting upon tentative conclusions. There will inevitably be periods of discouragement and depression. The well-balanced person regards the temporary disappointments incident to vigorous living for what they are—transient difficulties. Steps should be taken to remove the difficulty if it is remediable; if the source is beyond control, then attention should be directed to compensating activities.

The source of much of people's inability to enjoy life is, as Allport suggests in the above quotation, due to a direct seeking of happiness—making it a matter of too much concern. It follows, among other things, that one must solidly identify himself with his fellow men. Happiness is an outcome of activity, purpose, and usefulness. It is a by-product of work that results in achieving worthwhile goals. Certainly, reading about the subject is not enough. To pretend to be happy does not change the basic factors. The wise course is to seek the sources of unhappiness and do some constructive work to remove the causes.

SUMMARY

Philosophy is a way of looking at and of evaluating life so that better mental health may be achieved. There can be no satisfactory universal prescription for such a philosophy, but whatever it is, it should seek to exercise the major facets of personality—the physical, the mental, the emotional, and the spiritual.

The teacher's philosophy should include the fundamental mental hygiene values, which demands that the teacher exercise the various facets of personality and satisfy the fundamental human needs. The summarizing list below offers suggestions to the teacher.

[22] Gordon W. Allport, *Becoming: Basic Considerations for a Psychology of Personality*, New Haven, Conn.: Yale University Press, 1955, p. 68.

Attention should be given to the maintenance of good physical health.

One should seek insight into his own conduct through the study of psychology, sociology, and philosophy and of other human beings.

A sense of genuine security should be sought through the conscious development of skills and knowledge.

Time should be devoted to the improvement of relationships with others.

Confidential relationships should be established with a few selected and mature persons.

One should seek to develop the habit of facing inevitable stress and strain with a high degree of emotional poise.

Worry (as circular thinking) should be resolutely replaced with problem solving and the ability to act on tentative conclusions.

An integrated personality will be fostered by a sane balance between the roles of work and play.

While one should learn from past errors and plan for the future, the major emphasis should be placed on giving attention to the present situation.

Studied attention should be devoted to attuning ourselves to the humorous elements that are inherent in daily living.

While one need not subscribe to the doctrine of mediocrity, he should not be frustrated by the ideal of perfectionism. He should learn to do just the best he can.

Many persons have learned that exercising the spiritual aspects of life can contribute much to complete living.

Happiness is less a goal to be sought than it is an indication that one has achieved a philosophy that contributes to optimal mental health.

STUDY AND DISCUSSION EXERCISES

1. How can the danger of being too critical or too uncritical of one's own motivations and conduct be overcome?

2. What are the weaknesses in the proposition that developed skills form the basis for feelings of security?

3. Recall some events in the past year which have caused you emotional stress. What evaluation do you place on them after a lapse of time?

4. What are some of the characteristics of a really worthwhile leisure-time activity?

5. What are some ways in which religion might serve as a handicap to achieving sound mental health? In what ways an asset?

SUGGESTED ADDITIONAL READINGS

Allport, Gordon W., *Becoming: Basic Considerations for a Psychology of Personality*, New Haven, Conn.: Yale University Press, 1955. 110 pp.

Considering scientific findings and theories, Allport looks at the complexity of human personality and draws a unified conceptual framework for understanding the ever-evolving personality.

Bonney, Merl E., *Mental Health in Education,* Englewood Cliffs, N.J.: Allyn and Bacon, Inc., 1960, pp. 394–423.

The importance of the teacher's adjustment is reviewed, and the characteristics of good teachers are summarized. Representative teacher problems are discussed.

Overstreet, Harry, and Bonaro Overstreet, *The Mind Goes Forth,* New York: W. W. Norton & Company, Inc., 1956. 384 pp.

Amid personal and international suspicions and hostilities, one of man's great needs is to meet others' minds at least half way.

Sorokin, Pitirim A., *Altruistic Love,* Boston: The Beacon Press, 1950. 253 pp.

This study investigates the origins, experiences, and status of individuals who have become significant through their altruistic love.

Tibbits, Clark, and Wilma Donahue, *Aging in the Modern World,* Ann Arbor, Mich.: University of Michigan Press, 1957. 175 pp.

Attention is given to the need for changing values as one matures. Since today is a preparation for tomorrow, the points in one's present philosophy form the base for future growth.

NAME INDEX

Adams, Georgia S., 266, 282
Adler, Alfred, 43, 159
Alcott, Louisa M., 348
Allen, Charles M., 259
Allport, Gordon W., 133, 484, 485
Almy, Millie, 29
Alvord, Emory, 473
Amatora, Sister Mary, 113
Anastasi, Anne, 107
Anderson, Archibald W., 229, 445
Angelino, Henry R., 85
Applegate, Mauree, 352
Arbuthnot, Mary Hill, 349, 351, 352
Auld, Richard M., 195
Axline, Virginia M., 142, 148, 363

Baber, Ray E., 73
Baer, Max F., 62
Bampton, Ruth, 324
Barker, Roger G., 43
Barlow, Robert J. G., 271
Baron, Denis, 97, 145, 298, 302
Barr, A. S., 116
Barrie, James M., 348
Barton, Betty, 5
Baruch, Dorothy W., 153, 217, 234, 335
Barzun, Jacques, 462
Bassett, Clara, 123
Batchelder, Marjorie, 369, 373
Baxter, Bernice, 128
Beasley, Jane D., 259
Beers, Clifford, 24
Bender, James F., 430
Benne, Kenneth D., 229, 445

Berk, Fred, 370
Berman, Leo, 120
Bernard, Harold W., 60, 86, 97, 107, 145, 186, 234, 242, 286, 302, 471, 482
Bills, Robert E., 365
Blatz, William C., 37
Bloom, Benjamin S., 80
Bolton, F. E., 240
Boniface, Jenora, 356
Bonney, Merl E., 24, 192, 486
Boyd, Gertrude A., 354
Boynton, P. L., 124
Brandt, Richard M., 116
Bromley, Dorothy, 262
Brooks, Deton J., Jr., 259
Bruce, William F., 445
Bryan, Quentin R., 228
Buhler, Charlotte, 81, 150
Bullis, Edmund, 148, 254, 302
Buros, Oscar K., 290
Burton, William H., 105, 263
Butler, Katharine, 381

Cantor, Nathaniel, 219
Capa, Cornell, 197, 200
Carroll, Harbert A., 483
Churchill, Winston, 63
Claypool, Vincent, 65
Clift, David H., 468
Cole, Natalie R., 82, 144, 336, 337, 352
Coleman, James C., 385
Comer, Virginia, 369, 373
Conant, James W., 213, 280
Corey, Stephen, 99

487

SUBJECT INDEX